ACROSS THE DISCIPLINES

ACADEMIC WRITING AND READING

JAQUELINE McLEOD ROGERS
UNIVERSITY OF WINNIPEG

CATHERINE G. TAYLOR
UNIVERSITY OF WINNIPEG

Pearson Canada
Toronto

Thanks and love to Warren, Hartley, and Morgan—J.M.R.

For Janice with love—C.G.T.

Library and Archives Canada Cataloguing in Publication

Rogers, Jaqueline McLeod

  Across the disciplines : academic writing and reading/Jaqueline McLeod Rogers, Catherine Taylor.

Includes bibliographical references.
ISBN 978-0-321-46951-9

    1. English language—Rhetoric.   2. College readers.   3. Report writing.
I. Taylor, Catherine.   II. Title.

PE1471.R634 2010   808'.042   C2010-905515-2

ISBN 978-0-321-46951-9

Vice-President, Editorial Director: Gary Bennett
Editor-in-Chief: Ky Pruesse
Acquisitions Editor: David S. LeGallais
Signing Representative: Duncan MacKinnon
Marketing Manager: Loula March
Senior Developmental Editor: Patti Altridge
Project Manager: Richard di Santo
Production Editor: Avivah Wargon
Copy Editor: Claire Horsnell
Proofreaders: Kelly Coleman, Cheryl Cohen
Compositor: Integra
Photo Research: The Editing Company
Permissions Research: The Editing Company
Art Director: Julia Hall
Cover and Interior Designer: Jennifer Stimson
Cover Image: Getty Images/Southern Stock

    3 4 5   15 14 13

Printed in Canada

BRIEF CONTENTS

CONTENTS

PREFACE

This book assumes that there is no easy formula for writing well, but that successful academic readers and writers employ certain methods and conventions that greatly facilitate their work. We present suggestions and guidelines for each of the key activities involved in academic reading and writing in our opening chapters.

This book also assumes that post-secondary students need to understand how to begin the task of learning to think like a scholar if they are to do well in academic reading and writing, and that critical thinking is the basis for all academic work. Whatever discipline students work within, whether it be a "science," an "art," or an interdisciplinary combination of both, they need to be able to think critically in order to read and write academic texts. This perspective is evident from the first pages forward.

Why another textbook with interdisciplinary readings? We think our approach is innovative in several ways. First, the opening chapter speaks directly to the issue of how disciplinary approaches shape disciplinary knowledge. Rather than simply providing readings sorted into disciplinary areas on the basis of topic, we discuss how writings within a discipline often share methods and key concepts.

We are also committed to providing readings that are scholarly rather than popular, most being samples of the kinds of published academic work that our students are actually confronted with and asked to produce in university. Often in university writing assignments, our students are asked to gather scholarly material for their research, and we can prepare them to do this work if they confront similar material in their composition studies. By the same token, they are asked to write in ways that represent the disciplinary genre conventions enacted within scholarly publications. Because the readings are complex and demanding, we have chosen topic areas that are within the range of student experience—thinking about the body or Canadian identity, for example, provides students with an opportunity to engage in a topic that is important both in the academy and in everyday culture.

Each chapter opens with activation questions that prepare students for the chapter readings by asking them to make connections between their own experiences and the chapter theme. Following each reading, there are two categories of questions. The first aims at encouraging active reading—helping students identify key ideas and transitions—and the second, critical reading. The questions not only draw attention to rhetorical features of the readings as well as to issues of content, but also include suggestions for further writing such as summaries, critiques, research proposals and annotated bibliographies, and research essays. At the end of each chapter of readings, we include questions for further research activities based on chapter readings and on outside sources.

ACKNOWLEDGMENTS

First, we would like to thank the following reviewers who provided feedback that was invaluable in helping us to refine the manuscript:

Carol Acton	University of Waterloo
Katharine Bassett Patterson	University of British Columbia
Kina Cavicchioli	Langara College
Roger Farr	Capilano University
Kevin Flynn	University of Saskatchewan
Rick Gooding	University of British Columbia
Roxanne Harde	University of Alberta
Karen Inglis	Kwantlen Polytechnic University
Kent Walker	Brock University
Caroline Whitfield	Brock University

Of course, we want to thank the many wonderful and gifted students at the University of Winnipeg who have helped us think about how to teach writing. Their variety of interests and abilities remind us that expertise comes in many forms and that no one approach will be interesting or helpful to all.

We are particularly grateful to student research assistants and contributors: Victoria Maynard, Katie Murphy, Heather Roscoe, and Illana Isaacs.

We would also like to express our gratitude to the University of Winnipeg for generous funding assistance through their Work Study granting program.

At Pearson, many good and talented people have supported this work. We have longstanding relationships with our tireless Pearson representative, Duncan MacKinnon, our acquisitions editor, David Le Gallais, and with our extremely patient and resourceful editor Patti Altridge. We have been helped by the decisiveness of Michael Young, the brilliant efficiency of copy editor Claire Horsnell and production editor Avivah Wargon, and the meticulous care of project manager Richard di Santo and proofreaders Kelly Coleman and Cheryl Cohen.

One might not expect to say of writing a textbook that it has been a project long in the making and fraught with surprises, but in our case both are true. We hope that the book will be useful to many.

PEARSON
mycanadiancomplab

www.mycanadiancomplab.ca

Visit **MyCanadianCompLab** to access diverse resources for composition in one easy-to-use place:

- Sections on **writing**, **research**, and **grammar** cover all the key topics in the text, providing additional instruction, examples, and practice. **Exercises** offer the opportunity to practise the skills learned in class and include both self-grading quizzes and writing activities. **Model documents** provide examples of different types of writing and different documentation styles; some are annotated to highlight key aspects or to stimulate reflection and discussion. **Videos** illustrate aspects of the writing process through scenarios, or provide grammar and editing tutorials through onscreen revision.

- An online **composing** space includes tools such as writing tips and editing FAQs, so you can get the help you need when you need it, without ever leaving the writing environment. Within this space, you'll find access to **EBSCO's ContentSelect**, a database of articles from academic journals that can be used for research and reference.

- The **portfolio** feature allows you to create an e-portfolio of your work that you can easily share with your instructor and peers.

Use the access code packaged with new copies of this textbook to log on to MyCanadianCompLab, or inquire at your bookstore to purchase separate access.

CHAPTER 1

Critical Thinking and Active Reading

WHY IS THIS WRITING BOOK MOSTLY READINGS?

Imagine yourself walking into a classroom where 20 people have been engaged in heated debate about the best approach to fighting global warming. They have hashed out various theories on the causes of global warming, considered and rejected various technologies as ineffective, argued about whether taxpayers or business should finance the effort, weighed the ethical and practical merits of stifling economic growth in developing nations, and so on.

How do you get in on that? How do you speak in such a way that your words will be regarded as a contribution to the conversation?

The usual advice would be to listen for a while with a critical ear so that you can sort out what has already been said, what points have been considered and rejected, and what points have stood up to debate and been established as important to the topic—*then* present your perspective on what to do about global warming in such a way that everyone sees that you understand the situation accurately.

That's the situation facing the student who is asked to write a research essay. What makes the task daunting is that the other speakers in the conversation are not students, but scholars who are writing for other scholars in their subject areas, which are called *disciplines*. It can be difficult to understand them at times because they use words that work efficiently as short forms for key concepts that are familiar to other members of the discipline but that may not be familiar to you.

Fortunately, though, writing an essay is unlike speaking in class in one fundamental aspect: much of it is done in private, with lots of opportunity to investigate concepts and perfect your thinking before making your entrance, so to speak. The readings in this book provide conversations that you can enter to practise time-tested principles of writing critically sound essays.

WHAT IS IT TO BE "CRITICAL"?

First, let's clear some underbrush. "Critical thinking" in an academic sense does not mean "picky" or even "negative" thinking, although sometimes the result of critical thinking is indeed a negative judgment of something.

The kind of critical thinking valued in academic work is *reasoning* as opposed to guessing or just believing what you are told. Obviously, the things you will be reasoning about in an English Literature course are very different from those in an Auto Mechanics course. But no matter what subject you end up majoring in, you will need to reason well in order to do well.

To reason is to think and to think about our thinking. Are we leaping to conclusions without sufficient evidence that they are correct? Are we simply repeating as true what we have been told by teachers? Are we accepting false-hoods as common sense just because those errors have been so frequently repeated on television? Are we favouring a perspective because it is most flatter-ing to a group we identify with, such as Canadians, or perhaps a religious or ethnic group? Are we reducing a complicated situation to a simplistic black and white argument that distorts the facts and ignores the details? Reflective think-ing looks out for such flaws and holds us to a higher standard.

Many of these flaws are forms of *binary thinking*, which has been explained by psychologists and philosophers as a natural by-product of human conscious-ness, where the developing infant becomes aware of itself as separate from the rest of the universe. It perceives that there is "Self," and there is "Other"; one, two. Because thinking in twos is rooted in our own development, it can feel appropriate and psychologically satisfying to see the world in its "us/them," "either/or," "all/nothing," "black and white" terms. However, while binary thinking is useful in some applications, such as the on/off world of electrical circuitry, it is far too limited an approach for making rational decisions about complicated problems. Binary thinking predisposes us to make up our minds quickly and ignore any evidence that contradicts our decision. Governments frequently make use of binary thinking to encourage unquestioning patriotism in wartime.

Critical thinking requires a combination of patience, humility, and self-confidence: the *patience* to think an issue through in all its complexity instead of just leaping to a conclusion, the *humility* to hold one's own beliefs up to scrutiny and revise them if necessary, and the *self-confidence* to tackle tough problems and formidable opponents.

Why should critical thinking be so highly valued in academia? The traditional hope of the academic community is that careful, reflective reasoning will not only result in clear, accurate knowledge, but in well-ordered, humane societies.

EXERCISE

1. Write a paragraph using binary thinking ("us/them," "either/or," "all/nothing," "black and white") to justify the post–9/11 attack on the oil-rich dictatorship of Iraq. Then make a list of all the points that are ignored in your justification.

2. Can you think of any examples of binary thinking in the news, where politicians perhaps present an overly simplified view of an important problem? What important aspects of the problem are being ignored?

KEY MOVES IN EVERY DISCIPLINE

A great many books and websites have been produced on critical thinking, offering various mental exercises designed to help us become good at it. Some of these books break it down into dozens of components—for example, beginning by examining our pre-existing beliefs on a subject. Others categorize flawed thinking into dozens of mental slips and traps to be avoided, such as leaping to conclusions. There is a whole strand of the discipline of philosophy that studies a version of critical thinking called "formal logic." Thinking well in any discipline involves the following key activities:

- Having a purpose (or finding a purpose) for thinking
- Posing questions
- Gathering information to help answer those questions (often in the form of books and articles)
- Selecting the most relevant information
- Developing a perspective that answers our questions as clearly and accurately as possible
- Considering the viability of alternative perspectives
- Displaying reasoning in class dialogue and written assignments. (Even multiple-choice tests, when well designed, demand the exercise of critical thinking.)

Good critical thinkers conduct each of these activities carefully, reflecting on the quality of their decisions and judgments as they go along, and remaining open to changing their minds if the evidence or the reasons warrant. However, it can be counterproductive to make yourself follow each and every step in rigid sequence. You can get ample practice in all of these activities by doing the exercises and assignments in this book.

CRITICAL THINKING IN DIFFERENT DISCIPLINES

All disciplines involve critical thinking. Some disciplines emphasize it as a separate activity, as in the writing of book reviews. Others put the word "critical" in course names such as "critical social theory," "literary criticism," and "critical literacy." Sometimes, the actual word is not used. But in all disciplines, thinking well and writing well mean thinking critically:

- A chemist thinks critically when she uses her knowledge of the discipline to understand a lab result.
- A computer programmer thinks critically when he uses his knowledge of the discipline to write new software.

We can break this disciplinary knowledge down into two main components—concepts and methods:

■ A theology professor thinks critically when she applies key concepts in her discipline to the development of a moral position on a problem such as euthanasia.

■ A Women's and Gender Studies student thinks critically when he applies key concepts from feminist theory and gender theory to argue that X should or should not be done.

The key to critical thinking in a discipline, then, is to apply its concepts and methods to solve problems. The essays you will write are intended to display that kind of reasoning.

Key Concepts

In fact, *key concepts* are at the heart of all disciplines—and applying them is at the heart of critical thinking in the discipline. Scholars use them carefully, aware that on each occasion they are communicating a particular meaning to other scholars. Key concepts are so important that tests and exams very often ask students to define them and illustrate them, and essay topics are routinely phrased in such a way as to require students to use key concepts. What are the key concepts in the following topics?

■ Compare the use of metaphor in two or three poems.

■ Is the residential school system an example of a "total institution" in Erving Goffman's sense?

■ Describe the chemical processes at work in nuclear fusion.

■ Does standardized assessment penalize at-risk youth?

A key concept such as "at-risk youth" cannot be fully understood by looking up "at," "risk," and "youth" in the dictionary because key concept terms are used to convey specialized meanings within a discipline. They act as "super-terms" that help to unify and connect all of the books and journals in which the concept is discussed. Scholars might disagree on who are "at-risk youth," and what to do about it, but they all use the same term as a beacon, telling other scholars, "Over here! The topic of *young people between 14 and 21 who are at higher than normal risk of getting involved in gangs and drugs and dropping out of school because of social factors such as troubled home life and social marginalization* is under discussion in these books and articles." Apparent synonyms for "at-risk youth," such as "endangered adolescents" or "young people in trouble," have not been mobilized as key concept terms, and they do not have the same beacon effect. (Test this out by doing a library search on a key concept term such as "at-risk youth" and then on a plausible everyday synonym for it like "adolescents in danger.")

Key concepts are meant to be used. They are not just more terms to memorize, but

■ *analytical aids to think and see with*—tools in your *toolkit,* to use Wittgenstein's term.

- *beacons*, casting light on, or illuminating, the terrain. Scholars think critically by trying to understand X *in light of* the key concepts of the discipline. Key concept terms communicate complex ideas in compressed, efficient form.

- parts of the *blueprint*, to use Foucault's term. Key concepts of a discipline link together to provide a systematic view of a complicated field—not the *only* way of looking at X, but an enormously well-developed way that represents the combined efforts of scholars all over the world, over decades or in some cases centuries.

- *gravitational centres*, holding related books and articles in the same orbit.

Critical reading involves wielding key concepts that you already know, *and* figuring out what the writer's key concepts are. A critical reader might keep these questions in mind:

- What key concepts are mobilized in the text (or in the course)? Which ones are launched early on and recur throughout the text?
- What concepts is the writer (or professor) thinking with?
- What are the connections between the key concepts?

The philosopher Gerald Nosich argues that every discipline has a short list of "fundamental and powerful" ("f&p") concepts that underlie the whole discipline. In clinical psychology, for example, the concepts of diagnosis, cause, and treatment are three important f&p concepts. These are f&p concepts because they structure the thinking of psychologists very powerfully, no matter what kind of psychological situation the psychologists are trying to understand. Nosich advises students

- to identify the f&p concepts [of a course].
- to understand how they fit together.
- to learn them in a deep way.
- to use them in every important question or problem that arises in the course.
- to use them to begin to think through questions that lie beyond the scope of the course. (108)[1]

Similarly, every book has a few key concepts, and every essay, too. Figuring out what they are, and how well they light up the topic they are applied to, is critical reading.

Questions and Methods

Another way to think about a discipline (or a course, or a book, or an essay) is to ask, "What makes it tick?"—or in intellectual terms, "What question is being

---

[1] Nosich, Gerald. *Learning to Think Things Through: A Guide to Critical Thinking Across the Curriculum.* Columbus, OH: Pearson, 2009. Print.

asked?"—and "How do members of the discipline go about answering it?" In other words, "What methods does the discipline use?"

- What question is being asked in the discipline of history? How do historians go about answering it?
- What question is being asked in your organic chemistry textbook? How do the authors go about answering it?
- What question is being asked in that survey about homophobia in Canadian schools? How do the researchers go about answering it?
- What question is being asked in a book about the residential school system?
- What question is being asked in your friend's essay about *Macbeth*?

Each of the disciplines has developed powerful methods for answering its questions. Sociologists often use surveys and interviews. Anthropologists typically use field notes, ethnography, and a technique called *participant observation.*

Scholars in many different disciplines are focusing on the topic of climate change, but their questions and methods are different:

- Business: Can we afford not to fight global warming? (Do a cost-benefit analysis.)
- Ecology: Is global warming occurring? (Compare natural data today to past data.)
- Engineering: What technologies might be developed to fight global warming? (Propose a new technology based on scientific studies.)
- Ethics: Do we have a moral duty to oppose global warming? (Compare the arguments for and against.)
- Religion: Does religious belief influence people's perceptions of global warming? (Interview believers.)
- Sociology: Who cares about global warming and why? (Do a survey and interviews.)

Whether we are thinking in macro terms of a whole discipline or micro terms such as one short essay, all academic work comes down to asking a question about some aspect of the universe—"X"—and trying to answer it.

The most powerful answers are the ones that illuminate X best by following methods that are known in the discipline to produce trustworthy results. It is for this reason that professors look for "methodological rigour" in each other's work and in their students' work, too. Little value is placed on eloquence and insight in the absence of methodological rigour, beyond providing possible inspiration for someone else to do the job right in future.

EXERCISE

1. Different disciplines call for different reasoning. What questions would scholars in different disciplines ask to explore the following subjects? What concepts and methods would they use to answer those questions?

   • Taxation of polluters
   • Internet predators

- Religious conflicts in the Middle East
- Year-round opening of the Northwest Passage
- Failures of banks around the world

2. Different disciplines have different writing conventions. Look at three articles (one science, one humanities, one popular) and describe some of the ways they differ—for example, in terms of questions being asked, methods being used to ask them, what counts as evidence, and documentation.

3. There is often variety within a discipline. Look at three articles from one discipline and check them for disciplinary consistency.

What Is the Key to Academic Success?

Academic writing does not exist in a vacuum. It is almost always an attempt to get in on a scholarly conversation that is already under way. That conversation occurs orally, when scholars present research papers at conferences, and in print, in the form of published articles and books. When students write essays, or professors write books and articles, the quality of their work depends in large part on how well they fit into the conversation and how much they contribute to it. In order to write well, students need to learn to think like members of the discipline they are writing for: that is, to ask the kinds of questions the discipline has focused on, and to use the key concepts and methods the discipline has developed to answer them. We do not use the term "disciple" for people who have learned to do this, but members of academic disciplines and religious disciples do share the characteristic of having focused their minds intensely for a long time on developing a particular way of thinking.

It is a sign that you are beginning to think like a member of the discipline when you start seeing examples of it everywhere; you are seeing the world through the discipline's eyes. Perhaps you have taken a year of engineering, and suddenly see all the buildings and bridges you pass in terms of how they were built, or you have studied microbiology and start seeing everything in your home as a breeding ground for bacteria. Perhaps you have studied history long enough to have habitually started seeing every current event in relation to the past. Has this ever happened to you? It has happened to all of your professors, and the sooner it happens to you, the easier you will find it to write excellent essays. Get in the habit of trying to answer questions like the following, and try to apply them to real-life situations in your everyday experience:

1. What is the one big question being asked in this course (or book, or article, or lecture)?
2. What are the two or three biggest concepts in this course (or book, or article, or lecture)?
3. What are the main methods used to answer questions in this course (or book, or article, or lecture)?

ACTIVE READING

It is easy to develop some lazy reading habits. Many of us have become used to reading while doing something else—while listening to music, using the internet, or watching TV. Many of us consider multi-tasking a virtue, or at least a necessary way of getting on with our lives. But the complex material you are asked to read for university courses demands your full attention. If you try to read while doing other things, you risk misunderstanding or missing information. Rather than wasting time reading inefficiently, you can use the techniques suggested here to improve your grasp of main ideas as you make your way through a first-time reading of a text.

Being alert to the development of important ideas is called *active reading*. This is a preliminary stage that often precedes the sort of *critical reading* that we discuss briefly toward the end of this chapter and in the chapter about conducting a critique, for it is easier to develop a critical perspective after first becoming fully familiar with the material. If an active reader is engaged in finding out what the writer says, a critical reader is more interested in questions to do with why the writer speaks as he or she does.

An Active Reading Process

Rather than making your way through a text and trying to "get it" in one sitting, it can be helpful to approach reading as a process, so that you can tackle it in stages, much like it can help to think of writing as a staged process. Here is a way to manage your reading in stages:

1. **BEFORE** reading:
   - read the title to glimpse the topic and perhaps even the approach;
   - look at any attached author information to find out what else the author has written, when the piece was written, and for what purpose. This information provides you with a context, a way to think about what the writer was trying to do;
   - preview the opening passage to anticipate what the writer might say.

2. **WHILE** reading:
   - jot down key concepts and connections on photocopied pages, or jot down page numbers with points on a separate piece of paper. Use a highlighter to underline important points. An active reader keeps a pencil or pen in hand;
   - look for and highlight the writer's main point (and try writing it using a paraphrase);
   - pay attention to vocabulary, looking for unusual words and for key words.

3. **AFTER** reading:
   - reconsider whether you were correct in identifying what the writer wanted to say and in general reflect on what you learned;
   - discuss the reading (with peer group members or interested friends).

Preparing to Read Short Texts

To prepare to understand a short text, you should look it over before reading it. There are at least six things to check that will help you anticipate the writer's pattern of thinking.

1. Look at the *title* and at any *headings,* for these often announce topics and key concepts.
2. Look at any *visuals* (photographs, charts, illustrations, tables, maps, and diagrams), for each supports ideas and information in the text.
3. Read the *first paragraph* because openings announce what the text is about.
4. Skim the *first sentences of each paragraph* because these often reveal paragraph ideas, and thus skimming them can provide a sense of the whole.
5. Read the *final paragraph* to see if it provides a summary of the writer's important points.
6. Look for *key words* that may be highlighted in bold or italics.

EXERCISE *Look at the section explaining the thesis in this textbook (in Chapter 2). Preview it using all six steps. You will notice that making a preliminary assessment does not take long. You will probably also notice that doing this prepares you to read the text and actually helps you to "take in" the ideas and information.*

Preparing to Read Book-length Texts

Many of you consult textbooks as part of your coursework or work with book-length studies as part of your research for essays and assignments. These longer works often have organizational features that are not present in articles and chapters. Often you skip over this material, as if it were just a bunch of extra words, but often looking it over can help provide an overview of the whole book.

1. Table of contents: Look this over to see what each chapter explores. Looking at the topics gives you a sense of what the book is about, and looking at the page numbers, a sense of how much coverage each topic is given.
2. Preface or foreword: Look over what the author says about why he or she wrote the book, or what the contributor says about the book's importance, for often this illuminates what you are likely to learn from reading it. Sometimes authors provide an organizational tip, or draw your attention to special features.
3. Introduction: Read this opening section to gather background information and a sense of the importance of the topic and the author's approach.
4. Index: Look over the index at the back for a list of important topics, words, and names.
5. Bibliography or references section: Look over this list of sources related to the topic.

6. Special features (sometimes called "Knowledge Apparatus"), which may include the following:

- Glossary: Sometimes at the end of the book, there is a glossary defining key or new terms.
- Biographical note: At the beginning or end, there is often a paragraph about the author, sometimes even a picture.
- Appendix (or appendices): Sometimes extra information that supplements or updates information presented in the book is placed in an appendix at the end.

EXERCISE *Before reading this text, did you look over some of the special features listed above? If you did so, did you gain a sense of the topics and approach? Many of us ignore these pages, assuming that they are not particularly helpful or that they are meant for teachers. Yet they often convey information that helps to clarify and direct your reading enterprise. Not looking them over is like taking a trip into unknown territory without a map: you might not see the important things; you might even get lost.*

So look over (or look again at) this text to see how many of these six features are included. Take a moment to consider how they contribute to your understanding of what you will find in the text.

Reading for Main Ideas and Information

The exercises and information here prepare you to sort out main ideas from those that are less important, and thus to comprehend what you read more fully. Being able to identify main ideas is especially helpful when you tackle *summarizing* as a writing assignment (Chapter 4), for to write a summary requires you to separate main ideas from details.

1. Finding Main Ideas in Sentences

The key idea of a sentence usually names

- a person or thing (subject)
- an action: what's the person or thing doing? (verb)

Using the language of grammar, you are looking for the subject and verb, two essential sentence elements. Look at the following sentence to see what it is about and what is going on:

The small creature dashed out the door and into the woods last Saturday and never returned.

The sentence is about a *creature* that *dashed out* and never *returned*. The other words provide details to add clarity and specificity. But the key idea resides in the thing and the action. In scholarly writing, of course, where we are often writing about concepts rather than people and events, the subject is often more abstract and the verb less dynamic.

EXERCISE *Here are three sentences, taken from articles in different disciplinary areas in this book. In each case, try to identify the key idea.*

Psychology Professor Jean Twenge says this generation is more narcissistic than the previous one (Tapscott 405).

One fine morning in turn-of-the-century Alberta, a young newcomer from England, Abee Carter Goodloe, went out to sample some local culture at Fort Macleod, only to find herself overwhelmed by the sense that she was back in the Old Country (Francis 433).

In 2004, Angela Cheung and Stephen Hwang released a study on the mortality rates of homeless women in Toronto (Scott 205).

2. Finding Main Ideas In Paragraphs

A paragraph is a group of sentences addressing a particular topic, with each sentence developing an idea about the topic. When a new topic is introduced, usually writers shift to start a new paragraph. Identifying the topic—usually in a word or phrase—is not the same as identifying the topic idea, which is usually a statement about the topic. The *topic* of this paragraph, for example, is "topics in paragraphs," but the main *idea* is that paragraphs say something about the topic. Sometimes the main idea is expressed directly, and you can find it in a single sentence. Other times it is implied or tacit, and you have to decide what the paragraph is saying about the topic.

EXERCISE *In the following sample paragraph, identify the topic, and then the main idea. Is the main idea expressed in a sentence within the paragraph, or do you have to make a statement that ties points about the topic together?*

Perhaps writing teachers have encouraged you to use topic sentences when you write a paragraph, so that, say, the opening or closing sentence expresses or summarizes the paragraph idea. If you have been so instructed, you have probably found it difficult in many cases to write such a crystallizing sentence or to introduce it in a manner that avoids sounding reductive or repetitive. What we are learning here as readers is that many writers do not write a topic sentence that contains the paragraph idea whole; instead many paragraphs are consistent because each sentence addresses an aspect of the same topic.

3. Finding Important Facts and Details

Here are several suggestions to help you identify facts that are important to your reading:

- Find the main idea. Once you identify this, you are better prepared to recognize supporting facts and details.
- Identify the key concepts being used.
- Look for signal transition words that introduce key ideas, like "most important," "in fact," "finally," or "therefore."
- Try to differentiate between facts and the author's opinions; in general, facts are things we hold true, whereas opinions are ideas we construct from facts (see the box for extended definitions).
- Pause from time to time to make connections ("How does this idea extend the idea in the last paragraph?").
- If you are reading textbook material for the purposes of discussion or testing, think about questions that might arise from the information.

EXERCISE *Identify the main ideas in the first three paragraphs of Doris Lessing's essay "Group Minds." Are they expressed directly? Then identify important facts and details. In small groups or in a class discussion, compare your selection of details to that of other readers. If there are inconsistencies, do these occur because readers differ in how they define the overall main idea?*

Fact and Opinion

A *fact* is something known to be true or to have occurred. Often (especially in the natural sciences) facts are known through the senses and can involve counting or numeric value. (For example, the statement "Holocaust survivor Simon Wiesenthal was born in 1908" is a fact.) Yet even facts are subject first to the writer's interpretation and then to the reader's. Despite being comparatively stable, how they are understood can be affected by the author's position, interpretation, and powers of recall, as well as by the reader's subjectivities.

An *opinion* is a position one comes to hold, usually after giving due consideration to facts. (For example, the statement "Pierre Trudeau was our greatest prime minister. He lived a life of great courage, passing bold laws to support Canada's development into a just society" is an opinion.) Expressing this kind of opinion in academic writing is appropriate only if you provide supporting evidence.

1. Discern fact from opinion.
2. Question opinion by considering how it relates to facts and other information.

Underlining, Highlighting, Note-taking

When you were in high school, teachers may have asked you not to write in books, probably because the books were school property for others to use. However, when you own the books you are reading, you *can* write in them. If you are reluctant to mark up a book, you might photocopy the sections you need to read so that you are free to underline and annotate important parts. Or you can work with pencil, which allows you to erase all comments or those that don't really help. If you are reading a pdf, you may be able to use the software's "comment" function to make notes in the file. By making notes and highlighting, you can improve your understanding and memory of what you read.

Here are a few suggestions to help you mark up your text as usefully as possible:

1. Devise a system for differentiating between main ideas and details, perhaps by underlining main ideas twice and details once.
2. Circle key words.
3. If main ideas are implied rather than stated in full, write your version of the main idea in the margin. Use margins in general for making notes to yourself, and in particular for making connections, such as noting how one passage connects to another.

A more thorough way of summarizing what you read is *note-taking*. As you read, note down main ideas and supporting details. Being organized is important to success when you are taking and keeping notes. Decide where you plan to keep your reading notes—perhaps in a section of a binder or a separate computer file, or at the back of your course notes. Before you begin, write down the date, so your notes have a context, as well as the full bibliographical information you will need for your reference list if you use the information in an essay.

The following notation system can help you avoid inadvertent plagiarism by ensuring that you can distinguish between direct quotations from the text, paraphrases, and your own ideas when you reread your notes:

- Put direct quotations in quotation marks ("/") and record the page number.
- Put paraphrases in tildes (~/~) and record the page number.
- Put your own ideas in square brackets ([]).

ACTIVE LISTENING

So far we have been talking about actively reading written material, because the printed word (whether on paper or online) remains the single most common and important mode of scholarly work. However, it is not the only mode, and articles and books are not the only texts. Increasingly, students need to be able to read non-verbal texts.

It used to be that post-secondary education consisted mainly of listening in silence to a long lecture delivered by a professor, usually without visual aids (or even a chance to ask questions afterwards). The challenge facing students in such classes was (and to the extent that such lectures still occur, still is) to derive as much benefit as possible by listening actively and taking notes that captured the lecturer's main points and important details. Many conventional lecturers begin by describing the structure of their lecture in the first few minutes; try to jot down the key moves and listen for them as the lecture unfolds to help organize your note-taking.

READING VISUAL TEXTS ACTIVELY

Over recent years, it has become more common for instructors to run interactive classes where there is an opportunity to engage in dialogue and seek clarification. When instructors need to lecture, many make use of PowerPoint presentations, which allow them to display the overall organization of their talk and the main points by which it is developed, thereby making the student's "active reading" work something of a no-brainer. The new challenge for students is to integrate a set of concepts and information they have received passively so that all of this can become part of their intellectual equipment for completing assignments and tests in the course.

PowerPoint presentations often include non-verbal visual material as well: charts, graphs, photographs, drawings, and video clips that convey information and illustrate ideas. Again, the challenge for students is not to switch into passive television-viewing mode, but to read those non-verbal texts actively, looking for the information that the instructor is intending to convey by displaying those images, and identifying the connections between the images and the ideas that are the subject of the lecture.

READING STORIES AND ARGUMENTS IN IMAGES

Photographs and images decorate our world, adding colour and appeal. Yet they have a function beyond simply looking good—it is true that every picture tells a story, and/or even makes an argument. A billboard to sell a watch, depicting a beautiful young woman in a gold evening gown and diamonds, tells us that wearing this brand is connected to being elegant and rich; a sign showing a white-toothed smile with an arrow pointing to the door of a dentist office argues (albeit gently) that a bright and even smile goes hand in hand with dental care. Often we take for granted a sign welcoming us to a city or a photograph depicting student life on a university website, but both are products of designers' minds, a point not really surprising to those of us who have spent time choosing profile pictures or setting up blog sites.

You can learn a lot by training yourself to look more closely at the visual images that are used to influence our thinking about everything around us. Think about the barrage of images that represent products (ads, for example), people (politicians, yes, but also more everyday folks, from realtors to Facebook friends), programs (even your university has a logo and brochures meant to appeal), and places (new housing developments or provincial parks). If you make a conscious effort to look at some of the more interesting images around you, you can learn a lot about how images trigger emotions and connections, and how text and images work together.

EXERCISE

1. Look at the two ads (see glossy insert) depicting a living room—one from the '50s and one more contemporary. What story do they tell about how people live? Can you infer an argument? (For example, is colour represented as important to the design? Is comfort? Is simplicity?)

2. Look at the cover pictures from *Chatelaine* (see glossy insert). Point out how the fashion and female images differ. Can you infer a connection between fashion choices and decades?

READING IMAGES IN ACADEMIC TEXTS

The internet has influenced how we take in information and, in turn, influences how information is produced for our consumption. In general, text is briefer and there are more visuals. Many of us get our daily news on MSN. If you get a newspaper or weekly news magazine, you may have noticed a series of design changes, aimed at breaking up text and increasing visual representations and appeal.

Design innovation is also influencing textbooks, so that putting information in charts, boxes, or illustrations is encouraged as a way to break up long passages of text. Sometimes a picture simply complements the text, to help readers who are more receptive to visual learning. Sometimes, however, the visual adds layers of meaning, moving beyond the discussion to add depth or resonance. When you look at photos or illustrations in texts, it can help to ask the same questions of them that you might ask of print text: What is the purpose? Who is the "author" (or artist/photographer/illustrator)? Has this item been published before?

EXERCISE *Look through your texts for an example of an illustration included to reinforce a concept. Bring in the text so that you can compare your selection to those of your peers. Be prepared to answer these questions:*

1. What is the connection between text and picture?

2. Beyond breaking up the print, does the picture add anything?

READING THE WORLD ACTIVELY

The discipline called Cultural Studies reads the world itself as a series of texts—obvious texts such as stop signs and store signs, and less obvious ones such as how people dress, how they behave with each other, even how streets are laid out and buildings are designed. Banks, for example, can be read in a functional way as buildings organized to facilitate the saving and lending of money, or in a rhetorical way as buildings designed to convince us that it is safe to leave our money there. Old-fashioned classrooms with raised lecterns at the front and orderly rows of desks can be read functionally as sensible arrangement of furniture to facilitate lecturing and note-taking, or rhetorically, as rooms designed to convey the relative importance of instructors and students.

Whether or not we are fully conscious of the activity, we go through our days reading the world and making judgments about how to proceed based on the visual "texts" we encounter.

EXERCISE *Choose a space or place you have either been in or seen depicted on television or in the movies, and offer an active reading of it. Consider questions such as these:*

How is the space organized? What are the most important places in this space? What is the status of the different people in this place? What features of the space tell me these things?

READING AND WRITING ACROSS THE DISCIPLINES

Post-secondary education demands that students read a great deal more than they are accustomed to, and that they remain critically engaged while doing it. Using the active reading strategies in this chapter may seem mechanical at first, but doing so will soon become a habit that helps you avoid wasting valuable study time doing inefficient, inaccurate, and unreflective passive reading. Further, all scholarly work involves not just active reading but critical thinking. Scholars in the Arts and Sciences think critically when they (1) apply specialized disciplinary concepts and methods to their own knowledge-production processes, and (2) assess their own and other scholars' results using established methods and measures for ensuring accurate, valid, reliable answers to their research questions. Later in the book, we address this second aspect of critical thinking: the "critique" through which scholars assess the strength and usefulness of each other's knowledge-production efforts and thus contribute to the development of a sound body of knowledge in their disciplines.

CHAPTER 2

Thesis, Process, and Paragraphs

First-year students sometimes get the message from more experienced peers that essays are easy, that they can be written almost according to formula and still fetch reasonable marks from most professors. And it is true that many essays have in common a basic structure: each has an introduction, followed by an orderly series of claims and support, in turn followed by a conclusion, all held together by devotion to an overarching claim or thesis. Though the details change from subject to subject and occasion to occasion, our work, while tending toward a happier outcome, can be understood as resembling another complex form of text, the Greek tragedy, described by Aristotle as requiring a beginning, a middle, and an end.

However, if we could adequately master the art of writing essays simply by following structural principles, essays would not be the challenging enterprise their name (from the Old French *essaier*, to try, or to test—not necessarily to succeed) suggests they are.

First, the people who take a formulaic approach—believing, say, that five paragraphs are a magic number for successful compositions—underestimate the central role that must be played by the essayist him- or herself. The essayist must use his or her own imagination to find an interesting angle on the topic, develop a thesis or insight that makes sense of it, and explore that thesis through a paper long enough to unpack and test its logic. Writing about any topic, whether we have a personal interest in it or not, requires the probing, connecting, questioning, shaping activity of the individual mind—not only "essaying" previously unfamiliar ideas and connections between ideas, but reflecting on whether they make sense of the topic.

Of course, this demand that the essay actually make sense of things further complicates the task. Not only must the essay be a well-crafted line of argument with its own structural integrity; it must also accurately represent that portion of the universe that is its topic. Depending on the topic, the need for accurate representation might require essay writers to observe with extreme attentiveness the behaviour of grizzly bears first-hand, or examine distant galaxies through a telescope, or recollect a 10-year-old experience in detail, or intently read and reread a poem or philosophical treatise, or conduct interviews with survivors of a natural disaster. Care is required because essays collapse if they are based on faulty observation. For example, an eloquently argued essay on Shakespeare's

Macbeth is no good if its claims are based on misquotations and misreadings; an essay on the safety of genetically modified foods, no matter how beautifully constructed as a fluid series of logically connected claims, cannot work if it has the facts wrong, or relies on faulty sources, or fails to consider important aspects of the issue. Essays, then, demand a dual focus—on both claims and support, writing and reading, the mind's eye and what it sees.

Full engagement in the process of writing a successful essay—reading, thinking, and sometimes observing—involves much more time than students often expect, particularly if, as is often the case, the students became accustomed in high school to getting good grades for "night-before" efforts that were short on research and contemplation but perhaps spirited in opinion or manner. The single most important advice we can give you for doing well in university and college writing assignments is to give them the time they demand, and to spend that time productively.

EXERCISE *By the time students begin their post-secondary education and find themselves in an academic writing course, they are likely to have had a significant amount of writing instruction, perhaps starting with their primary school teacher's advice to begin their little paragraph on "What I did on my summer vacation" with something to catch the reader's interest. Some students attribute their success in their senior high school essays to the five-paragraph essay formula they were taught in Grade 10. Working alone or in groups, list rules or approaches you have been taught for writing essays, then reflect on the following: Which ones do you expect to be reliable in post-secondary writing situations, and why? Which ones do you suspect might not be up to the task of helping students write essays at more advanced levels of education, and why?*

How Will My Work Be Marked?

A mathematics instructor can identify the specific mistakes on a test that account for a specific number of points lost. When an essay is being evaluated, however, instructors seldom pin down exactly where students have lost marks, which strikes some students as unfair or unhelpful. To provide more guided feedback, some instructors quantify the marks given for different aspects of an essay, working with categories such as argument, research, style, and usage. Yet most would still be hard-pressed to point to particular missteps if a student were to ask a question along the lines of "Could you show me where I lost each of the 23 marks?" What holds them back is that the most important aspect of an essay is the argument it makes, and argument is a general property that arises from all the different parts working together to create a whole that is (to use the old saying) greater than the sum of its parts.

Marking an essay is analogous to judging an artistic performance such as figure skating or a painted canvas. Some marks are reserved for specific technical criteria, while others go to the overall "artistry" of the performance: to how well everything goes together. The judges in each case know a good piece when they see one, and are confident of their professional assessment, but often point to general attributes more than to specific moves to justify their marking.

EXERCISE *If you have already had essays marked this year, examine them to see if you can identify exactly how many marks you earned (or lost) for particular qualities. Have you ever had a low mark on an essay praised for its strong thesis? Have you ever had a high mark on an essay criticized for careless proofreading? Working in groups, come up with an essay-marking scheme that you think attempts to convey fair and clear criteria, and be prepared to explain it in class discussion. Consider the following:*

- The components that are of note (e.g., thesis, evidence, style)
- Whether essays should be marked "holistically" (i.e., with the components in mind, but the focus on the overall performance, resulting in one mark) or "analytically" (i.e., with a pre-established number of points for each component)
- Whether there is need for flexibility in applying the scheme (e.g., should an analytical marker always stick to the pre-established number of points for each component?)
- Whether your marking scheme could result in unfairness, with an excellent performance getting a low grade, or a mediocre one getting a high grade

---

THESIS AND THE STRUCTURE OF ARGUMENTS

All Good Things Do NOT Come in the Five-Paragraph Essay

The goal of the process that proceeds from initial planning through creating multiple drafts and proofreading is to produce an essay that communicates its thesis in a well-crafted structure of claim and support. Crudely put, an academic essay usually looks something like this:

Thesis (X) in an introduction

Claim 1 (often a claim that the opposition doesn't count)

Claim 2 (a reason for believing X)

Claim 3 (another reason for believing X)

Claim 4 (and so on)

Conclusion where X is reasserted in a larger context

Sometimes academic writing is so blatantly structured this way that the whole line of argument—the structure of claim and support that develops the thesis—can be picked up simply by reading the first sentence of each paragraph and stringing them together. If this works, it is likely that the writer was consciously developing a thesis by making a series of claims in the form of *topic sentences*: sentences that (1) announce the main idea of the paragraph and (2) support the thesis. An essay shaped like this has the advantage of clarity, but such dull repetition is likely a harbinger of oversimplification. Readers like variety, and complex ideas often need to be coaxed with the kind of detail that is not needed to express simpler points.

Whether the argument is readily apparent or more subtle and varied, a successful academic essay will, on closer inspection, invariably have a solid structure of claim and support. As the novelist Virginia Woolf says about painting, even if an essay is, "on the surface, feathery and evanescent, one colour melting into another like the colours on a butterfly's wing . . . beneath [it] must be clamped together with bolts of iron."[1] If the essay is not built on a solid "iron" structure, it will be a failed attempt because it will not be able to carry the weight of the thesis.

How many claims do you need to make to be convincing? There is no formulaic answer. Some topics are complex and require extended analysis, whereas simple ideas can be dispatched more quickly. The number of claims you need is responsive to the topic you are addressing.

Some students come to university convinced that there is something magical (or at least reliable) about the *five-paragraph essay*, so they begin with an introduction, follow that with three paragraphs of support, and then end with a conclusion. This can be effective if the topic is straightforward or if the assignment has length restrictions that translate well into a five-paragraph approach. But rather than defaulting to a five-paragraph structure—which is really quite arbitrary—you should make decisions about how to present your claims in a way that best mounts your case. Usually, this means using both short and long paragraphs for variety—rather than trying to bundle your ideas into three big boxes, which is often what happens when writers assume that the body or middle section permits only three points of support.

Do I Always Need a Thesis?

It is true that many professional and scholarly writers seldom use a thesis, and they might describe their writing process as a systematic attempt to answer a research question using the methods and concepts of their discipline. Often, we understand their perspective as a result of taking all their points into consideration. It is probably safe to say that if you know your main idea as you write, you may not need to set it out *directly* before the reader, since your thesis idea will be made *tacitly*, with everything you say supporting and exploring this idea.

Yet most writing teachers encourage students to work with a thesis in order to avoid rambling. Developing a working thesis helps you to identify your probable focus, which helps you to make practical decisions about how to treat your topic and boosts your confidence by making the task more manageable. A thesis sentence guides the reader, too, for it identifies exactly what is going on. If your reader is a busy professor who is grading a stack of papers, it is a good strategy to be clear about your perspective by declaring it in a thesis.

As a student in the process of learning about many subjects, you are sometimes in the position of writing about topics you have not entirely mastered. If

---

[1] Virginia Woolf, *To the Lighthouse* (Harmondsworth, U.K.: Penguin, 1968), 194.

you are at all uneasy about your topic, you will probably want the added security of working with a thesis statement—one you can consult and revise as you hit difficult patches. Indeed, once an essay is drafted, it is usually a wise practice to return to the thesis, to revise it on the basis of what you have learned or emphasized in writing your essay.

Thesis and Bias

A thesis is the claim you make about your topic. It can be strongly in favour of a particular view as long as the argument is supported by logic and evidence and stands up to opposing logic and evidence.

In scientific research, it is conventional to avoid all emotional language or even expressions of intense conviction: researchers write as though they are research machines without human emotion or any interest in seeing one outcome over another. In other forms of research, such as interviews with abuse survivors, it would seem strange to appear that detached, and expression of passionate conviction is the norm, not the exception.

This introduces the question of when conviction becomes bias.

A bias is a *prejudice* in a general or specific sense—usually in the sense of having a preference to one particular *point of view* or *ideological* perspective. Anyone who has developed stands on issues has biases.

However, we are generally only said to be *biased* if our powers of judgment are influenced by the biases we hold to the extent that we accept or deny the *truth* of a *claim*, not on the basis of the strength of the arguments in support of the claim, but because of the extent of the claim's correspondence with our own preconceived *ideas*. This is called *confirmation bias*.

A more specialized definition of the term *bias* indicates a built-in flaw that increases the probability of getting a certain result. For example, a standards-based math test is biased if it relies on knowledge only baseball fans would have. A speedometer is biased if it adds 10 kilometres an hour to the actual speed you're driving. A hiring committee is biased if it routinely prefers candidates of one gender over equally qualified candidates of another gender.

Topic vs. Thesis

Whereas "topic" (from *topos*, the Greek word for "place") is a neutral description of the territory you explore in an essay, "thesis" is opinionated: it is the main claim you make—or, if you will, the central organizing insight you offer—about that territory. For example:

Topic: the legal status of same-sex couples

Thesis (informative): Canadian governments have legislated full equality for same-sex couples, but homophobia still persists in some pockets of Canadian society.

> **Thesis (argumentative):** Because of the continued bigotry of some socially conservative pockets of Canadian society, same-sex couples are still far from enjoying the same rights as heterosexual couples.
>
> A thesis always *says something about the topic*, whether proposing to provide information or staking out an argument.

Writing a Thesis Statement

A thesis statement summarizes the idea of an essay, usually in one sentence. This summary often comes in the introductory paragraph, sometimes in the final sentence after the topic has been introduced and the context established. It helps you to decide what to keep out and let in, and prepares your reader to anticipate your direction. The thesis is not always stated conveniently in one sentence or in one place, but a successful essay always has an implicit thesis that can be deduced from the whole text.

Building a Strong Thesis Statement

There is no one formula for writing a strong thesis statement, but the following approach is well suited to any essay in which you are expected to develop a thesis that takes alternative views into account. In this approach, the writer starts with his or her basic claim about the topic, then expands on it to provide the rationale for the claim, then incorporates the likeliest opposition to the claim.

Simple: just state your main claim about the topic:

- a one-clause sentence: X

"College and university students are the hardest-working demographic group in Canada today."

Expanded: better for you and the reader because it *forecasts* your argument by providing the rationale for your main claim:

- a two-clause sentence: X *because* Y

"College and university students are the hardest-working demographic group in Canada today because they typically work part-time or even full-time while going to school."

Or use another clause (Z) to acknowledge the opposition to X. This works well in an argumentative essay where the position taken is likely to be attacked.

- *Although* Z, X or *Even though* Z, X

"Even though being a student is generally regarded as easier than working for a living, college and university students are the hardest-working demographic group in Canada today."

Better yet, do both. Acknowledge the opposition right away, and then support your claim:

- *Even though* Z, X *because* Y

"Even though being a student is generally regarded as easier than working for a living, college and university students are the hardest-working demographic group in Canada today because they typically work part-time or even full-time while going to school."

This one forecasts the movement of a whole essay. The thesis promises that the essay will compare the workloads of students to those of other demographic groups. The essay will support the main claim that students are the hardest-working group by showing that they are unique in combining the double workload of employment and study, and it will refute the common perception that being a student is easier than working.

Now, ask yourself: If I prove this thesis, will my reader be persuaded that X is true—that students are the hardest-working people in Canada? If not, revise the thesis. Finally, ask yourself, "So what?" If you question your thesis statement in this way and no good answer comes to mind, it still needs work.

EXERCISE

1. Choose one of the chapters from Part 2 and try to identify the thesis in the first paragraph of each of the readings.

2. Choose a topic and write a thesis statement for it, using the moves suggested above to develop and expand the statement. Now get some practice at expanding your options by writing three more thesis statements on the same topic, all of them significantly different in perspective and purpose from the first.

3. Read the following thesis statements and decide whether each one is weak or strong. Consider the following criteria to make your decision:

   - Is it clear? Is it brief enough to be held in mind as you write a paper? Is it logical? Does it avoid careless or sensationalistic language?
   - Does it go beyond mere topic description to make a claim about the topic?
   - Can that claim be proved? Would it be hard to research?
   - Is the claim ambitious enough to warrant an essay? Alternatively, is it so ambitious that its promises could not be fulfilled in the time and space typically available for an essay?
   - So what? What difference does it make whether the statement is true or not? Why would anyone care?

   If you have time, explain your evaluation and propose a better version.

1. This essay will examine the health risks of eating potatoes.

2. We have come a long way since human beings first crawled out of caves.

3. College and university students are the hardest-working demographic group in Canada today.

4. Although Canada's anti-Jewish immigration policy during the Holocaust has been blamed on the prejudice of a few officials, the main reason for its adoption can be found in Mackenzie King's sensitivity to the political climate of his country: anti-Semitism was a vote-getter.

5. Michael Jackson was murdered by the media.

6. There is no need to be overly concerned about street gangs. After all, human beings have gathered into groups based on shared interests since the dawn of time.

7. Globalization of the economy is happening all around the world. More and more governments take their orders from big business. Some companies have more influence on the course of history than governments do. Students have been in the forefront of demonstrations against globalization. One of these demonstrations was at Quebec City, where anyone who approached the security fence was tear-gassed.

8. Same-sex couples are still far from enjoying the same rights as heterosexual couples in Canada.

THE RECURSIVE WRITING PROCESS

Keep in mind that an essay is not finished when the required number of pages are full. On the contrary, essay writing is a "recursive" process—one that goes over the same territory many times in the interests of shaping the best possible expression of the material. The intense concentration involved is more akin to that of painting a canvas or carving a sculpture than that of running a 100-metre race. Although successful writers vary in the particular techniques they employ and the amount of time they devote to each one, generally the recursive process involves three main stages: *planning*, *drafting*, and *revising*.

Stage 1: Planning or Pre-writing

In this stage, writers analyze the requirements of the writing challenge before them. They might have to decide on a topic if it is not supplied, or choose one from a limited selection. They try to find an angle that interests them and work at "unpacking" the topic to explore possible approaches to writing about it. Sometimes they use techniques such as *freewriting* or creating *point-counterpoint* lists at this stage, as shown in the pages that follow.

Writers usually develop a "working thesis" at the planning stage (though they continue to fine-tune it in the next stage—the drafting stage) and they try to find whatever research sources they need. If they cannot find the sources they need to support their preliminary thesis, or if their view of the topic changes unexpectedly as a result of information and ideas encountered in the research process, they revise the thesis. (We discuss this important process of finding a topic and developing a thesis later in this chapter.)

Some writers develop a detailed formal outline that is almost a point-form version of their whole essay before they go on to the drafting stage. Often a point can be developed into a full paragraph, as details and support come to mind and settle into the draft. Others, often writers who like to conceptualize things in visual terms, use mind maps (also known as concept maps), while still others employ quite minimal lists of the five or six main points. Whatever the particular techniques you use, the overall aim of the pre-writing stage is to put the writer in an excellent position to begin drafting.

Focused Freewriting to Explore a Topic

Let's say you are asked to write about biotechnology in a biology class, and you are uncertain about how to start. "Freewriting" can often help you to narrow your topic and identify a "real" subject that interests you. In another instance, you might be trying to outline your thoughts for an essay about youth crime, but get stuck at the point of thinking about how revising the *Young Offenders Act* might create positive change. In this case, you could try freewriting to explore connections that come to mind, hoping by this process to discover that you know more about your topic when you relax and write than when you simply sit and think hard.

Think about a topic you are currently writing about (perhaps in your writing class). Time yourself, allowing for about 10 minutes of non-stop writing. Use this opportunity to write about whatever comes to mind, to capture in writing things you already know about the topic, as well as connections you might not have considered previously. Try not to stop to evaluate your ideas, since the whole point is to find out the flow and direction of your thinking; try not to stop to correct yourself as you go, since worrying about surface expression tends to block the flow of ideas.

Here is an example of freewriting to start generating ideas on the topic of biotechnology:

> What to say about biotech . . . I never think about it very much why would I since I don't need any radical cures thank goodness and my family is OK so we don't have experience with transplants or whatever extremes they experiment with. I did hear about operations on embryos and how Canada needs to pass laws to make it illegal to do stem cell research, like they just passed laws in Britain I think. But there's GM foods, too—that's something that affects me, all the alterations they are doing to crops and animals, at least to animals through the sort of feed they get, so that they say kids are maturing earlier with all the hormones or steroids that are in the feed that cows eat and that get into the meat and the milk. That doesn't sound quite right. That could be a place to start looking.

By the end of this passage, the writer begins identifying a point of interest and thus finds a possible beginning place to focus.

Freewriting Rules

1. Don't STOP.
2. Don't worry about CORRECTNESS.

Outlining

Another way to get started is to outline ideas. On the informal level, there are scratch outlines, containing key words and ideas that the writer wants to explore. Asked to write about new technology and classroom etiquette in an education class, a student could jot down preliminary ideas in a list like this:

New technology in the classroom
improving education using online learning and software packages
time-saving factor in using laptop for note-taking and drafting
safety factor in having cell phone and internet warnings during class

More formal outlines often list out all the main points of support. The following represents the start of a three-column outline. This kind of outlining helps you to generate ideas, since it invites you to list your points of support, arguments running counter to each of these, and justifications explaining why your points prevail or how they can be modified to reflect the counter position.

Working thesis: New technologies such as iPhones and laptops are part of normal daily life, and instructors should have an open-door policy allowing students to use them during class time.

Point/Counterpoint/Defence Outline

Points	Counterpoints	Defences
Using a laptop in class saves time spent on rewriting assignments started in class and allows students to work at their own pace.	It is unfair for some students to have the benefit of time-saving technologies when others cannot afford them. Classrooms should offer computers for all students or for no one.	Students come to the classroom with uneven advantages in many areas, including family attitudes to education, family literacy, financial support for their educations, and so on. Prohibiting technology will not level the playing field.
Safety is improved when students have immediate cell phone and internet warning about dangerous situations on campus.	The small gain in an increased sense of safety comes at the expense of classroom courtesy.	Even a small increase in safety is crucial, and most technology users are courteous.

Mind Maps, Topic Outlines, and Argument Outlines

A Strategy for Outlining

Writers use different outlining techniques. Some go directly from note-taking to outlining the basic logic of their whole argument, and they keep fleshing it out until their whole essay is written. Writers who find that they can work in this way are very fortunate. Writing becomes less stressful because everything is broken down into manageable steps, and the writer can be confident that the overall architecture of the argument is solid.

If you are not in that fortunate position, though, and find yourself stuck without a thesis after reviewing half a dozen sources, unable to visualize what the main parts of your essay will involve, it can be helpful to put your research question in the middle of a blank page and map the points and subtopics that you have uncovered in your research. Ask yourself, "What have I found out that will help me answer my research question?" Display all the ideas and bits of information on your map, looking for clusters and connections. The clusters become the sections of your topic-style outline and ultimately of your research essay. The connections help you decide what order to put things in.

After that, take a step toward making the sequence of your essay linear by moving the clusters into a little topic outline. See if you can think of a thesis statement that would correspond to the outline. You may have to cut some material or add a section you had not thought of at the mapping stage.

Flesh out the topic outline with subtopics, and sub-subtopics. Do a little more tinkering with the basic organization, then start converting the topic outline into an argument (sentence-style) outline. Once you start writing sentences, you have started to write your essay.

A sentence-style outline is a sketch of the argument you can make to prove your thesis, so take some time to think about the best order to put things in. Look for transition points (points that belong to two sections) and rearrange the outline to make use of them. (In the best essays, each section builds on what has gone before rather than just starting a fresh subtopic.)

Check the outline to get the best possible fit between your thesis and your plan for developing it. Keep fleshing it out, section by section, until you have your whole essay written.

Some writers never use formal outlines; some never use maps. It is a good idea to try different approaches early in your academic career so that you can find what works best for you.

Looking at the examples of these techniques for getting started may provide you with models to experiment with. Both represent a writer's efforts to get started writing a sociology essay exploring images of Canadian culture.

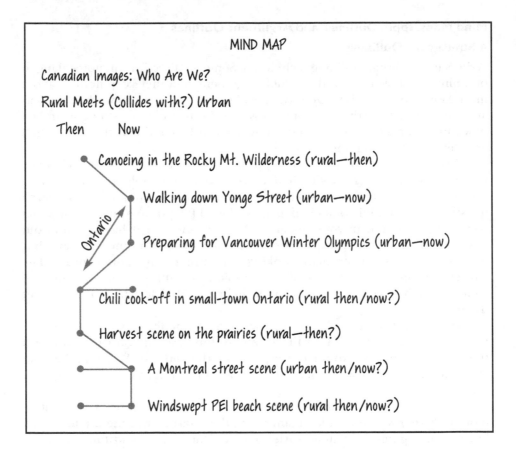

Formal Outline

    I. Introduce: Canada is still at a cultural crossroads, beginning to commit to urban over rural life, but still nostalgic for its rural past

    II. Images from our history that have appeal to our collective imagination are rural rather than urban
        A. the agricultural scenes
            i. a prairie harvest
            ii. orchards in the BC interior
            iii. market garden in the east
        B. wilderness scenes
            i. windswept rocky Newfoundland coast
            ii. windswept PEI sand beach
            iii. our Rockies, with turquoise lake
            iv. our "true" North
                a. the single arctic flower
                b. the windswept frozen sea

    III. Images of urbanization and modernization from the '60s
        A. Canadians at home: the vacuum and television
        B. Canadians at work: our "tall" buildings and lights

IV. Current images of our urban landscape
    A. homeless in our cities
    B. our Alberta oil boom cities
    C. core deterioration (and renewal) in Winnipeg
    D. Toronto the truly beautiful

V. Looking back with love and longing: Our rural roots
    A. the Maritime fishing village
    B. "Life in a Northern Town"
    C. back-to-the-land on Pacific Coast Islands
        i. artist communities
        ii. fishing villages
    D. Prairie peace
        i. the grain elevator
        ii. *Corner Gas*

VI. Looking back with anger
    A. animal hunts
    B. logging
    C. gas and oil production
        i. paving paradise
        ii. digging where deer and antelope play

VII. Conclusion

The writer with a formal outline like the one above has the advantage of writing with a plan. But this can turn into a disadvantage if the writer is inflexible, unable to revise or even tear up the plans if new directions arise.

EXERCISE

1. Pretend you are going to write an essay using the outline above, and revise it to add a new section. Make sure to use the right form of number or letter to signify the level of detail (moving from Roman numerals, to capital letters, to Arabic numbers, to lower-case letters). Why is the writer proposing to include section VI?

2. Revise the above outline into a sentence-style outline that clearly displays an argument that develops from the thesis.

Stage 2: Drafting and Redrafting or Revising

Again, successful writers approach this phase in different ways. For some, the first draft is very "drafty" indeed; it is written quickly and intensely, with the writer trying to plough through from beginning to end, knowing that there will be ample time for radical revision. In the example of the rough draft of the critique of "Language Crimes" below, the writer uses point form to move from beginning to end, so that the first draft looks more like an outline than an essay.

Other writers work and rework each paragraph or block of paragraphs as they go along, rather than separating their drafts out into different sittings, and then do one last reworking of the whole essay. The important thing at this stage is to ensure that the final draft ends up being the best possible execution of your thesis for your particular audience.

It is obvious that revising well involves effective rewriting of material; what is less obvious perhaps is that it involves particular troubleshooting skills, such as looking for gaps or repetitions in the argument, and identifying unsupported claims. Instructors provide you with an excellent opportunity to develop these troubleshooting skills when they set up peer feedback workshops to review drafts of your assignments. Such workshops also provide you with the opportunity to hear from real, live readers of your work before you submit it to be graded.

Here are two drafts of a critique of "Language Crimes." In this case, the first draft is an elaborate descriptive outline of the points that the writer intends to make. The second draft observes sentence and paragraph conventions.

DRAFT I

A Critique of Denis Dutton's "Language Crimes"

Introduction

- Passage: "Language Crimes: A Lesson in How Not to Write, Courtesy of the Professoriate," originally published in the *Wall Street Journal,* a large and influential US newspaper
- Author: Denis Dutton, an academic, an editor of the academic journal called *Philosophy and Literature* for two decades
- Dutton's main point: lots of contemporary academic writing in the humanities, especially within the departments of English Literature and Cultural Studies, is unnecessarily bad (i.e., "obscure," complex, technical . . .)

Summary

- Academic writing doesn't have to be "elegant."
- Much of the academic writing that is submitted to *Philosophy and Literature* is mediocre; some writing is horrible, excellent writing is rare.
- Student literacy is worse than in the past, and there has not been enough attention paid to professors' writing skills which have also been declining. (Dutton implies they are related.)
- Dutton cites an excerpt from a passage that made him realize how "bad" some contemporary academic writing had become.
- He evaluates the excerpt, determines that this writing is unacceptable coming from a professor of English, a professional who should model effective communication.

- He decides to assess the sorry state of contemporary academic writing with the Bad Writing Contest.
- He explains the rules of the Bad Writing Contest (e.g., excerpts of one to two sentences from academic texts, no translated texts . . .).
- He details the number of entries over past four years (70 each year), who judges the Bad Writing Contest (Dutton and coeditors), "winner" published each year in journal *(Philosophy and Literature)*.
- Writing in much of the humanities, especially within English departments, does not require a "technical" vocabulary; professors within English departments use a technical vocabulary ("theory"), which is inane; the vocabulary springs from critical theory, a feeble philosophy.
- Dutton gives example of writing described in previous paragraph; describes those who use "theory" as people "showing off."
- Within the field of Cultural Studies, the subject matter (as well as the writing about it with the lens of "theory") is "trivial"; Cultural Studies covers frivolous subjects (i.e. popular culture), and professors teach/study/write about it in an attempt to maintain student enrollment/interest in English departments because students have no interest in classics (e.g., Milton, Melville).
- He describes qualities of the "worst academic writing"—conceited, frivolous, superficial, hollow.
- He cites the winning excerpt from the most recent Bad Writing Contest, written by Judith Butler.
- He evaluates the winning excerpt: says Butler's style is ineffective and pretentious.
- He compares/contrasts writing of winners of the Bad Writing Contest with Kant, Aristotle, Wittgenstein; both groups of writers' writing is "obscure," but unlike Kant, et al., Bad Writing Contest–winning writers discuss trivial subjects and use difficult language to hide that they have unimportant ideas.

Analysis

1. Looking at professors' professional writing is important.
   - Dutton implies that the way professors use language could be a contributing factor in the "decline in student literacy."
   BUT
   - The connection between professors' writing in professional context and students' difficulties with literacy is unclear; Dutton ignores how professors communicate within the classroom, the type of writing students are assigned, social context for the "decline in student literacy" . . . .
   - It isn't clear that "bad" writing is widespread; Bad Writing Contest only receives 70 entries a year . . . Dutton doesn't prove "bad" writing is widespread among academia.

2. Bad writing is writing with a needlessly complicated style that addresses "trivial" ideas.
    - Dutton links bad writing with the use of "specialized vocabulary" within English Literature/Cultural Studies departments.
    - English Literature and Cultural Studies departments write about "trivial" subject matter (pop culture).

    BUT

    - Re: "specialized vocabulary" and "phony technicality": it is unclear why literature does not require a technical vocabulary; as subject continues to be studied, new terms develop to encompass what has been said about the topic, new ways of analyzing, new perspectives required for field to continue.
    - Re: "trivial" subject matter; why is popular culture not worthy of academic study? It permeates the world around us; how come it's trivial to look at mass culture and analyze it?

Response

- How would professors writing differently or about different subjects benefit me as a university student?
- There is no information cited by Dutton that supports Dutton's implication that how professors write in professional publications influences students.
- How does complicated writing make students less literate?
- "Straw man" argument? Is there really nothing redeeming about theory? Cultural studies?
- Shouldn't professors have freedom to persuade their interests (not just what DD thinks is important, or what has been important in the past—e.g., Milton, Melville)?
- "Specialized vocabulary"—from my perspective, as an undergraduate student, Dutton's critique of a specialized vocabulary doesn't make sense because in academic writing qualifications have to be made, specific descriptions are required—e.g., so many words describe different aspects of diction (asyndeton, sibilant sounds, polysyndeton, alliteration, anaphora).

Conclusion

- Dutton does not achieve his goal in this argument.
- My response to the argument is negative because of Dutton's *ad hominem* attacks (e.g., professors are more concerned with "showing off" than trying to communicate).
- Overall assessment: strengths (interesting/important issues raised, e.g., literacy in contemporary society, communication within universities), weaknesses (Dutton's use of evidence, his ethos).

DUCO colors shown: Dolphin Blue, Candlelight Ivory and White Semi-Gloss, Primrose Yellow Gloss. Ask your Du Pont Paint dealer about illustrated booklet "Color... Utensils and Stencils," show-ing 78 color schemes for your home or rent 25¢ to Du Pont Co. Finishes Division, Dept. 43E, Wilmington, Delaware. (Offer good only in U.S.A.)

In new, velvety Semi-Gloss or glistening Gloss . . .
DUCO enamel is "One-Coat Magic"

Here's color-scheming for a living room that lures you into a restful mood . . . and makes life easier on house-cleaning days, too! For the rich DUCO decorator colors are so easily kept fresh . . . just whisk over with a damp cloth!

A DUCO finish stays color-bright, color-*right* for years. For a soft, satin-smooth finish for walls and woodwork, use new DUCO Semi-Gloss. For the sparkling, tile-like finish so popu-lar on kitchen and bathroom walls, on outdoor or indoor furniture, use famous DUCO Gloss.

For every interior, DUCO enamel is "One-

Coat Magic"! From delicate pastels to dra-matic deep-tones, you'll find DUCO colors just right for your home. Ask your Du Pont Paint dealer about DUCO enamel today.

And remember...DUCO White, in Gloss or Semi-Gloss, stays brilliant white through the years.

* easy to apply—dries fast
* covers solidly without brush marks
* takes repeated washings—defies grease
* stands hard knocks, protects for years
* preferred by professional painters

Interior of Mastic Tan and White, Jonquil Yellow

A Grotto Green and White Semi-Gloss combination.

Save the Surface and You Save All!

DU PONT PAINTS
CHEMICALLY ENGINEERED
TO DO THE JOB BETTER
BETTER THINGS FOR BETTER LIVING . . . THROUGH CHEMISTRY

DUCO   DUCO   40 HOUSE PAINT   DULUX Trim & Shutter   DULUX VARNISH   HOUKOTE   PORCH & FLOOR

Chatelaine Magazine Cover, March 1955, copyright public domain. Courtesy of Rogers Publishing Ltd.

First for Canadian Women

Chatelaine

Fencer
SHERRAINE SCHALM, 33

EXCLUSIVE
How track star
**PERDITA FELICIEN, 27
picked herself up
after the fall**

Special
$2.99

Gymnast
ALEX ORLANDO, 21

OUR FABULOUS OLYMPIANS
CANADA'S ATHLETES SHOW THE WORLD
WHAT GIRLS ARE MADE OF

$2.99 | AUGUST 2008
WWW.CHATELAINE.C

08

0 74470 70002 9

DISPLAY UNTIL AUGUS
PM40070230R08251

THE *real*
WAY TO STAY
HEALTHY
FOR LIFE

+ **Fresh summer recipes**
Cooking with peaches,
salads that won't leave you
starving, and more

Where have all the guys gone? ALBERTA Meet Atlantic Canada's oil-patch widows

DRAFT 2

A Critique of Denis Dutton's "Language Crimes"

1   Denis Dutton is an academic and the editor of the scholarly journal *Philosophy and Literature*. In an opinion piece published by the newspaper the *Wall Street Journal*, "Language Crimes: A Lesson in How Not to Write, Courtesy of the Professoriate," Dutton explains his concerns about the quality of the academic writing produced by contemporary academics. Within this piece, Dutton also describes the rationale behind his decision to have *Philosophy and Literature* hold the Bad Writing Contest, which critiques examples from what Dutton sees as a trend towards the publication of "awkward, jargon-clogged" (Dutton 145) academic writing. The issues raised by Dutton's argument are important because the topics studied within academia as well as how academics write about them not only influence the scholarly community, but also society as a whole.

2   Dutton's piece begins with his concession that academic writing does not need to be aesthetically pleasing. Although academics have rarely produced texts with an aesthetic appeal, Dutton believes that a particularly unpleasant, vacuous, and incommunicative prose style has been emerging in published academic writing. Examining the writing published by professors in academic books and journals is important, Dutton argues, because of contemporary concerns about the literacy skills of students. To illustrate this point, Dutton quotes the introductory sentence of an academic work on education, and evaluates it as unacceptably convoluted because it is produced by a professional, an English professor, who should model effective communication.

3   In order to demonstrate the extent and excesses of such "deplorable writing among the professoriate" (145), Dutton explains that he decided to establish the Bad Writing Contest. Contest entries consist of excerpts from published academic works which have been submitted to Dutton and the other editors of *Philosophy and Literature*. Approximately seventy submissions had been received at the journal annually, and were judged by Dutton and his colleagues. Dutton cites several of these entries within the opinion piece. The submissions which receive criticism in Dutton's argument are largely those within the fields of Literary and Cultural Studies.

4   Dutton explains that his objections to the type of writing submitted to the contest are based on stylistic and epistemological reasons. The diction used by

these scholars—whose terminology largely stems from critical theory—is criticized for having a "vatic tone and phony technicality" (145). The topics studied by these scholars—such as popular culture—are criticized as "trivial" (145). The main reasons why this "bad writing" is undesirable, according to Dutton, are that it is "intellectual kitsch" (146), i.e., its "jargon-laden prose always suggests but never delivers genuine insight" (146), and that this obtuse style hinders communication on the subject it discusses.

5 "Language Crimes" concludes with Dutton comparing and contrasting the writing of the Bad Writing Contest winners with the writing of classic scholars such as Aristotle, Kant, and Wittgenstein. The writing of both groups, Dutton explains, is "obscure" (146), but the Bad Writing Contest winners discuss trivial issues and use difficult prose to hide that they have unimportant ideas. Aristotle et al., on the other hand, used complex language to further the pursuit of knowledge.

6 Some of Dutton's main points within "Language Crimes" lack supporting evidence that would improve the persuasiveness of his argument. At the start of the piece, Dutton implies that the way in which many contemporary professors use language could be a contributing factor in the "decline in student literacy" (145). However, the connection between professors' writing in professional publications and students' difficulties with literacy is unclear. How professors communicate within the classroom is not mentioned as relevant, nor are factors from outside the classroom mentioned as relevant factors by Dutton. Further, it is not clear that "bad writing" is widespread because as Dutton himself mentions, the Bad Writing Contest received only about seventy entries annually.

7 Dutton's definition of "bad writing" is writing with a needlessly complicated style about frivolous subjects. Bad writing, in Dutton's view, is associated with the rise of a particular type of "specialized vocabulary" within English departments, a vocabulary associated with "theory." Dutton fails to explain why theory is an "inept philosophy" other than from the reason that some scholars use it poorly; that argument could be applied to any field of intellectual endeavour. Dutton's argument that the subjects written about through the lens of "theory" are "trivial" is equally generic; his claim that professors are teaching Cultural Studies because it stimulates students' interests does not make the discipline frivolous.

8 Although I agree with Dutton that "awkward, jargon-laden" academic writing is undesirable, I strongly disagree with his contention that the "specialized vocabulary" employed in some university departments is harmful to university students. Dutton's implication that "obscure" writing within professional publications necessarily impedes students' ability to understand professors and write well is demeaning. As a university student, I understand that academic writing in the

humanities requires a great deal of complexity, often in the form of qualifications, specific descriptions, extended comparisons, and a resistance to conventional explanations. Dutton's argument is written for a mass audience, and it seems that he is misleading them about what academic writing demands.

9   Overall, Dutton's argument within "Language Crimes" does not achieve its stated goal of establishing that contemporary academic writing is in decline, or that it is placing students at a disadvantage. Although Dutton introduces his claims with the idea that he is concerned about students' literacy, he fails to make a cogent argument that theory and "intellectual kitsch" are hindering students' acquisition of skills and academics' expansion of knowledge. My response to Dutton's argument is largely negative because of the rhetorical technique of the *ad hominem* attack that he employs to support his claims. Dutton's statements about how academics whose writing is suitable for winning the Bad Writing Contest are more concerned with "showing off" than communicating are unfair; just because a writer has arguably bad prose does not mean they are intellectually dishonest. Unfortunately, Dutton's ostensible concern within this piece, addressing status of communication within the academic community, is not aided by his use of evidence or his ethos.

Work Cited

Dutton, Denis. "Language Crimes." In *Across the Disciplines: Academic Writing and Reading.* Ed. Jaqueline McLeod Rogers and Catherine Taylor. Toronto: Pearson, 2011. Print.

EXERCISE

1. Read the two drafts, and note five changes the writer makes to develop or improve the draft.

2. Discuss your notes in small groups, comparing the changes you see.

3. Can you identify places where the writer could do more work?

Stage 3: Editing and Proofreading

Time should be reserved at the end to attend to such micro-level issues as style (is the language used always appropriate for the audience? Is it as clear and dynamic as you can make it?), correct usage (are comma splices and sentence fragments avoided? Is everything spelled correctly?), typing (are there any typographical errors?), and complete documentation (is there a citation for every single usage of every single source, and a reference list at the end?). Because it is often hard to see your own mistakes, particularly if you have been working on an essay so long that you're feeling a bit stale about it, writing instructors often set up peer-editing workshops that focus only on this final stage of the writing process.

At this stage, access to a writing handbook that goes over matters of style and grammar can be helpful. In the box that follows we provide a list of common grammatical errors that may help to guide your proofreading work, but if an error is unusual you may need to ask for help identifying it and then consult a handbook to understand options for making corrections. The writing tools available in word processors (spell checker, thesaurus, grammar checker) provide another source of help, although they are not infallible in error-detection. All of these editing aids, including peer feedback, should be viewed as sources of possible improvements rather than correct answers. Writers know their work best and should always weigh their options carefully rather than obediently follow advice.

Here is the final draft of the critique we have observed in earlier draft stages:

FINAL DRAFT

Not Guilty: A Critique of Denis Dutton's "Language Crimes"

1   Denis Dutton is an academic and the editor of a small scholarly journal *Philosophy and Literature.* In an opinion-piece published by the newspaper *The Wall Street Journal,* "Language Crimes: A Lesson in How Not to Write, Courtesy of the Professoriate," Dutton criticizes the quality of the academic writing being produced by contemporary academics. Within this piece, Dutton also describes the rationale behind his decision to have *Philosophy and Literature* hold a Bad Writing Contest, a contest critical of professional, published academic writing. The issues raised by Dutton's argument are important because communication within academia not only influences the scholarly community, but also society as a whole.

2   Dutton's piece begins with his statement that although academics have rarely produced texts with an aesthetic appeal, a particularly unpleasant, vacuous, and incommunicative prose style has been emerging in published academic writing. Examining the writing published by professors in academic books and journals is important, Dutton argues, because of contemporary concerns about the literacy skills of students. To illustrate this point, Dutton quotes the introductory sentence of an academic work on education, and evaluates it as unacceptably convoluted because it is produced by a professional, an English professor, who should model graceful writing.

3   In order to demonstrate the extent and excesses of "deplorable writing among the professoriate" (Dutton 145), Dutton established the Bad Writing

Contest. Contest entries consist of excerpts from published academic works which have been submitted to Dutton and the other editors of *Philosophy and Literature.* Approximately seventy submissions had been received at the journal annually, and were judged by Dutton and his colleagues. The submissions which receive criticism in Dutton's argument are largely those within the fields of Literary and Cultural Studies.

4   Dutton objects to the type of writing submitted to the contest for stylistic and epistemological reasons. The diction used by these scholars—whose terminology largely stems from critical theory—is criticized for having a "vatic tone and phony technicality" (145). The topics studied by these scholars—such as popular culture—are criticized as "trivial" (145). The main reason why this "bad writing" is undesirable, according to Dutton, is that it is "intellectual kitsch" (146), i.e., it has more style than substance. As "Language Crimes" concludes, Dutton compares and contrasts the writing of the Bad Writing Contest winners with the writing of classic scholars such as Aristotle, Kant, and Wittgenstein. Dutton explains that the writing of both groups is "obscure" (146), but the Bad Writing Contest winners discuss trivial issues and use difficult prose to hide that they have unimportant ideas. Classic writers, on the other hand, use complex language to further the pursuit of knowledge.

5   Dutton's main points within "Language Crimes" lack enough supporting evidence to make his argument persuasive. At the start of the piece, Dutton implies that the way in which many contemporary professors use language could be a contributing factor in the "decline in student literacy" (145). However, the connection between professors' writing in professional publications and students' difficulties with literacy is unclear. Relevant issues, like how professors communicate within the classroom, the quality of the education that students receive before university, and social changes outside of the classroom are not mentioned by Dutton. Further, it is not clear that "bad writing" among academics is widespread because, as Dutton himself mentions, the Bad Writing Contest received only about seventy entries annually.

6   Dutton's definition of "bad writing" is writing that is needlessly technical and covers irrelevant subjects. Bad writing is associated with the rise of a particular type of "specialized vocabulary" within English departments, a vocabulary associated with theory. Dutton fails to explain why theory is an "inept philosophy" (145) other than for the reason that some scholars use it poorly; that argument could be applied to any field of intellectual endeavour. In addition, Dutton's argument that the topics discussed with theory are "trivial" (145) is

equally generic; his claim that professors are teaching Cultural Studies because it stimulates students' interests does not make the discipline frivolous.

7   Although I agree with Dutton that "awkward, jargon-laden" (146) academic writing is undesirable, I strongly disagree with his contention that the "specialized vocabulary" employed in some university departments is harmful to university students. As a university student, I understand that academic writing in the humanities requires a great deal of complexity, with frequent qualifications, specific descriptions, extended comparisons, and a resistance to conventional explanations. Dutton's argument is written for a mass audience, and it seems that he is misleading them about what academic writing demands.

8   Overall, Dutton's argument within "Language Crimes" does not achieve its goal of establishing that contemporary academic writing is in decline, or that "bad writing" is hindering students' education and academics' expansion of knowledge. My response to Dutton's argument is largely negative because of his use of *ad hominem* attacks to support his claims. Dutton's statements that the academics who are eligible for "winning" the Bad Writing Contest are more concerned with "showing off" (145) than communicating are unfair; because some writers have arguably bad prose, it does not mean that they are intellectually dishonest. Unfortunately, Dutton's ostensible concern within this piece, assessing status of communication within the academic community, is not aided by his use of evidence or his ethos.

Work Cited

Dutton, Denis. "Language Crimes: A Lesson in How Not to Write, Courtesy of the Professoriate." In *Across the Disciplines: Academic Writing and Reading.* Ed. Jaqueline McLeod Rogers and Catherine Taylor. Toronto: Pearson, 2011. Print.

EXERCISE

1. Identify several changes the author has made to move from draft to final stage.

2. If you were the writer (or advising the writer as a peer in a writing group), what further change(s) would you recommend?

3. Write a brief response to the writer, providing feedback to her the way you would to someone in your writing group. Consider these points:
   • what was most effective,
   • what sections/sentences need work,
   • what you think of her overall position (is it convincing/persuasive?).

Top Five Errors List

1. The Fragment

Sentences need both a subject and a verb. If one or both of these elements are missing, the words are not a sentence, but a mere fragment or phrase; for example, missing a subject: "Johnny was pure movement. *Always on the run.*"

When a subordinating conjunction (such as *because, after, when, which*) introduces a simple sentence (a main clause), it becomes a subordinate clause that cannot stand on its own—for example, "Johnny was pure movement. *Because he could never sit still.*"

2. The Comma Splice or Run-on

Complete sentences cannot be combined using a comma alone. Complete sentences can be combined using connecting words—coordinators (such as *and, or, but, yet*) or subordinators (such as *because, when, if*)—to link the two clauses together. Or you can use stronger punctuation—a semicolon to link or a period to separate ideas.

When a comma is used to connect two sentences, the result is a "comma splice" error. When sentences are run together with no punctuation or connecting words, the result is variously called a "run-on," "run-together," or "fused" sentence.

3. The Dangling or Misplaced Modifier

Modifiers are words and phrases that describe essential elements. They need to be beside the elements they are describing, to set up clear relationships. Otherwise, they "dangle" and are said to be "misplaced." For example, "*Serving the customers, the table* broke when the waiter picked up the plate."

4. Misplaced Commas

Commas group ideas together and tell readers where they can pause. If you're not sure about whether you need a comma, it's usually better to leave it out, so that you don't chop up ideas that need to go together.

In particular, avoid using a single comma to separate essential sentence elements. Never separate the subject from the verb; for example,

> *NO:*   Jordy dressed in designer junk, swaggered down the hall with a "look-at-me" rhythm.

> *YES:*   Jordy, dressed in designer junk, swaggered down the hall with a "look-at-me" rhythm.

5. Missing or Wrong Agreements

The agreement that gives us trouble usually occurs when we are trying to decide whether a singular or plural pronoun should replace a noun. Is it "A writer needs to sharpen his or her pencil" or "A writer needs to sharpen their pencil"? The correct version is the first one, using a singular pronoun, but using the masculine and feminine pronouns together is awkward. In cases like this, try changing the noun to the plural form: *Writers need to sharpen their pencils.*

PARAGRAPHS: FORMING AND SHAPING IDEAS

What Paragraphs Do

Paragraphs are made up of sentences that focus on a topic to develop an idea about it. The indentation that marks the start of a new paragraph is like a pause to tell your readers that there is some separation between the idea you have been developing and the one that you will develop in the paragraph ahead. Of course, the new paragraph is related to the previous one because both deal with some aspect of your thesis, but it is common for each paragraph to offer a fresh or altered approach.

Paragraph Variety: The Long and Short of It

As you have probably noticed when you are reading, paragraphs vary in length and complexity. Paragraph variety is often recommended as a way to appeal to readers. Yet the length of a paragraph is not entirely arbitrary, since it is often governed by the complexity of the concepts you are treating. Complex ideas sometimes require a long paragraph or even several paragraphs to explore their components adequately. If several paragraphs are needed to treat one idea, a shift to a new paragraph means that the writer is refocusing to take a new angle or present a new stage of thought.

Beginnings, Middles, Ends

The following sections provide guidelines to help you (1) think about shaping paragraphs and (2) make choices about developing details. Within composition circles, debate is beginning to grow about whether readers continue to expect academic writing to be well formed—connected and unified—since so much of our reading experience is shaped by jumping from site to site on the internet. We interrupt our own readings of source materials, often by juxtaposing several sources together in ways the authors never imagined. Over time, academic writing may begin to reflect some of these changes, but so far the requirements of connnectedness and consistency remain in place across disciplines.

Some writers are conscious of forming paragraphs even in early drafting stages. These writers often work from an outline of main, or topic, ideas, and thus approach essay writing by building a series of paragraphs that address different elements of the thesis. Other writers are more concerned with using their draft to explore ideas and they do not worry about paragraph structure until returning to the draft to make revisions. At some stage in the writing process, it can be useful to remember that most projects require three types of paragraphs—*introductory*, *concluding*, and *middle* paragraphs that build the body of the essay—and that helpful guidelines exist for shaping each of these.

Introductions: Some General Guidelines

Introductory paragraphs announce your topic and identify how you intend to approach it; to do this, this paragraph often includes your thesis sentence. This lets readers understand your intention from the outset—whether it is, for example, to explore, illustrate, or demonstrate your idea. Like other paragraphs, introductions usually contain some generalizations alongside more specific details. What makes an introduction different from paragraphs in the middle section is that its purpose is to announce the main argument or the "big idea."

Although there are many ways to build opening paragraphs, you may find it helpful in the drafting process to have a basic or conventional pattern in mind. Perhaps the most basic organizational pattern is to move from general to specific. You begin on relatively general grounds, often by telling the reader what the topic area is, what book you will examine, what controversy you will enter, or what situation you will analyze. The next few sentences often narrow or restrict your topic, so that you clarify some of your decisions about taking a specific approach to your topic. This sometimes involves sorting out why certain areas of the topic concern you and others do not. Sometimes when you are writing an argument using academic research, it involves locating your argument in the context of other academic commentary, so that you "create a research space" (see the discussion of the CARS-style introduction in Chapter 6). Finally, the last sentence of your opening paragraph often gives the reader your thesis—what you mean to say or contend about your specific topic.

One of the biggest problems with writing an opening paragraph occurs when writers try to cover too much. Remember that an introductory paragraph needs to familiarize readers with your focus and approach, and that substantive commentary presenting your evidence should come in the paragraphs to follow, which aim at developing your thesis idea. There is no rule concerning the correct length of an introduction. If you feel that a short introduction is appropriate, use one.

Some Advice about Getting Started: "GET STARTED!"

Sometimes handbooks and teachers say so much about captivating readers with lively openings and clear theses that students block and stall, waiting for the wonderful rather than beginning to work from a sensible, revisable starting place. Remember: Your thesis is a working thesis—a statement subject to reframing—until the essay is finished. Similarly, the first version of your introductory paragraph introduces an essay that does not yet exist, and probably needs to be revisited and revised as you draft your ideas.

In early drafting stages, it is not worthwhile to linger too long crafting a perfect introduction. Chances are you will need to return to the opening to rework it in light of new information and connections brought to light by the process of drafting.

See Chapter 6 (page 113) for a specialized type of introduction used by writers to create a research space.

Conclusions: Some General Guidelines

Your conclusion is a place to reiterate your thesis—briefly this time, since the reader should already have it in mind, although he or she may appreciate a prompt or reminder. You can sometimes pick up the key word or phrase from your thesis, creating a link between start and finish in this way. It is also the place to tell the reader why he or she should care, by making some broad connections or applications often to the human or world situation. Thus, the conclusion restates the thesis idea and usually expands on the idea.

While some writers want to summarize the whole essay in this last paragraph, this is usually overkill. An all-out summary is only helpful when an essay is long (say, over 25 pages) or extremely complex, so that the reader might benefit from a thorough recap.

If the form of an introduction at its most basic is like a funnel or top-heavy triangle, the conclusion can be pictured as an inversion of this—as an inverted funnel or bottom-heavy triangle. Usually the first sentence offers a recap of the thesis idea. This can be relatively brief, since your readers should be fairly clear about your main contention and expect the conclusion to offer a general reminder of the gist.

"I'm Done, Except for the Conclusion!"

Many students worry too much about the conclusion. The truth is, the conclusion should be relatively brief, for by this final stage it is too late to add anything substantive. Your conclusion will probably serve you well if it echoes your opening and provides an interesting connection between the world of your essay and the reader's world.

EXERCISE

1. Look at the final draft of the student-written model essay above. How would you describe the pattern of the conclusion?

2. Look at the concluding paragraphs of some of the professional essays in this book to see if you can find examples of several different approaches to writing conclusions.

Middle Paragraphs: Paragraphs of Support

While it is important to write carefully crafted introductions and conclusions because they catch readers both coming and going, paragraphs in the body or middle of the essay make up the remaining 98 percent of your essay and are therefore worth careful construction. Middle paragraphs are sometimes called paragraphs of support because they typically demonstrate or support some element of the thesis or main idea. Yet, common general purpose aside, middle paragraphs do many things—raise questions, provide examples, analyze arguments, develop interpretations—and take different shapes. Those that work best tend to be unified (focusing on one idea) and complete (providing enough detail about that one idea). Paragraphs also need to be presented in a coherent way, so that sentences are not choppy but smoothly linked together.

Unity

A paragraph should be about *one thing*. It should discuss one point rather than several or, if the point is complex, one aspect of the point. Paragraphs that try to cover too much ground can seem thin or underdeveloped, conveying the impression that the writer's thoughts have ranged far and wide but have not been deep.

One way to ensure that a paragraph is unified is to develop it from a topic sentence—a sentence that announces the general paragraph idea. This sentence controls the paragraph, since everything that follows it offers some level of support. For example, after announcing the paragraph topic in the topic sentence, the next sentence often restates the topic in a more refined or restricted version. From there we get the specific support—the facts, illustrations, statistics—that serve as evidence.

It helps some writers to think about the topic sentence as an "umbrella sentence" that "covers" the paragraph. In this way, it works like a small version of the thesis sentence, which can be seen as a bigger "umbrella sentence" that covers the essay as a whole.

Many paragraphs do not state a topic sentence directly, but convey the paragraph topic tacitly, by implication. If one of your paragraphs seems unmanageable and appears to lack unity, you might try to summarize it in a sentence, which can then function as an organizing topic sentence. You can decide whether to incorporate this sentence into the paragraph directly or just use it to help you focus and redirect the paragraph.

In the following example, the first paragraph builds from a direct topic statement, while the second paragraph implies the topic idea.

Direct Topic Sentence

Narrative writing has become increasingly influential across the curriculum in the last 10 years. Before that time, most disciplines favoured an objective tone and the recital of facts, but using the personal voice to treat the realm of material experience became more popular with the spread of postmodern skepticism toward the possibility of knowing truth. In the social sciences, ethnographies and case studies began to appear alongside more traditional quantitative studies, and personal essays began to be published with more frequency in journals in the humanities. In their recent text examining *Narrative Inquiry*, Clandinin and Connelly point out that while a narrative approach is appropriate to education research because it grants a human dimension to studying how humans think and learn, this approach is employed across disciplines, and they have consulted "other social sciences and humanities for insights" into how narrative inquiries can work (5).

Tacit Topic Sentence

About 10 years ago, ethnographies and case studies began to appear along-side more traditional quantitative studies in the social sciences, and personal essays began to be published with more frequency in journals in the humanities. In their recent text examining *Narrative Inquiry*, Clandinin and Connelly point out that while a narrative approach is appropriate to education research because it grants a human dimension to studying how humans think and learn, they recognize that this approach has an interdisciplinary appeal, for they have consulted "other social sciences and humanities for insights" into how narrative inquiries can work (5).

Note: The above paragraph cites material from D. Jean Clandinin and F. Michael Connelly, *Narrative Inquiry: Experience and Story in Qualitative Research.* San Francisco: Jossey-Bass, 2000. Print.

You also need to consider that sometimes complex topic sentences are multi-layered and control several paragraphs. To demonstrate the topic idea, that narrative inquiry is being used in many disciplines, a writer might decide to use three paragraphs to explore how there is evidence of this in the humanities, the social sciences, and, finally, the sciences.

Completeness

There is no formula to govern the length of a complete paragraph. However, to develop an idea fully, a paragraph usually requires a blend of general and specific information. On a general level, you state your topic sentence or paragraph point. More specific information follows this, serving as evidence to demonstrate your general point. For example, after an assertion, you might offer examples, facts, and/or statistics as supporting detail.

While there are no tests for paragraph completeness, many undergraduate writers struggle with the problem of leaving their ideas underdeveloped. It can sometimes help to remind yourself that two examples are probably more convincing than one and that readers expect you to explain or interpret the way in which an example demonstrates your point. Moreover, it is also a good strategy to use a variety of evidence, so that you can strengthen the effect of an example or observation from experience by giving it alongside a relevant statistic or a supportive quotation from an expert. In the sample paragraph demonstrating the use of a direct topic sentence, the writer's observations and interpretations gain resonance because they are echoed in "the expert testimony" of Clandinin and Connelly.

EXERCISE *Look over several readings in the "Canadian Identities" chapter to find examples of support paragraphs with overt and tacit topic sentences. Is it easier to read a paragraph when the topic sentence is directly stated? Could an author overdo this approach?*

CHAPTER 3

Representing Your Own Experience and Observations: Using Personal Voice in Academic Writing

THE GROUNDS FOR PERSONAL EXPERIENCE AS EVIDENCE

In most academic writing, writers consider the ideas of others in the course of developing their own position. The writer typically consults recognized experts in a field, and eventually forms a view that draws from the well of disciplinary knowledge. In these terms, it is easy to think of forming an opinion as a process that is driven by facts. And if you believe that your opinion can be proven by consulting the facts, it makes sense to present it in objective terms in order to confer upon your presentation the status of "facts-in-waiting."

Many researchers continue to conduct experiments that use scientific methodology and systematic techniques to build knowledge in a traditional and cumulative fashion. They believe that their research establishes factual evidence. But over the last few decades, as we have entered our postmodern period of thinking, many scholars—usually in non-science disciplines—have been more willing to acknowledge the role of interpretation in the meaning-making process. Many believe that much we hold to be true is culturally constructed rather than independently significant or essential.

For example, for many in our culture, the terms "masculinity" and "femininity" are associated with a set of behaviours we assume to be based in biological difference. Yet, according to vast and compelling social science research, "gender" is a cultural construct subject to change over time and place, so that, for example, our images of masculinity differ from those that prevail in less industrialized societies that offer different work and leisure opportunities. Images of masculinity also vary within our own contemporary culture, with many younger people considering hair dye and cosmetics part of masculine culture, and older people tending to associate these products with women. As a further illustration of how our thinking about gender changes, we might remember that historical analysts have pointed out that the words "homosexuality" and "heterosexuality" did not exist before the 1800s.

While facts about human experience may be hard to come by, the researcher sorts through negotiated ideas that a knowledge community has agreed to accept on the understanding that disciplinary knowledge is fluid and dynamic, always in the process of forming rather than final. In this light, conclusions of the best experts are still tentative constructs rather than immutable facts. A researcher takes these views into consideration in order, in turn, to represent a view rather than to prove a truth.

When writers are conscious of dealing with constructs rather than facts about human experience, they usually adjust their tone to abandon impersonality and neutrality. Rather than attempting to convey that they know best, once and for all, writers using a personal voice in their presentation invite readers to keep in mind that, while the text is informed by traditional expertise, it is a product of subjective understanding. To such writers, it would be negligent not to draw attention to that "fact."

EXERCISE   *Write a paragraph in which you identify your favourite band or song and argue that it is important in music history. As part of the evidence you use to develop your case, ask a friend or member of your writing group to comment on your musical choice. Refer to their comment to support your view if they agree or refute them if they disagree.*

First, write the paragraph using personal voice ("I") to express judgment or interpretation. Then, revise the paragraph so that it is written in the objective, third-person voice. How do the two versions differ? Which sounds more authentic and persuasive? Which sounds more fact-based and authoritative? Consider this: Some modern critical theorists hold that writers/researchers should enter their texts to clarify their position and experience explicitly, rather than attempting or pretending to be disinterested and without bias.

Where Does Personal Voice Fit in Academic Writing?

We are comfortable using the personal "I" voice in informal writing situations such as emails to friends or journal entries to ourselves. But many of us still resist using this voice in academic writing situations, which are usually characterized as more formal and serious.

When asked to write a personal-voice essay—in which the "I" pronoun plays a lead role—many students struggle because they have been trained in high school to abandon this way of presenting ideas. Perhaps you can remember your high school English teachers discouraging the use of personal voice and recommending instead that you adopt third-person objectivity. Instead of being encouraged to express your ideas using a personal pronoun—and writing, for example, "I believe that Holden Caulfield finds joy at the end of *Catcher in the Rye*"—you were encouraged to present your observations as objective statements—for example, "Holden Caulfield finds joy at the end of *Catcher in the Rye*." Even if you draft a sentence like "In my experience, the school system fails students who are smart," you probably revise it in later drafts to achieve impersonality, so that it eventually reads "The school system fails students who are smart." While the second version is more succinct and sounds more objective, what has been lost is the direct link between experience and claim. Adding the personal voice does not detract from the plausibility of the claim, but clarifies that it should be understood as grounded in human experience.

Of course, there are writing situations in which the personal voice is not appropriate or particularly helpful—when it is important to keep the focus squarely on the subject itself rather than on the activity of interpreting the subject. For example, if you are describing how something is done—such as the steps in an experiment—it is awkward and unnecessary to refer to yourself; instead of "I put the beaker on the burner" you would probably prefer to focus on the action itself with a sentence like "The beaker was placed on the burner."

Yet there is growing recognition that reading and writing are interpretive activities—that there are different ways to read and respond to texts and that the meanings we make are provisional rather than lasting. Replacing third-person objectivity with first-person subjectivity in non-scientific writing situations can be a move toward acknowledging the role of interpretation and reflection in knowing.

Writing in the first person often works when we are asked to interpret some element of human experience, given that each of us brings our own assumptions to the task. As part of the methodology of this type of research, writers are often encouraged to adopt an attitude of self-consciousness, in the sense of being willing to reflect on how their experience may be shaping their response to a text. Certainly, personal voice is the best choice when self-reflection is part of the research process, as it is, for example, when writers consider the influence of race or gender on their thinking about an issue. Personal voice can be used in a wide range of ways, from lengthy self-reflection to occasional use of "I." Whenever we write, we should always consider our situation—our purpose and audience—before making choices about matters of diction, detail, and overall voice. Whether to use first- or third-person voice is a rhetorical matter that scholarly writers need to consider in their disciplinary context.

We have suggested that a move toward personal-voice writing has coincided with the postmodern intellectual movement toward tolerating plurality, ambiguity, and dynamism as part of the process of knowing: there is no reason to strike a pose of objectivity if you believe you are presenting a situated understanding— an understanding that reflects a careful analysis of the conditions at work in a particular time and place.

Yet for many scholars, the position of the personal voice in academic writing is an unresolved issue. Some who have been trained in the tradition of using the third-person voice for all academic writing reject first-person writing as an unsuitable style. Others—who may be unhappy with the postmodern view of knowledge as changeable and responsive to particular contexts, rather than fixed—reject personal writing on serious methodological grounds. Knowing that many scholars continue to be uneasy with personal-voice writing, you need to make decisions about your audience and situation on a case-by-case basis.

EXERCISE

1. Write a sentence using the first person to respond to or explore an idea that you found interesting in the section above. Now, write a sentence summarizing the main idea in the section above, using an objective third-person stance. Is one task easier than the other?

2. Read your sentences aloud to your writing group. Because the responses explaining what writers find interesting are completely subjective, you will likely hear a lot of variety. By contrast, summaries are usually thought to be relatively objective reproductions of text. Yet there may still be some variety in the summaries as well because summarizing also involves a writer's decisions about main and important ideas.

3. Examine the readings in a scholarly journal in a subject that interests you. Is the personal voice used in some? How?

(When) Can I Use "I"?

One of the questions students ask most frequently about their writing is whether it is acceptable to use "I" to refer directly to themselves in their essay or assignment. Like many good questions, this one does not have a simple answer. Some high school teachers may have made restrictions against the use of "I." They may have argued that readers find objectivity more convincing, or that there is no need for writers to identify themselves ("It's your paper so of course you think such and such is true").

Increasingly, however, there are writing occasions across disciplines that call for personal voice and commitment. A research report to convey information may begin with an extended autobiographical passage to situate the researcher; within these reports, single sentences in which the writer conveys choices or interpretations can use personal voice. Reflective essays that depend on personal connections and insight are conducted entirely from a first-person perspective. So whether or not to use "I" is a decision to be made on a case-by-case basis. Personal reflections, autobiography, narrative argument, ethnography, and journals all call for the personal voice.

THE NARRATIVE ARGUMENT: TELLING STORIES THAT MAKE A POINT

The narrative argument is a common form of academic writing that involves writers directly by asking them to explore an idea or point by referring to their own experience. You may find it helpful to think about "narrative" as an academic word for "story." Using the term "narrative" is not just inventing jargon to make simple things seem complex, or known forms obscure. Typically, academic narrative is unlike what we normally think of as story in two ways.

First, a scholarly narrative—one written to address some level of academic audience—is usually based on the writer's experience, on some actual life scenes. While this does not mean that narratives are "true" reflections of what happened—that they are *necessarily* accurate accounts—they convey the writer's representation of reality as it was experienced rather than as it was imagined. Compared to the idea of "story" in its fictional variants, "narrative" is connected more closely to actual life.

The second element that distinguishes narrative from story is that the writer's commitment to making meaning—or more specifically, making a point—is central and not optional as it is to the fiction-teller. To build a narrative argument, the writer needs to make a clear connection between the personal experience and the public issue under discussion. To move from writer- to reader-based prose, the writer needs to show how his or her personal experience makes a point and is accessible to others who have had like experiences.

Making a point from experience does not in itself prove things or justify conclusions, but it can help to improve a reader's understanding. To accomplish this, your account of your experience should resonate with others, moving beyond the minutiae of particular events to strike a chord others recognize from their own experience. You will probably find it helpful to think about the personal argument as having twin components. As its name suggests, it is about a personal experience (or about several experiences, depending on the approach you pick) *and* it also makes an argument. In this way, the personal essay also has a thesis—the details support the point the essay makes about human experience.

EXERCISE   *Read the selections by Hoffman, McLeod Rogers, and Baker and compare how each uses personal experience in different ways. How does each put a public face on private experience? How does each use the details of personal experience to develop a thesis?*

Personal Voice in Writing Class Assignments: Life as Text

Many writing classes begin with a personal essay as a first assignment. In this assignment, you are often asked to make a point or explore an issue by telling a story drawn from your own experience. In other forms of writing—such as summary, critique, research argument—you look at written texts as the primary source of your ideas, but here it is your own experience that takes centre stage. Writing a narrative argument early in the term can be encouraging because it allows you to be the expert. You know more about your experience than your readers do, and your job is to help them understand its significance. Of all the assignments you write, you may find this one the most engaging because you have an obvious stake in reflecting on personal experience and understanding how it connects to and illuminates a public issue.

This form of writing is not really a holiday from the scholarly writing that lies ahead, for even if it does not, strictly speaking, involve research and textual analysis, it does prompt you to evaluate the "text "of your own life: your life history is the text you consult and evaluate in order to determine claim and support. And as always, you need to express yourself fluently and to decide what to omit, include, connect, and emphasize. This critical process is at the heart of most academic projects, which require writers to sort through the evidence to determine a pattern of development.

The personal essay comes in many varieties, so there is no one formula prescribing how you tell it—no rules, for example, for where you tell the story and where you stop to make your point. An important decision for you as the writer is whether to state your argument at the beginning, the end, or in both places. Experienced writers may even opt for making the point in a tacit or indirect way, so that all the details of the story work together to make a point, but no one sentence states the point in a nutshell.

If you make your point first, and then give your story, you are using the popular *deductive* pattern. Yet even in deductive narratives, the point of the story is seldom sharply separated from the telling of the story because good narratives usually interweave the two. Thinking about organizing a narrative according to a deductive framework can help you to connect this kind of writing to other forms of argument-based essays that announce their thesis in the opening. The point of the story is the thesis of the narrative argument, whereas a proposition or claim is the thesis in an analytical argument. Another basic way of developing a narrative is to use an *inductive* arrangement in which the story gets told first and the point of the story is directly addressed only in the conclusion. Sometimes this movement toward finding and refining the point of narrated experience is described as following an *exploratory* pattern, since the telling seems to replicate the writer's search for meaning. Because following a rigid pattern of induction or deduction can result in a story's being cut off from its broader implications, your teacher may recommend that you take an exploratory approach. Rather than announcing what your story will mean before you even begin telling it, or forcing it into a nutshell ending, an exploratory pattern allows meaning to accrue as you tell the story. For the reader, this has the effect of recreating the writer's sense of discovering or unfolding the connections and patterns in the events of experience.

Here are two samples of personal essays by students. The first, by Victoria Maynard, states as a general thesis at both the start and end that some stories are told to you and some you learn on your own, providing as the central narrative a story about being a victim of racism for the first time. The story conveys the writer's memory of pain and confusion, as well as the sense in which some things defy explanation. Thus it makes sense that the writer tells her story—which is about pain and the power of words to hurt—but does not try to grind a simplistic moral from it.

The second story, by Katie Murphy, is less personal and retrospective, since it describes current social changes that affect all of us. The writer reflects on how our expectations about what we can accomplish are changing, as technology continues to offer more possibilities. The writer tells us about changes she has experienced and observed, in order to encourage us to reflect on some of the attendant problems of thinking that we can buy programs to improve ourselves.

The Sweater: And Other Fables from My All-Canadian Childhood

by Victoria Maynard

1   There's one thing that almost every Canadian kid just knows. The Leafs: you either love 'em or hate 'em. That piece of Canadiana is one of the only things I can remember learning during elementary school. It wasn't in any sort of official lesson plan, but the word was out. In my grade 4 class, The Leafs were worse than wedgies. Looking back now, there are two types of stories I remember learning—stories I had told to me and the ones I learned on my own.

2   During my early years at school, one of my favourite things was when our whole class got to go to the library. Much of the time, our visits would consist of the librarian reading to us. My grade 4 year was the height of hockey-mania in the library. Everyone's absolute favourite story was Roch Carrier's *The Hockey Sweater.* We would listen to that story over and over again, even though our beloved Jets weren't in it. Each time I heard it, I got totally absorbed into the struggles of the little boy who was burdened with wearing the dreaded Leafs jersey. All his friends wore Habs jerseys. This situation seemed to be an almost unimaginable tragedy.

3   The boy asked his mother for a new jersey. She refused to buy him a new hockey sweater. She didn't know what the jersey meant. The boy couldn't explain its meaning in a way she'd understand. He couldn't bring himself to ask her again. His mom closed the argument by saying it was your insides that count anyways, not what you wear on the outside. Much like the little boy in the story, as a child I too missed the mother's moral of the story. As the librarian

read, my class would sit in the library listening, again and again. How could we not love this story? It was about hockey and how parents just don't understand. Years later, looking back, I have some sympathy for the mother. After all, she thought she was doing the right thing.

4   From my early years through high school, hockey always came up as a part of Canada. It's something we celebrate as a part of the nation's psyche along with our snowy winters, bilingualism, and colourful cultural mosaic. Hockey games are in the background as our lives play on. The suburb where I grew up was filled with French Immersion schools, which maybe accounted for most of us kids siding with the Habs. I went to a small French Immersion elementary school, so I remember listening to *"Le chandail de hockey."* Riding on the school bus, you could hear kids talking about hockey any time of year. Myself included, even though my dad wasn't like most of the other dads. He's from Barbados, a land without hockey. We didn't watch many hockey games in my family's house. Nevertheless, hockey was all around. Many of my friends played and I'd see them play at the local community centre. The radio at my maternal grandmother's house would be blasting out most games during my family's frequent visits. So my father too ended up hearing about hockey. Albeit at an uncomfortably loud volume.

5   When I got older, I learned that *The Hockey Sweater* could be read as a parable about the uncomfortable relationship between Canada's two solitudes. But back when I was listening to the story in the school library, I didn't hear anything about those differences. *Le Chandail* was so many nice words to me then. And as far as I knew, Canada had many faces by then, the 1980s, not just two. Usually, the story led to me spending a lot of time daydreaming about skating whenever I had a spare moment. One of my favourite spots to daydream was on the way to the bus stop. I'd wait for the school bus only a block from my parent's house. Because I was nine, I was allowed to catch the bus without my mom most days. I'd walk to the bus alone, sometimes cherishing my independence, but mostly lost in my childish reveries.

6   There was a kid around my age who would wait with me at the same bus stop for our ride to the same school. He was a boy, and therefore gross. We were kids of a certain age and the feeling was mutual. Nevertheless, we'd chat at the bus stop to pass the time. On many unfortunate days we'd end up getting assigned seats next to one another on the bus. Luckily, we lived in Winnipeg, which meant our parents had us bundled up tight in our snowsuits for most of

the year, so we weren't actually touching as we sat next to one another on the bus. In grade 4, sharing a seat with the opposite sex put you at risk for cooties, that miasma cast in turn by one sex on the other.

7 One morning this boy and I got into an argument at the bus stop. It had a most unexpected ending. I'd thought life couldn't get complicated until you hit double digits. So there we were, just two kids standing there, bickering. It got quiet when he said a word like it would cast a spell on me. It made sense that he could believe in magic, that he thought he could just "Abracadabra" me out of existence. I've forgotten what we had been arguing about. It couldn't have been too serious, we were only nine years old. I can still remember how his voice sounded when he said it. I never forget a voice. Earlier that year, my mom had my music teacher test me to see if I had perfect pitch. I didn't and still don't, but I've always had a good memory for sound.

8 In my mind's eye, I can replay that moment like a scene from a movie. We stood facing each other, me in my pink and grey snowsuit, him in an almost identical navy and red one. He says, "Shut up, shut up, shut up. You're stupid. Wrong and stupid." Almost two decades later I'm still surprised at what comes next. I hear: "I know what you are. My mom told me not to say it. But I know what you are. So shut up, you Nigger."

9 I'd never heard that word before. I asked him what it meant. So far, I'd only picked up on the change of topic. The usual taunts my schoolmates and I lobbed at one another were along the lines of "booger" or "snotbag." At worst, someone would throw out the still inscrutable, to me at least, insult of "dillweed." I asked him again what it meant. I didn't say the word, I was too scared to say it, because I knew it had to be a bad word. Back then, I thought that if I said "H-E-double-hockey-stick" out loud, that when I died, I wouldn't go to heaven. My schoolmate didn't answer at first. He just stared at me like he'd cast a spell on me that didn't entirely work. Eventually, he said something about how it meant something bad and I was something bad because I was the word. We didn't sit together on the bus that day.

10 After school, I asked my mom what the word meant while we sat eating our afternoon snack of apples and cheese. Mom asked me where I'd heard that word and I told her about that morning at the bus stop. She looked sad. For years after that, I still didn't know what the word meant. I'd wonder why my mother had told me to both forget the word and remember not to say it. I couldn't bring myself to ask her again. I was left to myself, wondering "Am I that thing?"

11   Years later, looking back I can sympathize with my mother. After all, she thought she was doing the right thing. I guess she couldn't explain the word's meaning to me in a way I'd understand. Or maybe she could have told me the truth—that sometimes it's not someone's insides that matter, some people just see what's on the outside—and the past isn't sealed off and far away. My mother didn't want some stories to become a part of my childhood, but they slipped in anyways. I learned some stories on my own because no one else would tell me.

12   The next morning I was alone at the bus stop. I guessed the word had some power after all.

Work Cited

Carrier, Roch. *The Hockey Sweater.* 1979. Trans. Sheila Fischman. Toronto: Tundra Books, 1984. Print.

Only Human: The Dawn of Human Enhancement

by Katie Murphy

1   I turned on *The Daily Show* the other night just as special correspondent Samantha Bee was finishing up her report on the future of robotics. A technologies expert said something that woke me from my half-watching-half-drifting-to-sleep trance: human *enhancement.* "Imagine being able to implant a chip into your brain that would allow you to understand calculus, for example." He suggested that in the future, advancements in robotics for enhancements in humans will be far more weird than *The Terminator.* Implied rampant lawlessness aside, I have not been able to stop wondering just how weird humans might be, or how *human* humans might be—I mean, look at how weird things are already: implants are not the future, but already a reality. Wireless communication technologies are implanted in human teeth, and now, can be transferred via electrical currents flowing through human skin. You can enhance your vision with eye laser technology, enhance hearing with hearing aids, if you lose a limb there are artificial robotic ones to replace them, even artificial antibodies being developed. I heard of a camera expert who lost an eye and is developing an eyeball-cam. I once saw a documentary that explored the computer technology used by two people in different cities to

have remote sex. Literally plugged in. Today, you can artificially inseminate an egg that has been extracted from its host, implant embryos into foreign hosts, or hell, why even go to all that trouble when you can just clone? Being pregnant is, like, *soooo* last year. Except for the humans in lab coats, technology can replace us even in making life. We don't even have to touch one another anymore. Which is ironic because we are obsessed with exploiting technologies that will make us more sexually attractive. More lips, and breasts, pecs and glutes; less fat, wrinkles and sagging: technologies are warp-speed in the field of plastic surgery. Beating cancer? We clearly have more important things to spend our money on.

2   So what will being human mean in the future? These days, we are driven by "better." Self-help books and seminars are all the rage, so we can become better people. Those Life Network programs dedicated to improving one's wardrobe, living space, diet and cuisine, interspersed with commercials persistently nagging us to look more attractive. Everywhere we look we are told to be better, be more educated, be more productive, be more constructive, be healthier, be better financial managers, better parents. Take it to the chorus, Kanye: work it harder, make it better, do it faster, makes us stronger. In a way, we can't help it; the entire narrative of human history compels us to wonder what we could be capable of, to imagine the possibilities—what are we missing out on without that calculus implant?

3   Technologically-enhanced humans are here. We are moments away from being not only everything-abled, but very, very, sexy.

4   I remember having a heated debate with my sister Sarah and her husband, Ian, when we'd heard of the news of the human ear they grew on a rat's back. Ian was excited—he could finally smoke all he wanted, fill his lungs full of boils and mucous, and just have a new pair grown in a lab and grafted in. Sarah and I jumped atop our high horse. We shouted down that he did not *deserve* new lungs if he couldn't even take care of the first pair he was given. Our point was valid (if vehement)—the ethics of responsibility continue to dog human enhancement projects—but Ian's was too: we all just want to eat our cake! Because unlike Kanye says, we do not really want to work it harder, we want to work smarter. Which really means not work at all. We want to push a button that will work for us.

5   But is it ever really that easy? Just push a button? What about the labour put into programming the computer to enable that magic button to do what

we want? What about the time and brainpower spent learning the software, so we can ably operate these technologies that make our lives so "convenient"? But again, we have trust in our inventiveness, our progressiveness that, yes it can be that easy: clap on a light, press the popcorn button on the microwave, command start your car. These technologies are second nature to the generation growing up with them. My daughter picked up her Polly Pocket the other day and asked, "Mom, how do I transform this?" She could hardly believe it to be *only* a doll . . . She believes it could be *anything*, and for kids these days, believing you can be anything doesn't mean a career choice, it means anything! A flower, a truck, a walking telephone. . . . This is not charming childish babble—this is what she sees. Once perfected, would there be anyone who would refuse the calculus implant? (Although, I'd put my money on someone perfecting the porn implant long before the educational variety.) Learning is so old school, so time consuming.

6   Will there be any only-human hold-outs? Rebel purists fighting the (techno-) Man, fighting the race forward, just like in *The Matrix*. It has all been imagined—from Orwell's *1984*, to *The Terminator* or *The Matrix*—and once imagined, it is only a matter of time before it is realized. Someone will figure it out.

7   The real question is who? Whom are we placing at the helm of mission control? In *The Matrix*, the One, the prophesized One who would save all the righteous rebels from the evil oppressors, was the guy *who could read and manipulate the computer operating systems.* Who is designing the implants that will become a part of our brain? Whose version of human will we trust? The efficient worker-bee version? The version who doesn't require nutrients to function? The artist version? Or would that be impossible, since our definition of art includes free, or different thinking? Then again, maybe we will program some humans to issue prototypes that the rest will have an implant to appreciate as art. Will there be choice? Diversity? If we rage right now, make our human voices heard, will we have an impact on the outcome of humanity? With all of the ethical debate, and Supreme Court rulings, have human cloning projects been dissuaded?

8   Maybe we'll end up a mushy sack of heart, bones, and brain lying around in heaps, our glazed eyes enhanced by wireless feeds of our newfound virtual paradise where we can fly, be beautiful, speak any language, go anywhere, do anything, be anything! The whole thing makes me rather depressed, but I'm sure I can find an implant to fix that.

EXERCISE *Begin by comparing the two personal narrative essays by students.*

1. How does each writer link his or her personal experience to a broader point? Structurally, how do the essays differ in terms of where the point or thesis emerges?

2. Compare the tone of the essays. Is one more colloquial? Why might the author choose a more colloquial tone to talk about the topic of our enhanced cyber futures?

3. Personal writing *needs to be as finely crafted as impersonal writing.* Can you find some examples of sentences that could still be improved in both essays?

4. Use your own personal experience to illuminate or demonstrate a point about the process of writing, reading, and/or learning. (Your experience can be drawn from lived life, or from your response to reading, for example, Baker or Hoffman.)

5. Use your personal experience to probe your identity. Draw from your education or other experience an event that explains your sense of who you are. To think of what to include, you might start by filling in the phrase "To know me, you need to know . . . "

Planning Strategies

Because narratives are stories made up of events that happen over time, a *horizontal timeline* is often a more useful planning device than a conventional outline that lists points from top to bottom. The line can be organized to collect several levels of information, for example, details of events can be noted along the top edge of the line, and their personal significance along the bottom. This technique can help writers to identify an event of sufficient complexity and significance to serve as the focus for a personal essay. In the final stages of working with timelines, the writer should begin to record a third level of information: the public significance of the events (see the sample timeline on the next page).

Another useful planning activity involves writing *lists* of "thick description" which itemize in minute detail all aspects of an event. While you will likely not use all of the descriptive details in your personal essay, you will find it helpful to have developed a generous array of consciously recollected detail from which you can choose the ones that best suit the purposes of your story.

Finally, using an *image* to convey an abstract idea or feeling can deepen your meaning. Rather than saying flatly "I felt sad," you could add vibrancy by using an evocative metaphor—"My sadness was like a grey November morning"—or add poignancy by personifying the feeling—"My sadness gripped my heart so hard I staggered." Contrary to the belief that images are the stuff of poetry, they often enliven clear prose. Even before drafting, you can focus your thoughts by writing several metaphors to describe key characters or visual images to convey emotional states.

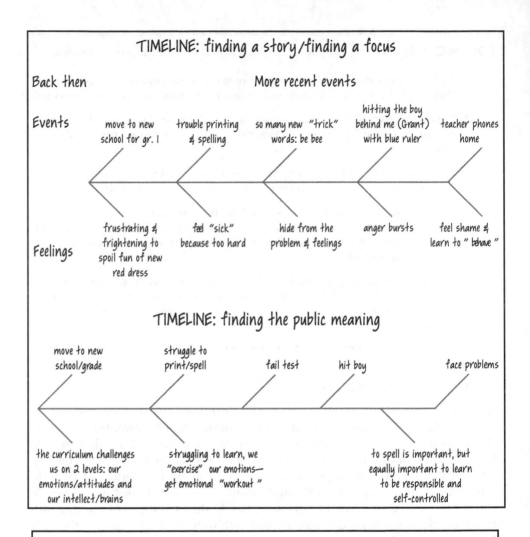

TIMELINE: finding a story/finding a focus

Back then   More recent events

Events | move to new school for gr. 1 | trouble printing & spelling | so many new "trick" words: be bee | hitting the boy behind me (Grant) with blue ruler | teacher phones home

Feelings | frustrating & frightening to spoil fun of new red dress | feel "sick" because too hard | hide from the problem & feelings | anger bursts | feel shame & learn to "behave"

TIMELINE: finding the public meaning

move to new school/grade | struggle to print/spell | fail test | hit boy | face problems

the curriculum challenges us on 2 levels: our emotions/attitudes and our intellect/brains | struggling to learn, we "exercise" our emotions— get emotional "workout" | to spell is important, but equally important to learn to be responsible and self-controlled

Sample Questions to Ask to Improve Drafts

In your peer-editing group, go around the circle and let each group member read his or her draft.

Before reading, the writer may ask listeners to pay attention to a "problem passage," so that follow-up discussion can centre on troubleshooting.

Focus

Is there a story and broader point?

Is the point tacit or explicit?

Does the point resonate with you (as listener)?

Is it a single point (message/lesson), or is the idea more layered? Is it connected to a theoretical perspective?

Is it plausible and coherent?

Is the title vibrant?

Style

Are there any sharp images in the narrative?

Does it use concrete words?

Is there sentence variety (short and long)?

What about passages of dialogue?

What about the writer's tone? Is the writer close and friendly, or cool and reflective?

Structure

Does the narrative follow strict chronological progression, or does it progress in fragments?

Does it use multiple perspectives?

Does it use sections to divide up the telling?

Does it use photos to complicate/illustrate the telling?

ETHNOGRAPHY: TELLING STORIES ABOUT OTHERS

Apart from its usefulness for presenting an argument based on our interpretation of our experiences, the "I" perspective is also a good way to present our observations of others, whether individuals or groups. An ethnography is a written account of a researcher's field experience, a text in which the researcher presents what he or she has learned about a group. As a way to explain and understand a group, ethnographic accounts were first used in anthropology, with the field worker travelling to an exotic location and recording observations about how others live in order to write an ethnographic account. More recently, this form has been used by sociologists, educators, and composition/rhetoric scholars to gain a better understanding of the discourse patterns of groups within our culture.

Although there is no formula to govern the relationship of the researcher to the group being observed, many researchers attempt to understand their subjects by taking on the role of "participant-observer." This term captures the way in which researchers view the group critically from the vantage point of an outsider, while cultivating empathy and understanding as an insider. This dual position enables researchers to get a more complete picture of the social relations or communicative patterns they observe.

Although most ethnographic accounts use the first person to some extent, this voice is especially strong in studies (or sections of studies) in which ethnographers reflect on their own methods and actions. In *Tales of the Field*, a study of ethnography as a form of writing, John Van Maanen calls this a "confessional" approach. Ethnographers use this approach, for example, to explain how emotions can affect observations. It can be challenging, for example, to present an informant in a positive light if he or she has been rude or dismissive in dealing with the researcher.

Van Maanen designates two other main ways of writing ethnography: the realistic and the impressionistic account. In the approach Van Maanen calls "realism," the role of the ethnographer is downplayed in order to foreground the observational field; the personal voice is relatively quiet, and rather than using "I" in accounting for the details, the writer often uses a third-person perspective.

If the ethnographer's voice is present in the ethnographic style that Van Maanen calls "impressionistic," the focus is more squarely on what happened and on the interactions of characters (of whom the ethnographer is one). In an impressionistic tale, the writer does not always provide interpretations of events but leaves the reader to form a response.

If you have not written ethnographies before, it can be helpful to think about taking one of the approaches Van Maanen outlines. That said, experienced ethnographers blend these styles, so it is often unproductive to try to label their work as conforming to one of these categories.

Writing an Ethnography

1. You need to pick a group or situation to observe. While your selection is probably motivated by your interest in knowing more about a particular aspect of the group, you need to maintain an open-minded attitude, since it is not unusual for the focus of your attention to change. The open-minded stance can be described as *exploratory*, rather than committed to looking for a specific thing.

2. Observe and make notes. Make sure you record dates and times.

3. Begin drafting the ethnography, the written account of your observations. Decide whether you want to place emphasis on yourself, or others, or a particular scene (and thus if you are working in a confessional or realist style).

A Note About Ethics

Because ethnography involves observing others, who are the "subjects" being studied, it is important to consider the ethical guidelines that pertain to these research conditions. If the project involves an "in-class" focus and is more of an exercise than an actual research study, then it may not be necessary to obtain formal permission to do this work from the research ethics committee or review board at your institution. If the project is an exercise rather than a full-scale research project, then your instructor may already have received approval for the assignment from your institution's ethics committee who have determined that individual project submissions are not necessary.

If you are going outside the classroom to do your observations and interviews, however, you will probably need to write a proposal for the Research Ethics Committee describing the measures you will take to protect the people you observe from potential harms such as breach of confidentiality. While these requirements often cause your ethnography assignment to be spread out over term—so that you propose it in the beginning of term, and write it toward the end, pending the approval of the ethics committee—you can learn a lot about methodological considerations by taking part in this process.

Apart from fulfilling formal ethical criteria established by a committee, you need to be responsive to the ethical considerations that arise as you collect information about others and begin to write about them. For example, if you are not a member of the group you are observing, you need to avoid such an ethical error as attempting to become the (unappointed) spokesperson of the group. While one currently popular response to this dilemma holds that ethnographers should belong to a group in question so that they have a genuine commitment to and understanding of this group, a more moderate view is that ethnographers should position themselves so that they are not simply observing, but participating in, the activity they are studying.

You need to be aware of the position you occupy in relation to the group you are studying and to identify your position as primarily insider or outsider. Being too firmly entrenched in either of these positions can make it difficult to construct a fair and full representation of the group, whereas moving between these positions can be conducive to developing a perspective that is both penetrating and empathic.

EXERCISE *Pick a school culture with which you are familiar (a team, individuals who work in a study area, a class). Write two versions of your observations: in one, use the third person and place emphasis on telling about others; in the other, use the first person, and explore your role as observer/ethnographer and the intersections between yourself and the others. As a variant, you can replace the third-person objective version of your observations with an impressionistic account, in which you bring to life a dramatic scene.*

In addition to observing, you may want to conduct some interviews. Please look at the two forms at the end of this chapter, one suggesting how to frame questions and the other providing a template of a permission form that indicates subjects are willing to participate.

Questions for Peer-Editing the Draft (Early Stages)

1. Is the writer insider or outsider? A participant and/or observer? Does he/she alternate between both perspectives?

2. Do you learn anything interesting about the group? What fascinates the writer? Does he/she indicate or begin to sketch "where the culture is," to use a phrase from ethnography; in other words, does the writer find a focus of particularly interesting cultural activity?

3. Does the writer know more about the group than you do? What do you think needs further exploration?

4. What artifacts might be part of the culture of this group? What sorts of interactions need to be observed?

5. Have you (the reader) had experiences with this group? Have you read about them before?

6. Is the writer biased in ways he/she does not note? Can you think of any logistical or ethical problems he/she could bump into by studying this group?

7. Does the writer convince you that he or she has found an interesting culture that (a) will be open to scrutiny and attention, and (b) can sustain it?

8. Does the writer begin the narrative by talking about the self, the group, or both? Do you have any suggestions for making the opening more dynamic?

9. Are there spots where the writer could provide more details or examples?

10. Are there places where the writer could use a passage of dialogue, rather than indirect conversation?

11. What sort of interview questions might help the writer to provide insight into members of the group?

12. Could the writer experiment with more descriptive language (modifiers, metaphors, concrete words)?

FORM 1

Conducting Interviews

Effective interviews are planned in advance so that you make good use of the occasion for your sake and for the interviewee's. *Ethical* interviews are planned in advance so that you can accurately inform interviewees of the topics you are asking them to consent to being questioned about and assure them that their wishes for anonymity and confidentiality will be respected.

Name of interviewee:_____

His or her connection to the topic:_____

Steps to follow in the interview

1. Explain the purpose and topic.
2. Explain provisions for confidentiality and anonymity.
3. Ask for consent and complete two copies of the form.
4. Begin the interview and record it or take notes as you go.

Question Framework

Questions should be mostly open-ended (i.e., not leading to one-word answers). It is all right to ask follow-up questions in response to what the interviewee says.

List your main questions here. They are the framework that will structure your interview.

1. _____

   _____

2. _____

   _____

3. _____

   _____

4. _____

   _____

5. _____

   _____

   _____

6. _____

   _____

FORM 2

Consent Letter for Interviews

If you are planning to interview anyone for your research essay, speak to your instructor about the research ethics requirements of your institution. The following sample "consent letter" covers the main elements of most academic research interviews: information about what you are asking the person to consent to, and anonymity, and confidentiality.

(Your university or college logo here)

Dear _____

I would like your permission to report on our interview in the research essay I am preparing for my (university or college name) course, "(course name)." I would like to ask you about

_____

_____

I will not refer to you by name in either oral discussion or written work unless you give me your permission to do so by signing below. You may decide at any time not to allow me to refer to all or part of our discussion. I will keep any recording and notes about the interview in a secure location.

The research ethics committee of the (name of department or university/ college) has approved this course research assignment. If you have any concerns about participating, you may discuss them with Dr. _____, Chair of the Research Ethics Committee, at ___-___-____, or with Dr. _____, my course professor, at ___-___-____.

Signature of student researcher: _____

Please check one:

____   I do agree to be interviewed for the purposes described above.

____   I do not agree to be interviewed for the purposes described above.

Please check one:

____   I would like to be credited by name in references to our discussion.

____   I would like to remain anonymous in references to our discussion.

Name (please print) _____

Date _____ Signature _____

CHAPTER 4

Representing Sources: Summary, Paraphrase, Quotation, and Documentation

THE ROLE OF REPRESENTING SOURCES

All intellectual work is a form of the human mind trying to understand the universe. In the course of doing this, the mind ventures a great many opinions, theories, hunches, claims, and theses—some of them dead ends, others well worth following through—but they are worth nothing if they are not grounded in an attempt to get it right: to see accurately and to represent what we see accurately. Without accurate representation of others' work on the subject, an essay can become little more than an intriguing rant, a series of unsupported claims that have not been tested against the phenomena they describe (a Mars launch, a short story, a three-toed sloth) or the studies of those phenomena completed by other scholars.

It is largely by representation of the work of other scholars that academic writing distinguishes itself from other kinds of writing. By situating our own perspectives in the existing body of scholarly work on the topic, rather than speaking alone as one, possibly brilliant, individual thinker, we work collaboratively toward the best possible understandings of our topic. (And by documenting our work as shown toward the end of this chapter, we make sure that our representations of others can be checked for accuracy by our readers; in this way scholarly writing provides a system of quality assurance that is unique in the publishing world.)

To represent others' work, you might offer a summary of a primary source that constitutes the topic of your paper (such as Leonard Cohen's *Beautiful Losers*), followed by references to secondary sources drawn from the existing body of scholarship on the topic (such as a critic's interpretation of *Beautiful Losers*). Whether the work is primary or secondary, it can be represented in three forms— summary, paraphrase, and quotation. The three forms cover a wide range from complete fidelity to the original, quoting it word for word, to drastic changes to the source, summarizing a whole book in a few sentences. Nevertheless, all three are forms of the original version and a faithful *re*-presentation of it. Though summarizing is the most ethically demanding of the three since it undertakes such a radical transformation of the original, all three require that writers put themselves at the service of the source they undertake to represent.

Together, summary, paraphrase, and quotation can occupy 50 percent or more of a research essay. For examples of the extent of representation in scholarly writing, look at the student essay in the argument chapter (Chapter 6) or at the scholarly articles in Part 2. Representing others is not just a humble rite of passage demanded of students. The tell-tale footnotes or in-text citations that signal the representation of a writer's sources are ubiquitous in writing by students and professors alike. The methods used vary to suit the aims of different disciplines: psychologists mainly use summary and paraphrase rather than quotation, for example, and literary scholars use quotations for primary sources and paraphrase for secondary ones, but all scholars use some form of representation in order to test their claims and integrate their work with that of others.

WRITING A SUMMARY

To summarize a few paragraphs or a longer passage, writers use their own words to represent the main ideas, leaving out minor details and personal opinions. Summaries can be brief—a sentence or two—or offer a more complete representation of the original source, often by condensing the main points. Summary can be thought of as a key technology of academic work. Summaries allow us as scholars to build on existing knowledge by importing other people's work into our own in condensed form. The summary we offer establishes our reading of the source work.

It should be acknowledged that even if you are careful to keep your own opinions out of your summary, chances are you are still using personal interpretation to decide what to include and leave out, and emphasize. While we attempt to be as objective as possible in writing summaries, often our interpretations are influenced by prior reading or experience, so that, for example, I might find certain ideas central that another reader would not. However, while it is probably true that no two summaries of a single source are identically worded, your goal as you summarize should be to reproduce the main ideas as faithfully as possible.

Summary as a Stand-alone Assignment

Writing a summary is sometimes required as an assignment in itself. For example:

- Find 10 books and articles on the topic of lesbian and gay rights legislation in Canada and produce a 100-word summary of each. (This is a form of annotated bibliography.)

> - Write a 200-word summary of your research essay and insert it between the title page and page 1 of your essay. (This is an abstract.)
> - Write a five-page summary of Michel Foucault's "Discourse on Language."
>
> Summaries show up in scholarly writing by professors, too:
>
> - as abstracts of proposed conference presentations
> - as abstracts of journal articles, inserted between the title and first paragraph of the article

A summary as a stand-alone piece of writing is often required in test-writing situations to demonstrate your grasp of material your professor already knows. Often, a summary is an element of a larger piece of work. In a research essay that requires the writer to synthesize many outside sources, a summary allows writers to do this efficiently without sacrificing accuracy. Summary information can also provide readers with a context for understanding an issue. If you were writing a paper about the creation of the territory of Nunavut in Canada's Arctic, for example, it would be a good idea early in the paper to summarize the Acts of Parliament by which the territory was created, for readers who may be unfamiliar with these provisions.

If teachers have criticized you in the past for writing a summary, it may be because they asked you to *analyze* rather than to *reproduce* the ideas. Make sure that you do not substitute summary for analysis.

Good Readers Write Good Summaries

You might think that grasping the meaning and identifying the main points of an argument is always what happens when you read. But across disciplines, as you proceed in your studies, the ideas you encounter in texts become more complicated and their presentation can be complex. Even careful readers need to reread challenging passages, highlight key points, and make notes, mobilizing many of the reading techniques suggested in Chapter 1.

Some theoretical texts are extremely complex. In the readings in Chapter 7, Dennis Dutton charges scholars with a mandate to write clearly, but influential scholar Judith Butler chides him by pointing out that surface clarity can misrepresent complex ideas—that some ideas resist oversimplification. If an assigned or important text is dense, you should gather what meaning you can, without becoming overly frustrated by or stuck on impenetrable passages. If you can place the writer's work within a general context, you are in a better position to make associations and interpretations (what view of the economy did Keynes usually espouse; was McLuhan known as an advocate or opponent of technology?).

The main exception: you need to read every word when reading directions. It makes a big difference whether you are asked to argue or explain. You could lose credit on an exam or paper because you failed to read carefully a crucial direction by your instructor.

How to Write a Summary: Four Steps

1. **Read the passage or text to understand what it is saying and how it is organized.** Look for the thesis and the series of main points used to advance that thesis as it moves along from one step to the next. Note where it shifts. (You may want to photocopy the passage, so that you feel free to label key ideas and section changes.)

   If you are summarizing a short article, you might consider each paragraph to be a separate unit or stage of development. In longer articles or books, you will need to group several paragraphs or pages as a single unit of development. In social science writing, the development of a new idea is often indicated by a subtitle. In other forms of writing, you can often identify where one stage ends and another begins by asking, "Where could a subtitle be inserted?"

2. **Reduce the piece to points and sum up the whole.** First, write a one-sentence summary of each main idea, or separate unit of thought. After you have summarized each section, go on to summarize the whole passage in a sentence or two, expressing what you have come to see as the central idea of the passage.

3. **Draft.** Begin drafting your summary by announcing the thesis first (the central idea of the whole), followed by the sentences summarizing the main ideas. Keep the main ideas in much the same order as they appear in the original text, for your summary should be able to guide your reader to ideas in the source.

4. **Revise.** Reread your summary against the original passage for accuracy and completeness. Because you are attempting to be brief, check that sentences are not incomplete and development between sentences is not choppy. Insert transition words to achieve flow.

Here is a summary of Doris Lessing's "Group Minds." (The full article appears in Chapter 10). It is an example of a longer, more complete summary that combines the thesis with section summaries.

In her short article "Group Minds," British author Doris Lessing argues that to provide those of us who live in western societies with real freedom and independence, we need to be educated from childhood to express our dissent against commonly held attitudes and opinions. Lessing claims that Westerners have cultivated a false vision of themselves as being free and independent. She argues that because of our social nature, the opposite is true, and that we actually adopt the attitudes and behaviours of those with whom we associate. Sociologists and psychologists have studied our tendency to conform and comply, but the results of their studies are not widely circulated or recognized by most people who continue defining themselves as freethinking.

She points to one experiment in which a group is convened and asked to describe a certain object. When the experimenter's confederates deliberately describe the object inaccurately, it does not take long for the subjects to abandon their authentic descriptions and adopt the inaccurate description endorsed by the others. When hearing about this experiment, most people claim they would never be so easily influenced by others. Lessing points out that it is difficult for us to face the fact that we partake of the human tendency to conform. She points out that this does not only occur in relation to small groups we choose to join, but is an aspect of our social order, since we adopt the views of our culture.

She recommends educating children to be more critical of predominant opinions and attitudes. She believes we Westerners need to learn from youth that conformity is part of our nature and that liberation depends on our learning how to examine behaviour and beliefs and exercise dissent.

Using this example, let's walk through the first two pre-drafting steps recommended for writing a summary:

1. Read

As you read the piece, think about how it is organized, and how each part contributes to shaping the whole. How do you determine where one stage of thought ends and the next one begins?

Look, particularly, for transitional sentences at the beginning of paragraphs. Such sentences generally work in one or both of the following two ways. (1) they summarize what has come before; (2) they set the stage for what is to follow. In "Group Minds," for example, Lessing opens paragraph 10 with the transition phrase "In other words." This is a signal to the reader that the sentence will offer a redefinition of a concept already developed. Obviously, then, paragraph 10 extends the idea of paragraph 9, and should be grouped with it.

Here is one way to divide Lessing's essay into sections of thought.

Section 1:   Introduction: The ideal—the idea we like to believe is that Westerners are free individuals (paragraphs 1–3).

Section 2:   The reality—we belong to influential groups (paragraphs 4–5).

Section 3:   Resisting reality—we have proof that people are influenced by groups, but we ignore the proof (paragraph 6).

Section 4:   The evidence—experiments document that most people adopt group attitudes and views, although most of us claim we would resist group pressure (paragraphs 7–10).

Section 5:   The solution—educate students to resist; the student can learn liberating critical thinking skills (paragraphs 12–14).

2. Reduce to points and sum the whole

Use your own words to summarize each stage of thought in a sentence, and then summarize the whole.

This step is important because it encourages you to use your own words to express the ideas of the original.

Section 1 notes: Introduction: The ideal—the idea we like to believe is that Westerners are free individuals (paragraphs 1–3).

- People in the Western world like to imagine that they are free to act as individuals pleasing themselves.

Section 2 notes: The reality—we belong to influential groups (paragraphs 4–5).

- People in the West belong to a variety of groups and maintain their group membership by complying with rules and sharing group values and attitudes.

Section 3 notes: Resisting reality—we have proof that people are influenced by groups, but we ignore the proof (paragraph 6).

- There have been experiments in sociology and psychology that prove we conform to group pressure, yet this information is not well known or widely circulated.

Section 4 notes: The evidence—experiments document that most people adopt group attitudes and views, although most of us claim we are able to resist group pressure (paragraphs 7–10).

- One particular experiment demonstrates that most subjects eventually adopt group opinion, even when that opinion is observably inaccurate; most people claim they would be able to resist this pressure, but most of us comply with cultural and group norms.

Section 5 notes: The solution—educate students to resist; a student can learn liberating critical thinking skills (paragraphs 12–14).

- Children should be taught that we are vulnerable to thinking like our neighbours, rather than for ourselves, if they are to learn to be more independent.

Now that you understand the components of Lessing's arguments, you are ready to **sum the whole** in one or two sentences that could be called the thesis of the piece:

- Thesis: We like to believe we are free and independent, but are actually controlled by shared values in a variety of social groups. Children need to be taught to think for themselves and resist group pressure.

The summary example given above, running 10 sentences in three paragraphs, is about one-fourth the length of the original. The example below shows it could be as short as two sentences. If you are referring to an article as a key document, you will likely need to provide a long and complete summary of the original. If you are making a brief reference to a work, a brief summary serves the purpose.

Here is a short summary of the essay:

> In the West, we like to believe we are free and independent, but experiments have shown we are actually controlled by the values we share with others in a variety of social groups. Children need to be taught to think for themselves and resist group pressure.

Whether writing a longer summary or a shorter one, concise writing is the key to capturing as much of the original meaning as possible in the available space.

Student Sample: Summarizing Bartholomae's "Inventing the University" in Three Drafts

Here are three drafts of a summary of the full-text version of David Bartholomae's "Inventing the University," an excerpt of which is included in Chapter 7. Notice that as the writer moves from the draft to the final version, she makes revisions that reflect her decisions about how to select and express the text to form the best representation.

FIRST DRAFT

A Summary of Bartholomae's "Inventing the University"

1   Bartholomae's essay, "Inventing the University," is written for fellow academics in the Humanities. His thesis is that when undergraduate university students compose academic writing, they "invent the university by assembling and mimicking its language" (149). According to Bartholomae, problems often arise during this process of inventing the university. Throughout this essay, Bartholomae examines why and how these problems occur in order to give professors and researchers insight into how they can help undergraduate students produce better academic writing.

2   Within this text, Bartholomae's argument follows four main stages of thought. First, Bartholomae introduces the concept of interpretive schemes and explains how students' difficulties with academic writing may arise from their inadequate interpretive schemes. Second, Bartholomae discusses the issue of audience awareness, and how in trying to achieve it, students are at a disadvantage because they lack the knowledge of the subject and the interpretive schemes used to discuss it that their professors have and expect of writing within their discipline.

3   Third, Bartholomae analyzes examples of student writing in order to demonstrate what makes some students' academic writing more successful than other students' academic writing. Bartholomae defines a successful student paper as one in which the student allows for complexity and recognizes that ideas are situated in prior understandings. Finally, Bartholomae concludes by repeating what he believes that undergraduate students

should aim for in their academic writing. Bartholomae suggests students should attempt to produce writing that acknowledges other sources, yet resists or contests these. The final suggestion that Bartholomae makes is to researchers studying the process of composition; he states that in the future, they should pay attention to the writing that students produce in order to better understand where and when problems occur during the writing process.

SECOND DRAFT

A Summary of Bartholomae's "Inventing the University"

1   In the essay "Inventing the University," David Bartholomae explains the challenges undergraduate students face when they learn to compose academic writing. For students to write successful papers, Bartholomae argues that they must "invent the university"(149) within their prose. This process of invention requires that students "appropriate (or be appropriated by) a specialized discourse" (149) which differs from discourses with which they are familiar. Problems often arise as students undertake this process. Bartholomae describes the nature of these difficulties, and explains how academics, whether they are teaching or doing research, can help students learn to invent the university. Bartholomae begins by explaining that in order to compose adequate academic writing, students must demonstrate not only the correct vocabulary and style of presentation, but also the correct interpretive scheme in their work. According to Bartholomae, students often use incorrect interpretive schemes within their academic writing because "academic" commonplaces are different from "everyday" commonplaces. A commonplace, as defined by Bartholomae, is a convention or a preconceived notion about the world (151). Inexperienced academic writers have difficulty asserting the type of authority required by academic interpretive schemes, and often conclude essays with an "everyday" commonplace—"a Lesson on Life" (151)—rather than the "academic" commonplace of an analysis of the issue being discussed.

2   The overall success of students' writing, Bartholomae argues, depends on how well they can "imagine and conform to a reader's goals" (152), but this achievement is difficult to attain in writing composed for a university

setting. The second section of Bartholomae's essay focuses on this issue of audience awareness that students need to confront within their writing. In trying to achieve audience awareness when writing for their professors, students are at a disadvantage because they lack the knowledge of a subject and the knowledge of the interpretive schemes used to discuss it that their professors have and expect of writing within their discipline. However, the imbalance of knowledge and power between students and the professors for whom they are writing assignments can be made less difficult for students to manage.

3   Professors could help students to invent the university, Bartholomae argues, by making it clear to their students that they do not expect their writing to be "new or original" (153), but rather "active and engaged" (153). This expectation entails that students be "continuously and stylistically working against the inevitable presence of conventional language" (153), and that students try to achieve an approximation of academic discourse. Successful students' papers, then, do not begin with a "moment of insight," but rather with "a moment of appropriation, a moment when they can offer up a sentence that is not theirs as though it were their own" (153). Professors, Bartholomae believes, can do more to help students learn academic writing than teach them the conventions of their discipline; they can also examine students' writing to determine how their approximations are inadequate. In the next section of his essay, Bartholomae undertakes the latter approach.

4   Throughout the third section of "Inventing the University," Bartholomae analyzes samples of students' writing in order to demonstrate what makes their academic writing successful or unsuccessful. Bartholomae judges a student's essay to be unsuccessful when it merely works with commonplace ideas from a non-critical perspective. In contrast, a successful essay challenges conventional schemes and interprets multilayered meanings in what has been observed and articulated. Bartholomae uses his analysis of students' writing to reinforce his claim that students do not understand their audience or feel in a position to move them. To accomplish their goal of inventing the university, Bartholomae shows that students must take on a new kind of authority—an authority skeptical of conventional thinking—and instead use an unfamiliar discourse with ease.

5   In the concluding section of his essay, Bartholomae reiterates that students must learn to invent the university by learning to establish their

own voice and authority by positioning themselves as both academic insiders and outsiders. Bartholomae also poses a "challenge" (158) to future researchers studying the writing process by asking that they pay attention to the writing that students produce in order to gain a more thorough understanding of how and when problems occur during the writing process.

FINAL DRAFT

A Summary of Bartholomae's "Inventing the University"

1   In the essay "Inventing the University," David Bartholomae explains the challenges undergraduate students face when they learn to compose academic writing. For students to write successful papers, Bartholomae argues that they must "invent the university" (149) within their prose. This process of invention requires that students "appropriate (or be appropriated by) a specialized discourse" (149) which differs from discourses with which they are familiar. Problems often arise as students undertake this process. Bartholomae describes the nature of these difficulties and explains how academics, whether they are teaching or doing research, can do more to help students learn to write well.

2   Bartholomae begins by explaining that in order to compose adequate academic writing, students must demonstrate not only the correct vocabulary and style of presentation, but also the correct academic interpretive scheme within their work. According to Bartholomae, students often use incorrect interpretive schemes within their academic writing because "academic" commonplaces are different from "everyday" commonplaces. Inexperienced academic writers have difficulty asserting the type of authority required by academic interpretive schemes. For example, students often conclude essays with an "everyday" commonplace—"a Lesson on Life" (151)—rather than the "academic" commonplace of an analysis of the issue being discussed.

3   The overall success of students' writing, Bartholomae argues, depends on how well they can "imagine and conform to a reader's goals" (152), but this achievement is difficult to attain in writing composed for a university setting. The second section of Bartholomae's essay focuses on this issue of audience

awareness that students need to confront within their writing. In trying to
achieve audience awareness when writing for their professors, students are at a
disadvantage because they lack the knowledge of a subject and the familiarity
with interpretive schemes used to discuss it that their professors have.
However, Bartholomae explains how the imbalance of knowledge and power
between students and the professors for whom they are writing can be made
less difficult for students to manage.

4   Professors could help students to improve their writing, Bartholomae
argues, by making it clear to their students that they do not expect their writing
to be "new or original" (153), but rather "active and engaged" (153). This
expectation entails that students resist conventional explanations and phrases,
and try to achieve an approximation of academic discourse. Bartholomae
describes successful papers and how they do not begin with a student having
a "moment of insight," but rather "a moment of appropriation, a moment when
they can offer up a sentence that is not theirs as though it were their own" (153).
Professors, Bartholomae believes, can do more to help students learn
academic writing than teach them the conventions of their discipline: they
can also examine students' writing to determine how their approximations are
inadequate. In the next section of his essay, Bartholomae undertakes the
latter approach.

5   Throughout the third section of "Inventing the University," Bartholomae
analyzes samples of students' writing in order to demonstrate what makes
their academic writing successful or unsuccessful. Bartholomae judges a
student's essay to be unsuccessful when it merely relates an unexamined
commonplace. In contrast, a successful essay challenges conventional
schemes and interprets multilayered meanings in what has been observed
and articulated. Bartholomae uses his analysis of students' writing to reinforce
his claim that students do not understand their audience or feel in a position
to move them. To accomplish their goal of inventing the university,
Bartholomae shows that students must both take on a new kind of authority—
an authority skeptical of conventional thinking—and use an unfamiliar
discourse with ease.

6   In the concluding section of his essay, Bartholomae reiterates that students
must learn to invent the university by learning. Students invent the university
by gradually discovering how to establish their own voice and authority by
positioning themselves as both academic insiders and outsiders.
Bartholomae's final suggestion is a "challenge" (158) to future researchers

studying the writing process. He asks that they pay attention to the writing that students produce, in order to gain a more thorough understanding of how and when problems occur during the writing process. As a result, there would be more research about how to help students as they learn to compose academic writing.

Work Cited

Bartholomae, David. "Inventing the University." In *Across the Disciplines: Academic Writing and Reading.* Ed. Jacqueline McLeod Rogers and Catherine Taylor. Toronto: Pearson, 2011. Print.

EXERCISE

1. Look at changes to the opening paragraphs in the three versions, and consider how the overall thesis is represented in each. Does the final draft succeed in presenting a more satisfying and complete version?

2. The first draft is vague in its wording. For example, the opening paragraph refers to students struggling with "problems." How does the writer clarify this point in the second and third drafts?

3. The rough draft of three paragraphs is developed into six paragraphs in the later drafts. Can you understand the writer's decision to arrange the material in this way? (Look at the transition phrases that are used to begin some paragraphs to see if they reveal connections between developing ideas.)

4. Read ahead to the essay by Eva Hoffman, "Lost in Translation." Write a longer summary of the article, following the directions in this chapter for dividing the article into sections, for writing a one-sentence summary of each section, and then for introducing section summaries with a thesis. Prepare for the summary by making notes in the margins. Your finished product should be the result of two or more drafts. Once you have completed a longer summary (about one quarter the length of the original), try to write a brief summary, capturing the essence in several sentences.

5. Ignore the example in the text and write your own summary of the article "Group Minds" by Doris Lessing. Your summary should capture the thesis statement and the main points of the article, and the most important details. Remember to "frame" the summary so that the author and title of the article are acknowledged early on and it remains clear that Lessing, not you, is the author of the material being summarized. Once you have completed your version, compare it to the version that appears earlier in this chapter.

The Role of Interpretation in Summarizing Narrative

Narratives are stories, whether in the form of creative fiction or non-fiction personal essays. Deciding how to represent the significance of the events is tricky, for five readers could interpret the narrative's significance in five ways. Yet while there will be differences based on experiences that lead readers to read from different points of view, there will also be agreement among them. Most authors present readers with a shared theme through the interactions of character and story, even if there is room for slight variations in the way individual readers interpret this theme.

In the case of "Finding Words" the author never says outright that writer's block is debilitating and difficult to eradicate, but the events she relates convey this dilemma. Moreover, her reference to herself as a writing teacher suggests she is interested in contributing something from her own experience to composition theory, helping readers to understand how writer's block can settle in if writers do not commit to a writing project. Yet the point of this narrative—like many others— is indirect or tacit, and requires some interpretation, whereas the point of an article or argumentative essay is relatively straightforward, and can usually be found stated in the text itself. The summary of Lessing's "Group Minds" presents Lessing's main idea or thesis as well as the most outstanding points of support. The following summary of the narrative "Finding Words" conveys not only what happened to whom, but also what the actions mean in relation to the theme.

In "Finding Words," Jaqueline McLeod Rogers tells about her experience with writer's block, as well as her eventual ability to overcome the frustrating pattern of resisting the writing process. She describes entering university hoping to pursue a career involving writing. Ironically, the more she read, the harder writing became, and she describes abandoning creative writing in tandem with experiencing an escalating struggle to perform academic writing. She eventually recaptured her voice when faced with the need to write up the results of her research into how young writers tell gendered stories. Once she had found a satisfying exigency (motive for writing), the right words fell into place. What she took from this experience to her teaching of writing was the recognition that there needs to be some connection between one's experience and the topic one is exploring if writing is to be motivated.

EXERCISE *Summarize and properly frame Eva Hoffman's chapter from* Lost in Translation. *Because there are narrative elements to this excerpt, you may be able to structure your summary using the storyline itself. Remember to refrain from personal judgment. Be prepared to discuss how your summary corresponds to and differs from those written by other class members.*

Summarize Figures and Tables in Your Text

The sciences and social sciences often depict data and concepts in non-text forms, such as figures and tables. Such visual devices offer a pictorial overview that conveys material more quickly than if it were framed as text. Even though visual data is not expressed in sentence form, it makes certain claims about the topic it represents. These claims can be summarized to help your reader understand what to look for in a figure; more often, though, the summary is offered in place of the figure.

Charts and Tables

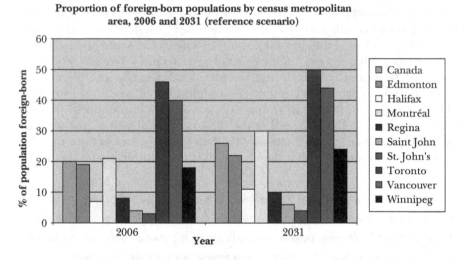

Proportion of foreign-born populations by census metropolitan area, 2006 and 2031 (reference scenario)

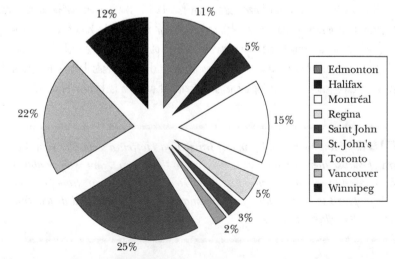

Proportion of foreign-born populations by census metropolitan area, 2031 (reference scenario)

Source: Adapted from Statistics Canada, Projections of the Diversity of the Canadian Population, 2006 to 2031 (91-551-X) March 9, 2010 http://www.statcan.gc.ca/pub/91-551-x/2010001/tbl/tbl013-eng.htm

Proportion of foreign-born populations by census
metropolitan area, 2006 and 2031 (reference scenario)

	Foreign-born	
	2006	**2031**
	% of population	
Canada	20	26
Edmonton	19	22
Halifax	7	11
Montréal	21	30
Regina	8	10
Saint John	4	6
St. John's	3	4
Toronto	46	50
Vancouver	40	44
Winnipeg	18	24

Source: Adapted from Statistics Canada, Projections of
the Diversity of the Canadian Population, 2006 to 2031
(91-551-X) March 9, 2010

http://www.statcan.gc.ca/pub/91-551-x/2010001/tbl/
tbl013-eng.htm

How to Summarize Figures and Tables

1. Study the figure to identify its logic and main claims, including general
   trends and striking results.
2. If the summary will be included in an essay, focus on the claims that
   relate to your topic.
3. Once you have composed the sentences that summarize the figure or
   table, check them against the original for fairness and accuracy.
4. Frame the summary properly by naming the source either in the summary itself or in a citation.

Illustrations and Photographs

In the humanities, where attention to visual texts has become common, you may
need to include illustrations or photographs. If so, do not leave them freestanding: each should be labelled and referred to in your written text, indicating what
the reader should look for.

WRITING PARAPHRASES

When you summarize a passage, your purpose is to shrink and import it into a
critique or a research essay, usually so you can build on existing knowledge.

When you paraphrase, your purpose is to refashion a passage in your own words, a process often meant not to save on number of words, but to provide increased clarity or streamlined style while retaining the entire meaning of the original passage. A particularly important source—if it is not too long—may rate a paraphrase. If it is less important, or peripheral to your central argument, you may choose to write a summary instead. And, of course, you may choose to summarize or paraphrase only part of your source—the part that is most relevant to the point you are making.

In a research essay, you need to include many references to outside sources, but using too many quotations can make the essay feel choppy and strung together. When you paraphrase, you turn the source material into your own words, and thus integrate it more smoothly into your argument. It can be a good idea to paraphrase material that is complex, abstract, or somehow difficult for readers to comprehend. Consider, for example, how an essay about Canadian identity could include a paraphrased version of this complex passage by Northrop Frye, a Canadian scholar and critic whose views helped to shape our thinking about the arts in our country over the last half of the twentieth century:

> It is not much wonder if Canada developed with the bewilderment of a neglected child, preoccupied with trying to define its own identity, alternately bumptious and diffident about its own achievements. Adolescent dreams of glory haunt the Canadian consciousness (and unconsciousness), some naïve and some sophisticated. In the naïve area are the predictions that the twentieth century belongs to Canada, that our cities will become much bigger than they ought to be, or like Edmonton and Vancouver, "gateways" to somewhere else, reconstructed Northwest passages. The more sophisticated usually take the form of a Messianic complex about Canadian culture, for Canadian culture, no less than Alberta, has always been "next year country." The myth of the hero brought up in the forest retreat, awaiting the moment when his giant strength will be fully grown and he can emerge into the world, informs a good deal of Canadian criticism down to our time. (221)
>
> Frye, Northrop. *The Bush Garden: Essays on the Canadian Imagination.*
> Toronto: Anansi, 1971. Print.

The following paraphrase captures Frye's point about how dreams of glory permeate the Canadian imagination in wording clear enough to appeal to generalist readers as well as disciplinary specialists:

> Northrop Frye believes that the Canadian sense of identity lacks full maturity, so that we vacillate between thinking of ourselves in modest or in grandiose terms. Moreover, the images we use to define ourselves are immature in differing degrees. For example, in the popular imagination our dreams of glory hold that the future belongs to us or that our cities are gateways to great places. Taking a Messianic

twist, a more sophisticated version of this dream holds that we have much to offer the world. Many of our critics write from the position that our superior strength is soon to be revealed to others. (221)

USING QUOTATIONS

A quotation is a word-for-word reproduction of the original source. Use quotations

1. when the writer has used stylistically engaging language,
2. when the writer has used remarkably clear and succinct language,
3. when the writer has unusual authority on the topic,
4. when you are analyzing the literary or rhetorical qualities of the quoted text.

Using Phrase, Sentence, or Block Quotations

By selecting a significant passage and quoting it in several ways, we can see the effect and structure of longer and shorter quotations. Suppose that while conducting research on Canadian history we come across the following, written by Gordon Laird, in his book *Slumming It at the Rodeo:*

> Cabot may not have discovered Canada but his main method of exploration, getting lost, is a persistent national theme. Even the nation's moniker has its beginnings in the missteps of early explorers. In 1535 two Indian youths told Jacques Cartier about the route to *kanata.* They were referring to the Huron village of Stadacona; *kanata* was simply the word for "village" or "settlement." Cartier assumed Kanata referred to an entire region, soon to be annexed by Europe's imperial powers. His initial mistake compounded as France and England made themselves at home. By 1547 maps designated everything north of the St. Lawrence River as "Canada." (8)
>
> *Slumming it at the Rodeo: The Cultural Roots of Canada's Right-Wing Revolution.*
> Vancouver: Douglas and McIntyre, 1998.

From this entire paragraph, we decide that this one sentence stands out for being both accurate and lively:

> Cabot may not have discovered Canada but his main method of exploration, getting lost, is a persistent national theme.

After selecting a phrase to quote, we build it into our own sentence smoothly, making sure that it makes grammatical sense:

> Gordon Laird, taking an ironic view of Canadian settlement patterns, points out that "getting lost . . . is a persistent national theme" (8). Gordon Laird refers

with disparagement to Cabot's "main method of exploration, getting lost," referring to indirection as a Canadian theme (8).

If including a longer quotation helps to make your case, you can choose to
quote an entire sentence:

> Gordon Laird, in an ironic analysis of Canadian settlement patterns,
> notes that indirection is part of our history: "Cabot may not have discovered
> Canada but his main method of exploration, getting lost, is a persistent
> national theme" (8).

Finally, there are times when you need to include a longer quotation, more
than 42 words, sometimes spanning several sentences.

> Gordon Laird's style of writing about our history engages the reader, since
> he finds humour in the way long-ago events nudge current-day life. Here he
> refers to Cabot's misadventures and wrong turns as thematic in the Canadian
> imagination:

> > Cabot may not have discovered Canada but his main method of
> > exploration, getting lost, is a persistent national theme. Even the nation's
> > moniker has its beginnings in the missteps of early explorers. In 1535 two
> > Indian youths told Jacques Cartier about the route to *kanata*. They were
> > referring to the Huron village of Stadacona; *kanata* was simply the word
> > for "village" or "settlement." Cartier assumed Kanata referred to an entire
> > region, soon to be annexed by Europe's imperial powers. His initial
> > mistake compounded as France and England made themselves at home.
> > By 1547 maps designated everything north of the St. Lawrence River as
> > "Canada." (8)

Using a block quotation is often necessary when you are analyzing the style
of a passage, but remember that too many block quotations can prevent your
voice from being heard and create a choppy or "strung-together" effect.

Ellipsis—Something Omitted

Sometimes writers want to quote the beginning and end of a sentence or short
passage, but not the middle. In these cases, some form of ellipsis is needed. If
you leave out words within a single sentence, three spaced dots are enough to
signal that a word or words are missing. If you leave out a sentence or more, then
you need to add a fourth dot, to indicate ellipses with a period. The period
comes immediately after the quoted text followed by the three spaced dots for
ellipses.

Here is the first paragraph of Doris Lessing's "Group Minds." Following that,
you will see use of ellipses for an omitted word and of a period and ellipses for
omitted sentence(s).

> People living in the West, in societies that we describe as Western, or as
> the free world, may be educated in many different ways, but they will all emerge
> with an idea about themselves that goes something like this: I am a citizen of a free
> society, and that means I am an individual, making individual choices. My mind

is my own, my opinions are chosen by me, I am free to do as I will, and at
the worst the pressures on me are economic, that is, I may be too poor to do as
I want.

Lessing says that those of us who live "in the West . . . may be educated in
many different ways" (226).

Lessing argues that we Westerners believe we are free. Each of us thinks "I am
an individual, making individual choices. . . . and at the worst the pressures on me
are economic, that is, I may be too poor to do as I want" (226).

When using ellipses, be careful to ensure that the resulting sentences are
grammatically sound and that you have not omitted material that you want the
reader to have in mind.

Square Brackets—Something Added

Sometimes you need to add or substitute words within a quotation. Letters,
words, and phrases within square brackets are those that do not appear in the
original passage, but which the writer has added for clarity or grammatical accuracy.

Imagine that you want to quote the last sentence in this passage:

The short story has also been the form that, before the present era, most
often crossed borders to bring international success to Canadian authors.
Thomas Chandler Haliburton, revered by the American story-teller Mark
Twain among others, was Canada's first writer to be widely recognized abroad.
So immense was his popularity that more than a hundred editions of his Clockmaker
sketches were printed in Canada, the United States, England, and, in translation, in
France and Germany (6).

> Brown, Russell, and Donna Bennett. Introduction. *Canadian Short*
> *Stories*. Eds. Russell Brown and Donna Bennett.
> Toronto: Penguin, 2005. Print.

If you want to quote this sentence, you need to tell the reader to whom the
pronoun "his" refers. This can be done using square brackets.

Haliburton's stories were widely printed and read not only in Canada but also
beyond our borders: "So immense was his [Haliburton's] popularity that more than
a hundred editions of his Clockmaker sketches were printed in Canada, the United
States, England, and, in translation, in France and Germany" (6).

Introduce Quotations Using Lively Verbs

Always provide some form of introduction when you build in a quotation. In the
following example, the quotation parachutes in with no introduction, which can
be disorienting for the reader:

Canadian settlement history has influenced how we think about being
Canadian today. "Cabot may not have discovered Canada but his main method of

exploration, getting lost, is a persistent national theme" (Laird 8). Many of the explorers contributed to our national character.

As you read the paragraph above, you find yourself in the midst of a quotation, without any introductory words; even with the parenthetical citation, the freestanding quotation jars the reader. Before beginning a quotation, it is a good idea to signal who the author is (and even to provide the name of the source and date of publication). The following versions provide this clarity:

> One cultural analyst has joked that "Cabot may not have discovered Canada but his main method of exploration, getting lost, is a persistent national theme" (Laird 8).
>
> Cultural analyst Gordon Laird points to the irony that early explorer John Cabot's "main method of exploration, getting lost, is a persistent national theme" (8).

Rather than using serviceable but unexciting verbs like "writes," or "says," to link speakers/writers to their quotations, try stronger verbs like "contends," "interrogates," "counters," even "imagines." Your writing will be more dynamic if you are as precise in your choice of verbs to denote speech acts as you are in choosing verbs to denote physical acts.

EXERCISE   *Write a short (one or two paragraph) essay to explain the ideas in Lessing's article or Hoffman's narrative excerpt using all the techniques of summarizing, paraphrasing, and quoting presented in this chapter. For the purposes of this exercise, your primary concern should be the accuracy of summaries and paraphrases and the correct quotation of well-selected material. Specifically, your little essay should include the following elements:*

- a one-sentence summary of the whole text
- a one-sentence paraphrase of a sentence from the text
- a long quotation in block form
- a sentence-length quotation
- a short phrase-length quotation

Use each of the following techniques at least once:

- square brackets to signify an alteration of the original
- ellipsis marks to omit unnecessary words

Make sure that you provide a citation in either MLA or APA form for each quotation and punctuate it correctly.

Finally, make sure that each quotation is somehow embedded into your own prose—never leave a quotation free-standing.

AVOID PLAGIARISM BY DOCUMENTING SOURCES

Documentation of outside sources is the most immediately identifiable foot-print of scholarly work. Commonly understood as a courtesy or perhaps legality by which we acknowledge our indebtedness to other writers, documentation is actually far more important than that: it is the system by which we anchor our claims in the existing body of worldwide scholarship on the topic. By making use of other scholars' work, we ensure that our own work builds on what is already known rather than reinventing the wheel. By documenting our use of others' work, we provide assurance to our own readers that we have drawn on sources that followed sound scholarly methods, and we give them the means to trace our research back to our original sources.

Documentation is a scholar's way of saying, "You can trust my claims. I didn't just make this stuff up." It is also completely compulsory.

Plagiarism is taking credit for someone else's words or ideas by reproducing them without proper attribution. Most students are eager to avoid this form of scholarly theft. On those occasions when it may seem tempting to borrow a pretty phrase or to include an idea without retracing your steps to locate the source, remember that instructors are often able to detect plagiarism—by hearing a shift in the writer's voice—and that they are professionally obligated to protect the integrity of academic work by dealing with plagiarism in ways that have serious consequences.

Avoid *plagiarism* when you are summarizing or paraphrasing someone else's ideas, by using your own words and providing a citation to credit the source. Remember, too, that it is essential to be accurate, so use square brackets or ellipses if you change any part of a quotation.

The following passage about writing narrative argument is reproduced from Chapter 3 of this book.

> Making a point from experience does not in itself prove things or justify con-clusions, but it can help to improve a reader's understanding. To accomplish this, your account of your experience should resonate with others, moving beyond the minutiae of particular events to strike a chord others recognize from their own experience. You will probably find it helpful to think about the personal argument as having twin components. As its name suggests, it is about a personal experience (or about several experiences, depending on the approach you pick) *and* it also makes an argument. In this way, the personal essay also has a thesis—the details support the point the essay makes about human experience.

> Here's a plagiarized presentation of this material that reproduces the original material without citation:

> Making a point from experience helps to improve a reader's understanding. Your account of your experience should resonate with others, moving beyond particular events to strike a chord others recognize from their own experience. The personal argument has twin components. It is about a personal experience *and*

it also makes an argument. The personal essay has a thesis—the details support the point the essay makes about human experience.

Here is a better version. The writer changes both the language and structure and directs the reader to the original source. This careful form of representation avoids plagiarism and enriches the writer's text by introducing what others have said:

> According to the authors of *Across the Disciplines: Academic Writing and Reading,* the narrative argument has the component of story, which involves telling about an event drawn from experience, as well as the component of argument, which makes a point that resonates with readers (McLeod Rogers and Taylor 49).

DOCUMENTING SOURCES

A paper in the humanities usually follows the Modern Language Association (MLA) format for citation. A paper in the social sciences usually follows the American Psychological Association (APA) format. In the brief outline of documentation procedures that follows, we focus on MLA and APA styles for the types of sources you are most likely to use in your academic writing. We have attempted to showcase the most commonly used citations in both MLA and APA formats. For a more complete listing, consult the *MLA Handbook for Writers of Research Papers,* the APA *Publication Manual,* or whichever style guide your instructor has specified. For example, history often follows the *Chicago Manual of Style (CMS)* and the sciences often follow the Council of Biology Editors (CBE) format.

In-text Citation

Provide a citation for any material from an outside source, whether quoted directly or paraphrased. Because inserting information in a pair of brackets interrupts the flow of text, keep the interruption as brief as possible by including only enough information to identify the source and the location within that source. In MLA style, the citation includes the author's last name and the page number; in APA, author and year (and page numbers for quoted material).

Final Source List

In MLA format, your list of sources is called "Works Cited." In APA format, it is called "References." Entries in this listing should be double-spaced, with second and subsequent lines of each entry indented five spaces; use the "hanging indent" function in the paragraph format menu of your word processor. In both styles, a single space follows the period or colon.

MLA and APA Compared

- In MLA style, the date of the publication follows the name of the publisher at the very end of the item; in APA style, the date is placed within parentheses immediately following the author's name.

- For titles in both MLA and APA systems, *italics* are preferred to underlining.

- In APA style, only the initial of the author's first name is indicated. In MLA style, the full name is given.

- In APA style, only the first word (and any proper noun) of a book or article title and subtitle is capitalized. In MLA style, all the words following the first word (except articles and short prepositions) are capitalized; in APA, only journal titles are capitalized this way. The first letter of any word after the colon in a title is capitalized in both styles.

- For APA style, do *not* place quotation marks around journal/magazine article titles. Do use "p." and "pp." to indicate page numbers of newspaper articles and book chapters (but not journal articles).

- In MLA style, publishers' names should be abbreviated; thus, "Oxford University Press" becomes "Oxford" or "Oxford UP." In APA, do not omit or abbreviate words such as "University" or "Press," but do omit trailing words or abbreviations such as "Limited" or "Inc."

- APA includes only sources available to the public in its reference list. Other material such as interviews done by the essayist are given in content notes. See the APA *Publication Manual* for details.

- MLA notes the medium of a source at the end of each entry in the "Works Cited" list (for example, if a source is print or from the web). These markers come at the end of each entry, but the word "Web" should be followed by the date of access. Include the URL only if it is unlikely that the reader can locate the source.

- APA includes the "Digital Object Identifier" (DOI) for electronic sources whenever they are available.

- MLA updates stipulate that if there are no page numbers, use the abbreviation "n.pag." If there is no publisher, or no place of publication available, use "n.p."

MLA Style: In-text Citation

This is an example of an MLA-style in-text citation:

> Many of those who have grown up using the net need "the educational system changed to embrace the way they learn, think, and process information" (Tapscott 118).

There is no punctuation or abbreviation for "page" between the author's name and the page number. In addition, if you name the author in your text, do not repeat it in the citation:

> Tapscott argues that many who have grown up using the net need "the educational system changed to embrace the way they learn, think, and process information" (118).

Provide page numbers for summaries and paraphrases, as well as for quotations:

> Tapscott argues that many who have grown up using the net need a form of education that reflects how they learn and think (118).

The parenthetical reference is placed before the final period unless it refers to more than the one sentence. In such cases, the citation *follows* the period ending the last paraphrased sentence, and it is your responsibility to make clear how many of the preceding sentences are involved. For example, you might use the source author's name at the beginning of the paraphrased material and use signal phrases ("she argues," "she goes on to say") to make it easy for the reader to identify all paraphrased material.

Always put the parenthetical citation after the period when using a block quotation:

> Amit Srivastava points towards troubling developments in her account of a recent visit to Canada:
>
>> Flying in from the San Francisco area where I live, I was on my way to give a speech about human rights and the environment in Calgary. I didn't get past the immigration desk. (25)

If reference to the source occurs only within the first part of the sentence, the parenthetical citation should be embedded within the sentence itself:

> Tapscott defends Net Geners by contending that the education system needs to be "changed to embrace the way they learn, think, and process information" (118), and dismisses arguments that this group has lost its intellectual edge.

Sometimes you need to alter the basic author/page number citation format. Here are some common variants:

Quotation cited in another source: Here, the quotation from Dennis Raphael appears in Susan Scott's article, and if you refer to Raphael, you will do so by citing Scott in the Works Cited.

> (Dennis Raphael qtd. in Scott 208)

An anonymous work: If no author is named, give the title.

> ("Reading" 101)

A work with two to three authors:

> (Skrobanek, Boonpakdee, and Jantateero 17).

Note: If there are more than three authors, use the phrase "et al." to refer to authors after the first.

(Belenky et al. 7)

A particular work by an author, when you list two or more works by that author in the Works Cited: Use a short form for the title of the work; the example here is a citation for a reference to Judith Butler's book, *Bodies That Matter*.

(Butler, *Bodies*, 96–97)

MLA Style: Works Cited List

Books

One Author

Mate, Gabor. *In the Realm of Hungry Ghosts: Close Encounters With Addiction.*
    Toronto: Knopf Canada, 2008. Print.

Include title and subtitle to provide complete information.

Two or More Books by the Same Author

Butler, Judith. *Bodies That Matter: On the Discursive Limits of "Sex."* New York:
    Routledge, 1993. Print.

—. *Gender Trouble: Feminism and the Subversion of Identity.* New York: Routledge,
    1990. Print.

Note: For MLA style, references are listed in order of publication, with the most recently published first.

Two or Three Authors

Skrobanek, Siriporn, Nataya Boonpakdee, and Chutima Jantateero. *The Traffic in
    Women: Human Realities of the International Sex Trade.* London: Zed Books,
    1997. Print.

More than Three Authors

Belenky, Mary Field, et al. *Women's Ways of Knowing: The Development of Self,
    Voice and Mind.* New York: Basic, 1986. Print.

A Book with an Editor

Sweetman, Caroline, ed. *Gender and Migration.* Oxford: Oxfam GB, 1998. Print.

A Selection from an Edited Collection or Anthology

Ng, Roxanna. "Finding Our Voices: Reflections on Immigrant Women's Organizing."
    Women and Social Change: Feminist Activism in Canada. Eds. Jeri D. Wine and
    Janice L. Ristock. Toronto: Lorimer, 1991. 184–97. Print.

Periodicals

An Article from a Scholarly Journal

Note: The revised MLA does not require differentiating between journals with continuous pagination and those that start on page 1 with each issue. In both cases give volume and issue (if available).

Rockhill, Kathleen. "The Chaos of Subjectivity in the Ordered Halls of Academe." *Canadian Woman Studies* 8.4 (1987): 12–17. Print.

A Signed Article in a Daily Newspaper

Landsberg, Michele. "Tory Policies Slowly Poison Public Education." *Toronto Star* 18 June 2000: A2. Print.

Electronic Sources

A Document on a Website

Bochenek, Michael and Widney Brown. "Hatred in the Hallways." *Human Rights Watch*. Human Rights Watch. 2001. Web. 12 July 2005.

A Journal Article on a Website

Lewis, Manfred. "Orientalism in Occidental Nations." *Post-colonial Studies in Canada* 2.3 (2003): 23–38. Web. 4 Apr. 2004.

A Journal Article from a Library Database

Lewis, Manfred. "Orientalism in Occidental Nations." *Post-colonial Studies in Canada* 2.3 (2003): 23–38. *Proquest.* Web. 12 Aug. 2004.

APA Style: In-text Citation

This is an example of an APA-style in-text citation:

> Many of those who have grown up using the internet need "the educational system changed to embrace the way they learn, think, and process information" (Tapscott, 2008, p. 118).

If you name the author and year of publication in your text, do not repeat it in the citation:

> Tapscott (2008) argues that many who have grown up using the net need "the educational system changed to embrace the way they learn, think, and process information" (p. 118).

When using the APA system, you are not required to provide page numbers for summaries or paraphrases unless your instructor requests that you do. If you do not refer to a specific page, simply indicate the date:

> Tapscott (2008) argues that many who have grown up using the internet need a form of education that reflects how they learn and think.

In the APA system, there is a comma between the author's name and the page number, and a "p." before the number (or "pp." for more than one page). The parenthetical citation is placed before the period ending the sentence (except, as explained for MLA, when the reference applies to more than the one preceding sentence).

In longer, block quotations, however, the parenthetical citation follows the period:

> Amit Srivastava (2000) points towards troubling developments in her account of a recent visit to Canada:
>
> > Flying in from the San Francisco area where I live, I was on my way to give a speech about human rights and the environment in Calgary. I didn't get past the immigration desk. (p. 25)

Place the parenthetical reference within the sentence if the reference to the source occurs only in the opening section:

> Tapscott defends Net Geners by contending that the education system needs to be "changed to embrace the way they learn, think, and process information" (p. 118), and dismisses arguments that this group have lost their intellectual edge.

There are times when you must modify the basic citation format that includes author's last name, year of publication, and page number. Depending on the nature of your source(s), you may need to use one of the following citation formats.

Quoted material appearing in another source: As with MLA, Scott, not Raphael, would appear in your final documentation list.

> (Dennis Raphael cited in Scott, 2007, p. 208)

An anonymous work:

> ("Reading," 2001, p. 32)

A work with two or more authors (notice the use of ampersand before final name):

> (Skrobanek, Boonpakdee, & Jantateero, 1997, p. 17)

For three or more authors, cite all authors the first time. In subsequent citations, cite only the last name of the first author, followed by "et al."

APA Style: References List

You might note that even though titles in an APA References list do not follow conventional rules requiring you to capitalize each main word, within your essay itself standard conventions do pertain. Even though you are to list Butler's book as *Bodies that matter* in the References list, within the essay itself you are to refer to it as *Bodies that Matter*.

Books

Book with One Author

Give the title as well as the subtitle to provide complete information.

Mate, G. (2008). *In the realm of hungry ghosts: Close encounters with addiction.*
    Toronto: Knopf Canada.

Two or More Books by the Same Author

Butler, J. (1990). *Gender trouble: Feminism and the subversion of identity.* New York:
    Routledge.

Butler, J. (1993). *Bodies that matter: On the discursive limits of "sex."* New York:
    Routledge.

Note: For APA style, references are listed in chronological order of publication.

Two or More Authors

Skrobanek, S., Boonpakdee, N., & Jantateero, C. (1997). *The traffic in women: Human
    realities of the international sex trade.* London: Zed Books.

Up to seven authors can be named. If there are more than seven, list the first six,
followed by an ellipsis, followed by the last author.

A Book with an Editor

Sweetman, C. (Ed.). (1998). *Gender and migration.* Oxford: Oxfam GB.

A Selection from an Edited Collection or Anthology

Ng, R. (1991). Finding our voices: Reflections on immigrant women's organizing. In J.
    D. Wine & J. L. Ristock (Eds.), *Women and social change: Feminist activism in
    Canada* (pp. 184–97). Toronto: Lorimer.

Periodicals

An Article from a Scholarly Journal with Continuous Pagination Throughout an Annual Cycle

Riger, S. (1993). What's wrong with empowerment. *American Journal of Community
    Psychology, 21,* 279–92.

An Article from a Scholarly Journal with Separate Pagination for Each Issue

Rockhill, K. (1987). The chaos of subjectivity in the ordered halls of academe.
    Canadian Woman Studies, 8(4), 12–17.

A Signed Article in a Daily Newspaper

Landsberg, M. (2000, June 18). Tory policies slowly poison public education.
    Toronto Star, A2.

Electronic Sources

For electronic sources, supply the same information as for print versions, followed by the "Digital Object Identifier" or "DOI" (if available). If the publisher has not supplied a DOI number, provide the name of the database instead—for example, Proquest. If you have neither a DOI nor a database, supply the URL. The date of retrieval is not required unless the document is likely to be removed or changed (e.g., if it is taken from a wiki).

A Document on a Website

Bochenek, M. & Brown, W. (2001). Hatred in the hallways. *Human Rights Watch.* Retrieved from http://www.hrw.org/reports/2001/uslgbt/toc.htm

A Document on a Website—Revision Likely

Anne of Denmark. (n.d.). In *Wikipedia.* Retrieved July 2, 2009, from http://en. wikipedia.org/wiki/Anne_of_Denmark

An Online Journal Article—Not from a Database, No DOI

Neil Pembroke. (2008). Narratives of silence: Availability in a spirituality of fathering. *Journal of Men, Masculinities and Spirituality, 2*(2), 82–94. Retrieved from http:// www.jmmsweb.org/

A Journal Article—from a Database, No DOI

Gilbert, E. (2005). The inevitability of integration? Neoliberal discourse and the proposals for a new North American economic space after September 11. *Annals of the Association of American Geographers, 95*(1), 202–222. Ebsco.

A Journal Article with a DOI

Gilbert, E. (2005). The inevitability of integration? Neoliberal discourse and the proposals for a new North American economic space after September 11. *Annals of the Association of American Geographers, 95*(1), 202–222. DOI 10.1111/j.1467-8306.2005.00456.x

---

EXERCISE

1. Figure out whether each of the following is a book, chapter of a book, journal article in print or on the web, or document on a website. Turn the unordered list into an alphabetized Works Cited list in proper MLA form. Then recast it as an APA References list.

   - James Miller, Is Bad Writing Necessary? in *Lingua Franca*, 2000, volume 9 issue 9 accessed by you 20 October 2005 on the web at http://www.linguafranca. com/9912/writing.html
   - Judith Butler, Bodies That Matter: On the Discursive Limits of "Sex," New York, Routledge, 1993.

- Beverly Daniel Tatum, Lighting Candles in the Dark, on pages 56–63 in Becoming and Unbecoming White, edited by Christine Clark and James O'Donnell, Westport, Connecticut and London, Bergin & Garvey, 1999.
- Diane Elam and Robyn Wiegman, editors, Feminism Beside Itself, New York, Routledge, 1995.
- Peter Newman, Living Dangerously, in Maclean's, December 20, 1999, pages 50–6.
- A.H. Grossman, A.R. D'Augelli, T.J. Howell, and S. Hubbard, Parents' reactions to transgender youths' gender nonconforming expression and identity, in *Journal of Gay & Lesbian Social Services: Issues in Practice, Policy, and Research,* 2005, *volume 18, issue 1, pages* 3-16, doi:10.1300/J041v18n01_02 S.

CHAPTER 5

Critiquing Sources: Writing Critiques and Reviews

As we noted in Chapter 1, academic writing typically involves entering into a pre-existing scholarly conversation about a topic. To write an essay that contributes to the conversation, we must

1. understand what has already been said,
2. decide what we think about what has been said,
3. develop our own perspective, and finally,
4. communicate that perspective and present it in the context of what others have said.

Many research essays (as discussed in Chapter 6) require the student to build an argument that draws on many sources, and every argument you read is an invitation to agreement or disagreement. To develop the required ability to enter into scholarly conversation, instructors often assign "critiques" or "reviews" that ask the student to write a detailed evaluation of a single text, usually an article or a book. Think of this task as engaging in dialogue with the author.

TECHNICAL TERMS

Critique and *review* are somewhat interchangeable terms for the task of commentary on a text. Critique is often used for an unpublished response to a text, and review for a published response to a published text, usually a book. Students are often asked to "critique" an article but "review" a book. Reviews sometimes include more summary and description than would be acceptable in a critique. Many scholarly journals include book reviews as a way of informing their readership about important new books in the discipline.

The *literature review* integrates a range of commentaries in order to provide a coherent picture of the state of scholarly conversation on a topic. Depending on the assignment, the literature review can be mainly descriptive or quite evaluative; it might end with an explanation of the writer's own position on the topic, or by identifying an angle that deserves more attention. (In the section on literature reviews later in this chapter, we refer to the process of creating a research space.) A literature review can involve reviewing anywhere from five or six texts in a first-year paper to a hundred or more in a Ph.D. thesis. The literature review is a standard feature of Social Science articles and is often assigned as a stand-alone paper in Social Science courses.

Response papers are related to critiques and reviews, but often, writers of response papers use a text as a springboard to develop their own perspectives on an issue, rather than closely evaluating the text.

When scholars write an article and ask a journal to consider publishing it, the journal editor sends the article out for *peer review* by several scholars who have expertise in the topic area. They evaluate the article for methodological rigour, importance, and originality, and based on whether it meets all three criteria, recommend for or against publishing it. The use of peer review (sometimes called blind review, because authors and reviewers are not identified to each other) as a quality control system makes scholarly journal articles an especially valued form of academic writing.

WRITING CRITIQUES AND REVIEWS

The specific instructions given can vary from discipline to discipline. This is because instructors use critique and review assignments to get students thinking in terms of the key concepts and methods of the course. For example:

- In history, you may be asked to comment on the types of *archival sources* used and not used in the text. You will be expected to describe what the text contributes to our knowledge of a historical *period* in a particular *region*.
- In sociology, you may be asked to comment on the methodology behind the text. For example, did the author conduct *survey* or *interview* research? How many *participants* were included? What were their *demographic* characteristics? You will also be expected to relate the text to broader *sociological issues* such as poverty, the welfare state, or racism.
- In physics, you may be asked to identify the methodology and *findings* of a study, then comment on how the research contributes to our understanding of a scientific *problem*, and how it relates to other research on the problem. For example, does it tackle the problem in a new way, or does it replicate other research? If so, does the study confirm or refute it? You may also be asked to comment on the possible future *applications* of the research.

Notice that in each example, the reviewer is asked to comment very specifically on the key aspects of the text, and then to step back and comment on what the text contributes to the larger scholarly conversation. While the specific content varies, the following box outlines the general structure of a review or critique.

General Format for Critiques and Reviews

Title

Bibliographic information

I. Introduction
    - Provide background material on text and author.
    - State the author's purpose and main argument.
    - State your thesis about the text and how you will develop it in the review.

II. Summary (this should take up no more than one-fifth of the whole paper)
    - Explain the author's argument.

III. Look closely at the text to figure out how the argument works
    - Main question: What is the core argument of the text? How skillfully is it argued?
    - Focus on rhetorical technique and methodological features.

IV. Step back to examine the text in the world
    - Main question: Do you agree or disagree with the author's perspective on the topic? Why?
    - Focus on the "politics" of the text, where you treat the text as an attempt to persuade members of the discipline or the public to view an issue in a particular way. Consider how else this problem/topic could have been analyzed.
    - How does the text contribute to scholarly knowledge/public discourse?

V. Conclusion
    - State your overall verdict on the author's views and his or her success in arguing them effectively.
    - Suggest what further research is needed (optional).

Parts of a Critique or Review

Here is a more detailed examination of the above approach:

Title

"A Review of X by Y," where X is the title of the book/article/video, and Y is the author or authors. In some disciplines, it may be appropriate to have a title and subtitle, where the title expresses the theme of the review, and the subtitle is written as above; for example, "Lost at Sea: A Review of X by Y."

Bibliographic Information

This is often put at the top of the first page, and written in note style; e.g., Sally Muntz, *Fishing* (Paris: Harvard University Press, 2006).

If the instructor has asked that it be put at the end, treat the bibliographic information as a one-item reference list; for example, Muntz, Sally. *Fishing.* Paris: Harvard University Press, 2006.

I. Introduction

- Introduce the text and the author.
- State the author's purpose for writing—what disciplinary question or public interest is he or she addressing? Who is the intended audience?
- State the main argument of the text. What perspective does the writer want the reader to accept?
- Provide background material to put the topic in context. This context could be discipline-specific or a public issue. What does the text contribute to the overall topic of your course? What course concepts does it engage with?
- State your thesis about the text and how you will develop it in the review.

II. Summary (this should take up no more than one-fifth of the whole paper)

- Explain the author's argument (thesis plus main stages of thought by which the thesis is developed).
- This can be done by reducing the original text to its main points, by describing it, or (more often) as a combination of both. The summarizing skills you practised in Chapter 4 will be useful here.

Some professors prefer a style in which summary is not separated, but included mainly to provide examples of points made in your analysis.

Movie reviewers and book reviewers in newspapers and magazines summarize the text under review because their readers will not have seen or read it yet. In contrast, instructors are normally very familiar with any text a student might be asked to review. The point of your summary is therefore not to inform the instructor of the argument made by the text, but to establish that you understand that argument accurately.

III. Look closely at the text to figure out how the argument works

(III and IV together should occupy about two-thirds of the essay and may be several paragraphs each, though depending on what you have to say, you may devote more space to III than to IV or vice versa.)

Most scholarly texts are meant both to inform and to persuade, though the balance varies widely from the provision of factual information about an uncontroversial topic with no apparent opinion involved, to making an impassioned argument that blatantly sets out to change the reader's outlook on an issue. But scholarly texts from one end of that continuum to the other share this characteristic: they all make an *argument*, mainly through logic and evidence, that their perspective on the topic is solid and that the reader should accept it. A scientist does this by presenting methodologically rigorous research in neutral language, with no adjectives or adverbs in sight; the text is nevertheless an argument that the findings are correct and the conclusions valid. Whatever the balance between informative and persuasive purpose in the text under review, however, the key to critique is to understand the argument: what it is, how it is conducted, and how well it is conducted.

The main focus of this section is to identify and assess the core argument of the text under review. This involves focusing on methodology and/or rhetorical features (logical solidity, ethical appeal, emotional appeal). Questions to be asked about *logic* might include

- How are key concepts defined?
- Is the structure of claim and support solid? Does one claim lead logically to the next? Are claims adequately supported with logic, evidence, and references to other scholarly sources?
- Is the information accurate? Peer-reviewed scholarly articles have been thoroughly checked for accuracy, but other texts may not have been. If the text has not been peer-reviewed, are you confident that the information is accurate? Why or why not?
- Is the information fairly interpreted? Does the author stick to conveying facts, or does he or she draw some conclusions from the facts? If the latter, what are these conclusions and are they justified?
- Does the author consider alternative perspectives on the topic? Are you convinced that the author's perspective is superior to the alternatives? Might a reflective reader be thinking, "Yes, but . . ."?
- What kind of evidence is used? (For example, does the author draw on primary or secondary material—see page 116—historical archives, survey data, interviews, literary analysis, and/or personal observation?) Is it adequate?

Does the author appeal to the reader's sense of ethics and emotion? How? How successfully?

Speakers and writers have never relied upon logic alone in advancing and supporting their claims. The Greek philosopher Aristotle (384–322 BC) lived at a time when public speaking was a key responsibility of citizens who were expected to participate in Athenian democracy. In *The Art of Rhetoric*, he analyzed the persuasive power of speakers ("*rhetors*") in terms of their success in appealing not only to the audience's sense of logic and evidence (logos), but to their sense of ethical substance (ethos) and to their emotions (pathos). Logic and evidence are obviously important to scholarly writing, but ethos, and often pathos, matter too.

- Ethos can be thought of as the ethical stature of a text. What gives it (or detracts from its) trustworthiness? If the text were a person, would it have *gravitas*—that combination of dignity and seriousness that leaders aspire to possess? For example, what are the author's credentials for writing on the topic? What is the stature of the journal or publisher? Is it well documented? What is the stature of the sources that the author cites as authoritative? Is the text written respectfully? Does it make you take the topic seriously? Does the author tie the argument to an important cause, such as saving the planet or reducing hunger?

■ Pathos might be attempted through anecdotes and other references meant to inspire such emotions as patriotism, compassion, or anger. The task of the reviewer is to identify such attempts and assess whether they are an appropriate emotional accompaniment to the logical case that has been presented, or are a substitute for logic instead.

Questions to be asked about *emotion* and *ethics* might include

■ Does the author appeal to emotion? If so, is emotion used effectively, or cheaply? Does it support a strong argument, or is it offered instead of logic and evidence?

■ Is the argument ethically sound? Is the author well qualified to write on the subject? Does he or she ally with noble causes (e.g., saving the planet, human rights)?

■ Are there stylistic or content issues that add to or detract from the ethos of the text? (For example, does it contain slang, profanity, or usage errors?)

The vast majority of texts that students are asked to review are scholarly articles and books that are intended to present a persuasive case for the value of the information presented, which means that comments on the entertainment value of the text are usually irrelevant. (It would be similarly irrelevant to review a movie negatively on account of its lack of scholarly evidence.) It is usually also true that scholarly texts are about complex topics and use a correspondingly complex form of expression that may not be immediately engaging to readers. If the language is impenetrable, a good review should warn readers of this. However, if the language is challenging because it is specialized (developed for the topic and discipline), the reviewer who complains may sound intellectually lazy—unwilling to put in the effort required to understand a difficult subject—rather than astute.

Logical Fallacies

Many common errors in argumentation have ancient Latin names, because people have been making the same mistakes for a very long time. Many of these errors are common journalistic techniques, and you can hone your logical skills by looking for them in ads and the news. Watch out for them in your own arguments and in other people's.

***Ad hominem* attacks**—the attempt to discredit a perspective by criticizing the character of a person associated with it instead of critiquing the perspective. (*X's views on sexual abuse by priests are irrelevant because he is just an ignorant atheist.*)

Bandwagon—asserting the superiority of a position on the basis of its popularity. (*Everyone knows capitalism is the best economic system.*)

Begging the question—claiming to address a problem without doing so, thus leaving the question "begging" for a response. Also known as circular reasoning, this technique often relies on *tautology* or stating the same thing in two different ways (defining X as X). (*Marijuana use is wrong; otherwise it would be legal.*)

Oversimplification—falsely reducing a complex situation to a simple one; sometimes called "reductionist" thinking. "Black and white" thinking and "either/or" thinking reduce the situation to two sides. (*Either we find more natural gas or we will freeze in the dark.*)

False analogy—claiming that one situation is similar to another when it is not. (*Barack Obama's health care reform is like Hitler's eugenics program.*)

Hasty generalization—drawing conclusions about a whole class on the basis of a limited number of examples. (*Molly is Polish; Molly is musical; therefore all Poles are musical.*)

Non sequitur—presenting one statement as following logically from another when it does not. (*Since we now have same-sex marriage in Canada, there is no homophobia in this country.*)

Post hoc, ergo propter hoc—falsely concluding that because something followed something else (*post hoc*), it was caused by it (*propter hoc*). (*Women went topless in April, and God punished us with an earthquake in May.*)

Slippery slope—falsely claiming that one event would lead inevitably to another, highly undesirable one. (*Legalizing same-sex marriage will destroy Canadian society.*)

Straw man—misrepresenting a perspective so that it is easier to attack. (*Environmentalists want us to freeze in the dark.*)

IV. Step back to examine the text in the world

- Main question: Quite apart from the previous question of whether the author has argued skillfully, to what extent to you agree or disagree with his or her perspective on the topic? If you agree, help the author do his or her work by offering good reasons for accepting the argument. If you disagree, explain why.

- Ask yourself what this text contributes to our understanding of a scholarly problem or social issue. Why is the problem or issue important?

- Ask, "So what?"

The always-useful "so what?" question directs us to think about what difference it makes—to individuals, to society, or to the discipline—whether we have this information or not.

To begin thinking about this, start by seeing what the author has to say about it. Scholarly writers usually try to answer the "so what" question in their introductions, where they review the existing scholarship and identify a gap that the text will fill, and in their conclusions, where they draw out the implications of their work.

Then think about whether the information presented, or the perspective offered, is as important as the author says it is. This can be thought of as focusing on the "politics" of the text, where you treat the text as a real-life participant in public discourse, not just black marks on white paper. The goal here is to read against the grain of the text, asking impertinent questions. What does this text contribute to our knowledge of the subject? What is the disciplinary importance of this work? If scholars were to act on its conclusions, what further research might they do? If people in society were to act on the basis of the argument made in this text, what would they do?

V. Conclusion

- Wrap up III and IV by stating your overall verdict on the author's views and his or her success in arguing them effectively.
- Briefly describe what further research is needed or what actions are called for.

CRITIQUING AIRTIGHT ARGUMENTS

Students sometimes feel that the text they are asked to evaluate for book reviews and other critical essays is so logically airtight, so solidly supported with scholarly references and impeccable logic, that they can find nothing to take issue with. The expertly constructed scholarly text seems like a shield designed to repel all attempts at negative judgment. Students can feel that they are reduced to the role of appreciative readers who can do little but point out the various strengths of the text. Such a reaction is understandable, given that the text was produced by an expert on the topic, and by the time it was published had been revised many times and reviewed by other similarly expert specialists.

But while it is theoretically appropriate to write an entirely positive critique in cases where the text offers no reasonable grounds for disagreement, more often the appreciative approach suggests an inadequate critical stance from which to identify problems, or at least, omissions in the text: after all, no single book or article can possibly have considered its topic from every conceivable angle, and what a text does *not* do can also be worthy of discussion.

Sometimes it is possible to develop a critical perspective on a text by stepping back to ask what it actually does and does not do, instead of asking how well it does what the author evidently meant it to do. In any case, the question of purpose, or authorial intent, can be seen as irrelevant since authors can change their minds or have ulterior motives we know nothing about; their texts can have effects very different from what they intended, and these effects can differ in different reading contexts. Further, if we focus on purpose, we allow the author to dictate the terms of discussion. Even if we shift our definition of purpose from "author's intention" to "thesis of the text," our frame of reference is pre-established.

Critical analysis that focuses on the purpose of the text or how well it defends its thesis mostly works "within the box"—first the big box of other scholarship on the subject, then the smaller box of the text itself. To address the former, traditional critical thinkers check to see if the author provides references to other trustworthy studies where any unproved statements *are* proved. To answer the second question, they ask pertinent questions that focus directly on the internal strength of the document:

- Does one claim lead logically to another? Are logical flaws avoided? (*logos*)
- Are appropriate methods used (e.g., statistical analysis, big enough sample size), and are they properly executed? (*logos*)
- Are all the claims backed up with solid evidence? (*logos*)
- Does the author ever try to get away with using emotion or personal experience instead of logic and objective evidence? (*pathos*)
- Does the author have the authority or credentials to speak on the subject? Does he or she seem trustworthy? (*ethos*)

In short, traditional critical thinking is rigorous and important, but it works in a limited context. It identifies an object of analysis (a text, an idea, an argument) and assesses its internal logic.

This method of thinking is "critical" in the sense of being necessary to find the "truth" by exposing and avoiding the mistakes of everyday common sense. As such, it is tremendously important to rigorous intellectual work and nothing is likely to get published in the scholarly press if it fails the test of critical thinking. However, traditional critical thinking is not a perfect method and in itself, it can tend to be intellectually conservative rather than conducive to new perspectives. The following statements reflect mainstream beliefs that have passed the test of traditional critical thinking either in our own or earlier times; they have all been fiercely defended as true by scholars using traditional critical thinking:

- Women should not attend university because studying diverts energy from the uterus.
- Women should not be allowed to vote or hold political office because they lack the rational capacities of men.
- It is acceptable to enslave people of other races because slavery helps the white race to prosper and spread Christianity worldwide in accordance with God's plan.
- It is in everyone's best interests to annihilate Aboriginal languages, religions, and traditions and assimilate Aboriginal people into Canadian culture.
- Human beings are the only living creatures that are conscious and have emotions.
- We are all completely free to think and do as we want in a Western democracy such as Canada. If we are poor, it's our own fault.

These statements, most of them generally rejected now as blatantly unjust constructions of reality designed to serve the interests of those in power, were produced by powerful social institutions such as universities, dominant religions, law, and medicine. Recognizing that to some extent—and the exact extent is the subject of fervent debate between constructionist and modernist intellectuals—traditional critical thinking has historically tended to serve the interests of the status quo, scholars in the field of critical literacy have developed a parallel method of critical thinking that is designed to open up new perspectives by asking whose interests are served by the text. This method is "critical" in the sense of "critical social theory": its focus is primarily on power rather than on "truth," and it looks for signs that a particular text is premised on versions of "truth" that serve the interests of dominant culture. These questions are pertinent when reading the articles in the chapter, for example, on Canadian identity, where the texts offer competing definitions of Canadian identity and national purpose that serve the interests of some groups (say, advocates of multiculturalism) at the expense of others (say, middle-class conservative defenders of the status quo).

Critical literacy involves becoming aware of the "box" constructed by the text itself (sometimes called "reading against the grain" of a text) by exposing the text's politics and drawing attention to its oppressive effects. It also involves developing alternative texts, alternative ways of understanding a topic. In order to get at what texts do, we can ask *impertinent* questions—ones the author does not invite. The text is analyzed as an attempt to persuade members of the discipline, or the public, to view an important issue in a particular way and act on that belief in their work and their lives. Critical literacy questions can be useful here, beginning with the key questions, "Whose interests are served by this text?" and "Whose interests are harmed?" Other questions include the following:

- What "problem" does this text address? What is defined as the problem? How else could the problem have been defined?
- Who benefits from the way this problem is defined and analyzed? Who is hurt by the way this problem is defined and analyzed?
- How are key terms defined?
- What is treated as a root cause?
- Who is telling the story? Whose voices are heard in this text? Whose are left out?
- What relevant factors are not considered?
- What kind of evidence is used? What kind of evidence could have been used?
- What does the text do for us? What does it contribute to the scholarly conversation? What does it contribute to public discourse? What does the text contribute to our understanding of an issue?
- What difference would it make if the argument were accepted and acted on? What political actions would this text support?

EXERCISE *To see how scholars conduct reviews within particular disciplines, browse published scholarly book reviews in disciplinary journals such as the* Canadian Journal of Education *or the* International Journal of Communication. *To see how reviews are written for a general educated public, look at periodicals such as the* London Review of Books *or the* New York Review of Books.

Model Demonstration: A Critique of the Article "Language Crimes" by Dennis Dutton (Chapter 2)

In Chapter 2 (pages 30 to 38), we provide a detailed outline and drafts for a critique on the article "Language Crimes" in which the student follows the format suggested in this chapter: an introduction that launches the thesis, a summary of the article, an analysis of the argument, a response to the argument, and a conclusion that briefly states the case for the thesis.

Note that the student is careful to acknowledge the merits of the article even though her assessment of it is largely negative. (Similarly, it would be important to acknowledge the weaknesses of an argument one admires and ultimately defends.)

EXERCISE

1. Do a rhetorical analysis of the final draft of the critique of "Language Crimes" to identify the author's use of the range of criteria discussed in this chapter.

   a) What types of information does she provide in the introduction? Where does she first state her thesis?

   b) How long is her summary? Could it have been condensed further? Are any details included that seem irrelevant to her argument?

   c) Which paragraphs involve a close-up analysis of the text? What techniques does she employ?

   d) Which paragraphs involve a contextual response to the text? What disciplinary or real-world issues does she discuss?

   e) How does she conclude her critique—by summarizing her argument? By opening up to a larger issue? Or by some other method?

   f) Is the critique mainly positive or negative, or a mixture of both? Are there places where the author acknowledges opposing perspectives? Does she manage to maintain a strong thesis without oversimplifying or misrepresenting the text?

2. Working alone or with another student, write a 500-word critique of "Language Crimes" that strongly supports the argument made in that text. Begin by coming up with a tentative thesis, then brainstorm points to support it and put them into a concept map or outline.

3. Working alone or in a group, find one or two journals in a particular discipline that publish book reviews and conduct a functional analysis that identifies the typical structure and content of reviews.

THE RHETORICAL CRITIQUE

When you are asked to write a critique in writing and rhetoric classes, you are often encouraged to provide a "rhetorical critique" aimed at discussing the style and arrangement of the text. You are asked to address large issues about how the writer defines his or her purpose and audience, as well as to shed light on smaller decisions about how he or she organized the presentation of ideas and selected diction. In the readings section (Part 2) of this book, every reading is followed by several questions designed to help develop your thinking about the writer's craft. Doing this sort of analysis is a reminder that all writers make choices, and that the published version of a text is the result of many decisions and revisions.

Analyzing the presentation and style is challenging. Experts who analyze style usually agree that a writer's style is crucial to how readers understand a text, yet a writer's style is difficult to pinpoint. Describing the historical significance of style, Ben Yagoda reminds us while Aristotle recommended a rather modest style, "emphasizing clarity, transparency and decorum," he devoted one of his three *On Rhetoric* books to style and defended it as more than "a series of ornaments or tricks but instead as an essential part of argument, investigation and communication" (5).[1]

Your analysis of style and presentation needs to be linked to your assessment of the author's overall position and accomplishment. It is not enough to dissect word choice and sentence style; this analysis is valuable when used to explain the writer's attitudes and approach. Remember, the point of a rhetorical critique, in common with most others, is to get you to participate in a scholarly conversation; thus, comments about whether you liked the text, found it boring or exciting, difficult to understand or easy, and so forth, are generally beside the point and should not be included unless you are specifically invited to comment on the motivational power or entertainment value of the text.

THE LITERATURE REVIEW

In the term *literature review*, "literature" does not have the common meaning of "works of fiction," but instead refers to scholarly publications about the topic at hand.

The literature review describes key articles and books related to a particular line of research. A literature review can be a stand-alone assignment, or

---

[1] Yagoda, Ben. *The Sound on the Page: Great Writers Talk about Style and Voice in Writing.* New York: HarperCollins, 2005. Print.

it can appear as a section of a research essay in many disciplines, typically coming right after the introduction. It can range in length from a paragraph or two to 10 or 20 pages. Its purpose is to establish the current state of research on a topic as found in the "literature," in order to do one of two things:

- In the case of a literature review at the beginning of an essay, the review creates a "research space" for the writer—establishing that the paper is not something that has already been done in the literature, but that it does build on what *has* been done. This is a standard section of research articles in many disciplines.[2]
- In the case of a stand-alone literature review, the review identifies implications and directions for future research. This sort of essay is often published in scholarly journals.

A successful literature review involves both summary and descriptive analysis; that is, it efficiently represents the arguments made in relevant texts and draws connections between them. Although some literature reviews argue strongly for a particular view of the scholarship under review, most are only mildly interpretive, and generally only to the extent required to find connections.

The literature review typically begins with an overview of the literature that summarizes the main themes. Subsequent paragraphs move from text to text, identifying the most important elements of each. This discussion can be organized by text, where you describe one text then move on to the next, or by your own sense of the key issues to address on the topic, moving from one issue to the next, and referring to the texts as appropriate. Depending on the discipline, it would be appropriate to highlight theoretical frameworks, methodological approaches, limitations, findings, and conclusions. It is important to identify commonalities and differences among the texts, and especially to identify major disagreements. Be sure to include a "Works Cited" or "References" list at the end of your review.

Options for Structuring a Literature Review

By text	By topic
Introduction	Introduction
Text A	Topic A
Text B	Topic B
Text C, and so forth	Topic C, and so forth
Future research	Future research

---

[2] John Swales analyzed this strategy as a key feature of scholarly research articles in his book *Genre Analysis* (Cambridge University Press, 1990).

Model Demonstration: A Literature Review on Obedience

The literature review below in APA style is structured by topic. Note how the author works to draw a picture of the scholarship on his topic. He makes connections as he moves from text to text, generalizing where possible and pointing out significant differences. Note also how he opens by introducing the research area and closes by identifying what further research is needed.

LITERATURE REVIEW ON OBEDIENCE

1   As one of the very first and most basic concepts learned as a child, obedience is the cornerstone of proper social etiquette. People and animals are rewarded for correctly following instructions and carrying out requests given by authoritative figures. However, the question of how far an individual will go in order to comply with the demands of a commanding person has been controversial in the academic world. Many researchers believe that most people are obedient to the extent where they can become harmful to other beings and to society in general.

2   Indeed, research conducted by Zimbardo (2007) drew shocking results, illustrating how average individuals would go as far as verbally, physically, and mentally abusing others if instructed to do so by a dictatorial person. Thus, he concluded that most people accept too easily roles assigned to them, not only in experimental settings, but in everyday life as well. Similar studies administered by Milgram (1974) support Zimbardo's (2007) claim, seeing participants knowingly inflict pain on one another, as instructed by the experimenter.

3   Although the research was an enormous breakthrough, the reactions that accompanied these findings were not entirely met with positive appraisal. Many psychologists found faults in Milgram's (1974) experiment and criticized his work. Baumrind (1964) asserts that Milgram's work is not justifiable, as it cannot be applied to everyday life settings. Furthermore, as a volunteer, the participant presumes that he must follow the instructions given throughout the experiment. The subject also finds himself in unfamiliar grounds, causing anxiety, which could ultimately affect the results of the experiment as well as traumatize the subject.

4   Other variables, such as whether the person is alone or part of a group, can also influence the outcome of the research. The writing of Lessing (1987) emphasizes that as a group, people are no longer thinking for themselves; rather, they tend to adopt the views of the group to which they belong. She

states that the pressures accompanying group situations play an important role as to why ideas and beliefs usually remain concealed. An example of how this type of conformism can be dangerous is found in the short story *The Lottery* (Jackson, 1972). In this scenario, a community continues to follow an annual tradition that involves stoning a randomly selected village habitant to death.

5   Fromm (1981) published an essay that focuses on the pros and cons of overly obedient behaviour, such as the example listed in the above paragraph. His work, much like the literature viewed earlier, argues that being excessively obedient can ultimately lead to the downfall of humankind. This begs the question of how much obedience is too much? Evidently, further research will have to address this question and determine a safe perception on how to be obedient within the right boundaries.

References

Baumrind, D. (1964). Some thoughts on ethics of research: After reading Milgram's "Behavioral study of obedience." *American Psychologist, 19*, 420–3.

Fromm, E. (1981). *On disobedience and other essays.* New York: Seabury.

Jackson, S. (1972). *The lottery.* New York: Avon Books.

Lessing, D. (1987). *Prisons we choose to live inside.* New York: Harper & Row.

Milgram, S. (1974). *Obedience to authority: An experimental view.* New York: Harper & Row.

Zimbardo, P.G. (2007). *The Lucifer effect: Understanding how good people turn evil.* New York: Random House.

EXERCISE

1. Working alone or in a group, find one or two journals in a particular discipline that publish stand-alone literature reviews and examine them to determine whether they are mildly interpretive or strongly so. Notice how the reviews conclude.

2. Again, working alone or in a group, examine the articles published in one or two journals to see whether they typically include a literature review that ends by creating a research space.

3. Choose one of the theme chapters in Part 2 of this book and analyze the scholarly articles to see whether they typically include a literature review that ends by creating a research space.

4. Choose one of the theme chapters in Part 2 of this book and write a three-page literature review that draws on all the articles in the chapter and ends with ideas for further research.

CHAPTER 6

The Research Essay: Integrating Sources into an Argument

The previous chapters have laid the groundwork for this one, which addresses the single most common and important assignment in academic writing: the research essay. Research essays draw on all the work you have done on approaching texts actively and critically; on representing texts through summary, quotation, and paraphrase; on critiquing and reviewing texts; and on developing a thesis.

The research essay is a student version of the articles that professors write, and as such is the most important genre, along with the book, for the production of scholarly knowledge. It is through the research essay that scholars build on each other's work and contribute to the growth of knowledge. Scholars therefore take the research essay very seriously, and their expectations are correspondingly high.

RESEARCH ESSAYS AS ARGUMENTS

The research essay can be defined as an evidence-based argument that a topic should be seen in a certain way, where the evidence used is mainly scholarly work published in journals and books.

Often this kind of essay is referred to as an academic argument. The term "argument" is commonly associated with heated disagreements, and certainly there are some scholarly topics that arouse intense debate. Yet academic arguments are often not oppositional and are seldom heated in tone. The best can be understood as subtle and layered attempts to get the reader to see a topic in a certain way. Indeed, most instances of written communication can be understood as arguments, if we think of an argument as an attempt to capture the reader's attention in order to shape his or her views. Summaries argue that they accurately represent the original. Critiques argue that they fairly and insightfully understand the worth of the text under review. Non-verbal texts can be seen as arguments, too: tables and charts make claims about data collected in a survey. Broadly speaking, any text, verbal or graphic, can be seen as an argument, insofar as it attempts to produce a specific response in the audience: ads, songs, and paintings can all be understood as arguments.

To think of "argument" in its most traditional scholarly sense is to recognize its specialized meaning: an argument is a *thesis*—a claim that something is true—plus a series of *claims* designed to lead to the *conclusion* that the thesis is indeed true.

In its simplest version, the thesis can be developed through a very short argument, as in the following syllogism:

Adam is mortal. All men are mortal. Adam is a man. Therefore Adam is mortal.
   [thesis]   [claim 1]   [claim 2]   [conclusion]

Our example is brief, but nevertheless illustrative of several common features of arguments:

- **The thesis is debatable**. It is not until we know more about Adam that we can say with certainty that he is mortal.
- **The claims support the thesis**. Irrelevant claims about Adam's character or appearance are not made.
- **The claims logically relate to each other, but they could be rearranged.** Claims 1 and 2 could be reversed and the conclusion would still be justified. Essays are filled with logical connectors such as *because, moreover, consequently* to help express the connection between claims.
- **The claims can be supported.** Evidence and explanations could be offered that Adam has the anatomy of a man, for example.
- **The conclusion mirrors the thesis.** Many research essays simply repeat the thesis in their conclusions. Philosophical and mathematical arguments traditionally end with the abbreviation "QED" (*quod erat demonstratum*: "what was to have been proved") once the conclusion has been stated: *Therefore Adam is mortal. QED.*

Research essays are typically the longest form of academic argument because they involve demonstrating not only that a thesis is logical, but that it is supported by the work of scholars. Ideally, the thesis of a research essay should emerge from a good knowledge of what has been written on various aspects of the topic, and the essay should refer to that literature to provide evidence for all of its claims.

In summary, then, a research essay is an argument supported by logic and evidence. The process of producing a research essay always involves

- finding a focused topic
- finding and familiarizing yourself with relevant sources
- developing the "angle" into a thesis that makes sense of what you are learning about the topic
- drawing on those sources to develop the thesis

Sometimes, depending on the instructor and perhaps the expected length of the essay, you may be asked to develop a research proposal before starting to work on the essay itself. Other times, the instructor may provide a topic. We offer guidance on the more elaborate process in this chapter, beginning with the tasks of selecting a topic and finding sources to develop a proposal.

FINDING A TOPIC THAT IS SPECIFIC AND RESEARCHABLE

Sometimes you are provided with a list of possible topics and asked to make a selection. Sometimes you are asked to choose your own topic. You have chosen a good topic for a research essay if there are a number of scholarly sources addressing it, and if these sources are current and accessible. If the topic remains contested, then you will be adding to the debate rather than simply repeating what has already been said. Often, researchers end an article or book by commenting on the way the debate may continue unfolding in further or future publications. By doing some preliminary research, you can usually identify how to focus on a topic in a fruitful way. Rather than expecting to look at the broad topic of homelessness, for example, you may decide on the basis of research directions to take a more specific look at homelessness and women.

Generally, AVOID Topics That Are

1. **Too new or current**, so that there is little or no scholarly publication in the area. Writing about the incidence of harassment on Twitter or Facebook might reveal something interesting about communication in our culture, but you will struggle to find published scholarship to support or challenge your argument. If you were writing a personal narrative reflection on this topic, limited research sources would not be a problem. But if you are writing a research argument, citing relevant sources is part of the assignment criteria.

2. **Too far off the scholarly radar,** so that all publication is in "popular press" sources. Writing about a fashion trend may be interesting (and might even be a way to review some element of our culture), but be sure that your topic has been addressed in scholarly publications rather than only in popular magazines like *Flare* or *Cosmopolitan* or newsmagazines like *Macleans* and *Time*. Such sources (funded by advertising, brightened with colour photographs, and without source attributions) are considered "popular" rather than "scholarly" because they are written for a generalist audience and do not employ scholarly methods of knowledge production. The information they provide might suggest some interesting research topics, but it is not suitable for inclusion in a research essay (unless you are using the material as a primary source—that is, one that you are analyzing as a cultural phenomenon).

3. **Too hackneyed,** so that no one really wants to hear about the topic again. If you wrote about a topic in high school, it is not a good idea to tackle it again. You may have some sources on hand, but you likely need to enrich these for university-level writing. Neither does it make sense to try to recycle your thesis because you have grown intellectually even if one year has passed since you wrote the original argument.

4. **Too dull,** so that even as a writer you are not really interested in exploring the arguments or proposing ways to resolve them. If you are not really interested, imagine how your reader/marker will feel. Of course, it is difficult to become engaged in every assignment, particularly when you are responding to several at once. But if you pick "any old thing" just to "get it done," you have to expect a similar lacklustre response in your reader. For example, if you argue that "abortion is a woman's right," chances are you will find sources to support your view and even that your marker may be poised to accept your views, but it will be very difficult to be engaging when writing about a topic so frequently visited.

FINDING AN ANGLE AND DEVELOPING A THESIS

Once you have a workable topic in mind, your next job is to move from a simple statement of your topic to a more focused statement of thesis—to your argument about your topic. For example, in a sociology course, you might choose to discuss whether there is a need for participants to be part of the research story. To focus this topic, you might select a particular text to examine—say, a text like Susan Scott's *Our Sisters, Ourselves* (represented in Chapter 8, on homelessness, in the excerpt "A Sick System Creates Sick People.") Your next step would be to decide what you might argue about the role of the case studies that present the lives of homeless women as individuals. You might want to criticize the approach: "The stories about particular people may be interesting, but prove nothing." Or you might decide to support this form of research: "The stories give voice to silenced women and pay attention to the details of their lives rather than theorizing their situations or bundling them together as statistics." The angle you take is your main argument or thesis.

As the example demonstrates, after narrowing the topic so that you can manage it in an essay, you need to decide what claim you want to make about the focused topic. (For a thorough discussion of moving from topic to thesis, see Chapter 2.) At this early stage, you might think about your claim as a "working" thesis, for you will need to adjust it by looking at the research and seeing what others have already said about the topic. The process of looking at the research actually affects the way you define your topic and approach. You want to find what some researchers refer to as a "research space"—a topic that others may have discussed in scholarly books and articles, but that still remains open for further speculation.

CREATING A RESEARCH SPACE (CARS)

Students are often advised to "try to engage the reader" in introductions to their research essays by supplying background information and spicing it up with an anecdote or quotation.

What scholars actually do to engage the scholarly reader is promise to fix a problem in the field. Rhetorician John Swales found in his analysis of the introductions to hundreds of journal articles that academic writers typically begin by creating a "niche" for themselves in the scholarly literature, and that they do it through three moves that have become known as the "CARS" model: "Creating a Research Space." Scholars make these moves in order to find a logical place in the conversation when they write research proposals, abstracts, introductions to articles, and literature reviews. To see an introduction that uses this CARS model, turn to Tracy Whalen's essay in Chapter 13. Her opening paragraph cites a series of sources, preparing the ground for the thesis that emerges in her second paragraph.

> **Move 1—establish the field.** "Wow!" Show that the field is of central importance—characterize it from the general level to the specific. Review relevant research that has produced knowledge of the field.

> **Move 2—find a problem in the field.** "Oh no!" Find some form of knowledge gap—a phenomenon no one has studied, an unsatisfying approach to studying it, a question about it no one has asked, an aspect that deserves more attention, an application that no one has made.

> **Move 3—respond to the problem.** "Whew!" Explain the purpose of this article or purpose of this research, and set out a plan for fulfilling that purpose, and thus filling the gap. By summarizing and citing previous research, the writer manages to show both that the field is important and that the field is deficient in some way. This is quite different from the usual assumption that writers cite merely to acknowledge debts or to get authority for their claims. Note that this gap-finding effort is not a hostile act designed to discredit the field—writers are often careful to show that they are part of the community of scholars that produced the knowledge and will use phrases such as "*our* knowledge in this area."

Find the 1-2-3 moves in the following paragraph:

> Researchers have been interested in the problem of group obedience since the 1950s when they first started to use social science methods to explore the mechanisms of what Doris Lessing calls our "Group Minds" (210–13). Phillip Zimbardo concluded from his "Stanford Prison Experiment" that almost everyone will succumb to group mentality given the right situation (253–67). Solomon Asch showed that even in a trivial matter like giving one's honest assessment of which pair of lines are the same size, people will change their behaviour to fit in with a group (213–21). Stanley Milgram's shock-treatment experiment showed that the majority of people will obey authority even if it means going against their own conscience (221–34). All of these experiments suggest that people lack courage, but they also show that some people had the courage of their convictions and did not succumb to authority. However, they are all laboratory experiments and do not really tell us how people have behaved in real situations when they are pressured to harm others. In my research I examine historical accounts of the behaviour of people who did not obey Nazi authority and risked their own lives to save other people, such as the hero of the film *Schindler's List*. By doing this, I hope to uncover some of the qualities they had that might explain their heroic behaviour.

Student essays that are not expected to fix a problem unnoticed by experts can still use the CARS model very successfully.

If lots of research is required, review the field and propose to explore an interesting angle that deserves further study instead of filling a gap in the whole body of knowledge. For example, "Many psychologists point to the problem of obedience to unjust authority as the single most important question for the future of the human race . . . [now start to review the literature]. Yet they disagree on whether fear for their own safety or sheer lack of empathy is the root cause [explain who thinks what]. In this essay I focus on the 'fear factor' and argue that only fear could account for the extreme callousness displayed towards other people's suffering."

If some research is required, you can refer to the work of one or two researchers on your topic instead of 10 or 20, and propose to explore an interesting angle not pursued by them instead of filling a gap in the whole body of knowledge. For example, "Psychologist A argues that the cause of events such as the Dawson College shooting can be found in the mental illness of the shooter. Psychologist B argues that we should look to the shooter's exposure to violent media for our answers. However, in this paper I want to explore a third possibility: that a contributing factor is the heartlessness of competitive societies." Or the student writer can use the placeholder technique: refer to a plausible approach to the topic and then say why the one you have chosen to research is worth investigating. For example, "The cause behind events such as the shooting at Dawson College might be thought to originate in mental illness or media violence, but it is plausible that such outbursts of rage are at least partly founded in the dog-eat-dog nature of capitalism. In this essay I will offer evidence that competition leads to violence."

FINDING SOURCES

Most instructors insist that students use mainly "peer-reviewed"[1] scholarly books and journal articles as sources for research essays, with supplementary use of government documents such as Statistics Canada census tables. Popular press sources can stimulate your thinking and give you ideas to search for in the scholarly literature, but for the most part they are not appropriate for use in an academic essay.

Most journal articles are now available in electronic form, though a few publish only on paper, and libraries continue to subscribe to paper versions of a limited selection of the more widely used journals. Journal articles can be found online using databases such as Ebsco, JStor, and Proquest to which university libraries subscribe. These databases are searchable by keyword, author's name, title, and other features, and often provide the full text of articles. If databases contain non-peer-reviewed material, they usually provide an option to restrict the search results to "scholarly" or "peer-reviewed" only.

Increasingly, publishers are releasing electronic copies of books that may be available through your library website. Most books, however, are still available in paper form only and are found by searching your institution's library catalogue.

---

[1]See Chapter 5, page 96, for an explanation of this term.

If your library does not have the book, it is often possible to request an "inter-library loan" from another institution, but it can take a few weeks to arrive. Government documents are often available in both electronic and paper form and can be found by searching the appropriate website; for example, Statistics Canada, Transport Canada.

Primary and Secondary Sources

Primary sources are those that provide readers with direct access to the topic under investigation. Secondary sources are scholarly books and articles about the topic. Here are some examples of primary sources in different fields:

Biology—lab reports and field observations.

Literature—novels, poems, plays, and any other analyzed texts, such as graffiti.

History—documents written at the time that is under study; for example, letters, diaries, newspaper accounts.

Sociology—interviews, survey responses, ethnographic field notes.

Taking Research Notes

Most students who struggle with research essays have not taken notes carefully and end up writing an essay that is inadequately supported by research and poorly documented. Your essay should weave back and forth between your claims about the topic and references to the scholarly literature (mostly to support your claims but also to represent alternative perspectives that you then proceed to argue are inferior to your own).

Whether you take notes on paper or on computer, this system is workable:

1. Maintain a "working bibliography." When you start to look at a new source, take down all the bibliographic information you will need if you decide to use it in your essay. When you come to write your essay, you will just need to delete any sources you ended up not referencing.
2. Use symbols to differentiate between direct quotations(" "), paraphrases (~ ~), and your own ideas([ ]) so that you do not end up giving a source credit for your own thoughts or unintentionally plagiarizing someone's work.
3. Keep track of the author's last name and page number for every note. (If you are using more than one work by the author, develop a short form to distinguish between them—e.g., Clifford A, Clifford B, etc.—and note the short form in the working bibliography.)

Students frequently end up with a great many more notes than they can use. Try to be selective as you take notes, thinking of your tentative thesis and the sections of your outline, and looking for material that directly relates. If you are unable to do this, you may need to change your thesis or outline.

Incorporating Material from Other Sources

There are various purposes for bringing in outside sources:

- To show that other scholars agree with your points
- To supply information in support of your points
- To represent the range of scholarly perspectives on your topic
- To show that you can answer the scholars who disagree with you
- To situate your work in the scholarly conversation on your topic

First-year students tend to cite only for the first two reasons, which marks them as outsiders to the scholarly world. To strengthen your writing and proceed in your education, move toward writing as though you are a scholar and have the right to orchestrate a conversation with other scholars. Every research essay is an opportunity to do that.

Do not lean too much on any one source. Look at the sample essays in this book to see how writers draw on sources and move on. It is very rare to use a single source uninterruptedly for more than a paragraph. Doing that makes you appear to be dependent on that source and lacking ideas of your own.

Decide whether to feature a source prominently or keep it in the background. If you want a source to be prominent, bring it into the argument by quoting directly and naming the author, as Ilana Isaacs does in the sample essay on page 124 by quoting Lloyd Axworthy directly and naming him in her prose.

To use a source prominently, you could

- Name the scholar in your prose, not just in a citation.
- Perhaps describe the scholar or his or her work.
- Quote him or her directly.

To draw on a source without sharing too much "stage time" with it, keep it in the background:

- Name the scholar only in a citation, not in your prose.
- Use the source for information only, not for the views or argument it expresses.
- Paraphrase rather than quote (but still provide a citation). (This suppresses the source so much that if you are using endnotes, the reader has to turn to the notes at the end of the essay to discover the source.)

HANDLING OPPOSING PERSPECTIVES

Confronting Opposing Views

Arguments are strengthened, not weakened, by confronting opposing perspectives and showing that the thesis can stand up to them.

There are three ways of presenting opposition. Each strategy has advantages and disadvantages.

- Debate style
- Debate style with a named opponent
- Monologue style where the opposition is pre-empted

Debate style would look like this in an essay:

> Principals need "Search and Seizure" authority because gang members have been known to stash drugs and weapons in school lockers. It could be argued that there is no precedent for this authority, because criminals stash drugs and weapons elsewhere in the community, too, but only police officers are authorized to conduct searches and seize property, and they have to get a warrant. However, airport and train station managers already have complete authority to search for drugs and weapons without getting a warrant or involving the police, and there is no reason why school principals should not, too.

Debate style with a named opponent (and perhaps a quotation from the opponent) increases the focus on the opposition.

> Principals need "Search and Seizure" authority because gang members have been known to stash drugs and weapons in school lockers. Fran Zimbardo (2001) has argued that there is no precedent for this authority, because criminals stash drugs and weapons elsewhere in the community, too, but only police officers are authorized to conduct searches and seize property, and they have to get a warrant (p. 205). However, airport and train station managers already have complete authority to search for drugs and weapons without getting a warrant or involving the police, and there is no reason why school principals shouldn't, too.

Monologue style keeps the focus on your own perspective. The writer figures out what the opposition would say, and responds without giving them a chance to say it. In other words, a monologue style pre-empts the opposition by omitting the counterpoint, leaving a point/defence structure, as in the following paragraph:

> Principals need "Search and Seizure" authority because gang members have been known to stash drugs and weapons in school lockers. Airport and train station managers already have complete authority to search for drugs and weapons without getting a warrant or involving the police, and there is no reason why school principals shouldn't, too.

Refute, Minimize, Concede

As noted above, to make your argument as strong as possible, you must show that it stands up to opposing perspectives and opposing information. Yet your challenge is not only to represent opposing points fairly, but to maintain your own position as persuasively as possible.

Therefore, try the following strategies:

- **Refute** the opposing point.
- If you cannot refute it, **minimize** it.
- If you cannot minimize it, **concede the point** (life is complex) and move on.

To use the "search and seizure" example, an opposing point could be:

> Criminals stash drugs and weapons elsewhere in the community, too, but only police officers are authorized to conduct searches, and they have to get a warrant.

Here are some of the strategies for responding to it:

- **REFUTING—"No."** The opposing point is not true.

  There are already many exceptions to the police officer/warrant rule in the interests of public safety—at airports, train stations, power plants, etc.

- **MINIMIZING—"Yes, but."** The opposing point is true, but not very important.

  The legalistic question of a signed piece of paper pales in comparison to our profound ethical responsibility to keep children safe.

- **CONCEDING—"Yes."** The opposing point is true and important.

  We must never compromise civil liberties lightly. However, in this case the compromise must be made because there is no other way to fight gang activity.

Here is another example:

Point: *Bullies should be severely punished.*

Counterpoint: *Being punished only makes bullies bitter and leads to even worse bullying.*

Defence:

- **REFUTING**—The opposing point is not true.

  Even though it is often claimed that punishment only makes bullies behave worse, the overwhelming weight of scholarly evidence shows that bullies respond to firm discipline.

- **MINIMIZING**—The opposing point is true, but not very important.

  Even though punishment can make bullies worse, this outcome is rare, and the worsening is very slight.

- **CONCEDING**—The opposing point is not only true, but important.

  Even though punishment makes bullies worse, and it is important to avoid aggravating bad behaviour, it is even more important to send the whole school population a strong message that bullying will not be tolerated.

ASSIGNMENT SEQUENCE: MOVING FROM RESEARCH PROPOSAL TO RESEARCH ESSAY

Here is an example of a proposal assignment—setting out the topic and thesis and listing relevant sources—followed by a sentence-style outline and a research essay. In the proposal, the writer wants to provide enough information to convince the reader that the topic is important and can be addressed in a research essay.

Note: This assignment conforms to APA documentation format.

RUNNING HEAD: CANADIAN IDENTITY AND U.S. BORDER RELATIONS

Draft Proposal

Working title:
Research Proposal on the Interplay between Canadian Identity and U.S. Border Relations

Topic and research question:
As I was reading Lloyd Axworthy's article about the need for Canada to be more assertive in its conduct with the United States, I started to wonder if the undefined Canadian identity had anything to do with pressure for intercontinental integration. What effect does the apparent lack of national Canadian unity have on our government's national and international policy-making?

Rough version of working thesis:
About Canadian identity and relations with our neighbour to the south, I believe that the nation of Canada is segregated into various geographical groups (e.g., "West Coasters," "Newfies," "Quebecois," "Prairies," etc.), *except* concerning our relations with the United States, where almost the whole nation is unified in its desire to be considered "separate" and "autonomous" from the States.

Revised version of working thesis:
The nation of Canada is segregated into various geographical groups (e.g., "West Coasters," "Newfies," "Quebecois," "Prairie Folks," etc.) and we derive our sense of identity based on regionalism, *except* concerning our relations with the United States, where most of the nation is unified in its desire to be considered "separate" and "autonomous" from the States.

Description:
In my paper, I intend to examine how Canadians define their political, socio-cultural, and national identity, as well as the firmness and frailties of this identity. I will then examine what role this identity, or lack thereof, plays in Canada/U.S. relations. Many theorists assume that Canadian identity has nothing to do with border relations and policy-making, while other, more liberal political theorists argue that autonomous policy-making cannot exist without a more con-crete definition of national unity in our country. While I agree more with liberal nationalists than I do with conservative integrates, I will try to find a balance in which an autonomous and unified Canada can take a firm but diplomatic and friendly stance in response to American pressures.

In this paper I will argue that Canadian identity is less than concrete in most areas except those concerning the United States; that our identity is to be "anything other than American." I will then describe how this has affected, and should affect, our national policy-making, as well as where this theory has faltered in the past and why. I believe this is a very relevant topic in today's society, especially with a new and "changing" government in place in the United States; the next few years will prove to be crucial in how both Canada and the United States will decide to move forward or back in terms of economic priorities, trade, and international relations.

In my research, I will include works by several political theorists, including University of Winnipeg president Lloyd Axworthy. Axworthy's article, "How to Make Love to a Porcupine," is articulate and appropriate to my topic; in it, he discusses the danger of complete integration with the United States in policy-making, trade relations, and continental security issues. Another article I will include is "Out of Ideas?" by Brian Bow. Bow outlines several ways in which Canada has tried, and continues to try, to influence American policies to a Canadian advantage. He provides a rather dour synopsis of Canada's influence in America, but nevertheless presents a thorough examination of Canada/U.S. relations. One of my non-academic sources, *Canada Eh to Zed*, provides a satirical account of the search for Canadian identity, and grants insight into the difficulties of our vast nation's quest for unity. I wish to find more academic literature on Canadian identity, as well as investigate further the correlation between this identity and North American relations. I would like to research more case studies about the American influence on Canadian policy-making, as well as the extent to which our international trade relations have changed in the last fifty or so years as a direct result of American pressure.

Annotated Bibliography

Axworthy, L. (2007). How to make love to a porcupine. In L. Behrens, L. J. Rosen, J. McLeod Rogers, C. Taylor (Eds.), *Writing and reading across the disciplines* (pp. 452–459). Toronto: Pearson Custom Publishing.

In this article, Axworthy describes the tenuous relationship between Canada and the United States in policy-making and trade relations. He stresses the importance of Canadian autonomy and provides many examples from his own experience as Minister of Foreign Affairs in the Liberal government in the 1990s. In particular, he discusses the increasing pressure from the United States to increase continental security, and the threat that this initiative poses to Canadian multiculturalism.

I will use this article for the case studies that Axworthy provides, as well as the clear argument that he presents. He raises several points that directly apply to my topic, and his cursory reference to Canada's lack of unified identity was what started my thought process for this topic.

Bow, B. (2006). Out of ideas? Models and strategies for Canada–US relations. *International Journal, 62*(1), 123–142. Ebsco.

Brian Bow makes several good observations regarding Canada/U.S. relations, and the challenge presented to Canadians with regards to influencing American policy. He outlines three different techniques that have been used to attempt to influence American politics to follow a more pro-Canadian agenda, and the challenges and risks associated with each, as well as if any have succeeded or will succeed.

I will use this article as a reference for what Canada has done and will continue to do in the future with regard to policy-making in past and present. His description of the tenuous relationship between Parliament Hill and the White House is directly applicable to my topic.

Coupland, D. (2007). End: Zed. In L. Behrens, L.J. Rosen, J. McLeod Rogers, C. Taylor (Eds.), *Writing and reading across the disciplines* (pp. 491–493). Toronto: Pearson Custom Publishing.

This short piece is a very stirring, albeit casual one, in which Coupland calls to attention the fact that Canadians have an identity which is synonymous with the great and beautiful land we live on. While this article is not scholarly, it provides very real imagery that serves as a wake-up call to the reader. I will attempt to incorporate some of that imagery in my paper.

Gilbert, E. (2005). The inevitability of integration? Neoliberal discourse and the proposals for a new North American economic space after September 11. *Annals of the Association of American Geographers, 95*(1), 202–222. Ebsco.

In this article, Emily Gilbert discusses the seemingly "inevitable" march towards economic and political integration with the United States. She outlines all the arguments which conclude with this troubling thought, and then continues on to describe how many of them ignore the important fact that many Canadians fear and resent the idea of deepening integration.

This article is perhaps the one that most directly supports my claim, but in a roundabout way. Although she discusses the link between Canadian attitudes and transnational policy-making, I will place her hypotheses in a different context to see if they still apply.

Huston, M. J. (1973). *Canada eh to zed: A further contribution to the continuing quest for the elusive Canadian identity*. Edmonton: Hurtig Publishers.

Huston provides the most interesting of the resources that I have found. His book is a humorous account of two men's search for Canadian identity, and through his humour Huston acknowledges the great difficulty of pinning down this definition. There are many quotes in the book that are so accurate as to make me feel uncomfortable. I intend to use some of this realistic material in my paper, even though this is not a scholarly book.

Meyer, K. E. (2003). Macho America, diffident Canada. *World Policy Journal, 20*(2), 103–106. Ebsco.

> Meyer's article is written from an entirely different perspective: that of an American regarding Canada with respect and a touch of condescension. He claims that America underestimates Canada with respect to international relations, quality of life, and general good governance, and misses the forest of Canada's good nature for the trees of political disagreement (such as Canada's refusal to participate in the Iraq War).

> I liked this article and will use Meyer's congenial discourse to highlight the aspects of Canadian identity that are often ignored by Canadians and other nations alike.

Sentence-style Outline

Thesis: Canadian identity is derived from our relations with the United States, where most of the nation is unified in its desire to be considered "separate" and "autonomous" from the United States.

I. Multiculturalism and regionalism have made it difficult to have a unified sense of what it means to be "Canadian."
   a. We need common ground or experiences (Howard-Hassmann quotation).

II. We are seen by others mainly as a good neighbour to the United States, but we have a strong international reputation.
   a. Quote Axworthy on this.
   b. Pearson and peacekeeping
   c. The United States still sees us as a quiet-mouse ally.
      i. We often support their political positions (Meyer).
      ii. Supporting them does not serve our interests.

IV. We should not aspire to a U.S.-style declaration of national accomplishments and identity.
   a. Canadians try hard to avoid being seen as Americans.
      i. Backpackers, etc.
      ii. Gilbert

V. Conforming to the United States can undermine our own identity.
   a. U.S. border restrictions on immigrants are in conflict with our multiculturalism policy.
   b. We should be a good neighbour but not at cost of our own principles.
   c. We need to retain our international stature.

The Interplay of Canadian Identity and U.S. Border Relations

Ilana Isaacs

Academic Writing: Social Sciences

Professor McLeod Rogers

April 28, 2009

The Interplay of Canadian Identity and U.S. Border Relations

As demonstrated in the introductory quotation in which two speakers circle around rather than define what it means to be Canadian, the quest for Canadian identity is tricky. Many countries view Canada as nearly synonymous with the United States, and many countries consider Quebec to be one step away from dividing Canada in half. Indeed, our identity seems to be faltering in terms of maintaining an autonomous image, particularly in our dealings with the U.S. However, I would argue that it is precisely the issues of cross-border relations and continental policy-making which are uniting Canadians in a desperate attempt to be regarded as an individual and completely independent and proud nation. I would argue that there is nothing that irks most Canadians more than to be considered the same as Americans, and that this sense of national pride will be what ultimately preserves the Canadian image at home and internationally.

Within Canada, the search for a national and unified identity has been a troubling one. In a way, Canada's significant land mass and ethnic diversity have both played huge roles in the challenge of defining what is "Canadian" (Howard-Hassmann, 2006, p. 222). There are many different people groups within Canada which contribute to our multicultural identity, but the question remains whether minority groups in Canada have helped or hindered the formation of a national identity. The problem lies not only with the minority groups, however. Canadians are also split into various groups based on their geographical location: the West Coast, the East Coast, Newfoundland, Quebec, and the Prairies are all examples of regions within Canada whose people can never identify fully with others simply because of the vast expanse between them. So what is necessary for a common and complete identity? Howard-Hassmann (2006) states that

> . . . [n]ational unity requires a Canadian community with a common, shared understanding of identity in all citizens. Such a community is based on common experiences in Canada and a common set of fundamental principles. Citizenship in Canada, as in any other country, must have more meaning than merely legal rights; it must imply shared ways of living, shared values, and loyalty to the country. (p. 222)

Therefore, a solution for Canadians is to identify that unique feature which sets Canadians apart from the rest of the world and highlights those shared values and fundamental principles.

In contrast, former Foreign Affairs Minister Lloyd Axworthy contends that the international community identifies Canada as the nation which is "next door to a very large, powerful neighbour" (2007, p. 452). However, over the last fifty years, Canada has made a very powerful impression on the global community through its peacekeeping efforts and international policies; indeed, Lester B. Pearson, Prime Minister of Canada from 1963–1968, received the Nobel Peace Prize for fathering the U.N. peacekeeping initiative after the Suez Crisis (Meyer, 2003, p. 104). Canada's international résumé is very important and should be considered a large part of its identity both at home and abroad; to do so would be to acknowledge Canada as an independent and prominent member of the world order.

The United States has a valuable neighbour and ally in the form of Canada. Canada supplies 25 percent of U.S. foreign trade, and about 87 percent of Canada's exports are to the U.S. (Gilbert, 2005, p. 203). In addition, since the September 11, 2001, terrorist attacks, Canada has provided substantial support in the U.S. effort in

Afghanistan, at no small cost to the Canadian people (Meyer, 2003, p. 103). Nonetheless, the American opinion of Canada seems to be one of slight condescension: Canada needs, as one American writer put it, "more recognition of its own virtues, more readiness to blow its own trumpet, a little less becoming diffidence, a bit more vulgar swagger" (Meyer, 2003, p. 105). Americans are known worldwide for their outspoken national pride; perhaps this is what Canada needs to firmly earn its southern neighbour's respect.

I would argue that this American-style, smug national identity is exactly the one which Canadians are desperate to avoid. Canadian backpackers sew flags on their luggage to avoid being mistaken for American travellers. Canadians pride themselves on their truly "multi-cultural" image and long to avoid a "melting pot" society— the preservation of individual cultures within Canada is emphasized in the *Canadian Charter of Rights and Freedoms* (Howard-Hassmann, 2006, pp. 217–18). To be identified as similar or analogous to Americans is a frightening prospect to most Canadians, both politically and socially. As Gilbert (2005) so aptly puts it, "the Canadian public appears to be apprehensive about deepening integration" (2005, p. 216). Although it is vital to maintain a healthy and respectful relationship with the U.S., it is vital to maintain a border between the two countries in political values, cultural preservation, foreign policy, and transnational policy-making. Axworthy (2007) has much to say on the subject of cross-border integration, claiming that "there is a delicate and difficult balance to be struck in our relations with the U.S. Tactical and temporary concessions may tip the balance in such a way that we permanently lose precious elements of our independence" (p. 456).

Pressure from Washington post-9/11 has increased to deepen security measures and restrict access to immigrants. This could "[undermine] distinctive elements of our multicultural society" (Axworthy, 2007, p. 458) if the Canadian public does not insist on more transparency in governmental decision-making; if the facts are laid clearly before the public and outline the ramifications of individual policies, Canadians would be much more likely to stand

CANADIAN IDENTITY AND U.S. BORDER RELATIONS 5

up for what they believe is a Canadian course of action. Elected officials may swing closer to or further away from U.S. policies (whether economic, foreign, domestic, or socio-cultural), but Canadians have the right to defend those decisions which they believe reflect their country and their country's values, and to reject those decisions which do not fit in the *Canadian* identity.

It is time for Canada to stand up for itself. While it is a nation which depends heavily on its southern neighbour economically, there is no reason why Canadians should surrender their own fragile international image in order to conform to U.S. principles and policies. The Canadian people know that they are different from Americans. Now they must use that difference to solidify how they define themselves and their country, and how they want themselves to be viewed on the international stage—as an independent and proud nation.

References

Axworthy, L. (2007). How to make love to a porcupine. In L. Behrens, L. J. Rosen, J. McLeod Rogers, C. Taylor (Eds.), *Writing and reading across the disciplines* (pp. 452–459). Toronto: Pearson Custom Publishing.

Gilbert, E. (2005). The inevitability of integration? Neoliberal discourse and the proposals for a new North American economic space after September 11. *Annals of the Association of American Geographers, 95*(1), 202–222. Ebsco.

Howard-Hassmann, R. E. (2006). "Canadian" as an ethnic category: Implications for multiculturalism and national unity. In S.P. Hier and B.S. Bolaria (Eds.), *Identity and belonging: Rethinking race and ethnicity in Canadian society* (pp. 217–232). Toronto: Canadian Scholars' Press, Inc.

Huston, M. J. (1973). *Canada eh to zed: A further contribution to the continuing quest for the elusive Canadian identity*. Edmonton: Hurtig Publishers.

Meyer, K. E. (2003). Macho America, diffident Canada. *World Policy Journal, 20*(2), 103-106. Ebsco.

MLA PAGES

Following are several key elements of the same paper recast using MLA format: the first page (MLA style does not require a title page) and some of the second (to show the required format for the first page as well as how in-text citations look in MLA style), and the final documentation of sources in a Works Cited list.

Ilana Isaacs

Academic Writing: Social Sciences

Professor McLeod Rogers

March 28, 2009

The Interplay of Canadian Identity and U.S. Border Relations

"As an opening gambit, let me pose the question, what is a Canadian?"

"A Canadian is like anybody else—only better."

"Why is he better?"

"Because he is a Canadian."

"That seems to have gone in a circle to bring us back to where we started."

"Good," said Mr. Zeppelin. "Then we haven't lost any ground." (Huston, 1973, p. 15)

As demonstrated in the introductory quotation in which two speakers circle around rather than define what it means to be Canadian, the quest for Canadian identity is tricky. Many countries view Canada as nearly synonymous with the United States, and many countries consider Quebec to be one step away from dividing Canada in half. Indeed, our identity seems to be faltering in terms of maintaining an autonomous image, particularly in our dealings with the U.S. However, I would argue that it is precisely the issues of cross-border relations and continental policy-making which are uniting Canadians in a desperate attempt to be regarded as an individual and completely independent and proud nation. I would argue that there is nothing that irks most Canadians more than to be considered the same as Americans, and that this sense of national pride will be what ultimately preserves the Canadian image at home and internationally.

Isaacs 2

Within Canada, the search for a national and unified identity has been a troubling one. In a way, Canada's significant land mass and ethnic diversity have both played huge roles in the challenge of defining what is "Canadian" (Howard-Hassmann 222). There are many different people groups within Canada which contribute to our multicultural identity, but the question remains whether minority groups in Canada have helped or hindered the formation of a national identity. The problem lies not only with the minority groups, however. Canadians are also split into various groups based on their geographical location: the West Coast, the East Coast, Newfoundland, Quebecs, and the Prairies are all examples of regions within Canada whose people can never identify fully with others simply because of the vast expanse between them. So what is necessary for a common and complete identity? Howard-Hassmann states that

> . . . [n]ational unity requires a Canadian community with a common, shared understanding of identity in all citizens. Such a community is based on common experiences in Canada and a common set of fundamental principles. Citizenship in Canada, as in any other country, must have more meaning than merely legal rights, it must imply shared ways of living, shared values, and loyalty to the country. (222)

Therefore, a solution for Canadians is to identify that unique feature which sets Canadians apart from the rest of the world and highlights those shared values and fundamental principles.

In contrast, former Canadian Foreign Affairs Minister Lloyd Axworthy has argued that the international community identifies Canada as the nation which is "next door to a very large, powerful neighbour" (452). However, over the last fifty years, Canada has made a very powerful impression on the global community through its peace-keeping efforts and international policies; indeed, Lester B. Pearson, Prime Minister of Canada from 1963–1968, received the Nobel Peace Prize for fathering the U.N. peacekeeping initiative after the Suez Crisis (Meyer 104). Canada's international résumé is very important and should be considered a large part of its identity both

Isaacs 3

at home and abroad; to do so would be to acknowledge Canada as an independent and prominent member of the world order.

Works Cited

Axworthy, Lloyd. "How to Make Love to a Porcupine." *Writing and Reading Across the Disciplines.* Ed. Laurence Behrens, Leonard. J. Rosen, Jaqueline McLeod Rogers, Catherine Taylor, Toronto: Pearson, 2007. 452–59. Print.

Gilbert, Emily. "The Inevitability of Integration? Neoliberal Discourse and the Proposals for a New North American Economic Space after September 11." *Annals of the Association of American Geographers,* 95.1 (2005): 202–222. Web. 9 March 2009.

Howard-Hassmann, Rhoda E. (2006). "'Canadian' as an Ethnic Category: Implications for Multiculturalism and National Unity." *Identity and Belonging: Rethinking Race and Ethnicity in Canadian Society.* Ed. Sean P. Hier and B.S. Bolaria. Toronto: Canadian Scholars' Press, 2006. 217–232. Print.

Huston, Mervyn J. *Canada Eh to Zed: A Further Contribution to the Continuing Quest for the Elusive Canadian Identity.* Edmonton: Hurtig Publishers, 1973. Print.

Meyer, Karl E. (2003). "Macho America, Diffident Canada." *World Policy Journal,* 20.2 (2003): 103–106. Web. 11 March 2009.

MAJOR RESEARCH PROJECT

The rest of this chapter provides detailed guidelines for working through a major research project. It takes you through the process of choosing a research topic, developing a formal proposal to do research in the area, developing a working bibliography of potential sources for use in that research, and finally writing a research essay that fulfills the proposal and makes use of at least six of the sources from your annotated bibliography. We also provide feedback sheets that can be used at key points in this project sequence, to help you work on revising your own work, and also to guide you in providing feedback to other students.

Your instructor may ask you to choose one of the research topics suggested at the end of the theme chapters in this book, or may ask you to think of your own topic within certain parameters, such as "history of Canada" or "environmental dangers." You may be required to use only articles in this book, or find your own sources, or use a combination of both.

If you are given completely free choice, try to find a topic that connects to an issue you are genuinely interested in or know something about. Although research essays rely on scholarly sources rather than personal experience, a personal connection to the topic can be a rich source of motivation and insight as you go through the various stages of research, planning, and finally writing the essay.

Whatever your topic, though, the following guidelines will prompt you to construct an argument rather than just a description of how something works.

RESEARCH PROPOSAL WITH ANNOTATED BIBLIOGRAPHY

Final version due _____

Weight _____%

Assignment description

The research proposal and bibliography can be thought of together as the planning stage of producing a research essay. Once you have finished this assignment, your last assignment in the course will be to write the essay itself.

The proposal assignment consists of two main parts: the proposal itself and an annotated working bibliography, which is a descriptive list of sources you have found on your topic.

Part One: Research Proposal

Your proposal should follow this format:

1. Working title. Don't be vague—a working title should zero in on your particular topic rather than wave toward a major subsection of the library. Use the heading "Research Proposal on X," where X is a fairly specific version of your topic; for example, "The Psychological Roots of Racist Bullying," not simply "Bullying."

2. Your research question—the answer to which will become the thesis of your research essay.

3. Short description (250 words) of your topic, including an introduction in which you create a research space by describing the general field you are examining and the particular issue or problem you are interested in.

4. Overall description of sources in your annotated bibliography and other sources of information you hope to find, such as scholarly presses, interviews, stats on your topic, first-hand experiences of it, historical background on it, and so forth.

Part Two: Annotated Working Bibliography

This assignment is designed to ensure that you find the resources you need to build a persuasive argument for your research essay. It also ensures that you develop the skills needed to find sources for your work in other courses. If you do this exercise well, you can feel very confident that your research skills are on par with those of successful senior students.

A working bibliography, in contrast to a Works Cited or References list, is a work in progress. It itemizes all sources that you consult in the course of doing research, including those that you decide, in the end, not to use in the essay itself. When it comes time to prepare the Works Cited list for your essay, you will be able to assemble it by copying the sources you actually used from the working bibliography and leaving the rest behind. Your annotated working bibliography should be in alphabetical order. It should look like an ordinary MLA, APA, or Chicago references list, but with an annotation following each item in the list.

One of the ways in which the working bibliography differs significantly from the Works Cited list is that, in the working bibliography, you need to annotate each source with a few sentences that indicate what the document covers, how relevant it is to your essay topic, and how strong it is as a scholarly source. Each annotation is an occasion to make strategic decisions about how to develop and support your argument. Here's a sample annotated entry for an essay on the mentality of terrorists:

Schnerd, Mortimer. "Osama bin Laden's Secret Ambition." *National Scandal Rag.* 24 Oct. 1995: 67–68. Print.

> Schnerd claims that bin Laden is a psychopath who is motivated more by a desire for personal power than by any kind of commitment to Islam. He quotes a Harvard psychologist who supports this theory. The theory is intriguing and directly relates to my topic, but the source is clearly inappropriate for an academic essay, and a lot has changed since it was published in 1995. I will look for stronger sources that follow this line of thinking, starting with articles by the professor named in the article.

Individual instructors will stipulate how many items you need to include in your bibliography. For example, you might be asked for ten items, at least eight of which should be scholarly journal articles and/or scholarly books. Your final two sources may include one or more of the following:

- news articles from web sources or newspapers
- documents from advocacy websites (or pamphlets from advocacy organizations)
- government documents
- films and documentaries
- articles from popular-press magazines
- articles from an encyclopaedia such as *Encarta* or the *Encyclopaedia Britannica*.
- interviews that you have conducted

RESEARCH ESSAY

Final version due _____

Weight _____%

The most important features of any research essay are (a) a strong, carefully constructed argument to illuminate its thesis, and (b) frequent references to research sources to incorporate the scholarly conversation on the topic and secure the claims made. This is the most common type of essay because it taps into the great strength of the academic method: by integrating outside sources, one voice acquires the power of many.

The challenge is to integrate or "synthesize" those external sources into your argument without letting them drown you out. Your voice should be just as strongly in control in a research essay as in a personal essay that uses no sources, or a critique that focuses on only one source. While you will be expected to refer to at least six sources from your annotated bibliography, the essay itself remains most importantly yours: a multi-level structure of claims and support in which you carefully develop or "unpack" your own view of the topic: your thesis.

Finding a Thesis Ask yourself, "what question do I most want to answer about my topic?" The answer you develop (by doing research and considering your findings) becomes the thesis for your essay. For example, if your research question is "Do we really need to worry about anti-hate groups gaining ground, or are they just a lunatic fringe?" your thesis might be "Although most of them stay at the level of a lunatic fringe, hate groups can become extremely dangerous and influential in times of social crisis, and we must therefore prosecute them diligently."

References Required Use the best sources from your working bibliography. Journal articles and book chapters are especially valuable. Try to find material that challenges your thesis as well as material that supports it: your argument will be stronger and more complex if, instead of presenting a one-sided view, you show the reader how it stands up to alternative interpretations.

Format The essay should begin with a title page followed by a one-paragraph abstract (summary) of the essay itself, and end with a Works Cited or References list in MLA, APA, or CMS (Chicago) style that includes all sources used in the essay. All usages of your sources must be cited, whether those usages are information only or summaries, quotations, and paraphrases of material from sources.

RESEARCH ESSAY DEVELOPMENT FORMS

The following forms offer heuristics aimed at getting peer readers to respond to your draft at different stages of development.

Form 1: Feedback on the Research Proposal

Form 2: Feedback on Sentence-style Outline

Form 3: Feedback on CARS-style Introduction—Creating a Research Space

Form 4: Feedback on the Argument

Form 5: Feedback to Troubleshoot the Draft of the Research Essay

Form 6: Copy Editing the Research Essay

While you may not have an opportunity to hear from others at each of these stages, you will find that comments from your peers help you to identify where your arguments are strong and where they may need further development or revision.

FORM I

Feedback on the Research Proposal

Name of writer: _____

Name of reader providing feedback: _____

 Writers, get at least two readers for your work. Get them to mark up your proposal if you like, and to write any comments on this sheet. Readers, please consider such issues as the following. Ask the writer about anything you don't understand.

Proposal

1. Is the working title precise, so that you know exactly what the research is about? Or is it so broad that you can't identify the particular focus of the research?

  _____

  _____

2. Is the research question clear? What will the writer be trying to find out?

  _____

  _____

3. Is the topic description concise—approximately 250 words? Does it help you understand why the writer thinks the topic is significant enough and complex enough to justify a research effort? Does it provide relevant background information? Summarize the topic description in the lines below.

  _____

  _____

  _____

  _____

4. Does the topic description clearly create a research space by (1) establishing an important field, (2) finding a gap or something worthy of attention in that field, and (3) explaining how the essay will fill that gap or devote that attention? Write a brief version of the CARS steps used in the topic description:

  a. _____

  b. _____

  c. _____

5. Why does this topic matter? (How would the author answer "So what?")

  _____

  _____

  _____

6. Does the plan for finding more sources of information seem reasonable? Can you think of additional sources, such as interviews, that would be helpful to the research effort?

  _____

  _____

  _____

Bibliography

1. Are there __ (required number and type) sources in the bibliography?

   _____

2. Are some sources from scholarly journal articles or scholarly books?

   _____

3. Does each annotation address all three required aspects—content, relevance, and scholarly strength?

   _____

   _____

   _____

4. What style is the bibliography in—MLA, APA, CMS, or CBE? Does it follow that style correctly? If not, what are the problems? (For example, are there problems with capitalization, italics, volume/issue format, etc.?)

   _____

   _____

Style

1. Is the proposal always clear? If not, help with the wording if you can.

   _____

   _____

   _____

2. Is it concise? (If not, point out wordy or repetitive patches.)

   _____

   _____

3. Does anything detract from the author's ethos (for example, slang, profanity, sensationalism, overly casual treatment of important subject)? Could the author do more to establish ethos (for example, argue in defence of an admirable cause)? Does the proposal appeal to pathos in any way? How?

   _____

   _____

4. Are quotations and paraphrases mechanically correct and properly cited in MLA, APA, or Chicago note style? If not, correct them.

   _____

   _____

5. Are there any usage issues (grammar, punctuation, or spelling) you can help with? What are they?

   _____

   _____

FORM 2

Feedback on Sentence-style Outline

This form can be used to test the structural soundness of the argument that is displayed in the outline prior to writing the essay.

1. Is there a thesis statement? Is it in claim form? (That is, the form is not "this essay will discuss X" but "X is . . .") Is it logical? Is it crystal clear?

_____

_____

2. Does each section have a main claim?

_____

_____

3. Does the outline develop the thesis adequately? If the writer proves the argument (the series of section claims) made in the outline, will the thesis have been proven?

_____

_____

4. If not, what needs to be changed: the thesis, or the section claims, or both?

_____

_____

5. Look at the thesis again. Does it forecast the direction the argument takes? Could it be revised to forecast the argument more fully?

_____

_____

6. Now look at the order of sections. Are they in the best possible order to develop the argument in a smooth, logical order with the fewest leaps from topic to topic? (For example, if X is talked about in sections 2 and 4, could section 4 be switched to section 3 in order to get a smoother transition?)

_____

_____

7. Now look at each section. Do the points under each section adequately develop the section claim? Do they fit properly under that claim? Are there too many, or too few?

_____

_____

_____

_____

FORM 3

Feedback on CARS-style Introduction—Creating a Research Space

For this project your essay introduction should be in CARS style. Use this form to itemize the moves by which you have created a research space.

1. Read the CARS-style introduction, asking yourself these questions:

   ■ What is the author's field?

   ■ What is the gap in that field (or important issue that the author will focus on)?

   ■ How will the author fill that gap or focus on that issue?

2. Put the numbers 1, 2, and 3 in the introduction where each move begins.

3. If you cannot clearly identify these three moves, explain why not below.

   _____

   _____

   _____

   _____

4. Does the introduction match the outline? Is the outline a plan for filling the knowledge gap?

   _____

   _____

   _____

   _____

FORM 4

Feedback on the Argument

Research essay writers can become mired in details. Asking readers for feedback can help writers to refresh their sense of what they are doing and get back on track.

Writer's name:_____

Your name:_____

Writers, teach your readers the argument you are making in your essay by walking them through your essay.

Readers, ask for clarifications and take notes as you listen. Make sure you know the author's thesis and pick up the main stages of thought through which the thesis is developed. If the writer's argument is clear, logical, and effective, you should be able to identify it easily. Put the argument to the test by seeing whether you can summarize it in point form below: First, identify the thesis of the whole argument and then list the main points of each stage of thought by which that thesis is developed.

Thesis statement: _____
_____

Main point (in sentence form) of each stage of thought (list in order—probably four to eight points):_____

_____

_____

_____

_____

_____

_____

_____

_____

_____

Comments on the clarity, logicality, and effectiveness of the argument:

_____

_____

_____

_____

_____

_____

_____

_____

_____

_____

FORM 5

Feedback to Troubleshoot the Draft of the Research Essay

Essays are not only wholes but parts. This heuristic focuses in on many of the details.

Writers, get at least one reader for your work. Get him or her to mark up your essay if you like, and to write any comments on this sheet. In addition, complete this form for your own essay. Staple both sheets to the back of your research essay when you hand it in.

Readers, please consider the issues below. Ask the writer about anything you don't understand.

Components of the knowledge apparatus

1. Is the title precise and accurate? Does it indicate both the topic and the author's perspective? If it is not already in title/subtitle form, could it be recast in that form?

   _____

2. Is there an abstract? Does it accurately summarize the thesis, stages of argument by which the thesis is developed, and conclusions?

   _____

3. Is there a citation for every quotation, paraphrase, and piece of information drawn from an outside source?

   _____

4. If the writer has used MLA or APA, is there a complete reference list containing at least six sources? Has the writer used mainly scholarly sources (i.e., scholarly books and journals)?

   _____

Introduction to the argument

1. Is the thesis clearly stated in the introduction? What is it? Does the writer agree that that is his or her thesis?

   _____

2. Does the introduction establish a research space using the CARS technique? Does the introduction accurately forecast how the argument develops in the essay?

   _____

Conclusion

Does the conclusion either recap the argument made in the essay or, better yet, more briefly recap the argument and make connections with the world beyond the essay? This could happen through recommendations, connection to current events, etc.

   _____

Logic

1. Look at topic sentences (the ones that begin a new paragraph). Does each topic sentence accurately state the main point of the paragraph it begins?

   _____

2. Does one point follow logically from another throughout the essay?

3. Is every claim backed up by evidence from sources or by logical explanation?

4. Look for opportunities to provide transition words or phrases ("similarly," "in contrast," "however," "therefore," etc.) between sentences and between paragraphs.

Opposition

1. Are important terms defined that might otherwise be interpreted differently by readers, making them unnecessarily skeptical of the argument?

2. Has the likeliest opposition to the argument been identified? Have those points been refuted or minimized, or has the damage caused by conceding to them at least been limited?

3. Are claims protected where necessary by appropriate hedging ("perhaps, X . . .," "it seems that . . .," "it is possible that X . . .") and limiting ("sometimes," "often")?

Use of sources

1. Are there enough quotations, paraphrases, and information to anchor claims in the scholarly literature on the topic?

2. Does the essay lean too much on a single source, making the essay seem at its service instead of the other way around? If so, look for ways of interspersing other sources that make the same points or other relevant points.

Style

1. Is "I" used appropriately, if at all? (That is, to describe the structure of the argument or to distinguish the writer's claims from the sources' claims, *not* as a "just my opinion" move.)

2. Is the essay always clear? If not, help with the wording if you can.

3. Is it concise? If not, point out wordy or repetitive patches.

4. Does anything detract from the author's ethos (for example, slang, profanity, prejudice, religious testimony, and casualness) or appeal to pathos (sensationalism, emotion in the absence of logic)?

FORM 6

Copy Editing the Research Essay

Finally, this heuristic lists the minor details of form and expression that should be checked before the essay is submitted.

Writers, get at least two readers for your work.

Readers, please consider the issues below. Ask the writer about anything you don't understand.

Components of the knowledge apparatus

1. Is the title page correctly formatted with the required information?

_____

2. Is there a single-spaced abstract in summary style?

_____

3. Are all quotations and paraphrases mechanically correct in terms of placement of quotation marks and punctuation? Are ellipses and square brackets used correctly?

_____

4. Is there a citation for every quotation, paraphrase, and piece of information drawn from an outside source?

_____

5. Is each citation or note in correct MLA, APA, or Chicago note style?

_____

6. If the writer has used MLA or APA, is there a complete reference list? Has the writer used mainly scholarly sources (that is, scholarly books and journals)?

_____

Style

1. Is the essay always clear? If not, help with the wording if you can.

_____

2. Is it concise? If not, point out wordy or repetitive patches.

_____

3. Does anything detract from the author's ethos (for example, slang, profanity, prejudice, religious testimony, casualness) or appeal to pathos (sensationalism, emotion in the absence of logic)?

_____

4. Are there any usage issues (diction, grammar, punctuation, or spelling) you can help with? What are they?

_____

CHAPTER 7

THE STRUGGLE FOR VOICE IN ACADEMIC WRITING

We are language users. Along with learning to walk in our early years, we learn to talk, then to read and write. As we grow, we like to think we gain control over the words we use. One of the reasons for enrolling in a composition course is to learn and practise practical strategies and techniques for making scholarly writing more vigorous and effective. It may surprise you to learn that much debate surrounds questions on how to teach students to improve their writing. Should we encourage students to write about what they know and expect them to learn through a process of feedback and practice? Or should we encourage them to think about academic writing as a distinctive form of discourse whose conventions need to be learned?

A number of pedagogical questions about teaching writing have arisen over the last few decades not only because writing instruction has been on the rise but also because the complex connections between language and thinking have been the subject of contemporary theorizing. While most scholars used to link clear thinking and writing and define good writing as a stable commodity across situations, influential structuralist theories changed mid-twentieth-century thinking. Rather than presuming that words represented things—that there was an essential link between word and thing—structuralist language philosophers (such as Ferdinand de Saussure) pointed out that words might be thought of as signs we associate with particular things. Post-structuralists (such as Jacques Derrida) pointed out that such meanings as we arrive at are interpretive and provisional. Rather than being understood as secure and stable, language and meaning became associated with struggle and change.

The writer and professor Denis Dutton presents a reassuring and common-sense view of language when he argues that we should all improve the clarity of our writing to make the job of readers easier. Yet understood against contemporary theories that help us define our postmodern world, identity, and language as constructed and continuously changing, his views seem a bit outdated and judgmental. It is true he writes clearly in this rather clipped journalistic piece, yet the question you might want to ask is whether his view of language is really rather conservative and ungenerous. He has no patience with students and scholars who do not express tidy thoughts in plain packages.

For her part, Judith Butler, a highly regarded feminist scholar and critical theorist to whom Dutton has awarded a bad writing "prize," has little patience with Dutton's finger wagging. She points out that clarity *is* linked to simplicity, and that while she can be clear in discussing mundane matters, she has no intention of attempting clarity when matters are complex and provisional and meant to provoke reflection and interpretation.

It is this sort of thinking that informs Donald Bartholomae's argument in "Inventing the University." If students want to learn new things, they need to leave behind the ways and means of common sense and folk wisdom, and attempt to learn how academics reason and talk—they need to become familiar with disciplinary *discourse*. He says that professors are wrong to encourage students to write with clarity and finality about matters that most of them accurately identify as still beyond their grasp. They need to mimic in order eventually to appropriate the elements of academic style.

Jaqueline McLeod Rogers and Eva Hoffman write narratives exploring problems with writing and language from the perspective of personal experience. Notice how both refer to outside sources and other writers in a way that conveys they are engaged in active reflection, rather than recording something whose meaning took shape in the past. McLeod Rogers speaks from a relatively privileged position as a language-user—working in her own language and pursuing academic studies—yet she struggles with the blank page as many students and writers do. Hoffman examines, even attempts to define, some of the obstacles of learning an entirely new and foreign discourse, weaving in subtle references to structuralist and psychoanalytic theory.

Activate

1. As a post-secondary student, you have by now been asked to read material that is very difficult to understand. Have you ever thought, "This could have been written much more simply"? Do you think you were right?

2. How easy has it been for you to adapt to the way language is used in your new educational setting? Do you ever find it impossible to contribute to class discussions because it feels like they are being conducted in a foreign language?

3. Do you have any experience of writer's block? What has caused it, do you think, and what have you done to get over it?

Language Crimes: A Lesson in How Not to Write, Courtesy of the Professoriate

Denis Dutton

(from the *Wall Street Journal*, February 5, 1999)

Denis Dutton is an American scholar (currently teaching in New Zealand) who ran the Bad Writing Contest from 1995 to 1998, years when he served as editor of the scholarly journal Philosophy and Literature. *In this brief news article (first published in 1999 in the New York* Times) *he alerts the public to his concerns about the sorry state of scholarly writing. He describes running a contest to pick out examples of particularly bad writing, hoping to embarrass acclaimed writers who he suggests rely on obscurity to cloak thoughtlessness.*

1   Pick up an academic book, and there is no reason to expect the writing to be graceful or elegant. Many factors attract people to the scholarly life, but an appealing prose style was never a requirement for the job.

2   Having spent the past 23 years editing a scholarly journal, *Philosophy and Literature*, I have come to know many lucid and lively academic writers. But for

every superb stylist there are a hundred whose writing is no better than adequate —or just plain awful.

3   While everyone moans (rightly) about the decline in student literacy, not enough attention has been given to deplorable writing among the professoriate. Things came to a head, for me, a few years ago when I opened a new book aptly called *The End of Education: Toward Posthumanism.* It began:

> "This book was instigated by the Harvard Core Curriculum Report in 1978 and was intended to respond to what I took to be an ominous educational reform initiative that, without naming it, would delegitimate the decisive, if spontaneous, disclosure of the complicity of liberal American institutions of higher learning with the state's brutal conduct of the war in Vietnam and the consequent call for opening the university to meet the demands by hitherto marginalized constituencies of American society for enfranchisement."

4   This was written by a professor of English. He's supposed to teach students how to write.

5   Fed up, I resolved to find out just how low the state of academic writing had sunk. I could use the Internet to solicit the most egregious examples of awkward, jargon-clogged academic prose from all over the English-speaking world. And so the annual Bad Writing Contest was born.

6   The rules were simple: Entries should be a sentence or two from an actual published scholarly book or journal article. No translations into English allowed, and the entries had to be nonironic: We could hardly admit parodies in a field where unintentional self-parody was so rampant.

7   Each year for four years now the contest has attracted around 70 entries. My co-editors at *Philosophy and Literature* and I are the judges, and the winner is announced in the journal.

8   No one denies the need for a specialized vocabulary in biochemistry or physics or in technical areas of the humanities like linguistics. But among literature professors who do what they now call "theory"—mostly inept philosophy applied to literature and culture—jargon has become the emperor's clothing of choice.

9   Thus in *A Defense of Poetry*, English Prof. Paul Fry writes: "It is the moment of non-construction, disclosing the absentation of actuality from the concept in part through its invitation to emphasize, in reading, the helplessness—rather than the will to power—of its fall into conceptuality." If readers are baffled by a phrase like "disclosing the absentation of actuality," they will imagine it's due to their own ignorance. Much of what passes for theory in English departments depends on this kind of natural humility on the part of readers. The writing is intended to look as though Mr. Fry is a physicist struggling to make clear the Copenhagen interpretation of Quantum Mechanics. Of course, he's just an English professor showing off.

10   The vatic tone and phony technicality can also serve to elevate a trivial subject. Many English departments these days find it hard to fill classes where students are assigned Milton or Melville, and they are transforming themselves into departments of so-called cultural studies, where the students are offered the analysis of movies, television programs, and popular music. Thus, in a

laughably convoluted book on the Nancy Kerrigan/Tonya Harding affair, we read in a typical sentence that "this melodrama parsed the transgressive hybridity of un-narratived representative bodies back into recognizable heterovisual modes."

11   The pretentiousness of the worst academic writing betrays it as a kind of intellectual kitsch, analogous to bad art that declares itself "profound" or "moving" not by displaying its own intrinsic value but by borrowing these values from elsewhere. Just as a cigar box is elevated by a Rembrandt painting, or a living room is dignified by sets of finely bound but unread books, so these kitsch theorists mimic the effects of rigor and profundity without actually doing serious intellectual work. Their jargon-laden prose always suggests but never delivers genuine insight. Here is this year's winning sentence, by Berkeley Prof. Judith Butler, from an article in the journal *Diacritics*:

> "The move from a structuralist account in which capital is understood to structure social relations in relatively homologous ways to a view of hegemony in which power relations are subject to repetition, convergence, and rearticulation brought the question of temporality into the thinking of structure, and marked a shift from a form of Althusserian theory that takes structural totalities as theoretical objects to one in which the insights into the contingent possibility of structure inaugurate a renewed conception of hegemony as bound up with the contingent sites and strategies of the rearticulation of power."

12   To ask what this means is to miss the point. This sentence beats readers into submission and instructs them that they are in the presence of a great and deep mind. Actual communication has nothing to do with it.

13   As a lifelong student of Kant, I know that philosophy is not always well-written. But when Kant or Aristotle or Wittgenstein are most obscure, it's because they are honestly grappling with the most complex and difficult problems the human mind can encounter. How different from the desperate incantations of the Bad Writing Contest winners, who hope to persuade their readers not by argument but by obscurity that they too are the great minds of the age.

Active Reading

1. What is a "language crime" according to Dutton, both by definition and example?

2. According to Dutton, which disciplines actually require difficult and specialized language? Which likely do not?

Critical Reading

1. Is "crime" a freighted (heavily charged) word for one academic to use against another? Is it fair to showcase single sentences as unclear, or should Dutton provide more context?

2. What are some of the ways Dutton attempts to build "ethos" by locating himself as an expert worthy of the project of judging the merits of the scholarly productions of others? Does he describe the project more as community service or as personal witch hunt/hobby horse?

3. Dutton says that a professor of English is "supposed to teach students how to write." Ask your composition professor to describe his or her job, and compare the two descriptions.

The Values of Difficulty

Judith Butler

Judith Butler is an American post-structuralist philosopher, who teaches at University of California, Berkeley. She has published many books and made influential contributions in areas such as feminism, queer theory, and ethics. This piece appeared in 1999 in the New York Times *as her response to Dutton.*

1   In the last few years, a small, culturally conservative academic journal has gained public attention by showcasing difficult sentences written by intellectuals in the academy. The journal, *Philosophy and Literature*, has offered itself as the arbiter of good prose and accused some of us of bad writing by awarding us "prizes." (I'm still waiting for my check!)

2   The targets, however, have been restricted to scholars on the left whose work focuses on topics like sexuality, race, nationalism and the workings of capitalism—a point the news media ignored. Still, the whole exercise hints at a serious question about the relation of language and politics: why are some of the most trenchant social criticisms often expressed through difficult and demanding language?

3   No doubt, scholars in the humanities should be able to clarify how their work informs and illuminates everyday life. Equally, however, such scholars are obliged to question common sense, interrogate its tacit presumptions and provoke new ways of looking at a familiar world.

4   Many quite nefarious ideologies pass for common sense. For decades of American history, it was "common sense" in some quarters for white people to own slaves and for women not to vote. Common sense, moreover, is not always "common"—the idea that lesbians and gay men should be protected against discrimination and violence strikes some people as common-sensical, but for others it threatens the foundations of ordinary life.

5   If common sense sometimes preserves the social status quo, and that status quo sometimes treats unjust social hierarchies as natural, it makes good sense on such occasions to find ways of challenging common sense. Language that takes up this challenge can help point the way to a more socially just world. The contemporary tradition of critical theory in the academy, derived in part from the Frankfurt School of German anti-fascist philosophers and social critics, has shown how language plays an important role in shaping and altering our common or "natural" understanding of social and political realities.

6   The philosopher Theodor W. Adorno, who maintained that nothing radical could come of common sense, wrote sentences that made his readers pause and reflect on the power of language to shape the world. A sentence of his such as "Man is the ideology of dehumanization" is hardly transparent in its meaning.

Adorno maintained that the way the word "man" was used by some of his contemporaries was dehumanizing.

7   Taken out of context, the sentence may seem vainly paradoxical. But it becomes clear when we recognize that in Adorno's time the word "man" was used by humanists to regard the individual in isolation from his or her social context. For Adorno, to be deprived of one's social context was precisely to suffer dehumanization. Thus, "man" is the ideology of dehumanization.

8   Herbert Marcuse once described the way philosophers who champion common sense scold those who propagate a more radical perspective: "The intellectual is called on the carpet . . . . Don't you conceal something? You talk a language which is suspect. You don't talk like the rest of us, like the man in the street, but rather like a foreigner who does not belong here. We have to cut you down to size, expose your tricks, purge you."

9   The accused then responds that "if what he says could be said in terms of ordinary language he would probably have done so in the first place." Understanding what the critical intellectual has to say, Marcuse goes on, "presupposes the collapse and invalidation of precisely that universe of discourse and behavior into which you want to translate it."

10   Of course, translations are sometimes crucial, especially when scholars teach. A student for whom a word such as "hegemony" appears strange might find that it denotes a dominance so entrenched that we take it for granted, and even appear to consent to it—a power that's strengthened by its invisibility.

11   One may have doubts that "hegemony" is needed to describe how power haunts the common-sense world, or one may believe that students have nothing to learn from European social theory in the present academy. But then we are no longer debating the question of good and bad writing, or of whether "hegemony" is an unlovely word. Rather, we have an intellectual disagreement about what kind of world we want to live in, and what intellectual resources we must preserve as we make our way toward the politically new.

Active Reading

1.   How does Butler define "common sense?"

2.   Butler quotes a dense sentence by Theodor Adorno and then helps us see how it can be interpreted or translated. What is she saying about the need for critical thinkers to use uncommon language?

Critical Reading

1.   What is the purpose of Butler's first two paragraphs? Is there a hint of anger in her tone? If so, is it appropriately expressed?

2.   Why do you think Butler never refers to Dutton by name? Why does she not work with the particular sentence from her own work that Dutton called into question?

3.   Is Butler's piece long enough to address Dutton's criticism? Is she convincing, or did she need to amplify her response?

4.   How might you apply critical questions such as "Who benefits from this text?" to analyze both Butler's and Dutton's position on the plain language issue?

Inventing the University

David Bartholomae

David Bartholomae is a professor of English at the University of Pittsburgh who has published widely in the field of composition, rhetoric, and pedagogy. Published in 1985, this influential essay argued that "basic writers"—writers entering university—do not benefit from practising general writing and thinking skills, but need to learn the conventions of academic writing so that they feel authorized to enter disciplinary debates. In this essay Bartholomae explains his view that student writers need to be discouraged from trying to be original thinkers and encouraged instead to begin the process of using the conventions of disciplinary discourse.

I.

1   Every time a student sits down to write for us, he has to invent the university for the occasion—invent the university, that is, or a branch of it, like history or anthropology or economics or English. The student has to learn to speak our language, to speak as we do, to try on the peculiar ways of knowing, selecting, evaluating, reporting, concluding, and arguing that define the discourse of our community. Or perhaps I should say the *various* discourses of our community, since it is in the nature of a liberal arts education that a student, after the first year or two, must learn to try on a variety of voices and interpretive schemes—to write, for example, as a literary critic one day and as an experimental psychologist the next; to work within fields where the rules governing the presentation of examples or the development of an argument are both distinct and, even to a professional, mysterious.

2   The student has to appropriate (or be appropriated by) a specialized discourse; and he has to do this as though he were easily and comfortably one with his audience, as though he were a member of the academy or an historian or an anthropologist or an economist; he has to invent the university by assembling and mimicking its language while finding some compromise between idiosyncrasy, a personal history, on the one hand, and the requirements of convention, the history of a discipline, on the other. He must learn to speak our language. Or he must dare to speak it or to carry off the bluff, since speaking and writing will most certainly be required long before the skill is "learned." And this, understandably, causes problems.

3   Let me look quickly at an example. Here is an essay written by a college freshman.

> In the past time I thought that an incident was creative was when I had to make a clay model of the earth, but not of the classical or your everyday model of the earth which consists of the two cores, the mantle and the crust. I thought of these things in a dimension of which it would be unique, but easy to comprehend. Of course, your materials to work with were basic and limited at the same time, but thought help to put this limit into a right attitude or frame of mind to work with the clay.

In the beginning of the clay model, I had to research and learn the different dimensions of the earth (in magnitude, quantity, state of matter, etc.) After this, I learned how to put this into the clay and come up with something different than any other person in my class at the time. In my opinion, color coordination and shape was the key to my creativity of the clay model of the earth.

Creativity is the venture of the mind at work with the mechanics relay to the limbs from the cranium, which stores and triggers this action. It can be a burst of energy released at a precise time a thought is being transmitted. This can cause a frenzy of the human body, but it depends on the characteristics of the individual and how they can relay the message clearly enough through mechanics of the body to us as an observer. Then we must determine if it is creative or a learned process varied by the individuals thought process. Creativity is indeed a tool which has to exist, or our world will not succeed into the future and progress like it should.

4   I am continually impressed by the patience and goodwill of our students. This student was writing a placement essay during freshman orientation. (The problem set to him was: "Describe a time when you did something you felt to be creative. Then, on the basis of the incident you have described, go on to draw some general conclusions about 'creativity.'") He knew that university faculty would be reading and evaluating his essay, and so he wrote for them.

5   In some ways it is a remarkable performance. He is trying on the discourse even though he doesn't have the knowledge that would make the discourse more than a routine, a set of conventional rituals and gestures. And he is doing this, I think, even though he *knows* he doesn't have the knowledge that would make the discourse more than a routine. He defines himself as a researcher working systematically, and not as a kid in a high school class: "I thought of these things in a dimension of . . ."; "I had to research and learn the different dimensions of the earth (in magnitude, quantity, state of matter, etc.)." He moves quickly into a specialized language (his approximation of our jargon) and draws both a general, textbook-like conclusion—"Creativity is the venture of the mind at work . . ."— and a resounding peroration—"Creativity is indeed a tool which has to exist, or our world will not succeed into the future and progress like it should." The writer has even picked up the rhythm of our prose with that last "indeed" and with the qualifications and the parenthetical expressions of the opening paragraphs. And through it all he speaks with an impressive air of authority.

6   There is an elaborate but, I will argue, a necessary and enabling fiction at work here as the student dramatizes his experience in a "setting"—the setting required by the discourse—where he can speak to us as a companion, a fellow researcher. As I read the essay, there is only one moment when the fiction is broken, when we are addressed differently. The student says, "Of course, your materials to work with were basic and limited at the same time, but thought help to put this limit into a right attitude or frame of mind to work with the clay." At this point, I think, we become students and he the teacher giving us a lesson (as in, "You take your pencil in your right hand and put your paper in front of you"). This is, however, one of the most characteristic slips of basic writers. (I use the term "basic writers" to refer to university students traditionally placed in remedial composition courses.) It is very hard for them to take on the role—the voice, the persona—of an authority whose authority is rooted in scholarship,

analysis, or research. They slip, then, into a more immediately available and realizable voice of authority, the voice of a teacher giving a lesson or the voice of a parent lecturing at the dinner table. They offer advice or homilies rather than "academic" conclusions. There is a similar break in the final paragraph, where the conclusion that pushes for a definition ("Creativity is the venture of the mind at work with the mechanics relay to the limbs from the cranium") is replaced by a conclusion that speaks in the voice of an elder ("Creativity is indeed a tool which has to exist, or our world will not succeed into the future and progress like it should").

7   It is not uncommon, then, to find such breaks in the concluding sections of essays written by basic writers. Here is the concluding section of an essay written by a student about his work as a mechanic. He had been asked to generalize about work after reviewing an on-the-job experience or incident that "stuck in his mind" as somehow significant.

> How could two repairmen miss a leak? Lack of pride? No incentive? Lazy? I don't know.

At this point the writer is in a perfect position to speculate, to move from the problem to an analysis of the problem. Here is how the paragraph continues, however (and notice the change in pronoun reference).

> From this point on, I take *my* time, do it right, and don't let customers get under *your* skin; If they have a complaint, tell them to call your boss and he'll be more than glad to handle it. Most important, worry about yourself, and keep a clear eye on everyone, for there's always someone trying to take advantage of you, anytime and anyplace. (Emphasis added)

We get neither a technical discussion nor an "academic" discussion but a Lesson on Life.[1] This is the language he uses to address the general question, "How could two repairmen miss a leak?" The other brand of conclusion, the more academic one, would have required him to speak of his experience in our terms; it would, that is, have required a special vocabulary, a special system of presentation, and an interpretive scheme (or a set of commonplaces) he could have used to identify and talk about the mystery of human error. The writer certainly had access to the range of acceptable commonplaces for such an explanation: "lack of pride," "no incentive," "lazy." Each commonplace would dictate its own set of phrases, examples, and conclusions; and we, his teachers, would know how to write out each argument, just as we know how to write out more specialized arguments of our own. A "commonplace," then, is a culturally or institutionally authorized concept or statement that carries with it its own necessary elaboration. We all use commonplaces to orient ourselves in the world; they provide points of reference and a set of "prearticulated" explanations that are readily available to organize and interpret experience. The phrase "lack of pride" carries with it its own account of the repairman's error, just as at another point in time a reference to "original sin" would have provided an explanation, or just as in certain university classrooms a reference to "alienation" would enable writers to continue and complete the discussion. While there is a way in which these terms are interchangeable, they are not all permissible: A student in a composition class would most likely be turned away from a discussion of original sin. Commonplaces are the "controlling ideas" of our composition textbooks, textbooks that not only insist on a set form for expository writing but a set view of public life.[2]

8   When the writer says, "I don't know," then, he is not saying that he has nothing to say. He is saying that he is not in a position to carry on this discussion. And so we are addressed as apprentices rather than as teachers or scholars. In order to speak as a person of status or privilege, the writer can either speak to us in our terms—in the privileged language of university discourse—or, in default (or in defiance) of that, he can speak to us as though we were children, offering us the wisdom of experience.

9   I think it is possible to say that the language of the "Clay Model" paper has come *through* the writer and not from the writer. The writer has located himself (more precisely, he has located the self that is represented by the "I" on the page) in a context that is finally beyond him, not his own and not available, to his immediate procedures for inventing and arranging text. I would not, that is, call this essay an example of "writer-based" prose. I would not say that it is egocentric or that it represents the "interior monologue or a writer thinking and talking to himself" (Flower, 1981, p. 63). It is, rather, the record of a writer who has lost himself in the discourse of his readers. There is a context beyond the intended reader that is not the world but a way of talking about the world, a way of talking that determines the use of examples, the possible conclusions, acceptable commonplaces, and key words for an essay on the construction of a clay model of the earth. This writer has entered the discourse without successfully approximating it.

10   Linda Flower (1981) has argued that the difficulty inexperienced writers have with writing can be understood as a difficulty in negotiating the transition between "writer-based" and "reader-based" prose. Expert writers, in other words, can better imagine how a reader will respond to a text and can transform or restructure what they have to say around a goal shared with a reader. Teaching students to revise for readers, then, will better prepare them to write initially with a reader in mind. The success of this pedagogy depends on the degree to which a writer can imagine and conform to a reader's goals. The difficulty of this act of imagination, and the burden of such conformity are so much at the heart of the problem that a teacher must pause and take stock before offering revision as a solution. A student like the one who wrote the "Clay Model" paper is not so much trapped in a private language as he is shut out from one of the privileged languages of public life, a language he is aware of but cannot control.

II.

[. . .]

11   . . . I think that all writers, in order to write, must imagine for themselves the privilege of being "insiders"—that is, the privilege both of being inside an established and powerful discourse and of being granted a special right to speak. But I think that right to speak is seldom conferred on us—on any of us, teachers or students—by virtue of that fact that we have invented or discovered an original idea. Leading students to believe that they are responsible for something new or

original, unless they understand what those words mean with regard to writing, is a dangerous and counterproductive practice. We do have the right to expect students to be active and engaged, but that is a matter of continually and stylistically working against the inevitable presence of conventional language; it is not a matter of inventing a language that is new.

[. . .]

12   . . . It should be clear by now that when I think of "knowledge" I think of it as situated in the discourse that constitutes "knowledge" in a particular discourse community, rather than as situated in mental "knowledge sites." One can remember a discourse, just as one can remember an essay or the movement of a professor's lecture; but this discourse, in effect, also has a memory of its own, its own rich network of structures and connections beyond the deliberate control of any individual imagination.

13   There is, to be sure, an important distinction to be made between learning history, say, and learning to write as an historian. A student can learn to command and reproduce a set of names, dates, places, and canonical interpretations (to "tell" somebody else's knowledge); but this is not the same thing as learning to "think" (by learning to write) as an historian. The former requires efforts of memory; the latter requires a student to compose a text out of the texts that represent the primary materials of history and in accordance with the texts that define history as an act of report and interpretation.

14   Let me draw on an example from my own teaching. I don't expect my students to *be* literary critics when they write about *Bleak House*. If a literary critic is a person who wins publication in a professional journal (or if he or she is one who could), the students aren't critics. I do, however, expect my students to be, themselves, invented as literary critics by approximating the language of a literary critic writing about *Bleak House*. My students, then, don't invent the language of literary criticism (they don't, that is, act on their own) but they are, themselves, invented by it. Their papers don't begin with a moment of insight; a "by God" moment that is outside of language. They begin with a moment of appropriation, a moment when they can offer up a sentence that is not theirs as though it were their own. (I can remember when, as a graduate student, I would begin papers by sitting down to write literally in the voice—with the syntax and the key words—of the strongest teacher I had met.)

15   What I am saying about my students' essays is that they are approximate, not that they are wrong or invalid. They are evidence of a discourse that lies between what I might call the students' primary discourse (what the students might write about *Bleak House* were they not in my class or in any class, and were they not imagining that they were in my class or in any class—if you can imagine any student doing any such thing) and standard, official literary criticism (which is imaginable but impossible to find). The students' essays are evidence of a discourse that lies between these two hypothetical poles. The writing is limited as much by a student's ability to imagine "what might be said" as it is by cognitive control strategies.[3] The act of writing takes the student away from where he is and what he knows and allows him to imagine something else. The approximate discourse, therefore, is evidence of a change, a change that, because we are teachers, we call "development." What our beginning students need to learn is

to extend themselves, by successive approximations, into the commonplaces, set phrases, rituals and gestures, habits of mind, tricks of persuasion, obligatory conclusions and necessary connections that determine the "what might be said" and constitute knowledge within the various branches of our academic community.[4]

16   Pat Bizzell is, I think, one of the most important scholars writing now on "basic writers" (and this is the common name we use for students who are refused unrestrained access to the academic community) and on the special characteristics of academic discourse. In a recent essay, "Cognition, Convention, and Certainty: What We Need to Know about Writing" (1982a), she looks at two schools of composition research and the way they represent the problems that writing poses for writers.[5] For one group, the "inner-directed theorists," the problems are internal, cognitive, rooted in the way the mind represents knowledge to itself. These researchers are concerned with discovering the "universal, fundamental structures of thought and language" and with developing pedagogies to teach or facilitate both basic, general cognitive skills and specific cognitive strategies, or heuristics, directed to serve more specialized needs. Of the second group, the "outer-directed theorists," she says that they are "more interested in the social processes whereby language-learning and thinking capacities are shaped and used in particular communities."

> The staple activity of outer-directed writing instruction will be analysis of the conventions of particular discourse communities. For example, a main focus of writing-across-the-curriculum programs is to demystify the conventions of the academic discourse community. (1982a, p. 218)

The essay offers a detailed analysis of the way the two theoretical camps can best serve the general enterprise of composition research and composition teaching. Its agenda, however, seems to be to counter the influence of the cognitivists and to provide bibliography and encouragement to those interested in the social dimension of language learning.

17   As far as basic writers are concerned, Bizzell argues that the cognitivists' failure to acknowledge the primary, shaping role of convention in the act of composing makes them "particularly insensitive to the problems of poor writers." She argues that some of those problems, like the problems of establishing and monitoring overall goals for a piece of writing, can be

> better understood in terms of their unfamiliarity with the academic discourse community, combined, perhaps, with such limited experience outside their native discourse communities that they are unaware that there is such a thing as a discourse community with conventions to be mastered. What is underdeveloped is their knowledge both of the ways experience is constituted and interpreted in the academic discourse community and of the fact that all discourse communities constitute and interpret experience. (1982a, p. 230)

One response to the problem of basic writers, then, would be to determine just what the community's conventions are, so that those conventions could be written out, "demystified" and taught in our classrooms. Teachers, as a result, could be more precise and helpful when they ask students to "think," "argue," "describe," or "define." Another response would be to examine the essays written by basic writers—their approximations of academic discourse—to determine more clearly where the problems lie. If we look at their writing, and if we look at it in the context of other student writing, we can better see the points of discord that arise when students try to write their way into the university.

III.

[. . .]

18   . . . In general, as I reviewed the essays for this study, I found that the more successful writers set themselves in their essays against what they defined as some more naive way of talking about their subject—against "those who think that . . ."—or against earlier, more naive versions of themselves—"once I thought that . . ." By trading in one set of commonplaces at the expense of another, they could win themselves status as members of what is taken to be some more privileged group. The ability to imagine privilege enabled writing. Here is one particularly successful essay. Notice the specialized vocabulary, but notice also the way in which the text continually refers to its own language and to the language of others.

> Throughout my life, I have been interested and intrigued by music. My mother has often told me of the times, before I went to school, when I would "conduct" the orchestra on her records. I continued to listen to music and eventually started to play the guitar and the clarinet. Finally, at about the age of twelve, I started to sit down and to try to write songs. Even though my instrumental skills were far from my own high standards, I would spend much of my spare time during the day with a guitar around my neck, trying to produce a piece of music.
>
> Each of these sessions, as I remember them, had a rather set format. I would sit in my bedroom, strumming different combinations of the five or six chords I could play, until I heard a series of which sounded particularly good to me. After this, I set the music to a suitable rhythm (usually dependent on my mood at the time), and ran through the tune until I could play it fairly easily. Only after this section was complete did I go on to writing lyrics, which generally followed along the lines of the current popular songs on the radio.
>
> At the time of the writing, I felt that my songs were, in themselves, an original creation of my own; that is, I, alone, made them. However, I now see that, in this sense of the word, I was not creative. The songs themselves seem to be an oversimplified form of the music I listened to at the time.
>
> In a more fitting sense, however, I *was* being creative. Since I did not purposely copy my favorite songs, I was, effectively, originating my songs from my own "process of creativity." To achieve my goal, I needed what a composer would call "inspiration" for my piece. In this case the inspiration was the current hit on the radio. Perhaps, with my present point of view, I feel that I used too much "inspiration" in my songs, but, at that time, I did not.
>
> Creativity, therefore, is a process which, in my case, involved a certain series of "small creations" if you like. As well, it is something, the appreciation of which varies with one's point of view, that point of view being set by the person's experience, tastes, and his own personal view of creativity. The less experienced tend to allow for less originality, while the more experienced demand real originality to classify something a "creation." Either way, a term as abstract as this is perfectly correct, and open to interpretation.

This writer is consistently and dramatically conscious of herself forming something to say out of what has been said *and* out of what she has been saying in the act of writing this paper. "Creativity" begins in this paper as "original creation." What she thought was "creativity," however, she now says was imitation; and, as she says, "in this sense of the word" she was not "creative." In another sense, however, she says that she *was* creative, since she didn't purposefully copy the songs but used them as "inspiration."

19   While the elaborate stylistic display—the pauses, qualifications, and the use of quotation marks—is in part a performance for our benefit, at a more obvious level we as readers are directly addressed in the first sentence of the last paragraph: "Creativity, therefore, is a process which, in my case, involved a certain series of 'small creations' if you like." We are addressed here as adults who can share her perspective on what she has said and who can be expected to understand her terms. If she gets into trouble after this sentence, and I think she does, it is because she doesn't have the courage to generalize from her assertion. Since she has rhetorically separated herself from her younger "self," and since she argues that she has gotten smarter, she assumes that there is some develop-mental sequence at work here and that, in the world of adults (which must be more complete than the world of children) there must be something like "real creativity." If her world is imperfect (if she can only talk about creation by putting the word in quotation marks), it must be because she is young. When she looks beyond herself to us, she cannot see our work as an extension of her project. She cannot assume that we too will be concerned with the problem of creativity and originality. At least she is not willing to challenge us on those grounds, to generalize her argument, and to argue that even for adults creations are really only "small creations." The sense of privilege that has allowed her to expose her own language cannot be extended to expose ours.

IV.

[. . .]

20   Problems of convention are both problems of finish and problems of substance. The most substantial academic tasks for students, learning history or sociology or literary criticism, are matters of many courses; much reading and writing, and several years of education. Our students, however, must have a place to begin. They cannot sit through lectures and read textbooks and, as a consequence, write as sociologists or write literary criticism. There must be steps along the way. Some of these steps will be marked by drafts and revisions. Some will be marked by courses, and in an ideal curriculum the preliminary courses would be writing courses, whether housed in an English department or not. For some students, students we call "basic writers," these courses will be in a sense the most basic introduction to the language and methods of academic writing.

[. . .]

21   Shaughnessy (1977) speaks of the advanced writer as one who often has a more facile but still incomplete possession of this prior discourse. In the case of the advanced writer, the evidence of a problem is the presence of dissonant, redundant, or imprecise language, as in a sentence such as this: "No education

can be *total*, it must be *continuous*." Such a student, Shaughnessy says, could be said to hear the "melody of formal English" while still unable to make precise or exact distinctions. And, she says,

> the pre-packaging feature of language, the possibility of taking over phrases and whole sentences without much thought about them, threatens the writer now as before. The writer, as we have said, inherits the language out of which he must fabricate his own messages. He is therefore in a constant tangle with the language, obliged to recognize its public, communal nature and yet driven to invent out of this language his own statements. (1977, pp. 207–208)

For the unskilled writer, the problem is different in degree and not in kind. The inexperienced writer is left with a more fragmentary record of the comings and goings of academic discourse. Or, as I said above, he or she often has the key words without the complete statements within which they are already operating.

22   Let me provide one final example of this kind of syntactic difficulty in another piece of student writing. The writer of this paper seems to be able to sustain a discussion only by continually repeating his first step, producing a litany of strong, general, authoritative assertions that trail quickly into confusion. Notice how the writer seems to stabilize his movement through the paper by returning again and again to recognizable and available commonplace utterances. When he has to move away from them, however, away from the familiar to statements that would extend those utterances, where he, too, must speak, the writing—that is, both the syntax and the structure of the discourse— falls to pieces.

> Many times the times drives a person's life depends on how he uses it. I would like to think about if time is twenty-five hours a day rather than twenty-four hours. Some people think it's the boaring or some people might say it's the pleasure to take one more hour for their life. But I think the time is passing and coming, still we are standing on same position. We should use time as best as we can use about the good way in our life. Everything we do, such as sleep, eat, study, play and doing something for ourselves. These take the time to do and we could find the individual ability and may process own. It is the important for us and our society. As time going on the world changes therefor we are changing, too. When these situation changes we should follow the suitable case of own. But many times we should decide what's the better way to do so by using time. Sometimes like this kind of situation can cause the success of our lives or ruin. I think every individual of his own thought drive how to use time. These affect are done from environmental causes. So we should work on the better way of our life recognizing the importance of time.

There is a general pattern of disintegration when the writer moves off from standard phrases. This sentence, for example, starts out coherently and then falls apart: "*We should use time as best as we can* use about the good way in our life." The difficulty seems to be one of extending those standard phrases or of connecting them to the main subject reference, "time" (or "the time," a construction that causes many of the problems in the paper). Here is an example of a sentence that shows, in miniature, this problem of connection: "*I think every individual* of his own thought drive how to use *time.*"

23   One of the remarkable things about this paper is that, in spite of all the syntactic confusion, there is the hint of an academic project here. The writer sets out to discuss how to creatively use one's time. The text seems to allude to examples and to stages in an argument, even if in the end it is all pretty incoherent. The gestures of academic authority, however, are clearly present, and present in a form that echoes the procedures in other, more successful papers. The writer sets himself against what "some people think"; he speaks with the air of authority: "But I think . . . . Everything we do . . . . When these situation changes . . . ." And he speaks as though there were a project underway, one where he proposes what he thinks, turns to evidence, and offers a conclusion: "These affect are done from environmental causes. So we should work. . . ." This is the case of a student with the ability to imagine the general outline and rhythm of academic prose but without the ability to carry it out, to complete the sentences. And when he gets lost in the new, in the unknown, in the responsibility of his own commitment to speak, he returns again to the familiar ground of the commonplace.

24   The challenge to researchers, it seems to me, is to turn their attention again to products, to student writing, since the drama in a student's essay, as he or she struggles with and against the languages of our contemporary life, is as intense and telling as the drama of an essay's mental preparation or physical production. A written text, too, can be a compelling model of the "composing process" once we conceive of a writer as at work within a text and simultaneously, then, within a society, a history, and a culture.

25   It may very well be that some students will need to learn to crudely mimic the "distinctive register" of academic discourse before they are prepared to actually and legitimately do the work of the discourse, and before they are sophisticated enough with the refinements of tone and gesture to do it with grace or elegance. To say this, however, is to say that our students must be our students. Their initial progress will be marked by their abilities to take on the role of privilege, by their abilities to establish authority. . . .

ACKNOWLEDGMENTS

Preparation of this chapter was supported by the Learning Research and Development Center of the University of Pittsburgh, which is supported in part by the National Institute of Education.

NOTES

1. David Olson has made a similar observation about school-related problems of language learning in younger children. Here is his conclusion: "Depending on whether children assumed language was primarily suitable for making assertions

and conjectures or primarily for making direct or indirect commands, they will either find school texts easy or difficult" (107).

2. For Aristotle, there were both general and specific commonplaces. A speaker, says Aristotle, has a "stock of arguments to which he may turn for a particular need."

> If he knows the *topic* (regions, places, lines of argument)—and a skilled speaker will know them—he will know where to find what he wants for a special case. The general topics, or *commonplaces*, are regions containing arguments that are common to all branches of knowledge .... But there are also special topics (regions, places, *loci*) in which one looks for arguments appertaining to particular branches of knowledge, special sciences such as ethics or politics. (154–155)

And, he says, "The topics or places, then, may be indifferently thought of as in the science that is concerned, or in the mind of the speaker." But the question of location is "indifferent" *only* if the mind of the speaker is in line with set opinion, general assumption. For the speaker (or writer) who is not situated so comfortably in the privileged public realm, this is indeed not an indifferent matter at all. If he does not have the commonplace at hand, he will not, in Aristotle's terms, know where to go at all.

[. . .]

3. Stanley Fish (1980) argues that the basis for distinguishing novice from expert readings is the persuasiveness of the discourse used to present and defend a given reading. In particular, see the chapter, "Demonstration vs. Persuasion: Two Models of Critical Activity" (pp. 356–373).

4. Some students, when they come to the university, can do this better than others. When Jonathan Culler says, "the possibility of bringing someone to see that a particular interpretation is a good one assumes shared points of departure and common notions of how to read," he is acknowledging that teaching, at least in English classes, has had to assume that students, to be students, were already to some degree participating in the structures of reading and writing that constitute English studies (quoted in Fish, 1980, p. 366).
   Stanley Fish tells us "not to worry" that students will violate our enterprise by offering idiosyncratic readings of standard texts:

> The fear of solipsism, of the imposition by the unconstrained self of its own prejudices, is unfounded because the self does not exist apart from the communal or conventional categories of thought that enable its operations (of thinking, seeing, reading). Once we realize that the conceptions that fill consciousness, including any conception of its own status, are culturally derived, the very notion of an unconstrained self, of a consciousness wholly and dangerously free, becomes incomprehensible. (1980, p. 335)

He, too, is assuming that students, to be students (and not "dangerously free"), must be members in good standing of the community whose immediate head is the English teacher. It is interesting that his parenthetical catalogue of the "operations" of thought, "thinking, seeing, reading," excludes writing; since it is only through written records that we have any real indication of how a student thinks, sees, and reads. (Perhaps "real" is an inappropriate word to use here, since there is certainly a "real" intellectual life that goes on, independent of writing. Let me say that thinking, seeing, and reading are valued in the academic community *only* as they are represented by extended, elaborated written records.) Writing, I presume, is a given for Fish. It is the card of entry into this closed community that constrains and excludes dangerous characters. Students who are excluded from this community are students who do poorly on written placement exams or in freshman composition. They do not, that is, move easily into the privileged discourse of the community, represented by the English literature class.

5. My debt to Bizzell's work should be evident everywhere in this essay. See also Bizzell (1978, 1982b) and Bizzell and Herzberg (1980).

REFERENCES

Aristotle. (1932). *The Rhetoric of Aristotle* (L. Cooper, Trans.). Englewood Cliffs, NJ: Prentice-Hall.

Barthes, R. (1974). *S/Z* (R. Howard, Trans.). New York: Hill & Wang.

Bartholomae, D. (1979). Teaching basic writing: An alternative to basic skills. *Journal of Basic Writing, 2*, 85–109.

Bartholomae, D. (1983). Writing assignments: Where writing begins. In P. Stock (Ed.), *Forum* (pp. 300–312). Montclair, NJ: Boynton/Cook.

Bereiter, C., & Scardamalia, M. (in press). Cognitive coping strategies and the problem of "inert knowledge." In S. S. Chipman, J. W. Segal, & R. Glaser (Eds.), *Thinking and learning skills: Research and open questions* (Vol. 2). Hillsdale, NJ: Erlbaum.

Bizzell, P. (1978). The ethos of academic discourse. *College Composition and Communication, 29*, 351–355.

Bizzell, P. (1982a). Cognition, convention, and certainty: What we need to know about writing, *Pre/text, 3*, 213–244.

Bizzell, P. (1982b). College composition: Initiation into the academic discourse community. *Curriculum Inquiry, 12*, 191–207.

Bizzell, P., and Herzberg, B. (1980). "Inherent" ideology, "universal" history, "empirical" evidence, and "context-free" writing: Some problems with E. D. Hirsch's *The Philosophy of Composition. Modern Language Notes, 95*, 1181–1202.

Coles, W. E., Jr,. (1978). *The plural I.* New York: Holt, Rinehart & Winston.

Fish, S. (1980). *Is there a text in this class? The authority of interpretive communities.* Cambridge, MA: Harvard University Press.

Flower, L. S. (1981). Revising writer-based prose, *Journal of Basic Writing, 3*, 62–74.

Flower, L., & Hayes, J. (1981). A cognitive process theory of writing. *College Composition and Communication, 32*, 365–387.

Hairston, M. (1978). *A contemporary rhetoric.* Boston: Houghton Mifflin.

Lunsford,. A. A. (1980). The content of basic writers' essays. *College Composition and Communication, 31*, 276–290.

Maimon, E. P., Belcher, G. L., Hearn, G. W., Nodine, B. F., O'Connor, F. X. (1981). *Writing in the arts and sciences.* Cambridge, MA: Winthrop.

Olson, D. R. (1981). Writing: The divorce of the author from the text. In B. M. Kroll & R. J. Vann (Eds.). *Exploring speaking-writing relationships: Connections and contrasts.* Urbana, IL: National Council of Teachers of English.

Perkins, D. N. (1985). General cognitive skills: Why not? In S. S. Chipman, J. W. Segal & R. Glaser (Eds.), *Thinking and learning skills: Research and open questions* (Vol. 2). Hillsdale, NJ: Earlbaum.

Ponsot, M., & Deen, R. (1982). *Beat not the poor desk.* Montclair, NJ: Boynton/Cook.

Rodriguez, R. (1983). *Hunger of memory.* New York: Bantam.

Rose, M. (1983). Remedial writing courses: A critique and a proposal. *College English, 45,* 109–126.

Said, E. W. (1975). *Beginnings: Intention and method.* Baltimore: The Johns Hopkins University Press.

Shaughnessy, M. (1977). *Errors and expectations.* New York: Oxford University Press.

Active Reading

1. What does Bartholomae's title phrase mean? Is it up to every student to "invent" the university? How is such invention a linguistic performance?

2. According to Bartholomae, how is mimicry a necessary stage a basic writer needs to move through in order to learn how to write like a scholar?

Critical Reading

1. For Dutton, good writing is clear writing; for Butler, language is more complex, and she argues that a writer needs to push against ordinary meaning to say something innovative and to engage readers in an interpretive process. Which view do you think Bartholomae would support? Language as tool or as construction and performance?

2. Bartholomae seems to say there is no place for everyday language and common sense in academic arguments. Do you think he would assign a personal argument, inviting students to reflect on experience and what they know and believe?

3. How do you think Bartholomae envisioned his audience: as composition instructors charged with teaching their students to become better academic writers, or as student writers at various stages of writing competency? Can you identify particular passages that might cause offence to some student readers? How would these passages need to be revised in order to address a student readership more successfully?

Finding Words

Jaqueline McLeod Rogers

McLeod Rogers teaches composition and rhetoric at the University of Winnipeg and is one of the authors of this book, aimed at helping student writers. In this short piece, published in Writing on the Edge in 2008, she discusses some of the differences between academic and creative writing, as well as some of the reasons students and scholars can struggle to produce words in either form. She also describes how fluency and motivation may be linked.

1   What I like best about writing is choosing words that say what I mean. I'm happy in the reassurance that there are words for feelings and knowings that will make fluent sense to me and others. Yet I didn't always have faith in these connections. At worst, I worried that the right words were elusive. Not much better was believing in critical thinking as a sort of magic meant to improve ideas by changing them into new shapes and forms.

BLOCKING AND STALLING

2   I spent years—maybe thirty—wanting to write, calling myself a writer when I was in some stage of composing and a failed writer when drafting stopped. As a creative writer without the drive for completion or perfection, I took a start-and-stop approach to writing poems and stories, never crafting them into mature pieces. As an academic writer, I was dogged by the opposite problem, often spending hours phrasing and revising an idea, refusing to go forward before I had every word in place.

3   Failed writer, indeed—undisciplined when writing raw from my imagination and blocked by paralyzing perfectionism when trying to think and write. Yet as I struggled with this two-headed monster—demon perfectionism and devil-may-care—I thought I was waging two separate battles. To do academic writing, you need to pay attention and be analytical whereas creative writing allowed for reflection and making connections. Writing about books was so hard that I couldn't get started, whereas writing about feelings and experience was only fun when it was spontaneous and exploratory, free of the tedium of revision.

4   Wanting to write is what led me to study literature in university. Hoping my own work would flourish in the company of greatness, I moved without break into graduate work. But as I became more immersed in studying literature and theory, my essays became more stilted and my story-making eventually stopped. Instead of trying to find help for this kind of trouble, I thought of myself as a failed writer and romanticized the special suffering. Peter Elbow is probably right when he reminds us that the urge to write is as natural as breathing to many (537); for me, writing was innate to self-identity, and I felt that failing was nobler than declaring myself a non-writer and moving on to more penetrable activities.

5   I think people in life and books tend to be either talkers or writers, and as a rapt student of literature I developed a preference for the writer figures. I appreciated Marlow and Nick for being less flamboyant and edgy than Kurtz and Gatsby. Instead of being busy getting adored in an exotic outpost or driving a glorious circus wagon of a car, the writer seemed admirably disciplined, living and learning rather than striding about. Surviving the horror, he was the one left to reflect on what happened and draw conclusions; living in the shadow of big adventure, observing or remembering, he was the one to conjure morality and magic into play.

6   And there was an attractive pathos to this writer-figure, who took himself and his sensibilities so seriously as he tried to make things mean something. I now see an element of repressed sexuality in the passionate attention I paid these characters. My favorite was D.H. Lawrence's Rupert Birkin, to whom I felt joined in being "damned and doomed to the old effort of serious living" (340)—although I missed the irony that serious living rewarded him with making art, whereas for me it meant not only being resolutely dour but reading about it. While many problems likely arise when a naive reader begins admiring art more than life, the biggest problem for me as a "reader in love" was that I stopped writing.

7   I am less enthusiastic these days about the literary portrait of the artist, having been alerted by post-modernist media critics like Norman Denzin to the twentieth-century malaise of their "I like to watch" stance. At that point, I admired their willingness to stand and reflect, and positioned myself more passively still in the posture of watching the watcher. I never gave up wanting to write, but my essays were always last-minute, late-night creations, and my motivation to finish—let alone rework—poems and stories dissolved.

STOP TELLING THAT STORY: FEELING WITHOUT THINKING

8   Being unable to finish a story about self-identity led me to give in to being blocked and give up self-expressive writing. In my story, I wanted the main character to begin the process of facing herself by going to the mirror to really look at herself. Her problem at the mirror was that a figure with no face looked back at her. My problem was that nothing seemed right as I tried to imagine ways for this girl to find a face.

9   Frustrated, I gave up my usual tack of working alone and decided to seek advice. The first available ear belonged to a friend whose life was happily unexamined, so she struggled to muster a response to something that must have struck her as an abstract waste of time.

10   "It's about a girl who thinks she's alright," I explained. "But when she goes to the mirror, she has no face. She's surprised and doesn't know how this happened. What I need to figure out is how she can change this."

11   "Poor you," she said, before brightening to suggest that I try finding a different story. "That one sounds a bit boring."

12   And for me, these words—mildly critical, mostly uninterested—ended my story writing. At the time, I thought I quit out of frustration at being unable to finish that particular story. Now, the quitting seems a bit more layered. The creative process I practiced was a carnival of emotion, fueled by feeling and aimed at exploring realms of caring and coldness, and this conception of creativity as non-intellectual left me defenseless in the face of criticism or negative emotions like self-doubt. When my friend questioned the value of my story, I caved in to feelings of self-doubt rather than calling up some self-discipline and carrying on. By separating the creative process from critical thinking and intellectual work, I had rendered myself unable to think through ways to solve problems. Hundreds of raw sketch "story starts" are still filed away in plaid three-ring binders, collecting dust in a basement cupboard.

BLOCK THAT ESSAY: OUTHINKING THOUGHT

13   At the same time as I withdrew from creative writing, I began struggling with scholarly writing projects, often looking for hours to find the words to build a sentence, only to give up after filling pages with false starts. The more I studied the writing of others, the less able I was to write about their work. If in my dualistic conception, creative writing was a sea of feeling, academic writing required using your head. So I would sit, concentrate on the act of thinking, write a phrase, cross it through, and go back to the effort of self-conscious thinking again. I was worried I had hit my intellectual limits. Even when convinced that I probably wasn't smart enough, I denied myself the right to give up or feel self pity in order to soldier on, determined that I'd find the right word by thinking harder or deeper. If "essay" means "from the Old French *essaier*, to try, to test— not necessarily to succeed" (Behrens et al, xxi), then I was working within the spirit of the original, to the extent of testing myself and not succeeding.

14   I was never quite ready to start writing because there was always more to read. And reading a book once barely counted as an accomplishment, since I had positioned myself as a student reader who could only know a text by a series of re-readings. I would never write an organized word until the night before the essay was due. Then, I would cajole myself into writing a paragraph by placing my watch beside the empty page to serve as a reminder that there were only, say, ten hours left before I would have to show up at my professor's door with a completed draft. It was a punishing process.

15   Many times a single paragraph could take hours to pinch and shape. Often a paragraph thus hard-won would fall on the cutting floor, no longer to the point at the end of a ten-hour marathon of thinking in circles. In one particularly difficult session while trying to write about *The Old Man and the Sea*, I had nothing salvageable to say about Santiago's heroism by four in the morning. Exhausted, I was reduced to inanities like, "Despite their different roles, Santiago establishes a bond of respect for the Marlin," which, on re-reading, seemed to be more about the antics of "The Odd Couple" than a description of Hemingway's characters. Following a fit of giggling, I almost convinced myself to slink off to bed but, full of coffee and inarticulate ideas and fears, I resolved to finish even if there was no hope of doing a good job.

16   It was fortunate that I wrote my Ph.D. on women's fiction, for I had read it for years and felt on more solid ground intellectually. This gave me a chance to consider whether I was really struggling with a thinking deficiency or resisting the writing task out of reluctance to risk saying something wrong. My thesis advisor alerted me to a writing tic. To present ideas, I would often provide several examples of the same thing, or repeat an idea several times before announcing the point I really wanted to make at the end of the paragraph.

17   "If I'm not sure what you're trying to say in a section, I just go to the last sentence of every paragraph. You usually like to bury your point there. Are you doing this on purpose?" she asked, in a joking tone. "Are you sure you're not tailoring your style to support your claim that women writers favor repetition and indirection?"

18   As soon as I recognized this pattern of repetition and delay in my work, I began thinking about what caused it. Since I was bound to the belief that

brilliant minds produce brilliant scholarship, I was terrified to go forward with an idea for fear of missing the mark. What if readers didn't understand me? Fear of being misunderstood also provoked me to endless reiteration. While most of us who have learned of Stephen Krashen's theory of the "affective filter" think of it as an explanation for the acquisition struggles of ESL students (qtd. in Clark, 206), I was a privileged first-language user with a full-blown fear filter preventing me from saying much and provoking me to say important things over and over again. Rather than thinking, as I do now, that with nudge and adjustment writing can say anything, at that point I believed that many things defied expression or eluded the comprehension of readers.

REPORTING QUANTITATIVE DATA: LEARNING TO LINK CREATIVE AND CRITICAL THINKING

19   I only began enjoying the process of scholarly writing about fifteen years ago, doing what I expected would be a dry and objective form of academic writing—presenting quantitative information about gender patterns in student writing. Once the design context was established, this was a task that needed to go forward independent of prior studies and claims and that required successive acts of interpretation and analysis: on-the-spot meaning-making. I was free to find connections not only in the data itself—in the student writing samples and in the reader responses to these samples—but also between the data and my experiences as a composition teacher. Instead of searching for things worth saying and then struggling to fashion reader-friendly points, I suddenly had things to say and a desire to say them well so that they might interest others. Thinking needed to take place in partnership with using memory, imagination, and feelings. It was as if I had introduced two powerful elements—"Work, meet life"—and they liked each other.

20   One incident crystallizes the experience of understanding ideas in the context of personal experience. A pattern I noticed while reading stories by elementary school writers was that not much happened in many stories by girls, especially in contrast to stories by boys that so often featured action figures and heroics along the lines recently outlined by Thomas Newkirk. In many of the girls' stories, not only were events few and non-dramatic, but several even made direct reference to non-eventfulness as a desirable thing. This story by a grade five writer still comes to my mind when I think about the tendency of girls and women to find reassurance in non-action and predictability.

> Once upon a time a boy and a girl were taking a walk. And their names were Bob and Tina and they were brother and sister. Bob always called Tina Sis, and Tina called Bob brother.
>
> They lived in a big white house with their Mom and Dad. Their names are Tanya and Ken. They were a very nice couple. Tina had a cat named Me and Bob had a dog named Ruff. They were nice and gentle pets. Their parents had six goldfish. They were very pretty.
>
> Tina and her brother Bob had a lot of friends on the block. Sometimes Tina and Bob would get into fights. But not very often.
>
> They wouldn't get hurt too much. But sometimes they would cry. But they loved each other.

> Every morning they would go for walks on the weekends. They even walked to school with their friends. So nothing happens to them. Their parents, Tanya and Ken, felt that they would be more safe walking with a lot of their good friends.
>
> They have a lot in common like they both like animals and they both like the same t.v. shows.
>
> They are just one big happy family.

21   All telling and no showing, a piece like this defies what many composition texts set out as the earmarks of lively narrative. Yet as a reader I found this story more powerful than the variants of "The Wrath of Robotman" written by boys. It seemed wrong to encourage girls to adopt male-friendly plots about epic conflict and calamity if doing so meant abandoning the potential subtleties of focusing on the unremarkable (and abandoning, too, staking new territory by finding words for the unremarked and unspoken).

22   As I tried to move beyond matters of taste to account for resisting the idea that plot and action are definitively linked, I remembered that as a girl I had shared the longing for predictability and inaction expressed by many girls. Raised in a house where my dad came home late, loud, and drunk many nights, by junior high I'd devised a code for making journal entries that turned on variants of the phrase "nothing happened." In lower-case, "nothing happened" meant things were good and dad had come home on time; beginning the same phrase with capital letters—"Nothing Happened"—meant things were relatively quiet even though he was late and drunk; a page with nothing written on it—a blank page— meant something ugly, noisy, violent had happened—something I had no urge to recreate. Writing about these events would not only mean reliving old trouble but also possibly revealing family secrets. I came to a felt understanding of how girls might choose to create worlds where "nothing happens (or nothing bad happens) to their characters, [for] in day-to-day life bad things all too often happen to girls and women." (McLeod Rogers, 122). What if what *was* there in so many female narratives needed to be there, as a beginning stage of writing? Rather than recommending that girls "trade up" to tales with more events, composition teachers might instead encourage female writers to flesh out more details in the relatively pacific stories they liked telling. Ignoring externally motivated events and exploring instead what the (usually) female character did or thought might help them move from a sense of victimhood toward agency. Finally, by asking them to find images to "show" feelings, we might bring the realm of caring in from the abstract by giving it shape or face.

23   At about the same time as I found voice and purpose by doing research that indirectly drew its life from my own experience, Jane Tompkins found a wide audience when she described her longing for a personalized form of criticism in "Me and My Shadow." She articulated the painful bind of so many female academics who worry that the self that thinks is not the same as the self who feels. While I like her overall claim that women need to link feeling and thinking—the realms of experience and text—I remain uncomfortable with advocacy of an open door between our personal and public lives. I prefer the somewhat variant view that self-reflection improves insight, but that the self need not be the center of attention. In his "iceberg theory" of fiction writing, Hemingway holds that

what readers see in printed stories is equivalent to the tip of the iceberg, with what is visible being supported by an unseen underlying mass; in his metaphor, the writer renders a point clearly to readers because of having taken full measure of the mass of supporting details that readers never see. This theory corresponds to my sense of the way scholarly writing is built on "silent knowledge"—built on the writer's awareness of the rootedness of abstract or scholarly ideas in personal experience, an awareness that, while best withheld from readers in many situations, enables the writer to grasp these ideas more firmly.

WRITING AND TEACHING WRITING

24   Recognizing how much my writing grows from consulting personal experi-
ence—and thus that my thinking is responsive to other ways of knowing such as feeling, imagining and remembering—has profoundly influenced my commitment to teaching personal forms of writing. Yet the question of whether we should teach personal writing doesn't strike me as either dry or done. I feel kinship with Janet Carey Eldred's recent book *Sentimental Attachments* on several counts: first is her assumption that how we write affects how we teach students to write and second is her commitment to continue actively inquiring into forms or genres that may offer opportunities to "fuse the personal and the academic" (vii).

25   Not so long ago, personal voice writing was out of favor. During the rush to epistemic rhetoric and disciplinary forms of academic writing, I found myself in the position of needing better arguments for keeping the practice of teaching personal writing. For reasons I didn't entirely understand, the exchange between those like me who wanted to hold on to expressive elements and those who wanted disciplinary models and immersion was oddly emotional, even "personal." I didn't know then that on a small-scale we were going through what would come to be called "the composition wars." In department meetings about curricular directions, I was angry at those who advocated the "no-nonsense" (non-expressive) writing-in-the-disciplines approach to composition; it was also uncomfortable being regarded as well-meaning but addle-headed in encourag-ing students to find a voice—as continuing an outmoded approach that was responsible for mystifying the process of academic writing and keeping students forever uninitiated in its ways.

26   Logic and momentum for learning disciplinary forms was strong. Yet, true to the change principle that governs the narrative course of life, the academic climate has warmed toward personal writing, and there is now a broad range of support. Wendy Bishop's was an eloquent voice connecting student writing to the writing practices of successful writers rather than to non-life-oriented *composing* activities; her book *Ethnographic Writing Research* emphasizes the interpretive, creative energy needed to "write up" results. Sherrie Gradin's *Romancing Rhetorics* points out that personal writing does not preclude writing for change and active social construction. Barbara Kamler explores the dynamism of narrative knowing, so that students move beyond reinscription of received ideas to "reframe personal writing, so that it is not simply con-fessional, not simply elided with self" (28). Recently, Nathan Crick revisits the constructivist-expressivist debate to suggest that besides these positions, we

need to remember the importance of time and experience in writing, so that more than merely representing what others have thought or what the individual writer thinks, writers draw from the complex relationship of "language, experience and meaning" (261). Looking back, he points out that the debate is really age-old, which may also be taken to suggest that, looking ahead, the debate will continue, and that when intellectual thought takes its next big turn, we need to be well versed in the variety of ways students are empowered by the personal.

27   I'm a writer who learned to write the hard way, trying to be smart and force my mind down a lonely intellectual path rather than strolling companionably with feelings and musings. Luckily, I've had an easier road as a writing teacher. I have been in position to help students make and strengthen the connection between the worlds of experience and ideas that I broke and have struggled to mend in order to like writing again. My experience testifies to the sense of Peter Elbow's call for the writing teacher to help students "to involve themselves personally"(538) in their research, to teach students to use "imaginative and metaphorical thinking" since the best essays are rooted "in the imagination rather than only in clear logical thinking and language" (539).

WORKS CITED

Behrens, Laurence, L.J. Rosen, Jaqueline McLeod Rogers, and Catherine Taylor. *Writing and Reading Across the Curriculum.* Canadian Edition. Toronto: Pearson, 2002.

Bishop, Wendy. *Ethnographic Writing Research: Writing It Down, Writing It Up, and Reading It.* Portsmouth, NH: Heinemann, 1999.

Clark, Irene. *Writing in the Center.* Dubuque: Kendall/Hunt, 1985.

Crick, Nathan. "Composition as Experience: John Dewey on Creative Expression and the Origins of 'Mind.'" *College Composition and Communication.* 55.2 (December 2003): 254–275.

Denzin, Norman. *The Cinematic Society: The Voyeur's Gaze.* London: Sage, 1995.

Elbow, Peter. "The Cultures of Literature and Composition: What Could Each Learn from the Other." *College English* 64.5 (May 2002): 533-46.

Eldred, Janet Carey. *Sentimental Attachments: Essays, Creative Non-Fiction and Other Experiments in Composition.* Portsmouth NH: Boynton Cook, 2005.

Gradin, Sheri. *Romancing Rhetorics: Social Expressivist Perspectives on the Teaching of Writing.* Portsmouth, NH: Boynton Cook, 1995.

Hemingway, Ernest. *The Old Man and the Sea.* New York: Scribner's, 1952.

Kamler, Barbara. *Relocating the Personal: A Critical Writing Pedagogy.* State University of New York Press, 2001.

Lawrence, D.H. *Women in Love.* London: Penguin, 1921.

McLeod Rogers, Jaqueline. *Two Sides to a Story: Gender Difference in Student Narrative.* Winnipeg, MB: Inkshed, 1996.

Newkirk, Thomas. *Misreading Masculinity: Boys, Literacy, and Popular Culture.* Heinemann, 2002.

Tompkins, Jane. "Me and My Shadow" in *The Intimate Critique: Autobiographical Literary Criticism.* Eds. Diane P. Freedman, Olivia Frey and Frances Murphy Zauhar. Durham and London: Duke University Press, 1995: 23–41.

Active Reading

1. What caused this writer to freeze up? Does she pinpoint a cause?

2. What allows her to take up writing again?

Critical Reading

1. According to this writer, once writer's block sets in, it gets worse. If you have experienced writer's block, compare your situation to hers. What are the similarities?

2. If you wanted to study writer's block more fully, what are some of the ways you might find out more about it (observation, interviews, etc.)?

3. Why should we read about someone's personal experiences? Are there places where the author makes an explicit connection between herself and others, so that her experiences might resonate with readers?

Lost in Translation

Eva Hoffman

Eva Hoffman was born in Poland in 1945 to Holocaust survivors. Her family immigrated to Vancouver in 1959, when she was 14. They eventually moved to the United States where she completed a Ph. D. In English literature at Harvard University and went on to work as a writer and editor of The New York Book Review. *The excerpt here is from* Lost in Translation, *a memoir about her experiences moving from one culture to another, emphasizing her sense of loss and displacement.*

1   Every day I learn new words, new expressions. I pick them up from school exercises, from conversations, from the books I take out of Vancouver's well-lit, cheerful public library. There are some turns of phrase to which I develop strange allergies. "You're welcome," for example, strikes me as a gaucherie, and I can hardly bring myself to say it—I suppose because it implies that there's something to be thanked for, which in Polish would be impolite. The very places where the language is at its most conventional, where it should be most taken for granted, are the places where I feel the prick of artifice.

2   Then there are words to which I take an equally irrational liking, for their sound, or just because I'm pleased to have deduced their meaning. Mainly they're words I learn from books, like "enigmatic" or "insolent"—words that have only a literary value, that exist only as signs on the page.

3   But mostly, the problem is that the signifier has become severed from the signified. The words I learn now don't stand for things in the same unquestioned way they did in my native tongue. "River" in Polish was a vital sound, energized with the essence of riverhood, of my rivers, of my being immersed in rivers. "River" in English is cold—a word without an aura. It has no accumulated associations for me, and it does not give off the radiating haze of connotation. It does not evoke.

4 The process, alas, works in reverse as well. When I see a river now, it is not shaped, assimilated by the word that accommodates it to the psyche—a word that makes a body of water a river rather than an uncontained element. The river before me remains a thing, absolutely other, absolutely unbending to the grasp of my mind.

5 When my friend Penny tells me that she's envious, or happy, or disappointed, I try laboriously to translate not from English to Polish but from the word back to its source, to the feeling from which it springs. Already, in that moment of strain, spontaneity of response is lost. And anyway, the translation doesn't work. I don't know how Penny feels when she talks about envy. The word hangs in a Platonic stratosphere, a vague prototype of all envy so large, so all-encompassing that it might crush me—as might disappointment or happiness.

6 I am becoming a living avatar of structuralist wisdom; I cannot help knowing that words are just themselves. But it's a terrible knowledge, without any of the consolations that wisdom usually brings. It does not mean that I'm free to play with words at my wont; anyway, words in their naked state are surely among the least satisfactory play objects. No, this radical disjoining between word and thing is a desiccating alchemy, draining the world not only of significance but of its colors, striations, nuances—its very existence. It is the loss of a living connection.

7 The worst losses come at night. As I lie down in a strange bed in a strange house—my mother is a sort of housekeeper here, to the aging Jewish man who has taken us in return for her services—I wait for that spontaneous flow of inner language which used to be my nighttime talk with myself, my way of informing the ego where the id had been. Nothing comes. Polish, in a short time, has atrophied, shriveled from sheer uselessness. Its words don't apply to my new experiences; they're not coeval with any of the objects, or faces, or the very air I breathe in the daytime. In English, words have not penetrated to those layers of my psyche from which a private conversation could proceed. This interval before sleep used to be the time when my mind became both receptive and alert, when images and words rose up to consciousness, reiterating what had happened during the day, adding the day's experiences to those already stored there, spinning out the thread of my personal story.

8 Now, this picture-and-word show is gone; the thread has been snapped. I have no interior language, and without it, interior images—those images through which we assimilate the external world, through which we take it in, love it, make it our own—become blurred too. My mother and I met a Canadian family who live down the block today. They were working in their garden and engaged us in a conversation of the "Nice weather we're having, isn't it?" variety, which culminated in their inviting us into their house. They sat stiffly on their couch, smiled in the long pauses between the conversation, and seemed at a loss for what to ask. Now my mind gropes for some description of them, but nothing fits. They're a different species from anyone I've met in Poland, and Polish words slip off them without sticking. English words don't hook on to anything. I try, deliberately, to come up with a few. Are these people pleasant or dull? Kindly or silly? The words float in an uncertain space. They come up from a part of my brain in which labels may be manufactured but which has no connection to my instincts, quick reactions,

knowledge. Even the simplest adjectives sow confusion in my mind; English kindliness has a whole system of morality behind it, a system that makes "kindness" an entirely positive virtue. Polish kindness has the tiniest element of irony. Besides, I'm beginning to feel the tug of prohibition, in English, against uncharitable words. In Polish, you can call someone an idiot without particularly harsh feelings and with the zest of a strong judgment. Yes, in Polish these people might tend toward "silly" and "dull"—but I force myself toward "kindly" and "pleasant." The cultural unconscious is beginning to exercise its subliminal influence.

9   The verbal blur covers these people's faces, their gestures with a sort of fog. I can't translate them into my mind's eye. The small event, instead of being added to the mosaic of consciousness and memory, falls through some black hole, and I fall with it. What has happened to me in this new world? I don't know. I don't see what I've seen, don't comprehend what's in front of me. I'm not filled with language anymore, and I have only a memory of fullness to anguish me with the knowledge that, in this dark and empty state, I don't really exist.

10   For my birthday, Penny gives me a diary complete with a little lock and key to keep what I write from the eyes of all intruders. It is that little lock—the visible symbol of the privacy in which the diary is meant to exist—that creates my dilemma. If I am indeed to write something entirely for myself, in what language do I write? Several times, I open the diary and close it again. I can't decide. Writing in Polish at this point would be a little like resorting to Latin or ancient Greek—an eccentric thing to do in a diary in which you're supposed to set down your most immediate experiences and unpremeditated thoughts in the most unmediated language. Polish is becoming a dead language, the language of the untranslatable past. But writing for nobody's eyes in English? That's like doing a school exercise, or performing in front of yourself, a slightly perverse act of self-voyeurism.

11   Because I have to choose something, I finally choose English. If I'm to write about the present, I have to write in the language of the present, even if it's not the language of the self. As a result, the diary becomes surely one of the more impersonal exercises of that sort produced by an adolescent girl. These are no sentimental effusions of rejected love, eruptions of familial anger, or consoling broodings about death. English is not the language of such emotions. Instead, I set down my reflections on the ugliness of wrestling, on the elegance of Mozart, and on how Dostoyevsky puts me in mind of El Greco. I write down Thoughts. I Write.

12   There is a certain pathos to this naïve snobbery, for the diary is an earnest attempt to create a part of my persona that I imagine I would have grown into in Polish. In the solitude of this most private act, I write, in my public language, in order to update what might have been my other self. The diary is about me and not about me at all. But on one level, it allows me to make the first jump. I learn English through writing, and, in turn, writing gives me a written self. Refracted through the double distance of English and writing, this self—my English self—becomes oddly objective; more than anything, it perceives. It exists more easily in the abstract sphere of thoughts and observations than in the world. For a while, this impersonal self, this cultural negative capability becomes the truest thing about me. When I write, I have a real existence that is proper to

the activity of writing—an existence that takes place midway between me and the sphere of artifice, art, pure language. This language is beginning to invent another me. However, I discover something odd. It seems that when I write (or, for that matter, think) in English, I am unable to use the word "I." I do not go as far as the schizophrenic "she"—but I am driven, as by a compulsion, to the double, the Siamese-twin "you."

13   My voice is doing funny things. It does not seem to emerge from the same parts of my body as before. It comes out from somewhere in my throat, tight, thin, and matt—a voice without the modulations, dips, and rises that it had before, when it went from my stomach all the way through my head. There is, of course, the constraint and the self-consciousness of an accent that I hear but cannot control. Some of my high school peers accuse me of putting it on in order to appear more "interesting." In fact, I'd do anything to get rid of it, and when I'm alone, I practice sounds for which my speech organs have no intuitions, such as "th" (I do this by putting my tongue between my teeth) and "a," which is longer and more open in Polish (by shaping my mouth into a sort of arrested grin). It is simple words like "cat" or "tap" that give me the most trouble, because they have no context of other syllables, and so people often misunderstand them. Whenever I can, I do awkward little swerves to avoid them, or pause and try to say them very clearly. Still, when people—like salesladies—hear me speak without being prepared to listen carefully, they often don't understand me the first time around. "Girls' shoes," I say, and the "girls" comes out as a sort of scramble. "Girls' shoes," I repeat, willing the syllable to form itself properly, and the saleslady usually smiles nicely, and sends my mother and me to the right part of the store. I say "Thank you" with a sweet smile, feeling as if I'm both claiming an unfair special privilege and being unfairly patronized.

14   It's as important to me to speak well as to play a piece of music without mistakes. Hearing English distorted grates on me like chalk screeching on a blackboard, like all things botched and badly done, like all forms of gracelessness. The odd thing is that I know what is correct, fluent, good, long before I can execute it. The English spoken by our Polish acquaintances strikes me as jagged and thick, and I know that I shouldn't imitate it. I'm turned off by the intonations I hear on the TV sitcoms—by the expectation of laughter, like a dog's tail wagging in supplication, built into the actors' pauses, and by the curtailed, cutoff rhythms. I like the way Penny speaks, with an easy flow and a pleasure in giving words a fleshly fullness; I like what I hear in some movies; and once the Old Vic comes to Vancouver to perform *Macbeth*, and though I can hardly understand the particular words, I am riveted by the tones of sureness and command that mold the actors' speech into such majestic periods.

15   Sociolinguists might say that I receive these language messages as class signals, that I associate the sounds of correctness with the social status of the speaker. In part, this is undoubtedly true. The class-linked notion that I transfer wholesale from Poland is that belonging to a "better" class of people is absolutely dependent on speaking a "better" language. And in my situation especially, I know that language will be a crucial instrument, that I can overcome the stigma of my marginality, the weight of presumption against me, only if the reassuringly right sounds come out of my mouth.

16   Yes, speech is a class signifier. But I think that in hearing these varieties of speech around me, I'm sensitized to something else as well—something that is a matter of aesthetics, and even of psychological health. Apparently, skilled chefs can tell whether a dish from some foreign cuisine is well cooked even if they have never tasted it and don't know the genre of cooking it belongs to. There seem to be some deep-structure qualities—consistency, proportions of ingredients, smoothness of blending—that indicate culinary achievement to these educated eaters' taste buds. So each language has its own distinctive music, and even if one doesn't know its separate components, one can pretty quickly recognize the propriety of the patterns in which the components are put together, their harmonies and discords. Perhaps the crucial element that strikes the ear in listening to living speech is the degree of the speaker's self-assurance and control.

17   As I listen to people speaking that foreign tongue, English, I can hear when they stumble or repeat the same phrases too many times, when their sentences trail off aimlessly—or, on the contrary, when their phrases have vigor and roundness, when they have the space and the breath to give a flourish at the end of a sentence, or make just the right pause before coming to a dramatic point. I can tell, in other words, the degree of their ease or disease, the extent of authority that shapes the rhythms of their speech. That authority—in whatever dialect, in whatever variant of the mainstream language—seems to me to be something we all desire. It's not that we all want to speak the King's English, but whether we speak Appalachian or Harlem English, or Cockney or Jamaican Creole, we want to be at home in our tongue. We want to be able to give voice accurately and fully to ourselves and our sense of the world. John Fowles, in one of his stories in *The Ebony Tower*, has a young man cruelly violate an elderly writer and his manuscripts because the legacy of language has not been passed on to the youthful vandal properly. This seems to me an entirely credible premise. Linguistic dispossession is a sufficient motive for violence, for it is close to the dispossession of one's self. Blind rage, helpless rage is rage that has no words—rage that overwhelms one with darkness. And if one is perpetually without words, if one exists in the entropy of inarticulateness, that condition itself is bound to be an enraging frustration. In my New York apartment, I listen almost nightly to fights that erupt like brushfire on the street below—and in their escalating fury of repetitious phrases ("Don't do this to me, man, you fucking bastard, I'll fucking kill you"), I hear not the pleasures of macho toughness but an infuriated beating against wordlessness, against the incapacity to make oneself understood, seen. Anger can be borne—it can even be satisfying—if it can gather into words and explode in a storm, or a rapier-sharp attack. But without this means of ventilation, it only turns back inward, building and swirling like a head of steam—building to an impotent, murderous rage. If all therapy is speaking therapy—a talking cure—then perhaps all neurosis is a speech disease.

Active Reading

1. Why does Hoffman say that words like "enigmatic" and "insolent" have mainly literary value?

2. Find the sentence where Hoffman calls herself "a living avatar of structuralist wisdom" in paragraph 6. Pay attention to the clause that follows the semicolon. It provides the main attribute of structuralist thinking. With this definition in mind, can you define what she means in the first part of her sentence, when she refers to herself as a language theory (structuralism) come to life?

3. How does she say that learning a new language and culture spoils dreaming?

4. Why does she decide to use English in her diary, and how does this constrict her written reflections?

Critical Reading

1. Do you think Hoffman's experiences are similar to others who leave a home culture to enter a new one? Is it likely true that language means more to Hoffman than to some others, given that she went on to get an advanced degree in literature at Harvard and to review and write books? If so, what is the value of her reflections?

2. Her story is painful and prismatic. Do you think she is something of a language pioneer, finding words for an experience with which other immigrants have struggled?

3. The genre of the personal essay is sometimes referred to as "creative non-fiction." Does Hoffman's paragraphing and writing style use more variety and play than is normally found in scholarly writing?

RESEARCH AND WRITING SUGGESTIONS

Chapter-based Research Questions

1. Look at how Butler and Bartholomae use the term "common sense." How do they revise the definition as it is understood in non-academic contexts?

2. Some writing teachers and tutors have argued that helping writers improve is as much a matter of building their confidence as of strengthening skills. How do you think it should be done? Can you find some research about how to approach teaching university students to write better?

3. What are some of the benefits and drawbacks of learning a new language, according to Hoffman?

Additional Research Questions

1. Write a short personal essay in which you tell about a turning point in your life at which your notion of what you needed to learn changed (something like "I never thought I would study psychology until . . ." or "I became a reader when . . .").

2. Find a memoir that describes a writer's journey. Is the memoir solely about the individual, or does the writer find ways to suggest that his/her experience resonates with others?

3. Rhetorician Kenneth Burke used what is sometimes referred to as a "parlour" metaphor to describe how many students feel about attempting to become involved in scholarly discussions. In the Burkean parlour, experts and scholars discuss the fine points of their theories and rebuttals and someone making a new entry into this scene might initially feel overwhelmed and unable to contribute anything sensible. Burke's point is that, over time, newcomers become participants as they gain confidence and insight. Do some online research into Burke's parlour and compare it to Bartholomae's description of the student writer being initiated into academic discourse.

CHAPTER 8
HOMELESS IN THE JUST SOCIETY

If it is true that "the poor are always with us," it is also true that people have different ideas about the causes of poverty and about the ways we might solve or respond to it. Part of the enduring legacy of Liberal prime minister Pierre Trudeau is the *Canadian Charter of Rights and Freedoms*, which attempts to enshrine conditions for citizenry in a "just society." As he imagined it, this society would ensure equal opportunities by providing those in need with the means to prosper: "The Just Society will be one in which all of our people will have the means and motivation to participate. . . . The just society will be one in which those regions and groups which have not fully shared in the country's affluence will be given a better opportunity. The just society will be one in which such urban problems as housing and pollution will be attacked through the application of new knowledge and new techniques."[1]

Even though we like to believe that ours is a just society offering equal opportunity, the number of people without sustaining jobs and permanent housing continues to grow in Canada. Many of the poor and homeless remain invisible, especially in the case of women and children. As the authors of "Voices from the Margins" point out, there are a chorus of reasons that young people find their way to the streets, and relatively few solutions to their dilemma. And as the authors of "Defining Girl Homelessness" observe, many girls are technically without a home even if they have found temporary places to rest, and they face life alone with no protection or security.

Susan Scott takes us into the lives of several poor and homeless women, to show us that while they may have poverty and illness in common, the details of their lives need to be understood on their own terms. No two people are similar, and we need to listen to their stories to develop empathy. Although she interviews individuals about the details of their lives, in this case the personal is indeed political because each story documents how individuals struggling with poverty and various forms of illness have been abandoned or mistreated by social agencies and representatives.

If Trudeau dreamed of a just society and attempted to create its political basis, these articles confront us with exclusion as a reality within Canadian society. Those who are poor struggle for simple sustenance, but their lives are further challenged by illness and violence. Perhaps because poverty tells a story of Canada that does not appeal to the relatively comfortable majority, these struggles remain undocumented or underrepresented. The authors of the paper "Defining Girl Homelessness" tell us directly that their topic needs to be further investigated, and some of the women Scott features in her case studies share their life stories because they are eager to break their silence.

---

[1] Pierre Elliot Trudeau, "The Just Society," in *The Essential Trudeau*, ed. Ron Graham (Toronto: McClelland and Stewart, 1998), 18–19.

Activate

1. Do you see homeless people on the street in your everyday life? How would you describe their demographic characteristics in terms of ethnicity, gender, and age?

2. No one dreams of becoming a homeless person as a child. How do you think people come to be homeless?

3. What kinds of comments have you heard other people make about homeless people? Do people tend to be sympathetic or judgmental? How do you suppose they developed their attitudes?

4. Have you or has anyone you know ever talked to a homeless person, besides saying, "Sorry, I don't have any change"?

The Canadian Charter of Rights and Freedoms

The Charter of Rights and Freedoms was part of the Constitution Act of 1982, which was a modernization of the original British North America Act of 1867. Passing this Act required the British Parliament to act on a joint address from the Canadian Senate and the House of Commons. As Dickerson and Flanagan point out in their book An Introduction to Canadian Politics, *the Act "not only lists and confirms the pre-existing parts of the written constitution but also introduces important new substance, particularly in the first thirty-four sections, known as the Canadian Charter of Rights and Freedoms" (p. 70).[2]*

The sections that we have reproduced are those that speak to civil liberties and to issues of equality rights.

Whereas Canada is founded upon principles that recognize the supremacy of God and the rule of law:

Guarantee of Rights and Freedoms

1. The *Canadian Charter of Rights and Freedoms* guarantees the rights and freedoms set out in it subject only to such reasonable limits prescribed by law as can be demonstrably justified in a free and democratic society.

> Rights and freedoms in Canada

Fundamental Freedoms

2. Everyone has the following fundamental freedoms:
   a) freedom of conscience and religion;
   b) freedom of thought, belief, opinion and expression, including freedom of the press and other media of communication;
   c) freedom of peaceful assembly; and
   d) freedom of association.

> Fundamental freedoms

---

[2] Dickerson, Mark O. and Thomas Flanagan. *An Introduction to Canadian Politics: A Conceptual Approach.* Toronto: Nelson, 1998. Print.

Democratic Rights

3. Every citizen of Canada has the right to vote in an election of members of the House of Commons or of a legislative assembly and to be qualified for membership therein.

4. (1) No House of Commons and no legislative assembly shall continue for longer than five years from the date fixed for the return of the writs of a general election of its members.

   (2) In time of real or apprehended war, invasion or insurrection, a House of Commons may be continued by Parliament and a legislative assembly may be continued by the legislature beyond five years if such continuation is not opposed by the votes of more than one-third of the members of the House of Commons or the legislative assembly, as the case may be.

5. There shall be a sitting of Parliament and of each legislature at least once every twelve months.

Mobility Rights

6. (1) Every citizen of Canada has the right to enter, remain in and leave Canada.

   (2) Every citizen of Canada and every person who has the status of a permanent resident of Canada has the right
      a) to move to and take up residence in any province; and
      b) to pursue the gaining of a livelihood in any province.

   (3) The rights specified in subsection (2) are subject to
      a) any laws or practices of general application in force in a province other than those that discriminate among persons primarily on the basis of province of present or previous residence; and
      b) any laws providing for reasonable residency requirements as a qualification for the receipt of publicly provided social services.

   (4) Subsections (2) and (3) do not preclude any law, program or activity that has as its object the amelioration in a province of conditions of individuals in that province who are socially or economically disadvantaged if the rate of employment in that province is below the rate of employment in Canada.

Legal Rights

7. Everyone has the right to life, liberty and security of the person and the right not to be deprived thereof except in accordance with the principles of fundamental justice.

8. Everyone has the right to be secure against unreasonable search or seizure.

9. Everyone has the right not to be arbitrarily detained or imprisoned.

10. Everyone has the right on arrest or detention

   a) to be informed promptly of the reasons therefor;
   b) to retain and instruct counsel without delay and to be informed of that right; and
   c) to have the validity of the detention determined by way of *habeas corpus* and to be released if the detention is not lawful.

11. Any person charged with an offence has the right

    a) to be informed without unreasonable delay of the specific offence;

    b) to be tried within a reasonable time;

    c) not to be compelled to be a witness in proceedings against that person in respect of the offence;

    d) to be presumed innocent until proven guilty according to law in a fair and public hearing by an independent and impartial tribunal;

    e) not to be denied reasonable bail without just cause;

    f) except in the case of an offence under military law tried before a military tribunal, to the benefit of trial by jury where the maximum punishment for the offence is imprisonment for five years or a more severe punishment;

    g) not to be found guilty on account of any act or omission unless, at the time of the act or omission, it constituted an offence under Canadian or international law or was criminal according to the general principles of law recognized by the community of nations;

    h) if finally acquitted of the offence, not to be tried for it again and, if finally found guilty and punished for the offence, not to be tried or punished for it again; and

    i) if found guilty of the offence and if the punishment for the offence has been varied between the time of commission and the time of sentencing, to the benefit of the lesser punishment.

    Proceedings in criminal and penal matters

12. Everyone has the right not to be subjected to any cruel and unusual treatment or punishment.

    Treatment or punishment

13. A witness who testifies in any proceedings has the right not to have any incriminating evidence so given used to incriminate that witness in any other proceedings, except in a prosecution for perjury or for the giving of contradictory evidence.

    Self-crimination

Interpreter

14. A party or witness in any proceedings who does not understand or speak the language in which the proceedings are conducted or who is deaf has the right to the assistance of an interpreter.

    Interpreter

Equality Rights

15. (1) Every individual is equal before and under the law and has the right to the equal protection and equal benefit of the law without discrimination and, in particular, without discrimination based on race, national or ethnic origin, colour, religion, sex, age or mental or physical disability.

    Equality before and under law and equal protection and benefit of law

    (2) Subsection (1) does not preclude any law, program or activity that has as its object the amelioration of conditions of disadvantaged individuals or groups including those that are disadvantaged because of race, national or ethnic origin, colour, religion, sex, age or mental or physical disability.

    Affirmative action programs

Active Reading

1. The *Charter* guarantees some rights to "everyone" in Canada, and others only to "citizens." Who is in Canada besides citizens? What is the apparent categorical distinction between the types of rights extended only to citizens and those extended to everyone?

2. Which sections pertain most directly to the rights of homeless members of Canadian society?

Critical Reading

1. Do certain points in the *Charter* guarantee that everyone in Canada has the right to expect a degree of economic security, or is the *Charter* vague about this?

2. If the *Charter* establishes that everyone deserves a basic level of comfort and safety, how does this "promise" hold up when read against one of the descriptions of homelessness and poverty in an article in this section?

3. After Trudeau, Prime Minister Jean Chrétien crafted an acceptance speech around the phrase "We have work to do." How does one (or any) of the articles in this section argue that there remains much political work to be done to help alleviate poverty and homelessness?

Voices from the Margins: Understanding Street Youth in Winnipeg

Susan Wingert, Nancy Higgitt, and Janice Ristock

In this article, the authors examine not only why youth become homeless, but also the struggles they face on the street and the obstacles to leaving this way of life. They point out that many youth do not have access to social services geared to adults and the very young.

The authors bring a variety of expertise to their research, Wingert as a sociologist at the University of Western Ontario, Higgitt as a member of the Department of Family Services at the University of Manitoba, and Ristock as a member of the Women's Studies Program and Associate Vice President (Research), also at the University of Manitoba.

Keywords: street youth, homeless youth, participatory research, service delivery, public policy.

1   While there is a lack of valid and reliable data on the number of homeless youth in Canada, there is evidence to suggest that the number of young people without adequate housing is growing. Novac, Serge, Eberle, and Brown (2002) identified four important trends among homeless youth: 1) the incidence is increasing; 2) an increasing number are chronically homeless; 3) the age at which youth become homeless is decreasing, especially for females; and 4) more identify as gay, lesbian, bisexual, or transgendered. Developing the

network of resources and supports to assist youth in the process of transitioning off the street is a challenge facing service providers and policy makers in most urban centres. Yet, many recent initiatives have served to make the street youth population less visible as opposed to addressing the root causes of homelessness. For example, Winnipeg's squeegee ban, which was passed with the ostensible intention of protecting youth, legally sanctioned one of the more socially acceptable ways in which youth earn money in order to survive without offering any alternative method for meeting basic needs. The Winnipeg by-law allows fines up to $1,000 and a jail sentence of up to six months if fines are not paid (National Anti Poverty Organization (NAPO) 1999). Other cities have instituted similar legislation. A number of municipal governments, including Vancouver, Ottawa, Edmonton, Winnipeg, and Saskatoon, have passed anti-panhandling by-laws, which prevents or places restrictions on the act of asking people on the street for money (NAPO 1999). The rationale for panhandling by-laws falls into one of three categories: "the preservation of economic vitality of city areas; the public's right to the peaceful enjoyment of public places; and the eradication of an unhealthy lifestyle" (NAPO 1999: 10). These by-laws coincided with the erosion of welfare benefits, which contributed to rising poverty rates and a greater depth of poverty.

2   Youth poverty rates indicate that a number of Canadian youth are at risk of experiencing difficulty in securing adequate, affordable, and suitable housing. Lee (2000) reported that, based on data from the 1996 Census, urban youth aged 15 to 24 had a 30.7% poverty rate, which varied by city between 10.6% in Burlington and 51.0% in Montreal. Winnipeg has a relatively high youth poverty rate at 30.4% (Lee 2000). The low status of youth in the labour market increases the risk of relative or absolute homelessness for youth who are unable or unwilling to continue living in home or in-care. Relative homelessness is the term used to describe housing that is inadequate, unsuitable, or unaffordable while absolute homelessness refers to a complete lack of stable housing, which includes those living in emergency shelters. The development of services and policies to address the issue of youth homelessness requires an understanding of street youth and life on the streets. The heterogeneity of this population precludes the possibility of a "one size fits all" approach. What works for one subgroup may be ineffective for or unacceptable to another. Furthermore, as the participants in this study describe, youth exercise agency in determining which resources and services they will use and which they will not. Even if services are available, they will not be accessed if they are perceived to be a threat to the safety and autonomy of the youth.

3   The purpose of this research was to explore the experience of being homeless from the perspectives of street-involved youth. The results of our study pertain primarily to younger, chronically homeless youth who represent a growing population. We wanted to know: (1) How youth became involved with the street? (2) What their lives were like on the street? (3) What barriers prevented them from leaving the street? and (4) What facilitated their transition off the street? A key feature of this study was that it was conducted from the perspective of street-experienced youth. This paper will discuss the findings of our research in order to inform initiatives aimed at eradicating youth homelessness.

LITERATURE REVIEW
Defining and Describing the Street Youth Population

4   Estimating the number of street-involved youth is challenging because there is no universally accepted definition of the term *street youth*. A common umbrella definition for this population is persons between twelve and twenty-four years of age without shelter or with inadequate or insecure shelter (Peressini and McDonald 2000). Street youth are primarily distinguished from the adult homeless population by their age, which has important consequences for their street experiences. Adolescence is the transitional period between childhood and adulthood where youth acquire the educational credentials needed to secure employment that will provide adequate income for independent living. Youth who leave home before achieving the milestones of adolescence are often unemployable or marginalized into low skill, low paying jobs, which precludes economic self-sufficiency. Due to their age, many homeless youth do not qualify for social assistance benefits or other income support programs. Antecedent family background, age, gender, race, and sexual orientation have been identified in the literature as sociodemographic characteristics that underlie the likelihood of youths becoming homeless and their street experiences.

5   Street youth have been found to come from a variety of family backgrounds in terms of family structure and social class (Ringwalt, Greene, and Robertson 1998). However, the family environment of most street-involved youth include high levels of dysfunction and/or abuse (CS/RESORS 2001; MacLean, Embry, and Cauce 1999; Ringwalt et al. 1998). Based on a sample of 602 runaway and homeless youth from the Midwestern United States, Yoder, Whitbeck, and Hoyt (2001) found that neglected and sexually abused adolescents were more than three times more likely to run away compared to their non-neglected and non-sexually abused counterparts. Similarly, MacLean et al. (1999) found relatively high rates of physical and sexual abuse among homeless adolescents regardless of whether they had run away, were kicked out, or removed from the home. Hyde (2005) found that while abuse and conflict within the home were central in youths' narratives about the decision to leave home, other factors, such as their own personal or emotional problems or desire to travel, were contributing factors. Not surprisingly, a significant number of street-involved youth have been involved with child welfare systems. In a study of 360 homeless youth in Toronto, Gaetz and O'Grady (2002) found that 43% had lived in foster care. MacLean et al. (1999) found that 17.7% of the 356 homeless youth in their study were removed from their homes by the authorities. More than half of the youth in this category had been sexually abused in their homes.

6   The likelihood of running away has been found to increase with age (Yoder et al. 2001). The challenges in accessing services and resources while on the street also vary by age. For example, youth in their late teen or early twenties often fall through the gap between systems meant for children and those for adults because they are too old for the former and too young for the latter (CS/RESORS 2001; Novac et al. 2002). On the other hand, youth under the age of fourteen who are not in care are particularly vulnerable on the street because

they cannot legally work and do not qualify for social assistance. They may be less aware of supports and services that are available.

7   In addition to age, gender is another variable that influences the risk of street involvement and street experiences. Females represented 58.7% (N = 53,459) reports of runaway children (National Missing Children Services 2003). Other studies have found that females represent one-third to one-half of the urban street youth population (Hagan and McCarthy 1997; Novac et al. 2002). There is evidence that the ratio of females to males is higher at younger age groups (Caputo et al. 1997; Novac et al. 2002). Males are more likely to become homeless after being kicked out of their homes due to deviant behaviour, while females, especially those who have been sexually abused, are more likely to run away (MacLean et al. 1999). Once on the street, females who engaged in substance use, illegal or out-of-the-mainstream subsistence strategies, and risky sexual behaviours were at risk for re-victimization (Whitbeck, Hoyt, and Yoder 1999). Of those youth who engage in prostitution, the majority are female (CS/RESORS 2001). U.S. data suggests that males and White youth are more likely to spend time on the street after running away (Yoder et al. 2001).

8   Aboriginal youth, especially Aboriginal women, are overrepresented (Beavis, Klos, Carter, and Douchant 1997; Kraus, Eberle, and Serge 2001; Novac et al. 2002). Adverse economic conditions, reserve-urban migration as a result of limited opportunities and poor housing on many reserves, racism and discrimination, and physical and mental health conditions have been cited as risk factors that are more prevalent among Aboriginal peoples (Beavis et al. 1997). The lack of culturally sensitive services and resources has been noted as a barrier (CS/RESORS Consulting 2001).

9   Gay, lesbian, bisexual, or transgendered (GLBT) youth are also at-risk for street involvement (Kraus et al. 2001; Gaetz 2004) as a result of rejection from peers at school and family members (Kreiss and Patterson 1997). Studies have shown that a significant number of non-street involved GLBT youth report being threatened with or experiencing verbal, physical, and/or sexual violence (Rivers and Carragher 2003), which may contribute to their alienation from their homes and schools. Whitbeck, Chen, Hoyt, Tyler, and Johnson (2004) found that gay, lesbian, and bisexual (GLB) street youth were more likely to report being kicked out or running away from their homes due to conflicts over their sexuality. GLB youth were more likely to report sexual abuse by a parent or guardian and physical abuse was more common among lesbians compared to heterosexual youth. Gay males engaged in survival sex more often than their heterosexual counterparts. Finally, GLB youth were almost twice as likely to be the victim of physical or sexual violence while on the street.

10   An additional challenge in estimating the street youth population is that Canada lacks national data and systemic measures of youth homelessness. As a result, estimates of incidence and prevalence vary widely. According to National Missing Children Services (2003), 53,459 reports of runaway children and youth were filed, which represents a smaller number of individuals since many left home more than once during the data collection period. However, these figures still underestimate the homeless youth population since cases where youth are evicted by parents or guardians ("throwaways") are not included, nor

are unreported cases of runaway youth. It has been estimated that there are as many as 150,000 homeless youth in Canada (Caputo, Weiler, and Anderson 1997).

STREET INVOLVEMENT

11   The experiences of youth on the street are another source of diversity. Caputo et al. (1997) developed a typology for classifying street-involved youth. At one end of the continuum are curbsiders who rotate between home and the street. Youth in this category tend to engage in more socially acceptable parts of the street lifestyle, such as hanging out and panhandling. On the other end of the spectrum are entrenched street youth with no connection to home. Entrenched youth are often involved in very dangerous aspects of street life, such as drugs, crime, or prostitution. The process of becoming enmeshed in the street lifestyle involves cutting ties with mainstream society, which makes intervention considerably more difficult. Intervention strategies must be tailored to the unique needs of street-involved youth depending on their sociodemographic characteristics, access to shelter, time spent on the street, and level of involvement in the street lifestyle.

12   Once on the street, day-to-day life becomes a constant struggle to meet basic needs, including shelter, safety, food, and money. Street-involved youth often lack the resources to get a job, including a fixed address, identification, education, and job related skills (Dachner and Tarasuk 2002). Those who are employed are usually in low wage and low prestige jobs, which can lead to disconnection from the traditional labour market (Baron 2001; Gaetz and O'Grady 2002). As a result, many youth turn to illegal activities such as prostitution, crime, squeegeeing, or flagging[1] for money (Kraus et al. 2001; Caputo et al. 1997; Gaetz and O'Grady 2002). These activities can create additional problems for youth, including criminal records and an increased risk of being the victim of violence (Ayerst 1999; Kraus et al. 2001; Novac et al. 2002).

13   Many youth turn to drugs, alcohol, and other substances to cope with the harsh realities of street life (Ayerst 1999; Novac et al. 2002). Not surprisingly, youth have a higher prevalence of depression (Ayerst 1999), suicide attempts, and self-harm (Novac et al. 2002) compared to other adolescents. Homeless youth have a higher than average number of health problems combined with a lack of medical attention. Both acute conditions, such as injuries, respiratory infections and dermatological problems, and chronic ailments, including HIV and depression, are more prevalent in this population (Barry et al. 2002; Novac et al. 2002). The literature has reported that many youth wait until health conditions become exacerbated before seeking medical attention. Usually, they turn to emergency medical facilities that are not equipped to provide comprehensive health assessments or preventative education (Deisher and Rogers 1991).

14   Caputo et al. (1997) reported that youth are most receptive to interventions within the first couple of weeks on the street. As they inhabit the street for longer periods of time, they become entrenched in the street lifestyle. Leaving the street is a difficult process because the freedom, power, excitement, and money

available to youth are alluring. In addition, youth learn how to survive on the street and report uncertainty about their ability to function in mainstream society. Youth who make the transition off the street, often encounter difficulties in reintegrating into society. Caputo et al. (1997) reported that stable housing, gainful employment, access to suitable services, and social supports were essential for long-term transition.

METHOD

15   The setting for the current study was Winnipeg, which has a population of approximately 650,000 (City of Winnipeg, 2005). Youth between the ages of 10 and 24 make up 20.4% of the city's population with slightly above average percentages living in non-inner city neighbourhoods (City of Winnipeg B, 2001). About 8.6% of Winnipeg's population identifies as Aboriginal. In inner city areas, Aboriginal peoples make up 19.2% of the population (City of Winnipeg A, 2001). The street youth population in Winnipeg face several challenges. One is that, unlike larger urban centres, Winnipeg has few resources available that are specifically targeted at street youth. At the time of the interviews, only two agencies provided non-shelter related services, such as meals, advocacy, and assistance in reuniting with family. Two agencies provided short-term shelter beds for youth; one was targeted at Aboriginal youth. One long-term transitional facility was being pilot tested at the time of the interviews, but subsequently closed due to a lack of sustainable funding. A second challenge is Winnipeg's cold winters. Most of the youth we interviewed reported that they would travel, usually by hitch hiking, to warmer cities, such as Vancouver, during the winter months and return in the spring. Although Winnipeg does not suffer from housing shortages compared to larger centres in Canada, much of the very low cost housing available on the private market is poor quality, inadequate, or located in undesirable areas (Kraus et al. 2001; Novac et al. 2002).

16   Our goal in undertaking this exploratory study was to gather information from the perspective of street-involved youth and to make policy recommendations based on their experiences, needs, and strengths. The objectives of this project were: 1) to build a working partnership with academic researchers, students, service providers, and at-risk youth; 2) to develop an effective methodology for collaborative research; and 3) to generate research data that will assist in the understanding of the causes and consequences of youth street involvement in order to inform policy and program planning in the area. We used the principles of participatory research to guide this study and meet these goals. Participatory research aims to break down the hierarchical relations between the researcher and the researched by including members of the population of interest as members of the research team. Specifically, we used the mutual engagement model in which academics collaborate with community members to carry out social research that generates results that can be used to effect change within the community or population (Petras and Porpora 1993).

17   In conducting this research from a participatory perspective, we partnered with Operation Go Home (OGH) [2], a not-for-profit agency mandated to provide services to street-involved youth. The research team consisted of two university

researchers, two staff members from OGH, a graduate and undergraduate student, and four street-experienced youth interns. Through a series of team meetings, we collaboratively developed and implemented this research project. During the process, the youth interns shared their experiences and knowledge of street life in order to guide what issues would be explored in the interview. For example, when we started the project, we were interested in exploring health care needs of street youth. However, the interns felt that health care was a less important issue compared to the barriers faced in meeting basic needs and accessing the resources and services needed to leave the street. During our interviews, we found that their perceptions were correct. When asked about their health, most youth said they were in good health; but in the process of discussing other issues most revealed acute and chronic health conditions, which suggests discrepancies in the definition, conceptualization, and contextualization of health and illness.

18   Following approval by the Joint Faculty Ethics Review Board at the University of Manitoba, the university researchers and one of the youth interns conducted in-depth interviews with twelve youth who had street experience. Interviews were conducted between May 22 and September 26, 2002. Each interview lasted about one hour and used a semi-standardized interview schedule. All of the interviews were conducted at a community agency with which the participant was familiar. Participants were recruited using a snowball sampling technique generated using contacts from OGH and the youth interns. Interviews were conducted until data saturation was achieved; that is, no new themes emerged from subsequent interviews. Since the goal of qualitative research is to provide rich description, small sample sizes are warranted. Interviews were audio taped and professionally transcribed. The university researchers and graduate student analyzed the data using thematic analysis. Upon completion of the data analysis, the youth interns were invited to review the findings and provide feedback. Given that we had worked closely with the youth in developing the study, the results of the research were congruent with their experiences and perceptions of street life. The primary goal of the interns who participated in the project was to raise awareness about the issue of youth homelessness since, in their experience, street youth are visible in society, but not well understood. Several youth attended the media launch for the final report of the project and the Winnipeg Street Youth Survival Guide, which was developed as part of the project at the request of our youth interns as a resource and service guide. The youth also reported that they were hopeful that their experience on the project would help them in finding work and educational opportunities.

PARTICIPANTS

19   Our sample was not representative of street youth; however, it did cover a range of youth and street-involvement with overrepresentation of females, those who were in early adolescence when they became street-involved, and youth from Winnipeg. At the time of the interview, half were actively street-involved, two were in the early stages of transition, and one was late in the transition and living independently. The remaining three had been off the street for a year or

more. Those who had transitioned off the street were, on average, older than those who were still street-involved and all were female. One was reunited with her family. Two got onto welfare with the assistance of a community agency. Three were accepted into a long-term transitional housing program operated by OGH. This group had severed their street ties and were unlikely to return, unlike those in transition who were still in a precarious position. Table 1 provides descriptive statistics about the youth in our sample.

Table 1 Sample Descriptive Statistics	
Characteristic	**n**
Sex	
Female	9
Male	3
Age at Interview	
15–17 years	8
18–27 years	4
Race	
Caucasian	7
Aboriginal/Metis	5
Socioeconomic Status	
Working class	5
Middle-class	4
Undisclosed	3
Place of Origin	
Winnipeg	8
Rural Manitoba	3
Vancouver	1
Age at Street-Involvement	
< 15 years	7
15–17 years	3
18 years	2
Duration of Street-Involvement	
< 1 year	2
1–2 years	2
3–4 years	8
Educational Attainment at Street-Involvement	
Not completed junior high	3
Not completed high school	8
Completed high school	1

20   Each of the youth we interviewed shared their stories about how they became street-involved, what their lives were like at that time, and the barriers they faced in leaving the street. Our participants also shared their beliefs about what was needed to transition off the street. Hagan and McCarthy (1997) used Rosenberg's theory of dissonant contexts to analyze the processes of becoming homeless and leaving the street. According to this theoretical perspective, when people find themselves in conflicting contexts as a result of their position in the social hierarchy or personal experiences, they will attempt to resolve the dissonant context by either changing their self-identity, altering their view of the context, or withdrawing from the context. The process of leaving home can be seen as choosing the latter path. For youth whose home lives are filled with dysfunction, conflict, and abuse, the street may offer more rewards and fewer costs.

REASONS FOR BECOMING STREET-INVOLVED

21   Based on their descriptions of the precipitants to leaving home three could be classified as runaways who chose to leave; the remaining nine were throwaways who were kicked out by their parents. The common cause in both groups was family conflicts over parental rules or values to parental substance abuse to physical and emotional abuse. For example:

> My family had a lot of problems and there's a lot of violence in the home, a lot of abuse. Basically, there were so many reasons why we would get kicked out.

> We had the choice of whether we wanted to stay or go back home, basically. And I didn't want to go home because I was having fun, you know. I was fighting with my parents and I felt like freedom.

22   When they first left home, all of the youth perceived that they had no alternative. They did not anticipate that ongoing conflicts would be resolved, which meant that disengagement from their families was the only way to reduce dissonance. However, a few felt that they would be able to return home after a cooling-off period. Usually, these youth had experienced neglect or verbal arguments with parents as opposed to physical or sexual abuse. Youth who had suffered more serious forms of abuse did not feel they could ever return home. In telling their stories, the youth did not portray themselves as victims. They saw themselves as survivors and agents who were in control of their lives.

23   The process of becoming homeless involved becoming increasingly alienated from the systems designed to support young people. Many struggled in school because the stress of their family conflicts inhibited their ability to concentrate on their studies. Several self-identified as having learning disabilities, being alienated by peers or experiencing racism within their communities. Others did not see school as relevant to their life situation. The following quotations reflect some of their experiences in the education system.

[Was school hard?] It wasn't hard as much as it was just not being able to concentrate on anything. Like I knew what I had to do and I knew I could do it and all that but I didn't see any point. [Because of all the trouble at home?] Because of everything, yeah.

They [teachers] didn't know how to teach me. They just didn't understand how to teach me. I have learning disabilities and they didn't understand how to get around them no matter how many times I explained it to them.

When I was in . . . elementary, I was in a predominantly White community so being Native I was like the outcast and people didn't like me and stuff.

24   Many of the young people in our study reported being let down by the child protection system. Those who had contact with the child protection system felt that it did not address their needs. Some were returned home when they felt it was unsafe. Others were shuffled through various living arrangements, including crisis stabilization facilities, foster care, and group homes. In other cases, the child protection system had no contact with youth who were experiencing family distress.

My grandfather still hit me. I ran away back to the city and CFS [Child and Family Services] put me back with my dad . . . My dad put on such a good face, like you know, "I never told my family to leave—I never." He loved me and blah, blah, blah. This is absolutely disgusting because he's mental.

I tried CFS and they just do nothing. They just fucked me over. Honestly, they are just a bullshit organization, and they should get rid of them. Fuck it, they should put some good people in there.

I was in grade eight when my dad starting doing crack and stuff. I didn't know at the time. Nobody really did. He would just sort of disappear for a few hours here and there and turned into a couple of days. And then he got fired from his job . . . I quit school. I got a job and started trying to take care of my brothers . . . And it didn't work. Lost the house. Hit the street.

25   It is evident that the facilitators of youth homelessness are complex. The results of this study suggest that youth become alienated from the systems that are meant to support them. Interventions that strengthen the connection between youth and one or more of these systems may have the potential to preclude street involvement.

LIFE ON THE STREET

26   Youth often experience cycles of being homeless and sheltered, but it is the instability of their housing arrangements that puts them at risk.

27   **Meeting basic needs.** Meeting basic needs was a daily struggle for youth on the street because most did not have reliable access to food and shelter. Food banks and soup kitchens were not widely used because of the perceived risk of food poisoning and an aversion to contact with the adult homeless population. Fast food restaurants and convenience stores were common sources of low-cost food.

To find food, we would do a couple of things. We would dumpster dive and sometimes we would know what time restaurants would be throwing out their food you know like even Tim Horton's when they're throwing out their donuts . . . Sometimes shelters, but not all the time because it depends on what city you're in cause you usually don't want to eat in soup kitchens. You would get food poisoning . . . because where they get their food from it's all like expired food like from Safeway or you know any grocery store . . . The soup kitchens would make slop.

I would eat once a day at 7-eleven. I think it was $2.50 or something to get a hot dog, a drink, and chips.

28   Many youth found shelter by "couch surfing," which involves sleeping on the couches of friends or acquaintances on a rotating basis. Some turned to youth shelters; however, the shelters in Winnipeg and some in other cities imposed maximum stays of less than a week. As a result, youth did not find the stability they needed to make more permanent housing arrangements. Cheap hotels were used by several youth when they had the money. These establishments were perceived as unclean and a haven for parasites. Sleeping outside was common in the summer months. Many youth slept under bridges, in parkades, abandoned buildings, and parks. Occasionally, youth were forced to sleep outside in the winter because they could not find shelter.

I was hanging around with the people I usually hang around with. I was like staying at their houses and then I had nowhere else to stay after that because their parents were getting fed up with me.

It [the shelter] was so scary and they took away everything like our bags and put us in a cubby-hole and stuff like that and we were like no we can't do this we'd rather sleep on the street than you know have some older man like practically on top of you . . . It's absolutely disgusting. So we left and we slept in a stairwell.

I've slept outside on a couch and it's like 35 below and I had a sleeping bag and I woke up later and my feet were just frozen. Just, "Oh my God!" And I ran to [a hotel and bar] and stayed in there for a while and ended up walking around all night so I didn't freeze.

29   **Making money.** None of the youth in our study were able to find and maintain stable employment while living on the street. Lack of education was a major hurdle in finding a decent job.

Squeegeeing makes me more than McDonald's.

I got the job and I lost the job and we lost the apartment and back on the street. And basically that's the pattern that I went through because it was quite obvious that I didn't have the math skills or anything like that. Even the last couple of years that I was in school, I wasn't fully there because of the traumatic things that had happened to me in my home.

30   For the youth in our study, panning, flagging, and squeegeeing were common sources of income. Many treated these pursuits like a job, which they dutifully performed until they had enough money to meet their basic needs. Saving for long-term goals was not common. Some of the entrenched youth turned to criminal activities such as robbery, theft, and drug dealing.

I tried it [panning]. Yeah and then it was embarrassing and felt really stupid . . . I felt really bad because, I don't know, I felt like a bum.

Basically, for money, I would just squeegee. That was before the squeegee ban. So sometimes you would make like fifty cents or like sometimes you would make a few dollars but basically you only made what you needed to eat and survive that day and then you left.

This guy wanted some crack, basically, and I refused to get it for him because, well, first of all, he was three dollars short and my dealer didn't like that. He didn't like being shortened at all so I refused to get it for him . . . He pulled a knife on me and he said I better call my dealer for him or he was going to stab me and I refused to call my dealer . . . And he stabbed me and then he just took off.

31   **Violence.** All of the youth with whom we spoke had witnessed or been the victim of violence while on the street. Street kids often had contact with other groups who spent time on the street, but were not necessarily homeless. Drug dealers, prostitutes, and gang members were a few of the people the youth in our study mentioned as part of their social networks. Often their association with these people led to violent encounters. In addition, stories of police brutality were also common in their narratives.

Yeah like there's a few times that I would go with her [friend who was involved in prostitution] . . . , but then she would leave me with the person and she would take off with the money and I wouldn't see her again and I'd be stuck dealing with this guy because she didn't do her trick or she would steal his wallet . . . And I have gotten beaten up by her clients because I was the second one with her.

Another guy from a gang . . . he was calling me a slut and stuff like that. So I called him a slob and they hated being called slobs. So I called this guy a slob and he pushed me down the stairs and stomped me right in the face, but I still got up and left them.

He [police officer] grabbed me by my leg and nearly suffocated me. Slammed my face against the cop car and then he had the fucking nerve to threaten me that if he ever caught me in the back lane at night ever again he's going to fucking kick the shit out of me.

32   **Substance use.** Using substances as a coping mechanism was a common theme in the youth's stories. Many used prior to becoming homeless, but all used substances to varying degrees while on the street.

When you're on the street, this is just my personal experience, life is the shits. The only thing you can think about is escaping it. How you do that, I think varies from person to person right. I did drugs.

[What makes your life easier or better?] Pot. Honestly, pot. It relaxes me on very, very stressful days. I normally go out and buy a gram and smoke a bowl and sit back and relax.

I'd been drinking all the time because that's about the time I was raped and I was also getting upset about that too and that's when I became an alcoholic.

33   **Health.** Many of the youth in our study described suffering from "street sickness," which was a constant feeling of malaise caused by exposure to the elements, sleep deprivation, lack of nutrition, and poor hygiene. When asked about major

health concerns, all said that they did not have any. Further probing revealed that most did have acute or chronic health conditions. We found that the youth in our study sought medical help only when it was absolutely necessary. Some youth turned to friends when they needed medical care, rather than trained professionals.

> I mean you always have street sickness no matter what. It's just a sickness that you always have like a constant cold and bronchial and feeling ugh from being . . . out all the time and just tired and worn out and stressed out . . . But you don't want to get sick on top of it because, you know, a lot of times you can't afford antibiotic.

> The crack makes you not want to eat so I lost a lot of weight . . . and I had mono once but other than that my health is actually just fine . . . Yeah, I ended up with chronic liver failure because of the crack.

> I would never go to the hospital. I don't like doctors. They don't know what they are doing. All they do is call the police and I don't need bullshit from the boys. I went to my buddy's place and had him sew it [stab wound] up.

BARRIERS TO LEAVING THE STREET

34   All of the youth in our study said that they wanted to leave the street at some point in their lives. Many had attempted to transition off the street, but had been either pulled back into the street lifestyle due to drugs or money or pushed back because they were unable to secure adequate and stable housing. Hagan and McCarthy (1997) found that youth experienced dissonant contexts during the process of transitioning off the street as well. For example, the contexts of work and the street are inherently incompatible. Early in the transition process, the demands of working may exceed the reward, which will lead to a return to the street.

> It is illegal to live on the street and all that, but I enjoy it. I like having a lot of adventures in my life. Everyday is like a new adventure for me.

> What I did is try to get a job . . . You save your money and you get an apartment, but it never worked for me because I was on crack . . .

35   The process of leaving the street was complicated by the lack of short-term and long-term shelter services for youth. In Winnipeg, at the time of the interviews, there were only two short-term shelters specifically for youth; one of which was targeted to Aboriginal youth. Our participants reported that the demand for shelter beds often exceeded the supply. Others chose not to use these services out of fear that they would be apprehended by Child and Family Services or their parents would be contacted. Long-term shelter usually involved going into foster care or a group home. Youth reported that they preferred to avoid services run by child protection agencies because their activities were too rigidly regulated. Some youth had been involuntarily placed in care at these agencies. Participants indicated that child protection agencies often contacted the youth's parents or the police. In some cases, youth were sent home with no ongoing support to correct the problems that had forced the youth to the street in the first place.

> I don't think there's enough cause there is a lot of people on the street. I think there should be more places for youth to go on the street.
>
> No, I couldn't have a cigarette—like that's gonna deal with me. They stick me in a place [crisis stabilization unit] where I can't smoke; I can't even go outside. Of course I'm going to snap.
>
> Yeah, most people think we do this as an option. I mean for me, it's not really an option. I don't want to go to CFS. I just don't like the idea. I like to do things on my own a lot.

36   Participants in our study also reported avoiding service providers who did not specifically cater to youth because they were uncomfortable with the adult clientele who they perceived to have mental health issues.

> I don't think the city realizes that fact that they may put money into, you know, soup kitchens and all these things, but they're more geared for older street adults and they don't recognize the separation.

37   When the youth did seek out services, they often encountered barriers to access. For example, many did not have identification, such as a health card, to access medical services. Many were unable to afford prescription medications. There was also the fear that the service provider would turn them into the police.

> You know some people don't even have ID, medical card to even, you know, see a doctor and most doctors won't accept you [without a medical card].
>
> I went to the hospital. They stitched me up. They said they were going to call CFS and I said I needed to use the washroom. And I went to the washroom and I waited until I could see the orderly's feet walk by cause he was watching me. He wasn't allowed to not watch me. Opened the door real fast and bolted . . . That was really painful though man cause I ripped out a couple of stitches.

38   The youth in our study experienced many barriers to leaving the street. They emphasized that they wanted to leave the street on their own terms and live independently. Many were cognizant of the fact that their lack of education and job skills would make the transition difficult. They struggled to find the stability they needed to begin to build a "normal" life.

> You can't take a kid off the street and put him in a place where they are going to have rules galore because they are not going to stay. It needs to be a stable place. No one's going to mind having a place where they can come and eat and sleep and stuff like that but it can't be a place like where you can't do anything.
>
> The only way it makes me a bit angry is because I wish . . . I did have all my schooling and I was like going forth with that and I could actually get a good job and actually go to university or college . . . but I can't because I still have to get my grade twelve and that affects me so much cause there is so much that I want to do and I won't be able to do that until X number of years so that's where it does make me bitter.

39   Despite the many barriers to leaving the street identified by the youth in our study, many had made progress in leaving the street.

FACILITATORS TO LEAVING THE STREET

40   Youth are often motivated to leave the street after a critical event such as the death of a friend, an arrest, or being threatened by others. Other motivators include disillusionment with street life, hitting rock bottom, fear, and taking on responsibilities (Caputo et al. 1997). Many of the youth in our study who had attempted or succeeded in transitioning off the street cited a particular event that made them decide it was time to leave the street.

> I had a baby and that baby saved me . . . I look back on him and say I'm glad I got pregnant even though his dad and I broke up like a month after I got pregnant. And I look at [him] everyday and know everyday that's why I stopped.

Given that the majority of our sample was female, we anticipated that pregnancy would be a prevalent issue; however, only one participant cited it as a trigger. Some of the youth in our study had a specific timeline during which they planned to leave the street.

> When I turn eighteen, I'm going to start settling down and getting my life back together. Until then, I'm probably going to keep myself lost in the system.

41   After making the decision to leave the street, those who began the process of transitioning did so with the assistance of another person who could help them secure stable housing and financial assistance. For example, one youth reported that he was "adopted" by a friend's mom, who was street-involved as a youth. She provided him with a stable home, food, and emotional support. Despite rejecting child protection agencies, many youth reported that a mentor or exceptional staff person within an agency was instrumental in their transition. One youth said that a social worker advocated for her to get on social assistance and rent an apartment. Several female youth who used services provided by a local street-youth outreach agency were chosen to live in a transitional housing facility that was being pilot tested. Once these resources were secured, the youth began reintegrating into society by seeking out educational, training, or employment opportunities.

> I was on social assistance and I worked with OGH with [an outreach worker]. [And how did you find out about OGH]? Through [a social worker] right after I was at her office, I went straight to OGH. She is with Child and Family Services . . . She's a wonderful woman. You would love her; a cool lady. Basically, that's what I did and [my outreach worker] helped me find an apartment.

> I'm a very independent person. I don't like asking for help. And I'd like die because of the street, you know, like even when I got pregnant and being at [supportive living facility for pregnant women], I put myself back in school and I learned about breastfeeding and doing just a bunch of stuff.

42   When asked about their ideal life, all the participants in our study listed things they wanted to accomplish. None of them saw themselves living on the street in the next few years; however, most said they did not plan for the future. This finding is

not surprising given that most were actively street-involved or had recently transitioned off the street. Youth who were still struggling to meet their basic needs for shelter, food, clothing, safety, and security were not able to develop concrete plans for making their dreams a reality. Youth who were further in the transitions process were working toward goals such as finishing school and starting a career.

> [So do you ever think about where you'll be in a couple of years?] I don't plan for the future. [No? How far ahead do you plan?] I don't.

> Two years, well, I plan to be graduated. Hopefully, I'll be working somewhere—where I'm going to save up for university cause student loans are just—I think they are bullshit. Student loans are bullshit. So I'll be working. Probably have my own apartment. You know, I'll be starting my adulthood in two years.

> I want a car and I want a big house one day. I want a nice house inside with couches and a whole bunch of furniture just to make it look nice and possibly another car. [Why is the house important to you?] Because . . . I've lived in so many houses. I want one of my own now—well not now, but pretty soon.

> I want to be a doctor or a nurse actually cause when my mom gets old and sick then she won't have to travel far to go to the doctor.

DISCUSSION

43   Using a participatory research framework, this study aimed to provide a forum through which homeless youth in Winnipeg could share their stories in order to inform policy and service provision. In-depth interviews with a small sample of participants provided rich description of the processes and experiences associated with becoming homeless, living on the street, and transitioning into mainstream society from the perspective of individuals with street experience. Qualitative research is especially well suited to addressing complex how and why questions that are difficult to explore using quantitative survey methods. Our sample is not representative of the street youth population in Winnipeg or Canada. However, the narratives of these youth can be used to inform future quantitative studies aimed at establishing frequencies, averages, correlational and causal relationships in order to determine to what extent the results of this research are typical or atypical. This type of research can also inform survey construction and design. For example, the use of self-rated health measures is called into question since youth in our study reported their health was good, despite the presence of acute and/or chronic conditions. Questions that ask specifically about symptoms or conditions may yield more valid results. The results of this study serve to inform policy makers and service providers about the needs and preferences of street-involved youth. Eradicating youth homelessness will require a multi-pronged approach that addresses intervention, transition, stabilization, and prevention.

44   Overall, what we learned from our interviews with street youth is consistent with the findings of many other researchers who have examined the issue of youth homelessness. Given that research conducted with samples of several hundred participants yielded similar results suggests that our findings are not unique to this group of homeless youth (although we do not imply that our findings

describe the "average" or universal experience). Homelessness is not a choice that they make freely or easily. Many youth perceive that they have no other alternative to leaving home. The results of this study suggest that homelessness is the outcome of a process whereby youth increasingly become disconnected from the systems that support them, such as family, school, and community. The literature has emphasized family breakdown as the primary cause of youth homelessness, which our findings support; however, some youth become homeless after experiencing school or community conflicts that lead to strained relations with family members. As documented in the literature, once on the street, meeting basic needs becomes the primary goals for most youth, which restricts the time, energy, and resources available to pursue long-term goals that enable youth to transition off the street. Recent policies, such as squeegee bans and panhandling by-laws have made meeting these needs increasingly difficult. In effect, these policies have served to further marginalize street youth from mainstream society. Further research is needed to assess the consequences of these by-laws on street youth. One inadvertent result of these policies may be to speed up the process of becoming entrenched in the street lifestyle. Youth may be forced to resort to crime in order to secure food, clothing, and shelter, which the literature has suggested increases the likelihood of victimization.

45   Research has shown that early intervention is vital in order to prevent entrenchment in the street lifestyle. Since life on the street is about survival, early intervention initiatives should assist youth in meeting their basic needs for food, clothing, and shelter. A finding of this study that is not widely cited in the literature is that street-involved youth portray themselves as agents, not victims. Service providers who were perceived as not respecting the autonomy of street-involved youth were often avoided unless absolutely necessary. Some youth chose to remain homeless instead of going into care in order to maintain their independence. All of the youth we interviewed said that they wanted to leave the street on their own terms; maintaining their autonomy was a critical issue for them. Operating from a philosophy of empowerment is critically important when serving the street youth population, which is a finding that emerges less often from large scale quantitative studies. Based on our interviews, street-involved youth preferred agencies that were not affiliated with child protection systems, which they perceived usurped their right to self-determination. In addition, services exclusively for youth are needed because of their aversion to contact with homeless adults. Drop-in services provide youth with a low-risk opportunity to try out an agency before becoming more deeply involved. Finally, once trust has been established, efforts can be made to link youth to long-term supports to assist with the transition home or into independent living.

46   Adequate and stable housing is the cornerstone of the transition process. Street-involved youth face numerous barriers in their attempts to leave the street, which include inadequate income assistance programs for minors, lack of education, job opportunities, identification, and supports to overcome addiction. A lack of long-term shelter services in Winnipeg was cited by our participants as a major barrier to leaving the street. Most of our interviewees did not want to live in group homes or foster care run by child protection or other agencies that controlled their daily activities. Instead, they wanted to live independently in a

facility with single occupant rooms and common areas for cooking and leisure activities where rules were minimal. The role of staff would be to serve as mentors who would oversee the functioning of the facility and provide support to residents while respecting the autonomy of residents. Operating from a philosophy of empowerment was the key criterion upon which youth decided whether a living facility was acceptable or not.

47   The literature on street youth and the findings of this study have shown that youth in transition also need a coordinated set of services to assist them in breaking free from the street lifestyle. The staff at the facility would be instrumental in providing referrals to other service providers with experience working with street youth. Counselling, legal advice, addictions treatment, and education upgrading were a few of the services our participants said they needed. In order for housing to be acceptable to street-involved youth, rules must be kept to a minimum. Involving residents in developing and maintaining the culture of the transition house was also seen as beneficial.

48   Youth who transition often return to the street several times before they are able to re-establish their lives in the mainstream. The process of stabilizing youth in transition involves the development of a comprehensive, coordinated system of services to assist youth in developing connections with mainstream society. A continuum of services from housing assistance to developing social networks to employment skills are needed over an extended period of time. Youth moving to independent living often face discrimination in the housing market. Some youth said they needed on-going counselling in order to heal from trauma they experienced in their homes and on the street. Several youth cited a lack of money management and budgeting skills as a reason for returning to the street. Connection to a life skills program could help youth develop these and other skills that are needed for independent living. Finding employment was another barrier for the youth in our study. They needed support in getting identification, such as a social insurance number, so they could be hired. Many needed employment skills training and preparation in addition to job search assistance. Finally, youth needed support in developing social networks within the community who could provide informal support during the stabilization process.

49   The final question that remains is: How do we prevent at-risk youth from becoming street-involved in the first place? The results of our study suggest that the contributing factors to homelessness are complex; however, all of the youth we interviewed experienced increasing alienation from their families and schools. Further research is needed to explore how problems within the family can be better addressed. Interviews with parents of at-risk or street-involved youth might reveal gaps in supports for parents of adolescents. In addition, our participants identified gaps within the school system that are worthy of further investigation. Our findings highlight the need for additional resources for students with special needs in school. Better mechanisms for identifying youth who are experiencing family problems and peer conflicts would also be beneficial.

50   A key finding of our study was that many youth fell between the cracks of systems meant to serve adults and those for children. For example, many youth rejected involvement with child protection agencies, but were ineligible for

social assistance, which left few alternatives to homelessness. It is evident that child protection agencies need to develop separate approaches to working with youth that respect their autonomy as decision-makers. Social programs could also help support youth if criteria were revised to include persons under the age of majority. Future studies might explore gaps in Canada's social safety net that exclude youth. These combined initiatives would strengthen the ties between youth and mainstream society by providing alternatives to homelessness.

51   At the heart of youth homelessness are larger issues of poverty, lack of afford-able housing, unemployment, gaps in social services, family violence, social isolation and a myriad of other social problems. These problems are not unique to street-involved youth; rather, they affect all marginalized and oppressed groups. It is beyond the scope of this research to make recommendations on these macro-level factors; however, broader social change is needed to completely eliminate the problem of youth homelessness. Finally, more specific research is needed to explore the experiences and needs of Aboriginal, GLBT, and female street youth in order to develop better prevention and intervention strategies.

ACKNOWLEDGMENTS

This research project was financially supported by the Winnipeg Inner-city Research Alliance (WIRA) which is funded by the Social Sciences and Humanities Research Council (SSHC) and Canada Mortgage and Housing Corporation (CMHC).

NOTES

1. Flagging refers to sitting or standing on the sidewalk or median of a street holding a sign asking for money.

2. In Spring 2005, Operation Go Home (OGH) changed its name to Resource Assistance for Youth (RAY).

REFERENCES

Ayerst, S. L. 1999. Depression and stress in street youth. *Adolescence 34* (135): 567–576.

Baron, S. W. 2001. Street youth labour market experiences and crime. *Canadian Review of Sociology and Anthropology 38* (2): 189–215.

Barry, P. J., J. Ensign, and S. H. Lippek. 2002. Embracing street culture: Fitting health care into the lives of street youth. *Journal of Transcultural Nursing 13* (2): 145–152.

Beavis, M. A., N. Klos, T. Carter, and C. Douchant. 1997. Literature review: Aboriginal peoples and homelessness. Ottawa: Canada Mortgage and Housing Corporation.

Caputo, T., R. Weiler, and J. Anderson. 1997. *The street lifestyle study*. Ottawa: Office of Alcohol, Drug, and Dependency Issues: Health Canada.

City of Winnipeg. 2005. Population of Winnipeg. Winnipeg: Author.

City of Winnipeg A 2001 Census data: Inner-city. 2001. Ottawa: Community Data Network, Custom Tabulation, Statistics Canada.

City of Winnipeg B 2001 Census data: Non-inner city. 2001. Ottawa: Community Data Network, Custom Tabulation, Statistics Canada.

CS/RESORS Consulting. 2001. Gap analysis of literature on issues related to street-involved youth. Ottawa: Research and Statistics Division, Department of Justice Canada.

Dachner, N. and V. Tarasuk. 2002. Homeless "squeegee kids": Food insecurity and daily survival. *Social Science and Medicine 54*: 1039–1049.

Deisher, R. W. and W. M. Rogers. 1991. The medical care of street youth. *Journal of Adolescent Health 12*: 500–503.

Gaetz, S. 2004. Safe streets for whom? Homeless youth, social exclusion, and criminal victimization. *Canadian Journal of Criminology and Criminal Justice 46* (4): 423–455.

Gaetz, S. and B. O'Grady. 2002. Making money: Exploring the economy of young homeless workers. *Work, Employment, and Society 16* (3): 433–456.

Hagan, J. and B. McCarthy. 1997. *Mean streets: Youth crime and homelessness.* New York: Cambridge University Press.

Hyde, J. 2005. Understanding young people's transitions into homelessness. *Journal of Adolescence 28*: 171–183.

Kraus, D., M. Eberle, and L. Serge. 2001. Environmental scan on youth homelessness. Ottawa: Canada Mortgage and Housing Corporation.

Kreiss, J. L. and D. L. Patterson. 1997. Psychosocial issues in primary care of lesbian, gay, bisexual, and transgender youth. *Journal of Pediatric Health Care 11*: 266–274.

Kurtz, R D. and G. L. Kurtz. 1991. Problems of maltreated runaway youth. *Adolescence 26* (103): 543–556.

Lee, K. K. 2000. Urban poverty in Canada: A statistical profile. Ottawa: Canadian Council on Social Development.

MacLean, M. G., L. E. Embry, and A. M. Cauce. 1999. Homeless adolescents' paths to separation from family: Comparison of family characteristics, psychological adjustment, and victimization. *Journal of Community Psychology 27* (2): 179–187.

National Anti Poverty Organization. 1999. Short changed on human rights: A NAPO position paper on anti-panhandling by-laws. Ottawa: Author.

National Missing Children Services. 2003. National missing children services 2003 reference report. Ottawa: Royal Canadian Mounted Police.

Novac, S., L. Serge, M. Eberle, and J. Brown. 2002. On her own: Young women and homelessness in Canada. Ottawa: Status of Women Canada.

Peressini, T., and L. McDonald. 2000. Urban homelessness in Canada. In *Canadian cities in transition: The twenty-first century*, ed. T. Bunting and P. Filion 2000, 535–545. Don Mills: Oxford University Press Canada.

Petras, E. M., and D. V. Porpora. 1993. Participatory research: Three models and an analysis. *The American Sociologist 24* (1): 107–126.

Ringwalt, C. L., J. M. Greene, and M. J. Robertson. 1998. Familial backgrounds and risk behaviours of youth with thrownaway experiences. *Journal of Adolescence 21*: 241–252.

Rivers, I. and D. J. Carragher. 2003. Social-developmental factors affecting lesbian and gay youth: A review of cross-national research findings. *Children & Society 17*: 374–385.

Whitbeck, L. B., X. Chen, D. R. Hoyt, K. A. Tyler, and K. D. Johnson. 2004. Mental disorder, subsistence strategies, and victimization among gay, lesbian, bisexual homeless and runaway adolescents. *The Journal of Sex Research 41* (4): 329–342.

Whitbeck, L. B., D. R. Hoyt, and K. A. Yoder. 1999. A risk-amplification model of victimization and depressive symptoms among runaway and homeless adolescents. *American Journal of Community Psychology 27* (2): 273–296.

Yoder, K. A., L. B. Whitbeck, D. R. Hoyt. 2001. Event history analysis of antecedents to running away from home and being on the street. *American Behavioral Scientist 45* (1): 51–65.

Active Reading

1. Notice that the article lists key words at the beginning. These are helpful in conducting library searches for similar articles, but they can also help readers to understand the meaning of the article at hand. Find the key words in the article and define each as it is used.

2. Look over the section labelled "Literature Review." Are the authors working with a variant of the CARS (create a research space) strategy recommended in Chapter 6 as a way to begin your research argument? Do they survey the field to locate a gap, and then propose to fill it? To how many sources do they refer?

Critical Reading

1. The study focuses on the situation of youth in Winnipeg. To what extent might the research extend to address the dilemma of street youth in other urban communities? (The method does not set out to establish generalizable patterns, but it does initiate the process of articulating themes or common threads.)

2. How do you think these authors might respond to calls from community members to make squeegeeing illegal or to increase surveillance and policing of homeless youth? To calls for increased social services and educational opportunities?

"Defining Girl Homelessness" from *More than Bricks & Mortar: A Rights-Based Strategy to Prevent Girl Homelessness in Canada*

Asia Czapska, Annabel Webb, and Nura Taefi

In this excerpt from a government report, the authors bring to light the situation surrounding girls who are homeless. They point out that many are invisible, because they seek safety from the streets by taking refuge in temporary places—on a friend's couch, in an older man's apartment. The authors point out that more research needs to be done on this group.

WHAT IS GIRL HOMELESSNESS?

1   Girl homelessness is any situation in which a teenage girl is living on the street, in a park or other outdoor environment, or in housing that is unstable, unsafe or otherwise inadequate. The United Nations has articulated that the right to adequate housing is not simply a roof over one's head. The UN Committee on Economic, Social and Cultural Rights has defined the right to adequate housing more broadly:

> The right to housing should not be interpreted in a narrow or restrictive sense which equates it with . . . the shelter provided by merely having a roof over one's head . . . . Rather it should be seen as the right to live somewhere in security, peace and dignity. [3]

2   The right to live in security and dignity is especially important in light of the fact that teenage girls who are homeless and otherwise inadequately housed are subject to extreme violence and degrading conditions of living.

COUCH SURFING

3   When girls are first on their own, many "couch surf" for days, weeks and months at a time. Girls we interviewed frequently started sleeping temporarily at friends' houses when they first left home. Girls would eventually be compelled to leave these temporary living arrangements as the friends they were relying on were also living in poverty and were not able to support an added person and/ or host parents became afraid of criminal sanction for housing them.[4]

4   Couch surfing does not always refer to staying on friends' couches, as one young woman describes:

> If I didn't have a place to stay, or a dealers' house to stay at, I slept anywhere I could. I'd get drunk and sleep at a strangers' house . . . I didn't feel safe, but when you're drunk and high you don't care if you wake up or not.

5   In 2004 the Wilder Research Centre found that "the number of homeless children and/or youth living 'doubled up' or in precarious housing situations was almost 2.7 times higher than the number of children or youth in emergency shelters." Certainly, the number of girls who are homeless and couch surfing is much higher than the number of girls who are staying in youth shelters.

ABSOLUTE HOMELESSNESS

6   Despite the perception that homeless teenage girls do not often "sleep rough," homeless girls in fact often sleep outside in parks, stairwells of buildings, or on sidewalks when they do not have a place to stay. They also sleep in abandoned derelict buildings ("squats"). Many girls we spoke to had experienced "absolute homelessness." One young woman talked about being sexually assaulted while sleeping in a park:

> I woke up one night and some guy was trying to feel me up in my sleeping bag.

Another young woman described:

> When I first slept in a park I was 10 years old. I ran away.

This young woman at age 20 is still sometimes forced to stay in parks. She described how her fear of attack prevents her from falling asleep when she is sleeping outside.

7   One young woman talked about how as a teenage girl she would burn free newspapers to stay warm on the street:

> I used to go to those free mail boxes, you know the ones with the free newspaper, and I'd take the newspaper out of there and lay it on the ground and then we'd burn some of it to keep warm or to sleep on it on the ground . . . in the park . . . .

Another young woman told us:

> If you have no place to go you just curl up and go to sleep and you wake up the next day.

8   Several of the girls described sleeping in squats (abandoned derelict build-ings). Girls described squats as extremely unsafe. One young woman who found herself living in a squat at the age of 15 or 16 described how bitterly cold it was inside during the winter, while another reported being in a squat fire where she almost lost her life, and another described living in a squat full of garbage and bloody needles.

9   Although one teenage girl described the conditions of the squat she had lived in as unsafe, she eventually became detached and desensitized from her surroundings:

> When you've been living with stuff for so long you're not scared, and don't think it's wrong that you're used to it.

10   Young women experience extreme male violence in squats that are dominated by male peers. The following is a poignant statement about the extreme conditions of violence and environmental hazards that young women are subject to in squats:

> In most of them, there was exposed asbestos, strangers coming and going, incidents of rape and theft, police brutality, rats, dead pigeons, animal and human feces and urine, broken glass, rusty nails, holes in the floors and ceilings, mould, extreme coldness and a number of other physical hazards.
>
> I can remember at least four times being badly beaten by men in "squats" and on the street. One time I was so badly beat that I could not move for three days, I have to have people pick me up and put me in a bath. A street worker finally noticed that both my eyes were red where the white was supposed to be and, fearful that I had a major head injury judging from the bruises on my head and face, took me to the hospital.[5]

LIVING WITH OLDER MEN TO HAVE A PLACE TO STAY

11   When governments fail to provide safe accessible housing for homeless girls, older exploitive men step in. Girls who are homeless "trade" sex with older men in exchange for a place to stay. The majority of the girls we spoke with had lived or were living with older males in order to survive. Activists who work with home-less girls explained that girls often end up living with older men because they don't have enough money from adult income assistance[6] to live on their own. Many girls described situations in which they were 14 or 15 and met a "boyfriend" in his 20s–30s (and sometimes much older) and began living with him because they didn't have a place to stay.

SINGLE ROOM OCCUPANCY HOTELS

12   Young women who live in poverty, especially those with addictions, are forced to live in the most deplorable environments in the form of Single Room Occupancy (SRO) suites. These single rooms in rooming houses are often infested with bed bugs, cockroaches and rodents, inhabited by violent predatory men, and toxic with environmentally hazardous chemicals, building materials and pesticides. Many young women live in these hotels.

13   The majority of SROs are privately owned and therefore are not commonly regulated by the government. SROs usually fail to meet even the most basic standards of sanitation and building services. Neglect of desperately needed building repairs has resulted in deaths, as fire escapes and emergency exits are barred or blocked making them inaccessible for tenants.[7] People living in SROs lack protection from the elements, access to safe water and sanitation, and affordable, safe and secure housing at the whim of their landlords.[8] In some cases, it has even been reported that building managers require tenants to leave their rooms for a day or two in order to circumvent the law that states that residents acquire permanent tenancy after thirty days. These evictions put young women on to the street for a day or two of every month, a practice which makes them the "relative homeless."

EXTENT OF THE PROBLEM

14   In May 2006, the UN Committee on Economic, Social and Cultural Rights reviewed Canada's housing and homelessness record and declared homelessness in Canada a "national emergency."

15   Teenage girls constitute between 30–50% of the homeless youth in big cities across Canada[9] and make up between 6–12% of all homeless people in large Canadian cities.[10] Federal, provincial and territorial governments are failing to respond to teenage girl homelessness. Income assistance and child welfare agencies' responses to violence against girls are dismal.

16   Most youth housing and shelters across Canada have not begun to deal with sexism and the issues that affect homeless girls. Indigenous girls are highly overrepresented among homeless girls. At the same time, lesbian and racialized girls are missing from homelessness research and their needs remain unmet within youth housing programs. Girls who flee male violence or homophobia in their family home, or the racism and alienation they experience in foster homes, do not get the housing they need or deserve. Despite all of this, reports on youth homelessness rarely discuss the specific experience of homeless girls. Most reports, youth shelters and government programs for homeless youth fail to respond to the needs of girls, and the needs of Aboriginal, racialized and lesbian girls in particular.

17   Homeless girls move between numerous unsafe living situations. The story of Zara is a common one: Zara's step-dad sexually abused her when she was a child. At school, she was teased by kids who called her "fat." She was holding in a lot of anger and pain from the sexual abuse and brought a knife to school thinking she could protect herself from the taunts. At age 13 her mom told her to leave home because she could not cope with the anger her daughter was feeling. The children's ministry moved Zara through group homes where she was teased, foster homes where she felt like a "paycheque," and "sterile" safe houses.[11] She slept in parks—where she was sexually assaulted—and couch surfed. At age 15 she met a 25-year-old boyfriend who "gave" her a place to stay and got her hooked on heroin. Now, at age 20, Zara is living in a rooming house in the Downtown Eastside, where her landlord recently tried to break into her room while she was changing.

18   The girls and young women we spoke with are continuously moving through unsafe living environments, negotiating their safety with predatory older men in exchange for a place to stay, and are constantly searching for a stable safe place to live.

19   The issue of teenage girl homelessness has only recently been explored.[12] *On Her Own*, the first Canadian report on young women and homelessness in Canada, concluded that very little was known and documented about girls' experiences of homelessness. Likewise, little had so far been discovered about prevention and what steps should be taken to provide teenage homeless girls with safe, accessible, affordable housing or what constitutes safe housing for girls.

20   Most of the girls interviewed by Justice for Girls became homeless (left or were made to leave their family home, foster home or group home) between the ages of 12 to 14. Almost all had become homeless between 11 and 19, with a majority becoming homeless before age 16. It has been noted by researchers that among younger youth (under 15) homeless girls outnumber homeless boys.[13]

21   Similarities in the experiences of the young women we interviewed include: experiences of sexual abuse, "couch surfing," living with an older boyfriend to have a place to stay, sleeping in a park, and distrusting the children's ministry. Many of the girls we interviewed made attempts to attend school even while homeless (including while couch surfing and sleeping in parks). Almost every girl we interviewed said that girl-only housing was important or very important. Girls named sexual harassment and sexual assault in co-ed housing as a primary reason for why girl-only housing matters.

NOTES

3. Office of the High Commissioner for Human Rights. General Comment Number 4, Article 11(1) International Covenant on Economic, Social and Cultural Rights. 1991.

4. Under Criminal Code Sections 280–283, it is a criminal offence to house a young person under the age of 16 without the consent of their parent.

5. Statement of Canadian Young Woman #1. "Memorandum of Justice for Girls Regarding the Right of Teenage Girls to Adequate Housing in Canada, For Consideration by Mr. Miloon Kothari, United Nations Special Rapporteur on Adequate Housing." Washington, DC. October 15–17, 2005.

6. Throughout this report we refer to the adult social assistance scheme as adult income assistance.

7. San Francisco Tenants Union. "2005 Hotel Fire Displacing Tenants." www.sftu.org (retrieved August 2005); Foley, D. "Hellish Conditions at Single-Room Occupancy Hotels." *The Body Positive.* 11(8) (1998):18–23. New York: Body Health Resources Corporation.

8. Shannon, Kate, Tomiye Ishida, Calvin Lai and Mark W. Tyndall. "The Impact of Unregulated Single Room Occupancy Hotels on the Health Status of Illicit Drug Users in Vancouver." *International Journal of Drug Policy.* 17(2) (2006):107–114.

9. Canadian Housing and Renewal Association. *On Her Own: Young Women and Homelessness in Canada.* Ottawa, ON. March 2002.

10. Ibid.

11. A "safe house" is a short-term coeducational emergency placement for youth who are homeless, similar to a youth shelter but situated in a house.

12. Most notably, the recent report *On Her Own: Young Women and Homelessness in Canada* has looked at homeless young women's experiences.

13. City of Vancouver Social Planning Department. *Homeless Street Youth in Downtown South: A Snapshot Study.* Vancouver, BC. 2002.

Active Reading

1. What elements are part of the condition of "absolute homelessness"?

2. Are girls particularly vulnerable to violence and sexual abuse?

3. How do Canadian and international laws offer different protections to children's rights?

Critical Reading

1. The article claims that teen girls constitute "between 30–50% of the homeless youth" and "between 6–12% of all homeless people" in big Canadian cities. These numbers are relatively low. How do the arguments in the article help us to appreciate their significance? If you wanted to argue that there is no crisis for girls, could you cite these same statistics? Discuss with reference to the demand that the writer attempt to be fair-minded in using source material (raised in the chapter on critiquing sources).

2. Another statement the article makes is that the subject of girl homelessness "has only recently been explored." Could the fact that research is just beginning mean that some of the data that the authors present may be revised, pending further, more in-depth studies?

"A Sick System Creates Sick People" from *All Our Sisters*

Susan Scott

In this article (from a full-length book studying different aspects of the lives of women living in poverty in Canada), Scott surveys what experts have said about the link between poverty and illness. She follows her analysis with several case studies that illuminate the struggles women undergo when they are challenged by mental and/or physical illness. Scott takes a case study approach to make the point that since no two lives are the same, we must avoid generalizing or stereotyping; she also wants to give a voice to people who are too often silenced in a system in which power and money are linked.

Susan Scott is a freelance writer who worked for many years at the Calgary Herald. She is the author of No Fixed Address: Tales from the Street *(Calgary Drop-in Centre). As a follow-up to* No Fixed Address, *which profiled the homeless in Calgary shelters, she released* All Our Sisters, *based on interviews with 60 women about the plight of homeless women in Canada.*

> *This is Wednesday. We are in a meeting. Please call back next week.*
>
> —Vancouver woman commenting on
> her mental health worker

1   Ask any homeless woman about her health and, depending on her stoicism, she will probably list a number of conditions that might include heart problems, fibromyalgia, sore knees and feet, breathing difficulties, hepatitis C, depression, osteoporosis, HIV/AIDS, and diabetes, to name but a few. Although most will not even bother to mention it, many also have severe gum and dental problems that are not only painful but that also contribute to heart disease, diabetes, breathing difficulties, and premature births. Of course, not everyone has all these problems, but health issues take their toll. Conditions are so bad on the street that at least one social housing complex on Vancouver's Downtown Eastside has lowered the qualifying age for a senior to 45 because homeless women at that age are in the same kind of physical shape as their middle-class sisters at 65.

2   In 2004 Angela Cheung and Stephen Hwang released a study on the mortality rates of homeless women in Toronto. It showed that in the 18–44 age bracket, they are 10 times more likely to die than women in the general population and that they are dying at about the same rate as homeless men of a similar age, losing women's universal advantage of greater longevity. No one should have been surprised; the wonder is that homeless women aren't dying even faster.

3   One problem is the quality and quantity of the food; scarcely a broccoli stalk is to be spotted in shelters where donuts are donated by the dozen. Another, as we learned in the last chapter, is violence. There is the exhaustion that comes from walking to numerous appointments in ill-fitting, second-hand shoes and the stress that comes from not having a home and from fearing the children will be taken away by social services. Some feel they have no choice but to give or sell their bodies in return for a bed or for cash to support a drug habit—and then there are all the risky behaviours associated with that. It's difficult to take meals and medication regularly when one is constantly on the move and has no safe place to store pills or insulin syringes. Without a fixed address, it's almost impossible to find a family doctor and the women are often reluctant to make appointments. And it's easy to pick up lice, colds, flu, tuberculosis, and other diseases in the crowded conditions of many shelters. This situation is exacerbated now that hospitals release people so much earlier, never enquiring whether the patient has a home to go to and the means to get there. They stumble back to shelters where bed rest is impossible, and then they proceed to infect everyone else.

4   On average, homeless people have eight to nine concurrent medical illnesses, says Dr. Martin Donohoe (2004). He lists dermatological conditions, respiratory infections, tooth decay, foot problems, vision problems, sexually transmitted infections, hypertension, asthma, diabetes, and mental illness, in particular depression, schizophrenia, PTSD, and personality disorders. He says that in the US, mental illness is reported in 30 per cent of homeless people, rising to 50 to 60 per cent in women. In conversation, staff at shelters across the country put that figure even higher, arguing that homelessness can trigger depression. It's tempting to separate mental health from physical health, because there is so much to say about both, but on the streets the two are even more obviously entwined than in the rest of the population.

5   Some of the factors that make it hard to treat homeless people include more vulnerability to crime and violence, prolonged standing, excessive outdoor exposure, overcrowding, risk of being robbed of medication, limited access to showers and dental care, inability to follow complex regimens, lack of privacy, and social isolation. On top of this, there may well be tobacco use, sleep deprivation, dehydration, drug use, and extreme long-term stress that creates physical and hormonal changes and physical and emotional trauma. Homeless women have little access to the media to lean about good nutrition and healthy lifestyles; even if they have such knowledge, it takes cash to buy fruit and a fitness club membership.

6   Homeless women are less likely to have a family doctor than other women, so they are apt to turn up at emergency departments after their situation has deteriorated into a medical crisis. They cite a number of reasons why they don't visit doctors regularly. They are ashamed of not having an address and feel intimidated; they don't have the bus fare or the phone money to make an appointment; they are unable to find a doctor; and, if they have been sexually assaulted, they fear flashbacks. Medical visits during pregnancy, or for mammograms and Pap smears (to prevent cancer of the cervix, more prevalent in women with multiple sexual partners), are all likely to trigger strong reactions in women who have been sexually abused. "It's heartbreaking because I know the fear they go through," says Cori Keating, a Vancouver outreach worker who has helped develop Pappaloosa, a program designed to make Pap smears less terrifying.

7   Women view health as a private matter, so it is very embarrassing for them to give physical details to receptionists in busy waiting rooms full of men also hoping to see the doctor, or to give personal information in front of a crowd waiting to enter detox. Once with a doctor or counsellor, women are reluctant to answer questions like "Were you ever sexually abused?" unless a rapport has been built up, which is difficult to establish during a brief assessment. Because there is no family doctor to monitor their health care, nor even a regular pharmacist, homeless women are very likely to be prescribed medications that react badly with each other or with street drugs that they might be taking, thereby compounding their problems.

8   In recent years many psychiatric beds across the country were closed down with the admirable aim of supporting people with mental illness "in the community." Those supports have failed to emerge in either sufficient numbers or in ways that are always helpful to consumers, as mental health patients are often called. Without a safe place, it is hard to deal with schizophrenia, bi-polar disorder, and depression, and many street workers say there just isn't the help available to deal with the deep trauma affecting many homeless women. Women also report that while they may be quite prepared and happy to stand by their man should he run into problems, they don't find the support is reciprocated. Men tend to disappear fast, often moving on to another relationship and leaving the woman at an even higher risk of becoming homeless. If their partner vanishes, the system seems at best ineffective and at worst downright harmful.

9   "The popular image of a person sitting on a couch receiving therapy makes me laugh. It's not therapeutic. It's about diagnosis, prescribing and monitoring,"

says a woman with a long experience of dealing with the mental health system, adding that visiting a psychiatrist is like "putting your head in a lion's mouth and expecting to be made well." She reported having to stand in line for the bathroom and for medication at psychiatric facilities and of being jumped on by guards, stripped naked, and locked in a room. Because she has never gone to hospital willingly, she also has the word "violent" attached to all her files. "If women are angry, it's a problem; there's more tolerance for men if they are angry," she says.

10   The physically sick, too, find there's one system for the rich and another for the poor. Some hospital staff and addictions workers seem to believe that the homeless are not entitled to confidentiality or respect like anyone else. Women recall hearing nurses say things like, "Don't worry, she's just a hooker." Toronto street nurse Kathy Hardill says one of the problems is that the current medical model does not look at patients as people nor at the context in which their illness occurs; therefore, homeless women are blamed for their poverty and when they inevitably become ill, they are blamed for not taking care of themselves even though the situation was not of their making.

11   As middle-class women strive to swallow their vitamins and to exercise regularly, it is worth reflecting on the huge body of research that clearly demonstrates that the greatest predictor of a healthy life is a decent income. In other words, poverty makes you sick. According to York University professor Dennis Raphael:

> The strong link between income and disease is one of the most well-established findings in the health sciences but the least publicized by health care and public health workers, and the media. The link occurs across a wide range of diseases, but the strongest association is with cardiovascular disease. It has been demonstrated time and time again—in Canadian, United States, and United Kingdom, and other studies—that the illness-producing effects of low income swamp the influence of medical and lifestyle risk factors such as cholesterol levels, hypertension, tobacco use, quality of diet, physical activity, and body/mass index among others. Yet, all we hear about from the medical and public health communities is about cholesterol screening, drug therapies and lifestyle changes. (Raphael 2002)

12   Raphael says it goes even further, that childhood poverty haunts one for life; the poor are much more likely to die at a younger age than people who were raised in comparatively wealthy homes. Poor families have much higher than average infant mortality rates and more low birth weight babies, frequently resulting in chronic problems. Poor children frequently lack nutritious food, and although their needs are greater, they make fewer visits to doctors, dentists, and other professionals. They can suffer stunted physical and mental development and have a low resistance to infection, often living in areas where there are environmental hazards like traffic emissions or lead paint. In addition, there is the shame of not being able to participate in organized sports or group activities, not having a lunch to take to school, wearing second-hand clothes, and not having the same books and toys as the other kids.

13   However, middle-class people should not be complacent that their bank accounts will enable them to lead if not the good, then the healthy life. The poor

are the canaries of society: societies with higher levels of poverty have higher mortality rates. Raphael (2000) cites a study that shows that, after years of increasing economic polarization, the richest people in Britain now have higher adult male and infant mortality rates than the poorest people in Sweden, a cautionary tale for Canadians as our poor become even poorer.

Naomi

14 *Naomi was left to fend for herself on the streets of Winnipeg because of her severe psychiatric condition. It wasn't until she met an outreach worker willing to support her on an ongoing basis that she finally found and was able to keep a home. In May 2005 she was silenced forever. Like so much in her life, the cause of death was not made known; it was speculated, however, that it might have been caused by an accidental overdose.*

15 Naomi walks into the filthy hotel coffee shop and greets the waitress boisterously. The greeting is not reciprocated. Naomi's noisy and erratic behaviour has caused her to be barred from many similar hotels on Winnipeg's Main Street that are happy to accommodate drunks, addicts, pimps and prostitutes, but not her. She is very loud, and the two or three other people in the coffee shop perforce listen in on the interview. She has recently returned from a hitchhiking trip to British Columbia and, as a result, has missed a couple of the monthly shots that keep her schizophrenia from swinging out of control.

16 Naomi, who is 48, wants to talk about Tony, her boyfriend. No one, apart from Naomi, has seen Tony—"he's shy, you see"—but her life revolves around him. She consults Tony before every move and does nothing unless it meets with his approval. Whether he is, or was, a real person, or a fantasy that has subsumed her is an open question. That he is important to Naomi is in no doubt. Like it or not, real or imagined, he comes first in her life and in her heart. Naomi says they met at the Salvation Army, although Tony has his own home. Sometimes she locates it in the country; at others it's in a different part of Winnipeg. At times she waffles on details, especially when pressed by social workers; at others she is very precise—his birthday, for instance, is February 26. She says that they meet daily for coffee or at a soup kitchen, and he gives her advice, frequently contradicting her outreach worker, although sometimes he can be in complete agreement with the caregivers.

17 Naomi's childhood was spent on a farm in Ontario. The first time she tells the story, she had a good childhood, but several versions later she says her mother spent most of her time in bed, emerging from her room only for meals. However, when she took Naomi and her sister to the cottage, she was just fine. It may be significant that her father was not present on these trips. Naomi's mother wanted to work but was forbidden to do so by the father. When she did eventually leave him to go to Toronto and a job, her fatigue disappeared and she thrived.

18 Naomi appears to have got along for the most part with both parents and is grateful to her father for instilling in her various interests. She makes frequent references to watercolour painting, singing in a choir, and most of all cooking—Thai

food, cabbage rolls, blueberry cake, and a chicken dish with mint and almonds. In fact, many of her hopes for the future revolve around creating the home she doesn't have and cooking for herself and Tony.

19   Naomi left school in Grade 10 because she couldn't concentrate and went to work in a Toronto bar where she says she did a variety of jobs from keeping bar to the night audit and cooking. It was while working there she met her husband. Although "a nice guy," the relationship lasted only a few months. Naomi left the bar, went to work as a teller at Green Road Race Track, and then trained as a chef, working her way up the culinary ladder to make good money in a three-star restaurant. She's glad she did it but wouldn't want to be in the food business again because the work is too hard for someone with multiple health problems.

20   At this point, her story takes a few confusing turns, involving several falls downstairs in which she seems to have broken her ankle at least twice. She rolls up her leggings to display the vicious scars where it was set with the help of pins. "I broke my ankle, hurt my back, and I'm incontinent, so they put me in a psychiatric hospital; they had to have a place to put me. I get needles now for my thoughts," she says, convinced that the hospitalization was all about her physical, not her mental health and that she ended up on a psychiatric ward because of a shortage of beds.

21   Naomi does recall some of the reasons why she is banned from so many of Winnipeg's cheap hotels, but in her version usually someone else started a fracas by pushing her or being lippy. She appears to have very little awareness of the effect of her penetrating voice and insistent conversational style, but for an observer it is easy to see how people lose patience with her and that she's not above losing patience herself.

22   After a lot of hunting, Naomi's outreach worker found her a small apartment where she seemed to be doing well. On a routine check, she found a note from Naomi saying she had left for Vancouver. This was considered progress, because previously Naomi would have gone with no communication at all. Naomi thumbed her way and lived at shelters while on the West Coast. Now that she's back, she wants her own room again before she and Tony move in together, but she's worn out her welcome at most of the places she can afford on social assistance. Finally, her outreach worker has found a cheap hotel with a manager who is warily willing to work with her to keep Naomi housed and stable.

23   The hotel appears quite clean, despite the drinking party going on in a nearby room at 10 a.m. The door is sturdy and the lock new. The bed is still unmade from the previous person; the toilet and the bath are down the hall. Naomi and her worker agree that it's better than many they have seen and decide to take it. The price, of course, is the maximum that welfare allows for a single person's rental accommodation. Tony will be okay with it, observes Naomi. The caseworker looks relieved. It's a sign that Naomi, too, will be okay with it. "Please, please let me know if you think she is running into trouble," says the outreach worker to the manager, "then we can head it off before anything happens."

24   Naomi is oblivious to their concerns. She's indignant that other places won't give her a room when she believes she is a model citizen. Her piece said, she turns to a practicum student working with the social worker. "You know Tony has

a friend called Garry. Would you like to meet him? He's nice, and I've told him that you are single." When the student says that she's leaving, Naomi replies, "You will have to come back and stay with Tony and me. We are going to get a little house and I can cook for you. It will be really nice."

Amy

25 *Although Amy hasn't had an epileptic seizure in four years, employers are reluctant to give her work. Amy and her husband, who has a back injury, have a hard time providing for their children. They would much prefer to be employed.*

I spoke with Amy and her two young daughters at a New Westminster drop-in centre.

26 It's spring break, and the family is at the drop-in because they have run out of food. They went to a food bank the previous day and, for two adults and two children, received two cans of soup, canned pumpkin pie filling, Rice Krispies, and some junk food. It was supposed to last three days. They don't blame the bank for the lack of nourishment, since they realize it can hand out only what comes in. At the same time, the food certainly wasn't enough to last three days, and no one even checked to see if they had a can opener.

27 Over the course of the week, the girls help out at the drop-in because Amy wants to make sure they grow up doing their bit for society. At other times she encourages them to draw pictures celebrating St. Patrick's Day and dresses them up in green, complete with shamrocks on their cheeks, to honour the Irish saint.

28 Amy's family arrived from England when she was three, but already she was plagued by ill health and required heart surgery. She also had something wrong with her eyes, which meant another operation a few years later. At school she was diagnosed with attention deficit disorder, but in the 1970s the family couldn't find help for her. She went to a vocational high school in Toronto where she took a hairdressing course.

29 Amy was the apple of her father's eye and the bane of her mother's life, and neither parent knew how to deal with a teenager who was testing them to the limit. Whenever there was a family row, her aunt and uncle jumped in too, compounding the situation. "I knew it all. My parents were wrong, they had never been there, never done it," says Amy, now wise at 32. "My parents didn't see I wanted to be a cool kid."

30 After a number of violent episodes, Amy made her break at 14. She hung out with bad kids and slept at friends' houses. She met her first husband, and they went to New Brunswick where she became pregnant. He then moved to Edmonton and Amy, 19, followed two weeks before the baby was due. There the beatings began. "In the beginning I thought it was my fault. I didn't know if it was normal or not. I phoned the police and they told me that he had to have a gun to my head before they could do anything."

31 Amy went to a shelter, but in a state of confusion and not knowing to this day if she was distraught or scared, she returned to her husband. At this point the authorities stepped in and took her daughter, fearing for the baby's safety. The father promptly blamed Amy for the loss. Devastated, Amy took all the Tylenol and penicillin in the house and then phoned for help. In hospital they told her

that she was lucky to have survived because of her childhood heart surgery. "I was trying to find a way out, but that escape route didn't work."

32   Four months later, she met her second husband, Rick, and in two weeks had moved in with him. Her first husband saluted her departure with a volley of baseball bats and a hail of threatening phone calls to her parents. Moving in with Rick was a turning point in Amy's life. It wasn't the end of her problems, but it signalled a time of growth and maturation. Rick is warm, friendly, loveable, huggable, gentle, and has a lot of compassion; most of all, "he never beats me." In fact, she instructs her two young daughters, "that's what you'll look for in men—your dad; his qualities." Nonetheless, Amy did leave Rick once for another man. Rick looked after the girls and patiently waited until she was ready to return. She is desperately ashamed of this episode because the new man made her work as a stripper, but it wasn't until he became addicted to crack and started to beat her that Amy saw the light and returned to her family. "It still hurts to talk about it. I made a mistake and could have lost all three kids . . . [Rick's] one in a million."

33   Health problems continue to plague Amy. She has had 29 surgeries, one abortion, 17 miscarriages, cancer of the cervix, and epilepsy. Although she hasn't had a seizure in four years, taking Dilantin to control the condition, it means she has trouble finding a job. She's become almost resigned to the situation, but it doesn't help the cash flow. "I've been turned down for four or five jobs because of the epilepsy. I don't care any more. I'm human, so what. I have a disorder. Big deal."

34   Currently Amy works on weekends as a dishwasher at a fast-food restaurant, earning $400 a month. In addition, the family receives $900 in social assistance and a $400 baby bonus. Rent is $680, leaving just over $1,000 a month for food, utilities, clothes, school supplies, and so on. They can't afford nutritional food, but most of the time they don't go hungry. There's not a big margin for emergencies.

35   Rick, who injured his back, is waiting to go back to school to retrain. The family hopes this will result in a lucrative job because, with the new British Columbia regulations, they will come off assistance in a year's time. Even if he does start to bring in real money, they don't know whether it will cover all the medication that Amy alone requires. There are many question marks in their future. Amy says there is an almost unbridgeable chasm between being on welfare and being financially safe and that it's very difficult to cross that divide because of the lack of support services. If she is ill and has to take a day off work, for example, all the family's calculations fall apart at the seams. "I want to get my life together and get off the system. My worker is really good and compassionate, but she does her job. We need more social workers who care about people instead of their paycheque. A lot just care about that cheque."

36   Amy sees increasing numbers of families hitting unacceptable poverty levels. Asked what she would do to change the system, laboriously she writes down this list:
- more family shelters;
- more training for parents-to-be;
- more support for kids so they can achieve their goals;

- action on domestic violence;
- the Canadian government has to put more money back into the community;
- social workers should come into homes to teach and to be a support system so children aren't apprehended as frequently;
- more subsidized day care.

37   "I'm not ashamed to say we are a low-income family. We get the free lunch program at school," says Amy, who blames "the government" for not helping people. "They turn around and give the money to something else. Basically, they are not helping our country. I've been on the streets long enough to know."

38   If Amy's not ashamed of telling strangers about her financial difficulties, she is also not ashamed of telling it as it is to her daughters. "I would rather my daughters see what is really happening to us because this is reality, it's not the fantasy in which most Canadians are raised. It makes them both stronger, and it shows them they do need schooling, that they can't give it up. My mother gave up on me, but I'm not giving up on my kids."

Pandora

39   *Pandora's mental illness catapulted her onto the streets, but she is one of the lucky ones who found help so that her life has taken several turns for the better. She has seen her share of chaos, but she defies every stereotype. It's worth noting that in the Greek myth the last quality released from Pandora's box was hope.*

40   "By any medical definition, I'm nuts," says Pandora, "but I can talk, I can work, and I have a normal life."

41   Pandora, who is 21, does, indeed, look like a very together young woman. She has her own apartment and a job she likes, she volunteers and looks forward to a good future. It's hard to imagine that she was ever accused of setting fire to a school, that she was heavily into drugs, that she went through boyfriends on almost a daily basis, and that she chose her street name as a deliberate reference to the young woman in Greek mythology who unleashed chaos upon the world.

42   Pandora has a mental illness—bi-polar disorder. A year ago she was re-diagnosed with borderline personality disorder. She says she has been seriously misdiagnosed three times and that one of her medications has just about wrecked her liver, but she's here to tell about her life on the streets of Toronto in extremely lucid terms.

43   Her family has strong values that they tried to instil into her at an early age. By 10 she was doing the cooking and laundry and saving her allowance. When puberty hit at 13, Pandora's body rapidly developed. Her brain chemistry as well as her hormones went into overdrive. Pandora began to pay visits to the juvenile psychiatric ward. As well, the rules at home started to chafe. She ran away to the streets, morphing into a "twinkie"—street slang for a new kid on the Yonge Street block where she panhandled. At the time she was on probation for arson. "I was on Paxil that had thrown me into a manic spin. They claimed I set fire to the school—me and another person. She said it was me and I said it was she."

44   Pandora and three of her street friends decided to hitchhike to the West Coast. Everywhere they stopped, they looked for outreach offices and used the facilities until they felt the urge to continue their journey. She had stolen an art book from school and kept notes on the services in each city. "In Winnipeg, there weren't many; in Regina, none. In Calgary we stayed longer, so I called my mom." Her mother sent her some money, and Pandora continued westward with a new bunch of youngsters, having several adventures on the way. After one, the RCMP took her to an aunt in Kelowna, who bought her a bus ticket to Vancouver where she arrived just as the sun was rising, a magical sight.

45   Pandora spent two weeks on welfare, moving several times until she met a friend, Philip, who "saw a broken soul and wanted to fix it." He invited her to live with him, his wife, and children. It was an unusual ménage in that the parents were "polyamourous." It was, however, a safe haven for Pandora and, although she didn't have a relationship with him, she made good money working for Philip.

46   After 18 months, she decided to return to Toronto and called her mother to let her know. "Are you coming home or home-home?" she asked. They agreed that it was probably better for all concerned for Pandora to stay at a shelter, but her mother sent cash for a plane ticket. Pandora quickly moved into transitional housing and acquired computer graphic skills. Two years ago she progressed into her own apartment in a complex run by a non-profit housing society. She has a job as the personal assistant to a company president who understands her ups and downs. "There are days when everything makes me angry," she says. "I isolate myself on those days. I'll let you know if it's a bad day. If I'm really quite bad, leave me be. My boss is really good about it."

47   Her life now is a far cry from her teens when her time was spent getting high, trying everything "minus heroin and coke." Once she passed out at a club. When she came to, she found her arm was bleeding, and it looked as though someone had given her an injection. She went to be tested for heroin, and the results came back positive. She entered a clinic for treatment because she didn't want to become an addict. She still has flashbacks from the acid she dropped and says, "I don't recommend drugs to anyone."

48   Speaking as a reformed drug-user, she says it would be very helpful if there were 24-hour drop-in centres for street youth because most facilities close in the early evening, just at the hour when the kids start using chemicals. "If they don't have a shelter and they are wandering around, there is a tendency to get into trouble." However, the greatest danger to young women on the streets is men. "I don't care what anyone says, it's not love. It's a guy who has duped you until he's finished using you. A lot want to chase tail and be drug dealers." She's not saying there are no successful relationships, but she's sized up the situation pretty realistically.

49   Many young women lose themselves, their minds, and their money, ending up pregnant, infected, or dead. "Girls have to be careful or they get a very nasty reputation. It's very hard to lose, I know. Formerly I had a bad reputation. I played the guys' game against them. I switched guys as often as most people switch their underwear. I switched before they did and a couple I used as a personal punching bag."

50   Pandora has been lucky enough to find Jackie, a mechanic and "a guy not like the other guys." They have been going together for a year and a half. She says Jackie's been her rock, seeing her through a serious breakdown last year that led to the borderline personality disorder diagnosis.

51   Pandora takes many of the new street kids under her wing, briefing them on survival skills and the unwritten code of the streets. She has taken some of them back to her apartment to help them pull their lives together. She's had her successes and her failures, She notes that 50 per cent of street kids will stay on the streets, 30 per cent will make a go of life, but will only earn $20,000 a year or less, and 20 per cent will be "truly truly successful. I want to fight for it [success]." She has her high school equivalency and is now working on college entry. Eventually, she wants to work with the deaf and dumb.

52   Few would suspect that mental illness has taken Pandora to the edge and back. She has also fought the prejudices and fears of the public about mental illness and about street kids. "They picture raving psychotics, the schizos, the worst-case scenarios. When it comes to homeless youths, they picture the dirtiest youth, the absolute worst."

Barb

53   *Childhood abuse and living rough on the streets have taken their toll on Barb's physical and mental health. She rarely complains about her conditions that include diabetes, a bad knee, dental problems, and dissociative personality disorder because she's too busy putting a new life together with the help of an array of professionals and her new friends.*

54   *A truly creative spirit, Barb writes the way most of us eat or breathe; it's a necessity. She can carve out an "office" on a busy outdoor pedestrian mall or in a corridor while waiting for an appointment. Stories pop out of her mouth in everyday conversation. There is no curbing her imagination.*

55   With a delightful sense of humour, a penchant for writing haunting children's tales, and her own idiosyncratic take on the world, Barb is not frightened to stand up for her beliefs. In fact, with multiple personality disorder (MPD), now known as dissociative identity disorder, she feels she's uniquely equipped to champion others: "I got 'alters' (alter egos) that do that. It's quite interesting."

56   Perhaps this sense of natural justice stems from the fact that Barb, 49, was routinely abused as a child. She is hesitant to talk about it because she's learning to live in the present and refraining from dwelling in the past. But occasionally the veil lifts, and she lets something fall—that her father offered her up to other men or that she didn't realize until she was an adult that it's not normal for a sister to have sex with her brother. At the age of six she revealed to her mother that her father was sexually abusing her. In retaliation, he beat her mother who, in turn, told her daughter not to be so silly: "Daddy says it's an awful thing you made up, but he will forgive you this time." Looking back, Barb says her father was a liar and her mother a manipulator who was quick to anger and equally quick to apologize without realizing that once the flower is picked "you can't put it back." In darker moments, she also hints at pedophile rings and ritual abuse.

One of the scariest things about this is that her father was a school caretaker with plenty of access to small children, and, as Barb remembers it, she was far from being the only child who was subjected to his deviancy, although she and her siblings were not encouraged to play with other kids in the neighbourhood. Her sense of isolation, on top of everything else, still haunts her and, like many others, it wasn't until she started living on the streets that she felt safe and that she made friends. "I wanted to be part of another family so bad. Everyone wants to fit in somewhere."

57   Barb explains that the trauma she experienced as a child caused the MPD by providing safe places in her mind. With more than 50 alters, at times it was quite a cacophony, and not all of those personalities have been benign. There have been mornings when she woke up covered in blood because one of them has urged her to slash herself. On the other hand, there have been occasions when a couple of the alters have stepped in to relieve her of pain, most notably when she slipped and smashed her front teeth, or they have taken charge in frightening situations.

58   Some doctors dispute the MPD diagnosis and have given her other labels, like schizo-affective, but whatever they choose to call her condition, two things remain clear: childhood abuse has traumatized her deeply and, despite everything, she's putting her life together and is, once more, a contributing member of society with a new circle of friends, several of them fellow writers.

59   Many of Barb's short stories are about transformations or about loving parents. She keeps her writing in a big briefcase under her bed in her small downtown apartment along with a few other precious possessions. "Just in case there's a fire and I can pick it up and run." This is not such an unlikely fear in a building where many residents have mental illnesses or addictions. Her collection of seashells is displayed on a small table, and her numerous stuffed animals are dotted around the room.

60   For many years Barb had no home, moving from a park bench to a stranger's bed when it grew cold, finding it easy to pick up men when she was in need. "I was a step lower than a prostitute because I didn't get paid. I didn't know how to have a relationship with a man without sex. I think I was pretty sick. Scared? No, because God will look after me. It was what I was used to, remember?"

61   Before moving into this apartment, Barb lived in a hostel for women in transition where she felt safe enough to begin tackling her issues. She continues to move forward, but wonders why there are not more similar facilities for women, pointing out that women like her may need special kinds of assistance. "We need long-term help . . . You just don't forget about it [the abuse]. We need lifelong help. We have got to find a new way, we've got to find new coping skills, and we need more shelters for women, but they have got to be safe, and you're not safe with guys."

62   Five years ago, Barb was a sullen, angry woman whose tougher alter egos were as likely to roar out of her mouth as she is to smile these days. If she spoke then, she talked only about the terrible things her parents had done and blamed them for her troubles. Or she would sit in a corridor, crying and staring into space. Now, she's much happier, describing her volunteer work with

children, the university courses she's taking, and her stories that appear in local publications.

63   The change was slow, but she began to get help at various agencies, not just for her addictions and mental health problems, but also for her physical illnesses. Formerly when Barb was taken to hospital, it was always an emergency—an overdose, a suicide attempt, or a collapse; now it's more likely to be a scheduled test. Despite the fact some health professionals have refused to treat her, Barb did find people who were ready and willing to stand by her. A year ago she made a dramatic turn for the better with new medication and cut herself off marijuana. "I had to give the meds a chance." Booze and drugs are a way for street people to cope, she explains, not to defend her own actions, but to explain those of others and why it is so hard for people to move on. "You have to give us back the hope we may never have had."

64   Barb is slowly acquiring hope for the future, especially now that her parents have died and can no longer touch her. She is learning techniques to cope with the terrible flashbacks and "not to react so much." As childhood episodes return, she patiently deals with them with the help of counsellors. She is also learning that self-mutilation isn't effective at quelling demons, and, as for all those personalities, she's beginning to integrate them into her life. "You think I want to get rid of that? No way." Her object is to have all the alters working for her, so that she can run them like a team, under the leadership of Anne whom she considers to be her real persona—Barb being the front woman, as it were. She would prefer that even the evil ones like Roberta and Tara—"one wears suede and the other leather"—join in rather than go away.

65   Certainly they all come together to speak out on behalf of sexually abused children. "We need more awareness of what's going on. Kids are not to blame. I don't care what they do, or who they do it with." She observes that those who are against protecting children are often perpetrators of the abuse.

66   Once the street appeared to be a safe and caring place; now Barb realizes that although she went there to relieve her pain and to find community, it has exacerbated the losses and accentuated the hurts. The prospect of returning to that way of life has, in turn, become frightening. "I'm terrified of going to the street again because I would lose my identity."

SOURCES

Cheung, Angela M., and Stephen W. Hwang. 2004. "Risk of Death among Homeless Women: A Cohort Study and Review of the Literature." *Canadian Medical Association Journal* (April).

Dental and Oral Health, Calgary Health Region. 2001. <http://wncalgaryhealthregion.ca/hecomm/oral/healthy.htm>.

Donner, Lissa, 2000. *Women, Income, and Health in Manitoba.* Winnipeg: Women's Health Clinic.

Donohoe, Martin. 2004. "Homelessness in the United States: History Epidemiology, Health Issues, Women and Public Policy." *Medscape* (July).

Hurtig, Mel. 1999. *Pay the Rent or Feed the Kids: The Tragedy and Disgrace of Poverty in Canada.* Toronto: McClelland and Stewart.

O'Connell, James. 2004. "Dying in the Shadows: The Challenge of Providing Health Care for Homeless People." *Canadian Medical Association Journal* (April).

Raphael, Dennis, 2002. Interview. Sunnybrook and Women's College Health Sciences Centre. <http://www.womenshealthmatters.ca>.

——. 2001. "Increasing Poverty Threatens the Health of All Canadians." *Canadian Family Physician* (September).

——. 2000. "Addressing Health Inequalities in Canada." *Leadership in Health Services* (October).

INTERVIEWS

Hardill, Kathy. Nurse practitioner, Regent Park Community Health Centre, Toronto. May 2004.

Hwang, Stephen W. Assistant Professor of Medicine, Division of General Internal Medicine, St. Michael's Hospital, University of Toronto, Toronto. May 2004.

Keating, Cori. Outreach worker, Downtown Eastside Women's Centre, Vancouver. April 2004.

Ricciardi, Josie. Community health worker, Regent Park Community Health Centre, Toronto. May 2004.

Active Reading

1. How many experts does Scott refer to in her opening section to explore the link between poverty and sickness?

2. Is Amy's epilepsy one of several factors causing Amy's poverty, or is it the chief cause?

Critical Reading

1. If Scott uses a case study approach to establish that every situation is different, can you explain how the cases differ or add a new element to our understanding of the ways poverty undermines health?

2. Does the long block quote from Dennis Raphael support Scott's reading, or provide a new perspective? How is it used?

RESEARCH AND WRITING SUGGESTIONS

Chapter-based Research Questions

1. Consider some of the reasons that the poverty and homelessness of groups like children, girls, and women have been overlooked.

2. Several of the articles rely on "participant-based" research to account for the lives of those they study. What motivates researchers to represent the "voices" of those they study rather than simply reporting what they found? What difference does it make to the reader?

Additional Research Questions

1. Choose a politician currently in office, and look up his or her record of statements on homelessness and poverty. You might choose a national or

provincial leader, for these individuals are expected to develop social policies. Alternatively, you might look at debate among civic figures, particularly if you were interested in some of the issues about the visibility of urban poverty in Vancouver leading up to the 2010 Winter Olympics.

2. Look up how the issue of women and poverty is treated in feminist literature and/or research. For example, look at a character like April Raintree (in the novel of that name, by Beatrice Culleton) to reflect on what happens to women who are poor in Canadian stories and novels. Or, turning to research based on actual lives and reported in case study or ethnographic form (such as in the books of researcher/activist Pat Capponi), develop an overview of what happens to women who live in poverty in Canada. (To shift the subject to children and poverty, you might consult as one of your sources the award-winning work of fiction *Lullabies for Little Criminals,* by Heather O'Neill, New York: Harper, 2006.)

3. Compile an annotated bibliography or full research proposal on the topic of homelessness that identifies relevant court cases in Canada and the provinces and territories that have invoked the *Charter of Rights and Freedoms.* You might begin by an open search on the internet to find newspaper articles and court decisions and then move to the journal databases to find scholarly articles on the subject.

CHAPTER 9

THE BODY UNDER CONSTRUCTION

Cultural Studies

Bodies matter. If I am a woman, if I am white, if I am old—these factors influence how I am treated.

When René Descartes declared "I think therefore I am," he articulated the rationalist split between the mind and the body that has persisted in Western society. In recent times, some have sought ways to integrate the mind and body (such as by using holistic therapies that offer to affect mind and spirit through body sensations). For others, the body is expressive of identity, a stage on which to perform self-discipline or self-enhancement. The first article in this section by Susie O'Brien and Imre Szeman provides a discussion of the ways the body is understood in our contemporary "postmodern" culture, which places high value on appearances; to conform to beauty standards, many regulate the body by extreme exercise or diet regimes. (Also note that these authors provide in a "Close-Up" box a smart extended definition of the term "postmodern.")

Apart from choosing clothes or costumes, we also modify our bodies by such means as tattooing or scarification. One of the questions several articles in this section raise is whether we are exercising agency in engaging these modifications of our own bodies, or whether we are simply conforming to cultural trends. Kathy Davis is interested in whether women in particular can use body modification to gain more control of their lives. Thomas Schramme takes a non-gendered look at extreme body modification, to ask philosophical questions about whether there ought to be limits on an individual's right to seek modifications that many would see as mutilations.

A recent debate over the gender of a runner who placed first in a women's meet had some calling into question whether the runner was a female, much to the surprise of the runner herself. One television commentator introduced a recent argument in biology that makes the case that there are not two but 32 genders. His sensible point was that we oversimplify by allowing for only two genders in the world of sport. Anne Fausto-Sterling looks at body construction in a sociological sense as well as a technological one and argues that the division of the population into male and female does not reflect the diversity found in nature but rather the medical world's deep investment in preserving our culture's rigid sex-gender-sexuality system.

Clearly, the days of feeling we are natural beings—at one with nature—are long past; from Aspirins to hair replacements, from gall bladder surgery to face-lifts, we rely on technology. The readings in this chapter investigate connections between the body and technology, between nature and culture.

Activate

1. How many people do you know who have undertaken body modifications? Have you had any yourself, or do you hope to some day? What kinds of modifications were performed by medical professionals? What kinds of modifications were performed outside the medical world? Can you categorize the medical modifications as elective or required? Are any in-between?

2. Have you ever found yourself passing judgment on whether someone else's body modification should have been done? If so, what reasons have you had for your judgments?

"Changing Our Bodies, Changing Ourselves?" from *Popular Culture: A User's Guide*

Susie O'Brien and Imre Szeman

This excerpt comes from the chapter "Identity and the Body" in a textbook (Popular Culture: A User's Guide) that examines the powerful impact of cultural practices on our daily lives and sense of identity. This chapter examines the ways our cultural values influence how we dress, walk, and talk, and perhaps more broadly how we define gender and human beauty. It looks at the interactive relation between nature and culture and at the many ways we currently alter nature by pursuing technological modifications, whether it be to seek relief from a headache with an Aspirin or the gratification of tattooing our ankle or changing the shape of our nose.

1   [. . .] [Q]uestions of identity cannot be pursued very far without reference to the body. The relationship between identities and bodies is the subject of this section, which looks at forms of body cultivation or modification in the context of such fundamental questions as: What role does the body play in the production of the self? Can we even define a "self" as distinct from the body? To what extent are our bodies the products of nature, and to what extent are they the products of our individual control? How are our bodies shaped or constrained by culture and vice versa? The answers to these questions all have significant bearing on the issue of *agency*: our power to act independently in the world, to determine our own meanings, our own actions, our own pleasures.

Embodied Selves

2   Descartes's famous formula, "I think therefore I am," informs the modern notion of identity as defined by the pre-eminence of mind (consciousness) over matter (the body). Descartes's elevation of the rational mind as the faculty that gives meaning to human life, granting it supremacy over other, non-rational forms of life, informs a dualist philosophy characterized by a series of closely overlapping oppositions—spirit vs. matter, mind vs. body, reason vs. passion, nature vs. culture—that map out relations of being and, more significantly, relations of power. Besides laying the groundwork for laws surrounding the protection of private property, this framework has underwritten such dubious social practices as slavery and the subjugation of women on the grounds of a division of living beings into knowing subjects—"man"—and knowable (and possessable) objects.

3   Postmodernist thought has posed significant challenges to the dualisms that inform the modern concept of identity—and indeed much of modern Western

philosophy (see Close-Up). In particular, postmodernism has blurred the scientific/philosophical certainty of distinctions between subjects and objects, consciousness and matter that allow us to know the world while remaining abstracted from, superior to it. The destabilization of philosophical dualisms associated with postmodernist thought is reflected by the more general breakdown of structure and hierarchy associated with contemporary social life. As old hierarchies dissolve—and with them any clear sense of identity based on birth, breeding, or old notions of class—the body becomes an increasingly important site for the negotiation of social meaning. In some ways, the new attention focused on the body reflects a move away from seeing bodies as simply containers for identity and toward recognition of the ways in which the self is embodied—at once natural and cultural, physical and psychological. This recognition is complicated, however, by the persistence of the modern notion of body and mind as somehow separate, with the latter being privileged as the home of substantial being.

4   This ambivalence about the relationship between self and body is highlighted in the 2001 movie *Shallow Hal*, a romantic comedy with a moral message about judging people by their inner qualities and not by outward appearance. With the help of a hypnotist, the hero, "Shallow Hal" (Jack Black), overcomes his obsession with beautiful women by losing his ability to perceive outward appearance entirely in favour of a focus on women's inner beauty. Thus, when he falls in love with Rosemary (Gwyneth Paltrow), he sees her not as she looks to others, and to herself—hugely overweight—but as a skinny goddess.

5   While the movie was cautiously praised for challenging stereotypes surrounding fatness—Rosemary is an extraordinarily (even unbelievably) energetic, selfless, and well-balanced person, despite insecurity about her weight—it inevitably upheld some problematic myths about body and identity. A critical component in the movie's success as a romantic comedy was the split between the images of Rosemary's outer and inner selves (unattractive vs. beautiful), conveyed by sporadic shots of Gwyneth Paltrow in a fat suit and much more frequent shots of Gwyneth Paltrow looking like, well, Gwyneth Paltrow. That Gwyneth Paltrow without the fat suit was meant to function as a metaphor for moral goodness is undercut by the overwhelming significance of her image as an icon of *physical* beauty. Our reading of Rosemary as a character is powerfully shaped by her embodiment as Paltrow.

6   Thus, the movie's overt message—that looks don't matter and that beauty is in the eye of the beholder—is compromised by the powerful myth of a correspondence between physical appearance and social and even moral worth. Moreover, to the extent that this myth is shaped by taboos against fatness—bodily excess— it expresses an ambivalent attachment to traditional ideas about the body, particularly the female body, as separate from, and essentially inferior to, the mind.

7   In spite of the contradictions just noted, it is tempting to take at least part of the message of *Shallow Hal* at face value, and to argue that, while we might sometimes confuse bodies and selves, we shouldn't. The relationship is purely a contingent one; there's no natural correlation between body weight and personality, or social value, only a culturally constructed one. It turns out, though, that it's not that easy to separate the two; not only do bodies shape identity, and vice versa, but the body itself is a complex amalgam of nature and culture.

The Human Body: Natural or Cultural?

8 Once we start to explore the entanglement of nature and culture in relation to the body, it becomes harder and harder to determine where one ends and the other begins. The body may be a material phenomenon, but the way we experience it is determined by culture. Concepts of health and disease are a case in point. Anthropologist Emily Martin has investigated the role of myth and metaphor in the way science understands the human body—for example by looking at it as a kind of machine, or by employing metaphors of war to describe the operation of the immune system in maintaining health. Thus, we "fight" disease; our white blood cells "seek out and destroy" pathogens. The metaphorical construction of the body has especially interesting social implications in relation to the representation of reproductive processes. Think, for example, of what it might mean for conventional gender mythology if we were to replace the familiar, almost cartoonish image of eager sperm competing to penetrate the docile, receptive egg—an image comically rendered in Woody Allen's 1972 movie *Everything You Always Wanted to Know About Sex (But Were Afraid to Ask)*—with what some scientists suggest is a more accurate image of a tiny wiggling sperm being *enveloped* by the much larger egg (Martin). (See Figure 1 on page 225)

Close-Up

Postmodernism

It has been said that postmodernism has come to have so many meanings that it is impossible to offer any simple definition. In the words of the critic Peter Brooker, postmodernism is "annoyingly elusive in its range of reference and attributions whether in academic debate or across the arts and culture" (174). Such variation in meaning has led many people to dismiss the term.

Generally, postmodernism refers to a phase in Western history that coincides with the information revolution and new forms of economic, social, and cultural life. Postmodernism names a period—the current era—and points to the fundamental differences of this era from even the recent past (i.e., modernism, ranging from roughly the mid-nineteenth to the mid-twentieth century).

One of the major changes in contemporary society lies in the character of the global economy. Rather than being based on the production of new things, economic transactions increasingly involve non-material commodities: stocks, information, the arts, and services (health care, fast food, tourism). The economy, then, is increasingly fuelled by culture, and culture, by extension, has become increasingly defined by economics. It is this development that Fredric Jameson refers to in his definition of postmodernism as "the cultural logic of late capitalism."

The economic circumstances Jameson highlights, along with recent historical developments such as decolonization, civil rights, and feminism have all contributed to intellectual and cultural changes now described under the heading of postmodernism. The concept is often used to describe a broad shift in approaches to truth and knowledge, away from the rationality and truth-seeking that emerged out of the Enlightenment. Since the late 1950s, the existence of such truths or laws has been challenged. Postmodernism views the search for truth as a project whose real aim is achieving social power and control, and is suspicious of any "grand narratives" or theories that seek to provide the single explanation of how human beings act (such as Freudian psychoanalysis) or how societies function (Marxism, for example).

The general public seems to share this skepticism to some degree: Where only a few decades ago people had faith in specialists (like doctors) and their political leaders, now there is widespread skepticism toward those who claim great expertise—as in Britain in February 2003, when the public simply did not believe what Prime Minister Tony Blair had to say about the threat posed by Iraq.

Postmodernism also refers to styles and movements in arts and culture that express this skeptical attitude, characterized by self-consciousness, formal and stylistic borrowing, irony, pastiche, parody, recycling, sampling, and a mixing of high and low culture. Films and novels today frequently highlight the fact that they are cultural constructions. For example, in the film *Adaptation* (2002) the screenwriter is also the film's main character. Cultural products today make self-conscious use of older forms to create new culture, such as Todd Haynes's film *Far From Heaven*, which mimics the Fifties melodramas of Douglas Sirk. Beginning with Andy Warhol, contemporary art has drawn on advertising (Jeff Wall), consumer culture (Jeff Koons), film (Cindy Sherman), and television. Irony and parody characterize the dominant modes of address on television (*Seinfeld, The Simpsons*).

For the French critic Jean Baudrillard, postmodernism is characterized by the culture of the "simulacrum"—a copy without an original, or a sign without a referent, defining a world in which representation quite simply is reality. Many find this disturbing, signalling the "emptying out" of history, the disappearance of nature, and the impossibility of defining a platform of belief from which to launch individual projects or political movement. For others, the erosion of traditional concepts of identity translates into exciting possibilities for the construction of new, multiply defined selves. In general, the way we respond to the breakdown of the old structures of meaning depends on whether our particular identities, defined by the traditional markers of class, gender, race, sexuality, and so on, were empowered or excluded by those structures.

9   Some theorists suggest that the physiological category of sex itself is not a natural given, but determined by culture. This is not to say that the physiological differences we refer to in assigning sexual identity do not exist; rather, that they operate much more variably and diffusely than the division of humans and other animals into mutually exclusive categories of "male" and "female" suggests. For example, the designation of sex hormones as male (testosterone) or female (estrogen) does not account for the fact that both hormones are released by men *and* women (Shilling 75).

Figure 1 A Traditional Image of Conception

Traditional images of conception owe less to scientific accuracy than to metaphorical representations of gender stereotypes.

10 Moreover, the presence of those hormones—along with other secondary sex characteristics such as the size and function of reproductive organs, facial hair, voice, and physique—alters with age and in response to environmental factors such as nutrition and stress. Even the seemingly clear-cut genetic markers of XX (female) vs. XY (male) chromosomes are complicated by the presence of other genes influencing physique and behaviour, not to mention the range of conditions that can affect the "normal" correspondence of genes to physiological characteristics. In short, humans are characterized by biological variances relating to reproductive capacity; however, the reduction of those variances to fixed, bipolar categories "male" and "female" comes about not through nature but through *culture*. The cultural basis of fundamental sex differences is highlighted by the different values and meanings accorded those differences in different times and places. In pre-eighteenth-century Europe, for example, women were viewed as biologically inferior to, but not fundamentally different from, men. The view of sexual difference as one of kind rather than degree arose in conjunction with the need to reconcile the continued disenfranchisement of women with new views about the universal rights of "man" (Laqueur 19).

11 **Learned "Body Techniques"** But culture does not influence only the way we understand bodies; it also becomes inscribed on bodies themselves. As sociologist and anthropologist Marcel Mauss (1872–1950) noted, the way we conduct such basic activities as sleeping, eating, sitting, walking, having sex, and giving birth should be understood not as natural, but as a series of "body techniques" that are learned in particular social contexts and are hence culturally and historically specific. One of the most striking examples Mauss provides is French women's characteristic style (or technique) of walking, which changed in the 1930s with the arrival of American cinema: the movies carried with them a whole repertoire of fashion comprising ways not just of dressing, but also of comportment, of holding and carrying the body.

12   While French women's imitation of styles of movement associated with Hollywood film might be prompted by an association of the U.S. with images of energy and freedom, most body techniques serve a much more utilitarian function in relation to the demands of a smoothly running society. In most societies, this means that considerable effort is expended in what Mauss calls "education in composure . . . a mechanism inhibiting disorderly movements" (474). Thus we learn not only how to move, but also how and when to inhibit movement, techniques that differ significantly by age and gender.

13   **The Self-Controlled Body** The idea that culture exerts a shaping and restraining effect on the body is carried further in the work of sociologist Norbert Elias (1897–1990), who documented the process by which centuries of Western civilization produced the modern, individualized, self-controlled body. Elias uses the concept of "civilization" not in the sense in which it is often used, to imply the progressive movement beyond the "backward" ways of the past, but rather to describe a series of specific historical changes in Europe, from the hardscrabble social world of the Middle Ages to the court society of the Renaissance, whose influence shapes our present-day culture. In particular, Elias focuses on the shift from a way of life in which physical strength, aggression, and indulgence of appetites were necessary to survival to one in which "polite society" defined by the court dictated increasingly complex social rituals, successful observance of which played a significant role in determining one's social status.

14   One of the critical aspects of this shift is a move toward interdependence, such that existence had to be negotiated with an increasing awareness of the effects of one's behaviour on others. Thus the civilized body is one that is subject to an expanding set of taboos and social codes, demarcating it sharply from the physical environment and from other bodies. Practices that were once widely tolerated, such as defecating in public or sharing beds with strangers, were subjected to increasingly strict social sanction as a new model of appropriate bodily conduct emerged. This new model was characterized by a broad repertoire of gestures—manners—that signified an observance of social relations, including an overall tendency toward self-restraint and a clear sense of separation between private and public.

Physical Capital and Social Status

15   Of course, body techniques and codes of civilized behaviour vary from social situation to social situation (for example, what's acceptable at a rave differs considerably from what's appropriate at your Great-Aunt Ethel's tea party) and depending on what position one occupies in society (class, gender, etc.). Sociologist Pierre Bourdieu (1930–2002) sheds light on these differences by expanding Mauss's concept of the *habitus*. A term connoting both living space and habit, **habitus** describes the way in which particular social environments are internalized by individuals in the form of dispositions toward particular bodily orientations and behaviours.

16   The concept of habitus thus allows us to talk about the way in which social differences are reproduced at the level of the individual body. Class, Bourdieu

suggests, plays a determining role in the development of bodies by influencing such factors as social location and taste (learned habits of discrimination influencing choice of lifestyle) as well as more physical aspects of habitus. These differences in turn contribute to the production of different kinds and degrees of social value attached to different kinds of bodies. Value corresponds more or less closely to class, with working-class bodies possessing less value than dominant-class bodies—value here is determined principally by the ability to translate what Bourdieu terms physical capital into other forms of capital: economic (money), cultural (education), and social (networks of belonging).

17   Of course, the different kinds of capital don't map perfectly onto one another: professional sport has traditionally offered a venue for men from under-privileged circumstances to convert physical capital into economic capital in a fairly direct way. However, the heavy toll professional sport—like most forms of physical labour—exacts on the body, combined with its relatively restricted access as a career path, diminishes its significance as an exception to the rule that "white-collar" bodies tend to enjoy more privileged access to forms of economic, social, and cultural capital than do "blue-collar" bodies.

18   A somewhat crude example of the relationship between taste and habitus and social and economic capital can be seen in the 1988 film *Working Girl*, in which Tess (Melanie Griffith), a secretary, employs her brains and ambition to land an executive position and an attractive, financially successful husband (Harrison Ford). An important component of her social and economic advancement is her successful cultivation of her appearance, voice, and gestures in order first to impersonate, and then truly to embody the image of a female executive. One scene has her pedalling frantically on an exer-cycle while trying to imitate phrases and intonations of speech from a tape of her boss (Sigourney Weaver) giving a speech. Perhaps the clearest sign of her progress—besides her successful business negotiations with and seduction of Harrison Ford—is the increasingly striking contrast throughout the film of Tess to her best friend (Joan Cusack), whose permanently entrenched position in the secretarial rank is signalled by her big hair, caked-on blue eye-shadow, and vampish clothes.

19   Premised on outrageous class (and gender) stereotypes, *Working Girl* clearly can't be read as a sociological comment on how class mobility operates in "real life." However, its tremendous popularity particularly among women, illustrates the pervasiveness of cultural myths about the role of physical appearance and behaviour in achieving—and, even more importantly, deserving—social and economic status.

20   In an interesting contrast with *Working Girl*, the 2002 movie *Maid in Manhattan* is much less conscious about the ways in which class and social position are articulated through bodily disposition or habitus. Unlike in *Working Girl*, where Tess has to unlearn her natural speech, gestures, and tastes to play the role of someone of a higher class, all it takes to transform Marisa (Jennifer Lopez) into a credible imitation of a rich socialite is a Dolce & Gabbana pantsuit. While both movies follow a fairytale format, *Working Girl* was arguably more realistic about the barriers to social mobility—barriers that are ingrained on the body.

Ingrained Habit—Culture Becoming Nature

21   One of the most obviously mythical elements of films like *Working Girl* and *Maid in Manhattan*—besides the stereotypes—is the assumption the films make that, through a combination of pluck and intelligence, it is possible for anyone to transform her- or himself, mentally and physically, into whomever she or he wants to be. *Maid in Manhattan* was perhaps less wildly unrealistic in this respect: while Tess catapults from secretary to senior executive, Marisa just rises through the ranks of the service industry, from maid to manager. This difference may simply reflect a change in ideologies of identity and work, particularly with respect to gender, from the late 1980s to the early twenty-first century.

22   While the message conveyed by *Working Girl* was a strongly feminist one, inflected by the emphasis on individualism and corporate success in Ronald Reagan's America, *Maid in Manhattan* offers a view of ideal femininity that, depending on your perspective, is either less progressive (economic equality with men isn't really important so long as you're feisty, beautiful, and a good mom), or more so (identity is not defined by work). Both movies, however, arguably downplayed the physical consequences of occupying particular social categories—consequences measurable in terms not just of appearance, but also of one's biological capacities, including health and bodily function. In many instances, learned behaviours have real physical effects that come to actually conform to the stereotype on which the behaviour was initially based.

23   For example, in an essay titled "Throwing Like a Girl," Iris Marion Young identifies a tendency in Western industrial societies for girls to move in ways that are more limited and constrained than the ways in which boys move. In effect, responding to a learned physical orientation that Young calls "inhibited intentionality" (145), girls and women are not inclined to use their bodies' full potential range of strength and motion. Thus what is often regarded as women's "natural" lack of physical strength and coordination is at least partly attributable to the way in which their bodies are socialized to move (or not) in particular ways. These learned behaviours, ingrained into habit, contribute to the transformation of women's bodies into the stereotypically "weak vessels" they were already imagined to be.

24   Nature and culture, then, are inextricably connected in the production of the body as a site of identity-formation. Naturally occurring biological variances are simplified and reduced to signs of absolute cultural difference, which themselves come to take on the appearance of nature. The ways in which we conceive of the body influence the way we look at, treat, and inhabit it. Most significantly, cultural influences on the body come to assume physical significance, both at the level of the individual physical body and of the social structures in which individual bodies are placed. Possibilities for modifying and even transcending the body thus become a highly charged cultural and political issue.

ALTERED STATES

25   While people at all times and in all places have sought to change their bodies in different ways, advances in science combined with the unique pressures of a consumer culture highly biased toward the visual have contributed to a growing trend toward body-cultivation and modification. Body modification describes

practices that include "piercing, tattooing, branding, cutting, binding and inserting implants," as well as less invasive practices such as exercise and diet, that seek to alter "the appearance and form of the body" (Featherstone 1). Whether these practices are motivated by health or by aesthetics, whether they uphold or challenge prevailing social norms, and whether they aim toward the accentuation or transcendence of the body—and few can be so simply classified—they demand examination in relation to the more fundamental questions of how they contribute to the production of individual and social meaning, identity and power.

Enhancing/Producing the Healthy Body

26   At the beginning of the twenty-first century Western cultures have come increasingly to see health as a matter of individual control and responsibility. This trend is reflected in such developments as the recent legislation passed in Canada on food labelling. The new law requiring uniform labelling on all packaged food, listing information such as fat content and potential health benefits, makes the assumption that health and fitness are largely dependent on wise consumer choices. A variety of factors have contributed to this development: individuals tend to have much more knowledge and confidence about health-related matters than they did a generation ago, leading to a much more proactive stance in managing their own health. At the same time, both fuelling and responding to this trend, a massive consumer industry has sprung up around personal health care, promoting everything from so-called "nutraceuticals" (drug-enhanced foods) to fitness clubs.

27   Finally, the rising costs of an increasingly technology-based medical system have led governments and insurance companies to search for ways to encourage less reliance on the system and greater responsibility on the part of individuals in addressing their health needs. This pressure is particularly acute in countries, such as Canada, that have a public health care system. The idea that health is a human right that should be protected by the entire community through taxation is increasingly hard to sustain in the face of a growing emphasis on the individual as largely in control of, and responsible for, his or her own health. Thus questions about whether individuals who smoke or don't wear seatbelts should be entitled to free health care have begun to appear with some frequency in the media. Increasingly, then, issues surrounding health are being shaped by rhetoric about consumer choice, at the same time as they convey more moralistic messages about individual responsibility.

28   The ambiguity of these messages is reflected in practices surrounding diet and fitness, where the general goal of "health" is overlaid with the complex and often contradictory values of physical and sexual attractiveness (generally associated with pleasure) and moral well-being (frequently defined by discipline and self-denial). In these mixed motivations can be detected the ambivalence about the relationship between self and body discussed at the beginning of this section. While the pursuit of exercise as a form of self-improvement might imply on one hand a recognition of an integral connection between body and identity, many practices associated with exercise, including dieting (and its more extreme pathological form, anorexia) are inspired by the idea of the body as an alien thing, separate and requiring discipline from the self.

What's Natural/Normal?

29 Many health practices are founded on ideas about a natural physical state, which regimes of diet or exercise seek to enhance. These ideas are troubled by the burgeoning popularity of cosmetic surgery that clearly aims less to preserve a "natural" state of health than to produce a "cultural" convention of beauty. Crossing the line from medicine to aesthetics, cosmetic surgery sheds unexpected light on the reliance of both discourses on concepts of *normalization.* Celebrated by many as a technology of self-expression that allows them to convey an outer image that is more in tune with their inner selves (ditching the fat suit to become Gwyneth Paltrow), cosmetic surgery is condemned by others as a biotechnological reinforcement of oppressive gender norms (Balsamo).

30 The operation of such norms is most clearly evident in such forms of cosmetic surgery as liposuction and breast enlargement. While these procedures may be seen—and, more importantly, may actually *work*—to enhance the self-confidence of those who seek them, they do so at the expense of conscripting them more fully into the prescribed roles of a patriarchal social order.

31 Some forms of body enhancement work more ambiguously. For example, female bodybuilding seems in one sense to challenge conventional gender codes by rejecting a feminine ideal of almost-anorexic thinness. Maximizing instead of minimizing the body—replacing weakness with strength—bodybuilding represents a form of physical feminine empowerment. On the other hand, the maxed-out body is achieved at a cost of punishing discipline and "self"-denial that, at its extreme, actually compromises the goals of health and fitness.

32 Of course, bodybuilding is about more than health and fitness: like most fitness practices, it is also about display. For women, whose relationships to their bodies have always been mediated by social codes that define them as objects-to-be-looked-at (see Mulvey in Chapter Three), display is at best an ambiguous form of empowerment (Grosz 224). At the same time as it accentuates strength, the culture of bodybuilding still draws attention to the female body as the repository of female worth. As this example demonstrates, body-modification practices may challenge social norms, but they cannot avoid negotiating them. Most practices, like bodybuilding, take place in complicated conversations with our historically ambivalent conceptions about mind and body—conceptions that are inevitably tied to ideas about gender and power.

33 **The Politics of Body Modification** Body modification practices also raise other issues of power and agency. As with highly gendered forms of body modification, the practice of surgically altering black or Asian features to give them a more Caucasian cast can be understood in terms of its promotion of empowerment and/or subjugation. The practice of blepharoplasty in which a fold is inserted to give the eyes a more rounded, open appearance, gained notoriety in Canada after the death of one patient from a botched, illicit operation. The incident sparked an unusual degree of media commentary on the powerful and damaging effect of myths of white normativity. A more nuanced perspective on the subject is expressed in Korean-Canadian Ann Shin's documentary *Western Eyes*, which mixes a critical analysis of racialized aesthetic conventions in pop culture with interviews with women who have undergone the procedure. The

women emerge from the film neither as victims of the dominant culture nor as models of self-empowerment, but as individuals struggling to define their identities through conflicting codes of physical beauty/normality.

34   These codes are not "natural"; neither are they solely cosmetic. The complexity of the issues surrounding medical/surgical body modification is evident in relation to sex-change procedures, in which transsexual individuals—those whose gender *identity* (masculine or feminine) conflicts with their chromosomal and physiological characteristics—undergo a series of surgical and medical treatments to transform them from male to female or vice versa. While aspects of gender are largely culturally determined, they are sufficiently deep and pervasive that gender identity disorders are considered by the medical community to constitute threats to physical health. Sexual modification blurs the distinction between culture and nature in the determination of what constitutes a "normal" identity. It also demonstrates the ambiguous political significance of body modification: fuelled by dominant codes of sex and gender identity, sex reassignment surgery also throws those codes into confusion, challenging society's deepest prejudices about what counts as normal.

Transcending the Body?

35   The possibilities of body modification are taken to their extreme, at the same time as they are critically challenged, in the work of performance artist Orlan, who has subjected herself to nine plastic-surgery operations—including the implantation of horns in her forehead—in order to explore (and explode) classical notions of beauty. Orlan's is a self-conscious parody of more conventional versions of plastic surgery (which themselves assume an extreme form in the more than twenty operations undergone by American talk show celebrity Cindy Jackson in an eerily successful bid to look like Barbie). Declaring "I don't want to be the Barbie Doll" (qtd. in Goodall 160), Orlan seeks instead to expose the arbitrariness, the unnaturalness, of the standards of beauty that have come to define Western femininity. She does this not in defence of the so-called "real" body, but in order to expose its non-existence. The body, Orlan observes, "is obsolete. It is no longer adequate for the current situation. We mutate at the rate of cockroaches, but we are cockroaches whose memories are in computers, who pilot planes and drive cars that we have conceived, although our bodies are not conceived for these speeds" (qtd. in Goodall 151).

36   Orlan's comment reflects the posthumanist position that the concepts "man," "self," and "body" that underwrite traditional ideas of human identity have become untenable as society confronts the inextricable entanglement of nature and technology, human and machine. This is not to say that the body *used* to exist in a more or less natural state that has been disrupted or corrupted by technology, but that the increasing difficulty of drawing distinctions between the human/natural and the technological highlights the inadequacy of the once-intelligible myth of an autonomous human identity.

37   **Cyborgs**   The figure of the cyborg, an amalgam of human and animal and/or living organism and machine, is not simply the imaginary creation of the producers of cyberpunk novels and movies but an everyday reality, embodied in

our use of computers and machines. In a significant way, we have not only come to inhabit technology, but technology has also come to inhabit us, as theorists such as Paul Virilio have pointed out; he cites as one example the medical use of micro-machines to view, diagnose, treat, and enhance the body. Such innovations have the potential to be socially useful, but also scarily invasive. University of Toronto professor and inventor Steve Mann highlights both the possibilities and the dangers of cyborg technology with wearable cameras and computers that turn the tables on such routine uses of surveillance as store security systems.

38   For many people, the prospect of an ever-closer relationship between humans and machines invokes utopian ideas of virtual reality, in which individuals and communities are able to transcend the limits of nature and their bodies to enjoy ever-greater freedoms. For others, the prospect of a progressive erosion of the integrity of principles like "humanity" and "nature" is deeply disturbing, heralding a night-marish world like the one represented in *Blade Runner*, in which the complexity and beauty of our existence is transformed into a bunch of animate machines.

39   As artists such as Orlan and cultural theorists such as Donna Haraway and Steve Mann have shown, however, neither of these visions is ultimately viable. The techno-utopian dream, an extension of the Enlightenment project of harnessing the physical world to human need, relies, like the techno-pessimist vision, on the old idea of a separation between body and mind, nature and culture, that is simply not sustainable. Both the technological and the natural ideal are myths forged out of culture, whose ideological frames limit the possibilities for human liberation.

40   Contrary to the promises of technophiles and purveyors of cosmetic miracles, "identity has not turned into a free option for all subjects in all situations and all contexts" (Klesse 20). Prevailing structures of gender, class, racial, and sexual inequality mean that everyone does not enjoy the opportunities for self-fulfillment. The limitations on our freedom to define ourselves as we will is also compromised by the fact—of which we are periodically reminded, by environmental catastrophes (some of them human-caused) and by the inevitability of death—that we are not just *in*, but also *of* nature. The critical issue, which we have tried to stress throughout this chapter, concerns not whether our identities are born or made, or whether they are defined through or against our bodies, but what they mean, in terms of our ability to enhance our own and others' power to act in a world not entirely of our own making.

SUMMARY

41   This chapter has advanced a number of arguments about the meaning and significance of individual identity some of which are picked up and extended in the next chapter, which looks at the role of identity and difference in the construction of community. Key points to remember include the following:

- Identities do not precede or transcend social formations, but are defined through them. Rather than essential truths, identities can be usefully conceived of as stories that fulfill particular purposes at particular times.
- Dominant categories of identity, particularly those relating to gender and sexuality, operate to uphold ideologies that support existing social inequalities.

- As vehicles of social power, identities can work to restrict or enhance possibilities for individual self-definition.
- The meaning of identity is inseparable from the significance of the body as a natural and social fact.
- The growing trend toward body management and modification functions to enhance and to restrict possibilities for the development of identity and agency.

WORKS CITED

Brooker, Peter. *A Concise Glossary of Cultural Theory.* London: Arnold, 1999.

Featherstone, Mike. "Body Modification: An Introduction." *Body Modification.* Ed. Mike Featherstone. London: Sage, 2000. 1-14.

Goodall, Jane. "An Order of Pure Decision: Un-Natural Selection in the Work of Stelarc and Orlan." *Body Modification.* Ed. Mike Featherstone. London: Sage, 2000. 149-170.

Grosz, Elizabeth. *Volatile Bodies.* Bloomington: Indiana University Press, 1994.

Klesse, Christian. "'Modern Primitivism': Non-Mainstream Body Modification and Racialized Representation." *Body & Society* 5 2/3 (1999): 16-38.

Mulvey, Laura. "Visual Pleasure and Narrative Cinema." *A Cultural Studies Reader.* Ed. Jessica Munns and Gita Rajan. New York: Longman, 1995. 322-332.

Young, Iris Marion. "Throwing Like a Girl: A Phenomenology of Feminine Body Comportment, Motility and Spatiality." *Human Studies* 3 (1980): 137-156.

Active Reading

1. What is the main argument developed in the section entitled "Physical Capital and Social Status"? Can you apply the term "habitus" to explain why you attend your writing class with certain books and supplies, dressed in a certain way, with expectations about how to act and speak?

2. Explain the connection among nature, culture, and gender, as it is developed toward the end of the section "Ingrained Habit—Culture Becoming Nature."

3. How do the authors define "body modification," and what makes it prevalent in our current culture?

Critical Reading

1. Look at the references to sources the authors make in a section like "Ingrained Habit." Do they blend popular and scholarly sources? How are they used differently? Does this emphasize that the study of popular culture has become a scholarly topic?

2. The authors refer to feminist performance artist Orlan, who is also discussed by Kathy Davis. Do some research to look at Orlan's work. Is it interesting art in your opinion? How is her performance different from that of someone who decides to have breast augmentation or to tattoo sleeves on her arms?

"My Body is My Art": Cosmetic Surgery as Feminist Utopia?

Kathy Davis

This is a particularly complex article, at times difficult to follow because the author is connecting her social science research work (which involves collecting data about subjects who have undergone plastic surgery) to the performance art of Orlan (which involves actual body modifications) and the philosophy of Kathryn Morgan (which advocates that plastic surgery may be a way for women to control their image by altering it). In arguing that plastic surgery can be used by women to control their identity and body image, both Orlan and Morgan are seeing it as a positive or "utopian" technology, rather than picking up the more common feminist critique of it as an instrument by which women are (self-) disciplined into conforming to patriarchal beauty standards. In this article, feminist researcher Davis ultimately disagrees with their position and doubts that cosmetic surgery can be used by women as a way to accomplish their own goals. She argues instead that we need to be concerned with the feelings of pain and unhappiness that drive women to seek this sort of surgical enhancement and with the physical pain it inflicts on them.

1   In August 1995, the French performance artist Orlan was invited to give a lecture at a multimedia festival in Amsterdam.[1] Orlan has caused considerable furore in the international art world in recent years for her radical body art in which she has her face surgically refashioned before the camera. On this particular occasion, the artist read a statement about her art while images of one of her operations flashed on the screen behind her. The audience watched as the surgeon inserted needles into her face, sliced open her lips, and, most gruesomely of all, severed her ear from the rest of her face with his scalpel. While Orlan appeared to be unmoved by these images, the audience was clearly shocked. Agitated whispers could be heard and several people left the room. Obviously irritated, Orlan interrupted her lecture and asked whether it was 'absolutely necessary to talk about the pictures *now*' or whether she could proceed with her talk. Finally one young woman stood up and exclaimed: 'You act as though it were not *you*, up there on the screen'.[2]

2   This may seem like a somewhat naive reaction. Good art is, after all, about shifting our perceptions and opening up new vistas. That this causes the audience some unease goes without saying. Moreover the young woman's reaction is not directed at Orlan the artist who is explaining her art, but rather at Orlan the woman who has had painful surgery. Here is a woman whose face has been mutilated and yet discusses it intellectually and dispassionately. The audience is squirming and Orlan is acting as though she were not directly involved.

3   I became interested in Orlan (and the reactions she evokes) as a result of my own research on women's involvement in cosmetic surgery (Davis 1995). Like many feminists, I was deeply troubled by the fact that so many women willingly and enthusiastically have their bodies altered surgically despite considerable hardship and risk to themselves. While I shared the commonly held feminist

view that cosmetic surgery represented one of the more pernicious horrors inflicted by the medical system upon women's bodies, I disliked the concomitant tendency among feminists to treat the recipients as nothing more than misguided or deluded victims. In an attempt to provide a critical analysis of cosmetic surgery which did not undermine the women who saw it as their best option under the circumstances, I conducted in-depth interviews with women who had had or were planning to have some form of cosmetic surgery. They had undergone everything from a relatively simple ear correction or a breast augmentation to—in the most extreme case—having the entire face reconstructed. Since the research was conducted in the Netherlands where cosmetic surgery was included in the national health care package, my informants came from diverse socioeconomic backgrounds. Some were professional women or academics, others were cashiers or home-helps and some were full-time housewives and mothers. Some were married, some single, some heterosexual, some lesbian. They ranged in age from a 17-year-old school girl whose mother took her in for a breast augmentation, to a successful, middle-aged business woman seeking a face lift in order to 'fit into the corporate culture'.

4   These women told me about their history of suffering because of their appearance, how they decided to have their bodies altered surgically, their experiences with the operation itself and their assessments of the outcome of the surgery. While their stories involved highly varied experiences of embodiment as well as different routes towards deciding to have their bodies altered surgically, they invariably made cosmetic surgery viewable as an understandable and even unavoidable course of action in light of their particular biographical circumstances. I learned of their despair, not because their bodies were not beautiful, but because they were not ordinary—'just like everyone else'. I listened to their accounts of how they struggled with the decision to have cosmetic surgery, weighing their anxieties about risks against the anticipated benefits of the surgery. I discovered that they were often highly ambivalent about cosmetic surgery and wrestled with the same dilemmas which have made cosmetic surgery problematic for many feminists. My research gave a central role to women's agency, underlining their active and lived relationship with their bodies and showing how they could knowledgeably choose to have cosmetic surgery. While I remained critical of the practice of cosmetic surgery and the discourse of feminine inferiority which it sustains, I did not reject it as an absolute evil, to be avoided at any cost. Instead I argued for viewing cosmetic surgery as a complex dilemma: problem and solution, symptom of oppression and act of empowerment, all in one.

5   Given my research on cosmetic surgery, I was obviously intrigued by Orlan's surgical experiments. While I was fascinated by her willingness to put her body under the knife, however, I did not immediately see what her project had to offer for understanding why 'ordinary' women have cosmetic surgery. On the contrary, I placed Orlan alongside other contemporary women artists who use their bodies to make radical statements about a male-dominated social world: Cindy Sherman's inflatable porno dolls with their gaping orifices, Bettina Rheim's naked women in their exaggerated sexual posings, or Matuschka's self-portraits of her body after her breast has been amputated. It came as a surprise, therefore, when my research was continually being linked to Orlan's project. Friends and

colleagues sent me clippings about Orlan. At lectures about my work, I was invariably asked what I thought about Orlan. Journalists juxtaposed interviews with me and Orlan for their radio programmes or discussed us in the same breath in their newspaper pieces. Our projects were cited as similar in their celebration of women's agency and our insistence that cosmetic surgery was about more than beauty.[3] We were both described as feminists who had gone against the feminist mainstream and dared to be politically incorrect. By exploring the empowering possibilities of cosmetic surgery, we were viewed as representatives of a more nuanced and—some would say—refreshing perspective on cosmetic surgery.

6   These reactions have increasingly led me to reconsider my initial belief that Orlan's surgical experiments have nothing to do with the experiences of women who have cosmetic surgery. In particular, two questions have begun to occupy my attention. The first is to what extent Orlan's aims coincide with my own; that is, to provide a feminist critique of the technologies and practices of the feminine beauty system while taking women who have cosmetic surgery seriously. The second is whether Orlan's project can provide insight into the motives of the run-of-the-mill cosmetic surgery recipient.

7   In this article, I am going to begin with this second question. After looking at Orlan's performances as well as how she justifies them, I consider the possible similarities between her surgical experiences and the surgical experiences of the women I spoke with. I then return to the first question and consider the status of Orlan's art as feminist critique of cosmetic surgery—that is, as a utopian revisioning of a future where women reappropriate cosmetic surgery for their own ends. In conclusion, I argue that—when all is said and done—surgical utopias may be better left to art than to feminist critique.

ORLAN'S BODY ART

8   Orlan came of age in the 1960s—the era of the student uprisings in Paris, the 'sexual revolution' and the emergence of populist street theatre. As visual artist, she has always used her own body in unconventional ways to challenge gender stereotypes, defy religion and, more generally, to shock her audience (Lovelace 1995). For example, in the 1960s, she displayed the sheets of her bridal trousseau stained with semen to document her various sexual encounters, thereby poking fun at the demands for virgin brides in France. In the 1970s, she went to the Louvre with a small audience and pasted a triangle of her own pubic hair to the voluptuously reclining nude depicted in the *Rape of Antiope*—a hairless body devoid of subjecthood, a mere object for consumption. In the 1980s, Orlan shocked Parisian audiences by displaying her magnified genitals, held open by means of pincers, with the pubic hair painted yellow, blue and red (the red was menstrual blood). A video camera was installed to record the faces of her viewers who were then given a text by Freud on castration anxiety.

9   Her present project in which she uses surgery as a performance is, by far, her most radical and outrageous. She devised a computer-synthesized ideal self-portrait based on features taken from women in famous works of art: the forehead of Da Vinci's *Mona Lisa*, the chin of Botticelli's *Venus*, the nose of

Fountainebleau's *Diana*, the eyes of Gérard's *Psyche* and the mouth of Boucher's *Europa*. She did not choose her models for their beauty, but rather for the stories which are associated with them. Mona Lisa represents transsexuality for beneath the woman is—as we now know—the hidden self-portrait of the artist Leonardo Da Vinci; Diana is the aggressive adventuress; Europa gazes with anticipation at an uncertain future on another continent; Psyche incorporates love and spiritual hunger; and Venus represents fertility and creativity.

10   Orlan's 'self-portraits' are not created at the easel, but on the operating table. The first took place on 30 May 1987, the artist's 40th birthday, and eight more have taken place since then. Each operation is a 'happening'. The operating theatre is decorated with colourful props and larger-than-life representations of the artist and her muses. Male striptease dancers perform to music. The surgeons and nurses wear costumes by top designers and Orlan herself appears in net stockings and party hat with one breast exposed. She kisses the surgeon ostentatiously on the mouth before lying down on the operating table. Each performance has a theme (like 'Carnal Art', 'This is My Body, This is My Software', 'I Have Given My Body to Art', 'Identity Alterity'). Orlan reads philosophical, literary or psychoanalytic texts while being operated on under local anaesthesia. Her mood is playful and she talks animatedly even while her face is being jabbed with needles or cut ('producing', as she puts it, 'the image of a cadaver under autopsy which just keeps speaking').[4]

11   All of the operations have been filmed. The seventh operation-performance in 1993 was transmitted live by satellite to galleries around the world (the theme was omnipresence) where specialists were able to watch the operation and ask questions which Orlan then answered 'live' during the performance. In between operations, Orlan speaks about her work at conferences and festivals throughout the world where she also shows photographs and video clips of her operations. Under the motto 'my body is my art', she has collected souvenirs from her operations and stored them in circular, plexi-glass receptacles which are on display in her studio in Ivry, France. These 'reliquaries' include pieces of her flesh preserved in liquid, sections of her scalp with hair still attached, fat cells which have been suctioned out of her face, or crumpled bits of surgical gauze drenched in her blood. She sells them for as much as 10,000 francs, intending to continue until she has 'no more flesh to sell'.

12   Orlan's performances require a strong stomach and her audiences have been known to walk out midway through the video. The confrontation of watching the artist direct the cutting up of her own body is just too much for many people to bear. Reactions range from irritation to—in Vienna—a viewer fainting.[5] While Orlan begins her performances by apologizing to her audience for causing them pain, this is precisely her intention. As she puts it, art has to be transgressive, disruptive and unpleasant in order to have a social function. ('Art is not for decorating apartments, for we already have plenty of that with aquariums, plants, carpets, curtains, furniture . . .').[6] Both artist and audience need to feel uncomfortable so that 'we will be forced to ask questions'.

13   For Orlan, the most important question concerns 'the status of the body in our society and its future . . . in terms of the new technologies'.[7] The body has traditionally been associated with the innate, the immutable, the god given or the

fated-ness of human life. Within modernist science, the body has been treated as the biological bedrock of theories on self and society—the 'only constant in a rapidly changing world' (Frank 1990: 133). In recent years, this view has become increasingly untenable. The body—as well as our beliefs about it—is subject to enormous variation, both within and between cultures. Postmodern thinkers have rejected the notion of a biological body in favour of viewing bodies as social constructions. Orlan's project takes the postmodern deconstruction of the material body a step further. In her view, modern technologies have made any notion of a natural body obsolete. Test-tube babies, genetic manipulation and cosmetic surgery enable us to intervene in nature and develop our capacities in accordance with our needs and desires. In the future, bodies will become increasingly insignificant—nothing more than a 'costume', a 'vehicle', something to be changed in our search 'to become who we are'.[8]

14   The body of which Orlan speaks is a female body. Whereas her earlier work explored gender stereotypes in historical representations of the female body, her present project examines the social pressures which are exercised upon women through their bodies—in particular, the cultural beauty norms. At first glance, this may seem contradictory, since the goal of her art is to achieve an 'ideal' face. Although she draws upon mythical beauties for inspiration, she does not want to resemble them. Nor is she particularly concerned with being beautiful. Her operations have left her considerably less beautiful than she was before. For example, in operation seven she had silicone implants inserted in her temples (the forehead of Mona Lisa), giving her a slightly extraterrestrial appearance. For her next and last operation, she has planned 'the biggest nose physically possible'—a nose which will begin midway up her forehead. Thus, while Orlan's face is an ideal one, it deviates radically from the masculinist ideal of feminine perfection. Her ideal is radically nonconformist. It does not make us aware of what we lack. When we look at Orlan, we are reminded that we can use our imagination to become the persons we want to be.

15   Orlan's project explores the problem of identity. Who she is, is in constant flux or, as she puts it, 'by wanting to become another, I become myself'. 'I am a bulldozer: dominant and aggressive . . . but if that becomes fixed it is a handicap . . . I, therefore, renew myself by becoming timid and tender . . .'.[9] Her identity project is radical precisely because she is willing to alter her body surgically in order to experiment with different identities. What happens to the notion of 'race', she wonders, if I shed my white skin for a black one?[10] Similarly, she rejects gender as a fixed category when she claims: 'I am a woman-to-woman transsexual act'. However, Orlan's surgical transformations—unlike a sex-change operation—are far from permanent. In this sense, Orlan's art can be viewed as a contribution to postmodern feminist theory on identity.[11] Her face resembles Haraway's (1991) cyborg—half-human, half-machine—which implodes the notion of the natural body. Her project represents the postmodern celebration of identity as fragmented, multiple and—above all—fluctuating and her performances resonate with the radical social constructionism of Butler (1990, 1993) and her celebration of the transgressive potential of such performativity.

16   For Orlan, plastic surgery is a path towards self-determination—a way for women to regain control over their bodies. Plastic surgery is one of the primary arenas where 'man's power can be most powerfully asserted on women's bodies', 'where the dictates of the dominant ideology . . . become . . . more deeply embedded in female . . . flesh'.[12] Instead of having her body rejuvenated or beautified, she turns the tables and uses surgery as a medium for a different project. For example, when Orlan's male plastic surgeons balked at having to make her too ugly ('they wanted to keep me cute'), she turned to a female feminist plastic surgeon who was prepared to carry out her wishes. The surgical performances themselves are set up to dispel the notion of a sick body, 'just an inert piece of meat, lying on the table'.[13] Orlan designs her body, orchestrates the operations and makes the final decision about when to stop and when to go on. Throughout the surgery, she talks, gesticulates and laughs. This is her party and the only constraint is that she remain in charge. Thus, while bone breaking might be desirable (she originally wanted to have longer legs), it had to be rejected because it would have required full anaesthesia and, therefore, have defeated the whole purpose of the project. Orlan has to be the creator, not just the creation; the one who decides and not the passive object of another's decisions.

ART AND LIFE

17   I now want to return to the issue which I raised at the outset of this article: namely, the puzzling fact that my research is continually being associated with Orlan's art. As one journalist noted after reading my book: the only difference between Orlan and the majority of women who have cosmetic surgery is one of degree. Orlan is just an extreme example of what is basically the same phenomenon: women who have cosmetic surgery want to be 'their own Pygmalions'.[14]

18   At first glance, there are, indeed, similarities between Orlan's statements about her art and how the women I interviewed described their reasons for having cosmetic surgery. For example, both Orlan and these women insisted that they did not have cosmetic surgery to become more beautiful. They had cosmetic surgery because they did not feel at home in their bodies; their bodies did not fit their sense of who they were. Cosmetic surgery was an intervention in identity. It enabled them to reduce the distance between the internal and external so that others could see them as they saw themselves.[15] Another similarity is that both Orlan and the women I spoke with viewed themselves as agents who, by remaking their bodies, remade their lives as well. They all rejected the notion that by having cosmetic surgery, they had allowed themselves to be coerced, normalized or ideologically manipulated. On the contrary, cosmetic surgery was a way for them to take control over circumstances over which they previously had had no control. Like Orlan, these women even regarded their decision to have cosmetic surgery as an oppositional act: something they did for themselves, often at great risk and in the face of considerable resistance from others.

19   However, this is where the similarities end. Orlan's project is not about a real-life problem; it is about art. She does not use cosmetic surgery to alleviate

suffering with her body, but rather to make a public and highly abstract state-ment about beauty, identity and agency. Her body is little more than a vehicle for her art and her personal feelings are entirely irrelevant. When asked about the pain she must be experiencing, she merely shrugs and says: 'Art is a dirty job, but someone has to do it.'[16] Orlan is a woman with a mission: she wants to shock, dis-rupt convention and provoke people into discussing taboo issues. 'Art can and must change the world, for that is its only justification.'[17]

20   This is very different from the reasons the women I spoke with gave for hav-ing cosmetic surgery. Their project is a very private and personal one. They want to eliminate suffering which has gone beyond what they feel they should have to endure. They are anxious about the pain of surgery and worried about the out-come. They prefer secrecy to publicity and have no desire to confront others with their decisions. While their explanations touch on issues like beauty, iden-tity and agency (although not necessarily using those words), they are always linked to their experiences and their particular life histories. Their justification for having cosmetic surgery is necessity. It is the lesser of two evils, their only option under the circumstances. They do not care at all about changing the world; they simply want to change themselves.

21   Thus, cosmetic surgery as art and cosmetic surgery in life appear to be very different phenomena. I, therefore, might conclude that there is little resem-blance between Orlan's surgical experiences and those of most women who have cosmetic surgery, after all. Orlan's celebration of surgical technologies seems to have little in common with a project like my own, which aims to pro-vide a feminist critique of cosmetic surgery. Consequently, comparisons between my research and Orlan's project can only be regarded as superficial or premature.

22   But perhaps this conclusion is overhasty. After all, it was never Orlan's inten-tion to understand the surgical experiences of 'ordinary' women. Nor is it her intention to provide a feminist polemic against the unimaginable lengths to which women will go to achieve an ideal of beauty as defined by men. Hers is not a sociological analysis which explicitly attacks the evils of cosmetic surgery and its pernicious effects on women (Lovelace 1995). Nevertheless, her project is an implicit critique of the dominant norms of beauty and the way cosmetic surgery is practised today. It belongs to the tradition of feminist critique which imaginatively explores the possibilities of modern technology for the empow-erment of women. As such, Orlan's project might be viewed as an example of a feminist utopia.

COSMETIC SURGERY AS FEMINIST UTOPIA

23   Feminists have often envisioned a future where technology has been seized by women for their own ends. Take, for example, Shulamith Firestone's *Dialectic of Sex* (1970) in which she fantasizes a world in which reproductive technology frees women from the chores and constraints of biological motherhood. In a similar vein, the novelist Marge Piercy depicts a feminist utopia in *Woman on the Edge of Time* (1976) where genetic engineering has erased sexual and 'racial' differences, thereby abolishing sexism and racism.[18]

24   More recently, the feminist philosopher Kathryn Morgan (1991) applies the notion of utopia to cosmetic surgery. She claims that refusal may not be the only feminist response to the troubling problem of women's determination to put themselves under the knife for the sake of beauty. There may, in fact, be a more radical way for feminists to tackle the 'technological beauty imperative'.

25   She puts forth what she calls 'a utopian response to cosmetic surgery': that is, an imaginary model which represents a desirable ideal that because of its radicality is unlikely to occur on a wide scale (Morgan 1991: 47). Drawing upon feminist street theatre, on the one hand, and postmodern feminist theory—most notably Judith Butler's (1990) notion of gender as performance—on the other, Morgan provides some imaginative, if somewhat ghoulish, examples of cosmetic surgery as feminist utopia.

26   For example, she envisions alternative 'Miss . . .' pageants where the contestants compete for the title 'Ms Ugly'. They bleach their hair white, apply wrinkle-inducing creams or have wrinkles *carved into* their faces, have their breasts pulled *down* and *darken* their skin. (Morgan 1991: 46). Or, she imagines 'beautiful body boutiques' where 'freeze-dried fat cells', 'skin velcro', magnetically attachable breasts complete with nipple pumps, and do-it-yourself sewing kits with pain-killers and needles are sold to interested customers.

27   These 'performances' can be characterized as a feminist critique of cosmetic surgery for several reasons.

28   First, they unmask both 'beauty' and 'ugliness' as cultural artefacts rather than natural properties of the female body. They valorize what is normally perceived as ugly, thereby upsetting the cultural constraints upon women to comply with the norms of beauty. By actually undergoing mutations of the flesh, the entire notion of a natural body—that linchpin of gender ideology—is destabilized.

29   Second, these surgical performances constitute women as subjects who use their feminine body as a site for action and protest rather than as an object of discipline and normalization. These parodies mock or mimic what is ordinarily a source of shame, guilt or alienation for women. Unlike the 'typical' feminine disorders (anorexia, agoraphobia or hysteria) which are forms of protest where women are victims, Morgan's actions require '*healthy*' (*sic*) women who already 'have a feminist understanding of cosmetic surgery' (Morgan 1991: 45).

30   Third, by providing a travesty of surgical technologies and procedures, these performances magnify the role that technology plays in constructing femininity through women's bodies. At the same time, they usurp men's control over these technologies and undermine the power dynamic which makes women dependent on male expertise (Morgan 1991: 47). Performances show how technology might be reappropriated for feminist ends.

31   Morgan acknowledges that her surgical utopias may make her readers a bit queasy or even cause offence. However, this is as it should be. It only shows that we are still in the thrall of the cultural dictates of beauty and cannot bear to imagine women's bodies as ugly. Anyone who feels that such visions go 'too far' must remind herself that she has merely become anaesthetized to the mutilations which are routinely performed on women by surgeons every day (Morgan 1991: 46–7). Where the 'surgical fix' is concerned, 'shock therapy' is the only solution.

DOES COSMETIC SURGERY CALL FOR A UTOPIAN RESPONSE?

32   The attractions of a utopian approach to cosmetic surgery are considerable. It enables feminists to take a stand against the cultural constraints upon women to be beautiful and dramatically exposes the excesses of the technological fix. It destabilizes many of our preconceived notions about beauty, identity and the female body and it provides a glimpse of how women might engage with their bodies in empowering ways. However, most important of all—and I believe this is why such approaches appeal to the feminist imagination— it promises the best of both worlds: a chance to be critical of the victimization of women without having to be victims ourselves.

33   While I am entertained and intrigued by the visions put forth by Morgan and enacted by Orlan, I must admit that they also make me feel profoundly uneasy. This unease has everything to do with my own research on cosmetic surgery. On the basis of what women have told me, I would argue that a utopian response to cosmetic surgery does not just open up radical avenues for feminist critique; it also limits and may even prevent this same critique. It is my contention that there are, at least, four drawbacks.

34   First, a utopian response discounts the suffering which accompanies any cosmetic surgery operation. One of the most shocking aspects of Orlan's performances is that she undergoes surgery which is clearly painful and yet shrugs off the pain ('Of course, there are several injections and several grimaces . . . but I just take painkillers like everyone else')[19] or explains that the audience feels more pain looking at the surgery than she does in undergoing it. ('Sorry to have made you suffer, but know that I do not suffer, unlike you . . .'.)[20] This nonchalance is belied by the postoperative faces of the artist—proceeding from swollen and discoloured to, several months later, pale and scarred. Whether a woman has her wrinkles smoothed out surgically or carved in has little effect on the pain she feels during the surgery. Such models, therefore, presuppose a non-sentient female body—a body which feels no pain.[21]

35   Second, a utopian response discounts the risks of cosmetic surgery. Technologies are presented as neutral instruments which can be deployed to feminist ends. Both Orlan and Morgan describe surgery as conceived, controlled and orchestrated by the autonomous feminine subject. She has the reins in her hand. However, even Orlan has had a 'failed' operation: one of the silicone implants wandered and had to be reinserted—this time not in front of the video camera. Such models overstate the possibilities of modern technology and diminish its limitations.

36   Third, a utopian response ignores women's suffering with their appearance. The visions presented by both Orlan and Morgan involve women who are clearly unaffected by the crippling constraints of femininity. They are not dissatisfied with their appearance as most women are; nor, indeed, do they seem to care what happens to their bodies at all. For women who have spent years hating their excess flesh or disciplining their bodies with drastic diets, killing fitness programmes or cosmetic surgery, the image of 'injecting fat cells' or having the breasts 'pulled down' is insulting. The choice of 'darkened skin' for

a feminist spectacle which aims to 'valorize the ugly' is unlikely to go down well with women of colour. At best, such models negate their pain. At worst, they treat women who care about their appearance as the unenlightened prisoners of the beauty system who are more 'culturally scripted' than their artistic sisters.

37   Fourth, a utopian response discounts the everyday acts of compliance and resistance which are part of ordinary women's involvement in cosmetic surgery. The surgical experiments put forth by Orlan and Morgan have the pretension of being revolutionary. In engaging in acts which are extraordinary and shocking, they not only entertain and disturb, but also distance us from the more mundane forms of protest.[22] It is difficult to imagine that cosmetic surgery might entail *both* compliance *and* resistance. The act of having cosmetic surgery involves going along with the dictates of the beauty system, but also refusal— refusal to suffer beyond a certain point. Utopian models privilege the flamboyant, public spectacle as feminist intervention and deprivilege the interventions which are part of living in a gendered social order.

38   In conclusion, I would like to return to the young woman I mentioned at the beginning of this chapter. At first glance, her reaction might be attributed to her failure to appreciate the radicality of Orlan's project. She is apparently unable to go beyond her initial, 'gut level' response of horror at the pictures and consider what Orlan's performances have to say in general about the status of the female body in a technological age. She is just not sophisticated enough to benefit from this particular form of feminist 'shock therapy'.

39   However, having explored the 'ins' and 'outs' of surgical utopias, I am not convinced that this is how we should interpret her reaction. Her refusal to take up Orlan's invitation may also be attributed to concern. She may feel concern for the pale woman before her whose face still bears the painful marks of her previous operations. Or she may be concerned that anyone can talk so abstractly and without emotion about something which is so visibly personal and painful. Or she may simply be concerned that in order to appreciate art, she is being required to dismiss her own feelings.

40   Her concern reminds us of what Orlan and, indeed, any utopian approach to cosmetic surgery leaves out: the sentient and embodied female subject, the one who feels concern about herself and about others. As feminists in search of a radical response to women's involvement in cosmetic surgery, we would do well to be concerned about this omission as well.

NOTES

1. This festival was organized by Triple X which puts on an annual exhibition including theatre, performance, music, dance and visual art. I would like to thank Peter van der Hoop for supplying me with information about Orlan. I am indebted to Willem de Haan, Suzanne Phibbs and the participants of the postgraduate seminar 'Gender, Body, Love', held at the Centre for Women's Research in Oslo, Norway in May 1996 for their constructive and insightful comments.

2. *De Groene Amsterdammer* (23 August 1995).

3. See, for example, a recent article by Xandra Schutte in *De Groene Amsterdammer* (13 December 1995) or 'Passages and Passanten' (VPRO Radio 5, 17 November 1995).

4. Quoted in Reitmaier (1995: 8).

5. *Falter* (1995, No. 49: 28).

6. Quoted in Reitmaier (1995: 7).

7. See Reitmaier (1995: 8).

8. Quoted in Tilroe (1996: 17).

9. *Actuel* (January 1991: 78).

10. Obviously, Orlan has not read John Howard Griffin's (1961) *Black Like Me* in which a white man chronicles his experiences of darkening his skin in order to gain access to African-American life in the mid-1950s. For him, becoming the racial Other was a way to understand the material and bodily effects of racism—an experiment which was anything but playful and ultimately resulted in the author's untimely death from skin cancer. See Awkward (1995) for an excellent discussion of such experiments from a postmodern ethnographic perspective.

11. While Orlan has been cited as a model for postmodern feminist critiques of identity, her project is, in some ways, antithetical to this critique. She celebrates a notion of the sovereign, autonomous subject in search of self which is much more in line with Sartre's existentialism than poststructuralist theory *a la* Butler. See, for example, the debate between Butler and others in Benhabib et al. (1995).

12. Quoted in Reitmaier (1995: 9).

13. *De Volkskrant* (5 June 1993).

14. *De Groene Amsterdammer* (13 December 1995: 29).

15. Quoted in Reitmaier (1995: 8).

16. Quoted in Reitmaier (1995: 10).

17. Quoted in Reitmaier (1995: 7).

18. See José van Dyck (1995) for an excellent analysis of feminist utopias (and dystopias) in debates on the new reproductive technologies.

19. Quoted in Reitmaier (1995: 10).

20. Statement given at performance in Amsterdam.

21. This harks back to the notion that women—particularly working-class women and women of colour—do not experience pain to the same degree that affluent, white women and men do. This notion justified considerable surgical experimentation on women in the last century. See, for example, Dally (1991).

22. It could be argued that in the context of the art business where success depends upon being extraordinary, Orlan is simply complying with convention. This would make her no more, but also no less, revolutionary than any other woman who embarks upon cosmetic surgery.

REFERENCES

Awkward, Michael (1995) *Negotiating Difference. Race, Gender, and the Politics of Positionality*, Chicago and London: The University of Chicago Press.

Benhabib, Seyla, Judith Butler, Drucilla Cornell and Nancy Fraser (1995) *Feminist Contentions. A Philosophical Exchange*, New York and London: Routledge.

Butler, Judith (1990) *Gender Trouble: Feminism and the Subversion of Identity*, New York: Routledge.

Butler, Judith (1993) *Bodies That Matter: On the Discursive Limits of 'Sex'*, New York: Routledge.

Dally, Ann (1991) *Women Under the Knife*, London: Hutchinson Radius.

Davis, Kathy (1995) *Reshaping the Female Body. The Dilemma of Cosmetic Surgery*, New York: Routledge.

Firestone, Shulamith (1970) *The Dialectic of Sex. The Case for Feminist Revolution*, New York: Bantam.

Frank, Arthur (1990) 'Bringing Bodies Back In: A Decade Review'. *Theory, Culture and Society* 7: 131–62.

Griffin, John Howard (1961) *Black Like Me*, New York: Signet.

Haraway, Donna J. (1991) *Simians, Cyborgs, and Women. The Reinvention of Nature*, London: Free Association Books.

Lovelace, Cary (1995) 'Orlan: Offensive Acts', *Performing Arts Journal 49*: 13–25.

Morgan, Kathryn Pauly (1991) 'Women and the Knife: Cosmetic *Surgery* and the Colonization of Women's Bodies', *Hypatia 6*(3): 25–53.

Piercy, Marge (1976) *Woman on the Edge of Time*, New York: Fawcett Crest.

Reitmaier, Heidi (1995) '"I Do Not Want to Look Like . . ." Orlan on becoming Orlan', *Women's Art 5* June: 5–10.

Tilroe, Anna (1996) *De huid van de kameleon. Over hedendaagse beeldende kunst*, Amsterdam: Querido.

Van Dyck, José (1995) *Manufacturing Babies and Public Consent*, London: Macmillan.

Active Reading

1. How does Davis describe the link between her interest in cosmetic surgery and her research study of it?

2. How has the view of the body changed, from modernist to postmodernist thinking?

3. Provide a brief summary of Morgan's utopian response to cosmetic surgery and the three ways it provides a critique of this medical technology.

Critical Reading

1. What do you think of Orlan's art project and of her definition of the purpose of art?

2. Considering the nature of Orlan's project, should we refer to the surgeries she undergoes as "modifications" or "mutilations"? Consider the connotations and denotations of these words, and how we use them to refer to various alterations.

3. The article is framed by references to a young woman who objects to the spectacle of Orlan's body mutilation/modification. What is the author's attitude to the spectator's concerns?

"Should We Prevent Non-Therapeutic Mutilation and Extreme Body Modification?"

Thomas Schramme

Thomas Schramme examines several arguments against body modification but ultimately concludes that because they are not convincing, body modification should be permitted. Schramme is a philosopher by training and specializes in the philosophy of psychiatry, concepts of health and disease and ethical issues in health care. He is course director of the MA Medical Humanities at the University of Swansea (UK) and teaches philosophy of medicine and medical ethics on undergraduate and postgraduate programs. Before starting his studies at Frankfurt University and Free University Berlin, he worked with people with intellectual disabilities and mental illnesses.

INTRODUCTION

1   Consider two cases: Ms A sees a doctor to get a breast amputated. She suffers from breast cancer. Her doctor has recommended the treatment and she has agreed. It is a straightforward case of a legitimate intervention into bodily integrity, because it is based on voluntary informed consent. Ms B also sees her doctor to get her breast amputated. She does not suffer from cancer but is a highly ambitious archer, who believes that her athletic abilities will be considerably enhanced by the amputation. She has read widely about the Amazons and therefore knows about the optimal preconditions of drawing a bow when the obstructing body part is removed. So in the case of Ms B we can also identify an example of voluntary mutilation. But the proposed intervention nevertheless does not seem to be justified. Why?[1]

2   We could argue that Ms B, in contrast to Ms A, does not have a valid claim to get her breast amputated, because the desired amputation does not serve a reasonable cause like preventing premature death. In order to argue this way we need an account of what can and what cannot be accepted as a justification of voluntary mutilation.[2] In the following, I want to scrutinise the considerations which might explain and possibly justify the common discomfort regarding non-therapeutic mutilation.[3] If we want to prevent or ban it, we need such a

---

[1] In order to be able to disregard obvious objections, which are not important for what I am trying to establish, I presuppose that Ms B is competent, medically informed and prepared to bear the costs of the intervention and possible consequential disadvantages. I also presume that the surgeon does not see the amputation as a violation of his professional duties.

[2] I do not distinguish between voluntary *self*-mutilation (maiming) and mutilation by others on grounds of informed consent.

[3] Since I am dealing mainly with non-therapeutic mutilations, I will not discuss the related example of Body Integrity Identity Disorder, which might justify the amputation of healthy limbs on grounds of an alienation of patients from these body parts (T. Bayne & N. Levy. Amputees By Choice: Body Integrity Identity Disorder and the Ethics of Amputation. *J Appl Philos* 2005; 22: 75–85). Although I see a relation of these cases to voluntary mutilation, I take the mentioned interventions to be therapeutic, because they aim at treating a peculiar symptom of a mental disorder. Whether amputation of healthy limbs is justified by that motive is, of course, a different issue.

justification, because in liberal societies any intervention into individual self-determination needs the support of a good reason.

3   Although my leading question is phrased in legal terms, we need to consider moral and prudential issues as well, i.e. whether it might be wrong or unreasonable to self-harm. Although the latter considerations are only a starting point and we might opt against legally preventing voluntary body modifications for other reasons, e.g. economic costs, they are significant in order to at least fulfil a necessary condition of banning non-therapeutic mutilations. If they cannot be shown to be immoral or at least irrational, it would be difficult to justify its legal prevention.

4   I believe that the case of extreme body modification is an ultimate test-case for liberal bioethics. It directly confronts two characteristics of a liberal attitude, namely to accept competent decisions even where they seem to be clearly unwise (anti-paternalism) and not to impose particular conceptions of the good on other people (neutrality). It seems that liberals need to drop either belief if they want to prevent non-therapeutic body modifications.

5   The history of mankind is full of examples of bodily mutilation inflicted for ritual, or other cultural, reasons. It could even be argued that the very transgression of given bodily appearance is an instance of exclusive human freedom.[4] Animals do not mutilate themselves for reasons other than saving their lives. Accordingly, tattoos and ear piercings are agreed to almost universally, and so too are more severe interventions into bodily integrity, like circumcision, accepted in many cultures. Some body mutilations or modifications, e.g. sterilisation or sex change, have become available in recent years through medical technology and are now also widely established and often acclaimed.

6   More contested examples of interventions specific to cultures are body stretchings, which can be found in many African tribes. Stretchings of the earlobes and lips to the size of a saucer, considerably elongated necks and even skull deformations are practised. And of course there is the well-known tradition of bound feet in some East Asian countries, which had been performed at least until the 20th century and seemingly still today in some rural areas.[5] What seems morally controversial in these cases is the lack of informed consent, since they are often carried out on infants or little children. But since similar or the same bodily modifications are done today on adults with their consent, common disgust provoked by them needs to be based on concerns other than the absence of competence to consent.

7   One of the most noticeable examples of mutilations which are widely condemned, on the other hand, is clitorectomy (or female genital mutilation for an evaluative expression), which is practised in some Islamic countries. I believe that this very case illustrates that the rejection of at least some body modifications is not based on lack of consent alone but on implicit value-judgements, which supposedly serve to set limits on legitimate alterations of bodily appearance.[6]

---

[4] G. Bataille. 1992. Orig. 1954. Sovereignty. Transl. Robert Hurley. *The Accused Share*, vol. 3, New York: Zone Books.

[5] S.R. Cummings & K. Stone. Consequences of foot binding among older women in Beijing, China. *Am J Public Health* 1997; 87: 1677–1679.

[6] The practice is illegal in Britain under the Prohibition of Female Circumcision Bill from 1985, even if performed on competent adults, cf. S. Sheldon & S. Wilkinson. Female Genital Mutilation and Cosmetic Surgery: Regulating Non-Therapeutic Body Modification. *Bioethics* 1998; 12: pp. 263–285.

8   However, it seems that value-judgements regarding interventions into bodily integrity, even the usage of terms like 'mutilation' versus the more neutral 'body modification', are based on nothing more than cultural and probably religious preferences. There seems to be no noticeable qualitative difference between, say, tattoos and aesthetic branding, and there is also no noticeable discrepancy in terms of the inflicted pain or health risk involved.

9   What many regard today as a repellent mutilation, e.g. tongue splitting, cuttings, subcutaneous implants and flesh staplings, have their precursors in piercings and other almost universally accepted modifications.[7] I therefore believe that the easy dismissal of the body modification community as a bunch of eccentrics or pathological cases ought to be rejected.[8] They have as their forerunners several tribal cultures, hence often refer to themselves as 'modern primitives', and some avant-garde artists, e.g. the Italian Futurists, who also perceived the body as material for the accomplishment of intended aims.[9] Grounds for rejecting body modifications are not as straightforward as many people would like to think.

10   There are five possible arguments against voluntary mutilation which I will discuss, though not all of them in detail: i) Self-mutilation is never really voluntary, but is caused by pathological beliefs and desires, or is a side-effect of mental disorder; ii) it violates moral duties to oneself; iii) it violates moral duties to others or harms other people; iv) it contravenes nature's purposes; v) it is unreasonable or irrational.[10]

1. PATHOLOGISATION

11   There is a lot of material on self-mutilation in the psychiatric literature. For example, self-cutting is identified as a common symptom in Borderline Personality Disorder. Self-mutilation is therefore usually regarded as a symptom or side-effect

---

[7] F. Musafar. 1996. Body-Play: State of Grace or Sickness? In *Bodies Under Siege: Self-Mutilation and Body Modification in Culture and Psychiatry*. Second Edition. A.R. Favazza. Baltimore: Johns Hopkins U.P.: 325–334. Examples of these practises can be seen on the website of the *Body Modification Ezine*. http://www.bmezine.com [Accessed: 21 March 2006].

[8] I am aware of only one serious scientific article on body modification, which does not set it in a psychiatric context from the outset: M. Benecke. First Report of Nonpsychotic Self-Cannibalism (Autophagy), Tongue Splitting, and Scar Patterns (Scarification) as an Extreme Form of Cultural Body Modification in a Western Civilization. *Am J Forensic Med Pathol* 1999; 200: 281–285.

[9] 'We believe in the possibility of an incalculable number of human transformations, and without a smile we declare that wings are asleep in the flesh of man.' F.T. Marinetti. 1991. Orig. 1911. Multiplied Man and the Reign of the Machine. In *Let's Murder the Moonshine: Selected Writings by F.T. Marinetti*. R.W. Flint, ed. Los Angeles: Sun and Moon Press: 90–93. Another famous slogan of the Italian Futurists reminds of Julien Offray de La Mettrie's study *Machine Man* (Cambridge: Cambridge U.P. 1996. Orig. 1747): 'We feel mechanically. We feel made of steel. We too are machines, we too are mechanized!' E. Prampolini, I. Pannaggi & V. Paladini. Mechanical Art: Futurist Manifesto (1922). Available at: http://www.futurism.org.uklmanifestos/manifesto57.htm [Accessed 31 March 2006].

[10] Apart from the bill on Female Genital Mutilation, I was not able to track down any legal regulations concerning extreme voluntary body modifications. Since so far most cases only concern minor interventions like piercing and tattooing, there still seems to be no need for regulation, besides already regulated issues of safety, hygiene, and consent. In Britain, and other countries, the common clause of 'grievous or actual bodily harm' may apply in some cases, because it even rules out interventions which are done by consent. Germany has a peculiar paragraph in its penal law (S228) that prohibits acts that 'offend good morals' *(wider die guten Sitten)*, i.e. are *contra bonos mores*. This paragraph also applies to consentient acts. The state of Illinois planned to ban tongue splitting unless performed for therapeutic or clinical reasons. This clause was dropped and the only proviso now is that a person from the medical profession performs the act. Available at: http://ilga.gov/legislation/publicacts/fulltext.asp?Name=093-0449. [Accessed 30 March 2006].

of pathological processes. But these psychiatric cases are not relevant to my concerns in this article, since they are clearly instances of non-voluntary or compulsive behaviour. It seems straightforward that many cases of self-mutilation can indeed be perceived as a 'morbid form of self help',[11] but it seems less obvious that *all* the examples I gave in the introduction can be pathologised in the same way.[12] If it would indeed be possible to show that every single instance of self-mutilation is caused by mental disorder, then we could deny the very reality of the phenomenon I am talking about. Voluntary, non-therapeutic mutilation then would not exist, it would be a contradiction in terms.

12   In order to reject this argumentation I would need to thoroughly scrutinise the criteria of voluntariness. I will not have the space to do so, but I want to stress that voluntary action and decision is usually established by the formal characteristics of lack of internal and external coercion or foreign control and not by the substance of the action or decision. Hence the *process* of decision-making and not the content of the decision itself is responsible for establishing its voluntariness. Therefore, there is no general reason to support the 'disorder' claim, but plenty of specific cases which, on investigation, at least seem to be obvious examples of voluntary mutilation, be they comprehensible and acceptable or not.[13]

13   One might object that the choice of self-mutilation cannot be regarded as voluntary, even under the formal approach, because social determinants coercively contribute to the will-formation of the possible self-maimers. Like anorectic adolescents, who seem to be strongly influenced by aesthetic ideals of their community, people contemplating body modifications may be manipulated by social pressure. But, firstly, all individual choices have a social aspect in being influenced by other people. It would need to be established when a social determinant becomes a normatively problematic case of manipulation or coercion. I do not see that this can be easily shown for the cases I am dealing with. Secondly, people who perform these body modifications hardly follow common social aesthetic ideals. On the contrary, they are still very often disrespected for their very appearance. So self-mutilation cannot be rejected for its alleged pathological or involuntary nature.

14   More positively, it can even be argued that the choice of body modifications coheres with the Western ideal of developing personality. One of the movement's main spokespersons, Erik Sprague, known as 'The Lizardman', says: 'Embrace your individuality: The unexamined life is not worth living because it is at best a pale imitation of life. So, examine your life. Devote time and consideration to your motivations, decisions, and goals. Take hard looks at them all. Actively engage in the process of self-definition. Make a concerted effort in all things to assert and express yourself as an individual rather than as a category or role.'[14] Since the body is an essential part of the self, it does seem to fit into the

[11] Favazza, *op. cit.* note 7; p. xix.

[12] V. L. Pitts. Body Modification, Self-Mutilation and Agency in Media Accounts of Subculture. *Body and Society*, 1999; 5: 291–303; V.L. Pitts. 2003. *In the Flesh: The Cultural Politics of Body Modification*, New York: Palgrave: 23ff.

[13] J. Feinberg. 1986. *Harm to Self*, Oxford: Oxford U.P.: 124ff.

[14] E. Sprague. Self-Definition and Body Modification & Ritual. Available at: hltp://www.bmezine.comlnews/lizardman/20031113.html [Accessed 31 March 2006].

ideal of self-development according to individual projects and life-plans. So why not shape the body according to individual tastes?

15   Having rejected the outright pathologisation of self-mutilation, I want to use the rest of the paper to inspect philosophical arguments which may be relevant for the evaluation of voluntary mutilation. Three important considerations are: duties to oneself (section 2), the value of autonomy vs. possible offence to others (section 3), and the concept of well-being and harm (section 4). I will conclude that none of these provides a firm justificatory basis for a rejection of voluntary body modifications.

2. DUTIES TO ONESELF

16   In the *Metaphysics of Morals*, Immanuel Kant attempts to justify duties to one-self.[15] Interestingly, he explicitly mentions self-maiming as an example of a vio-lation of this special kind of duty. If his argument succeeded we would indeed have a strong case for the rejection of many voluntary mutilations. But I contend that the notion of a duty to oneself is a non-starter, since the rights and duties are assembled in one and the same person. It seems obvious that a person (in the role of a rights-holder) could release himself from carrying out the duty. If so, there can be no binding of the individual will by the specific duty whatsoever. Therefore, the idea of self-regarding duties seems vacuous.[16]

17   It is to Kant's credit that he is aware of this problem and that he begins his analy-sis with an attempt to explain away the seeming contradiction. On one occasion he refers to the familiar rule *volenti non fit inturia*, which translates: no one is wronged willingly.[17] It is clearly an injustice to violate a duty, but if someone releases another person from acting according to a duty by consenting to the act which would violate the duty, then, according to the mentioned principle, no injustice is done. In the case of a self-regarding act or omission, the consent of the person affected has to be presumed by *definition*, because the subject and the object of the duty are one and the same person—hence the seeming antinomy in the idea of duties to oneself.

18   Kant solves the philosophical problem by splitting the personal union of human beings. He introduces two conceptions of man, the rational being (*homo noumenon*) and the natural being (*homo phenomenon*). According to him, there is no contradiction in duties to oneself, because a person as rational being binds the will of himself as a natural being. Although this solution looks rather obscure, I believe that Kant need not rely on this argument alone, because he could also maintain that on his account it is not (morally) permissible to release oneself (or another person) from the duty not to debase humanity.[18] So there might be specific duties, stemming from our respect for moral personhood, which cannot be waived; hence the idea of duties to oneself would make sense after all.

---

[15] I. Kant, 1996. Orig. 1797. *Practical Philosophy*. The Cambridge Edition of the works of Immanuel Kant. M.J. Gregor, transl. and ed. Cambridge: Cambridge U.P.: 543ff. [6:417ff.]. (Page numbers in square brackets refer to the pagination of the standard German Edition.)

[16] M.G. Singer. On Duties to Oneself, *Ethics* 1959; 69: 202–205.

[17] Kant, *op. cit.*, note 5, p. 547 [6:422.]

[18] A. Reath. 2002. Self-Legislation and Duties to Oneself. In: *Kant's Metaphysics of Morals. Interpretative Essays.* M. Timmons, ed. Oxford: Clarendon Press: 356.

19   But why is self-mutilation an instance of a violation of self-regarding duty? Self-maiming, according to Kant, contravenes self-preservation, which is a necessary condition of morality itself. Just as suicide is a (moral) crime, 'partial suicide', i.e. self-mutilation, is also morally wrong.

> A human being cannot renounce his personality as long as he is a subject of duty, hence as long as he lives; and it is a contradiction that he should be authorized to withdraw from all obligation, that is, freely to act as if no authorization were needed for this action. To annihilate the subject of morality in one's own person is to root out the existence of morality itself from the world, as far as one can, even though morality is an end in itself. Consequently, disposing of oneself as a mere means to some discretionary end is debasing humanity in one's person (*homo noumenon*), to which the human being (*homo phenomenon*) was nevertheless entrusted for preservation.
>
> To deprive oneself of an integral part or organ (to maim oneself)—for example, to give away or sell a tooth to be transplanted into another's mouth, or to have oneself castrated in order to get an easier livelihood as a singer, and so forth—are ways of partially murdering oneself.[19]

20   Even if we accepted Kant's dubious argumentation against suicide, his approach would still not suffice to morally condemn voluntary self-mutilation. After all, by mutilating oneself the conditions for the ability to act morally are neither threatened nor removed. Kant's own example of tooth-explantation makes this far too obvious. The reference to "partial suicide" does not help either, because we have to acknowledge a categorical, not merely gradual, distinction between self-mutilation and suicide.[20]

21   Alternatively Kant interprets self-mutilation as a threat to the purposes of human nature.[21] For there to be a categorical imperative at all, there must be, according to Kant, ends which are themselves duties.[22] The relevant (i.e. self-regarding) end, which is itself a duty, is self-perfection or the overcoming of human animality.[23] Self-perfection is explained in terms of abilities relevant for

---

[19] Kant, *op. cit.* note 15, p. 547 [6:4221.]. The formulation that a person, in committing suicide, is using himself as a mere means, is in line with the respective claim in the *Groundwork* (Kant, orig. 1785, *op. cit.* note 15, p. 80, [4:4293]). I refer to the *Metaphysics of Morals*, because his account of self-regarding duties in this later text is more detailed and because I fail to make sense of the idea that someone—while doing something *self-regarding*—may fail to treat himself (also) as an end.

[20] Denis (L. Denis. 2001. *Moral Self-Regard: Duties to Oneself in Kant's Moral Theory*. New York/London: Garland: 101) explains Kant's analogy between killing oneself and self-maiming by his premise that he 'considers the person to be a whole composed of physical and rational aspects'. But that does not make Kant's claim more agreeable, since the self-maimer is still a whole person after performing the act.

[21] The reference to human nature ought not to be interpreted in a biological way.

[22] Kant, *op. cit* note 15, p. 516ff. [6:38411.3]

[23] Kant seems to draw two distinctions which make the same point in analogous fashion: Firstly, he differentiates between negative worsening, or even removal, of the ability to morally self-improve, which is a violation of a perfect, negative duty to oneself, and the further enhancing of one's own moral abilities, which is an imperfect, positive duty to oneself (Ibid: p. 544f. [6:418f.] and p. 566f, [6:44&.]; Denis, *op. cit.* note 20, p. 110, also mentions Kant's notions of 'moral health' and 'moral prosperity' as objects of the respective duties). He secondly distinguishes between perfection in a quantitative (material) and a qualitative (formal) sense. I take it that the duty to perfection in the qualitative sense implies the non-neglect (negative) of specific capacities which are necessary for a certain end, i.e. becoming a moral person (see esp. Kant, op. cit. note 15, p. 517f. [6:3861.]). Kant explicitly says that moral perfection is—in terms of the qualitative interpretation—a perfect duty, but—in terms of its degree (i.e. quantitatively)—an imperfect one (Ibid: p. 241 [6:446]).

morality (e.g. understanding, the good will). Having the ability to act morally, again, means to be able to set one's own rational goals.

> The capacity to set oneself an end—any end whatsoever—is what characterizes humanity (as distinguished from animality). Hence there is also bound up with the end of humanity in our own person the rational will, and so the duty, to make ourselves worthy of humanity by culture in general, by procuring or promoting the *capacity* to realize all sorts of possible ends, so far as this is to be found in man himself. In other words, the human being has a duty to cultivate the crude predispositions of his nature, by which the animal is first raised into the human being. It is therefore a duty in itself.[24]

22   To be sure, this argument leaves open whether every form of self-mutilation threatens self-perfection and, if not, which do. Nevertheless, it may be argued in a Kantian spirit that every self-mutilation involves an impairment of bodily functional abilities, and that this equals a violation of duty, because, according to Kant, it is a self-regarding moral duty to obtain, preserve and possibly enhance these abilities.

23   I believe that even this putative reasoning applies to only a few cases of self-mutilation. Undeniably, Kant could claim that every mutilation entails a comparative deterioration of individual abilities to act, because bodily functional abilities are impaired or even removed. But it is not straightforward why a comparative restriction of abilities causes moral problems, as long as the ability to act morally is preserved in principle. Is there a duty to act (morally) as efficiently as possible? I believe that in order to answer this question in the affirmative one would need further premises, e.g. a different perfectionist approach to human capacities such as Aristotle's teleological *ergon*-argument.[25] But Kant's theory does not contain any premises of this sort; his claim that self-perfection is a *duty* (i.e. not merely something which is good for us), is nothing more than an unfounded assertion.

24   Even if we ignore the gradual problem—why is self-*perfection* a duty?—there is a further, qualitative problem: What are the abilities we need in order to act morally? Whatever they are, obviously not all of them are impaired by acts of self-mutilation. For example, it does not seem likely that someone weakens his or her moral capacities by ripping out a tooth or even by amputating a breast.

25   Last but not least there is a possible objection to Kant's condemnation of self-mutilation, which accepts his own premises. Kant is led by the belief that our specific human abilities generate autonomy of the will and hence the ability to give oneself a law upon which to act. The duty of self-perfection also has its foundation in this very characteristic. But the modification of our given body, the transgression of its natural limits, might be interpreted as the best accomplishment of human freedom. As I have stressed before, what is regarded by some as mutilation, others see as a perfection of their physical appearance. According to this line of argumentation, the manipulation of one's own bodily constitution is part of self-perfection. Kant's example of the castrato appears in a different light. He manifests the highest possible achievement of human ability to sing. Therefore,

---

[24] Ibid: p. 522f. [6:392].

[25] Aristotle. 2000. *Niconoachean Ethics*. R. Crisp, transl. and ed. Cambridge: Cambridge UP.

not every instance of voluntary mutilation need be seen as a violation of duties to oneself, even on Kant's own account.

26   It is possible that many readers will object to my careless identification of Kant's conception of autonomy with plain, unqualified self-determination. After all, his argument does not aim primarily at possible impairments of bodily abilities but at the renunciation of our own nature as moral beings in the case of—what he likes to call—partial self-murder. According to Kant, such a purpose cannot be chosen autonomously. But this defence is futile. It merely paraphrases his dubious assertions. Kant's supposition that voluntary mutilation violates our autonomy and debases our moral personhood simply begs the question.

3. THE HARM PRINCIPLE

27   There is another idea contravening the plausibility of preventing non-therapeutic mutilations, an idea that is widely accepted in liberal societies: the harm principle, most clearly stated by John Stuart Mill, which holds that only actions which harm or threaten to harm other people may be coercively prevented. If no other person is affected, we may not infringe liberty, though we may criticize a person for his behaviour. Hence the claimed individual liberty spans over almost the whole area of personal affairs. Nobody may be coerced into acting for his (alleged) own good. Mill explicitly holds that a person is sovereign over his own mind and body.[26]

28   Mill is mainly interested in legal issues. He restricts the sphere of possible legal interventions to acts which affect others. On this thesis we could argue that, because self-mutilation and body modifications merely affect the person in question, they are legally permitted.[27] If interventions into bodily integrity are done by other people, they are allowed if they are done on grounds of the voluntary consent of the affected person.[28]

29   To be sure, Mill does allow for critique of seemingly offensive behaviour, hence we should not view the private sphere as completely removed from any social influences on his account.[29] He might even be read in a way that allows for the moral (in contrast to legal) condemnation of self-regarding acts. However, we

---

[26] 'One very simple principle, as entitled to govern absolutely the dealings of society with the individual in the way of compulsion and control, whether the means used be physical force in the form of legal penalties, or the moral coercion of public opinion. That principle is, that the sole end for which mankind are warranted, individually or collectively, in interfering with the liberty of action of any of their number is [. . .] to prevent harm to others. His own good, either physical or moral, is not a sufficient warrant. He cannot rightfully be compelled to do or forbear because it will be better for him to do so, because it will make him happier, because, in the opinions of others, to do so would be wise or even right. [. . .] Over himself, over his own body and mind, the individual is sovereign.' (J.S. Mill. 1998. Orig. 1859. *On Liberty and Other Essays*. Oxford World's Classics. John Gray, ed. Oxford: Oxford U.P.: p. 13f). Mill explicitly refers to the concept of duties to oneself on p. 87.

[27] One might argue that other people may be shocked by seeing people with severe body-mutilations, hence are harmed. I agree that Mill's theory is not specific enough on cases like these, but I would like to mention two rejoinders anyway: Firstly, squeamishness is not a good basis for prohibitions. People also used to be shocked by gay people kissing in public. Secondly, there are people with severe disfiguration which also shock others by their mere physical appearance. Should they consequently be excluded from appearance in public?

[28] Mill extensively deals with the common objection that every act might affect other people by giving a bad example. To my mind, he rejects it convincingly, ibid: p. 88ff.

[29] 'Human beings owe to each other the help to distinguish the better from the worse, and encouragement to choose the former and avoid the latter.' Mill, *op. cit.* note 26. p. 84.

have already seen the problems of regarding self-mutilations as immoral acts. It is surely difficult to square the idea of self-regarding acts as part of morality with the modern idea of morality as a system of solving interpersonal conflicts of interest. Consequently Mill, for one, objects to moralisation and eventual legal prohibition of acts which only affect a person's own sphere. Since everyone is pursuing their own good life, a person is entitled to find out for themselves what they regard as good for them. Whoever is able to make their own judgements on these matters[30] may not be stopped, even if their chosen course of action ends in mishap.

30   Nevertheless, we might look for support of this argument against severe body modifications in Mill's own account, which is generally anti-paternalistic, but still seems to allow for interventions in cases where someone acts against his own very basic self-interest.[31] One example to be discussed here is voluntary enslavement, which Mill explicitly disapproves of.[32] Similar to Kant, he seems to use a transcendental argument at this point. According to Mill, it would be contradictory to apply a principle, which ought to secure individual freedom as far as possible, in a way which undermines the very conditions of making use of individual freedom. Consequently, one might try to make a case for interpreting specific forms of body modification as impairments of the very basis for self-determination, and therefore as acts which ought to be rejected.[33] I will scrutinise a variation of this argument in the next section.

31   We can conclude from the discussion of Kant's and Mill's theories that, although there are no grounds for *moral* disapproval of voluntary mutilation, there is still room for objections. After all, maiming oneself quite likely implies a serious impairment of individual health. So instead of counting on morals, objections should better relate to the self-interest of the self-mutilator. It seems plainly irrational to maim yourself voluntarily or let someone else mutilate you.

4. SELF-INTEREST

32   It is hard to deny that many cases of mutilation and other body modifications impair bodily functional ability. Almost all of these interventions cause pathological conditions, e.g. destroyed skin tissue. Since health is a precondition of the pursuit of our projects and goals it is an important prudential value. Therefore, we might reject mutilations, even where they are done voluntarily, for reasons of their irrationality.[34]

33   Hard-nosed anti-paternalists would not be impressed by this move, of course, because they do not take irrationality to be a sufficient criterion for paternalistic intervention. Unreasonable actions might, after all, be voluntarily chosen.

---

[30] This does not apply to children and mentally impaired people, according to Mill.

[31] D. Lyons. 1994. *Rights, Welfare, and Mills Moral Theory.* Oxford: Oxford U.P.: p. 132ff.

[32] Mill, *op. cit.* note 26, p. 113ff.

[33] The 'basis' referred to here is the material precondition of self-determination, namely a functioning body. It is not enough to reject this argument by referring to body modification as expression of one's own freedom.

[34] B. Gert, C.M. Culver & K.D. Clouser. 1997. *Bioethics. A Return to Fundamentals,* Oxford: Oxford U.P.: p. 26ff. and 93ff. The term prudential value stems from James Griffin (J. Griffin. 1986. *Well-Being: Its Meaning, Measurement, and Moral Importance.* Oxford: Clarendon Press).

However, people who are less committed on this issue might want to act paternalistically in these extreme cases. In order to justify their intervention they would have to show that self-mutilation is indeed an instance of harm, severe enough to justify its prevention. Surprisingly, this is not as easy to establish as expected.

34   The argument relies on the presuppositions that, firstly, severe body modifications can be defined as pathological conditions and, secondly, that they are necessarily bad for a person. While the first might be more or less straightforward, the second needs more treatment. If a person mutilating herself disagrees with the judgement that she is harmed by this very act, then—on this account—she has to be wrong about her own well-being. We might want to say that, at least in this respect, human well-being is objectively defined by a norm of health, which again is defined by normal functional ability. What is good for us, as regards bodily health, does not seem to depend on whether we subjectively regard it as good.

35   Many mutilations indeed worsen certain abilities like mobility. But it seems to me that the existence of a comparative disadvantage is not sufficient to justify an intervention. We do, of course, in many cases accept the worsening of abilities for idiosyncratic reasons, without even considering to prevent it. Consider for example the common unhealthy lifestyles which result in even graver impairments of motility than common mutilations. In addition, bodily health is only one aspect of our well-being and probably not even the most important one. If people voluntarily choose to mutilate their flesh, we better assume that they take it to be in their interest. I therefore believe that voluntary mutilation should be regarded non-pejoratively and labelled 'body modification'.

5. CONCLUSION

36   I have discussed several arguments against voluntary body modifications. Not all people who voluntarily opt for these interventions can be regarded as suffering from mental disorders. Voluntary body modifications do not violate self-regarding duties and they do not amount to instances of harm severe enough to justify interventions.[35] As long as there are no other, better, arguments available which may lead us to a different assessment, I conclude that severe body modifications ought to be permitted.[36]

Active Reading

1.   The article opens with two cases, Ms A and Ms B. How do these cases help Schramme to define his key terms?

2.   On what grounds does Schramme reject the argument that self-mutilation is never voluntary but caused by pathological beliefs and compulsions?

3.   How can Kant's argument that it is one's duty to seek self-perfection be used to make a case against as well as for self-mutilation?

---

[35] It is maybe worth stressing again that I do not argue in favour of public funding for these interventions, so there is no problem of unreasonable claims on resources involved. What is more, body modifications do not raise the issue of possible long-term unfairness, which is often seen in relation to other privately funded treatments, e.g. *enhancements*, since the interventions I discussed hardly bring about any individual advantages.

[36] I should like to thank Steve Edwards, Hugh Upton, and the anonymous reviewers for valuable suggestions and comments.

Critical Reading

1. What are some of the strongest arguments against self-mutilation?

2. Schramme is engaging in moral philosophy when he tries to reason what people ought to do. Who—what sorts of reading audiences—would be interested in the sort of reasoning in which he engages and the conclusions he draws? Could his sort of reasoning influence policy- or decision-makers?

3. Do you know people who engage in body modification and, if so, would they be receptive to Schramme's line of thinking?

How to Build A Man

Anne Fausto-Sterling

Fausto-Sterling invites us to consider that science writing is not a matter of dispensing facts but, like other forms of writing, an interpretive exercise conducted by individuals whose values reflect those of the culture at large. In the case of biologists who write about sex and gender, Fausto-Sterling argues that they actually base their definition of "normal" on exceptions and variations and often on uncritical assumptions about gender characteristics. She disputes the argument that a man can be made if a child is raised and socialized as a boy, and points out that, since gender identity goes through many stages and occurs on several levels, it is much more complicated than our binary gender system would suggest.

Anne Fausto-Sterling is a professor of Biology and Gender Studies at Brown University. She has written extensively on questions pertaining to biology of gender and sexual and gender identity.

1   How does one become a man? Although poets, novelists, and playwrights long past answered with discussions of morality and honor, these days scholars deliberate the same question using a metaphor—that of social construction. In the current intellectual fashion, men are made, not born. We construct masculinity through social discourse—that array of happenings that covers everything from the visuals on MTV rap lyrics, and poetry to sports, beer commercials, and psychotherapy. But underlying all of this clever carpentry is the sneaking suspicion that one must start with a blueprint—or, to stretch the metaphor yet a bit more, that buildings must have foundations. Within the soul of even the most die-hard constructionist lurks a doubt. It is called the body.

2   In contrast, biological and medical scientists feel quite certain about their world. For them the body tells the truth. (Never mind that postmodern scholarship has questioned the very meaning of the word *truth*.) My task in this essay is to consider the truths that biologists extract from bodies, human and otherwise, to examine scientific accounts—some might even say constructions—of masculinity. To do this, I treat the scientific/medical literature as yet another set of texts open to scholarly analysis and interpretation.

3   What are little boys made of? While the nursery rhyme suggests "snips and snails and puppy dog tails," during the past seventy years medical scientists

have built a rather more concrete and certainly less fanciful account. Perhaps the single most influential voice during this period has been that of psychologist John Money. At least since the 1920s, embryologists have understood that during fetal development a single embryonic primordium, the indifferent fetal gonad, can give rise to either an ovary or a testis. In a similar fashion, both male and female external genitalia arise from a single set of structures. Only the internal sex organs—uteri, fallopian tubes, prostates, sperm transport ducts—arise during embryonic development from separate sets of structures. In the 1950s, John Money extended these embryological understandings into the realm of psychological development.[1] He envisioned that while all humans start on the same road, the path rapidly begins to fork. Potential males take a series of turns in one direction, potential females in another. In real time the road begins at fertilization and ends during late adolescence. If all goes as it should, then there are two and only two possible destinations: male and female.

4   But of course all does not always go as it should. Money identified the various forks in the road by studying individuals who took one or more wrong turns. From them he came up with a map of the normal. This is, in fact, one of the very interesting things about biological investigators. They use the infrequent to illuminate the common. The former they call abnormal, the latter, normal. Often, as is the case for Money and others in the medical world, the abnormal requires management. In the examples I will discuss, management means conversion to the normal. Thus we have a profound irony. Biologists and physicians use natural biological variation to define normality. Once armed with the description, they then set out to eliminate the natural variation that gave them their definitions in the first place.

5   How does all this apply to the construction of masculinity? Money lists ten road signs directing a person along the path to male or female. In most cases these indicators are clear, but as in any large city these days, sometimes graffiti makes them hard to read, and the traveler ends up taking a wrong turn. The first sign is *chromosomal sex:* the presence of an X or a Y. The second is *gonadal sex:* when there is no graffiti, the Y or the X instructs the fetal gonad to develop into a testis or an ovary. *Fetal hormonal sex* marks the third fork: the embryonic testis must make hormones that influence events to come—most especially the fourth (*internal morphologic sex*), fifth (*external mophologic sex*), and sixth (*brain sex*) branches in the road. All of these, but most especially external morphologic sex at birth, illuminate the road sign for step number seven: *sex of assignment and rearing.* Finally, to become, in John Money's world, either a true male or a true female, one must produce the right hormones at puberty (*pubertal hormonal sex*), acquire and express a consistent gender identity and role, and, to complete the picture, must be able to reproduce in the appropriate fashion (*procreative sex*) (see Money & Tucker 1975; Money & Ehrhardt 1972).

6   Many medical texts reproduce this neat little scheme, suggesting that it is a literal account of the scientific truth, but neglecting to point out how, at each step, scientists have woven into the fabric their own deeply social preexisting understandings of what it means to be male or female. Let me illustrate this for several of the branches in the road. Why is it that usually XX babies grow up to

be female while XYs become male? Geneticists say that it is because of a specific Y chromosome gene, often abbreviated SDY for "sex-determining gene on the Y chromosome." Biologists also refer to the SDY as the Master Sex Determining gene, and say that in its *presence*, a male is formed. Females, on the other hand, are said to be the default sex. In the *absence* of the master gene, they just naturally happen. The story of the SDY begins an account of maleness which continues throughout development. A male embryo must activate its master gene and seize its developmental pathway from the underlying female ground plan.

7   When the SDY gene starts working, it turns the indifferent gonad into a functional testis. One of the first things the testis does is to induce hormone synthesis. It is these molecules that take control of subsequent developmental steps. The first hormone to hit the decks (MIS or Mullerian Inhibiting Substance) suppresses the development of the internal female organs, which otherwise lie in wait ready to unveil their feminine presence. The next, fetal testosterone, manfully pushes other embryonic primordia to develop both the internal and external trappings of physical masculinity. Again, medical texts offer the presence/absence hypothesis: Maleness requires the presence of special hormones; in their absence, femaleness just happens.[2]

8   At this point two themes emerge. First, masculinity is an active presence that forces itself onto a feminine foundation, Money (1992) calls this "The Adam Principle—adding something to make a male." Second, the male is in constant danger. At any point, male development can be derailed: a failure to activate SDY, and the gonad becomes an ovary; a failure to make MIS, and the fetus can end up with fallopian tubes and a uterus superimposed on an otherwise male body; fail to make fetal testosterone, and, despite the presence of a testis, the embryo develops the external trappings of a baby girl. One fascinating contradiction in the scientific literature illustrates my point. Most texts write that femaleness results from the absence of male hormones,[3] yet, at the same time, scientists worry about how male fetuses protect themselves from being feminized by the sea of maternal (female) hormones in which they grow. This fear suggests, of course, that female hormones play an active role after all; but most scientists do not pick upon that bit of logic. Instead they hunt for special proteins the male embryo makes in order to protect itself from maternally induced feminization. (It seems that mother is to blame even before birth.)

9   Consider now the birth of a boy-child. He is perfect—Y chromosomes, testes descended into their sweet little scrotal sacs, a beautifully formed penis. He is perfect—except that the penis is very tiny. What happens next? Some medical texts refer to a situation such as this as a social emergency; others, as a surgical one. The parents want to tell everyone about the birth of their baby boy; the physicians fear he cannot continue developing along the road to masculinity. They decide that creating a female is best. Females are imperfect by nature, and if this child cannot be a perfect or near-perfect male, then being an imperfect female is the best choice. What do physicians' criteria for making such choices tell us about the construction of masculinity?

10   Medical managers use the following rule of thumb: "Genetic females should always be raised as females, preserving reproductive potential, regardless of how

severely the patients are virilized. In the genetic male, however, the gender of assignment is based on the infant's anatomy, predominantly the size of the phallus" (Donahue, Powell, & Lee 1991, 527). Only a few reports on penile size at birth exist in the scientific literature, and it seems that birth size, in and of itself, is not a particularly good indicator of size and function at puberty. The average phallus at birth measures 3.5 cm (1–1.5 in.) long. A baby boy born with a penis measuring only 0.9 inches raises some eyebrows, while medical practitioners do not permit one born with a penis less than 0.6 inches long to remain as a male (Danish et al. 1980). (The medical name for this condition is "micropenis.") Despite the fact that the intact organ may provide orgasmic pleasure to the future adult, it is surgically removed (along with the testes), and replaced by a much smaller clitoris, which may or may not retain orgasmic function. When surgeons turn "Sammy" into "Suzanna," they also build her a vagina. Her primary sexual activity is to be the recipient of a penis during heterosexual intercourse. As one surgeon recently commented, "It's easier to poke a hole than build a pole."

11   All this surgical activity goes on to ensure a congruous and certain sex of assignment and sex of rearing. During childhood, the medical literature insists, boys must have a phallus large enough to permit them to pee standing up, thus allowing them to "feel normal" when they play in little boys' peeing contests. In adulthood the penis must become large enough for vaginal penetration during sexual intercourse. By and large, physicians use the standard of reproductive potential for making females and phallus size for making males, although Kessler (1990) reports one case of a physician choosing to reassign as male a potentially reproductive genetic female infant rather than remove a well-formed penis.

12   At birth, then, masculinity becomes a social phenomenon. For proper masculine socialization to occur, the little boy must have a sufficiently large penis. There must be no doubt in the boy's mind, in the minds of his parents and other adult relatives, or in the minds of his male peers about the legitimacy of male identification. In childhood all that is required is that he be able to pee in a standing position. In adulthood he must engage in vaginal heterosexual intercourse. The discourse of sexual pleasure, even for males, is totally absent from this medical literature. In fact, male infants who receive extensive penile surgery often end up with badly scarred and thus physically insensitive members. While no surgeon considers this to be a desirable outcome, in assigning sex to an intersexual infant or to a boy with micropenis, sexual pleasure clearly takes a back seat to ensuring heterosexual conventions. Penetration in the absence of pleasure takes precedence over pleasure in the absence of penetration.

13   In the world of John Money and other managers of intersexuality, men are made, not born. Proper socialization becomes more important than genetics. Hence, Money and Ehrhardt (1972, 118–123) have a simple solution to accidents as terrible as accidental penile amputation following infant circumcision: raise the boy as a girl. If both the parents and child remain confident of his new-found female identity, all will be well. But what counts as good mental health for boys and girls? Here Money and coworkers focus primarily on female development, which becomes the mirror from which we can reflect the truth about males. Money has published extensively on observations of XX infants born with masculinized genitalia (Money, Schwartz, & Lewis 1984; Money & Daléry 1976, 1977).

Usually such children are raised as girls, and receive surgery and hormonal treatments to feminize their genitalia and ensure a feminine puberty. He notes that frequently such children have a harder time than usual achieving clarity about their femininity. The signs of trouble include: engaging in rough-and-tumble play, and hitting more often than other toddler girls; thinking more about having a career, and fantasizing less about marriage than other adolescent girls; and having lesbian relationships as an adolescent and young adult.

14   The homologue to these developmental variations can be found in Richard Green's description of the "Sissy Boy Syndrome" (1987). Green studied little boys who develop feminine interests—playing with dolls, dressing in girls' clothing, not engaging in enough rough-and-tumble play. These boys, he argued, are at high risk for becoming homosexuals. Money's and Green's ideas work together to present a picture of normality. And—surprise, surprise—there is no room in the scheme for a normal homosexual. Money makes a remarkable claim: Genetics and even hormones count less in making a man or a woman than does socialization. In sustaining that claim his strongest evidence, his trump card, is that the child born a male but raised a female becomes a heterosexual female. In fact, Milton Diamond (1995) has followed up on Money's early case histories and found the outcomes to be far more complex. In their accounts of the power of socialization, Money, Hampson, and Hampson (1955b) define heterosexual in terms of the sex of rearing. Thus a child raised as a female (even if biologically male) who prefers male lovers is psychologically heterosexual, although genetically she is not.

15   Again. we can parse out the construction of masculinity. To begin with, normally developing little boys must be active and willing to push one another around; maleness and aggression go together. Eventually little boys become socialized into appropriate adult behavior, which includes heterosexual fantasy and activity. Adolescent boys do not dream of marriage, but of careers and a professional future. A healthy adolescent girl, in contrast, must fantasize about falling in love, marrying, and raising children. Only a masculinized girl dreams of a professional future. Of course, we know already that for men the true mark of heterosexuality involves vaginal penetration with the penis. Other activities, even if they are with a woman, do not really count.

16   This might be the end of the story, except for one thing: accounts of normal development drawn from the study of intersexuals contain internal inconsistencies. How does Money explain the higher-than-normal percentage of lesbianism or the more frequent aggressive behavior among masculinized children raised as girls? One could imagine elaborating on the socialization theme: parents aware of the uncertain sex of their children subconsciously socialize them in some intermediary fashion. Shockingly for a psychologist, however, Money denies the possibility of subconsciously driven behavior (Money, Hampson & Hampson 1955b). Instead, he and the many others who interpret the development of intersexual children resort to hormonal explanations. If an XX girl born with a penis, surgically "corrected" shortly after birth and raised as a girl, subsequently becomes a lesbian, Money and others do not look to socialization. Instead they explain this failure to become heterosexual by appealing to hormones present in the fetal environment. Excess fetal testosterone caused the masculinization of

the genitalia; similarly, fetal testosterone must have altered the developing brain, readying it to view females as appropriate sexual objects. Here, then, we have the last bit of the picture painted by biologists. By implication, normal males become sexually attracted to females because testosterone affects their brain during embryonic development. Socialization reinforces this inclination.

17   Biologists, therefore, write texts about human development. These documents, which take the form of research papers, texts, review articles, and popular books, grow from interpretations of scientific data. Often written in neutral, abstract language, the texts have the ring of authority. Because they represent scientific findings, one might imagine they contain no preconceptions, no culturally instigated belief systems. But this turns out not to be the case. Although based on evidence, scientific writing can be seen as a particular kind of cultural interpretation—the enculturated scientist interprets nature. In the process, he or she also uses that interpretation to reinforce old or build new sets of social beliefs. Thus scientific work contributes to the construction of masculinity, and masculine constructs are among the building blocks for particular kinds of scientific knowledge. One of the jobs of the science critic is to illuminate this interaction. Once such illumination has occurred, it becomes possible to discuss change.

NOTES

1. See Money (1952 and 1957); Money and Hampson (1955); Money, Hampson and Hampson (1955a).

2. The data do not actually match the presence/absence model, but this seems not to bother most people. For a discussion of this point, see Fausto-Sterling (1987, 1989, 1992).

3. I use the phrases "male hormones" and "female hormones" as shorthand. There are, in fact, no such categories. Males and females have the same hormones, albeit in different quantities and sometimes with different tissue distributions.

REFERENCES

Danish, Robert H., Peter A. Lee, Thomas Mazur, James A. Amthein, and Claude J. Migeon. 1980. Micropenis 11. Hypogonadotropic hypogonadism. *Johns Hopkins Medical Journal* 146:177–184.

Diamond, Milton. 1995. Presentation at meeting of the Society for the Scientific Study of Sex, San Francisco.

Donahue, Patricia, David M. Powell, and Mary M. Lee. 1991. Clinical management of inter-sex abnormalities. *Current Problems in Surgery* 28:513–579.

Fausto-Sterling, Anne. 1987. Society writes biology/biology constructs gender. *Dædalus* 116:61–76.

——. 1989. Life in the XY Corral. *Women's Studies International Forum* 12:319–331.

——. 1992. *Myths of Gender: Biological Theories About Women and Men.* New York: Basic.

Green, Richard. 1987. *The "Sissy Boy" Syndrome and the Development of Homosexuality.* New Haven: Yale University Press.

Kessler, Suzanne J. 1990. The medical construction of gender; Case management of intersexed infants. *Signs* 16:3–26.

Money, John. 1952. Hermaphroditism: An inquiry into the nature of a human paradox. Ph.D. diss., Harvard University, Cambridge.

——. 1957. *The Psychologic Study of Man*. Springfield, IL: Charles C. Thomas.

——. 1992. *The Adam Principle*. Elmhurst, NY: Global Academic Publishers.

Money, John, and J. Daléry. 1976. Iatrogenic homosexuality: Gender identity in seven 46, XX chromosomal females with hyperadrenocortical hermaphroditism born with a penis. *Journal of Homosexuality* 1:357–371.

——. 1977. Hyperadrenocortical 46, XX hermaphroditism with penile urethra. In *Congenital Adrenal Hyperplasia*, ed. P. A. Lee, L. P. Plotnick, A. A. Kowarski, and C. J. Migeon. Baltimore: University Park Press.

Money, John, and Anke A. Ehrhardt. 1972. *Man and Woman, Boy and Girl: The Differentiation and Dimorphism of Gender Identity from Conception to Maturity*. Baltimore: Johns Hopkins University Press.

Money, John, and J. G. Hampson. 1955. Idiopathic sexual precocity in the male. *Psychosomatic Medicine* 17:1–15.

Money, John, J. G. Hampson, and J. L. Hampson. 1955a. An examination of some basic sexual concepts: The evidence of human hermaphroditism. *Bulletin of the Johns Hopkins Hospital* 97:301–319.

——. 1955b. Hermaphroditism: Recommendations concerning assignment of sex, change of sex, and psychological management. *Bulletin of the Johns Hopkins Hospital* 97:284–300.

Money, John, M. Schwartz, and V. G. Lewis. 1984. Adult erotosexual status and fetal hormonal masculinization and demasculinization: 46, XX congenital virilizing hyperplasia and 46, XX androgen-insensitivity syndrome compared. *Psychoneuroendocrinology* 9:405–414.

Money, John, and Patricia Tucker. 1975. *Sexual Signatures: On Being a Man or a Woman*. Boston: Little, Brown and Co.

Active Reading

1.   What is "MIS"? How does the "The Adam Principle" depend on MIS?

2.   What is "intersexual" development, and how does it occur?

Critical Reading

1.   Fausto-Sterling is fluent in the discipline of biology, where articles are typically written in what she describes in her last paragraph as "neutral, abstract language." Yet aspects of her writing style seem rooted in the humanities. Choose a passage from her text and identify several examples of language that would not ordinarily be found in science writing. What might account for her writing style in this text?

2.   Are you surprised by any of Fausto-Sterling's claims about the high degree of medical intervention that occurs in assigning sex and gender? Can you cross-check some of her facts to see if others have made similar observations?

3.   John Money's insistence that gender is a matter of socialization affected many children, whose sex was altered according to criteria he established. One famous case is detailed in John Colapinto's *As Nature Made Him: The Boy Who Was Raised as a Girl* (New York: Harper Perennial, 2006),

where Canadian David Reimer describes his struggle to live as a girl when he felt like a boy. What arguments can be made for and against the common medical practice of altering infants' bodies to fit into the binary gender system?

RESEARCH AND WRITING SUGGESTIONS

Chapter-based Research Questions

1. Do some of the articles suggest that being human in our postmodern age necessarily involves forming an intimate relationship with technology? In what ways could it be argued that human beings remain independent of technology?

2. Write a literature review of the four readings in this chapter, concluding with a paragraph describing ideas for further research arising from your review.

3. Use the readings from this chapter as your sources for an essay in which you defend your own position on the ethics of body modification.

Additional Research Questions

1. Look at the references following one of these articles, and decide which ones appear to promise to expand the argument about the body in interesting ways. Get two of these articles and then choose one to critique.

2. Choose a particular form of body modification that interests you. How is it portrayed in current scholarly articles? Can you identify contested issues? If you know someone who has engaged in this form of body modification, can you interview them to add another perspective? (Refer to the two forms at the end of Chapter 3 about conducting interviews and seeking permission to interview *before* meeting your informant.)

3. Look at recent publications about gender and sex identity, including those in the fields of intersex and transgender studies. What are some current views about the role of nature and culture in the development of our sex identities as "male" or "female"? Do these discussions have relevance for the majority of people who may be quite comfortable with the binary gender system of our culture and their places in it?

4. In *I Am Charlotte Simmons,* American novelist and social commentator Tom Wolfe depicts contemporary youth culture by following the lives of several university students, depicting, among other things, how clothes influence identity and self-concept. Write a critical review of Wolfe's portrait of the body and self-concept in this novel.

CHAPTER 10
CONFORMITY AND COURAGE

Psychology

The character trait of courage has been extolled in countless tales of heroic action on the battlefield, and those who demonstrate it are recognized as extraordinary human beings. Sadly, it seems not to be a common characteristic, and history is filled with chilling examples of failures of courage. The collaboration of ordinary people with the Nazi regime (from roughly 1930 to 1945) has provided academic researchers with one of the biggest case studies of failure to stand up to an oppressive authority. The Nuremberg trials after the end of World War II revealed a mentality among senior Nazi military personnel that they bore no responsibility for the atrocities of the concentration camps because it was their duty to obey orders. We might imagine that people would obey orders made at gunpoint to hurt someone else. However, hundreds upon hundreds of thousands of people across Europe co-operated with the Nazi regime, and many would reveal in interviews afterwards that they were as often motivated by ambition as by fear.

The decades following the overthrow of the Nazi regime saw renewed interest among scholars in exploring the old question, "What makes so many people willing to hurt others?" and, perhaps the more interesting question, "How can we make ourselves more courageous in the face of pressure to be cruel?" The philosopher Hannah Arendt, reflecting on the Nazis' bureaucratic approach to brutal oppression, summed up her thesis with the phrase "the banality of evil." Other philosophers such as Isaiah Berlin explored the origins of prejudice and the attendant conviction that certain groups of people must be suppressed, no matter the cost. These questions have come to the forefront again as we try to understand some of the behaviours we have seen since the attack on the World Trade Center in 2001. What psychology is at work in the terrorist willing to murder hundreds of strangers to make a point? Or in the grinning American soldiers who were photographed humiliating Iraqi prisoners of war in Abu Ghraib?

The emerging discipline of social psychology investigated these questions in controlled experiments where the courage of individuals was put to the test. The prolific novelist and essayist Doris Lessing reviews the findings of these experiments in her essay, "Group Minds." The next reading in this chapter is Stanley Milgram's 1963 report on his landmark study of obedience, where he found that most people were willing to administer what they believed to be dangerous voltages of electrical shock when ordered to by someone in authority (in this case, a researcher in a lab coat: hardly an SS guard with a pistol). Studies achieve "landmark" status when they prove to have enduring explanatory power that is confirmed in a variety of subsequent studies. Thomas Blass reconsiders Milgram's work 35 years later in his review of the dozens of follow-up studies that ensued and finds that his conclusions about the propensity to obey remain valid. Philip G. Zimbardo conducted a related landmark study in 1971 using role play methodology in the "Stanford Prison Experiment," where he found that college students assigned to the roles of guards and prisoners in a simulated prison setting swiftly "became" the roles they were assigned, with guards enthusiastically mistreating prisoners, and prisoners turning on each other to comply with authority. In an excerpt from his 2008 book, *The Lucifer Effect*, Zimbardo reflects on the findings of a career spent investigating the banality of evil among people experiencing social pressure and explains that courage may be equally banal . . . and thus equally achievable by ordinary people. Finally, philosopher Martha Nussbaum argues that, knowing what we do about the human propensity for group mentality, people who care about social justice ought to be trying to harness the moral authority of patriotism, rather than allowing that authority to be monopolized by aggressive and brutal political movements.

Activate

1. Have you ever gone against your own conscience to follow the crowd? What calculations of personal cost went into your behaviour?

2. Conversely, have you ever acted courageously even though you feared the consequences? What considerations gave you the strength to do this?

3. Do you know of any current events in the news where people seem to be displaying group mentality? What makes you think so?

4. Can you think of any examples of people who demonstrated great courage at personal cost? What might have been the sources of their courage?

Group Minds

Doris Lessing

Doris Lessing explores the problem of people's tendency to "go with the herd" for the sake of fitting in. She begins by challenging us to view as a myth the personal freedom that is so proudly claimed as the birthright of people living in democratic countries. She then draws on the findings of the obedience experiments of the '60s and '70s to make her case that "we are group animals," and the better we understand that about ourselves, the stronger we might be in the face of pressure to conform. Lessing delivered this essay as one of her five lectures for the Massey Lectures series. She called her lectures Prisons We Choose to Live Inside.

Doris Lessing was born in Persia (now Iran) in 1919. She attended a Roman Catholic convent and a girls' high school in Southern Rhodesia (now Zimbabwe). From 1959 through to the present, Lessing has written more than 25 works of fiction. Her work has received a great deal of scholarly attention. Among her most distinguished works are Five: Short Novels *(1953),* The Golden Notebook *(1962), and* Briefing for a Descent into Hell *(1971). The jury that awarded her the Asturias Prize for literature in 2001 described her as "an impassioned freedom fighter, who has spared no effort in her commitment to Third World causes, through literature and the personal experience of a hazardous biography."[1] Lessing was awarded the Nobel Prize for literature in 2007.*

---

[1] Associated Press, "Top Literary Prize for 'Freedom Fighter' Lessing," *Winnipeg Free Press* B7, 9 June 2001.

1   People living in the West, in societies that we describe as Western, or as the free world, may be educated in many different ways, but they will all emerge with an idea about themselves that goes something like this: I am a citizen of a free society, and that means I am an individual, making individual choices. My mind is my own, my opinions are chosen by me, I am free to do as I will, and at the worst the pressures on me are economic, that is, I may be too poor to do as I want.

2   This set of ideas may sound something like a caricature, but it is not so far off how we see ourselves. It is a portrait that may not have been acquired consciously, but is part of a general atmosphere or set of assumptions that influence our ideas about ourselves.

3   People in the West therefore may go through their entire lives never thinking to analyze this very flattering picture, and as a result are helpless against all kinds of pressures on them to conform in many kinds of ways.

4   The fact is that we all live our lives in groups—the family, work groups, social, religious and political groups. Very few people indeed are happy as solitaries, and they tend to be seen by their neighbours as peculiar or selfish or worse. Most people cannot stand being alone for long. They are always seeking groups to belong to, and if one group dissolves, they look for another. We are group animals still, and there is nothing wrong with that. But what is dangerous is not the belonging to a group, or groups, but not understanding the social laws that govern groups and govern us.

5   When we're in a group, we tend to think as that group does: we may even have joined the group to find "like-minded" people. But we also find our thinking changing because we belong to a group. It is the hardest thing in the world to maintain an individual dissident opinion, as a member of a group.

6   It seems to me that this is something we have all experienced—something we take for granted, may never have thought about it. But a great deal of experiment has gone on among psychologists and sociologists on this very theme. If I describe an experiment or two, then anyone listening who may be a sociologist or psychologist will groan, oh God not *again*—for they will have heard of these classic experiments far too often. My guess is that the rest of the people will never have heard of these experiments, never have had these ideas presented to them. If my guess is true, then it aptly illustrates my general thesis, and the general idea behind these talks, that we (the human race) are now in possession of a great deal of hard information about ourselves, but we do not use it to improve our institutions and therefore our lives.

7   A typical test, or experiment, on this theme goes like this. A group of people are taken into the researcher's confidence. A minority of one or two are left in the dark. Some situation demanding measurement or assessment is chosen. For instance, comparing lengths of wood that differ only a little from each other, but enough to be perceptible, or shapes that are almost the same size. The majority in the group—according to instruction—will assert stubbornly that these two shapes or lengths are the same length, or size, while the solitary individual, or the couple, who have not been so instructed will assert that the pieces of wood or whatever are different. But the majority will continue to insist—speaking metaphorically—that black is white, and after a period of exasperation, irritation, even anger, certainly incomprehension, the minority will fall into line. Not always, but nearly always.

There are indeed glorious individuals who stubbornly insist on telling the truth as they see it, but most give in to the majority opinion, obey the atmosphere.

8 When put as badly, as unflatteringly, as this, reactions tend to be incredulous: "I certainly wouldn't give in, I speak my mind . . . ." But would you?

9 People who have experienced a lot of groups, who perhaps have observed their own behaviour, may agree that the hardest thing in the world is to stand out against one's group, a group of one's peers. Many agree that among our most shameful memories is this, how often we said black was white because other people were saying it.

10 In other words, we know that this is true of human behaviour, but how do we know it? It is one thing to admit it, in a vague uncomfortable sort of way (which probably includes the hope that one will never again be in such a testing situation) but quite another to make that cool step into a kind of objectivity, where one may say, "Right, if that's what human beings are like, myself included, then let's admit it, examine and organize our attitudes accordingly."

11 This mechanism, of obedience to the group, does not only mean obedience or submission to a small group, or one that is sharply determined, like a religion or political party. It means, too, conforming to those large, vague, ill-defined collections of people who may never think of themselves as having a collective mind because they are aware of differences of opinion—but which, to people from outside, from another culture, seem very minor. The underlying assumptions and assertions that govern the group are never discussed, never challenged, probably never noticed, the main one being precisely this: that it *is* a group mind, intensely resistant to change, equipped with sacred assumptions about which there can be no discussion.

12 But suppose this kind of thing were taught in schools?

13 Let us just suppose it, for a moment. . . . But at once the nub of the problem is laid bare.

14 Imagine us saying to children, "In the last fifty or so years, the human race has become aware of a great deal of information about its mechanisms; how it behaves, how it must behave under certain circumstances. If this is to be useful, you must learn to contemplate these rules calmly, dispassionately, disinterestedly, without emotion. It is information that will set people free from blind loyalties, obedience to slogans, rhetoric, leaders, group emotions." Well, there it is.

15 What government, anywhere in the world, will happily envisage its subjects learning to free themselves from governmental and state rhetoric and pressures? Passionate loyalty and subjection to group pressures is what every state relies on. Some, of course, more than others. Khomeini's Iran, and the extreme Islamic sects, the Communist countries, are at one end of the scale. Countries like Norway, whose national day is celebrated by groups of children in fancy dress carrying flowers, singing and dancing, with not a tank or gun in sight, are at the other. It is interesting to speculate: what country, what nation, when, and where, would have undertaken a programme to teach its children to be people to resist rhetoric, to examine the mechanisms that govern them? I can think of only one—America at its birth, in that heady period of the Gettysburg address. And that time could not have survived the Civil War, for when war starts, countries cannot afford disinterested examination of their behaviour. When a war starts,

nations go mad—and have to go mad, in order to survive. When I look back at the Second World War, I see something I didn't more than dimly suspect at the time. It was that everyone was crazy. Even people not in the immediate arena of war. I am not talking of the aptitudes for killing, for destruction, which soldiers are taught as part of their training, but a kind of atmosphere, the invisible poison, which spreads everywhere. And then people everywhere begin behaving as they never could in peacetime. Afterwards we look back, amazed. Did I really do that? Believe that? Fall for that bit of propaganda? Think that all our enemies were evil? That all our own nation's acts were good? How could I have tolerated that state of mind, day after day, month after month—perpetually stimulated, perpetually whipped up into emotions that my mind was meanwhile quietly and desperately protesting against?

16   No, I cannot imagine any nation—or not for long—teaching its citizens to become individuals able to resist group pressures.

17   And no political party, either. I know a lot of people who are socialists of various kinds, and I try this subject out on them, saying: all governments these days use social psychologists, experts on crowd behaviour, and mob behaviour, to advise them. Elections are stage managed, public issues presented according to the rules of mass psychology. The military uses this information. Interrogators, secret services and the police use it. Yet these issues are never even discussed, as far as I am aware, by those parties and groups who claim to represent the people.

18   On one hand there are governments who manipulate, using expert knowledge and skills, on the other hand people who talk about democracy, freedom, liberty and all the rest of it, as if these values are created and maintained by simply talking about them, by repeating them often enough. How is it that so-called democratic movements don't make a point of instructing their members in the laws of crowd psychology, of group psychology?

19   When I ask this, the response is always an uncomfortable, squeamish reluctance, as if the whole subject is really in very bad taste, unpleasant, irrelevant. As if it will all just go away if it is ignored.

20   So at the moment, if we look around the world, the paradox is that we may see this new information being eagerly studied by governments, the possessors and users of power—studied and put into effect. But the people who say they oppose tyranny literally don't want to know.

Active Reading

1. Why does Lessing refer to individualism as a myth?

2. What makes people so susceptible to group mentality?

3. Summarize the methods used in the obedience experiments.

4. Why is Lessing cynical about the school system ever teaching students about the human tendency to conform?

Critical Reading

1. Lessing refers to scholarly studies, but her own essay has more features of popular press writing than of academic writing. What are some of these features? What is missing that you would expect to see in a scholarly version of this essay?

2. What is Lessing's thesis? Describe the main stages of thought that she goes through to develop that thesis.

3. Lessing draws on the common experience of going to school to trigger her audience's memories of having succumbed to group mentality. Is there something about school or about students that makes them particularly vulnerable to group mentality?

4. Do you agree with Lessing that it is crucial to develop knowledge of the "social laws that govern groups"? What difference would it make to themselves or to the world if students understood the findings of the obedience experiments?

Behavioral Study of Obedience

Stanley Milgram

In his relatively short life (1933–1984), Stanley Milgram produced scholarship that is still foundational to our understandings of conformity and courage. Milgram was a social psychologist who taught at Yale, Harvard, and City University of New York. The work that he first reported in the article presented here led to various honours, including being named Guggenheim Fellow in 1972–1973 and being nominated for the National Book Award for Obedience to Authority. He authored several other books, including Television and Antisocial Behavior (1973), The City and the Self (1974), Human Aggression (1976), and The Individual in the Social World (1977).

It had been understood before Milgram that people tend to obey authority figures; Milgram's work showed researchers the depth of this tendency and identified several of its key mechanisms. Although most scientific articles are read for only a few years, landmark studies that change the way researchers understand the field can be referenced for decades. "Behavioral Study of Obedience" is one such study. It appeared in the scholarly periodical Journal of Abnormal and Social Psychology in 1963.

Behavioral Study Of Obedience[1]

Stanley Milgram[2]

Yale University

This article describes a procedure for the study of destructive obedience in the laboratory. It consists of ordering a naive S to administer increasingly more severe punishment to a victim in the context of a learning experiment. Punishment is administered by means of a shock generator with 30 graded switches ranging from Slight Shock to Danger: Severe Shock. The victim is a confederate of the E. The primary dependent variable is the maximum shock the S is willing to administer before he refuses to continue further. 26 Ss obeyed the experimental commands fully, and administered the highest shock on the generator. 14 Ss broke off the experiment at some point after the victim protested and refused to provide further

[1] This research was supported by a grant (NSF G-17916) from the National Science Foundation. Exploratory studies conducted in 1960 were supported by a grant from the Higgins Fund at Yale University. The research assistance of Alan C. Elms and Jon Wayland is gratefully acknowledged.

[2] Now at Harvard University.

answers. The procedure created extreme levels of nervous tension in some Ss. Profuse sweating, trembling, and stuttering were typical expressions of this emotional disturbance. One unexpected sign of tension—yet to be explained—was the regular occurrence of nervous laughter, which in some Ss developed into uncontrollable seizures. The variety of interesting behavioral dynamics observed in the experiment, the reality of the situation for the S, and the possibility of parametric variation within the framework of the procedure, point to the fruitfulness of further study.

1   Obedience is as basic an element in the structure of social life as one can point to. Some system of authority is a requirement of all communal living, and it is only the man dwelling in isolation who is not forced to respond, through defiance or submission, to the commands of others. Obedience, as a determinant of behavior, is of particular relevance to our time. It has been reliably established that from 1933–45 millions of innocent persons were systematically slaughtered on command. Gas chambers were built, death camps were guarded, daily quotas of corpses were produced with the same efficiency as the manufacture of appliances. These inhumane policies may have originated in the mind of a single person, but they could only be carried out on a massive scale if a very large number of persons obeyed orders.

2   Obedience is the psychological mechanism that links individual action to political purpose. It is the dispositional cement that binds men to systems of authority. Facts of recent history and observation in daily life suggest that for many persons obedience may be a deeply ingrained behavior tendency, indeed, a prepotent impulse overriding training in ethics, sympathy, and moral conduct. C. P. Snow (1961) points to its importance when he writes:

> When you think of the long and gloomy history of man, you will find more hideous crimes have been committed in the name of obedience than have ever been committed in the name of rebellion. If you doubt that, read William Shirer's "Rise and Fall of the Third Reich." The German Officer Corps were brought up in the most rigorous code of obedience . . . in the name of obedience they were party to, and assisted in, the most wicked large scale actions in the history of the world [p. 24].

3   While the particular form of obedience dealt with in the present study has its antecedents in these episodes, it must not be thought all obedience entails acts of aggression against others. Obedience serves numerous productive functions. Indeed, the very life of society is predicated on its existence. Obedience may be ennobling and educative and refer to acts of charity and kindness, as well as to destruction.

General Procedure

4   A procedure was devised which seems useful as a tool for studying obedience (Milgram, 1961). It consists of ordering a naive subject to administer electric shock to a victim. A simulated shock generator is used, with 30 clearly marked voltage levels that range from 15 to 450 volts. The instrument bears verbal designations that range from Slight Shock to Danger: Severe Shock. The responses of the victim, who is a trained confederate of the experimenter, are standardized. The orders to administer shocks are given to the naive subject in the context of a

"learning experiment" ostensibly set up to study the effects of punishment on memory. As the experiment proceeds the naive subject is commanded to administer increasingly more intense shocks to the victim, even to the point of reaching the level marked Danger: Severe Shock. Internal resistances become stronger, and at a certain point the subject refuses to go on with the experiment. Behavior prior to this rupture is considered "obedience," in that the subject complies with the commands of the experimenter. The point of rupture is the act of disobedience. A quantitative value is assigned to the subject's performance based on the maximum intensity shock he is willing to administer before he refuses to participate further. Thus for any particular subject and for any particular experimental condition the degree of obedience may be specified with a numerical value. The crux of the study is to systematically vary the factors believed to alter the degree of obedience to the experimental commands.

5   The technique allows important variables to be manipulated at several points in the experiment. One may vary aspects of the source of command, content and form of command, instrumentalities for its execution, target object, general social setting, etc. The problem, therefore, is not one of designing increasingly more numerous experimental conditions, but of selecting those that best illuminate the *process* of obedience from the sociopsychological standpoint.

Related Studies

6   The inquiry bears an important relation to philosophic analyses of obedience and authority (Arendt, 1958; Friedrich, 1958; Weber, 1947), an early experimental study of obedience by Frank (1944), studies in "authoritarianism" (Adorno, Frenkel-Brunswik, Levinson, & Sanford, 1950; Rokeach, 1961), and a recent series of analytic and empirical studies in social power (Cartwright, 1959). It owes much to the long concern with *suggestion* in social psychology, both in its normal forms (e.g., Binet, 1900) and in its clinical manifestations (Charcot, 1881). But it derives, in the first instance, from direct observation of a social fact; the individual who is commanded by a legitimate authority ordinarily obeys. Obedience comes easily and often. It is a ubiquitous and indispensable feature of social life.

METHOD

Subjects

7   The subjects were 40 males between the ages of 20 and 50, drawn from New Haven and the surrounding communities. Subjects were obtained by a newspaper advertisement and direct mail solicitation. Those who responded to the appeal believed they were to participate in a study of memory and learning at Yale University. A wide range of occupations is represented in the sample. Typical subjects were postal clerks, high school teachers, salesmen, engineers, and laborers. Subjects ranged in educational level from one who had not finished elementary school, to those who had doctorate and other professional degrees. They were paid $4.50 for their participation in the experiment. However, subjects were told that payment was simply for coming to the laboratory, and that the money was theirs no matter what happened after they arrived. Table 1 shows the proportion of age and occupational types assigned to the experimental condition.

Personnel and Locale

8   The experiment was conducted on the grounds of Yale University in the elegant interaction laboratory. (This detail is relevant to the perceived legitimacy of the experiment. In further variations, the experiment was dissociated from the university, with consequences for performance.) The role of experimenter was played by a 31-year-old high school teacher of biology. His manner was impassive, and his appearance somewhat stern throughout the experiment. He was dressed in a gray technician's coat. The victim was played by a 47-year-old accountant, trained for the role; he was of Irish-American stock, whom most observers found mild-mannered and likable.

Table I Distribution of Age and Occupational Types in the Experiment

Occupations	20–29 years n	30–39 years n	40–50 years n	Percentage of total (Occupations)
Workers, skilled and unskilled	4	5	6	37.5
Sales, business, and white-collar	3	6	7	40.0
Professional	1	5	3	22.5
Percentage of total (Age)	20	40	40	

Note—Total $N = 40$.

Procedure

9   One naive subject and one victim (an accomplice) performed in each experiment. A pretext had to be devised that would justify the administration of electric shock by the naive subject. This was effectively accomplished by the cover story. After a general introduction on the presumed relation between punishment and learning, subjects were told:

> But actually, we know *very little* about the effect of punishment on learning, because almost no truly scientific studies have been made of it in human beings.
>
> For instance, we don't know how *much* punishment is best for learning—and we don't know how much difference it makes as to who is giving the punishment, whether an adult learns best from a younger or an older person than himself—or many things of that sort.
>
> So in this study we are bringing together a number of adults of different occupations and ages. And we're asking some of them to be teachers and some of them to be learners.
>
> We want to find out just what effect different people have on each other as teachers and learners, and also what effect *punishment* will have on learning in this situation.
>
> Therefore, I'm going to ask one of you to be the teacher here tonight and the other one to be the learner.
>
> Does either of you have a preference?

10   Subjects then drew slips of paper from a hat to determine who would be the teacher and who would be the learner in the experiment. The drawing was rigged so that the naive subject was always the teacher and the accomplice always the learner. (Both slips contained the word "Teacher.") Immediately after the drawing, the teacher and learner were taken to an adjacent room and the learner was strapped into an "electric chair" apparatus.

11   The experimenter explained that the straps were to prevent excessive movement while the learner was being shocked. The effect was to make it impossible for him to escape from the situation. An electrode was attached to the learner's wrist, and electrode paste was applied "to avoid blisters and burns." Subjects were told that the electrode was attached to the shock generator in the adjoining room.

12   In order to improve credibility the experimenter declared, in response to a question by the learner: "Although the shocks can be extremely painful, they cause no permanent tissue damage."

13   *Learning task.* The lesson administered by the subject was a paired-associate learning task. The subject read a series of word pairs to the learner, and then read the first word of the pair along with four terms. The learner was to indicate which of the four terms had originally been paired with the first word. He communicated his answer by pressing one of four switches in front of him, which in turn lit up one of four numbered quadrants in an answer-box located atop the shock generator.

14   *Shock generator.* The instrument panel consists of 30 lever switches set in a horizontal line. Each switch is clearly labeled with a voltage designation that ranges from 15 to 450 volts. There is a 15-volt increment from one switch to the next going from left to right. In addition, the following verbal designations are clearly indicated for groups of four switches going from left to right: Slight Shock, Moderate Shock, Strong Shock, Very Strong Shock, Intense Shock, Extreme Intensity Shock, Danger: Severe Shock. (Two switches after this last designation are simply marked XXX.)

15   Upon depressing a switch: a pilot light corresponding to each switch is illuminated in bright red; an electric buzzing is heard; an electric blue light, labeled "voltage energizer," flashes; the dial on the voltage meter swings to the right; various relay clicks are sounded.

16   The upper left-hand corner of the generator is labeled Shock Generator, Type ZLB, Dyson Instrument Company, Waltham, Mass. Output 15 Volts–450 Volts.

17   Details of the instrument were carefully handled to insure an appearance of authenticity. The panel was engraved by precision industrial engravers, and all components were of high quality. No subject in the experiment suspected that the instrument was merely a simulated shock generator.[3]

---

[3] A related technique, making use of a shock generator, was reported by Buss (1961) for the study of aggression in the laboratory. Despite the considerable similarity of technical detail in the experimental procedures, both investigators proceeded in ignorance of the other's work. Milgram provided plans and photographs of his shock generator, experimental procedure, and first results in a report to the National Science Foundation in January 1961. This report received only limited circulation. Buss reported his procedure 6 months later, but to a wider audience. Subsequently, technical information and reports were exchanged. The present article was first received in the Editor's office on December 27, 1961; it was resubmitted with deletions on July 27, 1962.

18   *Sample shock.* Each naive subject is given a sample shock on the shock gener- ator, prior to beginning his run as teacher. This shock is always 45 volts, and is applied by pressing the third switch of the generator. The shock is applied to the wrist of the naive subject, and has its source in a 45-volt battery wired into the generator. This further convinces the subject of the authenticity of the generator.

19   *Shock instructions.* The subject is told to administer a shock to the learner each time he gives a wrong response. Moreover—and this is the key command—the subject is instructed to "move one level higher on the shock generator each time the learner flashes a wrong answer." He is also instructed to announce the voltage level before administering a shock. This serves to continually remind subjects of the increasing intensity of shocks administered to the learner.

20   *Preliminary and regular run.* Pretests revealed that the procedure of reading words and administering shocks requires some practice before it can be handled smoothly. Therefore, immediately preceding the regular run, the teacher is given a preliminary series of 10 words to read to the learner. There are 3 neutral words in the practice series (i.e., words that the learner answers correctly), so that shocks are administered for 7 of the words, with the maximum shock at 105 volts (moderate shock). Almost all subjects master the procedure by the time the preliminary run is over.

21   Subjects are then presented with a second list, and are told that the proce- dure is the same as for the first list; the experimenter adds, however:

> When you get to the bottom of the list, repeat it over again, and continue giving shocks, until the learner has learned all the pairs correctly.

22   The experimenter instructs the subject to,

> start from 15 volts and increase the shock level one step each time the learner gives a wrong answer.

23   *Feedback from the victim.* In all conditions the learner gives a predetermined set of responses to the word pair test, based on a schedule of approximately three wrong answers to one correct answer. In the present experimental condition no vocal response or other sign of protest is heard from the learner until Shock Level 300 is reached. When the 300-volt shock is administered, the learner pounds on the wall of the room in which he is bound to the electric chair. The pounding can be heard by the subject. From this point on, the learner's answers no longer appear on the four-way panel.

24   At this juncture, subjects ordinarily turn to the experimenter for guidance. The experimenter instructs the subject to treat the absence of a response as a wrong answer, and to shock the subject according to the usual schedule. He advises the subjects to allow 5–10 seconds before considering no response as a wrong answer, and to increase the shock level one step each time the learner fails to respond correctly. The learner's pounding is repeated after the 315-volt shock is administered; afterwards he is not heard from, nor do his answers reappear on the four-way signal box.

25   *Experimenter feedback.* At various points in the experiment the subject may turn to the experimenter for advice on whether he should continue to administer

shocks. Or he may indicate that he does not wish to go on. It was important to standardize the experimenter's responses to these inquiries and reactions.

26   If the subject indicated his unwillingness to go on, the experimenter responded with a sequence of "prods," using as many as necessary to bring the subject into line.

> Prod 1: Please continue, *or* Please go on.
> Prod 2: The experiment requires that you continue.
> Prod 3: It is absolutely essential that you continue.
> Prod 4: You have no other choice, you *must* go on.

27   The prods were always made in sequence: Only if Prod 1 had been unsuccessful, could Prod 2 be used. If the subject refused to obey the experimenter after Prod 4, the experiment was terminated. The experimenter's tone of voice was at all times firm, but not impolite. The sequence was begun anew on each occasion that the subject balked or showed reluctance to follow orders.

28   *Special prods.* If the subject asked if the learner was liable to suffer permanent physical injury, the experimenter said:

> Although the shocks may be painful, there is no permanent tissue damage, so please go on. [Followed by Prods 2, 3, and 4 if necessary.]

29   If the subject said that the learner did not want to go on, the experimenter replied:

> Whether the learner likes it or not, you must go on until he has learned all the word pairs correctly. So please go on. [Followed by Prods 2, 3, and 4 if necessary.]

Dependent Measures

30   The primary dependent measure for any subject is the maximum shock he administers before he refuses to go any further. In principle this may vary from 0 (for a subject who refuses to administer even the first shock) to 30 (for a subject who administers the highest shock on the generator). A subject who breaks off the experiment at any point prior to administering the thirtieth shock level is termed a *defiant* subject. One who complies with experimental commands fully, and proceeds to administer all shock levels commanded, is termed an obedient subject.

31   *Further records.* With few exceptions, experimental sessions were recorded on magnetic tape. Occasional photographs were taken through one-way mirrors. Notes were kept on any unusual behavior occurring during the course of the experiments. On occasion, additional observers were directed to write objective descriptions of the subjects' behavior. The latency and duration of shocks were measured by accurate timing devices.

32   *Interview and dehoax.* Following the experiment, subjects were interviewed; open-ended questions, projective measures, and attitude scales were employed. After the interview, procedures were undertaken to assure that the subject would leave the laboratory in a state of well being. A friendly reconciliation was arranged between the subject and the victim, and an effort was made to reduce any tensions that arose as a result of the experiment.

RESULTS

Preliminary Notions

33   Before giving an account of the experimental results, it is instructive to consider how persons predict others will perform when commanded to administer powerful shocks to another person. Fourteen Yale seniors, all psychology majors, were provided with a detailed description of the experimental situation. They were asked to reflect carefully on it, and to predict the behavior of 100 hypothetical subjects. More specifically, they were instructed to plot the distribution of obedience of "100 Americans of diverse occupations, and ranging in age from 20 to 50 years," who were placed in the experimental situation.

34   There was considerable agreement among the respondents on the expected behavior of hypothetical subjects. All respondents predicted that only an insignificant minority would go through to the end of the shock series. (The estimates ranged from 0 to 3%; i.e., the most "pessimistic" member of the class predicted that of 100 persons, 3 would continue through to the most potent shock available on the shock generator—450 volts.) The class mean was 1.2%. The question was also posed informally to colleagues of the author, and the most general feeling was that few if any subjects would go beyond the designation Very Strong Shock.

Result of Experiment I

35   *Subjects accept situation*. With few exceptions subjects were convinced of the reality of the experimental situation, that they were administering shocks to another person, and the most potent shocks were extremely painful. In the post-experimental interview subjects were asked: "How painful to the learner were the last few shocks that you administered to him?" Subjects were instructed to indicate their answers on a printed 14-point scale ranging from "Not at all painful" to "Extremely painful." The modal response was 14 (Extremely painful) with the mean at 13.42.

36   *Signs of extreme tension*. Many subjects showed signs of nervousness in the experimental situation, and especially upon administering the more powerful shocks. In a large number of cases the degree of tension reached extremes that are rarely seen in sociopsychological laboratory studies. Subjects were observed to sweat, tremble, stutter, bite their lips, groan, and dig their fingernails into their flesh. These were characteristic rather than exceptional responses to the experiment.

37   One sign of tension was the regular occurrence of nervous laughing fits. Fourteen of the 40 subjects showed definite signs of nervous laughter and smiling. The laughter seemed entirely out of place, even bizarre. Full-blown, uncontrollable seizures were observed for 3 subjects. On one occasion we observed a seizure so violently convulsive that it was necessary to call a halt to the experiment. The subject, a 46-year-old encyclopedia salesman, was seriously embarrassed by his untoward and uncontrollable behavior. In the post-experimental interviews subjects took pains to point out that they were not sadistic types, and that the laughter did not mean they enjoyed shocking the victim.

38   *Distribution of scores*. It had been conjectured that persons would not, in general, agree to administer shocks beyond the level designated as Very Strong Shock.

The distribution of maximum shocks for this experiment is shown in Table 2. The obtained distribution of scores deviates radically from the prediction.

39   Upon command of the experimenter, each of the 40 subjects went beyond the expected breakoff point. No subject stopped prior to administering Shock Level 20. (At this level—300 volts—the victim kicks on the wall and no longer provides answers to the teacher's multiple-choice questions.)

40   Of the 40 subjects, 5 refused to obey the experimental commands beyond the 300-volt level. Four more subjects administered one further shock, and then refused to go on. Two broke off at the 330-volt level, and 1 each at 345, 360, and 375 volts. Thus a total of 14 subjects defied the experimenter. It is instructive to reprint their remarks at the point of defiance, as transcribed from the tape recordings:

> [0124] I think he's trying to communicate, he's knocking . . . Well it's not fair to shock the guy . . . these are terrific volts. I don't think this is very humane. . . . Oh, I can't go on with this; no, this isn't right. It's a hell of an experiment. The guy is suffering in there. No, I don't want to go on. This is crazy. [Subject refused to administer more shocks.]

Table 2 Distribution of Breakoff Points

Verbal designation and voltage indication	Number of subjects for whom this was maximum shock
Slight Shock	
15	0
30	0
45	0
60	0
Moderate Shock	
75	0
90	0
105	0
120	0
Strong Shock	
135	0
150	0
165	0
180	0
Very Strong Shock	
195	0
210	0
225	0
240	0

(Continued)

Table 2 Continued	
Verbal designation and voltage indication	**Number of subjects for whom this was maximum shock**
Intense Shock	
255	0
270	0
285	0
300	5
Extreme Intensity Shock	
315	4
330	2
345	1
360	1
Danger: Severe Shock	
375	1
390	0
405	0
420	0
XXX	
435	0
450	26

[0123] He's banging in there. I'm gonna chicken out. I'd like to continue, but I can't do that to a man. . . . I'm sorry I can't do that to a man. I'll hurt his heart. You take your check. . . . No really, I couldn't do it.

41   These subjects were frequently in a highly agitated and even angered state. Sometimes, verbal protest was at a minimum, and the subject simply got up from his chair in front of the shock generator, and indicated that he wished to leave the laboratory.

42   Of the 40 subjects, 26 obeyed the orders of the experimenter to the end, proceeding to punish the victim until they reached the most potent shock available on the shock generator. At that point, the experimenter called a halt to the session. (The maximum shock is labeled 450 volts, and is two steps beyond the designation: Danger: Severe Shock.) Although obedient subjects continued to administer shocks, they often did so under extreme stress. Some expressed reluctance to administer shocks beyond the 300-volt level, and displayed fears similar to those who defied the experimenter; yet they obeyed.

43   After the maximum shocks had been delivered, and the experimenter called a halt to the proceedings, many obedient subjects heaved sighs of relief, mopped their brows, rubbed their fingers over their eyes, or nervously fumbled cigarettes. Some shook their heads, apparently in regret. Some subjects had

remained calm throughout the experiment, and displayed only minimal signs of tension from beginning to end.

DISCUSSION

44   The experiment yielded two findings that were surprising. The first finding concerns the sheer strength of obedient tendencies manifested in this situation. Subjects have learned from childhood that it is a fundamental breach of moral conduct to hurt another person against his will. Yet, 26 subjects abandon this tenet in following the instructions of an authority who has no special powers to enforce his commands. To disobey would bring no material loss to the subject; no punishment would ensue. It is clear from the remarks and outward behavior of many participants that in punishing the victim they are often acting against their own values. Subjects often expressed deep disapproval of shocking a man in the face of his objections, and others denounced it as stupid and senseless. Yet the majority complied with the experimental commands. This outcome was surprising from two perspectives: first, from the standpoint of predictions made in the questionnaire described earlier. (Here, however, it is possible that the remoteness of the respondents from the actual situation, and the difficulty of conveying to them the concrete details of the experiment, could account for the serious underestimation of obedience.)

45   But the results were also unexpected to persons who observed the experiment in progress, through one-way mirrors. Observers often uttered expressions of disbelief upon seeing a subject administer more powerful shocks to the victim. These persons had a full acquaintance with the details of the situation, and yet systematically underestimated the amount of obedience that subjects would display.

46   The second unanticipated effect was the extraordinary tension generated by the procedures. One might suppose that a subject would simply break off or continue as his conscience dictated. Yet, this is very far from what happened. There were striking reactions of tension and emotional strain. One observer related:

> I observed a mature and initially poised businessman enter the laboratory smiling and confident. Within 20 minutes he was reduced to a twitching, stuttering wreck, who was rapidly approaching a point of nervous collapse. He constantly pulled on his earlobe, and twisted his hands. At one point he pushed his fist into his forehead and muttered: "Oh God, let's stop it." And yet he continued to respond to every word of the experimenter, and obeyed to the end.

47   Any understanding of the phenomenon of obedience must rest on an analysis of the particular conditions in which it occurs. The following features of the experiment go some distance in explaining the high amount of obedience observed in the situation.

1. The experiment is sponsored by and takes place on the grounds of an institution of unimpeachable reputation, Yale University. It may be reasonably presumed that the personnel are competent and reputable. The importance of this background authority is now being studied by conducting a series of experiments outside of New Haven, and without any visible ties to the university.

2. The experiment is, on the face of it, designed to attain a worthy purpose—advancement of knowledge about learning and memory. Obedience occurs not as an end in itself, but as an instrumental element in a situation that the subject construes as significant, and meaningful. He may not be able to see its full significance, but he may properly assume that the experimenter does.

3. The subject perceives that the victim has voluntarily submitted to the authority system of the experimenter. He is not (at first) an unwilling captive impressed for involuntary service. He has taken the trouble to come to the laboratory presumably to aid the experimental research. That he later becomes an involuntary subject does not alter the fact that, initially, he consented to participate without qualification. Thus he has in some degree incurred an obligation toward the experimenter.

4. The subject, too, has entered the experiment voluntarily, and perceives himself under obligation to aid the experimenter. He has made a commitment, and to disrupt the experiment is a repudiation of this initial promise of aid.

5. Certain features of the procedure strengthen the subject's sense of obligation to the experimenter. For one, he has been paid for coming to the laboratory. In part this is canceled out by the experimenter's statement that:

> Of course, as in all experiments, the money is yours simply for coming to the laboratory. From this point on, no matter what happens, the money is yours.[4]

6. From the subject's standpoint, the fact that he is the teacher and the other man the learner is purely a chance consequence (it is determined by drawing lots) and he, the subject, ran the same risk as the other man in being assigned the role of learner. Since the assignment of positions in the experiment was achieved by fair means, the learner is deprived of any basis of complaint on this count. (A similar situation obtains in Army units, in which—in the absence of volunteers—a particularly dangerous mission may be assigned by drawing lots, and the unlucky soldier is expected to bear his misfortune with sportsmanship.)

7. There is, at best, ambiguity with regard to the prerogatives of a psychologist and the corresponding rights of his subject. There is a vagueness of expectation concerning what a psychologist may require of his subject, and when he is overstepping acceptable limits. Moreover, the experiment occurs in a closed setting, and thus provides no opportunity for the subject to remove these ambiguities by discussion with others. There are few standards that seem directly applicable to the situation, which is a novel one for most subjects.

8. The subjects are assured that the shocks administered to the subject are "painful but not dangerous." Thus they assume that the discomfort caused the victim is momentary, while the scientific gains resulting from the experiment are enduring.

9. Through Shock Level 20 the victim continues to provide answers on the signal box. The subject may construe this as a sign that the victim is still

---

[4] Forty-three subjects, undergraduates at Yale University, were run in the experiment without payment. The results are very similar to those obtained with paid subjects.

willing to "play the game." It is only after Shock Level 20 that the victim repudiates the rules completely, refusing to answer further.

These features help to explain the high amount of obedience obtained in this experiment. Many of the arguments raised need not remain matters of speculation, but can be reduced to testable propositions to be confirmed or disproved by further experiments.[5]

The following features of the experiment concern the nature of the conflict which the subject faces.

10. The subject is placed in a position in which he must respond to the competing demands of two persons: the experimenter and the victim. The conflict must be resolved by meeting the demands of one or the other; satisfaction of the victim and the experimenter are mutually exclusive. Moreover, the resolution must take the form of a highly visible action, that of continuing to shock the victim or breaking off the experiment. Thus the subject is forced into a public conflict that does not permit any completely satisfactory solution.

11. While the demands of the experimenter carry the weight of scientific authority, the demands of the victim spring from his personal experience of pain and suffering. The two claims need not be regarded as equally pressing and legitimate. The experimenter seeks an abstract scientific datum; the victim cries out for relief from physical suffering caused by the subject's actions.

12. The experiment gives the subject little time for reflection. The conflict comes on rapidly. It is only minutes after the subject has been seated before the shock generator that the victim begins his protests. Moreover, the subject perceives that he has gone through but two-thirds of the shock levels at the time the subject's first protests are heard. Thus he understands that the conflict will have a persistent aspect to it, and may well become more intense as increasingly more powerful shocks are required. The rapidity with which the conflict descends on the subject, and his realization that it is predictably recurrent may well be sources of tension to him.

13. At a more general level, the conflict stems from the opposition of two deeply ingrained behavior dispositions: first, the disposition not to harm other people, and second, the tendency to obey those whom we perceive to be legitimate authorities.

REFERENCES

Adorno, T., Frenkel-Brunswik, Else, Levinson, D. J., & Sanford, R. N. *The authoritarian personality.* New York: Harper, 1950.

Arendt, H. What was authority? In C. J. Friedrich (Ed.), *Authority.* Cambridge: Harvard Univer. Press, 1938. Pp. 81–112.

Binet, A. *La suggestibilité.* Paris: Schleicher, 1900.

Buss, A. H. *The psychology of aggression.* New York: Wiley, 1962.

Cartwright, S. (Ed.) *Studies in social Power.* Ann Arbor: University of Michigan Institute for Social Research, 1959.

---

[5] A series of recently completed experiments employing the obedience paradigm is reported in Milgram (1964).

Charcot, J. M. *Oeuvres complètes.* Paris: Bureaux du Progrés Medical, 1881.

Frank, J. D. Experimental studies of personal pressure and resistance. *J. gen. Psychol.,* 1944, 30, 23–64.

Friedrich, C. J. (Ed.) *Authority.* Cambridge: Harvard Univer. Press, 1958.

Milgram, S. Dynamics of obedience. Washington: National Science Foundation, 25 January 1961, (Mimeo)

Milgram, S. Some conditions of obedience and disobedience to authority. *Hum. Relat.,* 1964, in press.

Rokeach, M. Authority, authoritarianism, and conformity. In I. A. Berg & B. M. Bass (Eds.), *Conformity and deviation.* New York: Harper, 1961. Pp. 230–257.

Snow, C. P. Either-or. *Progressive,* 1961 (Feb.), 24.

Weber, M. *The theory at social and economic organization.* Oxford: Oxford Univer. Press, 1947.

Active Reading

1. How does Milgram "create a research space" for himself in the first part of the article?

2. What does Milgram mean by the term "naive subject"? How is this scientific meaning of the term different from popular usage?

3. Summarize Milgram's article in 500 words or less. Be sure to convey the main sections of the article.

4. What are Milgram's main conclusions?

5. After this article was published controversy erupted over the methods used. Are there any sections in which Milgram seems to be anticipating the objections that his "subjects" were mistreated in the experiment?

Critical Reading

1. Although he sometimes wrote for a general audience, Milgram wrote this article for fellow specialists in the field of social psychology. What are some of the features of the article that mark it as scholarly, and in particular as scientific? Distinguish between sections in which Milgram's "voice" is more prominent, and sections in which the disciplinary voice is the only one heard.

2. The *Journal of Abnormal and Social Psychology* was renamed the *Journal of Abnormal Psychology* in 1964. In 1965, the *Journal of Experimental Social Psychology* began publication. Look at research articles in a current issue of one or both journals. (Blass's article is one such example.) Are any of the rhetorical features of Milgram's article evident in current articles? For example, examine section headings, use of the passive voice, style of referring to participants ("S" for "subject" in Milgram), and so on. What might account for some elements having endured while others changed?

3. Milgram's experiment is not repeatable now because controversy about the methods used in his and other obedience experiments led to much stricter guidelines for the ethical conduct of research. The experiment did not actually involve administering electrical shocks to anyone: why would some researchers have criticized Milgram's treatment, not of the "learners," but of the "teachers" in this experiment? How might they have been harmed by participating in the experiment? Do you believe the results justify the methods?

4. Although moral codes such as religious teachings and criminal law stress the virtue of obedience, scholars such as Milgram made clear that disobedience could be just as virtuous. Do you believe both obedience and disobedience are important?

The Milgram Paradigm After 35 Years: Some Things We Now Know About Obedience to Authority[1]

Thomas Blass

Thomas Blass[2] is a professor of psychology and the leading authority on Milgram's life and work. He is the author of critically acclaimed works on Milgram, including the biography The Man Who Shocked the World *(New York: Basic Books, 2004), and an edited collection meant to "demonstrate the contemporary vibrancy of the obedience studies." A Holocaust survivor, Blass was a Hungarian child in 1944 when the Nazis invaded his country and subsequently murdered over half a million of his fellow Jews. Blass maintains a website devoted to Milgram studies at www.stanleymilgram.com.*

In this article from the Journal of Applied Social Psychology, Blass reviews 35 years of studies that have attempted to replicate, refine, and extend Milgram's obedience studies. He concludes that the results of this research uphold Milgram's findings. Viewers of the grainy black-and-white video of the experiment that can be found online might wonder whether people in our more technologically sophisticated age would be as easily duped as Milgram's "teachers" were; or whether people living now in the decades following mass civil disobedience in the anti-war movements and civil rights movements would be as inclined to obey an unjust authority. Blass concludes that the overwhelming message of the research is that we are as vulnerable now as Milgram's teachers were then.

Guided by the belief that we cannot make broad extrapolations from the obedience studies without first firmly establishing what has and has not been found using the paradigm itself, this article draws on 35 years of accumulated research and writings on the obedience paradigm to present a status report on the following salient questions and issues surrounding obedience to authority: (a) How should we construe the nature of authority in the obedience experiment? (b) Do predictions of those unfamiliar with the obedience experiment underestimate the actual obedience rates? (c) Are there gender differences in obedience? and (d) Have obedience rates changed over time?

What have I learned from my investigations? First, that the conflict between conscience and authority is not wholly a philosophical or moral issue. Many of the subjects felt, at the philosophical level of values, that they ought not to go on, but they were unable to translate this conviction into action.

[1]Quotes from letters and most information given without citation are from the Stanley Milgram Papers, Yale University Archives. I want to express my thanks to Annamarie Krackow for her help with some of the analyses presented in this article.

[2]Correspondence concerning this article should be addressed to Thomas Blass, Department of Psychology. University of Maryland Baltimore County. 1000 Hilltop Circle. Baltimore, MD 21250. e-mail: blass@umbc2.umbc.edu.

It may be that we are puppets—puppets controlled by the strings of society. But at least we are puppets with perception, with awareness. And perhaps our awareness is the first step to our liberation. (Milgram, 1974b, p. 568)

SAFER: . . . are you suggesting that—that it could happen here?
MILGRAM: I would say, on the basis of having observed a thousand people in the experiment and having my own intuition shaped and informed by these experiments, that if a system of death camps were set up in the United States of the sort we had seen in Nazi Germany, one would be able to find sufficient personnel for those camps in any medium-sized American town. (CBS News, *Sixty Minutes*, March 31, 1979)

1   Milgram conducted his obedience studies early in his professional career, and then went on to apply his innovative touch to a variety of other phenomena, such as the small-world method and the effects of televised antisocial behavior. Yet, clearly, the obedience work has overshadowed his other research—it remains his best-known and most widely discussed work. Of the approximately 140 invited speeches and colloquia he gave during his lifetime, more than one third dealt, directly or indirectly, with obedience. Milgram was still giving invited colloquia on the topic in 1984, the year he died—22 years after he completed them—one at LaSalle College on April 7, and the other at the University of Tennessee at Martin on April 26. In fact, it is somewhat ironic that his very last publications, both appearing posthumously in 1987, dealt with obedience. One was in the *Concise Encyclopedia of Psychology* (Milgram, 1987a), and the other in the *Oxford Companion to the Mind* (Milgram, 1987b).

2   Given the widespread familiarity with Milgram's obedience studies, it should not be surprising to find the obedience research discussed or referred to in publications as diverse as the *Archives of Internal Medicine* (Green, Mitchell, Stocking, Cassel, & Siegler, 1996) and the *Indian Journal of the History of Science* (Laurent, 1987), nor to see it brought into discussions of topics as wide-ranging as business ethics (Browne, Kubasek, & Giampetro-Meyer, 1995/1996; Ferrell & Gardiner, 1991; MacLellan & Dobson, 1997), military psychology (Guimond, Kwak, & Langevin, 1994; Spector, 1978), economics (Anderson & Block, 1995), Holocaust studies (e.g., Browning, 1992; Goldhagen, 1996; Katz, 1993), philosophy (Assiter, 1998; Morelli, 1983), and law (Koh, 1997). Perhaps it should not even be surprising to find it in the title of a song ("We Do What We're Told—Milgram's 37" by rock musician Peter Gabriel on his 1986 album titled *So*) or featured prominently in a French film, *I Comme I care* [I as in Icarus], starring Yves Montand. The obedience experiments were the focus of the Fall 1995 issue of the *Journal of Social Issues*, and they continue to fascinate the reading public (e.g., French, 1997; Masters, 1996).

3   The interest generated by the obedience research has crossed not only disciplinary boundaries but language barriers as well. Early on, Milgram's (1965b) article "Some Conditions of Obedience and Disobedience to Authority" appeared in translation in a German psychology journal in 1966 (Milgram, 1966) and in Hebrew in the Israeli journal *Megamot* in 1967 (Milgram, 1967). The book *Obedience to Authority: An Experimental View* (Milgram, 1974a) has been translated into 11 languages. During the past few years, a social psychologist at the Russian State University of the Humanities, Alexander Voronov, has

been introducing Milgram's work to Russian audiences through his teaching, newspaper articles (e.g.. Voronov, 1993), and Milgram's (1965a) documentary film, *Obedience*, with a Russian voice-over added.

4   The obedience research is clearly among the best-known and most widely discussed work in the social sciences. Undoubtedly, an important reason for this is that it has been a source of usable insights and lessons for both self and society. As Milgram's colleague, Irwin Katz, described the obedience studies at Milgram's funeral,

> After two decades of critical scrutiny and discussion, they remain one of the most singular, most penetrating, and most disturbing inquiries into human conduct that modem psychology has produced in this century. Those of us who presume to have knowledge of man are still perplexed by his findings, with their frightful implications for society. (Katz, 1984)

PURPOSE

5   The purpose of the present article is to provide a detailed examination of a number of salient questions and issues surrounding the Milgram obedience experiments which are still in need of systematic attention. (For reviews and analyses related to other aspects of the obedience paradigm and of other facets of Milgram's life and work, the reader is referred to Blass, 1991, 1992b, 1993, 1996b; see also Miller, 1986.) Specifically, I will draw on about 35 years of accumulated research and writings on the obedience paradigm to present a status report on four questions and issues. While each of the questions and issues could be addressed independently of the others, what unites them is that, in their totality, their answers should help to advance our knowledge of research using the Milgram paradigm and its implications.

6   First, I will address the question of how to construe the nature of authority in the obedience experiment. This is a fundamentally important question, since the kinds of authority–subordinate relationships to which the findings from the obedience experiments are generalizable hinge on the answer to that question. In pursuit of that answer, I will review the various views on this question. Then, in an attempt to provide at least an indirect resolution of the conflicting viewpoints, I will present the results of a person-perception experiment I conducted using an edited version of Milgram's (1965a) documentary film, *Obedience*.

7   Second, I will review the evidence regarding the apparent inability of naive respondents to predict the high degree of obedience Milgram found in his standard conditions. The tendency for those unfamiliar with the obedience experiments to vastly underestimate actual obedience rates reported by Milgram has contributed importantly to the revelatory power of the experiments. The prediction versus outcome dichotomy is also important because, as we will see, it is closely intertwined with a controversy regarding how to interpret the obedient subjects' behavior—as one representing destructive obedience, as Milgram saw it, or as one involving a more benign view centered on subjects' trust in the experimenter, as represented in Mixon's (1976) approach.

8   Third, I will present a review of all of the methodological replications of Milgram's standard or baseline conditions which allowed comparisons of males

and females in rates of obedience. As will be shown, the totality of the findings of my review are consistent with those of Milgram, although there are a couple of discrepant results which pose a challenge to understanding.

9   And finally, this article provides an empirical answer to the question of whether or not obedience rates have changed since Milgram first conducted his experiments in 1961–1962. The answer not only has practical usefulness for those of us who often have fielded this question from students when teaching about the obedience experiments, but it has theoretical importance as well: It provides data-based input regarding the validity of Gergen's (1973) *enlightenment effects* notion.

HOW SHOULD WE CONSTRUE THE NATURE OF AUTHORITY IN THE OBEDIENCE EXPERIMENT?

10   How to characterize the kind of authority embodied by Milgram's experimenter is a fundamentally important question, since the kind of authority-subordinate relationships the experiments have implications for depend on the answer to that question. We will first examine Milgram's view of the authority figure in his experiments, as well as the differing perspectives. Then, I will present the findings from an experiment which provides a rapprochement between the conflicting viewpoints, at least indirectly.

11   Milgram saw his experimenter as representing a legitimate authority, one who is seen as having a right to issue commands, and to whom one feels an obligation to obey. As Milgram (1974a) put it, "an authority system . . . consists of a minimum of two persons sharing the expectation that one of them has the right to prescribe behavior for the other" (pp. 142–143). He also notes that a legitimate authority is one who is "perceived to be in a position of social control within a given situation" (p. 138) and that "the power of an authority stems not from personal characteristics but from his perceived position in a social structure" (p. 139). And what is it about a legitimate authority that, according to Milgram, enables him to elicit destructive obedience, the kind that bears a kinship to the behavior of a Nazi storm trooper? First is the ability of a legitimate authority to define reality for the person who accepts his or her authority. As Milgram (1974a) put it, "There is a propensity for people to accept definitions of action provided by legitimate authority. That is, although the subject performs the action, he allows authority to define its meaning" (p. 145). Earlier, Milgram (1965b) had made the point even more strongly:

> With numbing regularity good people were seen to knuckle under the demands of authority and perform actions that were callous and severe. Men who are in everyday life responsible and decent were seduced by the trappings of authority, by the control of their perceptions, and by the uncritical acceptance of the experimenter's definition of the situation, into performing harsh acts. (p. 74)

12   The other factor that enables a legitimate authority to evoke destructive obedience, according to Milgram (1974a), is the shift of subjects into a different

experiential state—the agentic state—which enables them to relinquish responsibility to the authority and, therefore, to follow his or her orders without regard to their morality. As Milgram (1974a) stated, "The most far-reaching consequence of the agentic shift is that a man feels responsible *to* the authority directing him but feels no responsibility *for* the content of the actions that the authority prescribes" (pp. 145–146).

13   A main differing perspective on the nature of authority in the obedience experiment is to see him as an expert authority. Morelli (1983), a critic of Milgram, succinctly captures the difference between a legitimate authority and an expert authority via the difference between saying someone is *in* authority (i.e., in charge) or *an* authority (i.e., someone with expertise on some topic).

14   One of several writers (Greenwood, 1982; Helm & Morelli, 1925; Morelli, 1983; Penner, Hawkins, Dertke, Spector, & Stone, 1973) who expresses the authority-as-expert point of view is Patten (1977), a philosopher, and in so doing, he argues for a distinction between the obedience of a subject in the Milgram experiment and obedience to carry out mass killings. He argues that there is a difference between the type of authority represented by Milgram's experimenter and the kind wielded by a Hitler. The former possesses what Patten calls *expert-command authority*. That is, he is able to command obedience by means of his presumed expertise regarding learning and shock machinery. The latter, more worrisome, kind of authority wields what he calls a *simple-command authority*; namely, whose power to command and exact obedience is based on legal or quasi-legal considerations, not because of any special expertise regarding the task at hand. According to Patten, knowledge about how a person might react to expert-command authority cannot tell us about that individual's behavior in relation to simple-command authority.

15   Milgram clearly distinguished between his conception of his experimenter as a legitimate authority and authority based on expertise. In an interview conducted by Evans (1976, p. 349), he said, "When we talk about a medical authority, we're talking about someone with expertise. That's not quite the same as the kind of authority I was studying, which is someone perceived to have the right to control one's behavior."

16   What is interesting about this comment is that there is evidence provided by Milgram himself—though it is anecdotal—that for some of his own subjects, the authority's expertise may have been his salient attribute. In his book, he quotes an exchange between a subject (Mr. Rensaleer) and the experimenter. The subject had just stopped at 255 V, and the experimenter tried to prod him on by saying, "There is no permanent tissue damage." Mr. Rensaleer answers, "Yes, but I know what shocks do to you. I'm an electrical engineer, and I have had shocks . . . and you get real shook up by them—especially if you know the next one is coming. I'm sorry" (Milgram, 1974a, p. 51). What this subject seems to be doing is pitting his own expertise against the experimenter's expertise as a way of undermining the latter's power.

17   It is also worth noting that Milgram was not entirely consistent in his view about the source of his experimenter's power as an authority. Or, more precisely,

he seemed to have shifted his position somewhat, later in his career. In 1983, in one of the last things Milgram wrote about obedience before his death, here is what he said in reply to a critical article by Morelli (1983):

> In regard to the term *authority*, Morelli states I did not adequately distinguish between the expert knowledge of *an* authority and a person who is *in* authority (in the sense that he occupies an office or position). I fully agree with Morelli that this is an important distinction. . . . Within my own study, how would the experimenter be classified in terms of these two types of authority? As frequently happens, real life is more complex than textbooks: Both components co-exist in one person. The experimenter is both the person "in charge" and is presumed by subjects to possess expert knowledge. One could envision a series of experiments that attempt to empirically disentangle these two elements and I am all for such inquiry. (Milgram, 1983, pp. 191–192)

18   I recently conducted an experiment which was designed to assess the perceived roles played by expertise and legitimacy in the obedience experiment (Blass, 1992a). I studied my subjects' judgments about obedience rather than their own obedience, so it is not exactly the kind of experiment Milgram had in mind that would "empirically disentangle [the] two elements." Still, I had hoped that it would serve as useful input into the issue. (I should note that there is a study, a doctoral dissertation by Frederick Miller, 1975, that is probably closer to the kind that Milgram had in mind. It pitted the experimenter's expertise and legitimacy against each other in a factorial design, and obedient vs. defiant behavior of the subject served as the dependent variable. However, its focus was on self-inflicted pain, which probably involves different underlying dynamics than obedience to inflict pain on another person.)

19   The conceptual framework I worked with is French and Raven's (1959) classic formulation regarding the bases of social power. There is a natural affinity between French and Raven's schema and the obedience work, for a couple of reasons. First, many social psychology textbooks discuss them together. Second, Raven (1965; Raven & Rubin, 1983) in later publications actually cites the obedience experiment as an illustration of legitimate power, one of the types of power in French and Raven's system. (For a recent statement on the bases of social power, see Raven, 1992.) For my purposes, French and Raven's conceptualization is also useful because expert power is another one of their categories. A further potential benefit of using French and Raven's schema is that they actually distinguish among six different types of power: besides legitimate and expert power there are reward, coercive, referent, and informational power. So by using French and Raven's framework, we might also learn about the perceived role of other attributes besides expertise and legitimacy as determinants of the authority's power. They are listed, with their meanings, in the first and second columns of Table 1.

20   The college student participants in the experiment were shown a 12-min videotape, a shortened, edited version of Milgram's (1965a) documentary film, *Obedience*, similar to ones which I have used in other studies focusing on attributional processes in the Milgram experiment (Blass, 1990, 1995). The end of the

segment they saw shows a subject, referred to in Milgram's (1974a) book by the pseudonym "Fred Prozi" going through the shock sequence, beginning with his giving 90 V. In the full version of the film, he is shown ending up completely obedient (i.e., giving the 450-V shock). In the edited version shown to my subjects, the tape was stopped immediately after Prozi administered the 180-V shock.

21 Participants were then asked to indicate why they thought the subject they just saw kept on following the experimenter's instructions and continued to shock the learner. To answer that question, they were provided with a set of six cards, each of which contained a different explanation which was meant to capture a specific social power category. These are listed in the third column of Table 1.[3] The subjects were asked to indicate which reason they thought was the most likely one, then the next most likely one, and so on.

22 Subjects' choices were assigned rank scores, 1 through 6, with the most likely explanation receiving a rank score of 1. The data were analyzed by means of a one-way repeated-measures ANOVA, with social power category as the independent variable and assigned rank as the dependent variable, yielding a highly significant, $F(5, 170) = 42.77$, $p < .0001$. Dependent t tests, using the Bonferroni test correction, were then conducted to test for differences between pairs of mean rank scores. The mean rank scores are presented in the last column of Table 1. As can be seen, the expert power explanation was seen as most likely, followed very closely by legitimate power, while coercive power was seen as the third and informational power as the fourth most likely explanation. These differences, however, were not significant. Reward power comes next, and referent power is seen as the least likely reason for the subjects' compliance.

23 Several conclusions can be drawn from the findings, tempered by the obvious caution that they are based on data from external perceivers about 30 years after the fact, and not from actual participants in the Milgram experiments. First, it is reassuring to know that the experimental authority's two attributes seen as most salient by naive perceivers are the same ones that have been pointed to over the years by more scholarly perspectives; that is, legitimacy and expertise. Second, rather than deciding between legitimacy and expertise, the results suggest that both factors may have combined to give Milgram's experimenter the tremendous power that he had. Third, the fact that the coercive power explanation was ranked relatively high (as the third most likely explanation) is surprising, because it suggests that some subjects may have been reading things into the experimenter's words. Further, it leaves us with the gnawing possibility that many subjects may have been reading other things into the experimenter's words that we don't know about, which may have figured importantly as determinants of their behavior. And, finally, this study affirms—as do other studies (Blass, 1990, 1995, 1996a; Collins & Brief, 1993; Guimond & Kwak, 1995; Miller, Gillen, Schenker, & Radlove, 1974; Pearson, 1992) the value of using person-perception and attributional methodologies to advance our understanding of obedience to authority.

---

[3]I am indebted to Forsyth (1987) and Raven and Rubin (1983) for some of the ideas and wording that I used in developing the explanations.

Table 1 Mean Rankings of Bases of Social Power as Explanations for an Obedient Subject's Behavior in the Milgram Experiment

Power categories	Meanings: Subjects are influenced because …	Explanation	Mean ranks
Reward	they see the E as a potential source of rewards.	Because the experimenter is a figure of authority, his positive evaluations are especially rewarding, so the subject carries out the experimenter's wishes, thereby hoping to win his approval.	4.46_b
Coercive	they see the E as a potential source of punishments.	The experimenter urges the subject to continue, using such phrases as "The experiment requires that you go on." For the subject, such phrases seem to warn of negative consequences if he does not continue.	2.71_a
Legitimate	they believe that the E has a legitimate right to prescribe behavior for them.	Because the experimenter represents the authority of science and the subject agreed to be a participant, he believes that the experimenter has a right to control his actions, and so the subject feels obliged to comply with the experimenter's wishes.	2.40_a
Referent	they identify with, or like, the E.	The subject has respect and admiration for the experimenter, identifies with him, and would like to be such a person.	5.86_c
Expert	they perceive the E as having some special knowledge or expertise.	As a scientific expert, the experimenter has the faith and trust of the subject, so when the experimenter tells him that "although the shocks may be painful, they're not dangerous," the subject feels reassured and continues with the procedure.	2.31_a
Informational	the information the E provides is intrinsically compelling or convincing.	The introductory information, provided by the experimenter, about the goal of the experiment—namely, to learn more about the effect of punishment on memory—convinces the subject that the study has value and, therefore, that his cooperation is important.	3.23_a

Note. Means sharing a subscript do not differ significantly from each other.

DO PREDICTIONS OF THOSE UNFAMILIAR WITH THE EXPERIMENT UNDERESTIMATE THE ACTUAL OBEDIENCE RATES?

24   Milgram (1974a) found that they did, vastly, and much of the revelatory power of the obedience work is based on this contrast between our expectations of very little obedience and the actual result of a majority of subjects obeying in Milgram's standard or baseline conditions. Milgram considered this finding so centrally important that, according to one of his students (interview with Harold Takooshian, June 17, 1993, Fordham University at Lincoln Center), he would become furious if a student suggested that it was all common sense; that if you thought about it, you could have predicted the outcome. Incidentally, this feature of the obedience studies was dramatized very effectively in 1976 in *The Tenth Level*, a made-for-TV movie starring William Shatner, which earned its writer, George Bellak, an Honorable Mention in the American Psychological Foundation's 1977 National Media Awards. Specifically, Milgram (1963) found that a group of Yale seniors predicted an obedience rate of 1.2%, while a group of psychiatrists predicted that only 0.125% of subjects would be fully obedient. Here is how he described this latter finding in a letter to E. P. Hollander (September 24, 1962):

> Recently I asked a group of 40 Yale psychiatrists to predict the behavior of experimental subjects in a novel, though significant situation. The psychiatrists— although they expressed great certainty in the accuracy of their predictions— were wrong by a factor of 500. Indeed, I have little doubt that a group of charwomen would do as well.

25   While Milgram's powerful demonstration that normal individuals are much more willing to obey a legitimate authority's orders than one might have thought remains an enduring insight, subsequent studies suggest that it is in need of some qualification, since they show that greater accuracy in predicting the results of an obedience experiment is possible.

26   In studies using maximum voltages predicted on the 450-V scale as the dependent variable, mean estimates of others' obedience levels have been as high as 276.75 V (Miller et al., 1974), 225 V (Maughan, 1981), and 216 V (Maughan & Higbee, 1981) in specific conditions.

27   The gap between expected and obtained obedience narrows even more substantively when we consider studies which obtained predictions using obedience rates. Mixon (1971) read participants the Method section from Milgram (1963) and then asked them how "a hypothetical group of 100 American males" would behave. The percentage of subjects predicted to be fully obedient ranged from an average of 33.52% (naive females' estimates) to 44.3% (naive males' estimates). Kaufmann and Kooman (1967) gave subjects descriptions based on Milgram's (1963) procedures and found 27% of them predicting that the "teacher" would continue to the end of the 450-V shock scale. A similar finding was obtained in a more recent study by Guimond et al. (1994) involving a group of Canadian officer candidates. After learning about a baseline obedience experiment (without the outcome) from a short videotape, 23.9% of them predicted full obedience by other Canadians. Furthermore, Mixon (1971) was able to get

variations in predicted obedience by systematically modifying the details about the procedure that was read to subjects. These ranged from 0% of the subjects predicting complete obedience when the description they read clearly indicated that the learner was in danger of being harmed to 90% when indications of possible harm were minimized. Taken together, these findings not only point to greater accuracy in perceivers' predictions about obedience, but also to a different way of understanding underestimations of obedience.

28   An influential perspective on underestimations of obedience has been that of Ross (1977). According to his view, in attempting to predict obedience, people erroneously overlook the determining influence of the situation—the power of the authority—and place too much weight on the personal dispositions of the "teacher," exemplifying a tendency he labeled the *fundamental attribution error*. Mixon's (1971) findings suggest, however, that the discrepancy between predictions and findings takes place not because people do not give enough weight to the immediate situation, but because those who are asked to make predictions, on the one hand, and actual subjects in an obedience experiment, on the other hand, may be responding to different situations: The descriptions given in prediction tasks may convey a procedure that is potentially more harmful for the learner than the real subject in an obedience experiment typically found it to be. Thus, for example, Bierbrauer (1974) had participants learn about the obedience experiment by either watching, or serving as the "teacher" in, a reenactment of an experimental session which ends in complete obedience. Across two experiments and a number of conditions, his participants' subsequent estimates of the percentage of subjects who would give the 450-V shock averaged 11.5%.[4] In introducing the reenactment, however, Bierbrauer (1974) told his subjects that "Professor Milgram wanted to see whether subjects would obey an experimenter's instructions to deliver painful and *potentially dangerous* electric shocks to one of their peers" (p. 78; italics added). But, as Mixon (1976) has argued, both the scientific context and the experimenter's reassurances that the shocks may be painful but not dangerous probably led the actual participants in Milgram's experiments to anticipate that the "learner" would not be harmed.

29   In other words, Mixon's (1989) view of subjects' behavior in the obedience experiment is a more benign one than is Milgram's. If Mixon is right, then was Milgram wrong in referring to his obedient subjects' actions as "destructive"? This is how Mixon sees it, and for a long time, I saw Milgram's and Mixon's approaches as conflicting and irreconcilable. But then recently, in a review of Mixon's (1989) book, Hamilton (1992) presented a persuasive and insightful perspective that brings the implications of Mixon's viewpoint closer to Milgram's:

> I believe . . . that Milgram's work has a value beyond that accorded it in Mixon's account. True, perhaps Milgram's subjects suspended their doubts and disbeliefs in going along with experimental commands. Perhaps they did not really believe that damage and death could or should ensue from their actions. So what; they still did them. I see the actions of Milgram's subjects as more closely analogous to those of corporate employees who produce unsafe products and believe that the company could not really be endangering consumers just to

---

[4]This number was computed by averaging across the condition means in Tables 2 and E-4 in *Bierbrauer* (1974).

make a profit, than to the actions of a military subordinate ordered to shoot civilians. The fact remains that these employees—or Milgram's subjects—perform the deeds they are asked to perform. (Hamilton, 1992, p. 1313)

ARE THERE GENDER DIFFERENCES IN OBEDIENCE?

30   Although almost all of his subjects were men, Milgram had one condition (Experiment 8 in Milgram, 1974a) in which the participants were women. The result was exactly the same rate of obedience—65%—as for men in the comparable condition (Experiment 5). I found nine methodological replications in the literature which had both male and female participants. Consistent with Milgram's own findings, eight out of nine of these studies found no gender differences (Table 2).

31   As can be seen in Table 2, the one exception is a study by Kilham and Mann (1974), conducted in Australia, in which they found the obedience rate in men (40%) to be significantly higher than among women (16%). (The Kilham & Mann study is also noteworthy for another reason: Its overall rate of obedience—28%—is the lowest reported in the literature for a standard obedience condition.)

32   It is also relevant to mention two other studies in this context because they pose a challenge to understanding, though they were not included in Table 2: the first, because it lacked a comparison group of males; the second, because it used a real victim, an animal "learner." Ring, Wallston, and Corey (1970) conducted a voice-feedback replication using 57 female subjects. While the main focus of this study was the relative effectiveness of different debriefing methods, an important finding was that 91% of their subjects were fully obedient, the highest rate for a standard condition reported in the obedience literature. Sheridan and King (1972) conducted a unique Milgram-type study using a puppy as the "learner." Even though the cute puppy was visible to the subjects and enough actual shock was delivered to cause the puppy to yelp and jump in pain, 100% of the female subjects were fully obedient, while only 54% of the males were obedient.

33   Milgram (1974a) had also reported that, although the level of obedience in women was the same as in men, the self-reported tension of the obedient women was higher than among 20 groups of obedient male subjects. This result finds support in a study by Shanab and Yahya (1977) involving Jordanian children and adolescents. They reported that females were more likely to show visible signs of tension than were males.

34   Two consistencies emerge from the studies presented in this section. First, it is quite remarkable that 9 out of 10 comparisons (Table 2) showed no gender differences in obedience, despite the existence of between-experiment differences on such factors as country where the experiment was conducted, gender of experimenter, gender of learner, and specific details of the experimental procedures. Eagly's (1978) seminal review of gender differences in influenceability showed that the widely held assumption about women being generally more influenceable than men was wrong. She found no gender differences in the majority of the studies she reviewed. A tendency for women to be more susceptible to influence than men showed up in only one domain—the Asch-type

Table 2 Studies Using the Milgram Paradigm Which Have Compared Male and Female Subjects on Level of Obedience

Author and year	Country	Gender	Number of subjects	Author's name for or description of condition (when more than 1 in study)	Equivalent Milgram condition(s)	Percentage fully obedient
Milgram (1962)	United States	F	40	8. Women as subjects	N/A	65
Edwards et al. (1969)	South Africa	M F	10 6	—	2. Voice feedback	87.5
Bock & Warren (1972)	United States	M F	17 13	—	5. New baseline	?
Bock (1972)	United States	M/F	25	Scientific authority	5. New baseline	40
Kilham & Mann (1974)	Australia	M F	25 25	Executant	2. Voice feedback	28
Costanzo (1976)	United States	M F	48 48	"Retaliation" and "nonretaliation" conditions combined	1. Remote	81
Shanab & Yahya (1977)	Jordan	M F	48 48	Experimental	1 and 2. Remote and voice feedback combination	73
Shanab & Yahya (1978)	Jordan	M F	12 12	Experimental	1 and 2. Remote and voice feedback combination	62.5
Miranda, Caballero, Gomez, & Zamorano (1981)	Spain	M F	12 12	"Not watching" and "watching" conditions combined	2. Voice feedback 3. Proximity	50
Schurz (1985)	Austria	M F	24 32	—	1. Remote	80

Table 2 Continued

Subject gender differences

Gender of experimenter	Yes/No	Percentage fully obedient	Remarks
M	No	—	Compared to Milgram's Condition 5 (same condition using 40 male subjects) in which 65% were fully obedient. The data on women first appeared in Milgram (1974a), but all conditions were completed between the summer of 1961 and May 1962. The women's condition was carried out in 1962. Thus, the 1962 in the citation reflects the completion date, not the publication date.
F	No	—	The experimenter, a 19-year-old female, as well as her two male "technician" assistants, were college students. See also the note about this experiment in the Appendix.
M	No	—	Percentage of fully obedient subjects not reported. The measure of obedience was maximum shock level given.
M	No	—	Lack of subject gender differences reported only for total subject sample, that is, across three conditions, of which the scientific authority condition was one.
M	Yes	M 40% F 16%	Subjects assumed role of executants taking orders to shock from confederate transmitters who, they thought, were also subjects. Paired male executant with male learner and female executant with female learner.
F	No	—	Subject and learner paired in four conditions: M-M, M-F, F-M, F-F.
F	No	—	Subjects were children aged 6 to 16. Subject and learner paired in two conditions: M-M, F-F.
F	No	—	Subject and learner paired in two conditions: M-M, F-F.
M/F	No	—	When subjects were male, experimenter and learner were male. When subjects were female, experimenter and learner were female. The dependent variable was highest shock given, rather than percentage fully obedient. However, a graph in the report reveals indirectly that at least 50% were fully obedient.
F	No	—	Learner was female. Stimulus: "ultrasound waves" supposedly damaging to skin at higher intensities.

(Asch, 1956) group-pressure conformity situation, in which 34% of the studies found women to be significantly more conforming than men. Her review, although mentioning the Milgram studies and two replications that looked at gender differences (Kilham & Mann, 1974; Sheridan & King, 1972), did not include a systematic review of studies of gender differences in the obedience paradigm. The findings reported here complement Eagly's review by identifying yet another social influence paradigm in which the majority of studies show no gender differences.

35   Second, the consistency of Milgram's findings on gender differences in self-reported tension is also quite noteworthy, with obedient women reporting greater tension than the obedient males in 20 conditions. These findings have wide-ranging implications beyond the question of gender differences. In particular, the fact that the same observable behaviors—identical rates of obedience (65%), in men and women in a baseline condition—were accompanied by different levels of nervousness should alert us to the importance of trying to identify the underlying processes involved in acts of obedience and defiance, be they those involving the Milgram paradigm or not.

HAVE OBEDIENCE RATES CHANGED OVER TIME?

36   One of the questions I have posed to my social psychology classes when presenting the obedience studies is what they think the results would be if the research were conducted today. I collected systematic data relating to this and several other questions from students in 11 social psychology classes from 1983 to 1990. The results were as follows: 40% predicted less obedience today, 39% predicted the same amount, and only 11% predicted an increase in obedience (Blass & Krackow, 1991).

37   After completing this analysis, it occurred to me that it would be even more interesting to determine whether or not a change in obedience tendencies over time could be detected in the actual outcomes of obedience studies. So I took Milgram's standard or baseline conditions (i.e., in which the learner is physically separated from and not visible to the subject: Experiments 1, 2, 5, 6, 8, and 10 in Milgram, 1974a) and all of the methodological replications of these experiments carried out by others (there were 14 of these), and correlated the rank order of the year of publication of the study with the rank order of its obedience rate. The studies spanned a period of 22 years, from 1963 to 1985, which is the year of publication of the last methodological replication that I have found (Schurz, 1985). Although levels of obedience across studies ranged from a low of 28% (Kilham & Mann, 1974) to a high of 91% (Ring et al., 1970), there was no systematic relationship between when a study was conducted and the amount of obedience obtained: The Spearman rank-order correlation coefficient (r_s) was .002. A second correlation was performed, this time adding Milgram's Proximity condition (Experiment 3) and three proximity-condition replications by other investigators (for a total of 24 conditions or studies). These had been excluded from the first correlation because the rate of obedience in Milgram's Experiment 3 was significantly lower than those of his Experiments 1, 2, 5, and 8 (Blass, 1991), suggesting that methodologically and experientially they were distinct. However, as it turns

out, the addition of the Proximity studies leaves the correlation virtually unchanged: $r_s = -.008$. (See the Appendix for a listing of studies and findings which were used in the correlational analyses.)

38   An important implication of the findings of these correlational analyses is that they provide evidence—at least, indirectly—against the operation of enlightenment effects, which had been proposed by Gergen (1973). Gergen had argued that "sophistication as to psychological principles liberates one from their behavioral implications" (p. 313). If Gergen is right, the later studies should have found less obedience than the earlier ones since, with the longer passage of time, the participants in the more recent studies would have had more of a chance to hear about Milgram's work and thereby become enlightened about, and liberated from, the unwanted demands of authority.

39   Two unpublished studies attempted to provide more direct tests regarding the operation of enlightenment effects using the Milgram paradigm—one by Brant (1978) and the other by Shelton (1982). Brant had college undergraduates, who had first been familiarized with the obedience studies, participate in a "learning" experiment, similar to Milgram's Experiment 11, in which they could choose any shock level on a 390-V "shock" generator whenever the learner made an error. Brant reports that only 4 subjects out of 44 refused to participate in the study after they heard the instructions—a finding which he interprets as "seriously call[ing] into question" (p. 53) Gergen's thesis. However, the study suffers from a serious methodological flaw, precluding any firm conclusions about enlightenment effects: It is not clear how many of the subjects, if any, actually knew about the obedience studies prior to their own participation. This is because the attempt to inform them about it took the following form:

> Prior to their participation, subjects had been assigned readings in their classes concerning the obedience research as well as other psychological findings in conjunction with their coursework. In addition, these students had been lectured to on topics relevant to this investigation. (Brant, 1978, p. 19)

There was no attempt, however, to ascertain whether or not subjects had actually read the assigned readings or attended the relevant lectures.

40   Shelton's (1982) attempt to determine the validity of Gergen's claim that the acquisition of psychological information can change a person's behavior was not only a methodological improvement over Brant's study but also was quite clever in its conception. First, she gave all of her subjects a detailed synopsis of the obedience experiment to read and then asked them a set of questions about what they had read. She then asked them to serve as experimenters in a similar "learning" experiment. Their job was to oversee a subject (the teacher) who was supposed to teach a verbal-learning task to another subject (the learner) by using increasing voltages of shock as punishment on each subsequent mistake. The subject (experimenter) was told that the learner was a confederate, but unbeknownst to the former, the teacher was also a confederate, who, as the shock levels and the learner's expressions of pain increased, "expressed uneasiness, then became quite anxious, angry, on the verge of tears; cursed, complained of stomach pains, asked for a glass of water, and pleaded with the experimenter to stop the session . . ." (p. 31). In spite of this, 22 out of 24 subjects continued to

the end, commanding the teacher to keep increasing the shock to the maximum 450-V level. Apparently, subjects could not draw a parallel between their obedience to Shelton and the teacher's obedience to them.

41   How do we reconcile a finding like Shelton's with the life-changing testimonials of individuals who found the strength to resist the unwanted demands of authority after participating in, or otherwise learning about, the obedience experiments (e.g., Appendix I in Milgram, 1974a)? One possibility is suggested in an insightful letter written to Milgram in April 1982, by a former participant in a Milgram-type experiment at the University of Minnesota in 1967. He wrote: "I'm writing to thank you for making a major contribution to my understanding of myself and of the meaning of the values I have." He wrote that he learned a number of things from his participation in the experiment, one of which was "that it is easier for me (although hardly simple) to recognize and avoid situations in which authority and obedience play significant roles (e.g., the military, many government and business organizations) than it is to defy authority within such situations." That is, contrary to what is implied by Gergen's enlightenment-effects notion, knowledge does not or cannot always lead to action. Being enlightened about the unexpected power of authority may help a person to stay away from an authority-dominated situation, but once he or she is already in such a situation, knowledge of the drastic degree of obedience that authorities are capable of eliciting does not necessarily help to free the individual from the grip of the forces operating in that concrete situation; that is, to defy the authority in charge.

SUMMARY AND CONCLUSIONS

42   In this article I set out to present a status report on four important questions and issues surrounding the obedience paradigm, grounded in systematic analysis—something which had heretofore not been done with these questions and issues. My analyses involved a variety of methods: literature reviews, a person-perception experiment, and correlational analyses. On the basis of these analyses, I believe that the following conclusions are called for. First, in all likelihood, Milgram's experimental authority was perceived by subjects as embodying a combination of a legitimate authority and a scientific expert. Second, a review of prediction studies found that while naive subjects generally underestimate actual obedience rates, the gap between estimated and actual obedience rates is often quite a bit smaller than what Milgram found. Third, with one exception, in all studies permitting a comparison between male and female subjects, no gender differences in obedience have been found. And fourth, rates of obedience show no systematic change over time: Two correlational analyses between year of publication and obedience outcome showed no relationship whatsoever between when a study was conducted and how much obedience occurred. In each case, the wider implications of each of these findings were also discussed.

REFERENCES

Ancona, L., & Pareyson, R. (1968). Contributo allo studio della aggressione: La dinamica della obbedienza distruttiva [Contribution to the study of aggression: The dynamics of destructive obedience]. *Archivio di Psicologia. Neumlogia. e Psichiatria*, 29, 340–372.

Anderson, C. M., & Block, W. (1995). Procrastination, obedience and public policy: The irrelevance of salience. *American Journal of Economics and Sociology, 54*, 201–215.

Asch, S. (1956). Studies of independence and conformity: 1. A minority of one against a unanimous majority. *Psychological Monographs, 70*, 1–70.

Assiter, A. (1998). Communitarianism and obedience. In B. Brecher, J. Halliday, & K. Kolinska (Eds.), *Nationalism and racism in the liberal order.* Aldershot, UK: Ashgate.

Bierbrauer, G. A, (1974). Attribution and perspective: Effects of time, set and role on interpersonal influence. *Dissertation Abstracts International, 34.* 6232B. (University Microfilms No. 74–13,602)

Blass, T. (1990, June 8). *Judgments about the Milgram obedience experiment support a cognitive view of defensive attribution.* Paper presented at the annual convention of the American Psychological Society, Dallas, TX.

Blass, T. (1991). Understanding behavior in the Milgram obedience experiment: The role of personality, situations, and their interactions. *Journal of Personality and Social Psychology, 60*, 398–413.

Blass, T. (1992a, August 17). The nature of authority in Milgram's obedience paradigm. In H. C. Kelman (Chair), *Authority—crimes of obedience and disobedience.* Symposium conducted at the annual meeting of the American Psychological Association, Washington, DC.

Blass, T. (1992b). The social psychology of Stanley Milgram. In M. P. Zanna (Ed.), *Advances in experimental social psychology* (Vol. 25, pp. 227–329). San Diego, CA: Academic.

Blass, T. (1993). Psychological perspectives on the perpetrators of the Holocaust: The role of situational pressures, personal dispositions, and their interactions. *Holocaust and Genocide Studies, 7*, 30–50.

Blass, T. (1995). Right-wing authoritarianism and role as predictors of attributions about obedience to authority. *Personality and Individual Differences, 19*, 99–100.

Blass, T. (1996a). Attribution of responsibility and trust in the Milgram obedience experiment. *Journal of Applied Social Psychology, 26*, 1529–1535.

Blass, T. (1996b). Stanley Milgram: A life of inventiveness and controversy. In G. Kimble, A. Boneau, & M. Wertheimer (Eds.), *Portraits of pioneers in psychology* (Vol. 2. pp. 315–331). Washington, DC, and Hillsdale, NJ: American Psychological Association and Lawrence Erlbaum.

Blass, T., & Krackow, A. (1991, June 14). *The Milgram obedience experiments: Students' views vs. scholarly perspectives and actual findings.* Paper presented at the annual convention of the American Psychological Society, Washington, DC.

Bock, D. C. (1972). Obedience: A response to authority and Christian commitment. *Dissertation Abstracts International, 33*, 3278B–3279B. (University Microfilms No. 72-31,651)

Bock, D.C., & Warren, N. C. (1972). Religious belief as a factor in obedience to destructive commands. *Review of Religious Research, 13*, 185–191.

Brant, W. D. (1978). *Situational pressure, racial stereotypes, and conformity in laboratory aggression.* Unpublished master's thesis, Oregon State University.

Browne, M. N., Kubasek, N. K., & Giampetro-Meyer, A. (1995/1996). The seductive danger of craft ethics for business organizations. *Review of Business, 17*, 23–28.

Browning, C. (1992). *Ordinary men: Reserve Police Battalion 101 and the Final Solution in Poland.* New York, NY: Harper/Collins.

CBS News. (1979, March 31). Transcript of *Sixty Minutes* segment, "I was only following orders," pp. 2–8.

Collins, B. E., & Brief; D. E. (1993, August 20). *Using person perception methodologies to uncover the meanings of the Milgram obedience paradigm.* Paper presented at the annual convention of the American Psychological Association, Toronto, Ontario, Canada.

Costanzo, E. M. (1976). The effect of probable retaliation and sex related variables on obedience. *Dissertation Abstracts International, 37,* 4214B. (University Microfilms No. 77-3253)

Eagly, A. H. (1978). Sex differences in influenceability. *Psychological Bulletin, 85,* 86–116.

Edwards, D. M., Franks, P., Friedgood, D., Lobban, G., & Mackay, H. C. G. (1969). *An experiment on obedience.* Unpublished student report, University of the Witwatersrand, Johannesburg, South Africa.

Evans, R. I. (1976). [Interview with] Stanley Milgram. In R. I. Evans (Ed.), *The making of psychology: Discussion with creative contributors* (pp. 346–356). New York, NY: Knopf.

Ferrell, O. C., & Gardiner, G. (1991). *In pursuit of ethics: Tough choices in the world of work.* Springfield, IL: Smith Collins.

Forsyth, D. (1987). *Social psychology.* Monterey, CA: Brooks/Cole.

French, J. R. P., Jr., & Raven, B. (1959). The bases of social power. In D. Cartwright (Ed.), *Studies in social power* (pp. 150–167). Ann Arbor, MI: Research Center for Group Dynamics, University of Michigan.

French, S. (1997, May 21). Parents: Devil's seed. *The Guardian,* p. T14.

Gergen, K. J. (1973). Social psychology as history. *Journal of Personality and Social Psychology, 26,* 309–320.

Goldhagen, D. (1996). *Hitler's willing executioners: Ordinary Germans and Holocaust.* New York, NY: Knopf.

Green, M. J., Mitchell, G., Stocking, C. B., Cassel, C. K., & Siegler, M. (1996). Do actions reported by the physicians in training conflict with consensus guidelines on ethics? *Archives of Internal Medicine. 156,* 298–304.

Greenwood, J. D. (1982). On the relation between laboratory experiments and social behavior: Causal explanation and generalization. *Journal for the Theory of Social Behavior, 12,* 225–250.

Guimond, S., & Kwak, K. (1995, June). *Learning about Milgram's experiments II: Effects on impressions of the "teacher" and the "learner."* Presented at the annual convention of the Canadian Psychological Association. Charlottetown, Prince Edward Island, Canada.

Guimond, S., Kwak, K., & Langevin, P. (1994, June 30–July 2). *Obedience in the military I: Psychological effects of learning about Milgram's experiments.* Presented at the annual convention of the Canadian Psychological Association, Penticton, British Columbia, Canada.

Hamilton, V. L. (1992). Thoughts on obedience: A social structural view. [Review of "Obedience and civilization: Authorized crime and the normality of evil"]. *Contemporary Psychology, 37,* 1313.

Helm, C., & Morelli, M. (1985). Obedience to authority in a laboratory setting: Generalizability and context dependency. *Political Studies, 33,* 610–627.

Holland, C. D. (1967). Sources of variance in the experimental investigation of behavioral obedience. *Dissertation Abstracts International, 29,* 2802A. (University Microfilms No. 69-2 146)

Katz, F. E. (1993). *Ordinary people and extraordinary evil*. Albany, NY: SUNY.

Katz, I. (1984, December 22). Remarks delivered at the funeral of Stanley Milgram.

Kaufmann, H., & Kooman, A. (1967). Predicted compliance in obedience situations as a function of implied instructional variables. *Psychonomic Science, 7*, 205–206.

Kilham, W., & Mann, L. (1974), Level of destructive obedience as a function of transmitter and executant roles in the Milgram obedience paradigm. *Journal of Personality and Social Psychology, 29*, 696–702.

Koh, H. H. (1997). Why do nations obey international law? *Yale Law Journal, 106*, 2599–2659.

Laurent, J. (1987). Milgram's shocking experiments: A case in the social construction of "science." *Indian Journal of the History of Science, 22*, 247–272.

MacLellan, C., & Dobson, J. (1997). Women, ethics, and MBAs. *Journal of Business Ethics, 16*, 1201–1209.

Mantell, D. M. (1971). The potential for violence in Germany. *Journal of Social Issues, 27*(4), 101–112.

Masters, B. (1996). *The evil that men do*. New York, NY: Doubleday.

Maughan, M. R. C. (1981). The effect of four methods of subject recruitment on subjects' estimated compliance for themselves and others in role-playing situations. *Dissertation Abstracts International, 42*, 2134. (University Microfilms No. 8 1-24,785)

Maughan, M. R. C., & Higbee, K. L. (1981). Effect of subjects' incentives for participation on estimated compliance for self and others. *Psychological Reports, 49*, 119–122.

Milgram, S. (1963). Behavioral study of obedience. *Journal of Abnormal and Social Psychology, 67*, 371–378.

Milgram, S. (1965a). *Obedience* [film]. University Park, PA: Penn State Audio-Visual Services [distributor].

Milgram, S. (1965b,). Some conditions of obedience and disobedience to authority. *Human Relations, 15*, 57–76.

Milgram, S. (1966). Einige Bedingungen von Autoritätsgehorsam und seiner Verweigerung [Some conditions of obedience and disobedience to authority]. *Zeitschrift fur Experimentelle und Angewandte Psychologie, 13*, 433–463.

Milgram, S. (1967). Tnaim achadim shel tziut ve-itziut le-samchut [Some conditions of obedience and disobedience to authority]. *Megamot. 15*, 31–49.

Milgram, S. (1974a). *Obedience to authority: An experimental view*. New York, NY: Harper & Row.

Milgram, S. (1974b, October 31). We are all obedient. *The Listener*, 567–568.

Milgram, S. (1983). Reflections on Morelli's "Dilemma of obedience." *Metaphilosophy, 14*, 190–194.

Milgram, S. (1987a). Obedience. in R. J. Corsini (Ed.), *Concise encyclopedia of psychology* (pp. 773–774). New York, NY: John Wiley & Sons.

Milgram, S. (1987b). Obedience. In R. L. Gregory (Ed.), *Oxford companion to the mind* (pp. 566–568). New York, NY: Oxford University Press.

Miller, A. G. (1986). *The obedience experiments: A case study of controversy in social science*. New York, NY: Praeger.

Miller, A. G., Gillen, B., Schenker, C., & Radlove, S. (1974). The prediction and perception of obedience to authority. *Journal of Personality, 42*, 23–42.

Miller, F. D. (1975). *An experimental study of obedience to authorities of varying legitimacy.* Unpublished doctoral dissertation, Harvard University.

Miranda, K S. B., Caballero, R. B., Gomez, M. N. G., & Zamorano, M. A. M. (1981). Obediencia a la autoridad [Obedience to authority]. *Psiquis.* 2, 212–221.

Mixon, D. (1971). Further conditions of obedience and disobedience to authority. *Dissertation Abstracts International,* 32, 4848B. (University Microfilms No. 72-6477)

Mixon, D. (1976). Studying feignable behavior. *Representative Research in Social Psychology,* **7,** 89–104.

Mixon, D. (1989*). Obedience and civilization: Authorized crime and the normality of evil.* London, UK: Pluto Press.

Morelli, M. (1983). Milgram's dilemma of obedience. *Metaphilosophy,* 14, 183–189.

Patten, S. C. (1977). Milgram's shocking experiments. *Philosophy,* 52, 425–440.

Pearson, K. N. (1992, May 2). *Assessing the obedient: Effects of behavioral extremity and information medium on observers' social judgments.* Paper presented at the annual convention of the Western Psychological Association, Portland, OR.

Penner, L. A., Hawkins, H. L., Dertke. M. C.. Spector, P., & Stone, A. (1973). Obedience as a function of experimenter competence. *Memory and Cognition,* 1, 241–245.

Podd, M. H. (1970). The relationship between ego identity status and two measures of morality. *Dissertation Abstracts International,* 31, 5634. (University Microfilms No. 71-6107)

Powers, P. C., & R. G. (1972). Effects of the behavior and the perceived arousal of a model on instrumental aggression. *Journal of Personality and Social Psychology,* 23, 175–183.

Raven, B. H. (1965). Social influence and power. in J. D. Steiner & M. Fishbein (Eds.), *Current studies in social psychology* (pp. 371–382). New York, NY: Holt, Rinehart, & Winston.

Raven, B. H. (1992). A power/interaction model of interpersonal influence: French and Raven thirty years later. *Journal of Social Behavior anti Personality,* 7, 217–244.

Raven, B. H., & Rubin, J. Z. (1983). *Social psychology* (2nd ed.). New York, NY: John Wiley & Sons.

Ring, K., Wallston, K., & Corey, M. (1970). Mode of debriefing as a factor affecting subjective reactions to a Milgram-type obedience experiment: An ethical inquiry. *Representative Research in Social Psychology,* 1, 67–85.

Rogers, R. W. (1973). *Obedience to authority: Presence of authority and command strength.* Paper presented at the annual convention of the Southeastern Psychological Association (Abstract).

Rosenhan, D. (1969). Some origins of concern for others. In P. Mussen, J. Langer, & M. Covington (Eds.), *Trends and issues in developmental psychology* (pp. 134–153). New York, NY: Holt, Rinehart, & Winston.

Ross, L. (1977). The intuitive psychologist and his shortcomings: Distortions in the attribution process. In L. Berkowitz (Ed.), *Advances in experimental social psychology* (Vol. 10, pp. 173–219). New York, NY; Academic.

Schurz, G. (1985). Experimentelle Uberprufung des Zusammenhangs zwischen Personlichkeitsmerkmalen und der Bereitschaft zum destruktiven Gehorsam gegenuber Autoritäten [Experimental examination of the relationships between personality characteristics and the readiness for destructive obedience toward authority]. *Zeitschrift fur Experimentelle und Angewandte Psychologie,* 32, 160–177.

Shalala, S. R. (1974). A study of various communication settings which produce obedience by subordinates to unlawful superior orders. *Dissertation Abstracts International,* 36, 979. (University Microfilms No. 75-17,675)

Shanab, M. E., & Yahya, K. A. (1977). A behavioral study of obedience in children. *Journal of Personality and Social Psychology,* 35, 530–536.

Shanab, M. E., & Yahya, K. A. (1978). A cross-cultural study of obedience. *Bulletin of the Psychonomic Society,* 11, 267–269.

Shelton, G. A. (1982). *The generalization of understanding to behavior: The role of perspective in enlightenment.* Unpublished doctoral dissertation, University of British Columbia, Canada.

Sheridan, C. L., & King, R. G. (1972). Obedience to authority with an authentic victim. *Proceedings of the eightieth annual convention of the American Psychological Association* (pp. 165–166). Washington, DC: American Psychological Association.

Spector, B. J. (1978). *Military self-discipline: A motivational analysis.* Unpublished final report, CACI Inc.—Federal, Arlington, VA, Policy Sciences Division.

Voronov, A. (1993, September 8-14). Provenyemost kak prestuplenya [Obedience as a crime]. *Rossia,* 8.

APPENDIX

List of Obedience Studies and Their Findings (in Obedience Rates) Used in the Correlational Analyses Reported in the Article

Study	Country	Obedience rate (%)
Milgram (1963)[a]	United States	
Exp. 1		65
Exp. 2		62.5
*Exp. 3		40
Exp. 5		65
Exp. 6		50
Exp. 8		65
Exp. 10		47.5
Holland (1967)	United States	75
*Ancona & Pareyson (1968)	Italy	85
Rosenhan (1969)	United States	85
*Podd (1970)[b]	United States	31
Edwards, Franks, Friedgood, Lobban, & Mackay (1969)[c]	South Africa	87.5
Ring, Wallston, & Corey (1970)	United States	91
Mantell (1971)	West Germany	85
Bock (1972)	United States	40
Powers & Green (1972)	United States	83
Rogers	United States	37
Kilham & Mann (1974)	Australia	28

Study	Country	Obedience rate (%)
Shalala (1974)	United States	30
Costanzo (1976)	United States	81
Shanab & Yahya (1977)	Jordan	73
Shanab & Yahya (1978)	Jordan	62.5
*Miranda, Caballero, Gomez, & Zamorano (1980)	Spain	50
Schurz (1985)	Austria	80

Note. Studies preceded by an asterisk were included in the second, but not the first, correlation. (See the body of the article for an explanation.) Some studies listed consist of more than one condition. In such cases, the obedience rate reported is for the condition that represents the methodological replication of Milgram's standard or proximity conditions (i.e., Experiments 1, 2, 3, 5, 6, 8, or 10 in Milgram, 1974a).

[a]Although the numbers designating Milgram's experiments are the ones he used in his book (Milgram, 1974a), all of his obedience experiments (other than pilot work) were conducted between the summer of 1961 and the end of May 1962. In the correlational analyses, they were all designated by the year 1963, the year of the first publication of his obedience findings.

[b]The obedience rate found by Podd (1970) does not appear in his dissertation, but was provided by him in a personal communication.

[c]The study by Edwards et al. (1969) was conducted by third-year psychology majors for a course in Experimental Social Psychology at the University of Witwatersrand in Johannesburg, South Africa. Their instructor, L. Melamed, sent a copy of the report to Milgram on October 23, 1969. In his book, Milgram (1974a) mentions South Africa as one of the foreign countries where replications of the obedience experiments had been conducted, but gave no reference for it. Since in searching the literature I have not found any other South African obedience study, this is the one that, in all likelihood, Milgram had in mind.

Active Reading

1. Summarize Blass's article in 500 words or less. Be sure to convey the organizational structure of his article and how he reaches his conclusions.

2. Blass uses the term "conceptual framework." What appears to be meant by this common and important scholarly term?

3. What are the four questions Blass sets out to answer in his article, and what reasons does he give for focusing on them?

4. What are "enlightenment effects"? What is Blass's position on the value of understanding the "unexpected power of authority"?

5. How does Blass describe the impact of Milgram's work in the introduction to the article? How is this kind of assessment different from the assessment provided at the end of the article?

Critical Reading

1. As you did with Milgram's article, identify the sections of Blass's article where his own voice seems more prominent, and sections in which the voice of science dominates. Why would Blass vary his style in these ways?

2. How is the structure of Blass's article similar to Milgram's, and how does it differ? What factors might account for the similarities and differences?

3. How does Blass use "I"?

4. Are you convinced by Blass's argument that Milgram was right?
5. What is your position on the likely benefits of "enlightenment effects"? Do you agree with Blass?

Learning How to Resist Unwanted Influences

Philip G. Zimbardo

Philip Zimbardo is a social psychologist and professor at Stanford University, where he has devoted his career to investigating the ability of individuals to resist pressures to conform. He has served as president of the American Psychological Association and most recently has written extensively on the human capacity for evil and heroism in relation to terrorism.

Zimbardo's work first came to international prominence in the early 1970s when he published the results of "The Stanford Prison Experiment." In that study, Zimbardo created a simulated prison in the basement of the psychology building at Stanford, recruited college students as participants, and assigned them randomly to the roles of guard and prisoner. Within a few days the "guards" were abusing the "prisoners" and the prisoners were betraying each other to please the guards. Behaviour became so extreme and psychological states became so disturbed that the experiment had to be stopped. Zimbardo concluded from the experiment that the vast majority of ordinary people will conform to group pressure. This experiment became as famous and provoked as much controversy as Milgram's electric shock experiments. The experiment was filmed in a video called Quiet Rage *and reenacted in a German film called simply,* The Experiment.

In the following excerpt from his 2008 book, The Lucifer Effect, *Zimbardo draws on the findings of the obedience experiments to return to the question of how understanding social forces can help us resist them, and argues that nations should foster "heroic imagination" in their citizens in order to awaken the potential for courage that is dormant in ordinary people.*

1   People with paranoid disorders have great difficulty in conforming to, complying with, or responding to a persuasive message, even when it is offered by their well-meaning therapists or loved ones. Their cynicism and distrust create an isolating barrier that shields them from involvement in most social encounters. Because they are adamantly resistant to social pressures, they provide an extreme model for immunity to influence, though obviously at great psychic cost. At the other end of the scale are the overly gullible, unconditionally trusting people who are easy marks for any and every scam artist.

2   Among them are the many people who fall prey to frauds, scams, and confidence games at some time in their lives. A full 12 percent of Americans are defrauded by con-artist criminals each year, sometimes losing their life savings. It is likely that this figure is shared by people in most nations. Although the majority of those defrauded are over fifty years old, at a time of life when wisdom should prevail, many people of all ages are regularly duped by tricksters in telemarketing, health care, and lottery scams.[1]

3   Remember the phony authority hoax perpetrated on an innocent teenager at a McDonald's restaurant that was described in chapter 12? Surely you asked

yourself, "How could she and those adults duped by this caller be so stupid?" Well, this same hoax was effective in getting many other fast-food restaurant personnel to follow that false authority blindly. How many? Recall in a dozen different restaurant chains in nearly seventy different establishments, in thirty-two states![2] We noted that one assistant manager in a McDonald's restaurant, who was totally duped by the phony caller–con man, asks us all, "Unless you are in that situation, at that time, how do you know what you would do? You don't know what you would do."[3]

4   The point is that instead of distancing ourselves from the individuals who were deceived by assuming negative dispositional attributes in them—stupidity, naiveté—we need to understand why and how people like us were so completely seduced. Then we will be in a position to resist and to spread awareness of methods of resisting such hoaxes.

The Duality of Detachment Versus Saturation

5   A basic duality exists in the human condition of detachment versus saturation, of cynical suspicion versus engagement. Detaching ourselves from others in the fear of being "taken in" is an extreme defensive posture, but it is true that the more open we are to other people's persuasion, the more likely we are to be swayed by them. Nevertheless, open, passionate involvement with others is essential to human happiness. We want to feel strongly, to trust completely, to act spontaneously, and to feel connected to others. We want to be fully "saturated" in living. At least some of the time, we want to suspend our evaluative faculties and abandon our primitive fearful reserve. We want to dance with passion along with Zorba the Greek.[4]

6   Yet, we must regularly assess the worth of our social involvements. The challenge for each of us is how best to oscillate between two poles, immersing fully and distancing appropriately. Knowing when to stay involved with others, when to support and be loyal to a cause or a relationship rather than dismissing it, is a delicate question that we all face regularly. We live in a world in which some people aim to use us. In that same world are others who genuinely want us to share what they believe are mutually positive goals. How to tell which is which? That is the question, dear Hamlet and dear Ophelia.

7   Before we begin to deal with specific means for combating mind-controlling influences, we must consider another possibility: the old illusion of *personal invulnerability*.[5] Them? Yes. Me? *No!* Our psychological journey should have convinced you to appreciate how the array of situational forces that we've highlighted can suck in the majority of people. But not You, right? It is hard to extend the lessons we have learned from an intellectual assessment to affect our own codes of conduct. What is easily applied in the abstract to "those others" is not easily applied in the concrete to oneself. We are different. Just as no two fingerprints have identical patterns, no two people have identical genetic, developmental, and personality patterns.

8   Individual differences should be celebrated, but in the face of strong, common situational forces, individual differences shrink and are compressed. In such instances, behavioral scientists can predict what the majority of people will do knowing nothing about the particular people who comprise a group, only the

nature of their behavioral context. It should be clear that not even the best psychology can predict how each and every individual will behave in a given situation; some degree of individual variance always exists that cannot be accounted for. Therefore, you may reject the lessons that we are about to learn as inapplicable to yourself; you are the special case, the special end of the tail of the normal distribution. However, know that you do so at the cost of being caught with your defenses down and your tail twisted.

9   My advice about what to do in case you encounter a "dirty, rotten scoundrel," disguised as a nice guy or a sweet old lady, has been accumulated over many decades from many personal experiences. As a scrawny, sickly kid trying to survive on the mean streets of my South Bronx ghetto, I had to learn basic street smarts; these consisted of figuring out quickly how certain people would be likely to act in certain situations. I got good enough at the skill to become a leader of the gang, the team, or the class. Then I was trained by an unscrupulous boss, a Fagin-like character in drag, on how to deceive Broadway theatergoers into checking their hats and coats when they did not want to and to manipulate them into paying tips to get them back, when tipping was not required: As her apprentice, I became experienced in selling expensive show programs when free versions were available and in overdosing kids with loads of candy and drinks if their parents were not chaperoning them to our candy counter. I was also trained to sell magazines door to door, eliciting pity from, and thereby sales to, sympathetic tenement dwellers. Later on, I studied formally the tactics police use to get confessions from suspects, that state-sanctioned torturers use to get anything they want from their victims, and that cult recruiters use in seducing the innocent into their dens. My scholarship extended to studying the mind control tactics used by the Soviets and the methods used by the Chinese Communists in the Korean War and in their massive national thought reform programs: I also studied our own homegrown mind manipulators in the CIA, the state-sponsored MKULTRA program,[6] and Jim Jones's lethal charismatic power over his religious followers (described in earlier chapters).

10   I have both counseled and learned from those who survived various cult experiences. In addition, I have engaged in a lifetime of investigative research on persuasion, compliance, dissonance, and group processes. My writing on some of these topics includes a training manual for peace activists during the Vietnam War, as well as several basic texts on attitude change and social influence.[7] These credentials are offered only to bolster the communicator credibility of the information provided next.

Promoting Altruism via the Virtuous Authority Experiment

11   Let us first imagine a "Reverse-Milgram" authority experiment. Our goal is to create a setting in which people will comply with demands that intensify over time to do good. The participants would be guided gradually to behave in ever-more-altruistic ways, slowly but surely moving further than they could have imagined toward ever-more-positive, prosocial actions. Instead of the paradigm arranged to facilitate a slow descent into evil, we could substitute a paradigm for a slow ascent into goodness. How could we formulate an experimental setting in

which that was possible? Let us design such a thought experiment. To begin, imagine that we arrange for each participant a hierarchy of experiences or actions that range from slightly more positive acts than he or she is used to doing to ever-more-extreme "good" actions. The extremes of virtue push him or her upward all the way to engaging in actions that at first seemed unimaginable.

12   There might be a time-based dimension in the design for those busy citizens who do not practice virtue because they have convinced themselves that they just don't have time to spare for good deeds. The first "button" on the "Goodness Generator" might be to spend ten minutes writing a thank-you note to a friend or a get-well card to a colleague. The next level might demand twenty minutes of giving advice to a troubled child. Increasing the pressure in this paradigm might then entail the participant's agreeing to give thirty minutes of his time to read a story to an illiterate housekeeper. Then the altruism scale moves upward to spending an hour tutoring a needy student, then to babysitting for a few hours to allow a single parent to visit her sick mother, working for an evening in a soup kitchen, helping unemployed veterans, devoting part of a day to taking a group of orphaned children to the zoo, being available to talk with returning wounded veterans, and on and on upward, a step-by-step commitment to giving precious time every week to ever-more-worthy causes. Providing social models along the way who are already engaged in the requested task, or who take the initiative to ante up to the next level, should work to encourage obedience to virtuous authority, should it not? It's worth a try, especially since, as far as I know, nothing like this experiment has ever been done.

13   Ideally, our experiment in social goodness would end when the person was doing something that he or she could never have imagined doing before. Our goodness track could also include contributions to creating a healthy and sustainable environment that might go from minimal acts of conservation or recycling to ever more substantial activities, such as giving money, time, and personal involvement to "green" causes. I invite you to expand on this notion in a host of domains in which society would benefit as more citizens "went all the way"— doing good without any supporting ideology, for, as we know from dissonance theory, beliefs follow behavior. Get people to perform good actions, and they will generate the necessary underlying principles to justify them. Talmudic scholars are supposed to have preached not to require that people believe before they pray only to do what is needed to get them to begin to pray; then they will come to believe in what and to whom they are praying.

Research Supports a Reverse-Milgram Altruism Effect

14   As noted, this reverse-Milgram experiment has never been done. Suppose we actually attempted to perform such an experiment in the laboratory or, better yet, in our homes and communities. Would it work? Could we use the power of authority and of the situation to produce virtue? Based on what I know about human beings and the principles of social influence, I am confident that we could do a better job of bringing about righteousness in our world, employing basic principles of social influence (see Notes for some references).[8]

15   The reverse-Milgram experiment described here combines three simple influence tactics that have been extensively studied and documented by social psychologists: the

foot-in-the-door tactic, social modeling, and self-labeling of helpfulness. I've merely brought them together in one situation for promoting altruism. Moreover, researchers have found that these tactics can be used to promote all sorts of prosocial behavior—from donating one's hard-earned money to charity to increasing recycling and even to giving blood at the next Red Cross blood drive.

16 Our "slow ascent into goodness step by step" makes use of what social psychologists call the *"foot-in-the-door"* (FITD) tactic. This tactic begins by first asking someone to do a small request (which most people readily perform) and then later on to ask them to comply with a related but much bigger request (which was the actual goal all along).[9] The classic demonstration of this tactic was done more than forty years ago by Jonathan Freedman and Scott Fraser.[10] They asked suburbanites to put a big, ugly sign urging "Drive Carefully" in their nice suburban yard. Fewer than twenty percent of the homeowners did so. However, three fourths of the homeowners agreed to place that sign in their yards if two weeks earlier they had taken a small step and posted in their windows an unobtrusive three-inch sign urging safe driving. The same approach works with other prosocial behavior. For example, researchers have found that merely signing a petition leads to increased monetary support of the handicapped, filling out a brief questionnaire increases the willingness of people to donate their organs to others after death, conserving a small amount of energy induces homeowners to subsequently conserve more energy, and making a small public commitment increases the recycling of paper products.[11] What is more, this FITD effect can be enhanced by chaining together a series of increasingly larger requests, putting two feet in the door—just as in our reverse-Milgram experiment on promoting altruism.[12]

17 Our reverse-Milgram experiment would also employ *social models* to encourage prosocial behavior. In the SPE and Abu Ghraib Prison, there was an abundance of negative models that supported abusive behavior. Turning the power of social models around to enhance positive acts can be as effective in achieving the opposite, desirable outcomes. Researchers have found that altruistic role models increase the likelihood that those around them will engage in positive, prosocial behavior. Here is just a sampling of findings: social role models have been shown to increase donations to the Salvation Army; to promote helping a stranger with a flat tire; to lower rates of aggression and promote nonviolent responses; to reduce littering; and to increase donating money to poor children and a willingness to share one's resources with others.[13] But one word of advice: Remember to practice what you preach. Models persuade far more effectively than words. For example, in one set of experiments, children were exposed to an adult model that preached either greed or charity to them in a persuasive sermon. However, that adult then went on to practice either greedy or charitable actions. The results showed that the children were more likely to do what the model did than what the model had said.[14]

18 The wisdom of the Talmudic scholars previously mentioned is consistent with another social influence principle underlying our reverse-Milgram experiment: Give someone an *identity label* of the kind that you would like them to have as someone who will then do the action you want to elicit from them. When you tell a person that he or she is helpful, altruistic, and kind, that person is more likely to do helpful, altruistic, and kind behaviors for others. In the Stanford Prison Experiment, we randomly assigned young men to the roles of prisoner and guard, and they soon took on the manners and the behaviors of those roles. So,

too, if we tell someone that he or she is a helpful person, he or she will take on the manners and actions consistent with that identity label. For example, researchers have found that telling someone that he or she is "a generous person" increases compliance with a request to make a large contribution to prevent multiple sclerosis; giving people feedback that they are kind makes them more likely to help someone who has dropped a large number of cards; and those given a salient identity as "blood donors" are more likely to continue to donate their own blood to a stranger whom they don't expect ever to know or meet.[15]

19   One of the great advantages of our species is the ability to explore and understand our social world and then to use what we know to make our lives better. Throughout this book, we have seen the power of the situation to produce evil. I now argue that we can take those same basic principles and use the power of the situation to produce virtue. I fear for the future of humanity if my argument on this point is a failure or if I fail in making my argument acceptable to you. Might I suggest that you take a small step today in carrying out the reverse-Milgram experiment in your own life? I think you are just the person to do it and to serve as a role model for others in transforming our world to one with a more positive future. If not you, then who?

[. . .]

HEROIC CONTRASTS: THE EXTRAORDINARY VERSUS THE BANAL

Fame is no plant that grows on mortal soil.

—John Milton

20   To the traditionally accepted notion that heroes are exceptional people, we can now add an opposing perspective—that some heroes are ordinary people who have done something extraordinary. The first image is the more romantic and is favored in ancient myth and modern media. It suggests that the hero has done something that ordinary people in the same position would not or could not have done. These superstars must have been born with a hero gene. They are the exception to the rule.

21   A second perspective, which we might call "the rule is the exception," directs us to examine the interaction between situation and person, the dynamic that impelled an individual to act heroically at a particular time and place. A situation may act either as a catalyst, encouraging action, or it may reduce barriers to action, such as the formation of a collective social support network. It is remarkable that in most instances people who have engaged in heroic action repeatedly reject the name of hero, as we saw was the case with Christina Maslach.

22   Such doers of heroic deeds typically argue that they were simply taking an action that seemed necessary at the time. They are convinced that anybody would have acted similarly, or else they find it difficult to understand why others did not. Nelson Mandela has said, "I was not a messiah, but an ordinary man who had become a leader because of extraordinary circumstances."[73] Phrases like this are used by people at all levels of society who have acted heroically: "It was nothing special"; "I did what had to be done." These are the refrains of the "ordinary" or everyday warrior, our "banal hero." Let's contrast such positive banality with what Hannah Arendt has taught us to call "the banality of evil."

On the Banality of Evil

23 This concept emerged from Arendt's observations at the trial of Adolf Eichmann, indicted for crimes against humanity because he helped to orchestrate the genocide of European Jews. In *Eichmann in Jerusalem: A Report on the Banality of Evil,* Arendt formulates the idea that such individuals should not be viewed as exceptions, as monsters, or as perverted sadists. She argues that such dispositional attributes, typically applied to perpetrators of evil deeds, serves to set them apart from the rest of the human community. Instead, Eichmann and others like him, Arendt says, should be exposed in their very ordinariness. When we realize this, we become more aware that such people are a pervasive, hidden danger in all societies. Eichmann's defense was that he was simply following orders. Of this mass murderer's motives and conscience, Arendt notes:

> As for his base motives, he was perfectly sure that he was not what he called an *innerer Schweinehund,* a dirty bastard in the depths of his heart; and as for his conscience, he remembered perfectly well that he would have had a bad conscience only if he had not done what he had been ordered to do—to ship millions of men, women, and children to their death with great zeal and the most meticulous care.

24 What is most striking in Arendt's account of Eichmann is all the ways in which he seemed absolutely normal and totally ordinary:

> Half a dozen psychiatrists had certified him as "normal"—"More normal, at any rate, than I am after having examined him," one of them was said to have exclaimed, while another had found that his whole psychological outlook, his attitude toward his wife and children, mother and father, brothers, sisters, and friends was "not only normal but most desirable."[74]

25 Arendt's now-classic conclusion:

> The trouble with Eichmann was precisely that so many were like him, and that the many were neither perverted nor sadistic, that they were, and still are, terribly and terrifyingly normal. From the viewpoint of our legal institutions and our moral standards of judgment, this normality was much more terrifying than all the atrocities put together, for it implied . . . that this new type of criminal, who is in actual fact *hostis generis humani,* commits his crimes under circumstances that make it well-nigh impossible for him to know or feel that he is doing wrong.[75]

26 Then came her punch line, describing Eichmann's dignified march to the gallows:

> It was as though in those last minutes he was summing up the lesson that this long course in human wickedness had taught us—the lesson of the fearsome, word-and-thought-defying banality of evil.[76]

27 The notion that "ordinary men" can commit atrocities has been more fully developed by the historian Christopher Browning, as we noted earlier. He uncovered the systematic and personal annihilation of Jews in remote Polish villages that were committed by hundreds of men in Reserve Police Battalion 101, sent to Poland from Hamburg, Germany. These middle-aged, family men of working-class and lower-middle-class backgrounds shot thousands of unarmed Jews—men, women, the elderly, and children—and arranged for the deportation to death

camps of thousands more. Yet Browning contends in his book that they were all "ordinary men." He believes that the mass-murder policies of the Nazi regime "were not aberrational or exceptional events that scarcely ruffle the surface of everyday life. As the story of Reserve Battalion 101 demonstrates, mass murder and routine had become one. Normality itself had become exceedingly abnormal."[77]

28   The psychologist Ervin Staub holds a similar view. His extensive research led him to the conclusion that "Evil that arises out of ordinary thinking and is committed by ordinary people is the norm, not the exception."[78] Cruelty should be attributed to its social origins more than to its "characterological" determinants or "faulty personalities," according to Zygmunt Bauman's analysis of the horrors of the Holocaust. Bauman believes further that the exception to this norm is the rare individual who has the capacity to assert moral autonomy in resisting the demands of destructive authorities. Such a person is rarely aware that he or she possesses this hidden strength until put to the test.[79]

29   Another quality of the banality of evil ushers us into the torturers' den to consider whether such people, whose mission is to use all means necessary to break the will, resistance, and dignity of their victims, are anything other than pathological villains. The consensus among those who have studied torturers is that in general they were not distinguishable from the general population in their backgrounds or dispositions prior to taking on their sordid job. John Conroy, who studied men involved in torture in three different venues in Ireland, Israel, and Chicago, concluded that in all cases "unspeakable acts" were committed by "ordinary people." He maintains that torturers act out the will of the community they represent in suppressing its foes.[80]

30   From her in-depth analysis of soldiers trained by the Greek military junta to be state-sanctioned torturers (1967–1974), my colleague the Greek psychologist Mika Haritos-Fatouros concluded that torturers are not born but made by their training. "Anybody's son will do" is her answer to the question "Who will make an effective torturer?" In a matter of a few months, ordinary young men from rural villages became "weaponized" by their training in cruelty to act like brute beasts capable of inflicting the most horrendous acts of humiliation, pain, and suffering on anyone labeled "the enemy," who, of course, were all citizens of their own country.[81] Such conclusions are not limited to one nation, but are common in many totalitarian regimes. We studied "violence workers" in Brazil, policemen who tortured and murdered other Brazilian citizens for the ruling military junta. They too were "ordinary men," based on all the evidence we could amass.[82]

On the Banality of Heroism[83]

31 We may now entertain the notion that most people who become perpetrators of evil deeds are directly comparable to those who become perpetrators of heroic deeds, alike in being just ordinary, average people. The banality of evil shares much with the banality of heroism. Neither attribute is the direct consequence of unique dispositional tendencies; there are no special inner attributes of either pathology or goodness residing within the human psyche or the human genome. Both conditions emerge in particular situations at particular times when situational forces play a compelling role in moving particular individuals across a decisional line from inaction to action. There is a decisive decisional moment when a

person is caught up in a vector of forces that emanate from a behavioral context. Those forces combine to increase the probability of one's acting to harm others or acting to help others. Their decision may or may not be consciously planned or mindfully taken. Rather, strong situational forces most often impulsively drive the person to action. Among the situational action vectors are: group pressures and group identity, the diffusion of responsibility for the action, a temporal focus on the immediate moment without concern for consequences stemming from the act in the future, presence of social models, and commitment to an ideology.

32   A common theme in the accounts of European Christians who helped the Jews during the Holocaust could be summed up as the "banality of goodness." What is striking over and over again is the number of these rescuers who did the right thing without considering themselves heroic, who acted merely out of a sense of common decency. The ordinariness of their goodness is especially striking in the context of the incredible evil of the systematic genocide by Nazis on a scale the world had never before experienced.[84]

33   I have tried to show throughout our journey that the military police guards who abused prisoners at Abu Ghraib and the prison guards in my Stanford Prison Experiment who abused their prisoners illustrate a *Lord of the Flies*–type temporary transition of ordinary individuals into perpetrators of evil. We must set them alongside those whose evil behavior is enduring and extensive, tyrants such as Idi Amin, Stalin, Hitler, and Saddam Hussein. Heroes of the moment also stand in contrast to lifetime heroes.

34   The heroic action of Rosa Parks's refusal to sit in the "colored" section in the back of an Alabama bus, of Joe Darby's exposing the Abu Ghraib tortures, or of the first responders' rush to the World Trade Center disaster are acts of bravery that occur at particular times and places. In contrast, the heroism of Mohandas Gandhi or Mother Teresa consists of valorous acts repeated over a lifetime. Chronic heroism is to acute heroism as valor is to bravery.

35   This perception implies that any of us could as easily become heroes as perpetrators of evil depending on how we are influenced by situational forces. The imperative becomes discovering how to limit, constrain, and prevent the situational and systemic forces that propel some of us toward social pathology. But equally important is the injunction for every society to foster a "heroic imagination" in its citizenry. It is achieved by conveying the message that every person is a hero in waiting who will be counted upon to do the right thing when the moment of decision comes. The decisive question for each of us is whether to act in help of others, to prevent harm to others, or not to act at all. We should be preparing many laurel wreaths for all those who will discover their reservoir of hidden strengths and virtues enabling them to come forth to act against injustice and cruelty and to stand up for their principled values.

36   The large body of research on situational determinants of antisocial behavior that we reviewed here, bookended by Milgram's investigations of authority power and the SPE's institutional power, reveals the extent to which normal, ordinary people can be led to engage in cruel acts against innocent others.[85] However, in those studies and many others, while the majority obeyed, conformed, complied, were persuaded and were seduced, there was always a minority who resisted, dissented, and disobeyed. In one sense, heroism lies in the ability to resist powerful situational forces that so readily entrap most people.

37   Are the personalities of the resisters different from those of the blindly obedient?[86] Are they like Clark Kent, whose normal appearance conceals Superman's extraordinary powers? Not at all. Rather, our banality of heroism conception maintains that doers of heroic deeds of the moment are not essentially different from those who comprise the base rate of the easily seduced. There is not much empirical research on which to base such assertions. Because heroism is not a simple phenomenon that can be studied systematically, it defies clean definitions and on-the-spot data collection. Heroic acts are ephemeral and unpredictable, and appreciation of them is decidedly retrospective. Because heroes are usually interviewed months or years after their heroic behavior has occurred, there are no prospective studies of what the photographer Henri Cartier-Bresson might call the "decisive moment" of heroic action.[87] Generally we do not know what the decision matrix for heroes is at the time they elect to engage in risk-laden activities.

38   What seems evident is that heroic behavior is rare enough not to be readily predictable by any psychological assessments of personality. They measure individual differences between people in their usual, standard behavioral settings, not in the atypical settings that often elicit heroic deeds.

39   Lieutenant Alexander (Sandy) Nininger is a case example of a heroic soldier who engaged in extraordinarily fearless and ferocious fighting during World War II's infamous Battle of Bataan. This twenty-three-year-old West Point graduate volunteered to go hunting for Japanese snipers where the fighting was most intense. With grenades, a rifle, submachine gun, and bayonet, Nininger killed many Japanese soldiers single-handedly in intense close combat, and kept fighting although repeatedly wounded. Only after he had destroyed an enemy bunker did he collapse and die. His heroism earned him the Medal of Honor, posthumously, the first given in that war.

40   What makes this hero an object of our concern is that nothing from his past would have predicted that he would engage in such killing. This quiet, sensitive, intellectual young man had gone on record as saying that he could never kill anyone out of hatred. Yet, he had done so repeatedly without regard for his own safety. Had he been given all available personality tests, would they have helped predict this unexpectedly violent behavior? In his review of personality testing, the author Malcolm Gladwell surmises that Nininger's file might be as thick as a phone book, but "his file will tell us little about the one thing we're most interested in. For that, we have to join him in the jungles of Bataan." In short, we have to understand the Person in the Situation.[88]

NOTES

1. These and related data are found in an important resource book published by the American Association of Retired People (AARP), based on extensive research by the social psychologist Anthony Pratkanis of hundreds of audiotapes recorded of con men and swindlers pitching their wares to potential victims. See his important book filled with specific advice about how to detect hoaxes and not be taken in by them: Anthony Pratkanis and Doug Shadel, *Weapons of Fraud: A Source Book for Fraud Fighters* (Seattle: AARP Press, 2005).
2. Andrew Wolfson, "A Hoax most Cruel," *The Courier-Journal*, October 9, 2005.
3. Quote by former assistant manager Donna Summers in "The Human Behavior Experiments," Jigsaw productions, Sundance TV, June 1, 2006.

4. *Zorba the Greek* is Niko Kazantzakis's classic novel, written in 1952. Alexis Zorba was portrayed by Anthony Quinn in the 1964 movie of the same name, directed by Michael Cacoyannis, and co-starring Alan Bates as the shy, intellectual boss who is the foil to Zorba's boundless extroversion and devotion to living life with unbridled passion.

5. B. J. Sagarin, R. B. Cialdini, W. E. Rice, and S. B. Serna, "Dispelling the Illusion of Invulnerability: The Motivations and Mechanisms of Resistance to Persuasion," *Journal of Personality and Social Psychology* 83 (2002): 526–41.

6. The MKULTRA program, secretly sponsored by the CIA in the 1950s and '60s, is well presented in John D. Marks, *The Search for the Manchurian Candidate: The CIA and Mind Control* (New York: Times Books, 1979). A more detailed scholarly presentation is found in Alan W. Scheflin and Edward Opton, Jr., *The Mind Manipulators* (New York: Grosset and Dunlap, 1978). See Alex Constantine's *Virtual Government: CIA Mind Control Operations in America* (Los Angeles: Feral House, 1997) for a fuller exposition of many other CIA-sponsored programs, such as Operation Mockingbird, designed to influence the American press and program public opinion.

7. A sample of my work in these diverse domains of social influence can be found in these publications: R. P. Abelson and P. G. Zimbardo, *Canvassing for Peace: A Manual for Volunteers* (Ann Arbor, MI: Society for the Psychological Study of Social Issues, 1970); P. G. Zimbardo, "Coercion and Compliance: The Psychology of Police Confessions," in *The Triple Revolution Emerging*, eds. R. Perruci and M. Pilisuk (Boston: Little, Brown, 1971), pp.492–508; P. G. Zimbardo, E. B. Ebbeson, and C. Maslach, *Influencing Attitudes and Changing Behavior*, 2nd ed. (Reading, MA: Addison-Wesley, 1977); P. G. Zimbardo and C. E. Hartley, "Cults Go to High School: A Theoretical and Empirical Analysis of the Initial Stage in the Recruitment Process," *Cultic Studies Journal* 2 (Spring-Summer 1985): 91–147; P. G. Zimbardo and S. A. Andersen, "Understanding Mind Control: Exotic and Mundane Mental Manipulations," *Recovery from Cults*, ed. M. Langone (New York: Norton Press, 1993), pp. 104–25; P. G. Zimbardo and M. Leippe, *The Psychology of Attitude Change and Social Influence* (New York: McGraw-Hill, 1991).

8. To learn more about basic social influence principles, see R. B. Cialdini, *Influence*, 4th ed. (Boston: Allyn & Bacon, 2001); A. R. Pratkanis, "Social Influence Analysis: An Index of Tactics," in *The Science of Social Influence: Advances and Future Progress*, ed. A. R. Pratkanis (Philadelphia: Psychology Press, 2007, in press); A. R. Pratkanis and E. Aronson, *Age of Propaganda: The Everyday Use and Abuse of Persuasion* (New York: W. H. Freeman, 2001); Robert Levine, *The Power to Persuade: How We're Bought and Sold* (New York: Wiley, 2003); Daryl Bem, *Beliefs, Attitudes, and Human Affairs* (Belmont, CA; Brooks/Cole, 1970); Richard Petty and John Cacioppo, *Communication and Persuasion: Central and Peripheral Routes to Attitude Change* (New York: Springer-Verlag, 1986); Steven Hassan, *Combatting Cult Mind Control* (Rochester, VT: Park Street Press, 1988); Brad Sagarin and Sarah Wood, "Resistance to Influence" in *The Science of Social Influence: Advances and Future Progress*, ed. A. R. Pratkanis (Philadelphia: Psychology Press, in press, 2007).

9. J. M. Burger, "the Foot-in-the-Door Compliance Procedure: A Multiple-Process Analysis and Review," *Personality and Social Psychology Review* 3 (1999): 303–25.

10. J. Freedman and S. Fraser, "Compliance Without Pressure: The Foot-in-the-Door Technique," *Journal of Personality and Social Psychology* 4 (1966): 195–202.

11. For some references to prosocial applications of the foot-in-the-door tactic, see J. Schwarzwald, A. Bizman, and M. Raz, "The Foot-in-the-Door Paradigm: Effects of Second Request Size on Donation Probability and Donor Generosity," *Personality and Social Psychology Bulletin* 9 (1983): 443–50; B. J. Carducci and P. S. Deuser, "The Foot-in-the-Door Technique: Initial Request and Organ Donation," *Basic and Applied Social Psychology* 5 (1984): 75–81; B. J. Carducci, P. S. Deuser, A. Bauer, M. Large, and M. Ramaekers, "An Application of the Foot in the Door Technique to

Organ Donation, " *Journal of Business and Psychology* 4 (1989): 245–49; R. D. Katzev and T. R. Johnson, "Comparing the Effects of Monetary Incentives and Foot-in-the-Door Strategies in Promoting Residential Electricity Conservation," *Journal of Applied Social Psychology* 14 (1984): 12–27; T. H. Wang and R. D. Katsev, "Group Commitment and Resource Conservation: Two Field Experiments on Promoting Recycling," *Journal of Applied Social Psychology* 20 (1990): 265–75; R. Katsev and T. Wang, "Can Commitment Change Behavior? A Case Study of Environmental Actions," *Journal of Social Behavior and Personality* 9 (1994): 13–26.

12. M. Goldman, C. R. Creason, and C. G. McGall. "Compliance Employing a Two-Feet-in-the-Door Procedure," *Journal of Social Psychology* 114 (1981): 259–65.

13. For references on the prosocial effects of positive models, see J. H. Bryan and M. A. Test, "Models and Helping: Naturalistic Studies in Aiding Behavior," *Journal of Personality and Social Psychology* 6 (1967): 400–7; C. A. Kallgren, R. R. Reno, and R. B. Cialdini, "A Focus Theory of Normative Conduct: When Norms Do and Do Not Affect Behavior," *Personality and Social Psychology Bulletin* 26 (2000): 1002–12; R. A. Baron and C. R. Kepner, "Model's Behavior and Attraction Toward the Model as Determinants of Adult Aggressive Behavior," *Journal of Personality and Social Psychology* 14 (1970): 335–44; M. E. Rice and J. E. Grusec, "Saying and Doing: Effects on Observer Performance," *Journal of Personality and Social Psychology* 32 (1975): 584–93.

14. J. H. Bryan, J. Redfield, and S. Mader, "Words and Deeds About Altruism and the Subsequent Reinforcement Power of the Model," *Child Development* 42 (1971): 1501–8; J. H. Bryan and N. H. Walbek, "Preaching and Practicing Generosity: Children's Actions and Reactions," *Child Development* 41 (1970): 329–53.

15. For referencences on social identity labeling, also known as "altercasting," see R. E. Kraut, "Effects of Social Labeling on Giving to Charity," *Journal of Experimental Social Psychology* 9 (1973): 551–62; A. Strenta and W. DeJong, "The Effects of a Prosocial Label on Helping Behavior," *Social Psychology Quarterly* 44 (1981): 142–47; J. A. Piliavin and P. L. Callero, *Giving Blood* (Baltimore: John Hopkins University Press, 1991).

[. . .]

73. Brink, "Leaders and Revolutionaries."

74. H. Arendt, *Eichmann in Jerusalem: A Report on the Banality of Evil* (rev. and enlarged edition) (New York: Penguin, 1994 [1963]) pp. 25–26.

75. Ibid., p. 276.

76. Ibid., p. 252.

77. C. R. Browning, *Ordinary Men: Reserve Police Battalion 101 and the Final Solution in Poland* (New York: HarperPerennial, 1992), p. xix.

78. E. Staub, *The Roots of Evil: The Origins of Genocide and Other Group Violence* (New York: Cambridge University Press, 1989), p. 126.

79. Z. Bauman, *Modernity and the Holocaust* (Ithaca, NY: Cornell University Press, 1989).

80. J. Conroy, *Unspeakable Acts, Ordinary People: The Dynamics of Torture* (New York: Knopf, 2000).

81. M. Haritos-Fatouros, *The Psychological Origins of Institutionalized Torture* (London: Routledge, 2003).

82. M. Huggins, M. Haritos-Fatouros, and P. G. Zimbardo, *Violence Workers: Police Torturers and Murderers Reconstruct Brazilian Atrocities* (Berkeley: University of California Press, 2002).

83. This conception of the banality of heroism was first presented in an essay by Zimbardo on *Edge* Annual Question 2006, an annual event sponsored by John Brockman inviting a range of scholars to reply to a provocative question, which that year was "What is your dangerous idea?" See www.edge.org.

84. See Francois Rochat and Andre Modigliani, "Captain Paul Grueninger: The Chief of Police Who Saved Jewish Refugees by Refusing to Do His Duty," in *Obedience to*

Authority: Current Perspectives on the Milgram Paradigm, ed. T. Blass (Mahwah, NJ: Erlbaum, 2000).

85. Stanley Milgram, *Obedience to Authority: An Experimental View* (New York: Harper & Row, 1974). Also see Philip Zimbardo, Craig Haney, William Curtis Banks, and David Jaffe, "The Mind Is a Formidable Jailer: A Pirandellian Prison," *The New York Times Magazine,* April 8, 1973, pp. 36 ff.

86. Research on the personality correlates that differentiate "obedients" from "defiants" points to only a few significant predictors. Those who are high scorers on a measure of authoritarian personality (F-scale) were more likely to obey authority, while defiants had lower F-scores. See A. C. Elms and S. Milgram, "Personality Characteristics Associated with Obedience and Defiance Toward Authoritative Command," *Journal of Experimental Research in Personality* 1 (1966): 282–89.

   A second variable that may influence the tendency to obey or disobey is one's belief in external controlling influences on one's life versus internal control, with greater obedience among those who accept the notion of their behavior as being controlled by external forces. In a similar vein, among Christian research participants, obedience was greatest among those who believed in divine control of their lives while those who were low on measures of belief in external divine control tended to reject scientific as well as religious authority. See Tom Blass, "Understanding Behavior in the Milgram Obedience Experiment: The Role of Personality, Situations, and Their Interactions," *Journal of Personality and Social Psychology* 60 (1991): 398–413.

87. E. Midlarsky, S. F. Jones, and R. Corley, "Personality Correlates of Heroic Rescue During the Holocaust," *Journal of Personality* 73 (2005): 907–34.

88. Malcolm Gladwell, "Personality Plus: Employers Love Personality Tests. But What Do They Really Reveal?" *The New Yorker* (September 20, 2004): 42. Available online at www.gladwell.com/2004/2001_09_20_a_personality.html.

Active Reading

1. What are the fundamental concepts in this text?
2. What evidence does Zimbardo provide that people who succumb to situational forces are ordinary people? What purpose is served by making this point at the beginning of the section, "Learning How to Resist Unwanted Influences"?
3. What is a "Reverse-Milgram" authority experiment?
4. Summarize Zimbardo's argument for the banality of heroism.

Critical Reading

1. This text is drawn from a book written for a general audience. How does it differ in voice, structure, and documentation from the Milgram and Blass articles? How is it more like the Lessing lecture?
2. Pretend you are Philip Zimbardo and want to revise this text for publication in a scholarly journal. Working with a partner or in a small group, identify all the claims made that would need to be supported by reference to published scholarly works, and then find that support by searching in journal databases.
3. Do you find Zimbardo's action plan for learning how to resist unwanted influences convincing? Working with a partner, identify the strengths and weaknesses of his approach and suggest a revised plan.
4. Do you agree with Zimbardo that no one possesses intrinsically good or evil dispositions, and that anyone can be trained to be a torturer or a hero? Give reasons for your answer.

Toward a Globally Sensitive Patriotism

Martha Nussbaum

Martha Nussbaum is a prolific scholar who has been honoured many times for her books and essays and for distinguished service to the international community. She is currently the Ernst Freund Distinguished Service Professor of Law and Ethics at the University of Chicago, where she is cross-appointed to the Philosophy Department, the Law School, and the Divinity School. This inter-disciplinary scholar is an Associate in the Classics Department and the Political Science Department, a member of the Committee on Southern Asian Studies, a board member of the Human Rights Program, and founder and coordinator of the Center for Comparative Constitutionalism.

Nussbaum's work is in the liberal tradition but stresses the need to enrich liberal thinking with feminist and other anti-oppression perspectives in order to achieve liberalism's promise of dignity and respect for all people. She writes on the big themes that are at the core of the humanities: compassion, happiness, dignity, justice. In this essay, Nussbaum examines the nature of patriotism, which calls us to our better selves in some ways and turns us against our neighbours in others. She argues that patriotism is a form of love and that nations could contribute to global justice by promoting a humane version of patriotism.

1   In 1892, a World's Fair, called the Columbian Exposition, was scheduled to take place in Chicago. Clearly, it was gearing up to be a celebration of unfettered greed and egoism. Industry and innovation were to be its central foci, as America planned to welcome the world with displays of technological prowess and material enrichment. Gross inequalities of opportunity in the nation were to be masked by the glowing exterior of the buildings that came to be called the 'White City.'[1]

2   Advocates for the poor, upset by the plan, got together to think about how the celebration might incorporate ideas of equal opportunity and sacrifice. A group of Christian socialists finally went to President Benjamin Harrison with an idea: at the Exposition the president would introduce a new public ritual of patriotism, a pledge of allegiance to the flag, which would place the accent squarely on the nation's core moral values, include all Americans as equals, and rededicate the nation to something more than individual greed. The words that were concocted to express these sentiments were: "I pledge allegiance to the flag of the United States of America, and to the republic for which it stands: one nation, indivisible, with liberty and justice for all."[2]

3   As so often happens with patriotic sentiment, however, the Pledge soon proved a formula of both inclusion and exclusion. Francis Bellamy, the Pledge's author, was himself both a socialist and a xenophobe, who feared that our national values were being undermined by the flood of new immigrants from southern Europe. By the 1940s, required by law as a daily recitation in schools in many states, the Pledge became a litmus test for the 'good' American; and those who flunked the test faced both exclusion and violence. Jehovah's Witnesses, who refused to recite the Pledge for religious reasons, seeing it as a form of idolatry, soon found their children expelled from school for noncompliance. Then, in a Catch-22, the parents were fined or jailed for "contributing to the delinquency of a minor" because their children were not in school.

4   Patriotism is Janus-faced. It faces outward, calling the self, at times, to duties for others, to the need to sacrifice for a common good, to renewed effort to fulfill the promises of equality and dignity inherent in national ideals. And yet, just as clearly, it also faces inward, inviting those who consider themselves 'good' or 'true' Americans to distinguish themselves from outsiders and subversives. Perhaps more dangerous yet, it serves to define the nation against its foreign rivals, whipping up warlike sentiments against them. (It was for precisely this reason that Jean-Jacques Rousseau thought that a good nation needed a patriotic 'civil religion' in place of the dogmas of Christianity, which he found too meek and pacifistic.[3])

5   For such reasons, people committed to the twin goals of a world in which all human beings have a decent set of life opportunities, and a world in which wars of aggression do not mar people's life chances, typically turn a skeptical eye on appeals to patriotic sentiment. They see such sentiments as binding the mind to something smaller than humanity; and, in a way, they are not wrong.

6   Patriotism is a species of love that, by definition, is bounded rather than global, particularistic rather than universal. Although it calls the mind to many aspects of humanity that lead the mind beyond its domestic confines—for example, human need or the struggle for justice and equality—patriotism is also irreducibly attached to particular memories, geographical features, and plans for the future.

7   If, then, our political doctrine included the thought that duties to all humanity should always take precedence over other duties, or the thought that particular obligations are correctly understood to be derivative from universal obligations (as a way of fulfilling, locally, those general obligations), it would be inconsistent with giving a large role to patriotism.

8   In my earlier writing on cosmopolitanism, I tentatively endorsed those two claims.[4] In the meantime, however, my ideas have changed in two ways.

9   First, having come to endorse a form of Rawlsian political liberalism, I now think it crucial that the political principles of a decent society not include comprehensive ethical or metaphysical doctrines that could not be endorsed by reasonable citizens holding a wide range of comprehensive doctrines. Clearly, a strong form of cosmopolitanism that denied legitimacy to nonderivative particular obligations could not be the object of an overlapping consensus in a political-liberal state. Many of the reasonable comprehensive religious and secular doctrines that citizens hold do insist on the importance of particularistic forms of love and attachment, pursued for their own sake and not just as derivative from universal duties to humanity. (Indeed, duties to God, in most religions, are particularistic in this way.) So even if I had continued to endorse cosmopolitanism as a correct comprehensive ethical position, I would not have made it the foundation of political principles for either a nation or a world order.

10   I do not, however, even endorse cosmopolitanism as a correct comprehensive doctrine. Further thought about Stoic cosmopolitanism, and particularly the strict form of it developed by Marcus Aurelius, persuaded me that the denial of particular attachments leaves life empty of meaning for most of us, with the human psychology and the developmental history we have. The dark side of Stoic thought is the conviction that life contains merely a sequence of meaningless episodes, once particular attachments have been uprooted; and the solution to problems of particular attachments ought not to be this total uprooting, so destructive of the human personality.

11   It should be, instead, an uneven dialectical oscillation within ourselves, as we accept the constraints of some strong duties to humanity, and then ask ourselves how far we are entitled to devote ourselves to the particular people and places whom we love.

12   This, then, is my current comprehensive ethical position, and it makes plenty of room for patriotism, especially in a form that accepts the constraints of global justice.

13   As it happens, this position allows me to incorporate—both in my political doctrine and in my comprehensive ethical doctrine—an insight firmly grasped by thinkers of the late eighteenth and nineteenth centuries that national sentiment is also a way of making the mind bigger, calling it away from its immersion in greed and egoism toward a set of values connected to a decent common life and the need for sacrifices connected to that common life.

14   Italian revolutionary and nationalist Giuseppe Mazzini, seeing the many ways in which the rise of capitalism threatened any common project involving personal sacrifice, believed that national sentiment was a valuable "fulcrum," on which one could ultimately leverage universal sentiment toward the goal of a just world. He doubted that the immediate appeal to love all humanity could motivate people deeply sunk in greed, but he thought that the idea of the nation might acquire a strong motivational force even when people were rushing to enrich themselves.

15   Mazzini' s argument for patriotic sentiment goes something like this.

1. It is good, ultimately, for all human beings to care strongly about the good of all humanity.

2. Human beings are, by nature, somewhat narrow and particularistic in their concerns, and are not able to form a strong attachment to all humanity directly.

3. Human beings are, however, able to form a strong attachment to the nation, seen as the embodiment of both memory of past struggles and commitments to a common future.

4. The nation, because of its connection with common memory, episodes of suffering, and common hopes, is the largest unit to which such strong attachments can be directly formed.

5. Such national sentiments, if rightly targeted on things of genuine importance, such as human liberty and human need, will give people practice in caring about something larger than themselves, jolting them out of the egoism that is all too prevalent and preparing them for enlarged concern for the liberty and well-being of all humanity.

6. Human beings ought to cultivate patriotic sentiment, as a basis for global concern.

16   Mazzini offers an attractive route out of egoism to global concern through a rightly focused nationalism. These days, however, one might doubt premise 4. In the nineteenth century, nations looked very large. As Germany and Italy were unifying, pulling nations together out of disparate regional entities and the loyalties they had traditionally inspired, it seemed natural to think that calling the mind to the nation was already a way of calling it to something very vast. The success of that call seemed, to many people, to show that global concern was only a step away. John Stuart Mill even said that the world was simply a "larger country,"[5] and that the strength of patriotic feeling showed that his "religion of humanity" was possible.

17   Today, we are much more skeptical about the nation. We think of it as smaller, not larger, as confining the mind rather than enlarging it. Many people believe that nations should not exist in a future decent world order, and many more doubt that the nation is the largest unit to which human beings are capable of feeling a strong and vivid loyalty. Any contemporary argument for sentiments that give the nation a special place must begin, then, by explaining why it ought to have any place at all.

18   My own argument for patriotism is rather different from Mazzini's, but reaches a similar conclusion: national sentiment can play a valuable role in creating a decent world culture. I contend that:

1. The nation-state, including a strong form of national sovereignty, is an important good for all human beings, if the state takes a certain (liberal, democratic) form. Any decent world culture should promote the continued sovereignty and autonomy of (liberal and democratic) nation-states and protect the rights of citizenship associated with them.
2. Nation-states of the sort described cannot remain stable without moral sentiments attached to their institutions and their political culture.
3. The sentiments required cannot be supplied merely by allegiances to smaller units, such as families; cities; regions; and ethnic, racial, or gender groups: they must have the nation (under some description) as their object.
4. So, there is a good reason for nations of the sort described to engender sentiments of love and support in their citizens.
5. National states of the sort described need the moral sentiments even more if they are going to undertake projects that require considerable sacrifice of self-interest, such as substantial internal redistribution or copious foreign aid, the overcoming of discrimination against traditionally marginalized groups, or the protection of allies against unjust domination.
6. Such projects are good projects for nations to undertake. Therefore, we have even stronger reasons for the cultivation of nation-directed moral sentiments.

19   How would one defend premise 1? The classic defense is Grotian: a legitimate national state provides people with a role in creating the institutions and laws that govern them. It is thus a key expression of human autonomy. One may have a lot of autonomy elsewhere in one's life, but if one has no voice in the choice of policies affecting one's society's 'basic structure,' i.e., the set of institutions that governs one's life chances pervasively and from the start of a human life,[6] one is cut off from an extremely important good.

20   Of course, other institutions might do this job equally wall, or even better: the world state; the large NGO; the United Nations; the multinational corporation; the ethnic group; the state, the city, the family.[7] All of these can be decisively rejected, however, on grounds of access and accountability. The contenders that have not been eliminated are a federation of nations, such as the EU, and smaller self-governing units within a federal nation, such as the states of the United States and of India. Such political entities do offer some reasonable degree of access and accountability. Both, however, ultimately fall short of the nation state in accountability and protection of basic rights, at least at the present time. We should keep reexamining these cases as new information becomes available. But currently, and

for the foreseeable future, nations are critical for the promotion of people's well-being and life opportunities.

21   As for my premise 2, Rawls defends this in *A Theory of Justice*, especially since his state is very ambitious in the sacrifices it asks of its members in the name of justice.[8] Habermas offers a similar moralized account of supportive sentiment, in his defense of a "constitutional patriotism."[9]

22   It is plausible, however, that the moral sentiments on which Rawls relies are a bit too transparently rationalistic to do the job he assigns to them. He fails to consider (although he does not deny) that an essential motivational role, in connection with the love of just institutions, may be played by more indirect appeals to the emotions, using symbols, memories, poetry, narrative. People are sometimes moved by the love of just institutions presented just as such; but the human mind is quirky and particularistic, more easily able to conceive a strong attachment if these high principles are connected to a particular set of memories, symbols, narrative, and poetry.

23   My claim is that the emotions of citizens in a Rawlsian well-ordered society are, or should be, like this: that is, fixed on the moral meanings of the political conception (thus attaining stability for the right reasons, and not merely a tradition-governed type of stability), but held to those meanings by rituals and narratives of a kind that must be more particular, more uneven, more aesthetic, more tragic, and more silly than anything explicitly envisaged in Rawls's text.

24   These rituals and narratives might possibly be confined to what Rawls calls the "background culture"—but on the other hand, inasmuch as they are essential vehicles of public reason, there is no reason to confine them to that role. Candidates for election, legislators, and even judges might use such symbols and poetic references, and songs and stories, if they do so in a way that reinforces and deepens the moral meaning of the political conception. We just need to be sure that citizens develop a type of 'purified' patriotism that is reliably linked to the deeper principles of the political conception, that does not exalt the United States (for example) above other nations, and that focuses on suffering humanity wherever it occurs.[10]

25   In order to talk about the sentiments of a 'purified' patriotism, we need to have a normative conception of a decent society, since it is the institutions and entitlements of such a society that such sentiments would support. Let me, for the sake of argument, stipulate that the (national) society has committed itself to my capabilities approach, which guarantees to all citizens a threshold level of ten central opportunities, or capabilities, and that also assigns to the richer nations some definite, and rather exigent, duties of foreign aid in the pursuit of global justice. Since my conception requires a high degree of sacrifice, it will need to call patriotism to its aid. If the patriotism in question is to be of the right sort, much thought must be given to questions concerning which sentiments should be fostered and which avoided.

26   Before I discuss these sentiments, I must add two preliminary notes. First, since the society I take as my starting point is a classically liberal one, with ample protections for freedoms of speech and association,[11] the public cultivation of sentiment will not be a form of coercive enforcement; later on I shall insist on a key role for a vigorous critical culture as part of what will make the whole enterprise work. So what I am talking about is public persuasion, about the many ways in which public leaders and educators cultivate sentiments through rhetoric and example.

27   Second, any nation is a narrative, a story in which memory of the past and aspiration for the future are salient. But any national narrative is an interpretation. Some past events are made salient and others are not. Some aspects of founding documents are brought forward and others are left behind. The moral form of patriotism that I am trying to articulate here will need to attend carefully to issues of interpretation, selecting from the many versions of a nation's history the one that makes best constructive sense against the background of the core moral commitments of the decent society. If the nation is a new one, the interpreter has somewhat more freedom of selection; nonetheless, this freedom is not total, since the creator of patriotism for a new nation still needs to link the nation to the past of its people, their memories of struggle, and their religious and ethnic traditions.

28   Which moral sentiments will help and which will hinder the creator of a purified patriotism for the decent society envisaged in the capability approach? There is a limit to how useful any general answer to this question can be, in advance of knowing what historical materials we have to work with, and what problems the patriot is facing. Patriotism, like and as a species of love, is particularistic. Nonetheless, we can say something about what is generally helpful or harmful—just as we can in the case of familial or romantic love.

29   Johann Gottfried Herder, in the eighteenth century, wrote well about the moral sentiments a wise leader would need to create.[12] Revealingly, he called these "dispositions of peace." These dispositions, he said, would include a horror of war; a "reduced respect for heroic glory"; a loathing of a "false statecraft" that connects national glory to warlike expansionist projects; a "purified patriotism" that would breed contempt for aggression against other nations and, equally, for internal hatreds and group animosities; "feelings of justice towards other nations," including sentiments of pain when another nation is disparaged or treated badly; humane feelings about international trade relations, so that people would feel upset when weaker nations "get sacrificed . . . for a profit that they do not even receive"; and, finally, a love of useful activity on behalf of human well-being, together with a dislike of attempts to promote well-being through war.

30   On one point, however, a modern patriotism must to some extent diverge from Herder: we must not base patriotic sentiment on any ethnolinguistic homogeneity, or on any religious sentiments that are divisive. It must appeal to sentiments that bind together the citizens of modern democracies that are diverse in religion and ethnicity, all of whom must be treated as fully equal citizens.

31   Moreover, we need to say much more than Herder does concerning the specific moral sentiments that a true statecraft and a purified patriotism should call to its aid. Central to the stability of any society that asks people to make sacrifices will be the sentiment of compassion, together with an ability to imagine vividly the predicaments of others. People will not be moved to address poverty constructively, or to give copious foreign aid, without a carefully constructed and moralized compassion that addresses the predicaments of the poor, seeing them as both serious and not caused simply by laziness or bad behavior. This compassion must learn a lesson from ancient Greek tragedy in the following sense: it must combine compassion for the plight of the suffering person with respect for that person's agency, treating the person not as a passive victim of fortune, but as a human being striving, often heroically, against great obstacles.

32   Because compassion is not intrinsically reliable—for example, people usually feel compassion more strongly toward the near and dear than toward the distant—it must therefore be carefully constructed in connection with the nation's moral norms.

33   Two other useful sentiments—within proper limits—are anger and hope. Anger may be misdirected, but no struggle against injustice can do without it. Leaders will need to try to construct an anger that is targeted at injustices, not at people; that is firmly linked to nonviolent political struggle; and that offers, in the distance, possibilities of mercy and reconciliation. Hope is an essential comrade of a reasonable anger, since people will only stick with nonviolence, and hope for reconciliation, if they do not despair.

34   What, by contrast, does a wise statecraft need to watch out for and try hard not to construct? In *Hiding from Humanity* I argue that two of the most dangerous moral sentiments for a decent society are disgust and shame. Both arise in early childhood in a primitive form and both take as their first object the insufficiencies of the human body, its necessary mortality, weakness, and dependency. These features of human life are difficult for ambitious and intelligent beings to endure, and are the source of much instability in the moral life. In disgust, people initially reject the effluvia and decay of the animal body. Usually, however, things don't stop there, as people find a group of humans onto whom they can project the discomfort they feel about their own bodies, calling them smelly, slimy, disgusting, and so forth. Much racial hatred, and most misogyny, has such elements, as does the hatred of homosexuals. A politician who appeals to disgust in the public realm is a dangerous person, one who is seeking to exploit for divisive purposes the discomfort that people feel at having a body that will die and decay.

35   Shame is more complex, since shame can sometimes call us to high ideals that we have let slide through laziness or obtuseness. But there is a type of shame, or 'primitive shame,' that focuses on the alleged shamefulness of the very fact of needing others, that seeks a rockhard type of invulnerability and calls that manliness. A 'real man,' so we are told, is able to be totally self-sufficient. Any kind of weakness or need is a sign of compromised masculinity. Studies of disturbed adolescents in the United States show how this sort of shame, in connection with diseased norms of manliness, leads to aggression against the weak and against women.[13]

36   In my recent study of religious violence in India,[14] I found that shame was a key element in the violence of militant Hindus against Muslims, in the 2002 Gujarat pogrom and elsewhere. Hindu males tell themselves a story of centuries of humiliation—first at the hands of the Muslims, then at the hands of the British. Out of this collective sense that their virility has been compromised emerges a narrative of the shame-free nation of the future, one that will be so successfully aggressive, so efficient in cleansing the land of the ones who are blamed for the humiliation, that Hindu pride will reign supreme and inviolate. This story is a large part of what fuels violence against Muslims, as well as sexual violence against Muslim women.

37   So the good sort of patriotism will have to attend carefully to shame and to images of masculinity, seeking to cultivate an acceptance of bodily vulnerability as a part of daily life and to prevent the formation of diseased stereotypes of the real man. These ideas converge, clearly, with Herder's ideas about the need to discourage people from seeing glory in aggressive military exploits.

38   As my story of the Pledge of Allegiance shows, even a purified patriotism has its dangers. Although we turn to patriotism to render good institutions stable (for the right reasons), the good in patriotism may itself be unstable in times of anxiety. Law and institutional structure are therefore essential props to the good in patriotism. Five factors contribute to our getting the good out of patriotism without the bad.

39   The first is constitutional rights and an independent judiciary. Constitutional rights are bulwarks for minorities against the panic and excess of majorities. Because minorities are always at risk from patriotism, which can often stir majority sentiment against them, a purified patriotism needs to be advanced in conjunction with a firm and comprehensive tradition of constitutional rights protecting all citizens, and an independent judiciary, detached from public bias and panic, as these rights' interpreter.

40   A second factor is a separation of powers that makes going to war more difficult. Herder thinks of a horror of war as the very core of a purified patriotism. But a people's horror of war will not stop leaders from making war in the absence of political structure. War-making powers should reside in the legislature, and executive authority to initiate and continue wars should be severely contained.

41   Next, protections for the rights of immigrants are necessary. Patriotism always risks veering into xenophobia, and xenophobia often takes new immigrant groups as its targets. In addition to protections for minorities who already enjoy citizens' rights, a purified patriotism needs to be advanced in conjunction with firm protections for the rights of legal immigrants who are not (or not yet) citizens, and decent arrangements for illegal immigrants.

42   Fourth, getting the good out of a purified patriotism requires education about foreign cultures and domestic minorities. Panic and xenophobia are always more difficult to sustain when people are acquainted with complex historical facts regarding the groups they encounter. For example, if schools in Europe and the United States were doing their job teaching people about the varieties of Islam, the current atmosphere of panic would be far more difficult to sustain.

43   Finally, purified patriotism requires a vigorous critical culture. Kant emphasized perhaps the most important factor: protection of the freedom of speech and dissent, and of the voices of intellectuals who play leading roles in shaping a critical public culture. Schools need to foster this critical culture from the earliest years, by teaching children that the ability to think critically is one of the most essential abilities of the democratic citizen, and that learning by rote and thinking by habit are the marks of the bad citizen.

44   Indeed, although the United States is far from having as vigorous a critical culture as it ought to have, my story of the Pledge of Allegiance owes its relatively happy denouement to the critical culture it does have. After the Supreme Court decision upholding the constitutionality of the laws mandating the daily pledge recitation and flag salute[15]—notice that even the independent judiciary was led astray by patriotic fervor—there was a tremendous outburst of protest from the public, led by journalists and intellectuals, but joined by people of goodwill all over the nation. The Court reacted to the public critique of its arguments by hearing, only a short time later, a similar case, taking that occasion to change its

mind. In Board of Education v. Barnette, Justice Jackson observed that nationalism often seeks to "coerce uniformity of sentiment," and insisted that we must be vigilant against all such attempts.[16]

45   History contains countless examples showing how bold projects requiring sacrifice derive support from moral emotions directed at the nation and its history. Let us look at two different cases: the attempt to end the injustice of slavery and racial discrimination in the United States, and the attempt to forge a new Indian nation dedicated to combating economic inequality. In each case I shall focus on political rhetoric—not because I do not believe that sculpture, music, public parks, and many other things are also important, but simply because political rhetoric is the easiest to describe in an essay. In the case of Gandhi, however, some description of his self-dramatization and his use of theater will prove essential.

46   Abraham Lincoln's speeches insistently focus on the history of the United States, offering a constructive account of its core values that underwrites his request for continued sacrifice. The Gettysburg Address, for example, begins with memory, with the mention of "fourscore and seven years," reminding people that the nation, so imperiled at present, had a beginning. It was "a new nation," with a distinctive set of ideals focusing on liberty and equality. Lincoln observes that the present war tests whether any nation of this sort "can long endure." Praising the sacrifice of those who died (in a battle that was one of the war's bloodiest), he then says that the living cannot hallow the ground: only the bravery of the fallen can do so. Living people are thus led toward an attitude of reverential emulation of the sacrifice of the fallen. Lincoln then asks that dedication of them: we are all to be dedicated to the task of preserving the American democracy, and to giving it "a new birth of freedom." He ends on the note of urgency he has sounded throughout: the struggle is really over whether democracy itself can exist.

47   Lincoln's speech contains appeals to a constitutional patriotism that would have pleased Rawls and Habermas. But it does much more: in its vivid invocation of the founding, its heartfelt mourning for the fallen soldiers, its appeal to renewed commitment, it puts historical and contemporary flesh on these moral bones.

48   Lincoln's Second Inaugural Address is another interesting Herderian document, because it carefully positions the Union as the side that wanted and desperately tried to avoid war. The survival of the nation is the starting point: the South would "make war" rather than see it survive, while the North was willing to "accept war" rather than see it perish. The two sides are asymmetrical in their relationship to the nation: the secessionist struggle of the South is a war of aggression against the body of the nation, and the Union's response is a just response to aggression. Thus the speech does what Herder wanted, nurturing a horror of war and a reluctance to make war.

49   The situation of the slaves now enters the picture, and the fact that the South is motivated by greed is emphasized. On one side, then, we have people motivated by self-interest, who "wring their bread from the sweat of other men's faces" and even ask God to help them do it. On the other are those who would include the slaves as human beings and citizens who count, "one-eighth of the

whole population." The nation is now allied with respect and inclusion, the secessionist movement with egoism and false religion.

50   Finally, however, the speech appeals, famously, to mercy and forgiveness "With malice toward none, with charity for all"—since the nation is wounded and its wounds must be "bound up." Mercy does not compromise "firmness in the right," but it gives us a way of going on together into an uncertain future.

51   This speech contains admirable principles, but its use of image and narrative, and its rhythmic cadences of language, are what make the moral principles come alive, in ways that could be internalized by children, forging their deepest images of what their nation is. Said together in schools by black and white children together, it reminds them of the history of pain and struggle, but also of Americans' capacity for respect, love, and sheer endurance. It constructs an interpretive patriotism, using general ideals to criticize historical wrongs.

52   The speech ends on a strongly universalistic note : "To do all which may achieve and cherish a just and lasting peace among ourselves and with all nations." This comes easily, because when a nation is conceived around ideas of inclusion and human dignity, it can easily lead to a struggle for these ideas everywhere.

53   The Emancipation Proclamation was signed in 1863. One hundred years later, its promise was not fulfilled. Martin Luther King's great "I Have a Dream" speech, delivered in Washington, D.C., on August 28, 1963, is another of the most formative documents of American education: all young Americans have heard it thousands of times, in King's extraordinary voice. Nobody could doubt that it is a masterpiece of rhetoric, and that its achievements go well beyond the abstract sentiments that it conveys. Its soaring images of freedom and revelation, and its musical cadences, all give the bare ideas of freedom, dignity, inclusion, and nonviolence wings, so to speak. What I want to study more closely here is the way in which King appeals to the history and traditions of the nation, and to sentiments connected to an idea of America that is, once again, interpretive, using general ideals to criticize an unjust reality.

54   The speech begins with an allusion to the Gettysburg Address—"Five score years ago"—positioning itself as its next chapter. Just as Lincoln looked back to the founding as a moment of commitment to ideals that he sees as gravely threatened, so King looks back to Lincoln's freeing of the slaves as a moment of commitment whose promise is still unrealized. He uses a mundane, and very American, image for that failure. The Constitution and the Declaration of Independence were a "promissory note," but the nation has "defaulted," giving the Negro people a "bad check" that has come back marked "insufficient funds."

55   King constructs an image of America: the virtue of fiscal rectitude on which Americans pride themselves is inconsistent with their past and current behavior toward the country's Negro citizens. And it is the virtues that must and will win the battle with selfishness: "[W]e refuse to believe that the bank of justice is bankrupt. We refuse to believe that there are insufficient funds in the great vaults of opportunity of this nation."

56   Throughout the speech, King sounds a note of urgency: the "sweltering summer of the Negro's legitimate discontent" means that there will be no peace in America until justice is done. But he also cultivates in his followers a purified patriotism: they must, in Gandhian fashion, attain moral superiority by forgoing

violent deeds. Like Gandhi, he makes nonviolence seem "majestic," and violence sordid. ("Again and again, we must rise to the majestic heights of meeting physical force with soul force.") And he also, like Lincoln, appeals to trust between the races, reminding his followers that many white people are present and have joined the struggle for justice: "We cannot walk alone." By cultivating hope and trust, along with legitimate anger, he defuses the urge to violence. This is Herderian purified patriotism, based on a strong denigration of violence and a refusal to bow down before false idols of aggressive masculinity.

57   The visionary and well-known "I have a dream" section of the speech is central to its construction of an image of a morally decent nation, in which all may join together on terms of equality. But then, immediately following upon this vision of a new America, King returns to national memory and national tradition, by quoting in full the famous song "America," or "My Country 'Tis of Thee." Significantly, he now says, "And if America is to be a great nation, this must become true." In other words, the song, which people usually sing complacently, as the account of a reality, is itself prophecy, and its words of freedom must be made true by committed action for justice.

58   The next section of the speech can best be described in the language of jazz, as a series of riffs on the song, as freedom is asked to ring from a series of regions of America. The abstract image of America is being made concrete and physical by being linked to well-known features of geography. At the same time, geography is being moralized: the mountains of New York are now not just mountains; they are sites of freedom. Meanwhile, the body of the nation is being personified in a sensuous, indeed sexy, way: the "heightening Alleghenies of Pennsylvania," the "curvaceous slopes of California." Thus the invitations to disgust so ubiquitous in malign patriotism are replaced by an embrace of the sensuous reminiscent of Walt Whitman.

59   But also: the end of the Civil War is finally at hand, as freedom is asked to ring from a series of sites in the South. In a way reminiscent of the Second Inaugural, King expresses malice toward none and charity toward all. The note of sly humor, as he gets in his dig at Mississippi ("let freedom ring from every hill and every molehill of Mississippi") is a reminder that bad behavior has not been forgotten; it has, however, been transcended in a surge of joy whose object is the purified patriotic nation.

60   Like Lincoln's speech, King's ends on a global note: the victory of integration in America will "speed up that day when all of God's children" will enjoy freedom. Thus purified patriotism melds naturally into a striving for global justice and an inclusive human love.

61   Let us now turn to India's founding. When a new nation is founded, there are no canonical documents or traditions, no memories of long past struggles, that will command the agreement and sentiments of all. Indeed, to this day, a struggle continues over the proper image of the nation and its history, as partisans of the Hindu Right endeavor to characterize that history as one of indigenous Hindu peace and alien domination, first by Muslims and then by Christians. Gandhi and Nehru, setting out to forge the image of a pluralistic India, united by commitment to a truly shared history of struggle for self-rule and to the nation's people, had an uphill battle, since colonial humiliation bred in many a

strong desire to perform deeds of manly aggression. Their struggle involved, then, a conception of true manliness and truly strong patriotism that was controverted by a more warlike form of patriotism.

62   This struggle is neatly exemplified by the ongoing dispute over which of two songs should be India's national anthem. The actual national anthem, "Jana Gana Mana," was written (words and music) by poet, novelist, and theorist of global justice Rabindranath Tagore, a determined critic of most existing forms of nationalism.[17] Its addressee is an immortal spirit of righteousness, equivalent to the moral law, and the anthem describes all Indians as seeking the victory of that moral principle. Like King, Tagore enumerates all the regions from which Indians come together: people from all regions seek the blessings of justice.

63   The Tagore anthem puts beautiful sensuous poetry and music underneath inclusive and egalitarian moral sentiment. Its notion of victory is a moral, not a warlike, notion. Very different is the anthem preferred by the Hindu Right, known as "Bande Mataram," ("Hail Motherland"), taken from a novel by the nineteenth-century Bengali novelist, and early nationalist, Bankimchandra Chatterjee.[18] This anthem depicts the citizen as bowing down to the motherland, which is then identified with a series of Hindu deities. (Thus the not-too-subtle suggestion is that India is a Hindu nation, in which Muslims will always be outsiders.) This uncritical devotion ("Mother, I kiss thy feet") is closely linked to warlike aggression against the enemies of Hindu India: "Who hath said thou art weak in thy lands/When the swords flash out in twice seventy million hands/And seventy millions voices roar/Thy dreadful name from shore to shore?"[19]

64   This controversy about the national anthem is a debate between the form of patriotism Herder loathed and a form that would have been very congenial to him. There is a parallel debate about the Indian flag. The existing flag has at its center the wheel of law, a symbol associated with the Buddhist emperor Ashoka, who fostered religious toleration. It is, then, a symbol of religious inclusiveness, nonviolence, and the supremacy of law. The flag preferred by the Hindu Right is the saffron banner of the eighteenth-century Maharashtrian hero Shivaji, who conducted a briefly successful rebellion against Muslim rule. It is an aggressive and exclusionary symbol, a symbol that says that Hindus will strike back against centuries of humiliation and seize power for themselves, subordinating others.

65   The world has known no more canny creator of purified patriotism than Mohandas Gandhi. Gandhi wrote copiously, but his success in forging a purified patriotism for the new nation, a vast majority of whose inhabitants could not read and write, owes little to his writings. What Gandhi brilliantly did was to make his own body a living symbol of a (purified conception of the) nation. This self-fashioning expressed his idea that the essential site of national struggle is inside each person, a struggle to conquer greed and anxious desires for domination of others.

66   Gandhi did not fashion himself in a vacuum: he relied heavily on traditional Hindu images of asceticism, and he therefore had to be very careful lest his image of the nation seem Hindu in an exclusionary way. He took care to put Muslims in central positions in his freedom movement, and to turn to them at what we might call key ritual moments. His famous fast unto death in 1947, for example, was broken when he turned to Maulana Azad, a Muslim cleric and

Congress Party leader, asking him for some orange juice and some bread. He thus broke with traditional Hindu ideas of purity, which were exclusionary along lines of both caste and religion. Wielding the enormous power of traditional asceticism, he diverted it to an utterly new cause.

67   At the same time, Gandhi constructed his body as a symbol of unity across lines of wealth and caste. If one examines the change in his physical appearance between the early days in South Africa and the height of his influence in India, one sees a deliberately cultivated solidarity with the lowest and poorest, into which the force of his moral authority also led the elites around him. To see an elite Kashmiri Brahmin such as Jawaharlal Nehru spinning his own thread, or marrying his daughter Indira in a homespun sari, is to see the magnitude of the transformation Gandhi was able to accomplish. His half-naked persona, draped only in a loincloth and propped up by a walking stick, etched itself indelibly into the mind of the nation, and the world.

68   Gandhi constructed purified patriotism above all through his theater of civil resistance. Both supremely moral and strategic, Gandhi knew that when the eyes of the world were on India, dignified nonviolent behavior both seemed and was strong and self-governing, and that British thuggishness seemed and was puny and ugly by contrast. In the process, he made both his followers and countless others see manliness in a new way: the body that stood with dignity, taking blows, looked strong and proud. The body that kept dishing out the blows looked utterly at sea, hopelessly weak, not able to touch what it was trying to control.

69   Gandhian patriotism asked a lot of people. It asked the rich to live in solidarity with the poor and to make huge sacrifices of personal comfort. It asked all men to adopt a new type of nonviolent manliness that entailed a great deal of sacrifice, since revenge is pleasant. Only the use of symbols, Gandhi repeatedly said, could succeed in making people willing to take on these difficult tasks. Fortunately, he was a brilliant forger of symbols, symbols that moved because they were old and yet included because they were utterly new. He was also a brilliant wielder of humor, who found ways to include through a kind of loving childlike play. Thus, a common reaction to meeting him was to be surprised that he was not forbiddingly austere or saintly, but puckish and delightful.

70   Because Gandhi was so charismatic, his crusade on behalf of purified patriotism temporarily disabled the struggle of the Hindu Right on behalf of exclusionary patriotism. Gandhi's assassin, Nathuram Godse, justified the assassination for posterity in the name of a (correct) love of country. Godse remains a hero for the Hindu Right, not least for the Gujarati Hindus who, in December 2007, reelected by a large margin as chief minister Narendra Modi, a leader whose complicity in the killings of innocent Muslims during riots in 2002 has now been proven beyond doubt.[20]

71   Gandhi's version of patriotism, however, is the one that won out at the founding, enshrined in India's constitution and in the founding principles laid down in Jawaharlal Nehru's famous "tryst with destiny" speech on the night of India's independence, yet another example of the public construction of a purified patriotism of inclusiveness and equality. Imagining Indian citizens not as aggressive warriors, but as mothers laboring to bring forth a new and just nation ("Before the birth of freedom, we have endured all the pains of labor, and our

hearts are heavy with the memory of this sorrow"), Nehru drew a map that linked proper patriotism to a universal commitment to justice and the eradication of poverty and misery: "[A]s long as there are tears and suffering, so long our work will not be over."

72   For the popular idea of an aggressive warlike India, Nehru then substitutes the idea of an India at work, characterized by incessant labor and striving toward the goal of eradicating human suffering—not only in India, but everywhere: "And so we have to labour and to work, and to work hard, to give reality to our dreams. Those dreams are for India, but they are also for the world, for all the nations and peoples are too closely knit together today for any one of them to imagine that it can live apart."

73   Unfortunately, where patriotism is concerned, both India and the United States have recently taken a turn from the purified toward the malign. In today's India, patriotism shows her Janusfaced nature. The Hindu Right, building on sentiments of ethnic purity, has created a climate of violence and fear for minorities, especially Muslims. Although the Gandhi-Nehru vision in some ways prevailed in the 2004 elections, it is hanging on by its teeth, and still faces strong opposition from the malign patriotism of "Bande Mataram," egged on substantially by nonresident Indians in the United States, who made a large financial and emotional contribution to Narendra Modi's recent victory.

74   Meanwhile, a new technological middle class focuses on the patriotism of national enrichment, repudiating the Nehruvian ideas of striving and of solidarity with the poor. The Congress Party has tied itself into knots trying not to alienate these voters, and this has meant that only Sonia Gandhi continues to speak out resolutely in favor of sacrifice and against a patriotism that divides. On this account she is repeatedly attacked for her allegedly 'Italian' ideas. (Her Italian birth is a trope used to undermine her claim to represent the nation.) Every day, in the weeks leading up to the Gujarat state elections, I received e-mail denouncing her, from a group that calls itself "Indian media bias." Titles such as "Is Sonia Losing Her Marbles?" and "It is not Muslims, It is Islam, stupid!" show a malign exclusionary patriotism making its way, through mockery of ideals of peace and demonization of the different.

75   As for the United States, a politics of fear has convinced many Americans that they need to curb civil liberties in the name of a never-ending 'war on terror,' while politicians increasingly help themselves to a language that demonizes Islam and Muslims ('Islamofascism,' 'war against Islamic terrorism'). At the same time, political actors from Antonin Scalia to Mike Huckabee rally around an exclusionary vision of America, with Scalia holding, with Mitt Romney, that we should prefer the monotheistic religions and disfavor other religions and nonreligion, and Huckabee going so far as to assert that the United States is a Christian nation. Acute fear has typically led Americans to characterize the nation in narrow and exclusionary terms. As with Congress Party members in India, Democrats in the United States are not standing up for the Hindus, Buddhists, agnostics, and atheists whom the rhetoric of the Right invites us to consider second-class citizens. Nobody dares to alienate the powerful evangelical movement by pointing to the way in which current Republican rhetoric violates an idea of equal standing and fair play that lies deep in the history of the nation.

The demonization of illegal immigrants is yet another ugly part of this politics of anxiety.

76   Obviously, then, patriotism in and of itself is not a good thing; often indeed it is a very bad thing. It might, then, seem perverse of me, at such a time, even to mention the idea of patriotism.

77   What I have argued, however, is that a nation that pursues goals that require sacrifice of self-interest needs to be able to appeal to patriotism, in ways that draw on symbol and rhetoric, emotional memory and history—as Lincoln, King, Gandhi, and Nehru all successfully did. This is all the more true when a nation pursues not only internal justice but the goal of global justice as well. If people interested in economic equality, justice for minorities, and global justice eschew symbol and rhetoric, fearing all appeals to emotion and imagination as inherently dangerous and irrational, the Right will monopolize these forces, to the detriment of democracy.

NOTES

1. All of this is well portrayed in Erik Larsen's novel *The Devil in the White City*, a work of popular semifiction that has, at the same time, a serious historical thesis.

2. The history of the Pledge is exhaustively documented in Richard J. Ellis, *To the Flag: The Unlikely History of the Pledge of Allegiance* (Lawrence: University Press of Kansas, 2005). The words "under God" were added to the Pledge in 1954, during the Cold War. I discuss the Pledge and the legal conflicts surrounding it in *Liberty of Conscience: In Defense of America's Tradition of Religious Equality* (New York: Basic Books, 2008), chap. 5, 8.

3. Jean-Jacques Rousseau, *On the Social Contract*, book IV, chap. VIII ("On Civil Religion"). One good modern edition is in Jean-Jacques Rousseau, *The Basic Political Writings*, trans. Donald A. Cress (Indianapolis: Hackett Publishing, 1987), 220–227.

4. Martha Nussbaum, "For Love of Country," in *For Love of Country : A Debate on Patriotism and Cosmopolitanism* (Boston: Beacon Press, 1996). I am extremely grateful to Paul Weithman for comments that showed me the need for this clarification.

5. J. S. Mill, "The Utility of Religion," 1874 (posthumously published).

6. This definition of 'basic structure' is that used by Rawls in *Political Liberalism*.

7. On the world state, see Martha Nussbaum, *Frontiers of Justice: Disability, Nationality, Species Membership* (Cambridge, Mass.: Belknap Press of Harvard University Press, 2007), 313–314.

8. John Rawls, *A Theory of Justice* (Cambridge, Mass.: Harvard University Press, 1971), 479–504. Although Rawls came to doubt the specifics of this section by the time he wrote *Political Liberalism*, he continued to assert that the just society needed to operate with a "reasonable political psychology."

9. Juergen Habermas, "Citizenship and National Identity: Some Reflections on the Future of Europe," *Praxis International* 12(1992–1993):1–19.

10. David Miller, *On Nationality* (Oxford: Clarendon Press, 1995).

11. See Nussbaum, Frontiers, chap. 1, 3.

12. In "Letters for the Advancement of Humanity" (1793–1797), translated by Michael Forster in Forster, ed., *Herder: Philosophical Writings* (Cambridge: Cambridge University Press, 2002), Letter 119, 404-409.

13. Dan Kindlon and Michael Thompson, *Raising Cain: Protecting the Emotional Life of Boys* (New York: Ballantine, 1999).

14. Martha Nussbaum, *The Clash Within: Democracy, Religious Violence, and India's Future* (Cambridge, Mass.: Harvard University Press, 2007), chap. 6.

15. Minersville School Dist. v. Gobitis, 310 U.S. 596 (1940).

16. Board of Education v. Barnette, 319 U.S. 624 (1943).

17. See Rabindranath Tagore, *Nationalism*, lectures delivered in 1917. "Jana Gana Mana" was not written as the national anthem; it was written much earlier, as Tagore's form of indirect protest against the visit of George V to India. What he was basically doing is to state that India's diverse citizens owe their ultimate loyalty not to the colonial ruler, but to the moral law. I discuss the anthem's history in the introduction to *The Clash*.

18. Chatterjee is one of the targets of Tagore's mordant critique of warlike nationalism, in his 1916 novel *Ghare Baire*, or *The Home and the World*. Its hero, who favors an inclusive conception of citizenship based upon justice, declares himself unable to understand the spirit of "Bande Mataram."

19. I cite the well-known translation by nationalist philosopher Sri Aurobindo.

20. On the evidence that led to a denial to Modi of a visa to enter the United States, see Nussbaum, *The Clash Within*, chap. 1; since that time, interviews by the investigative magazine *Tehelka*, conducted with hidden camera, have given even more overwhelming evidence of his guilt; see the special issue of *Tehelka*, "The Truth Gujarat 2002, In the Words of the Men Who Did It," *Tehelka* 4(43) (November 3, 2007).

Active Reading

1. Why does Nussbaum call patriotism "Janus-faced"?

2. Why is Nussbaum concerned with finding a route out of egoism to global concern? Explain her proposal for achieving this through patriotism.

3. Why does she see Lincoln, King, Gandhi, and Nehru as having inspired a purified form of patriotism?

4. How does Nussbaum see the roles of shame and fear in producing a dangerous form of patriotism?

Critical Reading

1. Nussbaum is highly literate in the sense of having read and reflected widely in many fields of study. Do you find that there are times when it is difficult to follow her because she "presupposes" that her readers share her knowledge base? Or does she successfully provide enough information about the context that she does not leave you behind? Find examples of both presupposition and contextualization.

2. Although she is very interdisciplinary, Nussbaum works mainly in the humanities: religion, law, philosophy, and classics. What features of her writing mark her work as part of the humanities tradition and not the social sciences?

3. Does Canada need a "globally sensitive patriotism"? Do you think Canadian patriotism is as Janus-faced as the American version?

4. Are you aware of any figures in Canadian history who might be added to Nussbaum's list of leaders who inspire the finer sort of patriotism? If not, why not?

READING AND WRITING SUGGESTIONS

Chapter-based Research Questions

1. Compare styles between authors in this section. First, identify the tradition they are writing in (humanities or social sciences) and whether they are writing for other scholarly specialists or for a general readership. Then identify discipline, thesis, methodology, type of evidence supplied, language styles, and documentation.

2. Rewrite part of Lessing's article as a research article in APA style. Rewrite part of Milgram's article as a popular press essay with no scholarly documentation.

3. Write a critical review essay on courage and conformity that refers to all five texts in this chapter.

4. Each of the authors in this chapter responds to some degree to the question, "How can we make ourselves more courageous in the face of pressure to be cruel?" Write an essay that develops your own response to this question in the course of analyzing the merits of each approach.

Additional Research Questions

1. The obedience experiments remain important not only because of what they contributed to our knowledge of the impact of social forces on individual behaviour, but because of controversy over the methods employed. Produce an annotated bibliography of scholarly articles, books, book chapters, and ethics documents (available online) that could form the research base for an essay on the ethical issues raised by the methods used in Milgram and Zimbardo's studies.

2. All scholarly research in Canada that involves human participants is required to adhere to the guidelines set out in a document called *Tri-Council Policy Statement: Ethical Conduct for Research Involving Humans* (often abbreviated as TCPS). If you ever work as a research assistant for a professor who is doing such research, or conduct your own research project involving human beings for a senior course or graduate thesis, you will have to follow these guidelines as well. Reflect on the issues of psychological distress and deception involved in the obedience documents and explain how the *TCPS* responds to such issues in its rules for research done today.

3. YouTube and Google reveal that the obedience experiments continue to resonate within popular culture. A BBC documentary in 2009 and a French television show called *The Game of Death* in 2010 each reenacted elements of the Milgram experiment. Do contemporary reenactments cover new ground or simply point out that group thinking continues to flourish?

CHAPTER 11
POWER AND PRIVILEGE IN SCHOOL CULTURE

Whatever else schools might be, they have always operated as instruments of normalization, servants of the state whose primary responsibility is to take five-year-olds through a 10- or 12-year character-building process that will make them into citizens who share behaviours and values compatible with the smooth functioning of the state: loyalty, obedience, hard work, and self-reliance. Historically, this mission has been visible in such practices as reciting the Lord's Prayer and the national anthem, and, now notoriously, in the establishment of the residential school system, which was designed to assimilate Aboriginal children into mainstream culture by annihilating their own language, traditions, and family bonds.

Canadians often think of excesses of citizenship as being a U.S. phenomenon, and it is true that there are comparatively fewer proponents of the "My country, right or wrong" form of patriotism here. But while we may like to think that our school systems are now organized around dedication to all children achieving their potential, there is a large body of scholarship that indicates otherwise. Studies in the sociology of education analyze the many ways (inappropriately standardized testing, greater resources for schools in prosperous neighbourhoods) in which schools effectively serve to reproduce the existing hierarchies of society, where social inequities are manifested along lines of race, gender, class, sexual identity, and other differences. Ironically, as Doris Lessing argues in her essay "Group Minds,"[1] education does this in part by teaching people that if they are poor, or harshly treated, it is their own fault, and not the result of any injustice in our social arrangements. Given the personal conflicts built into the school system, it should not be surprising, then, that individuals within it can be caught up in their own power struggles. In this chapter, we bring together readings that approach various issues of power and privilege in school culture.

The first is excerpted from Shaheen Shariff's book on cyber-bullying. Bullying is arguably the most pressing issue of power in schools today, and we are just beginning to understand its electronic forms. Shocked into rethinking the significance of bullying after a string of retaliatory shootings across North America, most of us now agree that it is wrong to dismiss complaints of bullying with a "kids will be kids" attitude. Teachers and school officials who used to reply to the complaints of victimized students with the message that bullying was wrong, but that tattling was even worse, are now trying to learn how to recognize bullying and take responsibility for intervening in it. Some are wondering how the culture of schools participates in the production of bullying: Are children just showing they've learned their lessons well when they bully those who are somehow different from the norm? Shariff explains what makes cyber-bullying particularly damaging: cyber-bullies often torment their victims anonymously, leaving victims in a state of generalized fear, not knowing where the abuse is

---

[1] See Lessing's essay in Chapter 10.

coming from, and undermining their attachment to the school community. For Shariff, this situation is a denial of the right to learn that calls for a more vigorous response than has typically been the case.

In a related article, Catherine Taylor examines the response of Winnipeg School Division to the problem of homophobic bullying. Rather than restricting their efforts to punishing bullies and consoling victims after the fact, the Division ultimately decided to implement a system-wide "anti-homophobia initiative" aimed at building consensus around the proposition that opposing homophobia means defending human rights.

Next we have a reading about the residential school system in which Aboriginal children experienced prolonged, systematic, cultural shaming (and sometimes physical and sexual abuse) at the hands of White teachers, many of whom felt that they were performing a noble service by teaching Aboriginal children to assimilate into White society. Regardless of their motives, they are now seen by many as having obeyed orders from unjust authorities and conformed to the racist group mentality of colonial Canada. Judges Murray Sinclair and A.C. Hamilton analyze both state-sanctioned and systemic abuses of power in residential schools, and the traumatic effects of abuse that persist in Aboriginal communities today.

The chapter concludes with an article that examines plagiarism, a dishonest practice that abuses the privilege of having access to other people's work. Plagiarism is abusive in that it involves stealing other people's work, and getting unearned rewards that other students work hard for. However, some practitioners of plagiarism regard it as being, at worst, a victimless crime. Peggy Pittman-Munke and Michael Berghoef offer a "typology of plagiarists" in university settings and discuss a range of possible responses to the problem. At the centre of their discussion is the question, is plagiarism as much a function of the sometimes impersonal nature of contemporary education as it is a function of technical ability to do it easily?

As you read the texts in this chapter, you may find yourself thinking back to Chapter 10, with its focus on the influence of social forces such as group mentality and obedience to authority, and the importance of finding effective ways to encourage people to respond more ethically when we are tempted to sideline our own consciences for personal advantage.

Activate

1. Were you aware of the occurrence of bullying in high school? Who seemed to be the targets? Do you know anyone who has been targeted by cyber-bullying?

2. Now that you are out of high school, are you in a bully-free zone? What is it about high school that might foster bullying behaviour?

3. Was "That's so gay!" used as an insult when you were in school? If so, did anyone point out that this expression is hurtful and unacceptable when used to mean "stupid"?

4. How widespread is the practice of plagiarism (presenting other people's written work as your own) among your peers?

5. What kind of person did your schools try to make you become?

"Bullying Today" from *Cyber-Bullying: Issues and Solutions for the School, the Classroom and the Home*

Shaheen Shariff

Shaheen Shariff is Associate Professor in the Faculty of Education at McGill University and has achieved international prominence for her expertise on cyber-bullying. She is the author of several books on cyber-bullying. Her work investigates what she sees as a policy vacuum on the topic that threatens the safety and well-being of children. Her work therefore engages with law, policy, and human rights to make the case for parents' and teachers' responsibility to supervise children and adolescents and intervene when bullying occurs.

In this excerpt from her book, Cyber-Bullying: Issues and Solutions for the School, the Classroom and the Home, *Shariff defines cyber-bullying and explains the behavioural and ethical consequences that flow from the opportunity to torment others anonymously, and the psychological impact on the victims of being targeted by such abuse.*

1   In the wake of the Columbine and Montreal (Dawson College) shootings and, more recently, the mass random shootings at Virginia Polytechnic University (Agence France Presse, 2007) and Dawson College in Montreal in 2006, and the media attention to those and other serious bullying cases, many parents and stakeholders are concerned that school violence is on the rise[13] and possibly even out of control. Easy access to guns and the high population in the United States might contribute to the current rates of violence there. Students in Canada, Australia, China, Japan or the UK, for example, may not experience cases of extreme violence as often because there is less ready access to guns. This does not mean, however, that bullying is not prevalent in schools in those countries, nor that it is not a serious concern. It is an issue in many countries, but it usually does not involve extreme violence nor result in death. Given the media attention to bullying, however, it is important to consider it in context.

2   Canadian and US researchers (Dolmage, 2000; Roher, 1997; Tanner, 1996) concur that a very small number of young people (4 to 6 per cent) actually engage in serious acts of violence.[14] DiGiulio, in fact, contends that schools are the 'safest places in the world' (2001, p. 23). He notes that violent deaths from murder and suicide in American schools declined by 40 per cent between 1995 and 2001, whereas the risk of violent death for students who dropped out of school, were expelled or suspended increased 'several hundredfold' (ibid.).[15] These statistics, although less recent than those I provide on cyber-bullying in the next chapter, are crucial. Let me repeat the fact that the risk of violent death for students who were expelled or suspended increased 'several hundredfold' (ibid., p. 23). When we consider school and government responses to bullying and cyber-bullying in later chapters, these statistics will play an important role. DiGiulio also provides data that disclose a 14 per cent reduction in physical fights in US schools between 1991 and 1997—another positive finding; however, as we will see in Chapter 3, it may be simply that the physical bullying has moved into the covert realm of cyberspace with far wider reach.

3   In the meantime, it is notable that typically only extreme bullying cases are reported by the media, thus giving an inaccurate picture of its frequency and seriousness. According to Dolmage (2000), media-reported statistics that reflect a rise in youth violence are rarely presented in context. The numbers may instead reflect higher rates of overall violence because of a growing population[16] or because schools now report incidents of a less serious nature to police more frequently.[17] Put another way, it is important to question critically the statistics presented by the media that are often geared to sensationalize and draw attention to aspects of a story without attention to the context. This in turn has significant impact on the policy and practice response by schools and education ministries.

4   I spend quite a bit of time addressing the influence of the media in creating fear and shaping the public's perceptions about bullying, cyber-bullying and the dangers of communication technologies in later chapters. For now, it is notable that a lot of bullying is psychological — both in terms of how it is carried out and its effects. In contemporary society, much of it flows between physical and cyber-space as 'cyber-bullying', and it is to this form of bullying that I now turn.

DEFINITIONS OF CYBER-BULLYING

5   One of the problems I have always had with definitions of 'bullying' is that they were too simplistic and therefore invited reactions, policy and programmatic responses that failed to recognize its nuances and complexities. In the case of cyberspace, because of the range of possibilities, the fluidity with which it is possible to move from one form of technology such as email, MSN, Facebook, MySpace, web-blogs, chat rooms and so on, and the capacity for millions of people to read and participate in various forms of communication, any definition of cyber-bullying must be applied with a caveat. Cyber-bullying must be understood in the specific paradigmatic context in which it is presented.

6   More importantly, when we define a behaviour, it is important to remember it as an action that takes place in a particular context, at a particular time, with various influences operating on the individual(s) who take the action. Moreover, it is the particular lens or conceptual approach that we bring to our understanding of bullying or cyber-bullying that will determine our response. I began to hint, in my introduction to Chapter 1, that descriptions and definitions of reality can be deliberately framed to develop people's understanding of an issue by the words that are used to define it. So, for example, if the Internet is described as a 'gift from the devil' (Soloyon, 2005), or 'Web ensnares teens up to eight hours a day' (Soloyon, 2005) and if use of communications technology by young people is consistently described in this way, then it follows that no matter how they use it, there will be a negative connotation attached to it. For example, I gave the example of the teenage boys who testified at the Azmi Jubran human rights tribunal and explained that when they call someone 'gay' or a 'homo' and if the expression is directed towards someone they like, then they mean it as a term of endearment. When it is against someone they dislike, then it is meant to hurt.

7   With so much of popular teenage discourse infiltrated with words such as 'ho' (prostitute) and 'bitch' and quick communication codes such as 'omg' which means 'Oh my God', which have developed through MSN and text messaging, teenagers are increasingly blocking out the adults in their lives. Moreover, as Lankshear and Knobel (2006) point out, kids approach cyberspace with a very different understanding of its fluidity or capacity, whereas adults tend to see cyberspace as something that can be controlled in the same way as physical space.

8   For example, adults might perceive that online firewalls are like brick walls that cannot be hacked through. As adults have always had some kind of 'control' over the spaces that kids occupy, and over forms of knowledge young people access at home and school, they might define cyber-bullying as 'anti-authority', 'rampant' and 'out of control'. Although, in the last five years, numerous studies have reported on the forms, extent and impact of cyber-bullying, it is important to bear in mind that these findings may help us understand only one part of the puzzle, and that we ought to look at the range of influences that might tacitly condone cyber-bullying through the behaviour and responses we ourselves model.

9   We should also be cognizant of the very fine line between youth expression that we generally accept when they interact among themselves and that which is truly harmful and offensive. Here are some definitions of cyber-bullying that illustrate the forms it takes, the tools that are used to engage in it, and ways in which it is understood to differ from traditional bullying.

10   It is not clear whether the term 'cyber-bullying' was first coined by Canadian Bill Belsey (2005) or American lawyer Nancy Willard (2003). Belsey defined cyber-bullying as follows:

> Cyber-bullying involves the use of information and communication technologies such as email, cellphone and pager text messages, instant messaging, defamatory personal Web sites, and defamatory online personal polling Web sites, to support deliberate, repeated, and hostile behavior by an individual or group that is intended to harm others.
>
> (Belsey, 2005)

11   A more comprehensive, though shorter, definition is presented by Nancy Willard, Director for the Center for Safe and Responsible Internet Use, who describes cyber-bullying as speech that is 'defamatory, constitutes bullying, harassment, or discrimination, discloses personal information, or contains offensive, vulgar or derogatory comments' (Willard, 2003, p. 66). Remember that, if we adopt this definition, the defamatory nature of the expression would have to be first established in a court of law. According to Willard, other forms of cyber-bullying can include flaming (sending derogatory messages to a person), harassing and denigrating (put-downs), masquerading, outing and excluding (Willard, 2005).

12   The term 'cyber-bullying' describes forms of bullying that use technology. According to some reports, it is a phenomenon that children and adolescents seem to increasingly be using to harm others (Campbell, 2005), although there is also significant evidence (Media Awareness Network, 2005) that many adults are equally guilty of engaging in cyber-bullying. I will give examples of adult cyber-bullying as we go along.

13   There is no dearth of definitions of cyber-bullying. Elsewhere, and within the context of certain articles, I have defined peer-to-peer cyber-bullying (Shariff and Strong-Wilson, 2005) as comprising covert, psychological bullying, conveyed through the electronic media such as cellphones, weblogs and web sites, online chat rooms, 'MUD' rooms (multi-user domains where individuals take on different characters) and Xangas (online personal profiles where some adolescents create lists of people they do not like).

14   In 2007 I would add to that definition to include social communications networks such as Facebook, YouTube, Orkut, LinkdIn, MySpace and countless others that are surfacing on the Internet. Some researchers have defined cyber-bullying as 'willful and repeated harm inflicted through the medium of electronic text' (Patchin and Hinduja, 2006). Other researchers define it as an 'an aggressive, intentional act carried out by a group or individual, using electronic forms of contact, repeatedly and over time against a victim who cannot easily defend him or herself' (Smith, 2004).

15   It might be a good idea to check the description of cyber-bullying on Wikipedia. The definitions and explanation of cyber-bullying are comprehensive and helpful because they cover a range, although not all, of cyber-actions that could be included as cyber-bullying:

> Cyberbullying (also spelled Cyber-bullying, or online bullying) is the term used to refer to bullying and harassment by use of electronic devices through means of email, instant messaging, text messages, blogs, mobile phones, pagers, and web sites. Other terms for cyberbullying are 'electronic bullying', 'e-bullying', 'SMS bullying', 'mobile bullying', 'online bullying', digital bullying', or 'Internet bullying.'
>
> (Wikipedia, 2007)

Wikipedia goes on to explain that, in some countries, provinces and states, cyber-bullying is defined as a crime. As with the profile of traditional bullying presented earlier, cyber-bullying is described as:

> [W]illful and involves recurring or repeated harm inflicted through the medium of electronic text. According to R.B. Standler, bullying intends to cause emotional distress and has no legitimate purpose to the choice of communications, Cyberbullying can be as simple as continuing to send e-mail to someone who has said they want no farther contact with the sender. Cyberbullying may also include threats, sexual remarks, pejorative labels (i.e., hate speech). Cyber-bullies may publish personal contact information for their victims at web sites. They may attempt to assume the identity of a victim for the purpose of publishing material in their name that defames or ridicules them.
>
> (Wikipedia, 2007a)

16   These definitions all state in common the fact that communications technology tools and media are being used to engage in online bullying, that the communication is, as with general bullying, deliberate and wilful, repeated and exclusionary. So the question that arises is: Do we blame the medium or the message? (McLuhan, 1964). I would argue that the medium of cyberspace simply provides an avenue for expression of the message. As Campbell (2005) asks,

'is cyber-bullying, an old problem in a new guise?' (p. 68). The message is no different from that which is often expressed when bullying occurs in physical space (overtly or covertly). If we are to carry out Hamed Nastoh's goal of education effectively, then it is critical to focus on the message, but also important to understand the medium so that it too can be used to empower learning and convey an altogether different message.

17   Methods used in cyber-bullying include text messaging of derogatory insults on mobile phones, with students showing the message to others before sending it to the target; sending threatening emails, and forwarding a confidential email to all address-book contacts, thus publicly humiliating the first sender. Others gang up on one student and bombard him/her with 'flame' emails or set up a derogatory web site dedicated to a targeted student and emailing others the address, inviting their comments.

18   In the United States, high school student David Knight lived this nightmare. David had been teased, taunted, kicked, threatened and punched for most of his years in high school. In an interview with CBC National News (Leishman, 2002), David explained that the most devastating aspect of the bullying was the humiliation he suffered every time he logged onto the Internet. Students from his school set up a web site about him where they continued the threats, insults and gossip. The derision against David spread quickly and globally. He was told by peers to check out a certain web site originating in Thailand. To his horror, the web site was titled, 'Welcome to the page that makes fun of Dave Knight' — an extension of the web site that was set up by his Canadian peers. In an interview with CBC National News, David explained:

> Rather than just some people, say 30 in a cafeteria, hearing them all yell insults at you, it's up there for 6 billion people to see. Anyone with a computer can see it . . . and you can't get away from it. It doesn't go away when you come home from school. It made me feel even more trapped.
>
> (Ibid.)

It took the threat of litigation against the Internet provider and David's school before the web site was finally taken down — approximately six months after his family's initial request for removal (ibid.).

19   In addition, web sites can be set up for others to vote on the biggest geek, or sluttiest girl in the school (Campbell, 2005; Snider, 2004). In one instance, a video of a teenager masturbating for her boyfriend was uploaded and emailed to her entire class when the relationship soured (Harmon, 2004). . . .

20   The previous section presented a profile of traditional bullying as either physical or psychological, and overt or covert. Although I have described it as primarily 'covert', cyber-bullying can be as open, aggressive and 'overt' as other forms of psychological bullying — especially now that comments derogating teachers and persons in authority can be loaded on the Internet for everyone to see. Cyber-bullying generally takes the form of verbal and written bullying. Written forms of communication, especially online, can often be saved, reproduced and have an element of permanence, whereas the spoken word, if not recorded, is difficult to reproduce.

21   As I have mentioned several times and will continue to emphasize and expand upon throughout this book, cyber-bullying is not restricted to children and youths. The Internet and email, for example, have provided a medium for many adults to vent their anger and frustration, harass, threaten and exploit the reputations of other adults. Some take on virtual personalities in MUD rooms and sexually harass other players. In Chapter 7, I will also highlight cases involving online harassment and cyber-libel against teachers by parents, and introduce examples of Internet web sites created by adults that perpetuate hate and violence.

22   Before presenting statistics drawing from a range of international studies to gauge the extent of technology use and cyber-bullying in various parts of the world, it is important to highlight some of the key characteristics of cyber-bullying that are not aspects of traditional bullying.

CHARACTERISTICS OF CYBER-BULLYING

23   Electronic media by their nature allow for traditional forms of bullying to take on characteristics that are specific to cyberspace.

Anonymity

24   The anonymous nature of cyberspace first made it attractive to young people, especially when there is a nexus to the school, because it allows for the targeting of classmates and/or teachers without being easily detected (unless they are using social networking sites on which it is easier to identify those who post comments). Most cyber-bullying is anonymous because perpetrators are shielded by screen names that protect their identity. Anonymity in cyberspace adds to the challenges for schools (Harmon, 2004). Furthermore, although cyber-bullying begins anonymously in the virtual environment, it impacts learning in the physical school environment. The consequences can be psychologically devastating for victims and socially detrimental for all students (Gáti *et al.*, 2002). Fear of unknown cyber-perpetrators among classmates and bullying that continues at school distracts all students (victims, bystanders and perpetrators) from schoolwork. It creates a hostile physical school environment where students feel unwelcome and unsafe. In such an atmosphere, equal opportunities to learn are greatly reduced (Devlin, 1997; Shariff and Strong-Wilson, 2005).

An Infinite Audience

25   Second, and as I mentioned earlier in this chapter, research on general bullying finds that 30 per cent of onlookers and bystanders support perpetrators instead of victims (Boulton, 1993; Salmivalli, 2001). The longer it persists, the more bystanders join in the abuse (Henderson *et al.*, 2002), creating a power imbalance between victim and perpetrators. Isolation renders victims vulnerable to continued abuse, and the cycle repeats itself. What might begin in the physical school environment as friendly banter can quickly turn into verbal bullying that

continues in cyberspace as covert psychological bullying. The difference in cyberspace is that hundreds of perpetrators can get involved in the abuse, and classmates who may not engage in the bullying at school can hide behind technology to inflict the most serious abuse.

26   I have already used the well-known example of an abusive web site designed to insult David Knight, which found its way into Thailand. A similar situation occurred with a Trois Rivières, Québec teenager, Ghislain Reza, who became known worldwide as the 'Star Wars kid'. Ghislain had taped himself playing a Star Wars character and doing a dance with a light sabre. He mistakenly left the tape in the media room at his school. The tape was stolen by two classmates who uploaded the video onto a web site. The web site received approximately 15 million hits and over 106 clones of the video were made. This resulted in Ghislain becoming known as the 'Star Wars kid'. He was teased everywhere he went at school. The Hollywood director of the Star Wars movies, George Lucas, heard about Ghislain. The American corporate mentality kicked in, and some entrepreneurs began to produce 'Star Wars kid' memorabilia and souvenirs. At his school, students would jump up on tables and dance chanting 'Star Wars kid!' everywhere he went. His parents eventually sued the two classmates who uploaded the tape and settled out of court for approximately C$360,000 in April, 2006. Ghislain had to move to another school to avoid the teasing. Although the settlement was good for Ghislain because it took him out of the public eye, if the case had proceeded to trial it would have been the first of its kind on cyber-bullying. Most of the court cases that are instigated for bullying and cyber-bullying seem to get settled out of court because legal costs are generally too high for parents, and school insurance companies use all kinds of delay tactics to avoid trial. Moreover, courts are reluctant to hear cases of cyber-bullying because of the definitional challenges and their concern of opening up the floodgates to litigation. David Knight's situation is a case in point. His claim was delayed for at least three years by the school's insurers and is now under settlement negotiations.

Prevalent Sexual and Homophobic Harassment

27   A third concern is that sexual and homophobic harassment is emerging as a prevalent aspect of cyber-bullying, and this may be related to the gender differences in the way that males and females use the Internet and cellphone technologies. Certainly, the international findings that I discuss later on are very interesting in this regard.

Permanence of Expression

28   Fourth, online communications have a permanence and inseparability that are very difficult to erase. Cellular phones are generally carried all the time, making them difficult for victims to ignore, and computers are generally used every day. Although, of course, a cellphone can be ignored, text messages and emails can be sent so that every time the phone or computer is turned on, the nasty messages are waiting. Most people have a cellphone and need their computer for learning and

work activities. Moreover, emails and defamatory material or modified photographs about a person on the Internet are extremely difficult to remove once posted, as millions of people can download and save it immediately. These forms of expression can then be forwarded on to hundreds of other people and saved in their desk or laptop computers.

Myspace, Facebook and YouTube

29   Online social communications tools such as MySpace for pre-teens and teenagers began to surface approximately five years ago and caught on like wildfire. Especially for girls, who engage in more social and verbal forms of communication, MySpace was the perfect way to connect with friends, but also exclude peers, harass, and demean them. Disney has recently created a MySpace of its own to capitalize on its popularity. Until this year, incidents of cyber-bullying involving MySpace were generally restricted to peer-to-peer cases. However, with the advent of Facebook and YouTube, the world of social networking entered entirely new realms.

30   Facebook was launched on 4 February 2004, at Harvard University, by twenty-two-year-old Mark Zuckerberg. It was developed to be a social networking tool for Ivy League university students, and, within two weeks, one-half of Harvard students were members. By 30 May 2004, students at Stanford and Yale had joined, and, by September 2005, Facebook was opened to high school students. By June 2006, the site was opened to business networks with more than 20,000 networks of employees. Within a span of three years, Facebook gained over 19 million registered users: It is the sixth most trafficked site in the United States, and 1 per cent of all Internet time is spent on facebook.com (Roher, 2007). One of its attractions is that it is a photo-sharing site on the web. Six million photographs are uploaded daily and are expected to bring Zuckerman US$100m in revenue in 2007. Yahoo offered to purchase Facebook for US$1bn and was turned down.

31   According to a California ethnographer, danah boyd (her legal name is in lowercase), the competition between Facebook and MySpace is based on class. In an article entitled 'Facebook is for "good" kids — MySpace is for freaks' (Harris, 2007), *The Gazette* reports boyd's research that Facebook teens tend to be from families who are wealthier and emphasize a college education, are predominantly white, take honours classes and 'live in a world dictated by after school activities'. The young people who communicate on MySpace, however, are described as 'geeks, freaks or queers' from lower-income families and are expected to get jobs after graduating from grade 12. The reason for this divide according to boyd is that people tend to gravitate to social groups where they feel most comfortable. This was verified in a survey by Comscore (an Internet data collection company) that found almost 50 per cent of Facebook users — compared with the overall web average of 40 per cent — live in households in which the annual income is higher than US$75,000. The media article notes that, although boyd's findings were presented as a 'blog essay' rather than an academic article, her reputation as a leading analyst of online behaviour makes her study convincing.

32   I agree with other academics who found boyd's study interesting because it identifies the online subtleties of discrimination, which are difficult to recognize. In light of this study, it is not surprising that the US military prevented their soldiers from accessing MySpace but allowed access to Facebook, which is preferred by officers.

ONLINE SOCIAL COMMUNICATIONS TOOLS

33   In a recent interview, boyd described MySpace and Facebook as follows:

> MySpace and Facebook are social network sites where individuals create profiles and link to others ('friends') within the system. The profile serves as an individual's digital representation (similar to homepages) of their tastes, fashion, and identity. In crafting this profile, individuals upload photos, indicate interests, list favorite musicians and describe themselves textually and through associated media. The social network feature allows participants to link themselves to others within the system, revealing their affiliations and peer group. These sites also allow friends to comment on each other's profiles. Structurally, social network sites are a cross between a year book and a community web site.
>
> These sites also provide numerous communication tools. Both have a messaging system similar to email; MySpace also has a bulletin board where people can post messages that all friends can read and a blogging service where people can post entries for either friends or the public at large. When youth log in, their first task is typically to check messages in order to see who has written to them. While email is still used to communicate with adults and authorities, MySpace is the primary asynchronous communication tool for teens. After checking personal messages, youth check friend additions, bulletins board posts, event announcements and new blog posts by friends. They visit their friends' pages to see new photos or check out each other's comments. The vast majority of social network site use amongst youth does not involve surfing to strangers' profiles, but engaging more locally with known friends and acquaintances.
>
> (boyd and Jenkins, 2006 (May 26))

According to boyd, MySpace has over 78 million registered accounts, and Facebook has approximately 8 million. Although over 85 per cent of college students participate on Facebook if it exists on their campus, she explains that MySpace is a cultural requirement for American high school students. She quotes one teenager as saying: 'If you're not on MySpace, you don't exist' (ibid.). Not all MySpace users are teenagers but most American teenagers have MySpace accounts.

34   boyd explains that these sites play a key role in contemporary youth culture:

> These sites play a key role in youth culture because they give youth a space to hang out amongst friends and peers, share cultural artifacts (like links to funny web sites, comments about TV shows) and work out an image of how they see themselves. They also serve as digital publics, substituting for the types of publics that most adults took for granted growing up, but are now inaccessible for many people — neighborhood basketball courts, malls, parks, etc.—and allow them spaces *where they can escape adult culture* [emphasis added].
>
> (Ibid.)

I ask readers to make note of boyd's remarks because they are important to my discussion of how we supervise student spaces in Chapter 5.

35   Because of its more elitist status and the fact that its enrolment is popular with so called brighter and more educated youngsters, prospective employers have begun to check applicant's profiles on Facebook to see what kinds of friends they have; how much they drink (as evidenced by photographs of themselves either posted or tagged by friends); what kinds of personal conversation they have with friends on their walls; how they generally dress, behave and so on (Sankey, 2007).

36   As more teens join Facebook, this social networking web site has run into problems relating to high school and middle school students posting anti-authority cyber-expression about teachers and school officials. What is surprising is that many of the kids who post the online comments argue that their conversations should not be accessed by adults (even if those adults are on Facebook and can see their postings through other people's profiles). This fuels the debate about private and public spaces, and the argument by students that they are not 'wilfully bullying' their teachers but simply having conversations among themselves that are not meant for their teachers' or school officials' eyes. They argue that they do not intend to harass, threaten and generally bully their teachers and that they have every right to a free conversation. I return to an analysis of these issues later in the book. In the meantime, other networks, such as YouTube, are also drawing their share of problems.

37   YouTube allows for the downloading of videos for all to see. Internationally, YouTube has caught on as a site where all kinds of videotapes can be posted. In some cases videotapes are modified and placed on YouTube. Examples include videotaping student fights, filming peers undressing in gym changing rooms and washrooms; filming angry teachers in classrooms; and students dancing at a school dance (Roher, 1997).

38   Other social networking tools include Orkut, the equivalent of MySpace in India, and Freevote.com. Using Freevote.com, students can set up a web page for an individual school that permits students to vote on issues at their school. Although the philosophy is positive, this site also allows students to make personal, degrading and offensive anonymous comments about others. Similarly, RateMyTeacher.com and RateMyProfessor.com sometimes invite vitriolic comments when students are angry with teachers or professors for a variety of reasons. Bebo.com is popular in New Zealand, Australia, the UK and Ireland and contains categories such as 'people search', 'background check', 'find friends', 'find people', 'chat room', 'black dating', 'photo album', 'online photo albums'. Although it is important that the web site has background checks, Bebo has also had its share of young people engaging in cyber-bullying on its site.

39   These online social networking tools are both public and private to a limited extent, opening up important debates about which stakeholders have the authority (and responsibility) to intervene in cyberspace to monitor young people's social communications. The jury is still out on this issue as the courts have yet to provide clear direction on these issues. The social communications networks present an exception to the anonymity of cyber-bullying, because the names of those who post comments can be made visible and accessed by others who join the same network. Because of the overwhelming global reaction to

these social communication networks, I deal with them in upcoming chapters through detailed analysis, because it is through these issues that we can sift through and tease out some of the boundaries of responsibility that at present remain unclear.

ONLINE SEXUAL DISCRIMINATION

40 In 2005, I wrote several articles and book chapters with a graduate student, Rachel Gouin, on the prevalence of sexual and homophobic harassment in cyberspace. I reiterate here some of the findings we reported. This form of cyber-bullying is largely influenced by both biology (hormonal and prepubescent influences) and environment (gender socialization).

41 The research suggests that, although both genders engage in cyber-bullying, there are differences (Chu, 2005; Li, 2005). It has been argued that children who engage in any form of bullying are victims. They are influenced by biological and environmental forces, including intersecting and interlocking systemic barriers of oppression based on race, gender, sexual orientation, (dis)abilities, cultural hegemony, androcentrism and Eurocentrism, that continue to pervade many institutions, including schools and courts (Razack, 1998; Shariff, 2003). I expand on these influences in Chapter 4.

42 Numerous scholars have written about online gender harassment (Brail, 1996; Finn, 2004; Cáti *et al.*, 2002; Herring, 2002; McCormick and Leonard, 1996). Some have outlined categories such as gender harassment, unwanted sexual attention and sexual coercion (Barak, 2005). Others have written about virtual rape (Dibbell, 1993; MacKinnon, 2001), cyberstalking (Adam, 2001; 2002; Spitzberg and Hoobler, 2002; Tavani and Grodzinsky, 2002), identity theft (Finn and Banach, 2000), cyber-bullying (Shariff, 2004; Ybarra and Mitchell, 2004a,b) and cyber-violence more generally (Herring, 2002). The studies highlighted below illuminate ways in which gender-based cyber-bullying or violence differs from, and is linked to, what occurs in physical (non-virtual) space.

Female Victims

43 Barak (2005) defines three categories of sexual harassment:

1. gender harassment;
2. unwanted sexual attention; and
3. sexual coercion.

She divides the first category into four subcategories:

1. active verbal sexual harassment, which includes offensive sexual messages from harasser to victim, gender humiliating comments and sexual remarks;
2. passive verbal sexual harassment, which includes offensive nicknames and online identities (such as wetpussy, xlargetool);
3. active graphic gender harassment, which includes unwanted erotic and pornographic content through mail or posting in online environments; and
4. passive graphic gender harassment, including pictures and movies published on pornographic sites (such as forced pop-up windows).

The second category, unwanted sexual attention, 'refers to uninvited behaviours that explicitly communicate sexual desires or intentions toward another individual' (ibid., p. 78). Finally, sexual coercion entails the use of various online means to pressure the victim into sexual co-operation. Even though the use of force is not possible online, the threats can be perceived by the victim as being as realistic as a face-to-face situation. This is illustrated by the telephone threat that caused Canadian teenager Dawn Marie Wesley to commit suicide. The words 'You're f—g dead!' from a classmate caused her to believe real harm would come to her. Her perpetrator was convicted of criminal harassment because the court observed that perceived harm by the victim amounts to the same thing as actual harm (Shariff, 2004).

44   This perspective that electronic threats are as real as, or even more frightening than, those made face-to-face, is supported by Herring (2002), who explains that online behaviour that leads to assault against the physical, psychological or emotional well-being of an individual or group in effect constitutes a form of violence. She distinguishes four types of cyber-violence:

1. online contact leading to offline abuse (misrepresentation leading to fraud, theft, unwanted sexual contact);
2. cyber stalking, which comprises online monitoring or tracking of users' actions with criminal intent;
3. online harassment, which consists of unwanted, repeated and deliberate threats, abuses and alarms; and
4. degrading online representations of women through words or images that invite disrespect or put-downs.

Adam (2001) observes that cyber-violence studies disclose that the majority of perpetrators are men and the majority of victims are women. He reports that as many as one in of three female children reported having been harassed online in 2001 alone. Among children, girls appear to be targeted twice as much as boys (Finkelhor *et al.*, 2000).

45   According to Herring (2002), 25 per cent of Internet users aged ten to seventeen were exposed to unwanted pornographic images in the past year. Eight per cent of the images involved violence, in addition to sex and nudity. The Alberta study of middle school children referred to earlier (Li, 2005) disclosed that boys owned up to cyber-bullying more frequently and girls were more frequently victimized. Furthermore, Mitchell *et al.* (2001, as cited in Barak, 2005), in a survey of American teenagers, found that 19 per cent of these youths (mostly older girls) had experienced at least one sexual solicitation online in the preceding year.

Female Perpetrators

46 Although girls may be more likely targets of cyber-violence because of their location along a hierarchy of power, adolescent girls are increasingly surfacing as active instigators of cyber-bullying. Although Ybarra and Mitchell (2004a) found that males and females were equally likely to report having harassed someone online, a recent study of 3,700 adolescents (Kowalski, as cited in Chu [2005]) found that, in a two-month period, 17 per cent of the girls surveyed confessed to

online bullying compared with 10 per cent of the boys. Given that girls aged twelve to eighteen have been found to spend at least 74 per cent of their time on chat rooms or instant messaging (Berson *et al.*, 2002), this is not surprising. It is even less surprising when considered in the context of the biological and environmental (socializing) influences that are addressed in Chapter 4.

47   Given that preliminary research on cyber-bullying discloses a significant amount of sexual harassment and gender differences in the way Internet harassment is carried out, we cannot ignore the role of gender and its manifestations of online violence. Later, I will present examples and statistics that impact and motivate young men and women and show how this in turn affects learning environments (both physical and virtual). These examples will set the stage for introductions of judicial and legislative responses to legal claims of sexual harassment in cyberspace in later chapters. For now, it is important to note that, although girls and women appear to be the primary targets in cyberspace, sufficient research suggests that girls, internationally, are increasingly found to perpetrate cyber-bullying in groups and are more frequent users of social networking tools.

Male Targets and Perpetrators

48   Sexual orientation also features heavily in general and cyber-bullying. Cases of general bullying include the devastating suicide of Hamed Nastoh, the pouring of acid and four-year-long homophobic bullying of Azmi Jubran by his classmates at Handsworth High school. In Azmi's case, his perpetrators retestified at the human rights tribunal that, when friends are teased about being gay, it is a term of endearment; however, when the insult is directed at someone who is disliked, the words are meant to hurt. Based on the persistent, long drawn out and deliberate nature of homophobic bullying endured by Azmi Jubran and David Knight, the words were meant to hurt. In David Knight's case, he was described as a homosexual paedophile, with invitations to an infinite audience to write insults and comments below his photograph.

49   A study conducted by Tolman *et al.* (2001) at the middle school level in the United States made important observations relating to sexual harassment and homophobic bullying at the adolescent level. What they found was that sexual harassment significantly increased at pre-adolescence and adolescence. It was largely perpetrated by male students, who also engaged in homophobic bullying of their less aggressive male peers. Tolman *et al.* suggest two reasons — first, the raging hormones and interest in females and second, the need by adolescent males to prove their manhood. In doing so they engage in sexual harassment of females and put down males who are either perceived to be competitors or perceived to have more 'feminine' characteristics, resulting in the homophobic bullying. These issues are addressed in greater detail in Chapter 4.

Intersecting Forms of Discrimination

50   To complicate matters, in each of the cases discussed here, it is not simply the sexual orientation that invites the derision. Each of the victims I have mentioned

were teased for something else as well — in Hamed and Azmi's case, it was the fact that they were also of Iranian heritage, although both were born in Canada. In David Knight's case, his intelligence and good looks might have played a role. In Ghislain Reza's case, his weight certainly played a role.

THE INTERNATIONAL CONTEXT

51   Although there have been limited studies over the last few years, and many new studies have either yet to be completed or are emerging as this book goes to print, it is nonetheless important to summarize them here, and underscore the fact that cyber-bullying is emerging as a global concern. Although significant media and research attention has been paid to addressing it in countries such as Britain, New Zealand, the Netherlands, Australia, the United States and Canada, research in South Asia is just getting underway, as the use of technologies begins to proliferate among young people in those countries. My own research project, which includes collaborators in Japan, India, China, New Zealand, Australia and the United Kingdom (www.cyberbullying.co.nr/) is a two-year project that will culminate in a conference in New Zealand in July 2008 to disseminate findings. For the purposes of this book I present preliminary data as they trickle in from my international colleagues and research assistants in Japan, India and China, and also briefly discuss what is taking place in the West. The South Asian countries are interesting from the perspective of understanding the impact that technologies are having on their respective cultures and the way in which their young people are beginning to break traditional roles through online communication.

NOTES

13. Seventy-five per cent of Americans interviewed thought school shootings were likely to happen in their community.

14. These authors also agree that most young people who engage in crime are not dangerous. They engage in petty thefts, break and enter or play truant from school.

15. Providing American statistics, he notes that, in 1992 and 1993, a total of seventy-six students were murdered or committed suicide at school — an average of about thirty-eight a year. Six years later, a total of sixty-nine students suffered school-associated, violent deaths (murder and suicide) in a two-year period. The number also decreased 40 per cent from 1998 to 1999, from forty-three to twenty-six. DiGiulio argues that, when compared with the rate of youth murders occurring outside the school context, in 1992–1993 young persons between the ages of five and nineteen were over 100 times more likely to be murdered away from school than in school according to a report from the Office of Juvenile Justice and Delinquency Prevention.

16. This is a result of the baby-boomers having children.

17. Doob et al. (1995) observe, for example, that, whereas previously schoolyard fights were simply reported to school administrators, they are now more frequently reported to police.

REFERENCES

Adam, A. (2001). Cyberstalking: Gender and computer ethics. In E. Green and A. Adam (eds), *Virtual gender: Technology, consumption and identity*. New York: Routledge, pp. 209–24.

Adam, A. (2002). Cyberstalking and internet pornography: Gender and the gaze. *Ethics and Information Technology*, 4: 133–42.

Agence France Presse (2007). Foreign students don't fear backlash. *The Gazette*: A4.

Barak, A. (2005). Sexual harassment on the Internet. *Social Science Computer Review*, 23(1): 77–92.

Belsey, B. (2005). Internet usage: Facts and news. Web page. Retrieved 8 July 2005 from www.cyberbullying.ca/facts_st.html.

Berson, I. R., Berson, M. J. and Ferron, J. M. (2002). Emerging risks of violence in the digital age: Lessons for educators from an online study of adolescent girls in the United States. *Journal of School Violence*, 1(2): 51–71.

Boulton, M. (1993). A comparison of adults' and children's abilities to distinguish between aggressive and playful fighting in middle school pupils. Implications for playground supervision and behaviour management. *Educational Studies*, 19(3): 193–203.

boyd, d. and Jenkins, H. (2006). MySpace and Deleting Online Predators Act (DOPA) [electronic version]. *MIT Tech Talk*, 26 May. Retrieved 13 August 2007 from www.danah.org/papers/MySPaceDOPA.html.

Brail, S. (1996). The price of admission: Harassment and free speech in the wild, wild west. In L. Cherny and E. R. Weise (eds), *Wired women: Gender and new realities in cyberspace*. Toronto, ON: Seal Press.

Campbell, M. (2005). Cyberbullying: An old problem in a new guise? *Australian Journal of Guidance and counselling*, 15(1): 68–76.

Chu, J. (2005). You wanna take this online? Cyberspace is the 21st century bully's playground where girls play rougher than boys. *Time, Canadian Edition*, 8 August: 42–3.

Devlin, A. (1997). Offenders at school: Links between school failure and aggressive behaviour. In D. Tattum and H. Graham (eds), *Bullying: Home, school and community*. London: David Fulton Publishers, pp. 149–58.

Dibbell, J. (1993). A rape in cyberspace or how an evil clown, a Haitian trickster spirit, two wizards, and a cast of dozens turned a database into a society. *Village Voice*, 21 December, 38: 36–42.

DiGiulio, R. C. (2001). *Educate, mediate, or litigate? What teachers, parents, and administrators must do about student behavior*. Thousand Oaks, CA: Corwin Press.

Dolmage, W. R. (2000). Lies, damned lies, and statistics: The media's treatment of youth violence. *Education and Law Journal*, 10: 1–46.

Doob, A. N., Marinos, V., Varma, K. N. and University of Toronto, Centre of Criminology (1995). *Youth crime and the youth justice system in Canada: A research perspective*. Toronto, ON: Centre of Criminology, University of Toronto.

Finkelhor, D., Mitchell, K. and Wolak, J. (2000). *Online victimization: A report on the nation's youth*. Retrieved 12 August 2007 from www.unh.edu/ccrc/pdf/Victimization_Online_Survey.pdf.

Finn, J. and Banach, M. (2000). Victimization online: The downside of seeking human services for women on the Internet. *Cyberpsychology and behaviour*, 3(5): 785–96.

Finn, J. (2004). A survey of online harassment at a university campus. *Journal of Interpersonal Violence, 19*: 468–83.

Gáti, A., Tényi, T., Túry, F. and Wildmann, M. (2002). Anorexia nervosa following sexual harassment on the Internet: A case report. *The International Journal of Eating Disorders, 31*(4): 474–7.

Harmon, A. (2004). Internet gives teenage bullies weapons to wound from afar [electronic version]. *New York Times*, 24 August. Retrieved 26 August 2004 from www.nytimes.com/2004/08/26/education.

Harris, M. (2007). Facebook is for 'good' kids – Myspace is for freaks. *The Gazette*, 29 June.

Henderson, N. R., Hymel, S., Bonanno, R. A. and Davidson, K. (2002). *Bullying as a normal part of school life: Early adolescents' perspectives on bullying and peer harassment*. Paper presented at the Safe Schools Safe Communities Conference (Poster session), Vancouver, British Columbia.

Herring, S. C. (2002). Cyberviolence, Recognizing and resisting abuse in online environments. *Asian Women*, 14: 187–212.

Lankshear, C. and Knobel, M. (2005). *Digital literacies: Policy, pedagogy and research considerations for education*. Opening plenary address. Paper presented at the ITU Conference, Oslo, Norway. Retrieved 9 August 2007 from www.geocities.com/c.lankshear/Oslo.pdf.

Leishman, J. (2002). Cyber-bullying: The Internet is the latest weapon in a bully's arsenal [electronic version]. *CBC News. The National*, 10 October. Retrieved 27 January 2003 from http://cbc.ca/news/national/news/cyberbullying/index.html.

Li, Q. (2005). Cyber-bullying in schools: The nature and extent of adolescents' experience. Paper presented at the American Education Research Association (AERA) Conference, Montreal.

MacKinnon, R. (2001). Virtual rape. *Journal of Computer Mediated Communication, 2*(4): n.p.

McCormick, N. and Leonard, J (1996). Gender and sexuality in the cyberspace frontier. *Women and Therapy, 19*(4): 109–19.

McLuhan, M. (1964). *Understanding media: The extensions of man*. New York: Mentor.

Media Awareness Network (2005). Kids' online activities: Key findings [electronic version]. *Young Canadians in a wired world: Key findings*. Retrieved 10 January 2006 from www.mediaawareness.ca/english/resources/special_initiatives/survey_resources/students_survey/key_findings/kids_online_key_findings.cfm.

Patchkin, J. and Hinduja, S. (2006). Bullies move beyond the schoolyard: A preliminary look at cyberbullying. *Youth Violence and Juvenile Justice*, 4(2): 148–69.

Razack, S. (1998). *Looking white people in the eye: Gender, race, and culture in courtrooms and classrooms*. Toronto, ON: University of Toronto Press.

Roher, E. (1997). *An Educator's Guide to Violence in Schools*. Toronto, ON: Canada Law Books.

Salmivalli, C. (2001). Group view on victimization: empirical findings and their implications. In J. Juvonen and S. Graham (eds), *Peer harassment in school: The plight of the vulnerable and victimized*. New York, London: Guilford Press, pp 398–419.

Sankey, D. (2007). Beware: Your prospective boss could see you naked on the Net. *The Gazette*, 18 July: B6.

Shariff, S. and Strong-Wilson, T. (2005). Bullying and new technologies: What can teachers do to foster socially responsible discourse in the physical and virtual school environments? In J. Kincheloe (ed.), *Classroom teaching: An introduction*. New York: Peter Lang Publishers, pp 219–40.

Shariff, S. (2003). A system on trial: Identifying legal standards for educational, ethical and legally defensible approaches to bullying in schools. Unpublished doctoral dissertation. Burnaby, BC: Simon Fraser University.

Shariff, S. (2004). Keeping schools out of court: Legally defensible models of leadership to reduce cyber-bullying. Educational Forum. *Delta Kappa Pi, 68*(3): 222–3.

Smith, W.J. (2004). Balancing security and human rights: Quebec schools between past and future. *Education and Law Journal, 14*(1): 99–136.

Snider, M. (2004). Stalked by a cyberbully. *Maclean's*, 24 May, *117*:76.

Soloyon, C. (2005). A gift from the devil: Worry about on-line activities. *The Gazette*, 2 February: A2.

Spitzberg, B. and Hoobler, G. (2002). Cyberstalking and the technologies of interpersonal terrorism. *New Media and Society, 4*: 71–92.

Tanner, J. (1996). *Teenage troubles: Youth and deviance in Canada*. Toronto, ON: Nelson Canada.

Tavani, H. and Grodinsky, F. (2002). Cyberstalking, personal privacy, and moral responsibility. *Ethics and Information Technology, 4*: 123–32.

Tolman, D. L., Spencer, R., Rosen-Reynoso, M. and Porches, M. (2001). 'He's the man!' Gender ideologies and early adolescents' experiences with sexual harassment. Paper presented at the American Educational Researchers Association (AERA) Conference, Seattle, Washington.

Willard, N. (2003). Off-campus, harmful online student speech. *Journal of School Violence, 1*(2): 65–93.

Willard, N. (2005). Educator's guide to cyber bullying: Addressing the harm caused by online social cruelty [electronic version]. Retrieved 10 December 2005 from www.cyberbullying.org.

Ybarra, M. L. and Mitchell, K. J. K., Finkelhor, D. and Wolak, J (2007). Internet prevention messages: Targeting the right online behaviors. *Archives of Pediatric and Adolescent Medicine, 161*(2): 138–45.

Active Reading

1. Summarize Shariff's text in 250 words organized around the similarities and differences between cyber-bullying and face-to-face bullying.

2. Why are bullies less likely to feel empathy for their victims when the bullying is done online than when it is done face-to-face?

3. How does the anonymity of cyber-bullying create a hostile environment in the physical space of the school?

4. Explain why Shariff does not see cyber-bullying as simply an extension of traditional bullying, but rather a new phenomenon with distinctive causes, characteristics, and effects.

Critical Reading

1. How does Shariff use stories and references to the popular press (for example, news stories and Wikipedia articles) to advance her argument? Have you encountered instructors who forbid the use of such evidence in your own essays? Why would Shariff have made use of sources that she might prohibit in her own students' writing?

2. Unlike face-to-face bullying, cyber-bullying does not involve a possibility of direct physical harm (although it may involve threats of subsequent physical harm). Yet victims of cyber-bullying have committed suicide. What unique characteristics of cyber-bullying might account for its devastating effects?

3. The author points out that the internet is often blamed for the occurrence of cyber-bullying, and she invokes the Canadian communications theorist Marshall McLuhan's famous phrase "The medium is the message" in arguing that the medium is merely the vehicle for the message. Do you agree with her position?

4. Discuss the behaviour of cyber-bullies with reference to the psychology of group mentality as discussed in the readings in Chapter 10.

A Human Rights Approach to Stopping Homophobic Bullying in Schools

Catherine Taylor

Catherine Taylor is Associate Professor at the University of Winnipeg, where she is cross-appointed to the Faculty of Education and the Department of Rhetoric, Writing, and Communications. She did her Ph.D. in cultural studies and critical pedagogy at the University of Toronto. Her interest in the field of anti-oppressive education is reflected in her courses, "Critical Pedagogy and Student Diversity" and "Critical Literacy for Empowerment." She has published widely on issues of social justice, such as research ethics, refusals of empathy, and anti-homophobia education. She was principal investigator for the First National Climate Survey of Homophobia in Canadian Schools, which reported on students' perceptions and experiences of homophobic elements in their high schools.

In this article, Taylor examines the process by which Winnipeg School Division overcame public controversy about implementing anti-homophobia education in its 80 schools by systematically insisting that opposing homophobia was synonymous with defending human rights.

ABSTRACT. *This article examines the development of Winnipeg School Division's groundbreaking program to oppose homophobic bullying by making that struggle synonymous with the defence of human rights. The analysis draws on interviews with key players in the development of the program, committee minutes, newspaper accounts, workshop evaluations and court rulings. The Division's approach involves a range of actions, the mainstay of which is compulsory workshops for all employees, and is supported by various initiatives undertaken by stakeholders outside the Division. The article assesses the strategic merits of the Division's human rights approach to stopping homophobic bullying and argues that curriculum development is still required to achieve the full potential of that approach.*

1   The effects of homophobic bullying have been well documented in studies that show disproportionately high levels of depression, dropping out, suicidal ideation and suicide attempts among queer teenagers (GLSEN, 2004; Kosciw & Diaz, 2005; Morrison & L'Heareux, 2001), and a correspondingly high incidence of school-based homophobic experiences that include name-calling, threats, social and curricular exclusion, cultural and religious-based condemnation, and physical assault (Human Rights Watch, 2001; Kosciw & Diaz, 2005; McFarland, 2001; Plummer, 1999). This article examines the development of a groundbreaking initiative in a large school division in Winnipeg, Canada, now in its eighth year, where grassroots provocation led to the establishment of a program to oppose homophobic bullying by making that struggle synonymous with the defence of human rights. I draw on interviews with key players in the development of the initiative, committee minutes, newspaper accounts, workshop evaluations, and recent court rulings as a way to assess the strategic merits of addressing the problem of homophobic bullying through a human rights framework.[1]

2   The flagship of Winnipeg School Division's (WSD) initiative is a "Human Rights/Anti-Homophobia" workshop for all current and incoming staff. This key strategy is complemented by other Division initiatives and by those of other stakeholders in the educational community, including library resources, Gay-Straight Alliance groups (GSAs), professional development workshops and conferences, pre-service teacher education, and online resources. Despite this system-wide effort by diversely situated stakeholders to fight homophobia, the Division has not yet mandated anti-homophobia content for the curriculum. I argue that development of anti-homophobia curriculum is legally, logically, and ethically supported by the human rights framework and that a radically effective program to stop homophobic bullying must ultimately engage students at the level of everyday classroom experience.

BACKGROUND

3   Winnipeg is a city of 700,000 in a province of 1.1 million people. Winnipeg School Division is a system of 77 schools covering kindergarten through high school, with over 5000 employees and 33,000 students (WSD, 2006a). As an urban division, WSD brings together people of different ethnicities, cultures, religions, and sexual and gender identities. WSD also has a large population of Aboriginal people and of people living in poverty (WSD, 2006a). All of this provides opportunities for openness to diversity but also potential for conflicts.

4   The city has both progressive and conservative qualities. For example, in 1999, when WSD tackled the issue of anti-homophobia education, Winnipeg had elected and would re-elect Glenn Murray, an openly gay man as mayor. But River East, a school division adjacent to WSD, had since 1989 been prohibiting classroom discussion of homosexuality (along with abortion, birth control, and masturbation) and directing teachers to send students with questions about homosexuality to counseling (Marlowe, 1999).

5   The impetus for the initiative came in spring 1999 when a group of students, upset that some principals were refusing to allow the staging of a play about homophobic bullying, approached Kristine Barr, a Trustee of the Division, asking, "The Board of Trustees is supposed to protect our rights. What are you going to do about it?" Barr, an out lesbian who had stood for election to the Board in part because she recognized the need for anti-homophobia education, asked the Board to strike a large, broad-based committee of trustees, students, parents, teachers, and other community members to advise the Board on the development of anti-homophobia education for WSD classrooms. The Board formed a "Special Committee on Anti-homophobia Education," not to proceed outright with development, but to identify the need for such education, areas where it might be appropriate, and existing models.

6   Public uproar ensued, fanned by inflammatory talk-radio rhetoric claiming that the Special Committee would be stacked in favour of the development. At its next meeting, the Board turned the matter over to its standing Policy/ Program Committee. Although Barr later regretted how that move distanced the Board from grassroots support for curriculum development, at the time she believed it would effectively bypass public controversy and supported assigning the issue to the more powerful Board committee. Meanwhile, a grassroots committee, the "Coalition for Anti-homophobia Resources and Education" (CARE) organized. Consisting of people who would have been the natural constituency for the disbanded Special Committee, it strategized about how best to represent the cause in what had become a volatile situation.

7   The Board held hearings every two weeks to which the public were invited to make presentations, with attendance averaging 500 people. Many delegations spoke for the motion, including teachers, academics, religious leaders, parents, and students, who presented strong and often eloquent arguments. What consistently made the headlines, however, was the vehement opposition expressed by adherents to conservative faith traditions who were bussed in from suburban and rural churches. The behaviour of religious homophobes became so threatening that police were called to escort delegates speaking in favour of the proposal. Their behaviour descended to the level of screaming in the face of an eight-year-old girl that her lesbian mother was prostituting her (Martin, 1999).

8   Meanwhile, the CARE committee was holding to the strategy discussed in their founding meeting, of upholding civil discourse and "appeal[ing] to the best in people" by keeping to the message, "It could be your kid." Its strategy was simple:

> It is important to remain strong in our presence at the school board meetings. . . . We must agree to do the whole meeting "by the book." By not falling into the clapping, noise making, etc. we will be seen as the sane and reasonable ones. . . . Keep the message solid—whatever the others are saying, don't take the bait. We want safe and accepting places for our youth to go to school. . . . When doing media interviews, remember that we are not, for the most part, talking to the trustees or to the fringe right, we are speaking to the average person sitting at home over dinner in front of the tv set. (CARE minutes, April 21, 1999)

9   The tactical principle that homophobes do human rights supporters a favour by revealing the depth of their animosity proved true in this case. Trustees had

already been moved by LGBTTIQ students' accounts of homophobic bullying. Barr reported that some who had been wavering in their support changed their minds when they saw how ugly and aggressive the homophobia was. Karl Ridd, a Religious Studies professor who had spoken in support of the initiative told a reporter, "The meetings themselves had turned into a demonstration of the need for this" (Bray, 1999). The Board restricted future hearings to Division residents and implemented ongoing anti-homophobia training for all staff. It did so with some trepidation about further protest from religious groups, but there have been none in eight years.

10   The Board's deliberations concluded with a joint public statement from the Chair of the Policy/Program Committee and the Chief Superintendent of WSD equating anti-homophobia education with human rights education. They announced that workshops would be held "to ensure that the Board's expectations regarding harassment and racism are known and that existing policies are being enforced" (Santos & Smyth, 1999). However, they stated categorically that "At no time has the Board of Trustees agreed to including anti-homophobia education in the school curriculum."

11   Thus, "anti-homophobia" education as embraced by WSD had been boldly defined as "human rights" education and less boldly as *not* change and *not* curriculum. Although the CARE committee kept up its efforts to persuade the Board to mandate or at least sponsor the development of anti-homophobia curriculum materials, it was unsuccessful.

THE HUMAN RIGHTS/ANTI-HOMOPHOBIA EQUATION

12   WSD had long been committed to creating safe schools where diverse children learn in an atmosphere of respect for cultural differences, and the Division had human rights policies in place. However, protection on the grounds of sexual orientation was not explicit and staff were not reading it in, with the result that homophobic insults were being dismissed as harmless, or "not even meaning gay." By making the "Human Rights/Anti-Homophobia" equation explicit, WSD tied the initiative to a noble principle with the force of law.

13   When the Canadian *Charter of Rights and Freedoms* was proclaimed in 1982 it did not specify same-sex rights, but since that time a succession of Supreme Court of Canada decisions had resulted in "sexual identity" having been legally read into the meaning of "sex" in the *Charter*. As a result, by 1999, there were few lawful grounds for discrimination on the basis of sexual identity in Canada. Discriminatory laws and Human Rights Codes across the country were being judged unconstitutional and amended to include sexual identity, including the *Canadian Human Rights Act*.[2] WSD had also brought its own sexual harassment policy into line with the Manitoba provincial Human Rights Code in 1994 to include sexual orientation. Thus, when the Board took up the anti-homophobia issue in 1999, it did so in the context of a federal, provincial, and divisional human rights legal framework that already supported the principle of protecting people from homophobic bullying.

14   That framework is a powerful tool in the struggle against homophobia. But at every level it has to be explicitly attached to homophobia since people working in heterosexist systems do not make the connection. The importance of explicit inclusion is underscored by GLSEN's (2004) finding that anti-bullying policies tend to be ineffective in reducing homophobic bullying because they do not provide educators with clear guidance or even a sense of professional responsibility to act. GLSEN (2005) found further that students report being bullied less often and are more likely to inform authorities of bullying incidents in schools that specifically include sexual orientation in their harassment policies. Further evidence that attachment to LGBT-inclusive human rights legislation is not enough to produce anti-homophobic school policies is River East (now River East Transcona), the division that prohibits discussing homosexuality in class. Its policy documents seldom specify any grounds of discrimination, perhaps to avoid having to include sexual orientation, but when they do become specific, the categories are racism, sexual harassment, and respect for different cultures. At no point do River East Transcona's policies acknowledge the existence of homophobic bullying or LGBTTIQ people, even though its Human Rights policy states (as by law it must) that it "believes in the principle of human rights as identified in the Manitoba Human Rights Code, [and] the Canadian Charter of Rights and Freedoms" (River East, 2007).

15   After the hearings, WSD undertook a number of actions to make the Human Rights/Anti-Homophobia equation explicit. It gives sexual identity the same status as other forms of diversity in all its key policies, including human rights, employment equity, harassment, hiring, recruitment, and staff abuse. WSD's (2006b) *Code of Conduct* requires not only staff and students but parents and guardians to "show common courtesy and respect to all, regardless of race, religion, gender, age, or sexual orientation."

16   In making opposition to homophobia explicit, the Board of WSD seized the ethical authority for anti-homophobia education that is afforded, but not automatically conferred, by the human rights framework. In that strategic intervention, it acquired a powerful shield from public criticism of anti-homophobia education and moved the debate from whether or not LGBTTIQ people have morally defensible lifestyles to whether or not Division employees are prepared to defend the law and fulfill their obligations.

WSD PROGRAM COMPONENTS

17   WSD's public articulations have been important in signaling its ethical and legal authority to oppose homophobia. Nevertheless, the slow pace of progress in achieving compliance with women's rights and anti-segregation law illustrate the socio-cultural lag between new ideas and laws on the one hand and widespread social change on the other (Brinkman & Brinkman, 1997). Prejudices are difficult to dislodge because they are reinforced by so many social institutions and practices (McCaskell, 2005). New laws need not only to be explained and enforced but reinforced with knowledge and experiences that allow people to integrate change into their lives and adjust their beliefs.

18   McCaskell and Russell (2000) describe the system-wide efforts undertaken in Toronto, Canada, to help staff and students of the former Toronto Board of Education unlearn homophobia and heterosexism, ranging from developing curriculum materials for optional use to having Division staff participate in the annual Pride parade. Capacity-building in WSD's case involves similarly diverse efforts to reach every person in the system. Importantly, WSD's capacity-building efforts are not a top-down engineered product but the accrual of many initiatives from stakeholders across the system inside and outside the Division hierarchy. This range of sites and initiators brings the advantages of authenticity, broad-based investment and ownership, mutual support, and autonomy; it would be impossible to undo the capacity by unilateral directive.

Mandatory Workshops

19   The main plank of the WSD program is a workshop for all employees including administrators and secretaries, teachers and resource consultants, counselors and psychologists, bus drivers, engineers and pipe fitters, cafeteria staff, janitors and groundskeepers. The workshops put homophobia squarely in the context of human rights legislation and anti-harassment policies with the clear message that employees have a legal and professional obligation to combat homophobic intolerance and discrimination. Because of time constraints, the workshops are conducted in a 2.5 hour session, relying on lecture format.

20   As conventional as the instructional method employed is, the workshop is a radically capacity-building initiative. First, it attaches the fight against homophobia to the defence of human rights. Second, no matter what their job, employees know they are important in the capacity-building effort and that the Division will support them when they act against homophobic bullying.

21   The workshop is also the Division's most authoritarian initiative. It is mandatory. It lays down the law by invoking the power of federal and provincial legislation and professional ethics. It provides no avenue of escape or room for dissent. Whatever their personal beliefs, workshop participants know it is their professional responsibility and legal obligation to support the policy. Conflict with religious beliefs is specifically addressed as not being grounds for exemption; people are told that they are not being asked to change their beliefs, but they are being required to treat everyone with full and equal respect. Paradoxically, the mandatory status of the requirement has quelled opposition by providing religiously-opposed people with a way of resolving an otherwise painful conflict with their conscience.

22   Even with the pedagogical limitations of a half-day format and mandatory attendance, the workshop seems to have been positively received by the vast majority of the 6000+ employees who had participated by April 2005. The Division reports positive feedback from nine out of ten participants (WSD, 2005) with evaluation comments like: "a valuable presentation that will change what happens in schools over time"; "very useful for first year employees—reinforces the responsibility and accountability employees have within the school environment"; "thank you for the powerful messages—they really made me think"; "I feel very proud to work

for such a progressive, respectful division." Most learned valuable information, had not thought about the issue carefully before, and felt they now had a clear rationale for intervening against homophobic intolerance and discrimination.

23   Although there is permission to implement anti-homophobia education into one's teaching, there is no advice offered on how to do it. The closest the workshop comes to teaching technique is GLSEN's excellent one-page handout, "How to Handle Harassment in the Hallways in 3 Minutes!" Further, while the workshops correctly identify teachers as key players in the production and disruption of homophobic school culture, there is nothing in the workshops that necessarily leads to the classroom apart from interventions to disrupt bullying. Homosexuality is still unspoken in front of the children.

WSD Resource Development

24   The second plank of the WSD program is resource development. The cash-strapped Division allotted $25,000 or $300 per school library for anti-homophobia and LGBTTIQ-inclusive books. Between 15 to 25 age-appropriate titles are now available to every student in every school. WSD has also developed a strong collection of books and videos on anti-homophobia education for teaching and counseling staff. Once again, the Division asserts the Human Rights/Anti-Homophobia connection by categorizing these resources as part of its larger human rights collection. Other resources include a Human Rights/Anti-Homophobia poster, which is displayed throughout schools and administration buildings, and a pamphlet distributed to all students.

25   In 2002, the Division produced a 225 page *Human Rights/Anti-homophobia Resource Guide* and provided it to administrators of every school. It covers human rights obligations, the obligation to participate regardless of personal beliefs, information about LGBT people, and guidelines for starting a GSA. Importantly, the guide provides extensive advice on how to respond to incidents of name-calling and other homophobic assaults by applying strategies of "zero indifference." No administrator in WSD can say that he or she is unaware of the obligation to work at creating an anti-homophobia school culture or how to go about doing that. However, while the guide says that teachers should look for opportunities to integrate LGBT-inclusive or anti-homophobic content into the curriculum, it offers no advice on how to do this or where to find teaching resources.

PROGRAM COMPONENTS IN THE BROADER COMMUNITY

26   While WSD situated its work within the Human Rights/Anti-Homophobia framework, community and university educators have been working on their own initiatives.

27   The two-person staff of the local Rainbow Resource Centre has been involved in many of these efforts, organizing the CARE coalition, making presentations, facilitating workshops, co-organizing conferences, facilitating a curriculum website project, and securing federal government funding to finance their work. Centre staff members also conduct compulsory anti-homophobia education

workshops for all University of Manitoba Education faculty and students. These workshops share the same time limitation as the Division ones, but they send a similarly strong message about institutional values.

28   It is crucial to reach teacher education students in order to get the message to passive supporters among them that their active support is needed, and to challenge those who are opposed to same-sex rights before they embark on their careers with their prejudices intact (Taylor, 2002; 2004). At the University of Winnipeg, I have integrated intensive work on anti-homophobia education into my courses, as have a few other people. Because the courses are elective, students can still become teachers without having encountered the issue. That being said, the efforts of the Education faculties and WSD are mutually supportive. Professors can explain that anti-homophobia education is policy in WSD, where most education students will be employed, and the WSD program is strengthened as new teachers are certified with a background in anti-homophobia education.

29   Other efforts are involved where stakeholders support the Division initiatives and derive resources, encouragement, and legitimacy from each other's work. Gay-Straight Alliances have formed at the Division's high schools, providing an empowering network and contributing to the creation of an anti-homophobic school culture (Lee, 2002). Several "Envisioning Equality" conferences for educators and students have been held with the support of the Education faculties, the Manitoba Teachers Society, and the Rainbow Resource Centre. Educators working with the Centre and supported by a grant from the Teachers Society have organized to identify teaching resources and make them available through their website (helpingout.ca).

LESSONS FROM THE WINNIPEG APPROACH

30   Winnipeg's multi-pronged approach was supported by federal and provincial human rights legislation but was not masterminded by government decree. Although its components support each other in practice, it has not been coordinated by an agency and developed organically from several parts of the education community. What lessons can be drawn from the Winnipeg case?

1. Appealing to the legal framework gives authorities support when they encounter resistance, or fear they will.
2. Homophobic bullying must be made an explicit part of bullying and harassment policies because most people will not read it in.
3. Much can be done through local efforts without massive funding. The most expensive initiative, the workshops, was financed without hiring by making use of existing personnel.
4. Relationships with key individuals should be nurtured. Although dozens of people participated in developing the WSD initiative and thousands are affected, it was achieved largely because of the efforts of a small number of people at a few key sites.
5. The power of empathy can change minds. Being right or logical or principled is less persuasive than the spectacle of someone in pain, particularly people for whom one has a fiduciary obligation. What most moved trustees

were the testimonies of LGBTTIQ students and the spectacle of them under attack by homophobic bullies.

6. Religious opposition is intense and ugly but not necessarily robust; anti-homophobia education does not require equally intense support. Polls show that most Canadians, especially young urban ones, think homophobia is wrong (CRIC, 2005). This may not constitute passionate commitment to the struggle, but perhaps it means that sexual identity has become a non-issue for many people. Barr was re-elected, as was Lori Johnston, the out lesbian trustee who chaired the Board during its tumultuous anti-homophobia hearings. As Winnipeg's anti-homophobia measures have been implemented, there has no doubt been some degree of grumbling, but no ongoing opposition.

31   Winnipeg is a mid-sized city in the prairie region where support for same-sex rights is lower than elsewhere in Canada (Robinson, 2005). In bigger and richer cities, such as Toronto and Vancouver, there are more anti-homophobia educators and better-funded activists. But Winnipeg's experience of implementing a capacity-building approach to anti-homophobia education was not duplicated anywhere else in the country until the Vancouver School Board (2006) recently moved to implement a similar system-wide professional development program. Elsewhere, school boards have limited their efforts to policy-making and resource provision. There might be curriculum materials available, but all components remain optional and no professional development is required. The Winnipeg experience would indicate that more ambitious capacity-building programs that undertake to transform school culture by insisting on human rights can be achieved without government edict, massive funds, or large activist populations.

HOMOPHOBIC BULLYING AS A LEGAL AND COMMUNITY ISSUE

32   Since the establishment of WSD's program in 1999, a number of high-profile court rulings have fortified the Division's legal position by confirming the obligation of school authorities to provide a learning environment free of homophobic bullying. Rulings have also made more explicit what this means for classroom teachers.

33   In Marc Hall's suit against Durham Catholic School Board (*Hall v. Powers*, 2002), the Ontario Superior Court ruled that the Board had no right to bar a gay student from attending prom with his boyfriend. This ruling is significant because it confirms WSD's position on the limits of freedom of religious expression when it comes to discrimination:

> If individuals in Canada were permitted to simply assert that their religious beliefs require them to discriminate against homosexuals, without objective scrutiny, there would be no protection at all from discrimination for gays and lesbians in Canada because everyone who wished to discriminate against them could make that assertion. (*Hall v. Powers*, 2002, para. 31)

The Supreme Court of Canada had already affirmed that religious freedom does not include freedom to discriminate in the case of *Trinity Western University* (2001), a fundamentalist Christian college in British Columbia that requires its students and teachers to pledge to refrain from homosexual activity on the grounds that it is a "sexual sin" and "biblically condemned" (¶ 4). In its decision, the Court ruled that teachers, like everyone else, are entitled to hold sexist, racist, or homophobic beliefs (¶ 36),[3] but not to act on them (¶ 37). In ruling that teachers can think what they like, but must treat every student equally and with respect, the Court referred to Section 15 of the *Charter of Rights and Freedoms* and the *Human Rights Code of British Columbia.*

34   The most significant and directly relevant ruling for homophobic bullying, though, is the landmark Jubran case (*School District No. 44*, 2005). School officials in North Vancouver had dealt with the homophobic bullying of a high school student by punishing his tormentors. The British Columbia (B.C.) Human Rights Tribunal, in a decision upheld by the B.C. Court of Appeal, found that while school officials had *re*acted appropriately to the bullying, they had failed to protect the student's constitutionally enshrined human rights to an education free of harassment by neglecting to take *pro*active measures to make school culture unhomophobic. To do that, they needed to have provided "resources to adopt a broader, educative approach to deal with the difficult issues of harassment, homophobia and discrimination" (¶ 96). In making its ruling, the Court of Appeal recognized that reactive measures, while important, leave undisturbed the larger homophobic culture that produces and rationalizes homophobic bullying in the first place.

35   Reactive measures can be seen as sufficient only in an individualistic model that presumes the problem of homophobia resides merely in whoever is showing symptoms of having it or suffering from contact with it, rather than in a culture that produces it. Homophobia is a community issue that involves the culture that tolerates and produces it, not just the individual who expresses it or becomes its target. The message from the courts to school officials is clear: "You are teachers; teach people about this."

36   The WSD initiatives, as important as they are, leave homophobia largely unchallenged in any proactive sense. Making homophobia explicit in school policies is important, but GLSEN's (2005) survey shows that the effect, while significant, does not prevent most homophobic bullying. WSD's workshops may embolden educators to do anti-homophobia education knowing that they have legal and administrative support, but they do not offer much to educators who recognize the importance of curriculum and want teaching support. As positive as response was to the workshops, teachers consistently commented in their evaluations that they left not knowing what to do in their classroom. Since need for curriculum is implied in WSD's Human Rights/Anti-Homophobia message, teachers are surprised when the workshop ends and it has not been addressed. Predictably, few teachers discuss LGBTTIQ issues in their classrooms.

37   The problem is not lack of curricular resources. Teaching units and materials including videos have been developed for implementation at all grade levels from kindergarten through high school, and resources are readily available through the websites of organizations such as GLSEN, GALE BC, and the Safe Schools Coalition. WSD's own library has a solid collection of teaching

resources, and basic principles of inclusive education can be readily adapted to anti-homophobia education (Taylor, 2003). The bottleneck preventing the widespread implementation of anti-homophobia curriculum is not that authorities do not know that it is important, or that pedagogical and curricular resources are unavailable, nor even lingering prejudice, but the reluctance of school authorities to mandate it for fear of public outcry.

38   This returns us to where Kristine Barr found herself in the spring of 1999: realizing that to fight homophobic bullying, we need to implement anti-homophobia curriculum. WSD seized an opportunity to fight homophobic bullying by linking it to human rights. The strategy has since been vindicated as legally, ethically, and politically sound by the many court decisions demanding that sexual identity be read into human rights policies. Ironically, the Division described as "leading the way" for Canadian school boards in 1999 (McCaskell, 2000) has fallen behind others (Egale, 2007b). The Vancouver School Board (2006), for instance, has developed a policy that promises to fulfill the spirit of the Jubran decision by explicitly mandating not only anti-homophobic but LGBT-positive curriculum and pledging to provide the appropriate resources and professional development.

39   Until WSD mandates a truly inclusive curriculum and provides teachers with the resources to develop professional competence in it, teachers can take advantage of teachable moments simply by intervening whenever homophobic incidents occur during class, while doing hallway and cafeteria monitoring, and at other times during the school day. Every one of WSD's 5200 employees has been taught how to do that in the Human Rights/Anti-Homophobia workshop. They can relay the information—news to many students—that homophobia has no place in a respectful community and will not be tolerated. But without a system-wide anti-homophobia curriculum in place, students will still be learning from their pointedly silent teachers that homophobic bullying is not all that bad, because "Human Rights" does not, after all is said and left unsaid, mean "Anti-Homophobia."

40   Homophobic bullying is the inevitable product of the pedagogy of institutional and popular culture: the countless messages from a variety of sources by which people are taught to condemn homosexuality, and the absolute demand to do so in certain pockets of society such as fundamentalist faith communities, hypermasculine sports, and, almost always and almost everywhere, the education system. LGBTTIQ people have achieved full legal equality in Canada and it is possible to live quite openly without experiencing much blatant discrimination. Most schools, however, are in the land that time forgot, where homosexuality is still the Victorian-era "love that dare not speak its name." Dislodging the homophobic student attitudes that have resulted from all of this formal and informal mis-education will take more than the spectacle of teachers scolding homophobic bullies with what, in the absence of an LGBTTIQ-positive counter-discourse, amounts to "Don't be mean to the fag."

NOTES

1. This study was approved by the Research Ethics Committees of Winnipeg School Division and the University of Winnipeg.

2. Transgender rights are currently less solidly entrenched because of the lack of court challenges to date but are often included in institutional human rights

policies such as WSD's, and activists are working to ensure that gender identity is ultimately read into human rights law (Egale, 2007a).

3. The Court also ruled that the B.C. College of Teachers was unjustified in barring graduates of the college from candidacy for teaching positions. The suit did not ask the Court to rule on whether the College was violating Human Rights law in discriminating against its own students on the grounds of sexual orientation.

REFERENCES

Bray, A. (1999, May 20). Debate rivals approve cooling off period. *Winnipeg Free Press*, A16.

Brinkman, R., & Brinkman, J. (1997). Cultural lag: Conception and theory. *International Journal of Social Economics, 24,* 609–627.

CRIC. (2005). New Canada revisited: July 1, 2004. Centre for Research and Information on Canada. Retrieved April 5, 2007, from http://www.cric.ca/pwp_re/new_canada/new_canada_2003_slides_eng.ppt#295,39,Homosexuality

Egale. (2007a). Background on human rights protection for trans people. Egale Canada. Retrieved April 19, 2007, from http://www.egale.ca/index.asp?lang=E&menu=34&item=1256

Egale. (2007b). Egale education webpage. Egale Canada. Retrieved April 5, 2007, from http://www.egale.ca/index.asp?lang=&menu=1&item=1350

GLSEN. (2004). *A state of the states report: A policy analysis of lesbian, gay, bisexual and transgender safer schools issues.* New York: Author. http://www.glsen.org/binary-data/GLSEN_ATTACHMENTS/file/338–3.PDF

GLSEN. (2005). *From teasing to torment: School climate in America, A survey of students and teachers.* New York: Author. Retrieved April 5, 2007, from http://www.glsen.org/binary-data/GLSEN_ATTACHMENTS/file/499–1.pdf

Hall v. Powers. (2002). Ontario Superior Court of Justice 1803. Retrieved April 5, 2007 from http://www.samesexmarriage.ca/docs/MacKinnon_Hall.pdf

Human Rights Watch. (2001). *Hatred in the hallways: Violence and discrimination against lesbian, gay, bisexual, and transgendered students in U.S. Schools.* Retrieved April 8, 2007 from http://www.hrw.org/reports/2001/uslgbt/toc.htm

Kosciw, J., & Diaz, E. (2005). *The 2005 national school climate survey: The experiences of lesbian, gay, bisexual and transgender youth in our nation's schools.* New York: Gay, Lesbian and Straight Education Network. Retrieved April 5, 2007, from http://www.glsen.org/binary-data/GLSEN_ATTACHMENTS/file/585-1.pdf

Lee, C. (2002, Feb/Mar). The impact of belonging to a high school Gay/Straight Alliance. *The High School Journal, 85*(3), 13–26.

Marlowe, T. (1999, Mar 7). Gay play ban defended. *Winnipeg Sun*, L3.

Martin, N. (1999, May 12). Meeting boils over, police called to school. *Winnipeg Free Press*, A1, A4.

McCaskell, T. (2000). Winnipeg takes the lead. *The Rainbow Classroom Newsletter, 5*(3). Retrieved April 5, 2007, from http://www.dezines.com/rainbow/current.htm

McCaskell, T. (2005). Blueprints for an invisible future. In *Race to equity: Disrupting educational inequality* (pp. 242–254). Toronto: Between the Lines.

McCaskell, T., & Russell, V. (2000). Anti-homophobia initiatives at the former Toronto Board of Education. In T. Goldstein & D. Selby (Eds.), *Weaving connections:*

Educating for peace, social, and environmental justice (pp. 27–56). Toronto: Sumach Press.

McFarland, W. (2001). The legal duty to protect gay and lesbian students from violence in school. *Professional School Counseling, 4*(3), 171–179.

Morrison, L., & L'Heareux, J. (2001). Suicide and gay/lesbian/bisexual youth: Implications for clinicians. *Journal of Adolescence, 24*, 39–49.

Plummer, D. (1999). *One of the boys: Masculinity, homophobia and modern manhood.* Binghamton, NY: Haworth Press.

River East School Division. (2007). Human rights. [Policy statement]. Retrieved April 5, 2007, from http://www.retsd.mb.ca/site/about/policy/pol_index.pdf

Robinson, B. (2005). Same-sex marriage: Canadian public opinion polls 1996–2002. Retrieved April 5, 2007, from http://www.religioustolerance.org/hom_marz.htm

Robinson, B. (2006). Same-sex marriage: Canadian polls during 2006. Retrieved April 5, 2007, from http://www.religioustolerance.org/homssmpoll06.htm

Santos, M., & Smyth, J. (1999). Public statement on anti-homophobia education. Winnipeg School Division.

School District No. 44 (North Vancouver) v. Jubran. (2005). BCCA 201 (British Columbia Court of Appeal). Retrieved April 5, 2007, from http://www.courts.gov.bc.ca/jdb-txt/ca/05/02/previous%20judgment/2005bcca0201err1.htm

Taylor, C. (2002). Beyond empathy: Confronting homophobia in critical education courses. *Journal of Lesbian Studies, 6*(3/4), 219–234.

Taylor, C. (2003). Building community through anti-homophobia education. In D. Sutherland and L. Sokal (Eds.), *Resiliency and capacity building in inner-city learning communities* (pp. 127–146). Winnipeg, MB: Portage & Main Press.

Taylor, C. (2004). Queering teacher education: Failures of empathy and their uses. *Inter-cultural Studies Journal, 4*(1), 19–31.

Trinity Western University vs. British Columbia College of Teachers. (2001). SCC 31 (Supreme Court of Canada) (CanLII). Retrieved April 5, 2007, from http://www.canlii.org/en/ca/scc/doc/2001/2001scc31/2001scc31.html

Vancouver School Board. (2006). Lesbian, gay, bisexual, transgender, transsexual, two-spirit, questioning. Foundations and basic commitments, Policy ACB. *Policy Manual.* Retrieved April 5, 2007, from http://www.vsb.bc.ca/districtinfo/policies/a/ACG-Lesbian_Gay_Bisexual.htm

Winnipeg School District. (2002). *Human rights/anti-homophobia resource guide.* Winnipeg, MB: Author.

Winnipeg School District. (2005). Human rights/anti-homophobia initiative. Fact sheet. Winnipeg, MB: Author. Retrieved April 5, 2007, from http://ww.wsd1.org/parents/documents/HumanRightsAntiHomophobiainitiatives.pdf

Winnipeg School District. (2006a). In profile: 2005–06. Winnipeg, MB: Author. Retrieved April 5, 2007, from http://www.wsd1.org/communications/WSD%20in%20Profile0506.pdf

Winnipeg School District. (2006b). *A code of conduct for safe and caring schools for students, staff and parents/guardians.* Winnipeg, MB: Author. Retrieved April 5, 2007, from http://ww.wsd1.org/parents/documents/Code%20of%20Conduct%202006.pdf

Active Reading

1. What kinds of evidence does Taylor use as primary and secondary sources? How are the two categories of sources used differently?

2. Summarize the argument presented by the author that "anti-homophobia" equals "human rights."

3. Why does the author conclude that homophobia must be addressed in the curriculum?

4. What purpose is served by using the acronym "LGBTTIQ" in this article? Why would someone writing about discrimination not just use the more familiar term "gay"?

Critical Reading

1. Canadian society is increasingly diverse, not only because of advances in same-sex rights, but because of immigration, leading inevitably to cultural conflicts. Practices that mean freedom in one culture, such as women appearing in public without male escorts, can mean immorality in another; conversely, practices that signify virtue in one culture, such as women veiling their hair or faces, can mean oppression in another. Apply the argument that opposing prejudice means defending human rights to the topic of cultural conflicts such as these.

2. It is fundamental to the Criminal Code of Canada that "your right to swing your fist ends at my nose." Apply this principle to the question of what limits should be placed on personal freedom in a democratic country.

3. Do some research on the internet to find other examples of Canadian school divisions that have tackled the issue of homophobia and summarize your findings in a short essay organized around comparing different approaches.

4. Do you agree with Taylor that homophobia needs to be addressed in the curriculum, even if some students are from families that oppose the idea?

The Residential School System

Murray Sinclair and A.C. Hamilton

Although Aboriginal people have long said that the justice system of Canada was racist, it was not until 1988, in the aftermath of high-profile cases involving the violent deaths of Aboriginal people, that the province of Manitoba instituted the Aboriginal Justice Inquiry (AJI). When the massive report was released in 1991, it included an analysis of the racist mentality behind the development of the residential school system, with its explicit goals of assimilating Aboriginal people by destroying their culture. The system, together with other aspects of European colonization of Canada, had disastrous effects, one of them being the over-representation of Aboriginal people in the courts and prisons. The entire report can be found at www.ajic.mb.ca/.

The two authors of the report are the Honourable Murray Sinclair and Associate Chief Justice A.C. Hamilton. Sinclair was appointed a Judge of the Manitoba Court of Queen's Bench in 2001, having served since 1988 as Associate Chief Judge of the Provincial Court of Manitoba, an appointment that made him Manitoba's first Aboriginal Judge, and Canada's second. Murray now serves as the new chair of Canada's truth and reconciliation commission on the residential schools. Hamilton was appointed to the Manitoba Court of Queen's Bench in 1971, and as Associate Chief Justice of the Family Division (Manitoba's new Unified Family Court) in 1983; he retired from the Bench in 1993 to focus on mediation work and Aboriginal issues.

1   Since the time of earliest contact, Aboriginal people and European settlers have seen things from vastly divergent points of view, because their attitudes and philosophies differed. The interaction of the two groups has been characterized as one of "cooperation and conflict but, more importantly, by misconceptions and contradictions."[4] One of the first, and perhaps the most enduring, of these misconceptions was that:

> Europeans assumed the superiority of their culture over that of any Aboriginal peoples. Out of that misconception grew the European conviction that in order for the Indians to survive, they would have to be assimilated into the European social order.[5]

2   At first, these differences had minimal impact upon most Aboriginal people. The missionaries tried to convert Aboriginal people and to mold them into their religious ideal, often with mixed results.

> The Indians [. . .] had no more idea of religious authority, as opposed to personal beliefs, than they had of a coercive political hierarchy. The individual freedom that was fundamental to Indian culture ruled out both the idea of heresy and of subordinating one's will to priestly guidance. The concept of authority and the respect for it that was inculcated into all civilized peoples provided the missionary and the civilized non-Christian with a common basis of understanding that was totally lacking between the missionary and the Indians of Eastern Canada. The fundamental problem that the Recollets saw impeding their work was that the Indians were too "primitive" to be converted. From this they drew the devastatingly simple conclusion that if they were to convert the Indians they had first to find ways of "civilizing" them.[6]

3   This was an impossible task as long as Aboriginal people continued to live in vibrant, self-sufficient communities often far removed from the missionaries' influence. However, this did not prevent the missionaries from forming opinions about the ways Aboriginal people raised and taught their children, or from laying the foundation for future misconceptions of Aboriginal child-rearing methods. In view of current ideas about child-rearing, it is interesting to reflect that no aspect of behaviour shocked the French more than their refusal to use physical punishment to discipline their children. On general principles, the Huron considered it wrong to coerce or humiliate an individual publicly. To their own way of thinking, a child was an individual with his or her own needs and rights rather than something amorphous that must be molded into shape. The Huron feared a child who was unduly humiliated, like an adult, might be driven to commit suicide.[7]

4   Aboriginal parents taught their children

> . . . to assume adult roles in an atmosphere of warmth and affection.
> Learning emphasized such values as respect for all living things, sharing,
> self-reliance, individual responsibility, and proper conduct. Children also had
> to learn how to utilize the environment most effectively for economic survival.
> Integral to all aspects of the education of the young was the spiritual, and
> events in the life-cycle from birth to death were marked with ceremonies
> stressing the individual's link to the spiritual and sacred. Cultural continuity
> was thus ensured.[8]

5   The early missionaries also condemned Aboriginal child-rearing methods as
being negligent, irresponsible and "uncivilized." This stereotype was to endure even
after Aboriginal people had lost much of their independence and "in the point of
view of the European, the Indian became irrelevant."[9] From then on, the relationship between Aboriginal people and Europeans became even more one-sided and
paternalistic. Aboriginal people were reduced to being "wards of the state."[10] All
relevant decision-making power on financial, social or political matters, and even
education, came to rest in the hands of the federal government. Eventually, the
cause of "civilizing" Aboriginal people to European cultures and values evolved into
the government policy of "assimilation," and education became "the primary
vehicle in the civilization and advancement of the Indian race."[11]

6   The federal government had little previous experience in "civilizing"
Aboriginal people so it turned to the United States for an example. It sent
Nicholas F. Davin to study the Americans' "aggressive civilization policy,"[12] based
on sending Indian children to large, racially segregated, industrial schools.
Davin was convinced the Americans were correct in their approach and the only
way to "civilize" Aboriginal people was to remove them from the disruptive influences of the parents and the community. His final comment in the report to
Ottawa was representative of attitudes of the time that ". . . if anything is to be
done with the Indian, we must catch him very young."[13]

7   The federal government delegated the job of "civilizing" and "educating"
Aboriginal people in Canada to religious organizations and churches. It encouraged the opening of large, industrial residential schools far from reserves and,
later, of boarding schools for younger children nearer to their homes. There,
every aspect of European life, from dress and behaviour to religion and
language, was impressed upon the Aboriginal children. The belief was that
Indians were a vanishing race and their only hope of surviving was to assimilate.
Their uncivilized and pagan ways would be replaced by good Christian values.

8   The residential school system was a conscious, deliberate and often brutal
attempt to force Aboriginal people to assimilate into mainstream society, mostly
by forcing the children away from their languages, cultures and societies. In
1920, during debates in the House of Commons on planned changes to the
Indian Act, Duncan Campbell Scott, the Deputy Superintendent of Indian
Affairs, left no doubt about the federal government's aims:

> Our object is to continue until there is not a single Indian in Canada that
> has not been absorbed into the body politic and there is no Indian question,
> and no Indian department, that is the whole object of this Bill.[14]

9   The experience of residential schools is one shared by many Aboriginal people all across Canada. That experience was marked by emotional, physical and sexual abuse, social and spiritual deprivation, and substandard education. "Even as assimilation was stated as the goal of education for Native people," one researcher wrote, "the assimilation was to take place under conditions which would cause no threat to the surrounding business and farming community."[15] Few Aboriginal people achieved more than a grade five level of education.

10   The main goal of residential schools and the assimilation policy, however, was not further education, but, rather, to remove Aboriginal children from the influences of their parents and communities, and to rid them of their languages and cultures. The methods, as one former residential school student explained, often were brutally effective:

> The elimination of language has always been a primary stage in a process of cultural genocide. This was the primary function of the residential school. My father, who attended Alberni Indian Residential School for four years in the twenties, was physically tortured by his teachers for speaking Tseshaht: they pushed sewing needles through his tongue, a routine punishment for language offenders. . . . The needle tortures suffered by my father affected all my family (I have six brothers and six sisters). My Dad's attitude became "why teach my children Indian if they are going to be punished for speaking it?" so he would not allow my mother to speak Indian to us in his presence. I never learned how to speak my own language. I am now, therefore, truly a "dumb Indian."[16]

11   After the Second World War, the federal government began to reconsider its assimilation policy. It wanted a more effective means of accomplishing the ultimate aims of the policy. This coincided with yet another revamping of the *Indian Act* and another set of hearings at the House of Commons. This also allowed another famous Canadian, noted anthropologist Diamond Jenness, to unveil his "Plan for Liquidating Canada's Indian Problems Within 25 Years." Jenness proposed abolishing Indian reserves, scrapping the treaties and integrating Indian students into the public school system. For the time being, the federal government shelved most of Jenness' proposals. It did, however, heed his suggestion to change the *Indian Act* to allow Indian children to be enrolled in public schools. This event signalled "the beginning of the end for many residential schools." [17]

12   The effects upon Aboriginal societies of the federal government's residential school system, and its policy of assimilation, have been astounding. Residential schools denigrated Aboriginal cultures, customs and religions, and disrupted the traditional practices of Aboriginal child-rearing and education. They tore apart families and extended families, leaving the children straddling two worlds, the European one and that of their own Aboriginal societies, but belonging to neither. These policies have caused a wound to fester in Aboriginal communities that has left them diminished to this day. In testimony to our Inquiry, Janet Ross said:

> I'd like to begin at the boarding school. The boarding school is where the alienation began. Children were placed there, plucked out of their homes. The bond between parents and children was fragmented severely—some lost

forever. Some searched for the love between parent and child endlessly, searching for it in other ways, never to be restored. The boarding schools taught us violence. Violence was emphasized through physical, corporal punishment, strappings, beatings, bruising and control. We learned to understand that this was power and control. I remember being very confused when someone told me that my natural mother had died. Hence growing up for me not knowing whether my mother was really mine always created some more confusion. I searched for that love in [foster] parents, but that bond had been broken; you felt that it just wasn't there. The boarding schools were extremely influential towards our poor self-image and low self-esteem, because we were continuously put down by the use of text books portraying negative images of Indian people.

13   The loss of successive generations of children to residential schools, the destruction of Aboriginal economic bases, the decimation of their populations through diseases and the increasing dependence on government welfare have led to social chaos. This manifests itself in Aboriginal communities through staggering poverty rates, high unemployment rates, high suicide rates, lower education levels, high rates of alcoholism and high rates of crime. In individuals, the legacy of the residential schools has been lowered self-esteem, confusion of self-identity and cultural identity, and a distrust of, and antagonism toward, authority.

14   The residential school experience also resulted in a breakdown in traditional Aboriginal methods of teaching child-rearing and parenting. Entire families once took part in the raising of children. Young parents, like young parents everywhere, learned how to raise their children from their own parents, by example. Traditionally, they also drew upon the examples and advice of their extended families, their grandparents, uncles, aunts and siblings. The residential schools made this impossible. Without that example, many Aboriginal parents today feel that they have never learned how to raise their own children.

15   Aboriginal communities have not yet recovered from the damage caused by the residential schools. It is only in recent times that children are again being taught close to home. For the first time in over 100 years, many families are experiencing a generation of children who live with parents until their teens. The readjustment to this new situation has been difficult for both the parents and their children. The current generation of parents does not even have its own experiences as children growing up in a unified family upon which to draw.

16   The damage done by these schools is still evident today, as Aboriginal people struggle to recapture their cultural practices and beliefs. The return of self-identity and self-esteem is a slow process.

NOTES

4. Jean Barman, Yvonne Hebert and Don McCaskill, eds., *Indian Education in Canada, Vol. I: The Legacy* (Vancouver: University of British Columbia Press, 1986), p. 2.

5. *Ibid.*

6. Bruce G. Trigger, *The Children of Aataentsic: A History of the Huron People to 1660* (Montreal and Kingston: McGill-Queen's University Press, 1976), p. 378.

7. *Ibid.*, p. 47.

8. Barman, Hebert and McCaskill, *Indian Education in Canada*, p. 3.

9. E. P. Patterson, T*he Canadian Indian: A History since 1500* (Don Mills: Collier-Macmillan, 1972), p. 72.

10. Kahn-Tineta Miller and George Lerchs, *The Historical Development of the Indian Act* (Ottawa: Treaties and Historical Research Branch, Department of Indian Affairs and Northern Development, 1978), p. 114.

11. Canada, Department of Indian Affairs and Northern Development, *Annual Report* (Ottawa, 1976), p. 6.

12. N. F. Davin, "Report on Industrial Schools for Indians and Halfbreeds" (Ottawa: Public Archives, 14 March 1879), PAC RG 10, Vol. 6001, File 1-1-1, Part 1.

13. *Ibid.*

14. Cited in J. R. Miller, *Skyscrapers Hide the Heavens: A History of Indian-White Relations in Canada* (Toronto: University of Toronto Press, 1989), pp. 206–7.

15. Celia Haig-Brown, *Resistance and Renewal: Surviving the Indian Residential School* (Vancouver: Tillacum Library, 1988), p. 67.

16. Randy Fred, "Introduction," in *Ibid.*, pp. 1–2.

17. Haig-Brown, *Resistance and Renewal*, p. 28.

Active Reading

1. Explain why French colonizers were shocked by Aboriginal child-rearing practices and why this is ironic in light of current-day parenting styles.

2. Summarize the authors' argument that the residential school experience caused "social chaos" among Aboriginal people.

3. The authors use lengthy block quotations. What kind of material do they quote, and what do they gain by doing this rather than paraphrasing?

4. The authors use the key terms "assimilation," "education," and "civilization" often in this piece, and almost always in quotation marks. What does this use of quotation marks signal to the reader?

Critical Reading

1. What assumptions about the nature of civilization would have served to justify the Canadian government's decision to annihilate "Indian" culture?

2. Has mainstream Canadian society progressed from the clearly racist days in which the residential school system was implemented? Or are there still signs of old beliefs in the superiority of British culture?

3. Do you agree with this thesis statement: "The curriculum of modern-day public schools and private schools continues to serve the interests of dominant culture by marginalizing minority cultures." How could you support (or refute) this thesis based on your own experience?

4. Prime Minister Stephen Harper apologized to First Nations people on behalf of the government of Canada, clearly signalling that even conservative politicians acknowledge that nations are accountable for abuses committed by earlier generations, especially when people are still suffering the effects of those actions. In what sense are current citizens of Canada responsible for acts that were committed by earlier generations?

5. Investigate other Canadian government apologies in recent years, such as the apology for the Chinese "head tax" and the Japanese internment during World War II. Compare the wording of the apologies and the rationales offered for apologizing. Also find out whether the apologies were accompanied by financial compensation or other actions.

Tackling Plagiarism: Linking Hi-Tech, Low-Tech and No Tech Methods for Detection

Peggy Pittman-Munke and Michael Berghoef

Peggy Pittman-Munke teaches social work at Murray State University, where she pursues a number of research and teaching interests, including community organizing; parenting education; social work practice with children, adolescents, and chronically mentally ill clients; domestic violence, substance-abuse prevention education, training in adolescent suicide prevention education; social work education accreditation; and finally diversity issues. In addition to her work within higher education, Pittman-Munke has worked as a therapist for chronically mentally ill clients, and conducted program and organizational evaluations. Co-author Michael Berghoef specializes in clinical social work including mental health, substance abuse and clinical and educational technology.

Their experience in social work, as they point out in the following article, makes them keenly aware of the ethical dimensions of relationships: how to conduct relationships in such a way that misconduct does not occur, and how to respond when it does. In the following article, they turn their attention to the problem of plagiarism.

I. INTRODUCTION: THE EVOLUTION OF PLAGIARISM

1   The origins of plagiarism are rooted deeply in history. *The Oxford English Dictionary* (OED, 1982, p. 932) informs us that the term likely originated sometime in the 1600s. The term originally referred to kidnapping children or slaves. This usage transformed over time into a metaphor for stealing "intellectual children." In more recent times, the metaphor of a viral plague has been employed to capture the ease and self replicating nature of plagiarism coupled with advances in information technology, notably word processing and the Internet. Legal and popular conceptions of what constitutes plagiarism also have changed greatly over time.

2   Whereas the idea that plagiarism is stealing has remained constant over time, several questions about the concept of plagiarism and its evolution over time are important for us to consider as we frame this discussion. The first question asks, "Can plagiarism, to some extent, be unconscious?" The corollary to this question asks, "If plagiarism is not consciously intended, is it still stealing?" The next question asks, "If plagiarism is unconscious, is it still unethical?" These questions offer the beginning of a more sophisticated analysis of the issue and one more relevant to teaching social work values and ethics than is usually offered.

3   The profession of social work has a unique set of tools that can be brought to bear on the issue of academic honesty generally and plagiarism specifically. When we consider the Person in the Environment Approach, the Strengths Perspective, Developmental Thinking, Systems Perspective, the Advocacy Role, and our highly developed *Code of Ethics*, we realize that we are more equipped than most to address issues of academic honesty. In fact, social work may be in a unique position to develop highly effective prevention strategies for academic dishonesty by creating a professional culture where root causes are differentiated and dealt with successfully.

4   One example from the mid-seventies that many may remember involved the highly publicized case of musician George Harrison defending himself with an unconscious plagiarism defense. The gravity of this case indicated that the courts at that time took a dim view of plagiarism, whether conscious or unconscious. George Harrison was successfully sued by the publisher of the Chiffons' 1962 hit "He's So Fine," which was claimed to be the basis of Harrison's hit "My Sweet Lord" (Bright Tunes Music v. Harrisongs Music, 1976). The case turned on fairly technical musical analysis of the distinctive "grace notes" contained in the song. A strong case was made that if plagiarism occurred, it was the unconscious result of his listening to music rather than a deliberate attempt to copy it (DeCurtis, Henke, & George-Warren, 1992; Miller, J., 1980). The key question raised by this case was, "Can someone plagiarize someone else's work without being aware that this is happening?" The judge's decision was clear. Plagiarism, even if unconscious, is still plagiarism. This case also underscored that plagiarism can be criminally connected to copyright infringement and intellectual property laws.

5   Since that time, the practice of sampled music, sometimes parody, sometimes homage, has blurred the lines both legally and ethically (Bridgeport Music/Southfield Music v. Dimension Films/No Limit Films, 2004; Campbell v. Acuff-Rose, 1994). The rise of peer-to-peer networking has further changed the climate of copyright violation for what might be called the Napster generation. The social environment surrounding plagiarism and copyright is further complicated by the creation of hundreds, by some estimates thousands, of term paper mills furnishing generic term papers for free and customized papers for a fee (Kimbel Library, 2006).

6   As technology becomes more available and more powerful, the ease of committing plagiarism has increased, and as a result, more plagiarism routinely appears in student assignments as well as in scholarly writing and other media. For many, the attitudes around these ethical issues become a bit hazier. However, for the most part, today we see a change in degree of plagiarism, not a change in type of plagiarism.

2. THE PROLIFERATION OF PLAGIARISM

7   The evolution of plagiarism is fueled by one aspect of modern technology, the copy and paste option. This option makes plagiarism far easier and less time consuming than before. However, earlier generations of students also had versions of copy and paste, involving scissors, correction fluid and tape, or extensive retyping, a less sophisticated version of copy and paste. A variety of sources report exponential growth in plagiarism (Szabo & Underwood, 2004). However,

this raises questions about how much plagiarism has truly grown, how much awareness has grown, and how much have anti-plagiarism software tools improved the chances of detection. Although the Internet makes plagiarism easier and less complicated, the Internet also provides tools for easier detection of some types of plagiarism.

8   Let us consider the following "varieties of plagiaristic experience" that are familiar to all of us who teach:

- A student purchases a paper from a site such as www.cheathouse.com, a popular source for acquiring papers, and turns it in exactly as purchased.
- A student "tweaks" the purchased paper to make it less detectable.
- A student copies and pastes from a variety of sources and weaves an "original" collection.
- The student says, "I don't know why you are so upset with me. I've always done it this way!"

3. A TYPOLOGY OF PLAGIARISTS

9   Clearly, from the few preceding examples, there is a range of plagiarism from which one can develop typologies of plagiarists. Many authors have attempted to analyze what motivates plagiarism and distill a universal typology (Baggaley & Spencer, 2005).

10   One possible typology of plagiarists might include the following:

- The Unconscious Plagiarist

     Thought Process: "I didn't remember that I read it somewhere."
     Thought Process: "Isn't this all just common knowledge?"

- The Ignorant Plagiarist

     Thought Process: "I changed some words [the "and"s and "the"s]"
     Thought Process: "I put the citation in the reference list at the end."
     Thought Process: "I didn't know."
     Thought Process: "I didn't know that I couldn't quote from myself without attribution."

11   These first examples of plagiarists are difficult for most professors. If the student is genuinely ignorant or unconsciously plagiarizing, the professor often asks, "Does this justify heavy penalties that are often mandated by departments or universities?" and can be torn about how to best handle the situation.

12   The next group of examples generally produces less angst in faculty and often produces anger and frustration in students.

- The Con Artist as Plagiarist

     Thought Process: "I can change the paper enough that no one will figure out the source." This manifestation and subsequent detection of the "Con Artist" generally produces no angst in faculty.
     Thought Process: "I suckered someone else into writing my paper, my parent, significant other, or friend, by telling them if they don't

help me out, I'll fail the class, flunk out, or won't get into an MSW program"

- Subcategory: The Con Artist Enabler
  This subcategory raises for faculty the issue of how to handle the fellow student enabler. In other words, should the fellow student suffer the same penalty as the "Con Artist," especially when it is clear to the faculty member that there is a power imbalance or the "Con Artist" preyed on someone vulnerable and may even have framed this in a way that presented the failure to help a classmate as a violation of collegiality?

■ The Thoughtful Thief

Thought Process: "I knew they wouldn't mind if I used their paper." Usually the original author was not asked for permission.
Thought Process: "Oh, I would not have used it without permission if I knew it mattered that much." In this case, the original author is usually asked for permission, and if the original author does not bluntly deny the right to use the paper, the "Good Thief" assumes permission.

■ The Big Spender

Thought Process: "I bought it; it is my property." This student has no apparent guilty conscience over the plagiarism.
Thought Process: "I can't believe you don't believe I wrote this." This student attempts to place the faculty member in a defensive position by attacking. Some students add tears to the attack, while others threaten to complain about the faculty member to the administration, hoping to trump the situation by adding anxiety.

■ The Opportunistic Plagiarist

Thought Process: "My organization has files of papers . . . it would be a shame not to use them." Sometimes this thought process is supplemented with the thought "If I don't make a good grade on this paper and in this course, I will pull down the GPA of my organization," or "I am just using the papers to get some ideas."
Thought Process: "After all this is a free paper site on the Web . . . why not."

■ Other Plagiarist Enablers

There are a number of types of enablers. Faculty, administration, and fellow students can all appear in this category. Students in this category are generally not identified by faculty, either because they are not detected or because they deny complicity, so one half of the plagiarism often is undetected or unproven. Plagiarist enablers can appear in several subcategories, the "See No Evil" enabler, and the "Let's Not Make a Hassle Over Nothing" enabler.

13   The first subcategory, the "See No Evil" enabler, includes the following two enablers: the peer who says, "Go ahead, use my work, no one will ever know," and the professor who says, "I know that this is not something you would do knowingly." These two examples of enablers generally are not consciously complicit in encouraging plagiarism. Both are likely to see this as an exceptional circumstance calling for mercy, rather than an acceptance that plagiarism should be challenged or ignored.

14   A second subcategory, the "Let's Not Make a Hassle Over Nothing" enabler, includes the following situations: The professor who turns a blind eye to work that does not fit with the student who turns it in, and the administrator who says, "Let's not make such a fuss over this," or "Aren't you overreacting?" Other versions of this category may include faculty members who say to colleagues who detect plagiarism: "Don't you think you are being too hard on the student?" or "Do you know what that student is experiencing in his/her life?" or "I don't think this is a big enough problem to jeopardize his/her standing in the program, or mar a perfect GPA, or delay graduation," or "Are you sure you were clear in your assignment?" This second subcategory is the more pernicious of the two categories. In these examples, the enabler is likely aware at some level that s/he is complicit in the plagiarism. Faculty and administrators who are unwilling to deal forthrightly with the problem promote an atmosphere in which plagiarism becomes the norm rather than isolated instances.

15   Other common errors made by students may include:

- Only citing sources used at the end of the paper
- Not citing on PowerPoint slides
- Changing a few words and not attributing the source as an "almost" quote
- Giving the source as a Web site rather than the specific part of the Web site used
- Giving a primary source obtained from a secondary source without crediting the primary source (as: as cited in)
- Not citing pictures and graphics
- Not citing conversations, classes, and so forth that contribute heavily to the ideas developed by the student
- Not citing from previous work done by the student
- Turning in a paper written for another class without instructor permission
- Copying and pasting and dropping the source as the material is transferred into the new document
- Not So Unintentional (i.e., buying a paper from a Web source). These sources vary: papers written to order, purchasing a prewritten paper on a topic
- Copying a friend's paper, with or without the friend's permission
- Copying a paper in an organization's files (fraternities and sororities are notorious for paper files)
- Getting substantial help from a friend or another instructor on the paper
- Copying a published paper
- Our favorite: getting parents to write the paper but not removing telltale comments, such as, "Hope this helps you get a better grade. Be sure to bring your laundry home this weekend."
- Submitting work done as a team/group for another class as one's own work and without permission of the team/group

16   Faculty responses to this increase in plagiarism can be seen to form a continuum, ranging from plausible denial to career cynicism. Many faculty who have not yet detected much plagiarism ask, "Is it really that big of a problem?" Other jaded faculty will reply, "They all do it, and you can't catch them, so why bother trying?" But what is the proper response to waking up during an avalanche? And more to the point, what is the unique social work educator response?

4. EXAMPLES OF ANTI-PLAGIARISM SOFTWARE

17   Turnitin.com (www.turnitin.com) is perhaps the most well known brand of anti-plagiarism software and seems to have the greatest market share at this point in time. Other companies that offer this service include Ithenticate (www.ithenticate.com/) and WCopyfind (www.plagiarism.phys.virginia.edu/Wsoftware.html). In most of these services, an account is created that allows a professor (and in some cases a student) to submit a paper for review. An "originality report" is generated consisting of a graphic summary of the percentage of the paper that was found in other sources from the company's database. In the case of Turnitin.com, this database includes not only scholarly works, but also an archived record of all previously submitted student papers.

18   Some faculty liken using anti-plagiarism software to testing for illegal drug use. The drug testing analogy is interesting in that many testers, like many employers, find themselves surprised by the results, exclaiming, "That's not who I expected to or meant to catch!" The advantage to using software to identify plagiarized papers is that it provides a fast technological solution to the technological aspects of plagiarism by screening for content that has been copied from the Internet or previously published papers. It quantifies how much content came from specific sites. Ideally, it allows for a reasonably objective confrontation when a student has copied and pasted from uncited sources, such as, "This report demonstrates that 75% of your paper came from the following five Internet sites."

19   However, there are disadvantages to using anti-plagiarism software. For example, in these originality reports, proper citations are also highlighted, so faculty will still need to determine which quotations are valid and which are not properly cited. Anti-plagiarism software also misses a lot of territory in the literature, for instance, gray literature. For example, government produced brochures are often not included in the database against which papers are checked. This means that material copied and pasted from a source like this will not be detected by anti-plagiarism software.

20   As with any new technology, there is an investment of time, a learning curve for faculty and students to use a particular product, the time involved in submitting and waiting for results, the cost of purchasing or licensing such software, legal issues related to intellectual property, and informed consent concerns. All the issues are considerations for adoption of a particular technology. To avoid some of these issues, some faculty use lower tech methods, such as using free search engines to take a suspected piece of text and seeing if a simple Internet search detects uncited material (McCullough & Holmberg, 2005). Others use anti-plagiarism software preventatively by allowing students to submit assignments for analysis before submitting them for grading, using the software to check for missed citations or excessive quotations. Some universities are turning away from services such as Turnitin.com because of legal challenges and are now using alternative proprietary software such as SafeAssign (www.SafeAssign. com), which only adds student papers to its database if the student gives explicit permission to do so.

21   Another concern raised with these high-tech strategies for detection is that surveillance technology is being substituted for relationships. Rather

than a professor knowing a student and his or her work, faculty rely on ever more sophisticated technologies to catch the ever increasingly sophisticated plagiarist, creating an escalating "arms race" of detection and evasion techniques (Szabo & Underwood, 2004). There are also concerns about retention of student papers and the potential violation of intellectual property rights. All of these factors combine to create a process that feels more like surveillance and policing of students, rather than a respectful academic dialogue.

22   What then are faculty to do with such limited and potentially problematic tools? At this point, we may need to just accept them for what they are and what they can, and cannot, do and begin dealing with the thornier aspects of this issue. Proactively, we can identify and differentiate patterns of plagiarism as well as develop effective policies and differentiated responses as well as maintain an awareness of possible unintended consequences of our use of new technologies to identify academic dishonesty. It is also important to realize that detection is only the beginning. As is often the case with whistleblowing, no good deed goes unpunished. Once plagiarism is detected, and especially when multiple cases are detected, a response is required. This can range from turning a blind eye to expulsion from the university.

5. THE SOCIAL WORK RESPONSE

23   This leaves us with the rather daunting question: What is the best response, and indeed what is the unique social work educator's response, to this rise in academic dishonesty, specifically plagiarism? This will surely need to include the type of reflection in all directions we ask of our students—the best contextualization that we can muster. It will include an analysis of the person in the environment. It will include systems analysis. And it will include wrestling with and adhering to the social work code of ethics. It is crucial in this evolving discussion that wide ranging discussions from the social work community inform our collective practice in this area to answer these larger questions. To what extent is cheating in general, plagiarism in particular, and our response to it, an artifact of large classroom size, generic assignments, and a loss of knowledge of our students? To what extent is this a larger cultural issue, a relationship issue, an ethical issue? We will likely find that this is a much larger issue than just a few bad apples in the social work classroom.

24   However, there are some techniques that we have found helpful. To some extent, we need to become better at differentiating types and motivations for plagiarizing just as we would look at making such differentiations in our practice. If we start where the client/student is, we need to remember that all students who plagiarize do not consciously intend to cheat and that there are students who really do not understand that what they are doing is plagiarism. These are the relatively easy situations. We also need to examine our professional obligation in dealing with the more brazen versions of plagiarism and take the steps necessary to adequately address them. These can be far more challenging for most faculty.

6. AVOIDING PLAGIARISM: PREVENTION

25   One step that can be taken is to teach about plagiarism before there is a problem. For this purpose the syllabus can be used as a teaching moment. Sharing with students the definition of plagiarism and being clear about your classroom policies can head off many potential plagiarism situations. This is also an opportune time to reference college and university policies that deal with academic dishonesty generally and plagiarism specifically. This should include policy statements notifying students of the use of anti-plagiarism software and possibly may include an informed consent component (University of Windsor, 2005). Finally, tying in the social work code of ethics is an important aspect of teaching about expectations of professional integrity. These may go beyond university expectations for academic honesty and professional conduct and are an important element in acculturation to the profession.

26   Large class size can work against professors truly knowing their students. But there is only so far that relying on high tech methods of detection will carry us. We need to know our students well enough to be able to detect whether or not the work turned in belongs to the student who turned it in. A comparison of submissions with earlier writing can help detect unoriginal work. A student who writes in one style usually does not alter style drastically in subsequent sections of a paper. A student who usually writes with grammatical errors and slang generally does not abruptly change this behavior. A student who cannot organize thoughts easily usually does not suddenly produce a well organized paper.

27   Some practical ways to accomplish plagiarism prevention include assigning many different kinds of written assignments, such as creative free writing assignments, journals turned in regularly, and essay exams and requiring the rationale for selecting topic, notes, outline, and annotated bibliography from which the paper developed. Generally, written assignments that do not just deal with reporting facts but take higher order thinking skills are more difficult to plagiarize. Creating a unique, more involved step-by-step process of building an assignment can also aid in prevention. This may include requiring an application or an explanatory piece that is unique to the class.

28   Some faculty require student/professor conferences around written work, creating a dynamic in which sharing the process of creation with a professor makes it harder to take credit for work that is not one's own. This individualized attention allows for faculty to frame the assignment in such a way that it would be far more difficult to turn in someone else's work or a prewritten paper.

29   Well thought out assignment creation often also serves to thwart academic dishonesty. In general, it is advisable to avoid using the same assignments year to year. Careful explanation of the specifics of what is required in the work to be submitted and linkage back to the required content for the class for which it is to be submitted also helps discourage cheating. Generic assignments that broadly cover a topic can be an invitation to plagiarize, whereas idiosyncratic ones tend to prevent it.

30   Students who know that anti-plagiarism software will be employed may also be less inclined to use another's work. Again, some faculty have found great success

with the creative and effective proactive use of anti-plagiarism software. In this strategy, students must be given access to the service in order to check themselves against the originality report to evaluate how well they have done in regard to proper citation before final submission of an assignment.

7. CONSEQUENCES OF PLAGIARISM: TREATMENT

31   Clear consequences can also act as a deterrent to plagiarism. Intentional plagiarism can be considered to be a violation of the *Code of Ethics*. Potential consequences can include redoing the assignment; failing the assignment; failing the class; referral to the program, college, or university disciplinary committee; dismissal from the program; or dismissal from the university. Consequences should be consistent across situations and across faculty. The consequences of plagiarism should appear in student manuals and other program documents and should not be a surprise to any student. Student advisors can play a key role as a central person to monitor overall reports of plagiarism across courses and semesters. If a faculty member discovers that clear written policies are lacking at any of these levels, it is important to quickly initiate a process of review and policy development.

32   Wrestling through the consequences of a discovered plagiarism situation can be a painful experience. For this reason, faculty sometimes avoid dealing with it in a head-on straightforward manner. Remember, if the paper seems too good to be true, then it probably is not the student's work and it is best to follow up quickly with either a low tech check of references or a high tech utilization of anti-plagiarism software. As in many situations in life it is helpful to have a plan and follow the plan. This should include involving academic and program advisors in the determination, evaluation, and response to the plagiarism situation (Barnes, 2004).

8. CONCLUSION

33   In conclusion, it seems prudent for social work faculty to invest in prevention. It also seems that social work faculty should be on the forefront of developing fair, consistent, and effective policies to treat the problems of academic dishonesty. It is essential for social work educators to join the discussion and work toward more effective practice in the prevention and treatment of this social problem. More discipline specific studies need to be conducted to evaluate specific strengths as well as potential vulnerabilities to plagiarism within the social work community (Marsden, Carroll & Neill, 2005; Collins & Amodeo, 2005; Lambert & Hogan, 2004; Culwin, 2006). Careful evaluation should be conducted before adoption of any high tech solutions, such as anti-plagiarism software (Evans, 2006; Macdonald & Carroll, 2006; McKeever, 2006). We must also attempt to develop a holistic approach that embraces the tools with which we hope to equip our students to cultivate a culture of honesty, in academia and in practice settings (Leask, 2006). In an era that emphasizes and even glamorizes the distorted narrative of the

rugged independent individual researcher going it alone, our students need the social work reframe that the process of knowledge building is really building on the work of those who came before, and giving them proper acknowledgement.

REFERENCES

Baggaley, J., & Spencer, B. (2005). The mind of a plagiarist. *Learning, Media and Technology, 30* (1), 55–62.

Barnes, L. (2004). *Senate ad hoc committee on plagiarism, Dalhousie University*, Dalhousie University.

Bridgeport Music/Southfield Music v. Dimension Films/No Limit Films (2004). http://caselaw.lp.findlaw.com/cgi-bin/getcase.pl?court=6th&navby=docket&no=035738

Bright Tunes Music v. Harrisongs Music. (1976). http://ccnmtl.columbia.edu/projects/law/library/cases/case_brightharrisongs.html

Campbell v. Acuff-Rose (1994). http://ccnmtl.columbia.edu/projects/law/library/cases/case_campbellacuff.html

Collins, M. E., & Amodeo, M. (2005). Responding to plagiarism in schools of social work: Considerations and recommendations. *Journal of Social Work Education. Special Issue: Innovations in Gerontological Social Work Education, 41* (3), 527–543. PsycINFO database.

Culwin, F. (2006). An active introduction to academic misconduct and the measured demographics of misconduct. *Assessment & Evaluation in Higher Education. Special Issue: Plagiarism: Prevention, Practice and Policy, 31* (2), 167–182. doi:10.1080/02602930500262478

DeCurtis, A., Henke, J., & George-Warren, H. (1992). *The Rolling Stone illustrated history of rock & roll : The definitive history of the most important artists and their music* (3rd ed.). New York: Random House.

Evans, R. (2006). Evaluating an electronic plagiarism detection service: The importance of trust and the difficulty of proving students don't cheat. *Active Learning in Higher Education, 7* (1), 87–99. doi:10.1177/14697874060611

Kimbel Library. (2006). Coastal Carolina University Cheating 101: Internet Paper Mills http://www.coastal.edu/library/presentations/mills2.html

Lambert, E. G., & Hogan, N. L. (2004). Academic dishonesty among criminal justice majors: A research note. *American Journal of Criminal Justice, 29* (1), 1.

Leask, B. (2006). Plagiarism, cultural diversity and metaphor—implications for academic staff development. *Assessment & Evaluation in Higher Education. Special Issue: Plagiarism: Prevention, Practice and Policy, 31* (2), 183–199.

Macdonald, R., & Carroll, J. (2006). Plagiarism—a complex issue requiring a holistic institutional approach. *Assessment & Evaluation in Higher Education. Special Issue: Plagiarism: Prevention, Practice and Policy, 31* (2), 233–245.

Marsden, H., Carroll, M., & Neill, J. T. (2005). Who cheats at university? A self-report study of dishonest academic behaviours in a sample of Australian university students. *Australian Journal of Psychology, 57* (1), 1–10. http://www.fno.org/may98/cov98may.html

McCullough, M., & Holmberg, M. (2005). Using the Google search engine to detect word-for-word plagiarism in master's theses: A preliminary study. *College Student Journal, 39* (3), 435–441. PsycINFO database.

McKeever, L. (2006). Online plagiarism detection services—saviour or scourge? *Assessment & Evaluation in Higher Education. Special Issue: Plagiarism: Prevention, Practice and Policy, 31* (2), 155–165.

McKenzie, J. (1998). The new plagiarism: Seven antidotes to prevent highway robbery in an electronic age. *From Now on: The Educational Technology Journal, 7* (8).

Miller, J. (1980). *The Rolling Stone illustrated history of rock & roll* (Rev. and updated.). New York: Rolling Stone.

Pickard, J. (2006). Staff and student attitudes to plagiarism at University College Northampton. *Assessment & Evaluation in Higher Education. Special Issue: Plagiarism: Prevention, Practice and Policy, 31* (2), 215–232.

SafeAssign. www.SafeAssign.com. Corporate Web site.

Simpson, J. A., Weiner, E. S. C., & Oxford University Press. (1989). *The Oxford English Dictionary* (2nd ed. / prepared by J.A. Simpson and E.S.C. Weiner ed.). Oxford; New York: Clarendon Press; Oxford; Oxford University Press.

Szabo, A., & Underwood, J. (2004). Cybercheats: Is information and communication technology fuelling academic dishonesty? *Active Learning in Higher Education, 5* (2), 180–199.

Turnitin.com. www.turnitin.com, Corporate Web site.

University of Windsor. (2005). Policy on the use of Turnitin.com, http://athena. uwindsor.ca/units/senate/main.nsf/982f0e5f06b5c9a285256d6e006cff78/ a087aecb6b358d3e8525701f0053a1d8!OpenDocument

Active Reading

1. Summarize the entire article in one double-spaced page.

2. Like many social science articles, this one uses subheadings. If you were to revise this article for a humanities journal that did not allow subheadings, what transition sentences could you supply between sections to enable the reader to follow the structure of the article?

3. What do the authors mean by "plagiarist enabler"?

4. The authors conclude that knowledge-building needs to be reframed as "building on the work of those who came before" rather than "the rugged independent researcher going it alone." Explain why they see academic research and writing this way.

Critical Reading

1. Can plagiarism be unconscious? Is it still stealing if it is unconscious? Is our definition of plagiarism beginning to change, influenced by changes to communication technology that promote internet access and sampling?

2. The authors offer a "typology of plagiarists." Are any types missing? Is each type accurately described? Explain why or why not. What other "typologies" have you encountered in this course? What about in your other courses?

3. Explain how all of the items in the list of "other common errors made by students" could be seen as plagiarism. If you disagree with the inclusion of any item, explain why it should not be seen as plagiarism.

4.   What are the penalties in your university or college for plagiarism? Do you agree that they are fair? If not, explain how they should be revised.

5.   The authors point out that many classes are so large that instructors do not know their students' work well, and that "surveillance technology is being substituted for relationships." What role do you think weak student-instructor bonds play in the occurrence of plagiarism? Do you think the use of surveillance technology to detect plagiarized essays threatens the student-instructor relationship further? If so, how do you think individual instructors can discourage plagiarism?

READING AND WRITING SUGGESTIONS

Chapter-based Research Questions

1. Write an essay arguing for or against the thesis that the residential school system was a form of state-sponsored bullying.

2. Write an essay arguing for or against the thesis that homophobia, cyber-bullying, and assimilation are all examples of group mentality (with reference to Chapter 10).

3. Write an essay on electronically-enabled plagiarism and cyber-bullying as examples of new forms of human experience and new kinds of crimes, not just additional occurrences of traditional plagiarism and bullying.

Additional Research Questions

1. Investigate the current state of ongoing efforts to address the damage done by the residential school system by finding relevant news articles on such topics as the Truth and Reconciliation Commission and financial compensation hearings. Use these popular press documents as primary sources for an essay on the topic of representations of the issue in the popular press. Be careful *not* to use the sources as if they were secondary (scholarly) sources.

2. Any research involving communications technology needs to be updated to reflect current developments in the field. Develop an annotated bibliography of scholarly sources on the topic of cyber-bullying published after Shariff's book (2008). Alternatively, develop an annotated bibliography of scholarly sources on the topic of plagiarism published after Pittman-Munke and Berghoef's article (also 2008).

3. Taylor and Shariff address gender and sexuality as factors in school-based bullying. Write a research essay on this topic.

CHAPTER 12
MAKING OUR LIVES EASIER
OR MORE COMPLICATED?

Once we adopt a new form of technology, it often seems as though it has always been part of our lives. It is hard to imagine life without cell phones, but they were relatively uncommon fifteen years ago. Whether or not to adopt a BlackBerry was still a pertinent debate among business people only five years ago. How to deal with laptops and cell phones in the classroom remains a contested issue for educators. While there is no question that such technologies help students to access and organize information, their potential for misuse is also widely recognized. How many times have you seen the student in front of you Facebooking or watching a YouTube video that turns out to be an unwanted distraction to you? Since these technologies are still relatively new, how we manage their use in public settings is still evolving. Overall, it is fascinating to watch this social etiquette take shape, even if there are some awkward passages.

The term "Web 2.0" became popular in 2004 as a way of referring to overall changes in the way we conceive of the World Wide Web, understood now as user-centred and facilitating communication and information sharing. While this definition suggests that the web is a convenience which we all share, some cultural critics worry about the growing social and economic demands on us to stay "connected." Apart from conforming to expectations others may have that we should make ourselves available around the clock, many of us have noted our own growing appetite for keeping our phones on and checking our in-boxes.

Because the waves of new communication technologies have been so strong and recent in their impact, a number of scholars and critics have mapped out dangers and warnings. We often hear skeptics who worry about the influence of new technologies dismissed as Luddites, a reference to British textile artisans in the nineteenth century who protested against the introduction of mechanized looms. But most commentators who raise concerns are not so much opposed to technology as interested in curbing some of its misuses. For example, looking at Facebook, Carly Brandenburg examines issues of access to information and privacy rights from a legal perspective. She may hit a nerve with many students who are both Facebook users and job applicants. Her article examines whether employers have the right to look at online sites to conduct background checks on applicants and employees. Her question is, of course, part of larger concerns about the surveillance potential of technology, which may make it possible for those who want access to personal information to track our interests, contacts, and whereabouts.

Writer Jon Lorinc raises another area of concern. He depicts our world as one of jangling distractions. He suggests we are so busy learning about new applications and responding to emails and texts that we have no time left to pay attention to things that do not change: the need for astute writing, reading, and speaking.

The chapter ends on a note of relative optimism. Media and cultural analyst Don Tapscott challenges many conservative and critical assertions with his claims that the current generation of students, raised with home computers, conceptualize and perform reading and writing differently than their elders did. It is not that they do not write: they use a keyboard and screen and are online. He points out several ways in which critics are needlessly judgmental about the effects of the internet, as well as several critical thinking and character strengths he has identified as belonging to "Net Geners" (the generation raised with the internet, also referred to in other sources as "digital natives").

Activate

1. What stands out as the most recent news item you have heard or read about new communication technology? Is the report positive, alarming, or simply informational? Do you expect to hear updates? Is it true that social networking and communication technology often make headlines in popular media, but seldom sustain long-term coverage? Can you think of reasons that these topics tend to parachute into media reports and then drop from sight?

2. Think about how cell phones have changed in your lifetime. Can you speculate on the sorts of changes that may lie ahead? For people who tend to resist change, is the world of technology more challenging, even threatening? Apart from the question of how different personality types adjust to change, are there generational differences in attitudes toward technological innovations, so that older people as a group tend to resist new developments? Does it help to account for generational differences by thinking of younger people as digital natives, and older people as not?

The Newest Way to Screen Job Applicants

Carly Brandenburg

This article, recently published in the Federal Communications Law Journal *(2008), raises questions about whether the privacy rights of Facebook users can be ignored by potential employers looking for insight into the private lives and activities of potential employees. Brandenburg is a practising attorney who also holds a position with the Indiana University School of Law.*

I. SOCIAL NETWORKING: THINK TWICE

1   Web sites designed to promote shared information—like blogs, Facebook, Friendster, Xanga, and MySpace—may provide more than the opportunity to share stories and details of a college student's or graduate's life. To many students and graduates who are "nurtured in open, collegial situations, blogging and personal internet postings on social networking Internet sites such as

MySpace, Facebook, and Friendster . . . blur the line between personal and public."[1] Students and graduates today are getting more than they bargain for as they attempt to enter the workforce and realize their blogging and social networking ways can come back to bite them.

2   This Note discusses the potential ramifications of using shared information sites, focusing on the Facebook social network and its users. Employers who hire graduating students are steadily discovering that social networking sites allow them to learn more than they ever could from reading an applicant's resume and cover letter. This Note explores some of the legal issues raised when employers conduct social network background checks. Its primary focus is to determine what kinds of privacy expectations, if any, social networkers can anticipate.

A. Social Networks and Their Dangers

3   Social networks on the Internet have become increasingly popular among the general population, but these networking sites are still used most frequently by college students and recent graduates.[2] Most social networks merely require a user to register by providing basic information and a valid email address. Social network users can then post anything they wish on that particular Internet social Web site. Users can post their comments, upload photographs, join and form groups with other networkers, and share their personal information. They can also freely search other users' profiles in order to find and interact with other social networkers throughout the world.

1. The Messages Social Networkers Communicate

4   On Facebook, as is the case with many social networks, users create profiles to share basic information that will allow others to search for, find, and connect with them. However, some users provide information about themselves that "go[es] to the very edges of decency and legality."[3] For instance, a Facebook user can find more than 500 groups and more than 500 events that contain the search term "sex" using a basic Facebook search.[4] Some of the groups that can be located using this search term on Facebook are fairly tame, like the group referring to the popular television series with the title, "Alright . . . I admit it . . . I'm a Sex and the City addict." On the other hand, the vast majority of Facebook groups containing the word "sex" are far less innocuous with titles like "Casual Sex at IU,"

---

[1] *Is Your Company's Work Blogging Down?*, 4 No. 1 Fed. Emp. L. Insider (McGuire Woods LLP, Fortney Scott LLC), Sept. 2006, at 2 [hereinafter *Blogging Down?*].

[2] *What You Won't See on a Resume*, 18 No. 12 Ga. Emp. L. Letter (Ford, Harrison LLP), July 2006, at 5 [hereinafter *What You Won't See*].

[3] *Id.*

[4] *See* Welcome to Facebook, http://www.facebook.com/ (last visited Mar. 21, 2008). Once one creates a profile and gains access to Facebook through the main webpage, simply click on "search" and then select "all networks" under the "basic search" portion of the network. Then input the desired search term—in this instance, "sex"—to see how many names, profiles, groups, or events are yielded. Once a user begins searching, he or she can limit the search to his or her own social network or to all networks (including other universities, companies, geographic regions, etc.).

"Chances are I'm currently having Sex;" "Girls who Love Sex," "I Actually HAVE had Sex on Campus," and other similar groups.[5] By simply clicking on a group title and following its link to the group's members, Facebook users can find friends with similar interests, and employers can find potential hires with frighteningly questionable interests (and the propensity to share their feelings and interests with others). Similar results are yielded when searching for terms like "drugs," "porn," and "alcohol."

5   Beyond the groups social networkers can join and create, Facebook users can post anything they wish about themselves on their personal profiles. These profiles often contain pictures and also document Facebook users' interests and activities, political views, sexual orientations and proclivities, relationship status, religious beliefs, and any number of other bits of personal information that employers may find interesting or useful to their decision-making process.[6]

2. Employers Are Discovering Their Options

6   According to a National Association of Colleges and Employers ("NACE") study, approximately one in ten employers report they plan to review potential hires' profiles and information posted on social networks.[7] In addition, employers who admit to reviewing social networkers' profiles as they screen job applicants say the information available on these profiles has at least some influence on their hiring decisions. The NACE study does point out, on the other hand, that many employers say they do not review social networkers' online postings in order to evaluate potential hires; around forty percent of surveyed employers are still undecided regarding whether to use this sort of information as they seek the best candidates for jobs.[8]

7   Another study conducted by CareerBuilder.com yielded similar findings.[9] The study included 1,150 hiring managers nationwide, and about twelve percent of those managers surveyed said they have screened job candidates by searching for the potential hires' profiles on social networking sites. Of the employers electing to research candidates on social networking sites, sixty-three percent did not hire a prospective employee based on the information uncovered about the candidate online.[10] Beyond those managers surveyed who admitted to

---

[5] The titles of these groups were all found through the basic search on Facebook described *supra*, note 4. All are actual and current groups formed by Indiana University Bloomington students. Facebook users can find similar groups formed on many different college campuses by Facebook users at other universities.

[6] Many social networkers use Facebook or other similar sites to share the "idiosyncratic odds and ends of their lives, intended for viewing by other students . . . [but] the unintended consequences of overly comprehensive, brutally frank, or mischievous entries are surfacing." See Sarah Schweitzer, *Universities Ponder Facebook Etiquette*, The Tech, Sept. 27, 2005, *available at* http://www-tech.mit.edu/Vl25/N42/facebook.html.

[7] *See New "Background" Check*, 23 No. 21 Emp. Alert (National Employment Law Institute), Oct. 12, 2006, at 11 (highlighting the results from the NACE study).

[8] *See Id.*

[9] *See* CareerBuilder.com, One-in-Four Hiring Managers Have Used Internet Search Engines to Screen Job Candidates; One-in-Ten Have Used Social Networking Sites, CareerBuilder.com Survey Finds (Oct. 26, 2006), http://www.careerbuilder.com/share/aboutus/pressreleases.aspx (follow "2006" hyperlink; then follow "10/26/2006" hyperlink).

[10] *Id.*

searching for social networkers' information, an additional twenty-six percent of the managers reported they have used Internet search engines like Google to research prospective hires.[11]

8   Some sources recommend that employers search social networks and play it safe—why not check a potential candidate out using every resource available before making that critical hire?

> Online social networks provide you with a screening tool for job applicants. It's unlikely that a job applicant would ever attach provocative photos, detailed descriptions of sexual escapades, or a list of hobbies that includes funneling beer and recreational drug use on her resume. But with just a few clicks of the mouse, you can find out all sorts of revealing information about potential candidates.[12]

9   Employers are increasingly realizing that they have a choice when it comes to their hiring decisions. They may be more limited with disciplinary actions once employees are actually hired, and this makes an employer's decision to hire the right people particularly important.[13]

10   With the power and responsibilities many new employees can have in the workplace, many employers believe it is important that their hires possess a sense of propriety and an ability to separate their work life and behavior from their personal life. "[N]ew employees have access to a wide range of sensitive materials and information via the rise of the information economy and flattened workplace structures. Given the powerful communication tools in employees' hands, judgment or discretion are increasingly important characteristics for [employees to have]."[14]

B. Protecting Social Networkers' Privacy: An Impossible Task?

11   As employers discover the availability of social networkers' online information, can social network users protect themselves and their posted information? Users of Facebook may harbor the incorrect belief that other students and intended viewers are the only people able to view their profiles. Facebook's privacy settings state you can "control exactly who can see what by including or excluding certain friends or friend lists," as well as "[c]ontrol who can search for you, and how you can be contacted."[15]

12   According to Mark Zuckerberg, the man who created Facebook in 2004 while a sophomore student at Harvard University, "[T]he problem Facebook is solving

---

[11] *Id.*

[12] *What You Won't See, supra* note 2, at 5.

[13] *Blogging Down?, supra* note 1, at 2 (stating that "[o]nce employees are hired . . . it's usually better to address the problem by establishing specific guidelines and training them in the importance of observing the rules and exercising discretion and judgment").

[14] *Id.*

[15] Having created a Facebook profile, one may access privacy settings by clicking "Privacy." After accessing this section, users can choose whether everyone or only limited groups of people can access their profiles and information. *See* Welcome to Facebook, *supra* note 4.

is this one paradox. People want access to all the information around them, but they also want complete control over their own information. Those two things are at odds with each other."[16] Zuckerberg believe that Facebook is able to adequately address this problem because it lets its users activate privacy settings. Users can attempt to prevent strangers from viewing the profiles, pictures, and personal information they post on Facebook by enabling blocking techniques designed to limit outsiders' access to the information. College students, for example, can choose to block all persons not affiliated with their college or university. Those who use Facebook could also enable privacy settings that limit those who can view their profiles to people they accept as their friends or those connected to them through friends (friends of their friends).[17]

1. Facebook's Privacy Settings and Their Shortcomings

13   Despite the available technology that can potentially limit or block unwanted social network users from viewing students' and graduates' Facebook profiles, many Facebook users simply do not activate their privacy settings. Other social networkers enable their privacy settings, but fail to realize that employers nonetheless may be able to gain access to profiles seemingly protected by privacy settings.

14   Hiring companies can access potential hires' social networking profiles in a variety of ways. Not long ago, some of the employees now involved in making hiring decisions for their companies were students with their own Facebook profiles. Graduates can keep their profiles and maintain connections to their colleges' social networks, thereby maintaining connections to the college students who make up the next wave of employment hopefuls. This phenomenon may not be pervasive yet since Facebook and other social networking sites have only existed for a few years.[18] However, as Facebook and other social networking sites gain popularity among college students and as more student Facebook users graduate and join the world of employment, this trend may become increasingly prevalent. Even if employees never had Facebook profiles during their college years, many employees still retain their college email addresses or a valid alumni email address.[19] With a college or alumni email address, employees can create profiles and become affiliated with their undergraduate universities' networks, thereby acquiring access to current students. To those students, these employees will simply appear to be other students and alumni similarly interested in using Facebook as a social networking tool rather than as an employment screening tool.

15   Some companies also hire current students who can access their peers' social networking profiles and effectively circumvent any privacy settings a potential hire may have put in place to attempt to restrict unwanted persons from

---

[16] John Cassidy, *ME Media: How Hanging Out on the Internet Became Big Business*, New Yorker, at 56 (May 15, 2006), *available at* http://www.newyorker.com/archive/2006/05/15/060515fa_fact_cassidy.

[17] *See* Welcome to Facebook. *supra* note 4.

[18] A sophomore student at Harvard created Facebook in 2004. *See* Cassidy, *supra* note 16, at 50.

[19] *See* Alan Finder, *Online Persona Can Ruin Your Shot at That Job*, Seattle Times, June 11 2006, available at http://seattletimes.nwsource.com/html/nationworld/2003054004_recruit11.html.

accessing their profile.[20] For instance, an Indiana University ("IU") student seeking interviews may take extra precautions to keep his or her information safe by setting online privacy measures allowing only other IU students to access and view his or her Facebook profile. Not only would that student's information not be safe from a recent IU graduate who retains an IU student or alumni email address and now uses that address to aid his or her employer in seeking out the next wave of new employees, but the student also would not be shielded from a current peer instructed to research prospective employees for a particular company.

16   Many students discover their social networking profile or other information posted on the Internet has cost them a job opportunity after it is too late.[21] Others take a preemptive stance, attempting to keep their profiles clean and "Googling" themselves occasionally to ensure that unwanted material does not show up online for anyone to view.[22] Is self-censorship the only option available for social networkers hoping to keep their information restricted to intended recipients only?

2. Should a Right to Privacy on Social Networking Sites Be Recognized?

17   Could an employer's unauthorized use of the information on a social networker's profile for hiring purposes constitute an invasion of privacy? In order for a person's privacy to be invaded, that person must have a reasonable expectation of privacy.[23] Facebook tells its users that, "[a]t Facebook, we believe you should have control over your information and who sees it. So in addition to the basic visibility rules—only your friends and people in your networks can see your profile—we also give you granular control over the information you post to the site."[24] The site also provides in its December 6, 2007, adopted privacy policy:

> We built Facebook to make it easy to share information with your friends and people around you. We understand you may not want everyone in the world to have the information you share on Facebook; that is why we give you control of your information. Our default privacy settings limit the information displayed in your profile to your networks and other reasonable community limitations that we tell you about.[25]

---

[20] *See Id.*

[21] *See* Nate Anderson, *Google + Facebook + Alcohol = Trouble*, Ars Technica (Jan. 19, 2006), http://arsteclinica.com/news.ars/post/20060119-6016.html. This source and others also highlight the fact that social networkers can get themselves into trouble due to information posted on the Internet with persons other than prospective employers. Many colleges and universities have been able to access pictures and information on Facebook that provide evidence of underage drinking or other violations of school rules that can cause students to face disciplinary procedures within their academic institutions. *See Id.*

[22] *See Id.*; *see also*, Kate Bigam, *Employers May be Eying Students' Facebook Accounts*, Daily Kent Stater, Nov. 3, 2006, *available at* http://media.www.kentnewsnet.com/media/storage/paper867/news/2006/11/03/News/Employers.May.Be.Eyeing.Students.Facebook.Accounts-2437174.shtml.

[23] *See* Mitchell Waldman, Annotation, *Expectation of Privacy in Internet Communications*, 92 A.L.R. 5th 15 (2001).

[24] Facebook Site Tour, http://www.facebook.com/sitetour/privacy.php (last visited Mar. 21, 2008).

[25] Facebook Principles, http://www.facebook.com/policy.php (last visited Mar. 21, 2008).

18   From these statements, one can see why Facebook users may believe their information posted on the social networking site is secure. If one continues reading the Web site's privacy policy, he or she can also find this warning:

> You post User Content . . . on the Site at your own risk. Although we allow you to set privacy options that limit access to your pages, please be aware that no security measures are perfect or impenetrable. We cannot control the actions of other Users with whom you may choose to share your pages and information. Therefore, we cannot and do not guarantee that User Content you post on the Site will not be viewed by unauthorized persons. We are not responsible for circumvention of any privacy settings or security measures contained on the Site. You understand and acknowledge that, even after removal, copies of User Content may remain viewable in cached and archived pages or if other Users have copied or stored your User Content.[26]

19   From the statements informing Facebook users of their ability to use privacy protection measures to warnings about the unavoidable flaws inherent in any privacy protection system, it is difficult to determine whether Facebook networkers can have any reasonable expectation that the materials they post on the site will be safe from unwanted viewers.

3. The Reasonable Expectation of Privacy Requirement: Being Seen by Some Does Not Mean One Should be Seen by All

20   No clear answer can yet be gleaned from legal precedent as to whether the Facebook users and other social networkers have a reasonable expectation of privacy in their profiles and posted materials. According to court decisions, there is uncertainty as to whether a person retains a limited right to privacy and a reasonable expectation of privacy when the information that person intended to keep private was intentionally shared with some but also fell into the hands of unintended recipients. For example, the California Supreme Court stated in *Sanders v. American Broadcasting Co.* that:

> There are degrees and nuances to societal recognition of our expectations of privacy: the fact that the privacy one expects in a given setting is not complete or absolute does not render the expectation unreasonable as a matter of law. . . . The mere fact that a person can be seen by someone does not automatically mean that he or she can legally be forced to be subject to being seen by everyone.[27]

21   In *Sanders*, an ABC investigative journalist, Stacy Lescht, obtained employment as a telephone psychic and used a hidden video camera to record her conversations with her new co-workers. Sanders, an employee of the company, sued the undercover journalist after part of one of his conversations with her was broadcast on ABC's *Prime Time Live* television program. The ABC journalist

---

[26] *Id.*

[27] *See* Sanders v. American Brdcst. Co., 978 P.2d 67, 72 (Cal. 1999).

argued that because coworkers could overhear her conversations with Sanders, Sanders could have no reasonable expectation of privacy in the communication. The court disagreed, determining that Sanders retained a reasonable expectation of privacy during his workplace discussions with coworkers.[28]

22   Other cases also suggest that a plaintiff who reveals information about himself or herself to some people may have the right to keep that information private from other unintended persons for the purposes of privacy tort law.[29] This may be the case regardless of contractual or legal constraints placed upon those to whom the information is expressed.[30] In addition, a plaintiff may reasonably expect information to be kept private in a variety of situations involving different groups of people, such as persons close to the plaintiff,[31] coworkers,[32] or mere strangers.[33]

23   In *Y.G. v. Jewish Hospital of St. Louis,* the plaintiffs were a married couple who conceived twin children after their participation in an *in vitro* fertilization clinic. The couple's church condemned this form of conception, and the couple kept the information about their twins' conception limited to a few close friends and family members. The couple attended a party at the *in vitro* clinic for around forty people who were involved with the clinic, and a local news media crew covered the party and aired pictures of the couple on television. The media crew argued that the plaintiffs waived their expectation of privacy as to their involvement with the clinic when they attended the party, but the court disagreed. It held that by attending the party the couple "clearly chose to disclose their participation to only the other *in vitro* couples. By so attending this limited gathering, they did not waive their right to keep their condition and the process of *in vitro* private, in respect to the general public."[34]

24   Similarly, in *Multimedia WMAZ, Inc. v. Kubach,* the court determined that an HIV positive man retained a reasonable expectation of privacy as to his condition when it was disclosed by a television station. Mr. Kubach agreed to appear as a guest for a report the television station aired, but he agreed to do so only if his identity was kept private and his image distorted to render it unrecognizable. The distortion did not work as Kubach expected and as the station had promised, and Kubach was recognized by television viewers throughout his community. The television station argued that the plaintiff had no reasonable expectation of privacy as to the fact that he was HIV positive because he had disclosed the information to friends, some family members, and members of support groups. Many people were aware of the fact that Kubach was HIV positive. The court disagreed with the station and sided

---

[28] *Id.* at 79.

[29] *See Id.* at 67. *See generally* Y.G. v. Jewish Hosp. of St. Louis, 795 S.W.2d 488 (Mo. Ct. App. 1990); Multimedia WMAZ, Inc. v. Kubach, 443 S.E.2d 491 (Ga. Ct. App. 1994).

[30] In other words, whether the information one shares is with a doctor or lawyer (legally protected and private relationships) or with friends or acquaintances who are under no specific legal obligation to maintain the confidences shared with them is not determinative of whether the person can have an expectation of privacy.

[31] *See Kubach,* 443 S.E.2d at 491.

[32] *See Sanders,* 978 P.2d at 67.

[33] *See Y.G.,* 795 S.W.2d at 488.

[34] *Id.* at 502.

with Kubach, stating that the plaintiff had expressed news of his condition to some "because they cared about him and/or because they also had AIDS."[35] In addition, although Kubach did not tell his friends and relatives to keep his medical condition confidential, "there was also testimony that they understood that plaintiff's condition was not something they would discuss indiscriminately."[36]

4. The Reasonable Expectation of Privacy Requirement: Once Information is Provided to Some, it is Open to All?

25   On the opposite end of the spectrum, there are also cases that reject a plaintiff's invocation of a limited right to privacy regarding particular facts or information that the plaintiff disclosed to third parties. In *Nader v. General Motors Corp.*, the New York Court of Appeals set a very different precedent from the cases discussed previously.[37] Just before consumer advocate Ralph Nader published his best seller, *Unsafe at Any Speed*, General Motors allegedly tried to intimidate Nader by digging into his personal information and past. The company allegedly interviewed Nader's friends and relatives regarding Nader's interests, habits, political and religious beliefs, sexual history, and other areas under the false pretense that it was researching Nader for prospective employment purposes. The court determined that information already known to others could hardly be considered private, and Nader therefore could not expect to maintain his privacy despite the fact that he had shared personal information with select persons only.[38] Essentially, Nader was deemed to have assumed the risk that persons to whom he disclosed his information would spread that information to others. As a matter of law, facts shared with others are no longer private.[39]

26   The case of *Duran v. Detroit News, Inc.* also follows a similar hard-line toward privacy in information disclosed to third parties.[40] In this case, Consuelo Sanchez Duran was a Colombian judge who had indicted the drug lord Pablo Escobar. As a result of her ruling, Duran and her family received death threats that caused her to resign, flee Colombia, and take a job as the Colombian consul in Detroit, Michigan. Duran used her real name when shopping and dining out, and told a few neighbors of her reason for fleeing Colombia; however, she also took precautions to ensure that her relocation to Detroit was not otherwise advertised or widely known publicly (for instance, she kept an unlisted phone number, did not join clubs or organizations, and did not attend concerts or other public events). Duran sued when, after living in Detroit for a few months, local reporters exposed her history and disclosed her address. At least one reporter also publicized the $1 million bounty the Colombian drug cartel had put on Duran's head. The Michigan Court of Appeals determined that Duran's actions and disclosures to Detroit residents had rendered her identity "open to

---

[35] *Kubach*, 443 S.E.2d at 494.

[36] *Id.*

[37] *See Nader v. Gen. Motors Corp.*, 255 N.E.2d 765 (N.Y. 1970).

[38] *Id.* at 770.

[39] *See Id.*

[40] *See Duran v. Detroit News, Inc.*, 504 N.W.2d 715 (Mich. Ct. App. 1993).

the public eye,"[41] and Duran could enjoy no reasonable expectation of privacy as to her identity and background.

27   The final hard-line case of interest is *Fisher v. Ohio Department of Rehabilitation and Correction*.[42] In this case, the Ohio Court of Claims determined that a plaintiff who told four coworkers that some interactions between herself and her young son had "sexual overtones" could claim no reasonable expectation of privacy as to her statements.[43] The plaintiff's disclosure to the coworkers rendered the information nonprivate, and the plaintiff's employer was therefore free to disclose the information to the plaintiff's husband (who subsequently divorced her). The court stated that "the report merely recounts a conversation which the plaintiff publicly and openly conducted with her fellow employees. The plaintiff's discussion of her personal experiences was freely offered to the persons around her without concern of the impact it might have on her character."[44]

28   From the cases discussed in this section and the preceding section, it is clear that there is not a strong line of cases to direct a modern court's determination of whether a plaintiff has a reasonable expectation of privacy for the purposes of privacy tort law. The number of persons to whom a plaintiff voluntarily discloses information does not seem to be a determinative factor in deciding whether a plaintiff can claim an expectation of privacy. In *Kubach*, the plaintiff told around sixty people about his HIV positive condition, and the court determined that he could reasonably expect to maintain his privacy as to this fact;[45] on the other hand, the plaintiff in *Fisher* told only four coworkers of the "sexual undertones," but she could retain no expectation of privacy in her statements.[46] Why should particular disclosures waive privacy expectations while others do not?

[. . .]

6. The Internet: An Amazing and Unruly Medium

29   Because many courts have recognized how accessible the Internet is, how many people are able to effectively 'access the Internet,' and how difficult it is to keep track of who is involved in viewing particular Internet sites,[58] it is possible that a modern court faced with Facebook users' privacy dilemmas could determine that social networkers should not be able to reasonably claim an expectation of privacy in their Internet postings. While this may not be the correct response to the privacy problems online, it enjoys some precedential support.[59]

---

[41] *Id.* at 720.

[42] 578 N.E.2d 901 (Ohio Misc. 1988).

[43] *Id.* at 902.

[44] *Id.* at 903.

[45] Multimedia WMAZ, Inc. v. Kubach, 443 S.E.2nd 491, 494 (Ga. Ct. App. 1994).

[46] *Fisher*, 578 N.E. 2d at 902.

[58] "The nature of the Internet, however, is such that if a user enters the appropriate information (password, social security number, etc.), it is nearly impossible to verify the true identity of that user." *Konop*, 302 F.3d at 875.

[59] *Compare* Reno v. ACLU, 521 U.S. 844 (1997), *with* DoubleClick Inc. Privacy Litig., 154 F. Supp. 2d 497, 501 (S.D.N.Y. 2001) (pointing to the fact that the Internet allows millions of people across the world to share and exchange information and to communicate through the computer connections).

30   Just as the court in *Konop* tried to reconcile Congress's intent that the SCA protect electronically communicated materials from unauthorized viewers with the pervasiveness and easy accessibility of the Internet, a Pennsylvania court attempted to determine the privacy issues raised with regard to communication on an Internet Web site in *J.S. ex rel. H.S. v. Bethlehem Area School District.*[60] In this case the Commonwealth Court of Pennsylvania held that a middle school student could not have an expectation of privacy with regard to the materials he posted on his Web site. The student created a Web page at his home on his family's computer, and posted derogatory comments about his teachers and principal on this site. After discovering the site and deeming it to be threatening and harassing to a teacher and the principal, the school expelled the student.

31   In addressing the issue, the Pennsylvania court noted that the school district could not have violated the boy's right to privacy because "any user who happened upon the correct search terms could have stumbled upon [the] Student's web-site."[61] The court pointed out that the Web site in question was not a protected site—it was not the sort of site that could only be accessed by particular viewers with passwords or specific usernames. The court also compared the posting of a Web site to the sending of email messages or letters: once the message or letter is received, the sender can no longer control the information's ultimate destination or potential to spread to others. Similarly, a creator of a Web site controls the site until the time it is posted on the Internet. Once posting has occurred, the creator loses control of the Web site's final reach and audience, and that site becomes accessible to anyone on the Internet. "Without protecting the web-site, the creator takes the risk of other individuals accessing it once it is posted."[62] Accordingly, the court affirmed the trial court's decision that the student maintained no expectation of privacy in the comments he posted on his Web site.

32   The court's focus on the student's failure to implement privacy protection or security measures highlights its willingness to consider this particularly important issue as it addresses Internet users' privacy. Future courts' reliance on cases like *Konop* and *J.S.*, which discuss privacy settings and security measures at length, may help to create a future test and recognizable standards for determining a plaintiff's privacy expectations.

33   A court should be concerned with these privacy settings and security measures as it determines whether an expectation of privacy can exist. A number of factors could be relevant to determining whether a social networker can have a reasonable expectation of privacy in his or her information posted online. These factors include: (1) whether privacy settings are available; (2) whether the social networker attempted to or did enable the privacy settings; (3) the level of privacy the networker attempted to or was able to set with an eye to the spectrum of privacy settings and measures available to the social networker; (4) the kinds of people and groups to whom that networker chose to disclose the information he or she later claims to be sensitive and private; and (5) whether the unwanted or unauthorized person who accessed the networker's information was able to

---

[60] 757 A.2d. 412 (Pa. Commw. Ct. 2000).

[61] *Id.* at 425.

[62] *Id.*

happen upon the information or had to hack through security measures to find the information. While this list is by no means exhaustive, it builds on the principles established in some of the privacy cases discussed previously. A court facing this difficult question without the benefit of clear precedent and in the face of new technology will, no doubt, be faced with a daunting task.

C. Are Employers Violating Facebook's Terms Of Service?

34   In addition to the privacy issues that may arise when an employer uses Facebook to screen a potential hire, other legal difficulties may also occur. When a user registers for Facebook and creates a profile on the social networking site, that user must agree to particular terms of use. Any employer who retains, creates, or employs another to use their Facebook access and searching capabilities to locate information about the employer's prospective hires would also be bound by these terms of use. The terms state, in relevant part:

> You understand that . . . programs offered by us on the Site (e.g., Facebook Flyers . . .), the Service and the Site are available *for your personal, non-commercial use only. You represent, warrant and agree that no materials of any kind submitted through your account or otherwise posted, transmitted, or shared* by you on or through the Service will violate or infringe upon the rights of any third party . . .; or contain libelous, defamatory or otherwise unlawful material. . . . [Y]ou [further] agree not to use the Service or the Site to:
>
> > *impersonate any person or entity, or falsely state or otherwise misrepresent yourself, your age or your affiliation with any person or entity;*
> >
> > *intimidate or harass another;*
> >
> > *use or attempt to use another's account,* service or system without authorization from the Company, or *create a false identity* on the Service or the Site.[63]

35   The first portion of the terms of use is selected to emphasize that Facebook is not intended for commercial use. When employers use Facebook or similar social networks as a tool to screen job applicants, are the employers using the networks for commercial purposes? Certainly, employers would not screen potential applicants unless they did so in order to seek out the best human capital for hire and to make their businesses more profitable and successful. Commercial motivation may be one possible interpretation of employers' actions, but it may not be the only reasonable interpretation.[64] Just after stating that Facebook is to be used for noncommercial purposes, the terms of use focus "on materials submitted through your account," not on what one does with information he or she learns about others.[65] For this reason, "'non-commercial use only' could be interpreted as addressing only a prohibition on posting information for commercial gain, such as advertisements."[66]

---

[63] Facebook Terms of Use, http://www.facebook.com/terms.plip (last visited Mar, 21, 2008) (emphasis added). Scroll down to the heading titled "User Conduct." The portions of the terms that may affect an employer using Facebook as a background checking tool have been emphasized in italics. The "User Conduct" section of the Facebook Terms of Use are provided in full in Appendix B.

[64] *See* Lenard, *supra* note 48.

[65] *Id.*

[66] *Id.* (emphasis omitted).

36   While noncommercial use may be open for interpretation and, therefore, more difficult to prove, some employers' means of accessing applicants' information on Facebook may violate the terms of use more blatantly. Some employers may be engaged in misrepresentation in direct violation of Facebook's terms of service.[67] This might be the case where an employer pretends they are affiliated with a college in order to gain access to that college's students' profiles (this may include the example of the employee who uses her alumni email address to join her alma mater's network and thereby access enrolled students' posted information). An employee that uses another's Facebook account on a company's behalf (the example of the student "spy" hired by a company to research his or her peers) is also a clear violation of the terms of use policy.[68]

II. CONCLUSION: THINKING PRACTICALLY

37   As technology continues to advance and the Internet evolves, society can likely benefit from providing students, graduates, and the general population with the ability to access forums like Facebook and to interact in new and more meaningful ways with others in our communities. The Internet has the potential to break down geographic barriers and help people to feel connected to each other in ways they could not previously have imagined. It would be unfortunate indeed if we are all forced to mind our P's and Q's at every turn during our use of this promising medium.

38   Despite the potential promise of better connections, interactions, and open social communication forums, Facebook users and other social networkers cannot and should not ignore the current threat to their online privacy. Employers are free to use their best judgment as they choose their new employees.[69] Accessing Facebook or another social network to screen candidates is just one more tool the employers have discovered to help them learn as much as they can about the people who could become integral to the success or failure of their companies. Social networkers need to be realistic: their information is not, at the present time, safe from these unauthorized viewers. Privacy settings and blocking tools that limit other social networkers' access should be employed, at minimum, in order to attempt to protect a Facebook user's privacy. Beyond this imperfect attempt to protect information, the only sure way for a social networker to protect his or her private information is to ensure that he or she monitors postings and self-censors posted materials. Perhaps, with the development of technology and improved privacy measures, social networkers will be better able to enjoy the vibrancy and openness that social networks like Facebook can offer.

---

[67] As provided in the text, the Terms of Use state that one shall not "impersonate any person or entity, or falsely state or otherwise misrepresent yourself, your age or your affiliation with any person or entity." Facebook Terms of Use, *supra* note 64.

[68] *See Id.*

[69] Lenard, *supra* note 48 (pointing out that "like it or not, as a general proposition employers are free to make unfit, stupid, arbitrary, and wrongheaded hiring and termination decisions, even based on false information, as long as in doing so they do not violate some specific law.").

39   Perfect privacy settings may not be a realistic short term goal, however, and perfect privacy settings may prevent many of the social interactions that social networkers seek.[70] The solution to this privacy threat can best be resolved by the courts and the legislature. Should courts acknowledge that Internet users who attempt to limit others' access to their online information have an expectation of privacy in their information, the courts may be able to effectively discourage unauthorized snooping and prying by employers (and other unwanted viewers). If Congress clarifies that it is a priority to protect Internet communication from unauthorized viewers in acts like the Stored Communications Act, this may also create a clear standard of privacy protection.[71] Protecting social networkers' rights to privacy in their information could be the first step toward fostering and encouraging open communication on Internet public forums.

Active Reading

1. There are two major headings, marked by Roman numerals I and II. There are many subheadings under Roman numeral I (sections A, B, and C), but there are no subheadings following Roman numeral II. Does this structure indicate that the author does her work up front, and presents her conclusions as more or less self-evident?

2. Now look at the way the article is organized into sections by subheadings. There are three main subheadings, indicated by the capital letters A, B, and C. Under A, there are two subheadings, and under B there are five (one of the six sections in the original is not reproduced here). Section C has no subheadings. Write out these headings in the form of an outline. Do you think the author might have drafted the article using headings close to these in an outline?

3. Before you read the whole article, the title probably led you to believe that the author would actually have new revelations about the dangers of social networking. How do the three paragraphs in the conclusion soften the argument about dangers and even argue for the advantages of these social networking sites?

Critical Reading

1. As a reader, do you find the extensive use of footnotes a diversion from the main text? Can you think of some of the reasons why writing about legal matters might involve using footnotes?

2. Who is Mark Zuckerberg and how are his comments positioned in the author's argument? According to the way his views are represented here, does he seem

---

[70] Query: How can a social networker find strangers with similar interests with whom they can interact if their privacy settings effectively limit those who may view their information to those people they have expressly permitted to access that information (the people they already know)?

[71] For instance, if Congress removed the exception to the SCA that creates uncertainty as to whether an authorized user can share information with an unauthorized user, this would likely indicate to courts that the legislature's goal and priority is to protect stored communications from unauthorized viewers. Or, Congress could clarify this intention where a plaintiff's expectation of privacy is concerned. This would likely resolve issues, such as the one in *Konop*, where the terms of use clearly prohibited the manager from accessing the plaintiff's Web page.

to have a rather simplistic view of how to protect the privacy of Facebook users? Is it probable that he has produced a more thorough statement on privacy concerns? If you were writing a critique, you might want to look at full-text interviews with Zuckerberg, to see his extended position on privacy.

3. This article was published in a law journal. Can you find a passage where the author takes a legalistic view of the need to guard personal privacy?

4. The author shares the concern that social networking sites may reveal our "frighteningly questionable interests." Is she right to argue that a link to sex, drugs, and alcohol on a Facebook site is a dangerous self-revelation?

5. What is meant by the term "Note" in the first paragraphs? How is a "Note" different from an article in a scholarly journal?

Driven to Distraction

How our multi-channel, multi-tasking society is making it harder for us to think

Jon Lorinc

This article appeared in a Canadian magazine that explores contemporary issues and culture, The Walrus *(April 2007). John Lorinc considers how technologies like cell phones and BlackBerry devices keep us connected and informed, but how we pay a price by losing our privacy.*

Lorinc is a Toronto journalist who specializes in urban affairs. He wrote the politics column for Toronto Life *from 1995 to 2005, and contributes regularly to the* Globe and Mail.

1   In the late 1920s, a Russian-born psychologist named Bluma Zeigarnik found herself sitting in a crowded Viennese coffee house, wondering how the waiters could accurately recall the minute details of numerous orders without committing them to paper. That casual observation proved to be the basis of a paper published in 1927, in which she laid out what came to be known as the Zeigarnik Effect. Her now-famous thesis was that the human mind is better at remembering incomplete tasks, an insight that proved useful to generations of marketers and managers, who devised ways of leveraging our mental response to interruptions and manipulating individuals into buying products or completing tasks more efficiently.

2   I first learned about the Zeigarnik Effect on a fascinating website titled Interruptions in Human-Computer Interaction (*interruptions.net*), which gathers the work of a diverse collection of researchers—social scientists, software engineers, psychologists, and neuroscientists—who study what may well be the defining condition of the information age: chronic distraction.

3   During the past three or four years, quantum leaps in wireless digital technology have brought us to the point where high-powered portable devices permit us to be in constant contact with one another, to access vast storehouses of digitized entertainment, and to plug into the Internet virtually anytime, anywhere. The unveiling earlier this year of Apple's new iPhone anticipates an era dominated by a gadget that effortlessly functions as a cellphone, a personal digital assistant, and a camera; holds

hundreds of hours of digital music; streams high-resolution digital video; receives digital satellite radio and maybe even television; and offers full Internet access regardless of the time of day and where the user happens to be.

4   Even before this all-in-one technology makes its grand debut, we are revelling in the miracle of nearly ubiquitous connectivity. But all this access has not come without a psychological cost that is ultimately rooted in the way our brains function. If we now find ourselves adrift in an ocean of information, our mental state increasingly resembles the slivered surface of a melting glacier. As the dozens of studies at *interruptions.net* attest, we have created a technological miasma that inundates us with an inexhaustible supply of electronic distractions. Rather than providing necessary interruptions to assist us in focusing on the incomplete task at hand, as Zeigarnik proposed, the deluge of multi-channel signals has produced an array of concentration-related problems, including lost productivity, cognitive overload, and a wearying diminishment in our ability to retain the very information we consume with such voraciousness. It may be that our hyper-connected world has quite simply made it difficult for us to think.

5   The irony is that one of the fundamental promises of information technology— the radical improvement in the efficiency of our interactions with one another— is being undermined by the technology's enormous capacity to overwhelm us with information and thus short-circuit our need to concentrate. Cognitive psychologists are beginning to understand why the human brain isn't well suited to the sort of communications environment we've built for ourselves. Yet in post-industrial urban societies, few of us are willing or able to disengage, because going off-line in a wireless world is no longer an option. This raises a pair of tough questions: Do we control this technology or has it come to control us? And have we arrived at a point, fifteen years after the advent of the web, where we need to rethink our relationship with a technology that may well be altering the way our minds function?

6   This isn't going to be a Luddite rant. Like many people, I spend much of my working day in front of a computer screen. I have instant access to information I could never have obtained even a decade ago. At the same time, I find myself asking why phrases like "train of thought" and "undivided attention" are part of our linguistic geography, and what's become of the underlying mental states they refer to. It often seems as though the sheer glut of data itself has supplanted the kind of focused, reflective attention that might make this information useful in the first place.

7   The dysfunction of our information environment is an outgrowth of its extraordinary fecundity. Digital communications technology has demonstrated a striking capacity to subdivide our attention into smaller and smaller increments; increasingly, it seems as if the day's work has become a matter of interrupting the interruptions. Email for many people has become an oppressive feature of work life. MySpace, YouTube, chat rooms, and the blogosphere, for all their virtues as new mediums of political debate and cultural activity, have an amazing ability to suck up time. During this decade, executives and the political class became literally addicted to BlackBerrys, and these devices are now being taken up by consumers who obsessively check them while waiting for coffee or minding the kids at the playground. Information workers spend their days

pursuing multiple projects that involve serpentine email threads, thousands of files, and endless web searches. Paradoxically, the abundance of information begets a craving for even more, a compulsion that results in diminishing returns and is often remarkably undiscerning. Scientists at the Xerox Palo Alto Research Center have labelled this kind of online behaviour as "information foraging" and coined the pithy term "informavores" to describe this new species.

8   The technology, in theory, has the ability to emancipate individuals from tedious minutiae: we no longer need to memorize vast amounts of quotidian information (phone numbers, addresses, trivia of any sort) because a digital version is always retrievable. So, in principle, we should have more mental space to focus on the things that are important to us. And yet, the seductive nature of the technology allows us to sample almost anything and, when addicted to this foraging of bits and bytes, focus on nothing. The resulting cognitive overload has become the occupational hazard for the technorati.

9   Some years ago, researchers surveyed managers in the United States, the United Kingdom, Australia, Singapore, and Hong Kong. Two-thirds reported stress, tension, and loss of job satisfaction because of cognitive overload. "Information is relentlessly pushed at us, we need more, and of better quality and focus," wrote David Kirsh, a Toronto-born expert in cognitive science who runs the Interactive Cognition Lab at the University of California, San Diego. When I spoke to him recently, he said his basic concerns about information frag- mentation hadn't changed, and the problem may accelerate with the new portable technologies that have turbo-charged the data environment.

10   The mechanics of cognitive overload are similar to the problem of insuffi- cient RAM. "In most models of working memory and attention, everything has to go through a central executive processor before being passed into long-term memory," explains Frank Russo, an assistant professor of psychology at Ryerson University. Our built-in CPUs are found in the brain's frontal lobe. These cen- tres need time to "rehearse" or "scaffold" incoming information by building the neural circuits on which the data will eventually be stored. "If it is not rehearsed enough or elaborated upon," Russo told me, "the information never makes it to the long-term store." When someone is bombarded by data, the executive processor doesn't have the time or the resources to encode everything and starts to show signs of fatigue.

11   While "memory" is a word that has been appropriated by the information tech- nology world, human and digital memory function very differently. Absent cor- rupted documents or bugs, the act of saving a file means saving it in its entirety, with an understanding that when it is retrieved the file will be in the state the user left it. Human memory is much more error-prone and subjective. Our memories decay and reshape themselves over time. To appreciate the contrast, imagine if you saved a document and when you reopened it the text contained only the parts that pleased you.

12   Russo illustrates the point with an experiment he does for his students. He shows them a video of a group of young men and women tossing two basketballs among themselves quite rapidly. The students are asked to count the number of passes. At a certain point in the video, a man in a gorilla suit walks through the frame. After the video, when the students are asked if they noticed anything odd,

about a third say they didn't see this absurd disruption. "I use this experiment to demonstrate the point that perception and memory are not like running a tape," Russo says. "We do have selective attention and we miss things, especially if we're very focused on a particular task." As Jeffery Jones, an assistant professor of psychology at Wilfrid Laurier University, puts it, "There seems to be a limit to the amount of information we can process at one time."

13   It's not just a matter of quantity either. Kathy Sierra is a Boulder, Colorado-based educator who designed and created the bestselling "Head First" software-development guides, which are based on neuroscience research about cognition and human memory. In developing her approach, she pored over evidence that revealed how the human brain, from an evolutionary point of view, remains a machine programmed primarily to look out for its owner's survival, like the threat of an approaching predator. "Our brain cares about things that are very different than the conscious mind wants to learn," she says. It is geared to respond to novel, surprising, or terrifying emotional and sensory stimuli. Her conclusion: the fast-paced, visually arousing hit of video games is intensely captivating for the human brain, whereas the vast amount of text found on websites, blogs, and databases tends to wash over us.

14   The human mind, well-suited as it is for language, has always adapted to new information technologies such as the printing press and the telephone, so why should the latest generation be any different? It may be partly a matter of the quantity of information at our disposal, and the speed and frequency with which it comes at us. The research on cognitive overload and multi-tasking reveals that our brains are ill equipped to function effectively in an information-saturated digital environment characterized by constant disruptions. While there's much hype about how young people weaned on the Internet and video games develop neural circuits that allow them to concentrate on many tasks at once, the science of interruptions suggests our brains aren't nearly that plastic.

15   Russo cites epidemiological studies showing that drivers who are talking on a cellphone are four times more likely to be involved in an accident than those who remain focused on the road. Aviation experts have understood this phenomenon for years. A large proportion of plane crashes involving pilot error can be traced to cockpit interruptions and distractions. A 1998 study pointed out that when people are engaged in highly familiar or routine tasks—the things we say we can do in our sleep—they become vulnerable to distraction-related errors because the brain is, essentially, on autopilot and doesn't recover well when it is called on to respond to information that is unpredictable, even casual conversation. "Cognitive research indicates that people are able to perform two tasks concurrently only in limited circumstances, even if they are skillful in performing each task separately," concluded a recent NASA study on cockpit distractions. That's why pilots are required to keep banter to a minimum.

16   Multi-tasking, however, is the signature behaviour of the wired world. We spend our days ricocheting between websites, blogs, our own files, and the various communications devices demanding our attention. Ironically, humans have misappropriated the nomenclature of digital technology to describe this phenomenon. The phrase "multi-tasking," David Kirsh observes, was invented to describe a computer's capabilities, not a person's.

17   Yet wireless devices encourage ill-advised multi-tasking: driving and checking BlackBerrys; talking on the phone and reading email; working on two or more complex projects at once. In corporate meetings, participants discreetly text one another or check email while the boss is talking. University classrooms are now filled with students tapping away at their wireless laptops. They maybe focused on a document or a website related to the lecture or they may not. Digital technologies invite disruption and pose a daunting challenge to the possibility of a group of individuals applying their collective attention to a particular chore.

18   Not surprisingly, a growing body of scientific literature has demonstrated that multi-tasking in an office setting is a recipe for lost productivity—a message that runs directly counter to the way many companies want their employees to work. When someone is bouncing between complex tasks, he loses time as the brain is forced to refocus. An American Psychological Association study has found that those "time costs increased with the complexity of the tasks, so it took significantly longer to switch between more complex tasks." When multi-tasking, the brain's executive processor performs a two-stage operation: the first is "goal shifting" (e.g., shifting from editing a text file to checking email), and the second is "rule activation" (turning off the learned rules for editing on a word processing program and turning on the rules for managing the email program that's being used). According to the APA, Joshua Rubinstein, a psychologist with the US Federal Aviation Administration, determined that "rule activation itself takes significant amounts of time, several tenths of a second—which can add up when people switch back and forth repeatedly between tasks. Thus, multi-tasking may seem more efficient on the surface, but may actually take more time in the end."

19   Uncontrolled interruptions create a similar cognitive response. You're working on your computer and the cell rings, the BlackBerry buzzes, or the incoming email notification pings. Out of a sense of urgency, curiosity, or simply a craving for a distraction from an arduous task, you break away to deal with the interruption, which may be something very simple (a quick cellphone exchange) or something quite complex (a detailed email from a coworker that's been marked urgent). In other cases, the interruption leads you off on an entirely new tangent and you may not end up returning to the original project for hours. By that point, you have forgotten where you were or you may have closed windows that now need to be found and reactivated. It's like putting a novel down for days and then discovering you need to reread the last chapter in order to figure out what is happening.

20   When a large British company evaluated the emails sent by its employees, it discovered that almost 30 percent were unnecessarily copied, irrelevant, or difficult to understand. The annual cost in lost productivity was estimated to be about £3,400 per person, or almost £10 million across the firm. Those numbers don't include the time lost as employees try to get back on task.

21   The annual Computer-Human Interaction (CHI) conference, held last year at Montreal's cavernous Palais des congrés, was in many ways a classic nerdapalooza—hundreds of grad students, post-docs, professors, and software industry types networking and swapping business cards.

22   The Palais had set up hotspots throughout the building, which virtually guaranteed that the sessions would be a study in multi-tasking and fragmented

attention. The presenters plugged their laptops into digital projectors and fired up their PowerPoint presentations, while the conference delegates whipped out their PowerBooks and promptly went online. Almost everyone fiddled with some kind of portable device—laptops, BlackBerrys, Palms, or camera phones. One young woman played with an Etch A Sketch key fob.

23   Interestingly, many of the most popular sessions dealt with finding technological solutions to the daily problems precipitated by the combination of too much communication and too little time. Similar preoccupations have turned up at other information technology conferences in the past year or two, according to Sierra, who attends many techie gatherings. At one conference she went to last year, the dominant topic of discussion had to do with ways of filtering out unwanted information. "I've never seen that before and I've been going to these tech conferences for fifteen years."

24   Some groups debated the failings of recommender systems—software on movie, music, and book sites that purport to provide tips based on user profiles but typically generate unwieldy lists instead. Others deliberated on why it had become so difficult to electronically set up face-to-face meetings in the age of crushingly crowded schedules. At a session about text messaging, a young post-doc presented the results of a study on the costs of interruptions among MSN users.

25   But it was during an esoteric debate on "information architecture" that one participant drove right to the heart of the issue that seemed to be on everyone's mind. "If information is like the sea," this delegate asked, "what is seamanship?" The question seemed to me to be about as profound an observation as anything I've come across in all the discussions about the geography of the digital universe. "We don't talk about 'human-wind interactions,'" he continued. "We talk about sailing. We don't talk about 'human-saw interactions.' We talk about woodworking."

26   His point was that we don't have a relationship with a toaster because it is nothing more or less than an object we use to perform a discrete task. But information/communications technology is unlike any other human invention because it performs data processing tasks more adroitly than the human brain. What's more, the wireless advances of the past decade have created portable devices that purport to augment our minds. Whether or not they do, we have become more and more dependent on these fabricated cortexes. We have complex relationships with such gadgets because, increasingly, we can't really function without them. I could get along without a car but I can no longer earn a living without my browser.

27   When these technologies create an unintended consequence—i.e., a Google search that produces millions of hits that may not be ordered according to the user's needs and is therefore a self defeating solution to the problem of finding information on the Net—we seek to engineer our way out of the box. At the CHI conference, technical people debated technical solutions to the failings of a techno-culture that throws up too much information and too many distractions. While the participants were clearly preoccupied with this Catch-22, they largely believed that technology must deliver the solutions.

28   This orientation was glaringly obvious during a seminar entitled "Because I Carry My Cell Phone Anyway," by Pam Ludford, a Ph.D. candidate at the

University of Minnesota. She developed a prototype of a "place-based reminder system," dubbed "PlaceMail." Every day, she began, Americans spend about two-and-a-half hours doing chores at different places—the mall, the dry cleaners, the supermarket. But, she said, "people have imperfect practices for managing these tasks." We make lists, then misplace or forget to check them. By way of a solution to such common imperfections, she has devised a "location-based reminder system." In broad strokes, you key your to-do list into a web-interface feature on a cellphone or BlackBerry equipped with a global positioning system chip or other location-sensitive technology. Next, you input the locations of the places where said chores can be accomplished. Then, as you're driving around, the GPS chip will detect if you are close to the supermarket, say, whereupon the phone rings and an electronic message appears, reminding you to pick up eggs and toilet paper.

29　After the session, Victoria Bellotti, a principal scientist and area manager at the Palo Alto Research Center, told me that such aides may be "the next big thing." But she also seemed dubious. For most people, a mnemonic scribble—"Mother's Day" or "Beth blah blah"—is more than enough of a trigger to retrieve the memory necessary for an intended task, especially if it is stored in some kind of chronological context, such as an appointment book. "Your brain," Bellotti said, "is basically a pattern-matching instrument." Such memory prostheses may prove to be overkill, she added. But then she quickly noted that she herself has a dreadful memory. "Maybe we could stop worrying about certain things and focus on other things if we had that prosthetic device on us." On the other hand, it might simply prove to be yet another dispenser of interruptions that further atomize our capacity to concentrate.

30　PlaceMail, in fact, is evidence of the feedback mechanism in our over-connected culture. In our relentless drive for more data-friendly wireless communications, we have produced a surfeit of communication and information, the combination of which has a tendency to clog up our schedules, splinter our attention spans, and overwhelm our short-term memories. Given the way our brains actually function, it may turn out that what we need is more time and fewer distractions, even if that means less information.

31　Not all of us are looking to key our way out of this box. We are now witnessing the emergence of a non-technological response to the symptoms of an accelerated info-culture. In San Francisco, a writer and consultant named Merlin Mann runs a blog called 43 Folders, which is about "personal productivity, life hacks, and simple ways to make your life a little better." The popular site has become a focal point of debate about ways to manage the downside of too much digital communication, but from the perspective of users rather than technophobes.

32　The name of Mann's blog comes from an idea in *Getting Things Done: The Art of Stress-Free Productivity*, the bestselling 2001 time-management guide by David Allen, who has become a guiding light for people in BlackBerry twelve-step recovery programs. A hippie in dress pants, Allen is an Ojai, California-based consultant who was an educator and jack of all trades until the mid-1980s, when he set himself up as a productivity consultant. *Getting Things Done*—in the sturdy tradition of American marketing, he has trademarked the phrase and the acronym GTD—offers a smorgasbord of ideas about how to take back your life using a mixture of common sense, mind-clearing techniques, and self-discipline.

33   He's big on creating paper to-do lists and eliminating the minor sources of frustration that pollute the typical workday. The forty-three folders idea involves setting up a system of forty-three ordinary manila folders in one's office—one for each day of the month, and another dozen for the months—in which you place reminders of tasks that need to be completed and when. One of Allen's premises is that much of the stress associated with an information-saturated workplace is that we end up over-committing ourselves without quite knowing how much we're on the hook for. You have a vague sense of emails that have gone unanswered and interrupted projects dangling in digital limbo, going nowhere but nonetheless giving you grief.

34   By taking up the ideas in GTD, he contends, one can compile "a complete and current inventory of all your commitments, organized and reviewed in a systematic way [in which] you can focus clearly, view your world from optimal angles, and make trusted choices about what to do (and not do) at any moment." One of Allen's most popular ideas is the "Hipster PDA"—a little notebook or a sheath of index cards, which you keep on your person so you can make notations as they come to you, rather than committing them to some digital black hole or, worse, forgetting these fleeting thoughts as other sources of distraction muscle their way into your consciousness. It doesn't get any more low-tech than that.

35   The growing interest in such "solutions"—to borrow a favourite techie buzzword—indicates the way portable information technologies have unwittingly created new problems while solving old ones. The BlackBerry that doesn't stop pinging, the tsunami of email, the relentless subdividing and cross-posting of online data—these features of our daily information diet hint that something's gone awry. If we are to establish balance in our relationship with the digital information that envelops us, we must reconsider our understanding of the inner workings of our pre-existing mental machinery and the limits of its capacity to adapt to the electronic environment.

36   One approach is to recognize the futility of the compulsion to inundate ourselves with information in the hope of meaningfully processing everything that comes over the digital transom. Kathy Sierra says one of the most widely read and copied posts on her blog was a *cri de coeur* in which she confessed that she had stopped trying to keep up with all the technical reading she was supposed to be doing. The post brought an enormous sigh of relief in response from thousands of distracted bloggers who, she says, were grateful to be released from that treadmill of surfing, reading, forgetting, repeating.

37   The chronic memory loss prompted by such online behaviour is, in fact, the canary in the coal mine. Our information technologies have created an epidemic of engineered forgetfulness—a symptom of the massive quantity of data we attempt to cram into our minds each day. We inevitably fail, yet our social biases about forgetting are thoroughly negative. A great memory is still considered to be a sign of mental acuity while we associate forgetfulness with aging and decline. But, as Sierra points out, a healthy brain actively rejects much of the information we're trying to stuff into it; the brain is designed to be selective. "There's a lot of

chemistry in the brain devoted to stopping us from remembering things," she told me. "That means forgetting is pretty darn important. We feel guilty about it. But we should have a great deal of respect for that [mechanism]." Discarding information that is not urgent or relevant is crucial to our ability to think in ways that are efficient and creative.

38   The point is that we must acknowledge the self-inflicted memory lapses triggered by information overload, chronic interruptions, and relentless electronic multi-tasking. The need to be much more conscious of our information diet, in turn, is a reflection of the imbalance between our technical capacity to record information digitally and our neural capacity to remember it chemically. After fifteen years of web access, we haven't really tried to reconcile these unevenly matched features of our mental geography. Moreover, amid all the transformations, we have been devaluing those very neurological capabilities that technology has not been able to mimic, and none more thoroughly than the biological need to concentrate as a way of allowing long-term memory to transform into thought and, when necessary, action.

39   As a consequence, our perennially distracted Net culture seems programmed to eliminate time for thinking, which is not the same thing as time for finding and saving data. We have unleashed an explosion of digital media but, paradoxically, we have less and less opportunity to digest it, and then to allow all the information to, well, inform. Being online has become a state of being, while going off-line increasingly represents either an act of will or a tiny gesture of rebellion against the status quo. "We're at a point when we can't be alone," Wilfrid Laurier psychology professor Jeffery Jones told me as we talked about his research on technology and interruptions. We were sitting in his small office: the husk of an old computer sat on the floor, and there was a new wide-screen terminal on his desk, along with a joystick and his cellphone. Toward the end of the interview, someone knocked, but he ignored it. He said he now knows that if he wants to focus, he must make a point of not picking up the phone or answering his email—even though that failure to connect leaves him feeling vaguely guilty. "But I've learned," Jones reflected, "that you have to have some time when you are unavailable."

Active Reading

1. What is an "informavore" and what sort of behaviour is "information foraging"?

2. How do human and digital memories function differently?

3. Does "multi-tasking" come easily to most people?

4. Describe how "PlaceMail" would work, and provide reasons why it may or may not catch on with the public.

5. Describe the overall approach to getting organized that the author of *Getting Things Done* advocates.

Critical Reading

1. Because this article was published in a popular magazine, it adheres to journalistic conventions and does not provide a list of sources at the end. Yet

within the article, the author does refer to many experts—educators and theorists. Does this lead you to take his article more seriously? How would you characterize the readership of *The Walrus*, a magazine that publishes articles that are relatively dense and anchored in expert sources?

2. Did you notice when the author made direct references to himself and his own experiences? How does he contribute to the development of his overall argument by observing, for example, "I could get along without a car but I can no longer earn a living without my browser"?

3. When authors take a cautionary or discouraging approach to new technology, they need to cultivate an ethos that convinces us that they are authoritative and judicious, not reactionary and lazy. What are some of the moves Lorinc makes to seem open-minded and tech-savvy? Do his references to blogs and bloggers indicate that he is familiar with life online?

In Defense of the Future

Don Tapscott

This is the final chapter of Tapscott's recent book examining the characteristics of the net generation (those between the ages of 11 and 30 whom he describes in his title as Grown Up Digital). In an earlier book, he examined the previous generation: those who were Growing Up Digital. Tapscott is optimistic that the current generation raised with electronic media have not been weakened by their experience but have developed many strengths.

Tapscott is an internationally sought-after writer, consultant, and speaker on business strategy and organizational transformation, whose clients include top executives of many of the world's largest corporations and government leaders from many countries. The Washington Technology Report called him one of the most influential media authorities since Marshall McLuhan. He is the author of thirteen widely read books about information technology in business and society, and an Adjunct Professor of Management at the Joseph L. Rotman School of Management, University of Toronto.

1   To read the criticisms you might conclude the Net Generation are a bunch of dull, celebrity-obsessed, net-addicted, shopaholic exhibitionists with a taste for violence, online and offline. You might even want to follow the advice offered by Professor Bauerlein on the front cover of his book *The Dumbest Generation*: "Don't trust anyone under 30."

2   Net Geners themselves either laugh at the line (see some of their comments below), or respond in such a thoughtful way that the dumbness theory is invalidated. But when you add up all the charges and criticisms, they represent a serious critique of youth today. Throughout this book I have attempted to sort out what is true, what is false, and what is unknown. But when you scrutinize the situation—as the young people I've worked with would have us do—a shocking conclusion emerges. But it is not what most would think. Let us begin to do this now by addressing the top 10 Dark Side issues.

THE DARK SIDE REVISITED

I. The Dumbest Generation?

3   This line of thought suggests that because they spend so much time staring at the screen, the young people forfeit the ability to think deeply or creatively. Augmenting this sense of alarm is a survey suggesting that young people spend a lot less time reading literature than young people once did. If they only ingest bits and bites of online information, English neurobiologist Baroness Greenfield says, they will fail to develop intellectual skills needed for higher-order thinking. Some of them may even develop a digital version of attention deficit disorder—zigging and zagging from one idea to the next without really thinking about or finishing anything.

4   There's a lot we don't know about the brain, but it has become evident that this most complex of human organs can change its physical structure and its functioning throughout a person's life, far more than scientists thought it could when I was a teenager The brain is especially malleable during adolescence, which is just when teens are immersed in digital technology and spend hours playing games.

5   The typical boomer grew up watching more than 22 hours of TV a week. They just watched, zoned out. As I've explained, Net Geners watch less TV and when they do, they treat it as background Muzak while they hunt for information, play games, and chat with friends online. They spend a lot less time zoning out in front of the TV than their boomer parents did at the same age.

6   While the full impact of this digital immersion is still unknown, there is emerging evidence that the Net Gen brain is adapting to this wired world. Some of the early research is about the video games played by 8 out of 10 teenagers. Net Geners who play action video games can process information more quickly than non game-players. They can track more objects than can nonplayers too. Research on games suggests that video games might help players practice decision making. To become an expert player, you have to master many of the same skills that are essential for success in the educational system and later in life, such as understanding design principles, practicing, developing strategies, organizing information, and discovering. And when your success depends on collaborating with dozens of other people worldwide, you have to develop management skills that are not so different from the ones that the best corporate executives develop.

7   General online activity—hunting for information, reading, and responding—is far from mindless. Kids are, in fact, reading, but they're reading fewer books of literature and more nonfiction online. Online reading requires many of the same mental skills that are required to read a book—and then some. You are not led along every step of the way by the hand; you have to construct your own narrative and scenarios, and you must critique whatever it is you are reading along the way. You have to be able to detect a fraud—like the Pacific Northwest tree octopus that fooled most of the seventh grade students who participated in one of literacy expert Dr. Donald Leu's studies. You have to be able to keep the question in mind and not get distracted by all the interesting factoids out there. What's more, you're reading and writing as you go. That's why some people call Web 2.0 the "read-write Web." It's challenging. This is

why experts are talking about a new literacy that may be even more intellectually demanding than the old one.

8 Because the Internet gives young people a world of information at their fingertips, they have to struggle to understand and synthesize. It can be a great intellectual exercise. And yes, they do multitask, and switch from one stream of information to the next, with an ease that surprises their parents. Of course, they need to focus deeply to accomplish a complex task, but the rest of the time, they're developing multitasking skills that are very useful, even essential, in the modern digital world.

9 So is there any evidence that the Internet is making kids "the dumbest generation"? If anything, test scores suggest the opposite.

10 Although IQ scores are controversial and measure only one facet of intelligence, raw IQ scores have been going up three points a decade since World War II. Some researchers believe that the recent increase in IQ scores has been influenced by the complex media and technology environment.[1]

11 In the United States, average test scores have been improving in most subjects—especially in math. Yet this is no time to celebrate, not when so many young people are dropping out of school and college. That's why I say this is the story of two generations: the top students are doing fabulously and using the Internet to boost their academic accomplishments, but at the same time, the United States is facing a massive dropout problem, especially among city kids who are black or Hispanic. It's a scandal. Yet we shouldn't blame the Internet for this problem. Instead, let's fix class sizes, alleviate poverty, motivate teachers with better pay, improve childcare, and deal with the factors that directly cause kids to drop out and lose hope. In particular, let's get laptops and the Web into classrooms so that teachers can be freed to customize a learning experience rather than being forced to remain broadcasters of information. Don't make the Internet, a global system for communication and the sharing of knowledge, the scapegoat. That is like blaming the library for ignorance.

12 No one, by the way, has shown a shred of evidence that Net Geners are more ignorant than we were at their age. And when it comes to ignorance, remember the words of Samuel Johnson: "Knowledge is of two kinds. We know a subject ourselves, or we know where we can find information upon it."[2] Or, as Rob Cross and the authors of *The Hidden Power of Social Networks*, put it:" [Who] you know has a significant impact on what you come to know, because relationships are critical for obtaining information, solving problems, and learning how to do your work."[3] If Cross and colleagues are correct, and I believe they are, Net Geners' ability to network and access the world of information and appropriate people should put this generation in the driver's seat to be the smartest.

13 One of the executives who surely has one of the world's most insightful views of the Net Gen is Eric Schmidt, CEO of Google, the omnipresent search engine. He counts millions of Net Geners as customers, and has nearly 20,000 of them on the company payroll. In the spring of 2008, just after *The Dumbest Generation* was published, I asked him about the Net Geners he hires at Google. "Are they the dumbest generation? Do you have any other thoughts how this generation is different?" Schmidt e-mailed me within an hour: "This generation is the smartest, not the dumbest," he wrote. "They are quicker, more global, more savvy, and

better educated. The clear fact that they have been connected to each other since near birth through mobile phones, chat, and now social networks means they are the most connected generation, they care deeper about each other than we ever did. And you can quote me!"

I Don't Read Books . . .

14   In the spring of 2008, I was invited to lunch with the leaders of Florida State University to discuss the twenty-first-century university. Amid the deans and department heads who expressed profound thoughts about the future of the institution, was a 22-year-old student, Joe O'Shea. He was a handsome young man, dressed in a crisp white shirt and tie, as if he were headed for a high-priced job on Wall Street. It was his turn to speak:

15   "I don't read books per se," he told the erudite and now somewhat stunned crowd. "I go to Google and I can absorb relevant information quickly. Some of this comes from books. But sitting down and going through a book from cover to cover doesn't make sense. It's not a good use of my time as I can get all the information I need faster through the web. You need to know how to do it—to be a skilled hunter."

16   His perspective initiated, as you can imagine, a lively debate. "I don't know whether this portends the end of civilization," said Frank Patterson, the dean of the university's prestigious film school, "or a profoundly exciting and different future."

17   O'Shea is no slouch. It turns out that he was president of the student government, with a $10.1 million budget. He sat on dozens of university committees representing the students. With a couple of other friends he started Global Peace Exchange, which coordinates student collaboration in sustainable development projects. After Hurricane Katrina, he founded a free health clinic in the lower Ninth Ward of New Orleans that sees 10,000 people per year. He said he was impressed by how much other people were willing to give: "Human beings have innate compassion," he said. "A lot of times this is masked by society, but it can come forward with the right conditions. We're social beings; we live in communities. We care about others—that's our nature."

18   I was so impressed by O'Shea that I offered him a ride on a plane I had chartered for the day. It had been a very sad year for him. Both his parents had passed away. But now he gets together with his brothers online by playing video games, like World of Warcraft. "It's such a fun way to work together, to feel like a team together," he said. "Games provide great opportunities for people to work together and learn together. The three of us are a little team."

19   He was continuing his education, he told me, at Oxford: "I'm really looking forward to it. I'll have health care for the first time," he said. "We never did growing up. We just never went to the doctor."

20   I was impressed: Oxford sets an extraordinarily high bar for acceptance. I wondered, of course, whether he had funding. Yes, he had a scholarship, he said.

21   I pressed him for details.

22   "It's called a Rhodes Scholarship," he said.

2. Screen Addicted? Losing Social Skills?

23 I often hear pundits and even some parents express concerns that their kids are spending so much time online that they might not develop proper social skills. It's an understandable concern; we all want our kids to grow up with friends and a healthy ability to relate to other people. And young people should have balance in their lives. Addiction to anything—drugs, alcohol, sex, or video games—is a cause for serious concern.

24   But there is more to this issue than meets the eye. If in the past a young person spent a lot of time reading novels, no one would call her or him "reading addicted." So, assuming a young person has some kind of balance in his or her life, but still seems to spend a lot of time online, the underlying concern is over what exactly that young person is doing.

25   The fact is that young people are spending a lot of their time with social media—talking with friends and participating on social networks. The Net Geners are a community-minded generation, historian Neil Howe has observed; they are quite different from their individualistic baby boomer parents. They like to do things together. Some 81 percent of tweens (ages 8–12) and 53 percent of teens (13–18) say that the number one way they like spending time with their friends is in person. They're so social that they make sure all of their friends on Facebook know what's up with them day and night. Just watch them as they're walking down the street. Chances are they're talking to a friend on their cells or BlackBerrys.

26   True, interviews with Net Geners conducted by nGenera suggest that many of them prefer to communicate via instant messaging rather than in person for certain kinds of interactions. "It allows you to think about your responses, motives, and overall reduces the awkwardness of conversations," one of the young people told us. But this doesn't mean they are losing their social skills; after all, expressing one's feelings in writing was standard practice in the nineteenth century. In the end, look at what they do: instead of zoning out alone in front of the TV or bickering with siblings about what TV show to watch, they're interacting with friends, plenty of them, online or in person. The facts show that this is the most social generation ever, and from what I can see, they have all the social capabilities they'll need to be successful adults.

3. Are They Giving Up Their Privacy?

27 This is a very real problem. Net Geners *are* giving up their privacy without realizing it—or understanding the consequences. When I see what they're posting on Facebook or other social networking sites, I get really worried for them. Young people like to share pictures and stories about themselves, and they don't see any reason why they shouldn't. But they don't realize that this openness may come back to bite them when they're competing for the big job or a political post later in life. Everywhere I travel I meet recruiters who are already checking out the sites. "The term they've used over and over is 'red flags,'" says Trudy Steinfeld, executive director of the Center for Career Development at New York University. "Is there something about (a candidate's) lifestyle that we might find questionable or that we might find goes against the core values of our corporation?"[4]

28   Net Geners must wake up, now. For starters, they must use the privacy features on social networking sites like Facebook. They've got to be very careful about the pictures they post. If you tell something to 500 friends, you'd better assume you're telling everyone. This is not just about social networking sites either. Privacy is a huge and unresolved issue on the Internet.

4. Are They Coddled? Do They Lack Independence?

29   Friends of mine often raise their eyebrows when they hear that their kids or those of others are moving home—at age 24. It confirms their suspicions: these kids have been coddled all their lives. So who's surprised when they move home instead of striking out on their own, as baby boomers did? I think we have to look at this trend with a new viewfinder. Baby boomers couldn't wait to move out of the model of the family home because that was the only way they could seek freedom—away from the family hierarchy with the father in the ruling position. These Net Geners, on the other hand, were more likely to grow up in a family democracy, where they had their say. They don't have to move away to have freedom. They have it in their home, not only with the new more open family structure, but with their computer and their handheld device, which give them access to the Internet anywhere.

30   They're happy to move home because they have much closer relationships with their parents. It also makes sense because they're confronted with a massive student debt, which is eight times higher than it was for boomers (adjusted for inflation). No wonder 40 percent of Americans between the ages of 18 and 25 still live with their parents and 46 percent depend on family for financial help.[5]

31   So moving home might make a lot of sense for an energetic Net Gener who wants to save money while he or she is launching a career. It's not necessarily a sign of apathy or emotional weakness.

32   The real concern is whether Net Geners can think for themselves. They've been raised to be dependent on their parents, some experts say. Young people are subject to more than 10 times as many restrictions as mainstream adults, twice as many as active duty U.S. marines, and almost twice as many as incarcerated felons, according to Dr. Robert Epstein, West Coast editor of *Psychology Today*. The Net Generation were the most overscheduled generation in history.

33   So if now they're calling on the helicopter parents for help when they run into trouble, who should we blame: young people or their helicopter parents? There is an upside for employers, though. Yes, helicopter parents can be annoying, and they need to be confronted or ignored if they're insisting that a low performer get undue credit. But think of the other side of this coin: parents can be recruited to help nurture a better employee or student. Is that so bad? And don't think it will last. Most Net Geners simply ask their hovering parents to back off.

5. Does the Internet Encourage Youth to Steal? Are They Cheaters?

34   Our research shows that the Net Generation are big believers in integrity—honesty, consideration, accountability, and transparency. Yet, according to nGenera research, 77 percent of Net Geners have downloaded music, software,

games, or movies without paying for it. It sounds like a contradiction until you start talking to them. They don't see it as stealing and their assessment of the situation is pretty sophisticated. They think this is a case of a business model that needs to be changed. Net Geners, they say, pay more for music than ever—but not the old-fashioned way. They buy some music online and they spend a big chunk of their disposable income on concerts, ringtones, and artists' products.

35   This old model of owning and selling music makes no sense for this entire generation, or for anyone else for that matter. I don't think it is stealing. It's a classic example of a disruptive technology. For a decade I've described a model that would work. Music should be a service, not a product. Instead of purchasing tunes, you should pay a small monthly fee for access to all the songs in the world. They could be streamed to you when you want and where you want via the Internet. I call my vision of music bliss Everywhere Internet Audio. I'd listen to my own Don Channel. I could slice and dice the massive musical database anyway I liked—by artist, by genre, by year, by songwriter, by popularity, and so on. The Don Channel would know what I like, based on what I've chosen in the past. I could even ask my Everywhere Internet Audio service to suggest new artists that resemble my known favorites.

36   If Everywhere Internet Audio existed, no one would ever "steal." Why would they take possession of a song? Once again young people are showing how we need to change our business models—if we would only listen to them. Rather than build bold new approaches for digital entertainment, the industry has built a business model around suing its customers. And the industry that brought us the Beatles is now hated by its customers and collapsing. Sadly, obsession with control, piracy, and proprietary standards on the part of large industry players has only served to further alienate and anger music listeners.

37   What about intellectual property in the corporate world? Should employers be worried that the Net Geners will blog it to the world? This is not a complicated problem. Simply tell Net Geners what's confidential, and set rules about security. As for revealing corporate secrets, experience shows that they have good judgment. When Jonathan Schwartz became CEO of Sun Microsystems, he gave every employee the right to blog publically. They have never had a problem releasing inappropriate information.

38   It's a big issue in the university too. The Internet makes it easy to plagiarize, and, according to one 2003 survey, 38 percent of college and university students cut and paste information they find on the Internet.[6] Plagiarism appears to have gone up by eight percentage points since the early 1960s. But Don McCabe, a Rutgers Business School professor and expert on plagiarism, sees no widespread increase in plagiarism on campus. Rather, the students who are plagiarizing are using the Internet to do it more. It's not clear whether cheating overall has increased, either. Sixty percent of high school students admitted to cheating on an exam "at least once" on a 2006 survey conducted by the Josephson Institute—virtually the same number who admitted to cheating in 1992.[7]

39   Whether or not it's gone up, cheating is clearly a problem. The Internet cuts the cost of stealing or buying someone else's work, and young people are under

enormous pressure to score good grades so that they'll get into universities of their choice. So what's the answer? UCLA and other U.S. universities, as well as several others in Canada and elsewhere, are using an online program called Turnitin.com to detect plagiarism. The company claims it can cut "measurable rates" of plagiarism to "almost zero." My own kids say that online programs like this are an effective deterrent—because then most students wouldn't even think about trying to plagiarize when the penalty could be a failure or even a suspension. Yet the Center for Academic Integrity, a coalition of hundreds of educational institutions, does not think that technology can solve the problem completely. "Instead, we should be encouraging respect and fairness among the students," says the center's director, Dr. Stephen Satris.

6. Does It Encourage Bullying?

40   Every month we read appalling stories of online bullying, which can range from comments that aim to humiliate the target to outright physical violence. You can see the ugly evidence on YouTube or on the social networking sites. About 6 percent of respondents in one survey reported harassment incidents (threats, rumors, or other offensive behavior) during the past year. Another 2 percent of the surveyed youth reported episodes of distressing harassment (i.e., the incident made them feel very or extremely upset or afraid).[8]

41   But should we blame the Internet? Hardly. Bullying was a real problem when I was at school, but parents didn't know about it, and schools did nothing about it even if they did know. Now there's evidence—right there on YouTube—and parents, schools, and authorities can do something about it.

42   Bullies, experts tell us, need an audience, and the Internet provides an audience of millions, which amplifies the problem. It also allows people to bully targets while they're in the apparent comfort of their own homes.

43   But the bullies leave a permanent, searchable record; they can be detected, and confronted. It's going to be a lot harder to be a cyberbully, and get away with it. The response to bullying, experts tell us, needs to address the root of the problem. The bully needs to develop empathy. The target needs to develop a powerful sense of self to enable him or her to fend off attacks, in the playground or online. Only by addressing the human issues in a thoughtful way can we tackle this problem.

7. Does It Incite Youth Violence?

44   Sometimes the picture doesn't tell the story. In the spring of 2008, as we saw in Chapter 8, a group of teens posted an appalling video of several of them beating up a 16-year-old girl. It was all too easy for some commentators to jump to the conclusion that the desire to achieve notoriety on the Internet is driving some teens to violence. Fueling that concern is a 2007 book in which the authors argue that playing violent video games creates a significant risk factor for later aggressive and violent behavior.[9]

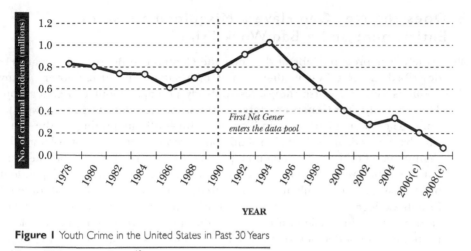

Figure 1 Youth Crime in the United States in Past 30 Years

Source: U.S. Department of Justice[10]

45   The research cited by this book is disturbing. One study randomly assigned elementary and college students to video games that were violent, or not. When they were later tested by a standard laboratory measure of aggressive behavior, the young people who had been playing violent video games displayed more aggression. That finding was bolstered by a survey and a longitudinal study.

46   This is cause for concern, especially when the video game *Grand Theft Auto IV* was such a mammoth hit when it launched in the spring of 2008. It's a violent action-adventure game: the protagonist has to commit multiple acts of mayhem while searching for the person who betrayed his army unit. In the first week it was released, it sold $500 million worth of games—more than 11 of the top movies in the past 13 years made in the entire year of their release. *Grand Theft Auto IV* is on track to becoming one of the biggest products in entertainment history. If Iowa State psychology professor Craig Anderson and his coauthors are correct, we could be in for trouble.

47   But there are many unknowns. It's very hard to prove that violent video games, and not early childhood violence by parents, poverty, neglect, genes, or other well-researched factors cause young people to be violent. It's not showing up yet in the number of actual violent acts. In fact, violence overall—including violent acts by youths—has been going down. Both violent crime and property crime have been dropping since the early 1990s,[11] and victim reports show that the number of serious violent offenses committed by persons ages 12 to 17 declined 61 percent from 1993 to 2005 (see Figure 1), while those committed by persons older than 17 fell 58 percent.[12]

48   More study is clearly needed. In the meantime, parents should be sensible. Impressionable youngsters should not be allowed to play games such as *Grand Theft Auto IV* that are clearly aimed at adult audiences—just as they're not allowed to view acclaimed but violent movies such as *Pulp Fiction* or *Silence of the Lambs.* It only makes sense.

8. Does the Net Gen Have a Misguided Sense of Entitlement and a Bad Work Ethic?

49   "Woefully ill-prepared" for work is how the Conference Board and its partners described the Net Gen in their results of a survey of 400 employers. Many boomers say even worse things, less publicly perhaps, about this generation. They think the Net Geners are entering the workforce with unrealistic expectations. They want to be rich and/or powerful—without putting in the work. They're hooked up with their friends on Facebook, and cannot tolerate the slightest bit of criticism from their employer—or they'll call their helicopter parent for help. "We are developing a generation that is going to be codependent on the parent," says Stephen Seaward, director of career development for Saint Joseph College. "Let's say they're at work, and they're working with a key account or a critical client: if they're on the spot, are they going to be able to make the kind of decision that you want them to make or are they going to get on the mobile phone and talk to mom or dad and see what they think?"

50   Yet I believe their concerns reflect something different. They don't like how this generation wants to work. Net Geners have seen the movie *Office Space* and a hundred YouTube videos that parody Dilbert Inc. They don't see why they should be stuck in a cubicle with the nine to five routine when they have technology that lets them work anywhere, anytime. This generation wants to be judged on its merits, not on its face time. They typically want to collaborate at work, not blindly follow the rules of an unproductive hierarchy. They want to use their tools of collaboration—like Facebook—while they're at work. They think that customized jobs and more regular feedback on performance makes sense, not just for them, but for their employers. They have ideas about how work could be more collaborative and innovative.

51   To some, this work ethos represents a threat to the old order. Yet other companies are finding ways to work with Net Geners. The smart companies are embracing not only this generation but their collaborative ways and are getting big results. Let me quote the head of the company rated as the best place to launch a career, Jim Quigley, CEO of Deloitte: "I have a simple measure for how capable this generation is—billings. Our new recruits deliver far greater value for clients than any previous generation—and this is reflected as a significant increase in the average revenue generated per employee. They do more good work and our clients are happier."

52   Case closed.

9. Are They Narcissistic?

53   Psychology professor Jean Twenge says this generation is more narcissistic than the previous one. They're Generation Me, a "little army of narcissists" that has been nurtured by the self-esteem movement. Twenge's study has been sharply criticized on many fronts—including by one group of researchers who found no evidence of narcissism rising at either colleges or universities.

54   But the bottom line is what they do. As you can see from the charts in this chapter (Figures 1 and 2), Net Geners are not self-centered risk takers.

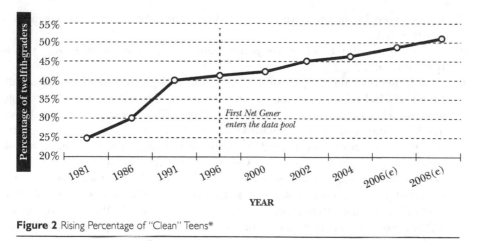

Figure 2 Rising Percentage of "Clean" Teens*

Source: Monitoring the Future Survey[13]
*The term "clean" indicates that the person has not used illicit drugs, smoked cigarettes, or consumed alcohol in the past 30 days.

They drink and smoke less than their parents did. They commit fewer crimes. They volunteer more than previous generations have. Their actions contradict Twenge's claim that they are the most narcissistic generation in history.

10. What About Their Values? Do They Just Want to Be Rich and Famous?

55   Yes, the Net Generation loves celebrities, and they love the idea that anyone can be a celebrity. There are lots more ways to be a celebrity now, compared to the days when boomer girls swooned over the Beatles and Elvis. It's no surprise that the most popular career choice for 13-year-old girls is to be an actress, while the boys want to be a pro athlete.

56   They do appear to be more interested in making money than boomers were at their age. According to U.S. Census data, 79 percent of freshmen in 1970 said an important personal objective was "developing a meaningful philosophy of life." In 2005, three-quarters of freshmen said their number one objective was to be "very well off financially."[14]

57   But who can blame them? Their college debt load and housing costs are much higher than it was for boomers. So, as the late William Strauss, founding partner of the LifeCourse Associates consulting firm, noted: it only makes sense to make money to pay off debt and pay the rent or the mortgage.

58   And yes, they shop. That's no surprise. The Net Generation has been exposed to more media and marketing than any other generation; this is the first generation to be targeted by marketers as a "tween" segment when they were between the ages of 8 and 13.

59   But what's wrong with loving choice, innovation, new products, and even fashions and brands? What's wrong with communicating with our friends on

social networks, or for having fun playing games? You can easily see it as a positive thing.

60   That is the glitter side of this generation. But they have another side that is quite different.

61   Volunteering, on the part of teenagers and college freshmen, has hit an all-time high. In high school, many of them are obliged to volunteer, but in college and in their early careers, they don't stop. About 36 percent of Net Geners age 15–25 volunteered in the previous year, slightly higher than the rate of volunteering for Americans over age 25.[15] (Older Americans were more likely to volunteer on a regular basis than Net Geners, though.) As we've seen in this book, Net Gen activists are using the power of the Internet to tackle some of the most dreadful problems on the planet. What's more, when Net Gens got political in 2008, they displayed their power by helping Senator Barack Obama to topple the Clinton powerhouse and rewrite the rules of contemporary political campaigns in America.

62   This is not a shallow, materialistic generation. On the contrary, this is a generation of community volunteers and activists. They actually want to make their world a little better.

Are You "The Dumbest Generation"? Does the Digital Age "Stupefy Young Americans and Jeopardize Our Future" As the Book with This Title Says?

63   "I'd like to better understand exactly how having a vast repository of knowledge and information at my fingertips somehow makes me dumber, or how being able to communicate with anybody else on the planet instantaneously somehow leaves me more ignorant of the world's workings?"

—Jonathan Wolf, 24, Worcester, Massachusetts

64   "A modern *Reefer Madness:* embarrassing for its creator, and unintentionally funny to its readers?"

—Alex Salzillo, 22, Atlanta, Georgia

65   "Our generation is awash in the present but we may be underinformed about the past. We are perpetually connected to events across the planet as they occur in realtime, making us self-important and complacent. Rather than get up and do something, we convince ourselves that by blogging about events we somehow affect their outcome."

—Mike Kanert, 29, Saitama, Japan

66   "I'm going to start handing this book out. It's great. A perfect way to manage expectations about what a loser I must surely be."

—Daniel Williamson, 27, Toronto

67   "Fiddlesticks! . . . or some other expression from the 'smartest' generation."

—Eva Szymanski, 24, London, Ontario

68   "I went online today, googled this book, found a short preview, read some reviews, read multiple bios of the author. Followed a link to the WSJ online, and read another one of his pieces. Then I stopped and laughed. The Internet is the driving force behind ignorance and apathy?"

—Brooke Rosenkrantz, 21, Boca Raton, Florida

69   "People believe what they read on the Internet without question when not all of it is true. A lot of it, namely blogging and other sources of personal posting, are opinions and ideas, not fact. One can be conditioned to believe anything, especially younger minds that soak up everything like a sponge."

—Nick Dubais, 25, Brooklyn, New York

70   "This diatribe is full of sound and fury, signifying nothing."

—Del McLean, 22, San Diego, California

71   "Sure I'm dumb. My role model on this is Socrates, who said: 'I know nothing save for the fact of my own ignorance.' Oh, that quote came from a book . . ."

—Graham Smith, 24, currently working in Rwanda

72   "My physics teacher came to class one day and told us that she had just looked at the physics tests from 30 years ago and that we had no chance of even imagining being able to complete the test correctly. She never directly explains why, but other times in class she talks about the negative effects on children today from technology."

—Alex Zajack, 15, Las Vegas, Nevada

73   "This is sensationalist nonsense—for one group or generation to categorize another as stupid or ignorant based on arbitrarily valued differences is baseless unproductive rhetoric."

—Eric Potter, 22, Waltham, Massachusetts

74   "I don't think we're the 'dumbest' generation, but in all that we have gained in this 'digital age' we may have lost something of ourselves. People are inherently different, always were, and always will be, so each will make use of the abundance of knowledge differently. As Sandra Carey said: 'Never mistake knowledge for wisdom. One helps you make a living; the other helps you make a life.'"

—Aditi Bakht, 23, New Delhi, India

75   "Bauerlein needs to be careful not to mix up stupidity with efficiency. Why would I waste my time memorizing hundreds of statistics and facts, when with the click of a mouse I can pull up just about anything I need to know?"

—Vanessa Kenalty, 25, Toronto

76   "We're destroying the English language? NFW [No F**king Way]!"

—Bobbi Munroe, San Francisco, California

77   "There is plenty of cause for alarm and/or optimism when it comes to my generation; even I can see that. Still I think the negative views of us come from a fear of the unknown, a fear of change. Our world is evolving at a rapid rate, and that can be scary for older generations."

—Savannah Jones, 17, Portland, Oregon

78   "Take a close look at what the baby-boom generation has left us: a bloated, unsustainable and selfish infrastructure of cars, homes, cities, and commerce. My Net Generation is critical of such development, largely thanks to the education and knowledge available at our 'lazy' fingertips (they didn't teach sustainability in high school)."

—Aaron Hay, 24, Toronto

79   "Ask a teenager what is the capital of Belgium, and he might not know the correct answer. But put that teenager in front of a computer, and he'll find Brussels, its population, geographic location, GDP, and all about its role as the administrative center of the European Union."

—*Ben Elrom, 17, Charlottesville, Virginia*

80   "I didn't walk 50 miles in the snow to school, but I've dealt with pop-up ads all my life. Just because information is at my fingertips and that's made me lazy, doesn't mean the wealth of accessible knowledge has made me dumb."

—*Matt Ceniceros, 29, Memphis, Tennessee*

81   "This generation is becoming more and more dependant on technology, but the effect is questionable. We cannot allow our basic skills to suffer at the cost of convienience. (I would also like to point out my dependance on wrod proccessors as I have had many gramatical and spelling errors above, and without the red underlines, I am none the wiser.)"

—*Nate Lewin, 16, Scarsdale, New York*

82   "Lazy is the mask for the entitlement we feel; the right to have access to endless information on the Internet, the drive to find our own innovative path, and the desire to see and understand the world. Sometimes the world gets so loud we need to cocoon ourselves in self-composed entertainment bubbles, but really we want to go places, enact change, and have our voices meaningfully heard above the cacophony."

—*Jen Shaw, 25, Hoboken, New Jersey*

83   "Ignorant and fearful—nothing less than a modern-day McCarthy in his campaign against youth."

—*Alex Tapscott, 22, Amherst, Massachusetts*

NOTES

1. Steven Johnson, *Everything Bad is Good for You: How Today's Popular Culture Is Actually Making Us Smarter*, New York: Riverhead, 2005. Clancy Blair et al., "Rising Mean IQ: Cognitive Demand of Mathematics Education for Young Children, Population Exposure to Formal Schooling and the Neurobiology of the Prefrontal Cortex," *Intelligence*, vol. 33, no. 1, January–February 2005, 93–106.

2. "Samuel Johnson," Wikiquote, en.wikiquote.org.

3. Robert L. Cross et al., *The Hidden Power of Social Networks*, Cambridge, Mass.: Harvard Business School Press, 2004, 11.

4. Alan Finder, "For Some, Online Persona Undermines a Resume," *New York Times*, June 11, 2006.

5. Anastasia Goodstein and Mike Dover, "The Net Generation 'Dark Side': Myths and Realities of the Cohort in the Workplace and the Marketplace," Syndicated Research Report, nGenera, July 2007, www.ngenera.com.

6. "New Study Confirms Internet Plagiarism Is Prevalent," Press Release, Rutgers University, August 2003, ur.rytgers.edu. The survey of 18,000 students was conducted in 2003 by Professor Donald McCabe, a management professor at Rutgers University.

7. "2006 Josephson Institute Report Card on the Ethics of American Youth: Part One—Integrity," Press Release, Josephson Institute, October 15, 2006, johnsoninstitute.org.

8. "Juvenile Offenders and Victims: 2006 National Report," U.S. Department of Justice, ch. 2, 38, 2006, ojjdp.ncjrs.gov.

9. Craig Anderson et al., *Violent Video Game Effects on Children and Adolescents: Theory, Research and Public Policy*, Cambridge, UK: Oxford University Press, 2007.

10. "The Proportion of Serious Violent Crimes Committed by Juveniles Has Generally Declined since 1993," U.S. Department of Justice, Office of Justice Programs, Bureau of Justice Statistics, www.ojp.usdoj.gov (accessed May 22, 2008). Data taken from the United States Department of Justice and extrapolated into 2006 and 2008 was not available at that time. The extrapolated points are estimated using the rate of decline starting at 1994; they are signified with an (e).

11. "The Decline in Crime: Why and What Next?" Urban Institute, October 2000, www.urban.org (accessed May 22, 2008).

12. "The Proportion of Serious Violent Crimes Committed by Juveniles Has Generally Declined Since 1993."

13. "Child Trends Databank," Table 3, www.childtrendsdatabank.org/tables/ 80_Table_3.htm (accessed May 26, 2008). Data taken from the Monitoring the Future Study was extrapolated out to 2008 using trends from 1991 to 2006.

14. "Nearly Half Our Lives Spent with TV, Radio, Internet, Newspapers, According to Census Bureau Publication," Press Release, U.S. Census Bureau, December 15, 2006, www.census.gov.

15. Mark Hugo Lopez et al., "The 2006 Civic and Political Health of the Nation: A Detailed Look at How Youth Participate in Politics and Communities," Center for Information and Research on Civic Learning and Engagement (CIRCLE), October 26, www.civic youth.org.

16. There is much discussion about who actually said this. Socrates is said to have been the most likely candidate.

17. Jean Twenge, *Generation Me: Why Today's Young Americans Are More Confident, Assertive, Entitled—and More Miserable Than Ever Before*, New York: Free Press, 2006, 226.

18. Adapted from the Amherst College charter: "Amherst College educates men and women of exceptional potential from all backgrounds so that they may seek, value, and advance knowledge, engage the world around them, and lead principled lives of consequence."

Active Reading

1. List three criticisms of the "Net Generation."

2. What does the word "narcissistic" mean, and why does Jean Twenge believe it describes the attitude of Net Geners?

Critical Reading

1. Do you like the way the main text is interrupted by a story ("I Don't Read Books")? Is this fragmentary and incoherent (a "distraction" of the type Jon Lorinc fears) or a welcome diversion?

2. Tapscott provides several graphs. Are they helpful in depicting information he is discussing? Does the text summarize the graphs in adequate details?

3. Tapscott would convince us that the internet is positive and those who criticize its effects on youth culture are wrong. The last passages above include quotations from young people reacting against another author's claim that the internet has assaulted the intelligence of young people. What is the value of these quotations? Are they evidence that the other author is wrong? Or does Tapscott include them to depict youth culture, and perhaps indirectly to convey the idea that young people are articulate and thoughtful rather than stupid as claimed?

RESEARCH AND WRITING SUGGESTIONS

Chapter-based Research Questions

1. Lorinc warns that new technology is disruptive. By contrast, Tapscott argues that we can benefit from the changes. Which argument seems most convincing? Is this a case where there is no need to attempt an "either/or" resolution, since there is room to accept both positions?

2. The articles by Tapscott and Lorinc appeal to generalist readers and develop according to conventions of popular rather than scholarly writing. What sorts of audiences do Tapscott and Lorinc likely have in mind? Do you think it is challenging to write about technology in layman's terms?

Additional Research Questions

1. Find a journal that specializes in publishing scholarly information about computers and technology. Look over the articles. Do most of the articles take a specific and technical focus that makes them too challenging for most non-specialist readers? Can you find one that would be appropriate in a reader like this one, whose purpose is to introduce academic conventions and debates?

2. Besides those mentioned in the articles in this section, what other forms of new communication technology are changing our lives? Write a research article citing four sources that document the influence of a particular innovation.

3. New technology and writing studies is an active and growing research field. See how many sources come up when you Google "Computers and Composition" or "New Media and Writing Studies." Can you identify some of the contested issues?

4. Writing teachers often ask students to write in a colloquial or personal way about their experiences with social networking and new technology. Can you find first-person opinion pieces on this issue? How could you build quotations from a blog response or personal essay into a research paper? Discuss possible contexts.

CHAPTER 13

STORIES OF CANADA—WHO DO WE THINK WE ARE? WHO DO WE WANT TO BE?

The topic of Canadian identity is always undergoing redefinition. It is a cliché that while Americans and Britons can be easily described, Canadians cannot, which makes us think that we must be a bland lot, lacking in distinctive qualities. The definition is indeed elusive, perhaps because it is plural and dynamic. The articles in this chapter explore various aspects of Canadian identity—or identities—and the reasons why we are so difficult to pin down.

Disciplines within the humanities (history, literature, philosophy, religion, rhetoric) study the construction of Canadian identity by examining the complex processes of "representation" by which people's world view is formed: how they see themselves and each other, how they see other people, how they define their values. We can think of these processes of representation as the stories we tell about ourselves. These stories get told in the form of history books, newspapers, photographs, paintings, songs, plays, and novels. Each of the writers in this chapter takes on the topic of the stories we tell ourselves and the language that we tell them in, and reflects on the consequences of living with those stories.

Tomson Highway draws our attention to the macro-level of representation, the sphere of what he calls "mythology," where grand narratives of human life circulate in a society and affect the world views of the people who live with them and through them. Next, Daniel Francis chronicles the construction of the "textbook Indian" through the representations and misrepresentations made of First Nations and Métis people in Canadian school books. Tracy Whalen reflects on photographs that have become part of the general environment of a society in her analysis of the popular images that represent Canada. In her article, "Resolution and Canadian Iconography," Whalen summons up memories of photographs that many Canadians have in common, and asks, what questions about Canadian identity are resolved, or rather not resolved, through these images. Finally, Marie Annharte Baker reflects on the costs of speaking and writing in an "enemy language" that conveys its own history of oppressive treatment of Aboriginal people, and on the possibilities of using a language of liars to tell the truth.

For each of these writers, representations make things happen. Far from being innocent stories and pictures we amuse ourselves with, representations can become the terms through which people's lives are lived, constructing not only our sense of self but our social and political lives. For example, while "race" is widely recognized as a fiction that was constructed to justify the oppressive practices of imperialist nations, the story of Canada is nevertheless a highly racialized story where white-skinned people end up being represented as real Canadians and everyone else as "other." Scholars within the humanities pay much more attention than in the past to the way that ethnicity, language, gender, class, and sexuality get represented in the interests of the status quo. The stories told in dominant culture tend to represent the way things have been rather than the way they should be, thus benefiting the status quo and opposing the aspirations of members of more marginalized groups.

The stories we tell tend to represent the way things have been as the way things should be. Sometimes the message is explicit, as in the same-sex marriage debate, and sometimes it is a little more subtle. Each of the authors in this chapter raises important questions about the stories we tell.

Activate

1. When you think "Canada" or "Canadian," what images or stories come to mind? Do they include diverse people (ethnicity, gender, sexuality, etc.) or are they mainly people who belong to dominant cultural groups (Caucasian, male, heterosexual, etc.)?

2. Do you think most Canadians have the same idea of Canada?

3. Did you find stories of Canadian history dull in high school? Why or why not?

Comparing Mythologies

Tomson Highway

Tomson Highway was born in a tent near Maria Lake, Manitoba, one of twelve children born to Joe and Pelagie Philomene Highway, from whom Tomson acquired his love of the oral tradition of storytelling in Cree culture. He attended residential school in The Pas, Manitoba, moving on to study music at the University of Western Ontario. Highway has helped to organize major Native music festivals in Canada and the United States, and has composed music for Native theatre. He is the award-winning playwright of The Rez Sisters *and* Dry Lips Oughta Move to Kapuskasing, *both of which take place on a reserve on Manitoulin Island in Georgian Bay. Highway has also published a novel,* Kiss of the Fur Queen, *which is based on the events leading to his brother René's death from AIDS.*

The text in this collection was delivered as the prestigious Bronfman lecture. In it, Highway explains the vital role of mythology in "the well-being, or the illness" of a people, and compares the world views imparted by three very different mythologies that live in Canadian culture: Greek, Christian, and Aboriginal.

1   Good evening, ladies and gentlemen. I am here to talk about mythology. I am here to talk about mythology because, after fifty years of living and watching—and studying—my people, my culture, my language, my land, go through the experience they have gone through since the year 1492, I have come to believe that if the well-being, or the illness, of a people and the environment they inhabit has its roots anywhere, then that's where those roots lie. I am here to talk about mythology because I believe that if the consciousness of a people has its roots anywhere, then that's where those roots lie. I am here to talk about mythology because I believe that if the language, just for instance, of a people, the very tool by which that people articulates life both inside it and life all around it, has its origins anywhere, then that's where lie those origins. I am here to talk about

mythology because I believe that if the very nerve pulse of the life of a people, the electrical impulse that sparks into action the life of a people, comes from anywhere, then that's where it comes from. I am here to talk about mythology because I believe that without mythology, we would be nothing but walking corpses, zombies, mere empty hulks of animal flesh and bone, skin and blood and liquid matter with no purpose, no reason for existing, no use, no point, nothing, mere flesh and bone and skin and blood with nowhere to go, and with no guide to guide it through a life path that, one imagines, has been given to us all by . . . what? Who? Why? And why here? These are the questions mythology answers, I feel very strongly, more so than theology, just for instance.

2   What, however, is mythology? What is it about the "discipline" of mythology that makes it stand quite unique as a discipline amongst an immense field of disciplines that can range anywhere from quantum physics to cellular biology to philosophy to anthropology to sociology to psychology to geography to history to theology and on and on and on *ad infinitum?* What is it about mythology that differentiates it, and differentiates it utterly, from any other field of intellectual activity?

3   The comparisons, of course, are limitless, but sociology, to pick one other discipline just to start with, tells the story of human interaction, the way people, communities, and societies interact with one another on a day-to-day, week-to-week, year-to-year basis, how they communicate, how they live together or against each other. Geography, to pick another, tells the story of a landscape; geography, that is to say, defines all the physical features of a land from its rivers to its mountains to its valleys to its fields to its forests to its towns and its cities. History tells the story of the *physical* movements of a people across that landscape. And mythology tells the story of the *spiritual* movements of that people across that landscape. If geography, in other words, were like looking at the photograph of a river, say, or a mountain or a hill or a forest or a valley or a city and if history were like looking at the photograph of the physical, exterior shape of a person, and sociology were like looking at the photograph of people in family and community groupings of one sort or another with their various modes of dress and of grooming and of tools, accoutrements, habitat and such, then mythology would be like looking at the negative of a person, an X-ray—that is to say, one, however, that outlines not the bone structure nor the internal organs of that person nor the veins nor the nerves (for these, too, are physical) but, rather, one that delineates the *spiritual* nervous system, as it were—and that system only—of that person, that tangle of electrical cords and wiring in all its wondrous, mystical, magical complexity. That, to me, is at least one definition of mythology that distinguishes it as a field of thought and of study from all others, including, most essentially, theology which I believe to be its nearest rival, so to speak, or its nearest cousin.

4   Mythology, of course, comes to us from the Greek word "myth," whose meaning is "narrative" or "story;" and "logos," whose meaning is "word" or "discourse," while theology comes, in the same language, from "theos," meaning "god" or "divinity" and, of course, the aforementioned "logos." So that the former ends up being a discourse on narrative, or the art of story-telling, including, most notably, a narrative on all three of humankind, animalkind, *and* god, the latter a discourse on god (or gods), and god only.

5   Now, in the language of my people, one that I knew way before I became conversant in the English or French languages, there are three distinct terms for the concept of narrative. The first term is *achimoowin*, which means "to tell a story" or "to tell the truth." The second is *kithaskiwin*, which means "to tell a lie," meaning "to weave a web of fiction," as it were. And the third, which lies at a point exactly halfway between these first two is *achithoogeewin*, which means "to mythologize." Meaning that the visionaries of my people, the thinkers who gave birth and shape to the Cree language as we know it today, chose the exact halfway point between truth and lie, non fiction and fiction, to situate mythology. And here I'll tell you a little story that illustrates this little principle:

6   One night, about twenty years ago, a most unruly and rather spectacular celebration was taking place at a hotel room in downtown Toronto that I, most unfortunately, was ignorant of at the time and so failed completely to attend, rats. As with most of our parties, this one was unruly and spectacular because a clown—a laughing deity, that is to say, one called, in English, the Trickster—lives inside our language and thus inside us, about which more shortly. So wild was the party, in fact, that the police eventually came calling. The thing, you see, was that my dear friend and colleague—Billy Boy Cutthroat, we shall call him, for purposes of concealing his true identity—had been fuelling the event with the liberal supply of some magical tobacco that he always seemed to have on his person all through those years, a substance that, by the way—and I must say this here—is infinitely, infinitely more conducive to the health of Indian reserves across this country than alcohol has ever, ever been. The knock on the door, at any rate, came and someone in the room yelled "Police." At which point, my friend Billy Boy Cutthroat rushed to the window, which was open, and jumped out. From the thirtieth floor! And it was said, for many years thereafter, that he hung on to a window ledge somewhere just below that thirtieth-floor window for "hours," all while the police searched the room inside out for evidence of criminal activity of the sort for which Billy Boy Cutthroat had gained, over the years, such glamorous notoriety. That the floor was the thirtieth was the lie. That was the fiction. That was outright *kithaskiwin*.

7   As I wandered my way across Ontario that next year (for that's the kind of job I had at the time), as I, *par hasard*, traced this story from city to reserve to town and back to city, that thirtieth floor in that hotel room became the twenty-fifth, then the twentieth, then the fifteenth, then the tenth, etc., etc., etc. until, about a whole year later, I got to Mr. Cutthroat himself, who, by the way, lived on a reserve way up in . . . well, somewhere in the north. At any rate, by the time I got to him, the source of the "myth," that is to say, that hotel room in Toronto, had been not on the thirtieth floor nor the twentieth nor the tenth, nor the seventh, not even the third. It had been the second! And he hadn't hung onto that window ledge for hours, he had merely dropped to the ground, suffered a few minor bruises, one sore ankle, and then sort of hobbled off down the alleyway, round the corner, and down the street to the nearest bar, which, of course, just happened to be there. That was the truth, that was the non fiction. That was *achimoowin*.

8   At a point exactly halfway between these two stories, or the two versions of this story, that is to say, at a point exactly halfway between the lie about this "narrative"

and the truth about this "narrative," of course, lies the narrative that I heard from who was perhaps the tenth teller of the tale (and way before I caught up with my friend up north). By this tenth telling of the story, that is to say, I had it firmly implanted in my mind—in my dream world, so to speak—that plain, old, ordinary human being Billy Boy Cutthroat not only had the fingernails of Superman himself but had sprouted the wings of an angel, which, of course, is how he managed to hover Holy Spirit-like high up in the air just outside that window on what I dreamt was the ninetieth floor of some extraordinary hotel in downtown Toronto. That was the myth. That was the dream. That was *achithoogeewin.* And that, ladies and gentlemen, is precisely the region of our collective dream world, our collective subconscious, where men sprout wings, horses sprout wings, creatures half-man and half-horse once walked this Earth, that is the region of our lives where people exist who are half-man and half-goat, half-woman and half-fish, half-man and half-coyote, half-woman and half-spider, snakes talk to women (but not to men), women give birth without having had sex, men—and women, too—are half-human and half-divine. And an old man up in the sky with a great white beard can part Lake Ontario right down the middle with one wave of his hand, so we Ontarians can shop in Rochester, New York, without having first to pass through Buffalo, Gananoque, or even Pearson Airport . . . and anyone pursuing us gets drowned to his death. That's another definition of mythology that, it seems to me, makes much sense.

9   The last definition that I wish to give of mythology, for the purposes of this lecture—which brings us round to the first quite neatly—is that mythology defines, mythology maps out, the collective subconscious, the collective dream world of races of people, the collective spirit of races of people, the collective spiritual nervous system, if you will, where every cord, every wire, every filament has a purpose and a function, every twitch a job in the way that collective human body, mind, and soul moves and operates from one day to the next to the next and to the next. Without this *mechanism,* that is to say, there would be no reason for getting up in the morning to go to work, to school, or to play. Life would have no meaning. And suicide would flourish.

10   The world, however, is filled with mythology—or, rather, mythologies—as who in their right mind doesn't know. Every race, every language; even every city, every town, every village has its own. Many hold immense similarity one to the other, many differ quite drastically, but the fact remains that each and every one of these mythologies defines the collective dream world, the collective subconscious of that people; it, in other words, is the principle, or driving force, that decides whether nature or our bodies, just for instance, are friends or foes, enemies to be conquered or lovers to be loved, gardens to be killed or gardens to be tilled.

11   To study each mythology extant on the planet, however, would take ten lifetimes, easy, to accomplish. With this lecture, we have time for three—and this with a superficiality and cursoriness so extreme you will probably laugh at me, rise from your seats, insult me, and leave—three, in any case, that I have selected if only for the reason that these, to my way of thinking, are the three that have had most to do with the development and the shaping of the society we know today, at the turn of the century, as North American society, the three that have

had most to do with the development and the shaping of this society as it thinks, this society as it lives, this society as it dreams. And these three "narratives," so to speak, are Christian mythology, Greek mythology, and North American Aboriginal mythology, specifically, in my case, Cree mythology, Cree *achithoogeewin*. I have, moreover, selected them because they offer, they teach, they promulgate three distinct ways of thinking, of relating to our planet, of relating to our universe, of relating to our bodies and ourselves; of relating to the very environment in which, and because of which, we live, breathe, and walk.

12   The first mythology of course—and by "first," I mean Christian mythology—defines a collective subconscious that is structured on, is governed and guided by, the principle of one straight line. In the beginning was this void, this endless soupy mass of matter that, according to the physicist Herr Heinz Pagels, pulsated and danced and swirled through the great dome of space. From this great swirl of nothingness emerged a God who, first of all, was male, and male entirely, one, moreover, who had seemingly no need of partnership from or collaboration with a female to give birth, by himself, to the universe with its planets and its stars and its moons and the Earth with its soil and its rock and its magic molecules. That was the beginning of time, the beginning of that straight line on the first day of which, of course, this male God gave birth to light, on the second day of which he gave birth to water, etc., until, on the sixth day he created man from a little ball of mud; woman came later; she wasn't necessary, not really. And the narrative goes on from there, the most salient feature to note being that this male God gave man the power to rule over nature, to exploit it, and to do with it as he pleased. The middle of time, of course—that is, the mid-point of that straight line—is when this male God's only son, a being half-human and half-divine, appears on the Earth—and on a very specific part of the Earth, one might add—with the purpose in mind of teaching man truth, love, and humble forgiveness, a project not entirely successful, it would seem, if one is to judge by events, today, in *that* part of the world. And at the end of that straight line, of course, comes Armageddon, the destruction of the universe by this same male God, the end of the Earth, the end of life, the end of time. I, for one, like to call this great "superstructure" the Book-of-Genesis-to-the-Book-of-Revelation straight line.

13   The first point to note about this particular mythology; of course, is that there is but one God; that is to say, the dream world it defines is monotheistic in structure, "mono" meaning "one" in ancient Greek, meaning that it is a monotheistic collective subconscious of which we speak here, a monotheistic universe. The second point to note is that this one God is male, and male exclusively. And heterosexual male, one must add here, one with not one conceivable speck of feminine attribute, physical, emotional, biological, or otherwise. The third point to note is that he is perfect, flawless; there is not one thing wrong with him; he knows everything, sees everything, feels everything, can do everything, including stop wars, one would think. The fourth point to note is that time, in this mythology, is of the essence and space, meaning the planet, the universe, our environment, meaning air and water, soil, vegetation, and all that sustains us, is of little to no consequence. And the fifth point is that this time functions according to the principle and structure of one straight line, a line that travels from point A to point B to point C. The sixth point? In the act of creating this universe, there was

no sexual act between two partners, no physical pleasure, no extended period of pregnancy; no biological process remotely conceivable; poof, the world just happened, in six short days. And, last, this male God gave us this Earth, and then snatched it away from us—the narrative of eviction from a garden, because of a woman's stupidity; is a narrative that, so far as I know, exists in three mythologies, and three mythologies only—Christian, Judaic, and Islamic—the only three mythologies extant on the Earth, so far as I know, that, not quite coincidentally, are monotheistic in structure, that have one God only. Space, in other words, was taken from us, and time is our curse.

14   The second mythology under discussion here, of course, differs quite dramatically on all these points. Greek mythology, first of all, defines a collective subconscious that is polytheistic in structure, "poly" meaning many in ancient Greek. In this universe, that is to say, there is not just one but many gods. And many, many goddesses. An epidemic of divine fecundity far too active, and far too exciting, to give fair treatment to, in a talk so very brief as this; suffice it to say that in this dream world, there was a god of the sky, for example, a god the father, if you will, whose name was Zeus (Jupiter in Roman mythology; a mythology which, by the way, came to appropriate this body of narrative round about the middle of the first millennium B.C.). There was a goddess of the Earth, a Mother Earth figure whose name was Hera (Juno in Latin). There was a goddess of love—a goddess of physical, sensual pleasure, that is to say, a goddess of, horrors, sex!—whose name was Aphrodite, from whence, of course, comes the term, in English, for aphrodisiac, among others. There was a goddess of grain whose name was Demeter (Ceres in Latin, from whence, of course, comes the English word for "cereal"). There was even a god of parties, of wild-downtown-Toronto-hotel-room-pagan-type celebrations, whose name, of course, was Dionysus (Bacchus in Latin, from whence, of course, comes the English word bacchanalia). There were messenger gods, gods of the sea, goddesses of the afterlife, a goddess of the home, a goddess of the hunt, gods of this, gods of that, gods of this, gods of that, *ad infinitum*—Apollo, Hestia, Athena, Hermes, Poseidon, Hades, Persephone, the list goes on; in fact, there seems not a single twitch of the human organism *and* of nature for which the Greeks didn't have a god or a goddess, much like, for example, Shinto mythology of Japan that has, to this day, over eight hundred gods *and* goddesses, including gods of trees and of wind and of such celestial bodies as the Sun.

15   The creation of the Earth, and of the universe, moreover, was made by a patently physical, biological act between an ancient male god, whom few have ever heard of but some accounts say was a wind called Ophion, others say was Boreas (from whence, of course, comes the English word for "boreal," as in "boreal forest")—a wind who wound his immense "physicality" around a female force of energy called Eurynome, which copulative connection gave birth to the universe, with its stars and its moons and its planets, including one that eventually came to be known as Earth, the goddess Eurynome, a female herself who eventually came to be known, by the Greeks, as Gaia, precursor to other Mother Earth goddesses through the centuries and eventually to the aforementioned Mother Earth goddess known as Hera. And Mother Earth Hera mated, through no time specified, with Father Sky Zeus and out of *that* union came all the other gods and goddesses, and so it goes. Trees were divinities named Dryads, rivers were

goddesses known as Naiads, reeds by the river were gods, sound was a god in the person of a cute little god called, in Greek as in English, Echo. And so it goes, a salient feature to note about these gods and goddesses being that none were perfect; all had the flaws of real-life, four-dimensional, flesh-and-blood human beings. Hera, for example, would traumatize the Earth with her great fits of jealousy whenever she got wind of the fact that her husband, Zeus-in-the-guise-of-swan, had made love to a princess of Sparta named Leda, to name but one Zeus dalliance, which human princess then gave birth to a demi-goddess whom we all know as Helen . . . of Troy. Aphrodite's amorous exploits were legendary. As were Pan's, in the garden of . . . well, more on that shortly.

16   There was, moreover, no sense of time—or at least no all-pervasive, obsessive sense of it—in this story of creation, or in Greek mythology as a whole. Nature came to fruition—as propelled by these divinities, forces of nature everyone of them—in no particular order; it just flourished, over an unspecified period of time, as one great act of pleasure, one great act of spectacular beauty. (Not, by the way, that pain and suffering didn't exist among the ancient Greeks but . . . more on this in the section on Aboriginal mythology.) Space, in other words, was much more important than was time. Interestingly enough therefore, if this mythology doesn't function according to the rigours of one straight line of time at the beginning, time in the middle, and time at the end, it also does not function quite like a complete circle, more like a circle interrupted and thus, at the very least a curve, a sort of grand semi-circle. And the reason for this interruption of the circle, of course, is because of what happened, historically, in that part of the world, round about the time of the birth of Christ, that point in time where Roman civilization—and thus Roman mythology—had taken over completely from the Greeks and Christian mythology in its turn, came to supplant Roman mythology. For mythologies, it would seem—as with the gods and goddesses that live therein—have limited life spans, limited periods of usefulness; they are born, they flourish, they fade, they die. Which is where new gods—and goddesses—spring from a battlefield covered, all too often, in blood, ashes, and empty hulks of temples, of churches.

17   Thus, the most important features to note about this second mythology, for the purposes of this lecture are: A) There is not just one god but many; this is a polytheistic universe, a polytheistic dream world that we speak of. B) God is not exclusively male or exclusively female, but is both at one and the same time. C) None of these gods, or goddesses, is perfect; they all have real emotions, they all have genuine physical sensations, desires, frailties, and such. D) Space is more important than is time. E) Time functions not according to the rigours of one straight line but as a sort of expansive curve, a grand semi-circle, a circle that has been punctured in the middle and then cut in half . . . of which more shortly. F) These were gods of pleasure; they got angry, yes, and they fought here and there but, first and foremost, what they were here for was a good time, a grand celebration of the fact of nature and its miraculous inner workings; the universe and its contents, in other words, were born out of an act of sex, an act of patent biological, and pleasurable, reality. G) As for Paradise or the Garden of Eden, the closest thing the Greeks had to it was Arcadia, a region of Greece still called Arcadia today. There was no eviction; humankind was not kicked out of the

garden of joy, that great space of pleasure, the garden of his fleshly desires, by an angry male god; rather was that space a gift from a benevolent—well, mostly benevolent—female god known as Mother Earth, a garden so very beautiful that one god from among the great pantheon of twelve forsook his residence on the airy heights of Mount Olympus to come and live, instead, a life of pleasure—including much sex—right there in the garden; half-goat, half-man in physical shape, an exciting, excitable, perpetually aroused deity, his name was Pan, from whence, of course, comes the English word for "panic," only in this context, the kind of "panic of pleasure" we all feel when sex is on the horizon . . . right there, smack dab in the middle of, precisely, *the garden.*

18   And the third mythology under discussion here, of course, as I promised, is North American Aboriginal mythology. Accounts vary widely across the continent, as they did in ancient Greece, as they did in the ancient Middle East, but the general consensus—at least in Cree—seems to be that the universe and its contents came into being as the result of the efforts of a female force of energy known as O-ma-ma, a miraculous entity eventually to be known, in the English language, as Mother Earth. Interestingly enough, moreover, in this particular account, there appears to be no overwhelming evidence of masculine involvement in the process of procreation. Hm, turkey basters must have existed back then, one may speculate, the point of the matter being that this girl was endlessly sexual, endlessly sensual, endlessly fertile, a creature of pleasure, a creature of the flesh who gave birth, in no particular order, with no great fixation on the concept of time, to many, many most wondrous and most, most beautiful things . . . including, at the start of her tale, this laughing, hysterically funny, totally outrageous clown called, in English, the Trickster—who, by the way, is half-human and half-god, like all superheroes in practically all mythologies on the planet. Mother Earth then, of course, also gave birth to women. And then men, as an afterthought. And mosquitoes, by the way. And blackflies. And little cells who don't quite always work out in the human bloodstream as cells and cause such illnesses as cancer. But then of course, there were trees, there were flowers, there were lakes, loons, whippoorwills, there was sunset and the wind.

19   The problem, however, with trying to describe such a concept of divinity in English, one would think, is the same problem one might encounter in attempting to describe Greek divinity and Greek concepts, in English, which is that it doesn't quite work. There is, for one thing—and most importantly—no concept of gender in the Cree language. In that language, we are all, in a sense, he/shes, trees are he/shes, ocelots are he/shes, budgie-birds in cages are he/shes, even rocks on the beaches of Rio are he/shes. And God—most essentially—is one big fat he/she. Meaning to say that God, even though she may be female in shape biologically in the context of Aboriginal mythology, is both male and female simultaneously, emotionally, spiritually, intellectually . . . as are we all, either to a greater or to a lesser extent, depending on who we are, and regardless of whether we are male biologically or female biologically, right? Right.

20   Second, this god/goddess known, again in English—damn that accursed language—is far from perfect. Yes, she is beautiful, yes, she is grand. And yes, she is generous, she is bountiful, she is kind and ever-loving and supportive and affectionate and all those good things. But she can, like the goddess Hera in Greek

mythology when tried to the limit by a masculine side of her that is not quite in working order, she can be one jealous, furiously angry bitch from hell. She kills with earthquakes, she destroys with hurricanes, she destroys with famine and starvation and drought and AIDS, tuberculosis, meningitis, all manner of disorders, physical, emotional, mental, spiritual and otherwise, she tortures with blackflies in July, snowstorms in February at least in Canada; one really has to be quite careful, but . . . in the end, she is beautiful and kind and, because of it, to be respected, revered, thanked. The point here being that, in Aboriginal mythology, there exists not one God as in Christian mythology, nor many gods, as in Greek mythology, but, rather, the concept of "God in all" or "God in everything"—in Aboriginal mythology that is to say, we speak not of "monotheism" or of "polytheism" but of "pantheism," the Greek word "pan" meaning all, as in "panorama," or in "pan-American." Meaning that all of nature—from leaves to soil to water to the cat in your living room to the heart inside your body to the woman, or the man, in your life—virtually pulsates with divinity. In the field of cellular biology they call the notion, I do believe, animism; in mythology *and* theology we call it pantheism. Same idea, same story.

21   Next, if time in Greek mythology took second place to space in the great scheme of things, then the distance or gap between that time and that space, in Aboriginal mythology, is of even greater width; in fact, that gap is one huge chasm that is all but unbridgeable, the same case—only in reverse—that exists in the sphere of Christian mythology. That is to say, if time lords it over space in Christian mythology, space lords it over time in Aboriginal mythology.

22   So that if time, in Christian mythology, is conceived of as one straight line, an arrow that travels with speed accelerating from point A to B to C, and ends there quite abruptly, then time, in Aboriginal mythology, is one vast circle. Or rather was, at one point in history, as was the case with Greek mythology before Judaic/ Christian mythology came along, in the thousand years between 500 B.C. and 500 A.D., to break it open and, out of it, make a semi-circle, as it were. And within that circle—of Aboriginal mythology—within that womb, to give the notion some visceral perspective, of course, lies the vast expanse of space, the vast expanse of land, the vast expanse of ocean, the vast expanse of air, the vast expanse of sunlight, of lakes—up here in Canada—of lakes unlimited, of forests unlimited, of wildlife unlimited, of a garden of pleasure, a garden of joy unlimited *and* of beauty unlimited and most, most wondrous. And on that circle—of time—moreover, there is no beginning, there is no middle, there is no end. Existence in the universe is merely one endless circle of birth and life and death and re-birth and life and death and rebirth and life and death so that those who lived in times before us—our mothers, our grandmothers, our great-great-grandmothers, those children of ours who have died, those loved ones—they live here with us, still, today, in the very air we breathe, in the shimmer of a leaf on that old oak tree, in that slant of sunlight that falls in through your window and lands on your wrist. They are here. Tears of sorrow are to be shed, yes, but tears of joy as well, tears of rampant celebration.

23   Last, of course, comes the notion of paradise, of the Garden of Eden. Keeping in mind that there are only three mythologies extant the whole world over at the very heart of which rests the tale of a woman talking to a snake and thus earning

all of us eviction from ourselves until the day we die, there is no such myth, no such narrative, in Aboriginal mythology (just as there is none in its Greek counterpart, just as there is none in all other world mythologies, that I know of anyway). According to that narrative, the way that dream world, that collective subconscious, is structured, in other words, we are *still* in that garden. The Sinai Peninsula, after all, may be a parched, treeless desert that has been cursed, and cursed most spectacularly, by an angry male God. And why angry, one may ask? Wouldn't you be angry if you hadn't had sex in five thousand years? Which reminds me . . . if he has no wife like Zeus did, or no girlfriend, of which the Trickster had very many, then just how did he get his rocks off . . . keeping in mind that you are looking straight at one of them legendary *retired* altar boys from hell, ouch! And keeping in mind that, at the very least, the Greek God the Father, Zeus—direct precursor to the Roman Jupiter, which name was subsequently shortened to Jove, which name was subsequently appropriated by Judaic and Christian mythology to Jehovah and thence to Yahweh and thus to the deity we know here today as God the Father—keeping in mind that the Greek God the Father, Zeus-in-the-guise-of-eagle made love to a boy named Ganymede, the sun god Apollo had a good friend in a young man named Hyacinth, the pleasure god Pan a good friend in a young man named Narcissus, that is, among his virtual army of Maenads, the point here is that, at the very least, the Greeks were honest about the biological reality both divine and human of the singular act of sex and of physical pleasure. Yes, the Sinai Peninsula may be a parched, treeless desert, cursed forever—very obviously—by an angry male god, but Canada, North America, our land, is not. North America, quite on the other hand, is the most spectacularly beautiful continent on Earth, as all who have seen it can attest. It is not a curse from an angry male. It is a gift from a benevolent *female* god. That is the difference. And the great Tree of Knowledge, which poor Eve had the bad luck to eat from, because of some overly-masculine narrator, perhaps? Well, in one mythology, we as a species are *not* to partake of such fruit. In the other two, *that's* why it's there; that tree of knowledge is there, right there in the middle of the garden for us to partake of, for us to enjoy, for us to celebrate every day, twice, thrice a day if we have to.

24   Therefore, ladies and gentlemen, just as Greek mythology came along at one point in the great turning wheel of gods and goddesses through the history of the world as we know it, Christian mythology arrived here on the shores of North America in October of the year 1492. At which point God as man met God as woman—for that's where she'd been kept hidden all this time, as it turns out—and thereby hangs a tale of what are probably the worst cases of rape, wife battery, and attempted wife murder in the history of the world as we know it. At that point in time, in other words, the circle of matriarchy was punctured by the straight line of patriarchy, the circle of the womb, was punctured, most brutally, by the straight line of the phallus. And the bleeding was profuse.

25   Circles, however, and fortunately, can be repaired. Or an erect phallus can be . . . um . . . doused with ice water? severed completely?—before it's too late. And perhaps, just perhaps what we're looking at today, as we see what's happening in the Middle East—*or* what's about to happen any minute now—perhaps what we're looking at is the death of the male god and the rebirth of the female.

We have, after all, very little choice, it seems to me. And, thankfully, as you look out all around you, just from the perspective of sociology alone, we may be seeing just *that*: genders formerly kept silent by the fury— some might say, by the fear—of the one very alone, and very lonely male god taking their lives and the lives of their communities into their own hands, into their own *healing* hands.

26   Science, after all, in all its brilliance—from quantum physics to cellular biology— has never, so far, yet been able to explain exactly where the impulse of that first cell in the universe came from. And neither has religion, in all its brilliance, in all its incredible complexity, been able to explain, adequately, just where the life force of the common human being originates, where the movement inside that first cell inside the human body comes from. A new language had therefore to be invented—by the visionaries, the priests, the shamans, of our respective societies—to articulate that origin. And that language is *mythology*, the dream world where exist, where thrive men with wings, horses with wings, creatures half-man and half-horse once walked this Earth, beings walk about who are half-man and half-goat just like the god Pan, or who are half-woman half-fish, half-man half-coyote, just like the Native Trickster, or who are half-woman and half-spider, again like the Native Trickster, snakes talk to women (but not to men), women give birth without having had sex, dead men rise from the grave. And men—and women, too—are human and divine at one and the same time.

27   Mythology: the exact halfway point between truth and fiction, mythology, the exact halfway point between science and religion, that most elaborate of all fictions. Truth, mythology, fiction. Science, mythology, religion, the ultimate, the original circle. And thereby hangs an enormous, and very long, story . . . of which more later.

28   Thank you.

Active Reading

1. Summarize Highway's view of the differences between Greek, Christian, and Aboriginal mythologies.

2. What difference does it make that Christian mythology is dominant in Canadian culture, according to Highway? How might our culture be different if Aboriginal mythology dominated instead?

3. In what sense is mythology a "discipline," and how is it different from other disciplines? How does mythology explain what the other disciplines cannot?

4. What is Highway's thesis, and what are the main stages of thought by which he develops it?

Critical Reading

1. Highway is an artist, not a scholar, but his lecture employs many references to scholarly knowledge. Identify some of these and analyze their likely effect on the audience.

2. Highway's lecture undertakes the very delicate task of critiquing Christianity as having been responsible for spreading some destructive seeds in our culture. How well does he walk the rhetorical tightrope between articulating his views and keeping a mainstream audience onside? For example, how does he

make it clear that he is critiquing a version of Christianity, and not Christianity itself? How does he avoid offending people who might normally object to hearing the term "mythology" applied to Christianity?

3. Do you find Highway's argument convincing?

4. If Highway is right that we need to be telling ourselves more humane stories in order to create a more compassionate society, what can we do about this?

"Your Majesty's Realm: The Myth of the Master Race" from *National Dreams: Myth, Memory and Canadian History*

Daniel Francis

Daniel Francis is a Vancouver-based freelance historical writer and researcher with a background in journalism and an M.A. in Canadian Studies from Carleton University. Francis is the author and editor of more than twenty books, including The Imaginary Indian: The Image of the Indian in Canadian Culture; Imagining Ourselves: Classics of Canadian Non-Fiction; Copying People: Photographing British Columbia First Nations; A History of World Whaling; Discovery of the North; Operation Orca: Springer, Luna and the Struggle to Save West Coast Killer Whales; Partners in Furs; *and* Red Light Neon: A History of Vancouver's Sex Trade; *as well as several textbooks published by Oxford University Press.*

The following excerpt from his book National Dreams: Myth, Memory, and Canadian History *traces the systematic construction of a myth of British superiority to all other cultures, in part through the equally systematic representation in school textbooks of Aboriginal culture as inferior.*

1 One fine morning in turn-of-the-century Alberta, a young newcomer from England, Abee Carter Goodloe, went out to sample some local culture at Fort Macleod, only to find herself overwhelmed by the sense that she was back in the Old Country. "In the morning there is polo," she wrote, "and one sees young English fellows in patent-leather boots and baggy khaki riding trousers, for which they have sent all the way to England, dashing up and down and 'running the whole show.' The Indians standing around look like aliens, like visiting strangers. The Englishman doesn't insult or bully the Indian. He simply ignores him, and by pursuing a life as nearly as possible like the one he would lead in England, and by appropriating whatever suits his interest or fancy, he makes the Indian understand that it is his country."[36]

2 Goodloe captures the arrogance of a colonial elite at its leisure, what Sid Marty calls the "Raj on the Range."[37] This vision of cowboys in polo helmets was replicated everywhere across the country, with regional variations, whether it was the tea-sipping, croquet-playing gentlefolk on Vancouver Island, or the colony of remittance men at Saskatchewan's Cannington Manor, or the ersatz Ontario gentry familiar from the best-selling Jalna novels of Mazo de la Roche. These were the self-confident purveyors of the British ideal who anticipated molding

the new dominion of Canada in the image of the Mother Country. Blacks, Jews, Asians of any type, Slavs, need not apply for membership in this elite. In the words of Professor W.G. Smith, an "expert" on immigration, "British-born Canadians" were "the elect of the earth."[38] This was the dark side of Canada's British inheritance, a virulent sense of racial superiority which placed beyond the pale anyone who was not English speaking, fair skinned, and devoutly Christian.

3   As Goodloe's description makes clear, one group which in particular suffered the fallout from this ethnocentric view of the country was the Aboriginal people, whom the newcomers pushed aside as if they hardly existed. The past three decades have seen an explosive growth in interest in the history and traditional culture of Canada's Native population. Treaty rights and land claims have shot to the top of the public agenda, and the century-long policy of assimilation has been discarded in favour of a formal commitment to some form of Native self-government. There has been nothing short of a revolution in the thinking of non-Native Canadians about the Aboriginal "question." Given such a changed climate of opinion, it is easy to forget how different the mainstream Euro-Canadian view was just a generation ago when Aboriginals, if they were considered at all, were dismissed as backward savages. No matter how familiar one is with the sad history of Aboriginal–white relations in Canada, one is not prepared for the sorry stew of smug, racist propaganda which, until quite recently, passed for informed opinion about Indians.

4   Just as school textbooks are an excellent place to examine the ideology of imperialism, they are also an excellent source for the kinds of stereotypes non-Native Canadians used when they thought about Aboriginal people. What emerges from the pages of these books is a cluster of images which might collectively be labelled the Textbook Indian. The Textbook Indian was the Indian in whom Abee Goodloe's polo-playing cowboys believed, the Indian which the anglocentric view of Canada invented in order to justify its own hegemony.

5   The earliest schoolbooks virtually ignored the Indian. A few pages at best, a few lines at worst, this was about all the attention Aboriginal societies received. W.H.P. Clement, for example, in his award-winning 1898 text, took eleven sentences to sum up the "character and habits" of the Indian. Another book concluded a brief discussion of the subject by dismissing its importance: "Much more might be said, but it would be tedious to do so in this place."[39] John George Hodgins's text, *A History of Canada*, in wide use in Ontario at the time of Confederation, included a nine-page chapter on "The Principal Indian Tribes," but prefaced it with the following note: "The Teacher can omit this chapter at his discretion."[40] Perhaps it was just as well that many teachers did, for the chapter is an appalling collection of stereotypes and misinformation. By the 1920s, the status of the Textbook Indian had improved to the point that most books presented at least some sort of an overview of Native societies. Still, as late as mid-century, the Canadian and Newfoundland Education Association, the national organization of educators, proposed a standardized outline of Canadian history that did not even include Native people as a topic worth studying.

6   Textbooks which did mention Native people adopted a fairly standard approach, beginning with a brief overview of the Indian Tribes, then moving on

to more important matters. Students could not help but notice that French and English colonists received far more attention than the indigenous people. At the same time as Clement devoted eleven sentences to the Indians, for instance, he took eight and a half pages to describe the career of Samuel de Champlain.

7   The material which was devoted to Aboriginal cultures focussed almost entirely on what they lacked. Texts made much of the fact that Indians did not have a written language and therefore had no books, no laws, no schools; that they did not have sophisticated technology; that they did not live in houses; that they had no discernible religions ("As they were heathens, of course, they knew not the true God of the Christians."[41]). Native people were portrayed as over-awed by the superiority of European technical achievements. Here is George Wrong, head of the history department at the University of Toronto, describing the sneering between Jacques Cartier and a party of Micmac: ". . . he scattered among them glass beads, combs and other trinkets for which they scrambled like eager children. They were a wretched company, and Cartier thought they must be the poorest people in all the world!"[42] Cartier may well have thought so, but the textbooks did nothing to suggest their readers might think otherwise. A relentless ethno-centrism pervaded all descriptions of the Textbook Indian.

8   The dominant theme of all these books was the expansion of European civilization in America. Given that way of framing the story, there was no real place for Native people, except insofar as they obstructed this process. History was something that happened to white people. "They had no history or written language," John Calkin assured his young reader.[43] Once the Iroquois wars end, the Indians go missing from the textbooks, reappearing briefly during the War of 1812 and again during the disturbances in western Canada in 1869 and 1885. Otherwise they have no role to play. By their very nature they were inimical to the main story line.

9   Until the 1960s, Textbook Indians were sinister, vicious figures, without history or culture. They inhabited the New World as wild animals inhabited the forest. They were introduced to young readers not as another civilization with which Europeans came into contact, but as part of the landscape, which had to be explored and subdued. Contact, a term familiar to modern readers, implies that two civilizations meet and interact. This was not the way youngsters thirty years ago, myself included, were taught to understand what took place. We were taught that the Indians were savages; that is, beings without civilization—and that the arrival of Europeans in America was a process of discovery and conquest, not contact.

10   Early texts portrayed Indians as bright-eyed animals peering out from their hiding places in the dark woods; "wolf-eyed, wolf-sinewed, stiller than the trees," as the poet Marjorie Pickthall put it. Descriptions focussed on their physical characteristics. The Indians were "a strange race," wrote Duncan McArthur. "They belonged to the country almost as the trees or the wild roaming animals."[44] They were "human wolves," wrote W.L. Grant.[45] Like animals, their senses were particularly keen. "They had bright, black eyes that could see ever so far, and ears that could hear clearly sounds that you would never notice."[46] And their strength was notable. "The Indians . . . were tall athletic people with sinewy forms . . . . They were capable of much endurance of cold, hunger and fatigue;

were haughty and taciturn in their manners; active, cunning, and stealthy in the chase and in war." [47] Their lodges were crowded and filthy like animal dens, and their ferocity was like the wild beasts tearing at the heart of the European settlements.

11   War was the favourite, almost the exclusive, pastime of Textbook Indians. "But to go to war was the most important part of an Indian's life," wrote J.N. McIlwraith in The Children's Study of Canada; "he cared for nothing else." [48] "The customs and character of the American aborigine turned, mainly, upon war," declared Castell Hopkins. [49] Before the arrival of whites, Textbook Indian life was taken up by fighting amongst themselves; afterwards they made a sport of preying on the colonists. And sport it seemed to be, since the textbooks never seriously paid attention to any rational motives Native people might have had for their behaviour. Colonists had political and economic objectives; Textbook Indians ("these forest tigers, these insatiable scalp-hunters" [50]) had only appetites and superstitions. Like beasts, they seemed to lack the ability to reason out their own best interests.

12   The double standard employed by Charles G.D. Roberts was typical. After condemning Iroquois bloodthirstiness for a hundred pages, he turns to a description of the expulsion of the Acadians from Nova Scotia by the British in 1755. Not surprisingly, Roberts finds reason to forgive this admittedly ruthless act. There was a war going on, he explains, and bad things happen in wartime. "If the step now decided upon seems to us a cruel one, we must remember to judge it by the standards of that day rather than this." [51] An excellent piece of advice but one which Roberts had not thought to give when he was portraying the Indians as "painted butchers," "shrewed red schemers." It was simply not admitted that Native people had a point of view worth trying to understand.

13   Textbook authors did admire certain martial qualities attributed to Textbook Indians, who were held to be fiercely brave in combat and when captured, "gloried in showing that they could not be made to heed pain." [52] As far as the texts were concerned, however, these qualities were corrupted by the Natives' whole approach to warfare: whereas Europeans fought honourably, out on the open battlefield, Textbook warriors skulked through the forest and attacked from ambush. They did not abide by the code of the gentleman; the textbooks use words like *ruthless, cunning, cruel, sinister, ferocious,* and *bloodthirsty* to describe their behaviour. Indians were not soldiers, they were predators. "War is not a pretty thing at any time," wrote Agnes Laut, a popular writer for children, "but war that lets loose the bloodhounds of Indian ferocity leaves the blackest scar of all." [53] Textbooks liked to linger over the hideous tortures inflicted on the colonists, entertaining their readers with the smell of burning flesh and the sound of tearing limbs.

14   The entire approach to the early history of Canada in these textbooks, both French and English, serves to demonize the Indians. The history of New France is depicted as the struggle of a small band of brave colonists to gain a toehold in the St. Lawrence Valley while fighting off first the Indians, then the English. The bold habitant farmers with a plow in one hand, a gun in the other. The founding colonists endure unspeakable suffering; Indians are the implacable foe which give meaning to this suffering. Every text highlights the same familiar

series of events as they review the history of New France for their readers. First, Adam Pollard des Ormeaux singlehandedly holds off an Iroquois war party at the Long Sault. This was "Canada's Thermopylae," declare the textbooks. Then Madeleine de Verchères, the teenaged farm girl, defends the family fort against marauding Iroquois; and the Iroquois attack on Lachine in 1689 is always presented as the worst instance of Indian depravity. It hardly matters that modern historians have shown that many of these events did not happen the way the textbooks say they happened. These stories long ago transcended mere fact to become the myths which explain the origins and survival of the country. Together they established what has been called our "trial-by-fire tradition," a tradition of suffering and sacrifice which animated, and to a great extent still animates, the textbook version of the earlier history of Canada.[54]

15   An important premise of the trial-by-fire tradition is that colonists were the innocent victims of Indian aggression. This premise is usually taken for granted. When made explicit, however, it shows how even the most glaring contradictions appear to make sense in the absence of an alternative point of view. In his *History of Canada*, J. George Hodgins spends about a hundred pages on the wars between the French colonists and the Iroquois, including the several attacks by French soldiers on Iroquois villages, after which he concludes, rather astonishingly, "that Canada was one of the few countries which was not originally settled by (or for purposes of) conquest. The pursuits of her inhabitants were always peaceful, not warlike. She has always acted on the defensive, and never as the aggressor."[55] Hodgins never offers his readers the opposite point of view, that Native people were fighting to protect their homelands against what amounted to an armed invasion by European soldiers and settlers. Instead, students were encouraged to believe that no colonist ever killed an Indian who wasn't asking for it.

16   At the centre of the trial-by-fire tradition is the figure of the Jesuit missionary. Textbooks pull out all the stops when they come to describe the efforts of these itinerant priests to convert the Native people not just to Christianity, but to civilization itself. "Their record among the savages is one of imperishable glory," wrote Charles Roberts, whose praise of the missionaries is bathed in eroticism. "Their faith was a white and living flame, that purged out all thought of self. Alone, fearless, not to be turned aside, they pierced to the inmost recesses of the wilderness."[56] The Jesuits were "pioneers of civilization," "a glorious army" sent to subdue the savage heart of America. The Indian represented the untamed, uncivilized essence of the New World. The Jesuits were special heroes because they went up against that essence armed only with a bible and a cross. Their suffering gave the colonial enterprise a moral purpose. And so it was described in gory detail, often purely imaginary: the necklace of red-hot hatchets, the dripping heart torn from the chest and devoured, the severed tongues and roasting flesh, the screams of agony. "The boys and girls who read these pages will never be called upon to witness such scenes in our country again," writes G.U. Hay in his *Public School History of Canada*; "but it is well that they should know of the toil, suffering and hardship of its founders, and be themselves willing to undergo, in a less degree trials that may come to them. This is the duty of the patriot."[57]

17   The deification of the Jesuits meant the demonization of the Indians. Native people were the villains of New France. As one historian has written, "martyrs must have murderers."[58] That was the role assigned to the Textbook Indians: they stood in the way of civilization, it was natural that they should be brushed aside. Textbooks constructed the story of New France in such a way as to justify policies of forced assimilation which the government had been practicing in Canada since Confederation. The derogatory image of the Textbook Indian was not created in a vacuum. It reflected the inferior status of Native people in Canadian society and Canadian historiography. In Quebec, prior to the Quiet Revolution of the 1960s, the Catholic Church exercised pervasive power and influence. The Church operated the school system and priests wrote the textbooks. Not surprisingly, the Catholic version of Canadian history disparaged Native people as superstitious savages and praised French colonists and missionaries for planting the One True Faith in the New World. To Catholics, which meant to the majority of Quebeckers, New France represented the triumph of Christianity over the dark forces of paganism. This was the meaning of Quebec's early history.

18   Until only recently, Native people everywhere in Canada were considered second-class citizens, and the declared aim of government policy was their assimilation. Most Canadians firmly believed that Indians had no future as Indians, that their culture was unsuited to modern, industrial civilization, that their only hope for survival was to join mainstream, white society. Natives were segregated socially, silenced politically, and marginalized economically. No wonder, then, that textbooks read back into history the inferior status of the Native which was everywhere evident in contemporary Canada.

19   When early textbooks turned their attention to the Métis of western Canada, it was usually with the same superficiality that characterized their treatment of the First Nations of New France. The Métis only appear in early textbooks when they clash with European settler society, so readers meet them for the first time at Seven Oaks on the Red River in 1816 when a party of Métis led by Cuthbert Grant skirmished with a party of Lord Selkirk's settlers. Responsibility for this event, which resulted in the deaths of twenty-two people, has been argued by historians ever since, but the textbooks show no hesitation in handing out blame. Seven Oaks was a "crime," declared A.L. Burt, committed by "half-civilized Métis" under the thumb of unscrupulous fur traders.[59] Chester Martin agreed that the Métis had no will of their own, that their "Indian blood" was "aroused to frenzy," that the "hideous massacre" was all their fault. It was "the worst orgy of bloodshed among men of British race that ever stained the western prairie," he told his readers.[60] The Selkirk settlement on the Red River represented an extension of European civilization into the wilderness; by opposing it, the Métis were seen to have put themselves beyond the pale. None of the textbooks admit that the Métis possessed a unique culture or played a pivotal role in the economy of the West. Charles G.D. Roberts was typical when he contemptuously dismissed their claim to be a "New Nation" as simply "vainglorious."[61]

20   The next textbook appearance of the Métis is the Red River insurrection of 1869-70. Most authors admit that the federal government was to blame for not dealing sooner with the legitimate fears of the Métis for the security of their

land tenure. But this did not mean that they condoned armed rebellion. To the contrary, they invariably portray the Métis and their leader, Louis Riel, as impatient, excitable, and unstable. Whatever cause the Métis may have had to complain about their treatment at the hands of an indifferent federal government, they are said to have had no cause to take the law into their own hands. What especially outraged the textbook authors, as it did most English-speaking Canadians at the time, was the death of Thomas Scott at the hands of a Métis firing squad. The execution was "cold-blooded murder," Scott was shot "like a dog." "It was not an execution," wrote Charles Roberts, "it was a murder, and a peculiarly brutal one."[62]

21   The North-West Rebellion in 1885 was similarly treated as an act of lunacy. While again admitting that the Métis may have had legitimate grievances, most authors concentrated on Louis Riel and the question of his stability. He was mad, they wrote, a wild fanatic. Chester Martin thought Riel was insane and raises the spectre of an Indian bloodbath. "None but a madman could think of bringing the savage Indians from their reserves on such a mission against settlers with their innocent women and children."[63] Others portray Riel as clever but "unstable" and "deluded." Once again the distinctive culture of the Métis is ignored, as are their claims to being a "new nation." In the early textbooks, the rebellion is important chiefly for the strain it placed on French-English relations; its implications for the West are largely ignored.

22   By the 1930s and 1940s the textbook view of the western rebellions were becoming a bit less black and white. The language used to describe the events was less hyperbolic, and more credence was given to the Métis point of view. Some books—not all, but some—began to lay a heavier weight of blame on the government of John A. Macdonald for not responding sooner to Métis grievances. Riel still emerges from the books as a highly erratic character, but his cause is considered just. "'With all his faults," admits Arthur Dorland somewhat reluctantly in 1949, "Riel's aims in standing up for the rights of the Métis and Indians were not entirely unworthy."[64] Evident in these books are the first glimmerings of the transformation of Riel into the folk hero he would become to later generations.

23   With the execution of Riel, Native people virtually disappear from the early textbooks, having served their purpose of providing a standard against which the superiority of Euro-Canadian civilization was measured. They had given Canadian youngsters like myself a reason to consider our country superior to the United States. And they had provided a rationale for the policy of forced assimilation which the government of our parents was implementing against Native people. No one cared that Textbook Indians were never really taken seriously as distinct cultures. Their contributions to Canadian history are not mentioned in the books. Issues which affect them are not discussed. There are almost no references to the contemporary land question, to the treaties, to life on the reserves. It is quite probable that as a student in high school during the 1960s I would not even have known that reserves existed. As in contemporary Canada, so in the textbooks, Indians are marginalized and silenced. Their spirituality is dismissed as nothing more than superstition. Their claims to their traditional territories are never even discussed.

24   Imagine for a moment the impact these ideas would have had on Native students when they encountered them in the residential schools which were established to accomplish their acculturation. Richard Nerysoo, a northern Native man, told Justice Thomas Berger at the hearings of the Mackenzie Valley Pipeline Inquiry in the mid-1970s: "When I went to school in Fort McPherson I can remember being taught that the Indians were savages. We were violent, cruel and uncivilized. I remember reading history books that glorified the white man who slaughtered whole nations of Indian people. No one called the white man savages, they were heroes who explored new horizons or conquered new frontiers . . ."[65] An analysis of social studies texts in use in Ontario schools during the 1960s concludes: "It is bad enough that any group should be subjected to prejudicial treatment, but the fact that Indians are the native people of this country and that their children are required to read these texts compounds the immorality of such treatment."[66]

25   Of course, the curriculum was not devised for Native students like Richard Nerysoo. Their discomfort, their shame, was incidental. The curriculum was devised for white youngsters like myself. It was supposed to teach us a view of history which rationalized the assimilationist policies being carried out by our government. In effect, we were being educated for racism. Textbook Indians were vicious children who did not have the good sense to recognize the superiority of the British heritage which could have been their rightful inheritance as citizens of Canada. Assimilation was presented as the only alternative to their extinction. We were taught that we were doing them a favour.

NOTES

36. From Abee Carter Goodloe, "At the Foot of the Rockies," *Alberta History*, vol. 34, no. 2 (1986); cited in Sid Marty, *Leaning on the Wind* (Toronto: HarperCollins, 1995), p. 78.

37. Marty, p. 78.

38. W. G. Smith, *A Study in Canadian Immigration* (Toronto: The Ryerson Press, 1920), p. 349.

39. Henry H. Miles, *The Child's History of Canada* (Montreal: William Dawson, 1910), p. 22.

40. J. George Hodgins, *A History of Canada and of the Other British Provinces in North America* (Montreal: John Lovell, 1857), p. 123.

41. Miles, p. 22.

42. George Wrong, et al., *The Story of Canada* (Toronto: The Ryerson Press, 1929), p. 14.

43. John Calkin, *A History of the Dominion of Canada* (Halifax: A & W MacKinlay, 1898), p. 3.

44. Duncan McArthur, *History of Canada for High Schools* (Toronto: The Educational Book Co., 1927), p. 2.

45. W. L. Grant, *History of Canada* (Toronto: T. Eaton Co., 1914), p. 51.

46. E. L. Marsh, *Where the Buffalo Roamed* (Toronto: Macmillan, 1923), p. 2.

47. William Withrow, *A History of Canada for the Use of Schools and General Readers* (Toronto: Copp, Clark & Co., 1876), p. 19.

48. J. N. McIlwraith, *The Children's Study of Canada* (London: Fisher Unwin, 1899), p. 6.

49. J. Castell Hopkins, *The Story of Our Country* (Toronto: John C. Winston, 1912), p. 52.

50. W. L. Grant, p. 48.

51. Charles G. D. Roberts, *A History of Canada for High Schools and Academies* (Toronto: Morang Educational Co., 1897), p. 129.

52. Miles, p. 20.

53. Agnes-laut, *Canada: The Empire of the North* (Toronto: William Briggs, 1904), p. 171.

54. James W. St.G Walker, "The Indian in Canadian Historical Writing," *Canadian Historical Assoc. Historical Papers* 1971, p. 37.

55. Hodgins, p. 144.

56. Roberts, p. 28.

57. G. U. Hay, *Public School History of Canada* (Toronto: Copp, Clark & Co., 1902) p. 218.

58. Walker, p. 36.

59. Burt, p. 200.

60. Wrong, et al., p. 263.

61. Roberts, p. 256.

62. Ibid., p. 364.

63. Wrong, et al., p. 293.

64. Dorland, *Our Canada*, p. 256.

65. Thomas Berger, *The Report of the Mackenzie Valley Pipeline Industry, vol. 1* (Ottawa: Supply and Services Canada, 1977), p. 91.

66. Garnet McDiarmid and David Pratt, *Teaching Prejudice* (Toronto: Ontario Institute for Studies in Education, Curriculum Series 12, 1971), p. 88.

Active Reading

1. What does Francis mean by "Textbook Indian"? Summarize Francis's description of the characteristics of the Textbook Indian.

2. Who benefited from the way First Nations and Métis people were represented in Canadian history textbooks? How? Did these representations do any real harm, in Francis's view? To whom, and what kind of harm?

3. How does "demonizing" one group of people help to "glorify" another group of people, according to Francis?

4. How did the content of the history books Francis discusses support the Canadian government's assimilationist policies toward Aboriginal people?

Critical Reading

1. Consider some of the ways in which the image of early British settlers as "cowboys in polo hats" aptly captures the misplaced confidence of colonialists.

2. Clearly the representation of Aboriginal people was unjust and inaccurate in the textbooks Francis describes. Use Francis's critiques of what is missing from school books to describe what he thinks should be covered. Do you agree with Francis about what should be taught, or do you have other suggestions?

3. Can you draw some connections between this reading and a) Sinclair and Hamilton's article on residential schools in the Education chapter and b) Baker's speech about enemy language in this chapter?

4. Francis is writing about textbooks up until the 1960s. How are Aboriginal people represented in textbooks used in recent years? Do you think Francis would be satisfied? Why or why not?

Resolution and Canadian Iconography: The "I-Canuck" Photograph?

Tracy Whalen

Tracy Whalen is Associate Professor in the department of Rhetoric, Writing, and Communications at the University of Winnipeg. Her research focuses on "the moment" and how such is communicated in language, gesture, and image. She has published articles about narrative moments in women's fiction, studying intensity and style and considering the politics of stylistic excess. This interest in significant moments fuels her research in the iconic photo-journalistic image, particularly as it relates to national identity. Whalen's research continues to engage with significant moments and key gestures in Canadian culture and how these encourage particular readings of citizenship in the public sphere.

In this article, Whalen reflects on the nature of the images that circulate in the imagination of Canadians, and on whether there might be better ones to have in mind.

1   Currently in Canada, the word *icon* or *iconic* is a popular epithet for cultural figures, events, locales, animals, and songs. A 2008 Ipsos-Reid survey documented by the CBC asked Canadians what best defined their country: "Trudeau was revealed as the person who most defines Canada. Niagara Falls was the defining place, Canada Day the defining event, Canadarm the defining accomplishment and the maple leaf was the defining symbol" ("Trudeau"). Canadian sociologist Patricia Cormack named the coffee chain Tim Hortons a "cultural icon," on par with "tuques, hockey sticks, canoes and beavers" (Proudfoot, *Winnipeg Free Press* A2). The most celebrated Canadian icons have, in fact, tended to be reified material objects. Douglas Coupland's *Souvenir of Canada*, which chronicles Canadian-ness through images, provides an assemblage of physical things including the stubbie, the vinegar bottle, the CN Tower, poutine, the inuksuk, and maple-walnut ice cream. Canadian media have designated writer-musician Leonard Cohen, artist Emily Carr, and red-haired Anne of Green Gables iconic. Equally iconic are Nova Scotia's racing boat, *The Bluenose*; the now defunct department store, Eaton's; the Avro Arrow; The Canadian National Exhibition; and CBC's former *Hockey Night in Canada* musical score. With the word's ubiquity have come critiques of its common, catch-all status. A blogger known as "Maxiumus," a New Zealander "interested in architecture and design" playfully asks the following:

> Do you reckon it might just be time to put an end to the use of the word Iconic? Once upon a time Icon was just a word meaning those painted portraits of Orthodox saints, then it became a symbol for a Mac application—and now they're everywhere. Damn icons! Enough with that word already! Does that make me an iconoclast? ("Icon Get No Satsifaction")

Closer to home, writer Gale Zoë Garnett, in a recent *Globe and Mail* book review, calls the term "a current lazy descriptor" ("Oh, he was more"). Whatever one's attitude, present-day public discourse suggests an urgent desire for, a strong pre-occupation with, and an occasional disavowal of the ubiquitous term *iconic*.

2   In this paper, I draw upon the work of rhetoric and communication scholars to closely examine the term *iconic* and to consider it in relation to one particular genre: the photojournalistic image. This essay centres on the idea of *resolution* to argue two things. First, it suggests, somewhat provocatively, that Canadians are not entirely resolved in their designation of The Iconic Image, even if there are many images—beautiful, significant, and dear—in Canadian circulation. Second, I demonstrate (using the "Standoff at Oka" picture as a primary example) that within many Canadian pictures, themselves, one often finds states of suspended resolution. This lack of resolution may entail a lack of visual focus or clarity; it may also involve a kind of unresolved tension between the participants in the photo. This lack of resolution *about* the pictures and *within* the pictures, I believe, reveals such to be a significant civic trait for Canadians. It's not that Canadians lack resolve or direction, but there seems to be national interest in moments of ambiguity and suspended tension. Ultimately, I view it as supremely productive—and not in the least troublesome—that Canada might need to stop and think about its superlative visual creations and to debate what constitutes its iconography. It is, in fact, the very commonplace, unreflective nature of visual icons that one should be wary of in the first place. In this respect, I believe Canadians are in a particularly instructive position to think, together, about what images are important to us and why.

3   Truth is, the label *iconic* cannot be empirically applied and then verified; there is necessarily some degree of subjectivity involved in the designation. There also has to be some degree of flexibility in assessment, which is why I am not suggesting that Canada lacks iconic photos entirely.[1] Such a proclamation, especially in a country anxious about its culture and its value, would likely prompt oppositional responses: *But what about that photo of Trudeau? What about that picture of Terry Fox running on the highway? Are you saying Canada lacks important pictures?* That angle would deflect attention from the images Canada does have and their considerable rhetorical work in constructing ideal citizenship in Canada's liberal democracy. Further, it might trigger defensive responses about the beauty of Canada's photography and, more importantly, Canada's value and visibility both within the country and without, visibility being a significant point of anxiety for Canadians. Writer Rick Salutin describes this "perpetual anxiety about Canadian culture": "Many Canadian writers and artists, when they sit down to produce a work, feel responsible not just for expressing themselves but for proving the country exists" (211). Political philosopher Will Kymlicka engages,

---

[1]Such binary framing characterized the media discussion of this research in June 2008. The *National Post* for instance, titled their story "Lacking Icons," and placed a picture of Henderson's 1972 summit goal above and against Rosenthal's U.S. image of Marines raising the flag on Iwo Jima. This emphasis, unfortunately, reduced the complexity and nuances of the discussion. Even more emphatically, the CBC, in an online piece entitled, "Iconic Canada: Is a Picture Worth Even One Word?" wrote: "In a paper to be presented to a conference in Vancouver this week, Tracy Whalen, a professor at the University of Winnipeg, says there are no real 'iconic' Canadian photographs."

too, with this idea of visibility, noting that Canadians "attach importance to how they are perceived by other countries. Indeed concerns about Canada's status in the world often affect the way the internal dimensions of Canadian identity are negotiated" ("Being Canadian" 357). That concern often centres on the gaze of the United States. In his article "Northern Enigma: American Images of Canada," Paul Gecelovsky argues that "for the most part, Canada is a country that excites little interest in the United States" (517). Sylvie Beaudreau seconds such an insight in her discussion of the difficulties *National Geographic* faced historically in trying to exoticize a country that was simply *too* familiar to American readers:

> Canada, for the most part, is a country that Americans don't think about a lot. When they do, they tend to think of it as America's "backyard"—as a kind of bigger, emptier, more natural and more polite version of the United States, peopled by lumberjacks, Mounties, ballerinas, hockey players and smiling Inuit. And Canada, a large, North American country whose inhabitants are mainly of European descent, is like the United States in many ways. So the challenge for *National Geographic* has been to convince Americans of Canada's unique, i.e. non-American identity. (518)

4   If one wonders, then, why iconic images have import in the first place, one might come back to such questions of perceived visibility and value. Canadians will, no doubt, cherish pictures of Terry Fox, images of Pierre Elliott Trudeau, "Standoff at," "The Last Spike," and glorious hockey moments, but a cherished picture is not, as this paper will explain, necessarily an *iconic* one. Definitions of such a term need to be more rigorous, especially now when this word has such widespread appeal. Further, this paper questions the social working of iconic images. We might consider whose interests are at play in the distribution of superlative national photos. What images are iconic for whom? What market factors drive the designation of such pseudo-sacred images? Icons are successfully commercialized artefacts. One might recall that Disney had exclusive control over the marketing of the Mountie image—arguably, the most Canadian of symbols—during a five-year contract in the 1990s. A Canadian national image was the property of an American corporation, which controlled its promotion and distribution.

5   This paper grounds itself in the work of American rhetoricians Robert Hariman and John Louis Lucaites, particularly their book *No Caption Needed: Iconic Photographs, Public Culture, and Liberal Democracy*. They study images like Dorothea Lange's "Migrant Mother" (1936), Joe Rosenthal's "Raising the Flag on Mount Suribachi" (1945), John Filo's "Kent State University Massacre" (1970), and Nick Ut's "Napalm" (1972) picture, among others. Hariman and Lucaites maintain that such images summon up powerful emotions and perform a kind of civic pedagogy, a teaching of what it means to be a citizen in a liberal democratic society. They emphasize, however, that they are discussing only U.S. public life and U.S. media, "as that is what [they] know." They write that "[i]t remains to be seen whether and how iconic photos operate in other national and transnational media environments" (7). This paper, then, steps in to apply their insights to Canadian photography. American scholars have produced

considerable theory about rhetoric and the public sphere and have paid close attention to their own public discourse. For that reason, I draw upon their theorizations and, necessarily, their examples, to ground my work. That's not to say American culture should always be the measure for studying Canadian public artefacts and that American definitions are always fitting. In this case, however, the American insights into visual iconography offer a rewarding place for Canadian explorations—and departures.

6   Although the topic of photojournalistic iconography in Canada has yet to be explored in scholarly work, Canadian photographers and Canadian photographs in general have received interdisciplinary critical attention. German Studies scholar Jill Scott, in her article "Photography and Forgiveness," studies the poignant work of Canadian photojournalist Robert Fleming, whose post–Second World War pictures of Germany, she argues, "provide a forum to think about the potential of visual culture to facilitate reconciliation and perhaps even forgiveness" (608). Sylvie Beaudreau, in the aforementioned piece above, notes how images of Canada in *National Geographic* magazine changed from a romanticized folk image in the 1960s to more gritty representations of social difficulties in the 1990s. Again from an historical perspective, visual culture scholar Keri Cronin documents the framing of interspecies encounters on postcards from The Rockies, studying how bears have become tourism commodities. The interest is certainly not limited to scholarly discussions: The August/September 2008 issue of *The Beaver*, a bimonthly publication that was renamed *Canada's History* in 2010, documented "10 Pictures that Changed Canada," featuring significant pictures in the nation's history.

LACK OF RESOLUTION IN LOCATING *THE* ICONIC PHOTOGRAPH

7   In their work, Hariman and Lucaites outline the iconic image as follows:

> We define iconic photographs as photographic images produced in print, electronic, or digital media that are widely recognized, are understood to be representations of historically significant events, activate strong emotional response, and are reproduced across a range of media, genres, or topics. Examples include the migrant mother staring past the camera while three children cling to her amid the Great Depression, John-John saluting his deceased father's passing caisson, the Vietnamese girl running in terror from a napalm attack, and the lone protestor staring down a tank near Tiananmen Square. ("Performing Civic Identity" 366)

They argue that visual icons are moments of "visual eloquence" ("Performing Civic Identity" 19). They are compositionally beautiful. Important to note, they are not simply famous pictures, but, as the term *icon* (with its religious history) suggests, iconic photos communicate—immediately and viscerally—a pseudo-spirituality or transcendence that attracts what the authors refer to as "civic piety." An iconic picture is a secular shot that elicits reverence. Further, these icons model a form of civic performance in the liberal-democratic society, what the theorists call "the murky gray area of guilt and freedom between self-interest and the common good" ("Performing" 16). In other words, these pictures show-case individual autonomy—the embodied person, the everyman—but working within the structures of a collectivity. They often emerge when times are chaotic and offer, visually, a way of understanding an often upsetting event. "Because all societies," they write, "and particularly democratic societies, are grounded in conflict, there is continual need for performance that can manage conflict. The stage is set for iconic circulation" ("Performing" 37). Iconic images like those of the *Challenger* explosion, the *Hindenburg* disaster, and the Kent State shootings (with Mary Ann Vecchio screaming next to the body of a dead student) offer visual resolution at a time of confusion.

8   When, in June 2008, a CBC poll asked Canadians what images they felt cap-tured Canada, results included the following: Paul Henderson's winning goal against Russia; "The Last Spike"; "Wait for Me, Daddy"; Bobby Orr's 1970 hori-zontal leap; the "Stanfield Fumble"; any number of Pierre Elliott Trudeau's shots; the liberation of The Netherlands in World War II by Canadian soldiers; "Standoff at Oka"; the Maple Leaf first being raised in Ottawa; a picture of Terry Fox running through Quebec; the Canadian flag lifted aloft after the Quebec referendum, and others. It would be interesting to know how many of these pic-tures the general Canadian reader could summon up in the imagination through title alone. Further, it would be interesting to discuss how many of these photographs elicit quasi-spiritual awe. This challenge is neither a test of IQ nor a measure of nationalism, but rather a suggestion of softer outlines and less emphatic tones around what constitutes The Iconic Shot in Canada.

9   The various responses on this CBC website illustrate the debate that charac-terizes this designation. Two figures frequently mentioned on the web forum are Pierre Elliott Trudeau and Terry Fox. I was struck by how many different pictures of these men were chosen as *the* iconic shot. One writer on the online forum, Joseph, labels as iconic the shot "[w]hen Prime Minister Trudeau is seen shak-ing hands with Chairman Mao in China. That was the day Canada truly went international." Another writer, Robert, opines: "To easily name only two [iconic shots]: Pierre Trudeau in his buckskin jacket paddling a canoe and the classic photo of Grey Owl (another buckskin jacket)." Sean feels that the iconic shot is "Pierre Trudeau giving the 'Trudeau salute' to protestors at Salmon Arm, BC." A contributor known only as h.w. adds the following:

> For me the single most iconic photo is that of Pierre Trudeau sliding down the banister. This picture of Canada's most charismatic (and polarizing) Prime Minister doing this very childish, charming and personal thing without regard for whatever others may think demonstrates his joie de vivre and passion while still being one step ahead of everyone else around him on any given topic.

10   Another writer, Tracey, selects "[t]he picture of Pierre Trudeau doing a pirou-ette after meeting the Queen" as her iconic moment. Robert Sibley of the *Ottawa Citizen* states, too, that the pirouette "is probably one of the more enduring images of the former prime minister embedded in the collective memory of Canadians" and expresses "his maverick anti-conformism, his democratic dis-dain for aristocratic pomp" ("Trudeau Deconstructed"). One might ask, given

this national conversation, *which* picture is the iconic one, the one that rises above the other representations.[2] The answer, I believe, comes back to the person in the photo rather than the photograph itself. I would argue that Trudeau is an iconic Canadian figure and that these various pictures take on the tincture of iconic through association. This argument is strengthened, in fact, by the postings about Terry Fox: James Papastamos writes on the web forum that "Fox is a Canadian icon." Len, on the same site, says that "[t]o me, Terry Fox is the ultimate Canadian icon." Ainslie, chiming in from Australia, observes that "Terry Fox is clearly an icon to Canadians." Again, what these writers are pinpointing is the iconicity of the person rather than the photograph. And this is, to my mind, a key distinction in this discussion.

11   When we imagine the iconic photograph of Terry Fox's journey from St. John's to Thunder Bay during his Marathon of Hope, what photograph do we have in mind, exactly? The cover of *The Beaver* depicts Terry Fox at night, outlined from behind by the lights of a trailing police car. This picture, taken by Peter Martin for the *Oakville Journal*, won a National Newspaper Award (Webb 23). If one looks at the Canadian coin commemorating Terry Fox[3], however, one will see Terry Fox in profile, with trees behind him. (Presumably, it would be difficult to depict nighttime on a coin, even if one wanted to replicate the exact image.) I recall many pictures of Terry Fox from my childhood, all with him facing the camera: one with a big truck coming up beside him on the highway, another with a police car behind him (during the day), as he wore his Marathon of Hope T-shirt. The iconicity of whatever shot one imagines comes back to Terry Fox and the TransCanada Highway, two salient symbols in the Canadian imaginary. Fox and Trudeau, in fact, are strong examples (for some Canadians, at least) of what rhetoricians call a "representative figure":

> "Remembered as product or story or some hybrid of the two," argued S. Paige Baty, a "representative character is a cultural figure" invested with "authority, legitimacy, and power," which functions "as a site on which . . . political culture is written and exchanged." Robert N. Bellah and others offered a similar perspective, suggesting that a "representative character" is a "public image that helps define, for a given group of people, just what kinds of personality traits it is good and legitimate to develop." (qtd. in Kimble and Olson 535)

Terry Fox represents many things for many Canadians: hope, tenacity, compassion, youth, strength, unification, what have you. Trudeau represents, for some, an international glamour, a charisma, official bilingualism and multiculturalism, an edginess (and sharp-edged intellect) that stood out against the mild-mannered backdrop of the nation.

12   Interestingly, Hariman and Lucaites discuss one moment of iconic ambiguity in U.S. photojournalism, that being NASA's "Explosion of the Challenger." They point out that there are a series of shots of the cumulus cloud after its explosion

---

[2] The issue of resolution becomes all the more complicated when we consider that this pirouette, which many believe to have been spontaneous, was (like many of Trudeau's antics) planned. *Ottawa Citizen* writer Robert Sibley notes that "it might well be our collective view of Trudeau is unfocused, even distorted." This lack of focus (or resolution) applies to my thesis, generally.

[3] This coin can be viewed at http://www.cbc.ca/canada/story/2005/03/14/terry-fox050314.html.

(the trajectory headed upwards and the tendrils of smoke falling downwards simultaneously): "They all are presented as if each one is the icon, the original, transparent photograph. Multiple images clearly are not being used to break iconicity, and they all draw on that symbolic power. That power is reinforced by their distribution" (*No Caption* 252). I would argue, too, that these numerous images of Trudeau and Fox work to reinforce their iconicity as Canadians, but I maintain that such a claim is different from designating one photograph as the iconic photograph. In the Terry Fox photos, however, there is a resolution into one recognizable body position: Terry facing forward, the strain of sustained effort showing on his face, his body leaning slightly to the side as he steps forward. Such a posture lends itself more, I maintain, to iconic *statuary* (if such a distinction is allowed), rather than an iconic photo *per se*. Canadians have a great deal of reverence for this young man in that pose, a pose that might remind some (given Terry's youth, his curls, and his strength) of Michelangelo's *David*.[4]

13   This quality of debate around iconicity played itself out, too, in one of my classes. I regularly teach a course called *The Rhetorics of Visual Representation* at the University of Winnipeg. On the day we began to talk about *The Flag Raising on Iwo Jima*, I asked the class what some of Canada's iconic images might be. I did not have a definite answer, but one image that flickered at the back of my mind was Frank Lennon's famous (and many call iconic) picture of Paul Henderson's winning goal against the Soviet Union in 1972. This picture won the National Newspaper Award and the CP Picture of the Year. As many Canadians of a certain age know, Henderson scored with 34 seconds left in the eighth game of a tied-series. On September 28, 1972, Canadians (many of whom took the day off work) watched the Moscow game in bars, universities, and public meeting places. Lennon's photo of the winning moment offers compositional interest with its slightly triangular configuration. The goalie Tretiak still lies on the ice in defeat, the horizontal of his sprawling body contrasting the triumphant vertical of Henderson's. Number 12 Cournoyer's raised stick provides a linear diagonal down the centre of the shot, a visual virgule that separates the joyful face of Henderson from the impassive visage of the Soviet player. With the embrace of Cournoyer, the photo celebrates collective effort. These players are the individual embodiment of co-operative victory—significantly, Western victory—and Canadian hockey prowess. An emotional image at the time, this picture taught Canadians, too, the place of emotion in a masculine representation of citizenship. As Morley Callaghan repeated in an interview after the game, the Canadians were like "Romantic figures" (their emotions were stirred up) while the Soviets were characterized (by Canadians) as "controlled," "impassive," "robotic," and "mechanical." This picture, in keeping with Hariman and Lucaites' definition of the iconic photograph, was widely circulated: it has been reproduced in books, and has appeared on hockey cards, coins, and postage stamps. One might assume, then, that this is an unproblematic image in the Canadian visual imaginary and that one might stop there.

---

[4]Readers might be interested in reading Marilyn Dahl's essay, "The role of the media in promoting images of disability." In that article, Dahl discusses the "selective coverage of disability" and critiques the "disabled as superstar" image favoured by the media.

14   When I mentioned this picture to my class of primarily twenty-somethings, however, their response surprised me. Some students knew of the picture, but not all. Some of the young men in the back nodded slightly, but did not seem excited about the photo or this historic event. When I spoke with a *National Post* journalist about this topic six months later, she had pulled up what she believed to be salient Canadian photos and this picture was not among them. I can only speculate that perhaps, for a post–Cold War generation, the picture has lost its oppositional intensity. This representation of hockey sportsmanship may not address the pluralistic and heterogeneous viewers of the 21st century. It may, instead, appeal to specific subcultures of people. Hariman and Lucaites understand famous baseball shots in American culture appeal to all under such a category: "They could be called icons within the subculture and they are salient without, but they don't do the same work for public life as they do for baseball" (*No Caption* 7). One CBC web forum contributor, JD, would agree with these critics, as she writes, "I don't believe the hockey photos are iconic Canadian photos. They should belong in a separate sports iconic photo category."

15   Which Canadian images, then, simultaneously illustrate all the elements Hariman and Lucaites outline as being necessary to the iconic image: one widely recognized, historically significant, strongly emotional, and compositionally pleasing? Some of the photos mentioned by CBC posters were not universally recognized (e.g. "Wait for Me, Daddy," the shot of Holland's liberation, the picture of Trudeau with Mao, for instance). The "Shawinigan Handshake" (with Jean Chrétien throttling a protestor) is not easily associated with any historical event, nor is Doug Ball's astonishingly eloquent 1974 shot of PC leader Robert Stanfield fumbling a football during an election stop-over (a picture Ball says he regrets taking), although some claim it cost Stanfield the election. This shot does not exactly inspire civic piety, either. "The Last Spike " is considered iconic by many Canadians, and though the photograph is historically resonant and significant, I wonder if it evokes strong emotions and veneration in present-day Canadian citizens (and if it is compositionally striking or dramatic enough to constitute this title). One might ask, even, if Canadians have a strong disposition towards secular veneration or if, instead, as Salutin argues, Canadians have an "ironic detachment . . . virtually the corpus of political and social satire in the American media in the past 25 years has been produced by Canadians" (214). In the introduction to *Fire and Ice: The United States, Canada, and the Myth of Convergent Values*, Michael Adams writes of Canada's "gift for irony and understatement in a world of exaggerated claims and excess" (2). As my examples in the next section demonstrate, a lot of the images younger Canadians cite as important to them involve subversion, irony, and antagonism and elicit responses of critique and humour more often than nostalgia or awe.

16   If one grants that the status of Canadian photos is complicated, one might ask why. Canada is a large country geographically, with a relatively small and dispersed population. Markets and media distribution companies are smaller in Canada than they are in the U.S. and distribution is crucial to recognizing an image nationally. Hariman and Lucaites stress that iconic photographs are "visual commonplaces . . . images you see again and again" (*No Caption* 2). Widely recognized, these images are "known for being known" (*No Caption* 12).

The United States has identified historically with images from the hugely influential *Life* magazine, *Time* magazine, and *National Geographic* and newspapers like *The New York Times*. By contrast, Victor Rabinovich sums up the "ecosystems" of distribution and circulation of cultural artefacts in Canada as follows:

> On balance, the Canadian cultural ecosystem remains breathtakingly fragile because the essential context of this country has not changed. Factors such as audience size, regionalism, linguistic divisions, under-financing, inadequate distribution, and the ubiquitous American presence continue to challenge potentially self-sustaining Canadian cultural undertakings. (230)

One might point to some notable Canadian pictures that have made it onto the cover of *Time* magazine, one being the picture of Maggie and Pierre Trudeau (photographed by Lynn Ball) after Trudeau's 1974 election victory. But in the main, the social realities of population, international status, and publishing in Canada can't help but affect the production and circulation of images in this country or the number of events believed to be powerful in collective memory on the international stage. And even in the U.S., iconic photos do not come along every day. Hariman and Lucaites acknowledge that they are a small set, "fifteen, twenty, maybe thirty at the most across a span of generations" (6). The circulation of iconic images does not stop, either, with those moments of civic piety and devotion, but are circulated further, in editorial cartoons and all manner of commercial goods (t-shirts, tattoos, mugs, mouse pads, posters, etc.).

17   This question of iconic images (or lack thereof) comes back, too, to white Canada's history of citizenship, which is still *en emergence*, given our recent status as British subjects. Iconic images are defined as domestic productions of model citizenship, and Canadians have not had a long time to develop these. As David Pearson tells us, dominions like "Australia, Canada and New Zealand . . . did not draw any formal distinctions between a British and local born 'European' identity until the late 1940s when a transnational British subjecthood was supplemented by the notion of a separate national citizenship" (994). In addition to citizenship identifications, there exist regionalisms in Canadian identity and anxieties around Canadian social cohesion. The integration of immigrant minorities in post-settler state Canada, for example, gets worked out in our evolving policies of multiculturalism. The different perspectives of Aboriginal populations (and the ethnoregionalism of Quebec) add further challenges in terms of shared photojournalistic images. Such complex political realities might prevent uncomplicated collective identification, then, with one photograph.

LOOKING *WITHIN* THE ICONIC IMAGE: AMBIGUITY AND LACK OF RESOLUTION

18   When I asked my students to select images that they believed to be even pseudo-iconic, they offered photographs like the "Shawinigan Handshake," Trudeau's aforementioned pirouette, and the "Standoff at Oka" picture. These images communicate moments of unresolved tension resolved compositionally within the frames of the pictures, themselves. I focus here on the "Standoff

at Oka" picture, which seems to approximate many of the criteria outlined by Hariman and Lucaites. The picture, taken on September 1, 1990 by Shaney Komulainen, symbolizes an historic moment during a 78 day standoff between the Mohawk nation at Kanehsatake and the Quebec town of Oka. Conflict was sparked when a private company successfully bid to expand its golf course on Mohawk burial grounds; the dispute centred on who owned the territory in question. The picture draws upon dominant ideologies and replicates ideas of public conduct and citizenship (for instance, the belief that war is waged by young men). It also locates Aboriginal people in the blurry space of the woods. The picture suggests that one important act of citizenship is to exercise self-control, emotionally. As Hariman and Lucaites write, "When public life appears emotional, it is assumed to be imperiled: either the political official is exhibiting a loss of the self-control essential for responsible administration of the state, or the public audience is succumbing to those irrational impulses that are amplified by massing bodies and can lead to demonstrations, riots, and the breakdown of social order" ("Dissent and Emotional Management" 5). A lot of the emotive power of this picture lies in its suggestion of an impending explosion of emotion and the possibility that this long-held suppression (both in the represented individuals and their nations) will explode into uncontainable violence. Private Patrick Cloutier, the Van Doo perimeter sentry in this picture, has come to represent civic order in his suppression of emotional display. We cannot know what Brad Larocque, an Ojibway student from Saskatchewan, is expressing, as his face is covered. Depending on one's stance vis-à-vis this shot, this picture might evoke disbelief, fear, satisfaction, anger, or aesthetic appreciation. Some might argue that this picture represents a most-Canadian trait: however much these men may oppose each other, within the framework of this picture, they will not touch, will not hit, will not kill. Important, too, pictures like this one provide figural resources for accompanying action, which in this case also involved opposition and antagonism: Canadians witnessed media footage of non-Aboriginal Quebecers burning Mohawk warriors in effigy next to the Mercier Bridge.

19   In terms of composition, the shot is striking: the profiles of these two men are foregrounded, in focus, against the blur of woods. A strong division along the vertical axis highlights rhetorical schemes of balance, specifically parallelism and antithesis. These men, centred in the picture, are close enough to the viewers that they allow for what Michael Warner in *Publics and Counterpublics* calls "stranger sociability." The viewer is close enough to Cloutier's face to see its expression. In fact, much of the power of the image lies in the range of readings one might bring to understanding his facial expression. The bodies of these men, which personalize this historical event and which constitute metonyms for Aboriginal and non-Aboriginal identity and interests, take up most of the picture. Their faces almost meet; intensity emerges, in part, from the depiction of two antithetical figures in so small a visual frame, two men whose clashing of visual directional substance constitutes head-on collision.

20   This image coordinates beautifully a number of different possibilities for identification and coordinates tensions in a manner that provides aesthetic balance. The photo's combination of close opposition, direct vector of eye contact, and contained (or concealed) emotion creates a strong sense of

moral crisis, a point at which viewers must decide where they stand. Does one identify with the Mohawk warrior and read Cloutier's face as afraid or full of barely concealed resentment? Along these lines, does one read the slightly higher stance of Larocque, his facial concealment, and his gun as triumphant in this frame?

21   Or does one identify with the non-Aboriginal Cloutier and read the Mohawk warrior as disruptive to social order, as a threat to national security? Do we read this face-to-face composition as a moment of visual ambiguity, a moment not of *either/or* but of a mediating *both/and*? This picture accommodates politically, too, the space of mediation, the viewer positioned in the fantasy space of potential peacekeeper or go-between. These men are not looking at us or directing their hostility at us; their antagonism is offered to us for reflection. At the centre of this picture is a white space, the line between the two men, a no-man's land of sorts. This picture instantiates a relation that is not entirely resolved; hierarchy seems slippery here in the crossing of visual space. One feels in the Oka picture the odd sensation of seeing two oppositionally positioned faces working together compositionally but occupying a space of political incommensurability on the debated territory of Kanehsatake woods. This is the space of unresolved tension.

22   It would appear this Canadian photo allows, in the safe space of a picture, an exploration of national limits to tolerance and diversity. The image not only communicates citizenship roles in the Canadian liberal-democratic state, but it also communicates the anxieties some Canadians feel about how one might go about reconciling the sometimes-divergent interests of the Canadian state and those of Indigenous Peoples. I am musing that such questions are important now in the Canadian imaginary. In a recent scholarly collection comparing Canada to fellow settler state Australia, Gilles Paquet argues that the Canadian government fails to directly address the issue of tolerance when it comes to managing social diversity:

> [P]ublic officials . . . claim to have no concern about defining any such set of expectations about the terms of integration for newcomers on the ground that one cannot ask anything from newcomers that one does not require explicitly from the native born . . . The result is not only a lack of debates in Canada about limits to tolerance and diversity, but a natural drift, as the jurisprudence cranks out case after case, towards a refusal to *recognize that there are any limits.* There is no longer pluralism but a leap of faith that if some form of limits proves necessary, it will emerge organically. (248)

This attitude of Canada just working it out "organically" emerges in a collection entitled *Uneasy Partners: Multiculturalism and Rights in Canada,* where one of the authors, Janice Gross Stein, writes that Canada is starting to recover what she calls its "*intuitive* sense of balance" (3). An "intuitive," ad hoc attitude towards everyday deliberation seems, in fact, to work for many Canadians, as much gets done through everyday negotiation. It might not be surprising, however, that some Canadians feel anxious about ad hoc, organic workings of integration and balance and are working out these anxieties in the store of national pictures.

CONCLUSION

23   This article has examined Canadian photojournalistic iconography through the lens of resolution. When one looks at the "Shawinigan Handshake" picture or the Trudeau pirouette, one might notice the poor visual resolution in these shots. In pictures, resolution can refer to the sharpness of an image: the greater the resolution or clarity, the sharper the image. Resolution also entails settlement or closure. When I think of Terry Fox shots, I think of a series of similar images that have not resolved into one picture. When I think of the Oka shot, I see a suspended state of unresolved opposition. When I have spoken informally with fellow Canadians about visual icons, I don't get a sense of resolved agreement about any one of them. Sharing icons is an act of identification, icons providing a reified object around which a culture can cohere and make sense of itself. Particularly in a country like Canada, where cultural anxieties around national identity and cohesion exist, one can understand the desire for icons. Such shared identifications come out of Canadian culture and, in turn, reflect back to Canadians the kind of nation they can recognize and celebrate. But this question is not a simple one.

24   Rather than lament or fault a society that debates its photographic icons, we might appreciate the richness of the debate. There are limits to iconic depiction, of seeing the world in a framed, simplifying shot. Because iconic images necessarily represent mainstream ideologies, they silence marginalized representations and alternate ways of understanding civic realities. As Hariman and Lucaites point out, for instance, the "Times Square Kiss" was between two white people. An image of interracial kissing would not have obeyed the necessary rules of decorum to unite mainstream public culture in this moment of post-war celebration. But the iconic image is problematic for other reasons, too. These images have an element of the transcendent about them. It is as if everyday experience were imbued with some quasi-religious meaning, some mystery, in these photos. Such transcendental meaning deflects society's attention from representations of the ordinary, from the less remarkable and less glorious elements of mundane living (the real experiences of living with a disability, for instance, instead of the transcendent heroism of Terry Fox; the realities of inner-city Aboriginal experience instead of the suspended equipoise of the "Standoff at Oka" picture). If we come to believe that life is lived with that condensed meaning, then we run the risk of overlooking images that do not fit the aesthetic mould of photojournalistic iconography (i.e. summoning up powerful emotions, quieting contradictions within the photo, offering peak moments as those worth regarding). These iconic photos, Hariman and Lucaites maintain, tend towards a repeated sameness (with strong vectors, for instance, or energies in the shot) that can diminish the variety of photojournalistic images that can story historic events. To push back against such aesthetic repetition and simplification, these rhetoricians suggest that "the better practice would be to feature more articulated coverage such as the photo-essay and more varied use of the archive to illustrate retrospective commentary" (*No Caption* 290). This recommendation of photo-essays is seconded by Stu, one of the web forum participants on the CBC icon website, who suggests that "maybe a montage is what is needed as an iconic symbol of this eclectic

country." Perhaps, as some on the CBC website suggested, what is most Canadian is our lack of resolution into one, definitive icon and (to risk a cliché) the photojournalistic multiplicity itself.

WORKS CITED

Adams, Michael. *Fire and Ice: The United States, Canada and the Myth of Converging Values.* Toronto: Penguin, 2003.

Ainslie. Online posting. 6 June 2008. Iconic Canada: Is a Picture Worth Even One Word? 1 May 2009 <http://www.cbc.ca/news/yourview/2008/06/iconic_canada_is_a_picture_wor.html>.

Beaudreau, Sylvie. "The Changing Face of Canada: Images of Canada in *National Geographic.*" *The American Review of Canadian Studies.* 32.4 (2002): 517–46.

Bielski, Zosia. "Lacking Icons." *National Post* 3 June 2008: A3.

Coupland, Douglas. *Souvenir of Canada.* Vancouver: Douglas and McIntyre, 2002.

Cronin, Keri. "'The Bears are Plentiful and Frequently Good Camera Subjects': Picture Postcards and the Framing of Interspecies Encounters in the Canadian Rockies." *Mosaic* 39.4 (2006): 77–92.

Dahl, Marilyn. "The Role of the Media in Promoting Images of Disability." *Canadian Journal of Communication* 18.1 (Winter 1993): 75–79.

Garnett, Gale Zoë. "Oh, he was more than a contender." *Globe and Mail* 8 Jan. 2009. 10 Jan. 2009. <http://www.theglobeandmail.com/servlet/story/RTGAM.20090108.wbkbrando10/BNStory/globebooks>.

Gecelovsky, Paul. "Northern Enigma: American Images of Canada." *American Review of Canadian Studies* 37.4 (2007): 517–36.

Gross Stein, Janice, et al. *Uneasy Partners: Multiculturalism and Rights in Canada.* Waterloo: Wilfrid Laurier UP: 2007.

Hariman, Robert, and John Louis Lucaites. "Dissent and Emotional Management in a Liberal-Democratic Society: The Kent State Iconic Photograph." *Rhetoric Society Quarterly* 31.3 (2001): 4–31.

——. *No Caption Needed: Iconic Photographs, Public Culture, and Liberal Democracy.* Chicago: U of Chicago P, 2007.

——. "Performing Civic Identity: The Iconic Photograph of the Flag Raising on Iwo Jima." *Quarterly Journal of Speech* 88.4 (2002): 363–92.

h.w. Online posting. 4 June 2008. Iconic Canada: Is a Picture Worth Even One Word? 1 May 2009 <http://www.cbc.ca/news/yourview/2008/06/iconic_canada_is_a_picture_wor.html>.

"Icon Get No Satisfaction." *Eye of the Fish: A wide-angle view of urban life, design, and architecture in Wellington, New Zealand.* 30 January 2009 <http://eyeofthefish.org/icon-get-no-satisfaction/>.

J.D. Online posting. 5 June 2008. Iconic Canada: Is a Picture Worth Even One Word? 1 May 2009 <http://www.cbc.ca/news/yourview/2008/06/iconic_canada_is_a_picture_wor.html>.

Joseph. Online posting. 9 June 2008. Iconic Canada: Is a Picture Worth Even One Word? 1 May 2009 <http://www.cbc.ca/news/yourview/2008/06/iconic_canada_is_a_picture_wor.html>.

Kimble, James J. and Lester C. Olson. "Visual Rhetoric Representing Rosie the Riveter: Myth and Misconception in J. Howard Miller's 'We Can Do It!' Poster." *Rhetoric & Public Affairs* 9.4 (2006): 533–70.

Kymlicka, Will. "Being Canadian." *Government and Opposition* 38.3 (2003): 357–85.

——. *Finding our Way: Rethinking Ethnocultural Relations in Canada.* Don Mills, ON: Oxford UP: 1998.

Len. Online posting. 6 June 2008. Iconic Canada: Is a Picture Worth Even One Word? 1 May 2009 <http://www.cbc.ca/news/yourview/2008/06/iconic_canada_is_a_picture_wor.html>.

Papastamos, James. Online posting. 6 June 2008. Iconic Canada: Is a Picture Worth Even One Word? 1 May 2009 <http://www.cbc.ca/news/yourview/2008/06/iconic_canada_is_a_picture_wor.html>.

Paquet, Gilles. "Governance and Emergent Transversal Citizenship: Towards a New Nexus of Moral Contracts." *From Subjects to Citizens: A Hundred Years of Citizenship in Australia and Canada.* Ed. Pierre Boyer, Linda Cardinal, and David John Headon. Ottawa: U of Ottawa P, 2004. 231–61.

Pearson, David. "Theorizing Citizenship in British Settler Socieities." *Ethnic and Racial Studies* 25.6 (2002): 989–1012.

Proudfoot, Shannon. "Tim Hortons an icon, says sociologist." *Winnipeg Free Press* 3 Nov. 2008: A2.

Reader, Robert. Online posting. 6 June 2008. Iconic Canada: Is a Picture Worth Even One Word? 1 May 2009 <http://www.cbc.ca/news/yourview/2008/06/iconic_canada_is_a_picture_wor.html>.

Salutin, Rick. "National Cultures in the Age of Globalization: The Case of Canada." *Queen's Quarterly* 106.2 (Summer 1999): 207–15.

Scott, Jill. "Photography and Forgiveness." *Queen's Quarterly* 113.4 (Winter 2006): 607–18.

Sean. Online posting. 5 June 2008. Iconic Canada: Is a Picture Worth Even One Word? 1 May 2009 <http://www.cbc.ca/news/yourview/2008/06/iconic_canada_is_a_picture_wor.html>.

Sibley, Robert. "Trudeau Deconstructed." *The Ottawa Citizen* 4 June 2006. 2 March 2009.<http://www2.canada.com/ottawacitizen/news/citizensweekly/story.html?id=e72eeda6-6d2f-4586-8f28-822719408b23>.

Stu. Online posting. 5 June 2008. Iconic Canada: Is a Picture Worth Even One Word? 1 May 2009 <http://www.cbc.ca/news/yourview/2008/06/iconic_canada_is_a_picture_wor.html>.

Tracey. Online posting. 5 June 2008. Iconic Canada: Is a Picture Worth Even One Word? 1 May 2009 <http://www.cbc.ca/news/yourview/2008/06/iconic_canada_is_a_picture_wor.html>.

"Trudeau, Niagara Falls among top Canadian Icons, Poll Finds." 26 June 2008. 30 January 2009. <http://www.cbc.ca/canada/story/2008/06/26/f-canada-poll1.html>.

Warner, Michael. *Publics and Counterpublics.* New York: Zone, 2002.

Webb, Chris. "Terry's Journey: A Story in Shadow and Light." *The Beaver* Aug./Sept. 2008: 22–23.

Active Reading

1. Whalen begins by offering operating definitions of two senses of one of her key concepts, "resolution." Put these definitions in your own words.

2. The author uses a number of informative footnotes, a practice used in several humanities disciplines such as rhetoric and history. What kinds of material is she putting in these footnotes? Why would they not have been appropriately placed in the main body of the text?

3. Whalen quotes scholars who argue that certain images "perform a kind of civic pedagogy." What is meant by this phrase?

4. Some or many of the images named as capturing Canada in a CBC poll correspond to events that may have occurred before you were born. (See paragraph 7.) How many of them can you "summon up"? What might this say about the "iconic" status of these images?

Critical Reading

1. Search the internet to find one or two of the photographs Whalen analyzes, as well as commentary on those photographs. Then write a short essay summarizing the range of commentary and comparing it to Whalen's comments.

2. Can you think of any other images that most Canadians would be able to "summon up"? Analyze the possible sources of their power by using Whalen's key concepts such as iconic qualities and lack of resolution.

3. Whalen concludes by suggesting that Canadian interests would perhaps be better served by a "montage" or "multiplicity" of images instead of single iconic ones. Why does she say this, and do you agree with her?

4. Many memorable images are photographs of people in pain: the victims of natural disaster and violence. Susan Sontag analyzes how the camera frames the viewer's response to images in her book, *Regarding the Pain of Others*, and reflects on the consequences: does our sympathetic response to the image of a person in pain make us feel unjustifiably free of any personal responsibility to do something to help? Why do both writers see the production and reception of images as activities with important consequences?

Borrowing Enemy Language: A First Nation Woman's Use of English

Marie Annharte Baker

Marie Annharte Baker is an Anishinabe poet, essayist, and storyteller whose interests include writings of women of colour, street poetry, and rap. Baker is the co-founder of the Regina Aboriginal Writers Group and the author of several books of poetry, including Being on the Moon, Coyote Columbus Café, Exercises in Lip Pointing, *and* Blueberry Canoe. *Baker combines art and activism in her work, as in her contribution to "five feminist minutes," commissioned by the National Film Board, in which she examined racial and sexual abuse of Aboriginal women.*

In this essay, originally given as a talk, Baker explores the colonizing effects of using "enemy language," which she sees as the situation of First Nation women speaking and writing in English.

1   If an elder apologizes for speaking in a "borrowed language," I take it to mean more than a simple announcement that the speech will *not* be made in an Indigenous language. While standard English is spoken in Native homes and workplaces, foreign spiel like bureaucratese is also heard around the kitchen table to communicate family matters. Even the most personal thoughts or intimate experiences may be articulated in the strange lingo of cultural outsiders. Some conversations are laced with words borrowed from A.A. meetings, government-sponsored conferences, educational workshops, and from a mere glancing through handouts or manuals.

2   My anger rises at the shaming mention of the loss of fluency in a mother tongue or the scolding talk that seems directed at a speaker who has not retained an Indigenous language or dialect — as if being a dispossessed person with fragments of culture, history, and land base was not enough tragedy. Now, I agree with apologies directed to ancestral spirits who preside at Indian ceremonies and gatherings, if a speaker concludes a prayer with "All my relations," it is to include preceding generations and even those yet to be born. The ancestor's language was not English. Even while some of us use English, attendant with its limited foreign meanings, the innate understandings might go beyond language. Maybe we actually do speak from the heart.

3   Native people frequently say that English is impersonal or, if used in translation, it fails to carry the spirit of what was said. The frequent repetition of the word "I" in English discourse gives the subject so much importance, and distances him or her from the humble listener. The colonial context of the replacement of English for First Nations languages in our communities results from a 500-year history of European occupation and attempted cultural domination. When the colonizers or settlers approached everything Native, natural, or necessary for North American survival as an enemy, English became an "Enemy Language." To "civilize" or "educate" was to take over a people's unique communication system.

4   As Indigenous peoples specify the relationship of Indigenous writing to the past and present destruction of both the environment and their lives, we should expect only tales of victimization and loss of culture. Especially when referring to the loss of Indigenous languages, the increased so-called literacy in the English language seems to bolster the idea of a "borrowed language" — one forced upon Indigenous peoples the world over. The death and mutilation of our peoples' spirits and bodies accompanied the teaching of English. Even today's educators want to hear "civilized" speech or the correct grammar and pronunciation of English words. One might recount horror stories of Native writers and educators who think their own people deficient in language skills because of a resistance to learn and use English the way it is taught in schools, where it is taught as a colonizer's language to communicate the words and symbols of the dominant society.

5   Thinking about English as the enemy's language is more than reversing the trend to overvalue English proficiency. The occasion to share experiences about subverting the English language is for me not just a discussion on First Nations' vernacular use in writing. I glibly mention that I "massacre" English when I write. Of course, I need to explain that I am deliberate about poetic language in my writing. Academic snobbery or cultural arrogance has adversely affected our ability to use catchy phrases. Anyone who gives an interesting talk is given accolades. The vulgarity of everyday expression is sacrificed for the deadness of scholarly language. Yet the ways to wring multiple meanings out of words still occur. The underclass English vocabulary is a source for my borrowing of language. "Sally Ann" was the way the Salvation Army was named in the neighborhood I grew up in. To help me "invent" or borrow English use for poetry, I listen to poor people speaking. As middle-class English starts to resemble more and more a computer language, and becomes an international business language, conversational English might just improve. Used by Indigenous peoples around the world to communicate, English may borrow from their struggle to maintain both land and cultural bases. I'm not suggesting further appropriation of ideas by ripping words and expressions out of a cultural context. I think borrowing does happen especially when reciprocity actually does happen.

6   Some of my poetry will appear in an anthology of Native North American women's writing, edited by Joy Harjo, called *Reinventing the Enemy's Language*. With more First Nations women writing in English, we must learn more about the kind of enemy that English literature pretends to be, or actually continues to be as its more oppressive forms are still promoted. Again, the history of Indigenous people in North, Central, and South America written in English texts may be inadequate. Translations of Indigenous thoughts on decolonization might eventually eliminate the practice of appropriating cultural icons and symbols described in English.

7   When I speak in English as the enemy's language, I see the enemy as being *within* the individual person — within one's own language use and how one is programmed to look at things. Those who see only the enemy outside are, fortunately, foolish; it's more difficult to detect the enemy within. A second language, or even one's first or mother tongue, might be the hiding place for a racist ideology. I do think of myself as a "word warrior" because I have a fight with words that demean my experience as an Indigenous person. I fight racist ideology or the ideas of white supremacy. Then again, I jokingly refer to myself as a "word slut." I find writing for me is a way to be sane in society. I make sense of my world through writing. If a writer does not question imposed language, then, to me, this writer is only passing on oppression to the reader or listener — we are hearing the "colonized Native" voice. The fight for land and language against the loss of our past generations has to be the priority for our survival. One very identifiable enemy to our survival is that shame that our people were not "civilized," and that our people used language differently than Europeans or other newcomers to this country. The shame of having been a holocaust survivor is what I hear and read of the "colonized Native" voice that has become even more popularized in Canadian literary circles. "White guilt" has been effectively

manipulated by some Native writers, especially when no attempt is being made to advance one's idea. Why not just reflect the "white people's ways"?

8   Sometimes, I meet Native people who seem to have a type of historical amnesia. I heard a Métis man who dismissed me as a writer because in his good old student days, John Donne's poetry was his particular expertise. I didn't perform the intellectual dual by saying that I'd read his favorite poet and even liked the old Anglican churchman. My own counter-plan was to immediately defend Indigenous writing. He put down not only our present efforts for recognition of Native writers, but also our significant oral traditional literary contributions. He might also have been sexist, so his attack on Native writing might have been directed against me personally, because I am a woman writer. He thought that with the credentials of a privileged white male, he might destroy my "illusion" of being a writer. I could have whipped out a booklist to show him his ignorance of the literature of his own people, but all I had was wit in my arsenal of word weapons. So instead, I gave him a "smart answer," or a riddle. I told him, "Well, to me, a pictograph is a novel." I realize many others might see a picture scratched on a rock or cave as being ritually painted. I was talking holy text, and my impromptu defence that pictograph might actually generate more writing than one novel probably struck him as pure cheek. As an Ojibway writer who stands in awe of the pictographs and petroglyphs of the Great Lakes region, the mysterious meanings of our ancestors' writings are still a mystery to be deciphered. I believe prophecies for our coming age have been left for us. Even for those of us who speak or write in a borrowed language — we have been left with symbols many of us "educated" Natives would be limited to understand. Our "whiteman's education" doesn't have a contingency plan for understanding the complexity of our own tribal teachings.

9   I venerate and respect all writing forms that are non-English. If I didn't win that dispute on the importance of native writing and reclaiming our history and identity, then I simply reaffirmed what I find to be challenging about writing in English. I am always searching for a simplicity and clarity in diction because English is an ultimate liar's language. I've heard Ojibwe speakers say it is easy to distort truth or reality in English. Harder to lie in an Indigenous language, some say.

10   Jimmie Durham, a Cherokee artist, has stated his position that Indigenous people shouldn't "educate the oppressor" because anything said or written in English will be used against us. Check any court record for quotes by anthropologists or other Indian experts. Sometimes, the words of our own elders are twisted out of context to support our so-called "non-occupation" of the environment. Obviously, our words will be used by "the enemy." Governments will want to take our land because too many of us speak English and are not "as Indian" or culturally pure as we are expected to be. I believe that is why some of our Ojibway people did not learn to speak English at all. I do appreciate why they don't want to use English: they prefer to speak their own Indigenous language because English is not superior.

11   The Ojibway language has now an achieved status of being a "sacred" language. It is a preferred spoken language at ceremonies. English, if used, is of minor importance. Speaking an Indigenous language is the better way of honoring the earth and the language of one's relatives. Our people know we respect this earth,

or Turtle Island, through our words. Poetic narratives are prayers that engage the spirits of both audience and environment.

12   Maybe the visual artists who depict traditional icons and symbols realize the almost routine "appropriation" of their representations by other artists. While some artists condone stealing ideas from each other, when they steal images from Indian people, they talk the rhetoric of "cultural borrowing," or reciprocal exchange. It's almost as if the oppressor says "speak to me in English about your exotic culture," and then he or she publishes the literary or documentary exclusive impressionistic evidence — for cultural superiority. With all the rip-offs in the art world, no wonder Native artists have made such strong statements to protect their works from the copying or trivializing of indigenous cultural materials and intellectual property.

13   Language retention is crucial for Indigenous cultural survival and representation. The lament about the loss of languages is pretty loud to the ears. The frightening prediction is that by the year 2000, only four Indigenous languages might be spoken. Whenever I get down in attitude about those statistics, I look at a map that depicts the geographic distribution of Ojibwe speakers. The picture is far from being limited to tiny and endangered populations in North America. The Ojibwe peoples' land base is about one-third of the continent. What I see is not a few dots to suggest reserves or communities around the Great Lakes. With the history of our migrations from coast to coast, we have spread out across the land. We have a language that is fairly consistent with the extension of our Ojibwe trading networks. The Caribbean and American Black writers refer to an African diaspora; Ojibwe speakers and those others from the Algonkian linguistic group also form large, distinct populations. Names such as Ojibway, Chippewa, Sauk and Fox, Menominee, Cheyenne, Blackfoot appear in the historical or anthropological travelogues or documents. Yes, it is true that our language is threatened, but I also hear many stories of how our people speak Ojibwe to their children. If the dire prediction — that only a few languages of a total of more than 300 will survive — comes true, I think it will because of the attacks on our land and population bases. I don't think it will be because the colonizer lucks out. The adaptability of Ojibwe speakers and their travels across this land have given us variation and incredible diversity. We were nations within nations. Our Ojibwe writers form probably the largest group of Native American or Native Canadian writers published in English. They write in Ojibwe, or may also display the current influence or infatuation with post-modernists and post-colonists. The Ojibwe language will survive because of our flexibility. England has been called the nation of shopkeepers, and English was used to develop an empire based on the slavery and the impoverishment of other Indigenous nations. Our Anishinabe nations also had a history of trading and were Argonauts of the inland watersystems of the continent. Have canoe, will travel.

14   If the future means that you will have to listen up to Ojibwe writers published in their language of choice, I refer you to the text on our language, *Anisbinababemodaa* or *Becoming a Successful Ojibwe Eavesdropper*. English has already borrowed many words from this language, such as "mooz" for moose, "mashkigg" for muskeg. Our language names rivers like the Mississippi, or cities like Winnipeg. Our word "doodem" is the source for totem. This book notes that

fluent speakers always seem to be laughing heartily when speaking the language. It's impossible to be "too serious," the language itself is picturesque. I particularly like the description that the Anishinabeg are a skeptical people: "We have so many words that mean 'maybe' . . . many ways . . . of saying 'I don't know'." When a speaker wasn't there to see the event he or she is describing, there is a word — "iinsan"— that is inserted into the sentence to indicate the uncertainty of relating information. Ojibwe speakers are still developing their terminology today and modernizing the language. They continue to make up words for things like "computer" or "insurance policy." The word for helicopter when written is huge, and sprawls halfway across the page:

GAA-GIZHIBAAYAAGOSEG ISHPAASIGIGAN

15　　Language retention is a passing on of the culture through the imagery of words. It is not enough to have the outer trappings of being Indian or Native, such as braids or beads. I claim my identity through my motherline. My mother was fluent in the language and spoke to me in it when I was a child. I identify as an Anishinabe because of the way I was treated by my mother and relatives. I don't take the racial designations to be as important. Some people even prefer *terms* for themselves and not *names*. I think terms such as "Aboriginal," "Métis," or even "First Nations" do not tell as much as the name of a people. In addition to the legal designations or anthropological terms applied to Anishinabeg, there are the many distinct names for the various bands, clans, or family groups that lived across the country. I am usually approached to identify myself racially because I am a mixed blood person. My father is a Celtic-cross, or comes from a Celtic confusion of Irish, Scottish, and English crofter origins.

16　　Cree writers have spoken about their language as being full of fun. I find that the speaking of English for some First Nations people presents moments of amusement. English has a strict idea that syntax is everything: for the sentence to have meaning, there is an order of separate words to be followed. We do certainly make different inferences. An example is me talking with my son, when he told me "Mom, I'm thinking of becoming celibate." I responded by saying "Well, don't think too much about it" — meaning I didn't want him to torture himself with thoughts of lust. The "thinking celibate" has an ambiguous meaning. The words don't always describe the activity or behavior, yet we are expected to believe the speaker's intent.

17　　Sometimes I find A.A. talk particularly horrible. We are forced to hear about everyone being "healed" or being in a state of "recovery." So much emotion or action is glossed over when someone refuses to give any detail of experience by saying simply that they are "healing." It's become so cliché that it is a type of code that silences the actual telling about a survivor's experience. We cannot find the word for genocide or holocaust because we are a "shame-based" culture. Other questionable phrases or buzz words such as "tricksters," "shaman," "traditional," "two spirit," "windigo," and "contrary"/"heyoka" are tossed around in conversations. Even upon meeting another Indigenous person these days, one is obliged to listen to the recounting of clan names.

While the common ancestry of tribal histories, or that of bands, has been replaced with the designation of First Nations, we still seem to know so little about actual differences among our own people. We are always lumped together. And, we are always pulling ourselves away from the generic terms that supposedly name us. Like if you claim to be an Aboriginal, then maybe you won't fit into Métis criteria. If you are non-status Indian, you might fit into one or both. We are inundated with these words. We also have logos like peace pipes, feathers, or other icons to represent us, whether or not our own ancestors or relatives engaged in these particular cultural practices. So much pretentiousness is exhibited by people's ability to manipulate these symbols to be "politically correct." Whenever I hear the word "shaman" I get apprehensive, because I think that whoever is using that word might be referring to a variety of performance art, or a New Age cult conversion, or even the equivalent of the English word "doctor." For me, I begin to distrust such speakers and their "loose" language. And I cannot always rely on other Native writers or readers to understand the disadvantage of using other people's names for us.

18   English has been the language used by what I call "settler lit." I sometimes include all the Canadian literature in my loose terminology. It's not Can Lit but "settler lit" to me. What I think of as Canadian literature and the inclusion of Native writings is a creation of a non-settler literature, or a decolonized approach to Indigenous literature, especially when people are writing about their history and their relationship to land. I think that what I call "settler lit" is literature that promotes the false identities or re-vision of the past.

19   I found this postcard in Victoria which says "Poverty in an age of affluence is being unable to write, and having others write about you." I find this explanation of the informant relationship similar to the one forced upon some Native writers. Native people have to suffer informant roles when movies, books, or plays are being written. When this type of cultural representation and its products are criticized, then the critics must bear the stigma of being called "reverse racists." They are seen to be intolerant of the white corrective procedures of producing a literature about us but not written by us.

20   English is the language that I've used in order to become a published writer. I might have tried other media or art forms to express my ideas rather than books. In that way, maybe words would not have been a focus of my work. Politics and community organizing were fascinating alternatives to writing poetry for me. I don't feel that it is my job entirely to fix "settler lit" or to apologize for the racist sexism that I experience with publishers and other writers. Or is it sexist racism? I hope that after 500 years of colonizer literature some of us will pursue a deconstruction of this mentality. In Ward Churchill's book, *Fantasies of the Master Race: Literature, Cinema, and the Colonization of American Indians*, are to be found analyses of the Euro-domination of our cultural and art forms. He's done a good job at starting us on our way toward understanding how cultural appropriation and racism are linked. Here he uses Vine Deloria's words:

> Underneath all the conflicting images of the Indian one fundamental truth emerges: the white man knows he is alien and he knows that North America is Indian — and he will never let go of the Indian image because he thinks that by some clever manipulation he can achieve an authenticity which can never be his.

21　I should add "hers," to include the many feminist or other women writers that have persisted in using their English commands as weapons against us to gain authenticity. Access to publishing doesn't always have to involve the paternalistic stance, or the pity, or the condescending approach to the study of Indigenous literature. I find now that all writers have a responsibility for cleaning up language use and if we understand that English may be used as an Enemy language by some, we might even have 500 years left to do the job of cleaning up the pollution of thought it has wrought. We don't have to keep on blindly repeating the folly of settler lit, or settler lit(ter).

Active Reading

1.　Baker is extremely critical of English as a language that conveys an oppressive relationship to Aboriginal people, yet she writes in English. How does Baker use critical reflection to resolve this contradiction?

2.　What are Baker's main criticisms of English?

3.　What is the difference between "settler lit(ter)" and "Canadian literature"?

4.　Identify the sources of optimism Baker expresses about the future of the Ojibway language and the possibilities of cleaning up English.

Critical Reading

1.　What are the stages of thought by which Baker builds toward her conclusion that "all writers have a responsibility for cleaning up language use"?

2.　Like Doris Lessing and Tomson Highway's pieces in this collection, Baker's essay began life as a speech. Identify aspects of the essay that seem intended for an audience of listeners. Are there places where you would have appreciated more explanation to clarify some concepts?

3.　Baker clearly sees language as more than a set of neutral labels for things, but instead as a vehicle for colonization. Why is she troubled by self-help jargon and "bureaucratese"?

4.　Compare Baker's view of English to Tomson Highway's view of Christian mythology.

READING AND WRITING SUGGESTIONS

Chapter-based Research Questions

1.　Highway, Francis, Whalen, and Baker take up related themes, but use very different concepts and methods. Explain the relevance of each text to the broad topic of "representations of Canada" and the different methodologies each author uses.

2.　Use the texts in this chapter as the research base for an essay on the values and dangers of "mythologizing."

3.　In a way, the writers in this chapter can be seen as participating in the same conversation as the writers in the chapter on psychology when the latter turn their attention to the question of how to become the more courageous people we would like to be. How do the writers in this chapter see the stories we tell ourselves as playing a role in the people we become and the way we treat each other?

Additional Research Questions

1. Many school divisions have developed progressive curriculum documents that respect diverse people, but financially challenged schools often continue to use outdated books that do not reflect current thinking. Examine two or three history or social studies textbooks currently used in Canadian schools and do a Francis-style analysis of their representations of a particular group of people. If you decide to analyze the representation of Aboriginal people, compare your findings to Francis's. Other groups you might focus on include women, immigrants, or disabled people. If you decide to focus on sexual diversity, you are likely to find that there is little or no representation of lesbian and gay people of any kind. You will need to do a different kind of analysis that focuses on how the representation of people generally represents all people as heterosexual, as though no one else even exists in Canada.

2. Write an essay about iconic images shared by most people in your age group. You could either follow Whalen's example in reflecting on images of Canada, or shift to another topic, such as iconic images of ideal beauty or sexuality or athleticism. Discussing the topic with other people will help you to identify images with possible iconic status.

3. Find creative works by Highway (plays) or Baker (poetry) and write an essay that draws comparisons with their work in this chapter.

TEXT

Marie Annharte Baker, "Borrowing Enemy Language: A First Nation Woman's Use of English," from *Words in Common: Essays on Language, Culture and Society*, edited by Gillian Thomas (Boston: Addison Wesley, 1999), 41–47. Reprinted by permission of the author.

David Bartholomae, "Inventing the University" from *When a Writer Can't Write: Studies in Writer's Block and Other Composing Process Problems*, edited by Mike Rose (New York: Guilford Press, 1985), 134–135.

Thomas Blass, "The Milgram Paradigm After 35 Years: Some Things We Now Know About Obedience to Authority," *Journal of Applied Social Psychology*, 29.5, May 1999. Copyright © 2006, 1999 V. H. Winston.

Carly Brandenburg, "The Newest Way to Screen Job Applicants: A Social Networker's Nightmare Preview," *Federal Communications Law Journal*, 60.3, June 2008, 597–626.

Judith Butler, "The Values of Difficulty." Reprinted by permission of the author.

Canadian Charter of Rights and Freedoms, Part I, Constitution Act, 1982 [en. by the Canada Act 1982 (U.K.) c.11, s.1], Articles 1–15.

Asia Czapska, Annabel Webb and Nura Taefi, "Defining Girl Homelessness," from *More than Bricks and Mortar: A Rights-based Strategy to Prevent Girl Homelessness in Canada* (Vancouver: Justice for Girls, May 2008). Copyright © 2008 Asia Czapska, Annabel Webb and Nura Taefi

Kathy Davis, "'My Body Is My Art': Cosmetic Surgery as Feminist Utopia?" *European Journal of Women's Studies* 4.1, 23–37. Copyright © 1997, SAGE Publications. Reprinted by Permission of SAGE.

Denis Dutton, "Language Crimes: A Lesson in How Not to Write." Reprinted by permission of Denis Dutton and The Wall Street Journal, © 1999 Dow Jones & Company. All rights reserved.

Anne Fausto-Sterling, "How to Build a Man," from *Constructing Masculinity*, edited by Maurice Berger, Brian Wallace and Simon Watson (New York: Routledge, 1995), 127–135. This work is protected by copyright and the making of this copy was with the permission of Access Copyright. Any alteration of its content or further copying in any form whatsoever is strictly prohibited unless otherwise permitted by law.

Daniel Francis, "Your Majesty's Realm: The Myth of the Master Race," from *National Dreams: Myth, Memory and Canadian History* by Daniel Francis (Vancouver: Arsenal Pulp Press, 1997).

Tomson Highway, "Comparing Mythologies," from the Charles R. Bronfman Lecture. Copyright © 2003. Reproduced with permission from the University of Ottawa Press.

Eva Hoffman, "Exile," from *LOST IN TRANSLATION* by Eva Hoffman. Copyright © 1989 by Eva Hoffman. Used by permission of Dutton, a division of Penguin Group (USA) Inc.

Doris Lessing, "Group Minds," from *Prisons We Choose to Live Inside*. Copyright © 1986 by Doris Lessing. Reprinted with permission from House of Anansi Press.

John Lorinc, "Driven to Distraction," *The Walrus*, April 2007, 50–59. Reprinted by permission of John Lorinc.

Jacqueline McLeod Rogers, "Finding Words." Reprinted by permission of *Writing on the Edge*, John Boe, editor.

Stanley Milgram, "Behavioral Study of Obedience," *Journal of Abnormal and Social Psychology* 67 (1963), 371–78.

Martha C. Nussbaum. "Toward a Globally Sensitive Patriotism," *Daedalus*, 137.3 (Summer, 2008), 78–93. © 2008 by the American Academy of Arts and Sciences. Reprinted by permission of MIT Press Journals.

Susie O'Brien and Imre Szeman, "Changing Our Bodies, Changing Ourselves?" from *Popular Culture: A User's Guide* (Toronto: Thomson Nelson, 2004), 184–98.

Peggy Pittman-Munke and Michael Berghoef, "Tackling Plagiarism: Linking Hi-Tech, Low-Tech and No Tech Methods for Detection," *Journal of Social Work Values and Ethics*, 5.1, 2008. http://www.socialworker.com/jswve.

Deborah Pollack, "Pro-eating Disorder Websites: What Should Be the Feminist Response?" *Feminism & Psychology*, 13.2, 246–251. Copyright © 2003, SAGE Publications. Reprinted by Permission of SAGE.

Thomas Schramme, "Should We Prevent Non-Therapeutic Mutilation and Extreme Body Modification?" *Bioethics*, 22.1, 8–15. Copyright © 2007, John Wiley and Sons. Reprinted by permission of John Wiley and Sons.

Shaheen Shariff, "A Profile of Traditional and Cyber-bullying," from *Cyber-Bullying: Issues and Solutions for the School, the Classroom and the Home* by Shaheen Shariff. Copyright © 2008, Routledge. Reproduced by permission of Taylor & Francis Books UK.

Murray Sinclair and A.C. Hamilton, *The Residential School System*. Excerpt from Chapter 14, "Child Welfare: Special Treatment for Aboriginal Children," from the Justice System and Aboriginal Justice Implementation Commission (Manitoba Government). Permission to reproduce this text is provided by the Queen's Printer for Manitoba. The Queen's Printer does not warrant the accuracy or currency of the reproduction of this information.

Susan Scott, "A Sick System Creates Sick People," in *All Our Sisters: Stories of Homeless Women in Canada.* © 2007 University of Toronto Press. Reprinted with permission of the publisher.

Don Tapscott, "In Defense of the Future," from *Growing Up Digital: How the Net Generation Is Changing the World* (New York: McGraw-Hill, 2009), 289–304.

Catherine Taylor, "A Human Rights Approach to Stopping Homophobic Bullying in Schools," *Journal of Gay and Lesbian Social Services*, 19.3/4, 2007, 157–172.

Tracy Whalen, "Does Canada Have National Icons?" Reprinted by permission of the author.

Susan Wingert, Nancy Higgitt and Janice Ristock, "Voices from the Margins: Understanding Street Youth in Winnipeg," *The Canadian Journal of Urban Research*, 14.1, Summer 2005.

Philip G. Zimbardo, "Resisting Situational Influences and Celebrating Heroism," from *THE LUCIFER EFFECT* by Philip G. Zimbardo. Copyright © 2007 by Philip G. Zimbardo, Inc. Used by permission of Random House, Inc.

IMAGES

Chatelaine Magazine Cover, August 2008. Photographer: Patrice Massé. Courtesy of Rogers Publishing Ltd.

Chatelaine Magazine Cover, March 1955, copyright public domain. Courtesy of Rogers Publishing Ltd.

"DUCO Enamel Paints." Courtesy of Du Pont.

"IKEA 2010 Brochure." Courtesy of Inter IKEA Systems B.V. 2010.